THE

DEFINITIVE TREATY

BETWEEN

GREAT BRITAIN,

AND THE

UNITED STATES OF AMERICA,

Signed at Paris, the 3ᵈ day of September 1783.

M. DCC. LXXXIII.

*The Definitive Treaty between Great Britain,
and the United States of America,* Title Page

THE PAPERS OF

Benjamin Franklin

VOLUME 40 *May 16 through September 15, 1783*

ELLEN R. COHN, *Editor*

JONATHAN R. DULL, *Senior Associate Editor*

KAREN DUVAL AND KATE M. OHNO, *Associate Editors*

ALICIA K. ANDERSON, ADRINA M. GARBOOSHIAN, MICHAEL SLETCHER, AND PHILIPP ZIESCHE, *Assistant Editors*

ALYSIA M. CAIN, *Editorial Assistant*

New Haven and London YALE UNIVERSITY PRESS, 2011

As indicated in the first volume, this edition was made possible through the vision and generosity of Yale University and the American Philosophical Society and by a substantial donation from Henry R. Luce in the name of Life Magazine. Additional funds were provided by a grant from the Ford Foundation to the National Archives Trust Fund Board. Subsequent support has come from the Andrew W. Mellon Foundation. Major underwriting of the present volume has been provided by the Packard Humanities Institute through Founding Fathers Papers, Inc., the Florence Gould Foundation, the Cinco Hermanos Fund, and The Pew Charitable Trusts. We gratefully acknowledge the bequest of Raymond N. Kjellberg, which will continue to sustain our enterprise. We offer particular appreciation to Richard Gilder, Charles and Ann Johnson, Mason Willrich, the Yale Class of 1954, Claude-Anne Lopez, and the Benjamin Franklin Tercentenary for generous donations that will insure the future of the edition. We are grateful for the generous support of Candace and Stuart Karu, Richard N. Rosenfeld, Phyllis Z. and Fenmore R. Seton, Malcolm N. Smith, Ralph Gregory Elliot, and Sheldon Cohen. Gifts from many other individuals as well as donations from the American Philosophical Society, Yale University, the New York Times Foundation, the Friends of the Franklin Papers, and the Saturday Evening Post Society help to sustain the enterprise. The Papers of Benjamin Franklin is a beneficiary of the generous and long-standing support of the National Historical Publications and Records Commission under the chairmanship of the Archivist of the United States. The National Endowment for the Humanities, an independent federal agency, has provided significant support for this volume. For the assistance of all these organizations and individuals, as well as for the indispensable aid of archivists, librarians, scholars, and collectors of Franklin manuscripts, the editors are most grateful.

Publication of this volume was assisted by a grant from The Pew Charitable Trusts.

Library of Congress catalog card number: 59–12697
International standard book number: 978-0-300-16546-3

⊗ The paper in this book meets the guidelines for permanence and durability of the Committee on Production Guidelines for Book Longevity of the Council on Library Resources.

Printed in the U.S.A.

Administrative Board

Contents

Foreign-language surnames and titles of nobility often run to great length. Our practice with an untitled person is to provide all the Christian names at the first appearance, and then drop them; a chevalier or noble is given the title used at the time, and the full name is provided in the index.

*Denotes a document referred to in annotation.

List of Illustrations

was visiting London in the latter part of 1783. Stuart failed to complete them, and when he left London several years later he gave them to a pawnbroker, from whom Trumbull retrieved them, presumably when he came to London in 1794 as Jay's secretary. Trumbull finished both portraits. He gave Jay the one reproduced here and kept the other for himself: Carrie R. Barratt and Ellen G. Miles, *Gilbert Stuart* (New York, 2004), pp. 121–2. Reproduced by courtesy of the Diplomatic Reception Rooms, U.S. Department of State, Washington, D.C. Photography by Will Brown.

Gold Pommel of Franklin's Walking Stick *facing page 346*

This walking stick, topped by a gold pommel in the shape of a liberty cap, was a gift to Franklin from the duchesse de Deux-Ponts. The duchesse did not make the presentation in person but inquired on July 20 (through a letter written by the chevalier de Kéralio) whether Franklin had received it. Whoever made the presentation wrote a verse upon the occasion, published below under the date of [before July 20]. Reproduced by courtesy of the Division of Political History, National Museum of American History, Smithsonian Institution.

Constitutions des treize Etats-Unis de l'Amérique, Title Page
facing page 377

French edition of *The Constitutions of the Several Independent States of America* . . . (Philadelphia, 1781), commissioned by Franklin and printed by Philippe-Denis Pierres, 1783. The translations were made by the duc de la Rochefoucauld and reviewed by Franklin. In addition to the thirteen state constitutions, the 1781 publication contained the Declaration of Independence, the Articles of Confederation, and the 1778 treaties between the United States and France. To these Franklin added the treaties that the United States had signed with Holland and Sweden. The title page displays the first printed version of the Great Seal of the United States, made from a block that Franklin would bring with him back to America in 1785. Reproduced by courtesy of the Yale University Library.

Balloon Rising over the Champ de Mars *facing page 543*

Anonymous engraving with the legend "Expérience de la Machine Aréostatique de Mrs. de Montgolfier, d'Anonai en Vivarais. / Reppetée à Paris le 27 Aoust. 1783. au Champ de Mars, avec un Balon de Taffetas enduit de Gomme élastique, de 36 pieds 6 pounces de Circonférence. / Ce Balon plein d'Air Inflamable a été exécuté par Mrs. Robert, en vertu d'une Souscription Nationale sous la direction de Mr. Faujas de Saint Fond. / Se vend à Paris chez Le Noir Md. d'Etampes au Louvre et rue du Coq. St. Honoré." Two versions of this engraving were issued, the

first of which was advertised in the *Journal de Paris* only three days after the experiment. No doubt in order to save time, the engraver adapted a plate used in 1782 for a satirical depiction of Jean-Pierre Blanchard's ill-fated flying machine (XXXVII, 246–7n), which also had been sold by Le Noir. The first version of the 1783 engraving features the same skyline of Paris (with the Ecole militaire incongruously replacing the Tuileries palace) and the same crowd of spectators. Blanchard's flying machine and Charles's balloon occupy the same spot in the upper right-hand corner. The artist erased from the sky a kite and the figure of Blanchard, both floating on strings, and added materials for generating hydrogen on the ground. In the second version, reproduced here, the crowd and balloon remain the same, but the cityscape is replaced by a view of the Champ de Mars with the Ecole militaire and Les Invalides in their proper place. Franklin sent a copy of one of these versions to Joseph Banks on September 16 by way of Richard Price. That example has never been located, but a copy of the legend indicates that Franklin added in pen "(& M. Charles)" after Faujas's name: W. Lockwood Marsh, *Aeronautical Prints & Drawings* (London, 1924), pp. vii–viii, 5–6, plates 2, 6, 7. Reproduced by courtesy of the Royal Aeronautical Society Library.

Definitive Peace Treaty between the United States and Great Britain, September 3, 1783 *facing page 566*

Official copy in the hand of William Temple Franklin, secretary of the American peace commission, signed and sealed on September 3, 1783, by David Hartley for Great Britain and John Adams, Benjamin Franklin, and John Jay for the United States of America. Reproduced by courtesy of the National Archives.

Contributors to Volume 40

The ownership of each manuscript, or the location of the particular copy used by the editors of each rare contemporary pamphlet or similar printed work, is indicated where the document appears in the text. The sponsors and editors are deeply grateful to the following institutions and individuals for permission to print or otherwise use in the present volume manuscripts and other materials which they own.

INSTITUTIONS

American Philosophical Society
Archives du Ministère des affaires
    étrangères, Paris
Archives of the Congregatio de
    Propaganda Fide, Rome
Bibliothèque de Genève
British Library
William L. Clements Library,
    University of Michigan
Columbia University Library
Dartmouth College Library
Harvard University Library
Historical Society of Pennsylvania
Henry E. Huntington Library
Library of Congress
Massachusetts Historical Society
Musée de l'Air et de l'Espace,
    France
Musée de Blérancourt
Nationaal Archief, The Hague

National Archives
New-York Historical Society
New York Public Library
North Carolina State Department
    of Archives and History
Princeton University Library
Public Record Office, London
Royal Mail Archive, London
Royal Society, London
Sächsisches Hauptstaatsarchiv,
    Dresden
Scottish Record Office, Edinburgh
Sotheby's, New York (1985)
South Carolina Historical Society
University of Pennsylvania
    Library
University of South Carolina
    Library
Yale University Library

INDIVIDUALS

Descendants of the Rawle and Corning Families, Connecticut
Mrs. Arthur Loeb, Philadelphia, Pennsylvania
E. Marie Lorimer, Melrose, Pennsylvania
James M. Osborn, New Haven, Connecticut
Mrs. James A. de Rothschild, England

Statement of Methodology

Arrangement of Materials

The documents are printed in chronological sequence according to their dates when these are given, or according to the date of publication in cases of contemporary printed materials. Records such as diaries, journals, and account books that cover substantial periods of time appear according to the dates of their earliest entries. When no date appears on the document itself, one is editorially supplied and an explanation provided. When no day within a month is given, the document is placed at the end of all specifically dated documents of that month; those dated only by year are placed at the end of that year. If no date is given, we use internal and external evidence to assign one whenever possible, providing our explanation in annotation. Documents which cannot be assigned a date more definite than the entire length of Franklin's stay in France (1777–85) will be published at the end of this period. Those for which we are unable to provide even a tentative date will be published at the conclusion of the series.

When two or more documents have the same date, they are arranged in the following order:

1. Those by a group of which Franklin was a member (*e.g.*, the American Commissioners in Paris)
2. Those by Franklin individually
3. Those to a group of which Franklin was a member
4. Those to Franklin individually
5. "Third-party" and unaddressed miscellaneous writings by others than Franklin.

In the first two categories letters are arranged alphabetically by the name of the addressee; in the last three, by the name of the signatory. An exception to this practice occurs when a letter to Franklin and his answer were written on the same day: in such cases the first letter precedes the reply. The same rules apply to documents lacking precise dates printed together at the end of any month or year.

Form of Presentation

The document and its accompanying editorial apparatus are presented in the following order:

1. *Title.* Essays and formal papers are headed by their titles, except in the case of pamphlets with very long titles, when a short form is substituted. Where previous editors supplied a title to a piece that had none, and this title has become familiar, we use it; otherwise we devise a suitable one.

Letters written by Franklin individually are entitled "To" the person or body addressed, as: To John Adams; To John Adams and Arthur Lee; To the Royal Society.

Letters to Franklin individually are entitled "From" the person or body who wrote them, as: From John Adams; From John Adams and Arthur Lee; From the Committee of Secret Correspondence.

Letters of which Franklin was a joint author or joint recipient are titled with the names of all concerned, as: Franklin and Silas Deane to Arthur Lee; Arthur Lee to Franklin and Silas Deane. "Third-party" letters or those by or to a body of which Franklin was a member are titled with the names of both writers and addressees, as: Arthur Lee to John Adams; The American Commissioners to John Paul Jones.

Documents not fitting into any of these categories are given brief descriptive headings, as: Extract from Franklin's Journal.

If the name in the title has been supplied from external evidence it appears in brackets, with a question mark when we are uncertain. If a letter is unsigned, or signed with initials or an alias, but is from a correspondent whose handwriting we know, the name appears without brackets.

2. *Source Identification.* This gives the nature of the printed or manuscript version of the document, and, in the case of a manuscript or a rare printed work, the ownership and location of the original.

Printed sources of three different classes are distinguished. First, a contemporary pamphlet, which is given its full title, place and date of publication, and the location of the copy the editors have used. Second, an essay or letter appearing originally in a *contemporary* publication, which is introduced by the words "Printed in," followed by the title, date, and inclusive page numbers, if necessary, of the publication. Third, a document, the manuscript or contemporary printed version of which is now lost, but which was printed at a later date, is identified by the words "Reprinted from," followed by the name of the work from which the editors have reproduced it. The following examples illustrate the distinction:

Printed in *The Pennsylvania Gazette*, October 2, 1729.
Reprinted from William Temple Franklin, ed., *Memoirs of the Life and Writings of Benjamin Franklin* . . . (3 vols., 4to, London, 1817–18), II, 244.

The Source Identification of a manuscript consists of a term or symbol (all of which are listed in the Short Title List) indicating the character of the manuscript version, followed by the name of the holder of the manuscript, as: ALS: American Philosophical Society. Because press copies replicate the manuscripts from which they were made, we indicate the character of the original manuscript, as: press copy of L. Since manuscripts belonging to individuals have a tendency to migrate, we indicate the year in which each private owner gave permission to publish, as: Morris Duane, Philadelphia, 1957. When two or more manuscript versions survive, the one listed first in the Source Identification is the one from which we print.

3. An editorial *Headnote* precedes some documents in this edition; it appears between the Source Identification and the actual text. Such a headnote is designed to supply the background of the composition of the document, its relation to events or other writings, and any other information which may be useful to the reader and is not obtainable from the document itself.

4. The *Text* of the document follows the Source Identification, or Headnote, if any. When multiple copies of a document are extant, the editors observe the following order of priority in determining which of the available versions to use in printing a text: ALS or ADS, LS or DS, AL or AD, L or D, and copy. An AL (draft) normally takes precedence over a contemporary copy based on the recipient's copy. If we deviate from the order set forth here, we explain our decision in the annotation. In those instances where multiple texts are available, the texts are col-

lated, and significant variations reported in the annotation. In selecting the publication text from among several copies of official French correspondence (*e.g.*, from Vergennes or Sartine) we use the version which is written in the best French, on the presumption that the French ministers used standard eighteenth-century spelling, grammar, and punctuation.

The form of presentation of the texts of letters is as follows:

The place and date of composition are set at the top, regardless of their location in the original manuscript.

The signature, set in capitals and small capitals, is placed at the right of the last line of the text if there is room; if not, then on the line below.

Addresses, endorsements, and notations are so labelled and printed at the end of the letter. An endorsement is, to the best of our belief, by the recipient, and a notation by someone else. When the writer of the notation has misread the date or the signature of the correspondent, we let the error stand without comment. Line breaks in addresses are marked by slashes. Different notations are separated by slashes; when they are by different individuals, we so indicate.

5. *Footnotes* to the Heading, Source Identification, Headnote, and Text appear on the pages to which they pertain. References to documents not printed or to be printed in later volumes are by date and repository, as: Jan. 17, 1785, APS.

Method of Textual Reproduction

1. *Spelling* of all words, including proper names, is retained. If it is abnormal enough to obscure the meaning we follow the word immediately with the current spelling in brackets.

2. *Capitalization and Punctuation* are retained. There is such variety in the size of initial letters, often in the same manuscript, that it is sometimes unclear whether the writer intended an upper or lower case letter. In such cases we make a decision on the basis of the correspondent's customary usage. We supply a capital letter when an immediately preceding period, colon, question mark, exclamation point, or dash indicates that a new sentence is intended. If a capital letter clearly indicates the beginning of a new thought, but no mark of punctuation precedes it, we insert a period. If neither punctuation nor capital

letter indicates a sentence break, we do not supply them unless their absence renders comprehension of the document nearly impossible. In that case we provide them and so indicate in a footnote.

Dashes were used for a variety of purposes in eighteenth-century personal and public letters. A dash within a sentence, used to indicate a break in thought, is represented as an em dash. A dash that follows a period or serves as a closing mark of punctuation for a sentence is represented as an em dash followed by a space. Occasionally correspondents used long dashes that continue to the end of a line and indicate a significant break in thought. We do not reproduce the dash, but treat it as indicating the start of a new paragraph.

When there is an initial quotation mark or parenthesis, but no closing one, we silently complete the pair.

3. *Contractions and abbreviations* are retained. Abbreviations such as "wd", "honble", "servt", "exclly", are used so frequently in Franklin's correspondence that they are readily comprehensible to the users of these volumes. Abbreviations, particularly of French words, that may be unclear are followed by an expanded version in brackets, as: nre [navire]. Superscript letters are brought down to the line. Where a period or colon is a part of the abbreviation, or indicates that letters were written above the line, we print it at the end of the word, as: 4th. for 4.th. In those few cases where superscript letters brought down to the line result in a confusing abbreviation ("Made" for "Mad^e"), we follow the abbreviation by an expanded version in brackets, as: Made [Madame].

The ampersand by itself and the "&c." are retained. Letters represented by the "y" are printed, as: "the" and "that". The tailed "p" is spelled out, as: "per", "pre", or "pro". Symbols of weights, measures, and money are converted to modern forms, as: *l.t.* instead of ₶ for *livres tournois*.

4. *Omissions, mutilations, and illegible words* are treated as follows:

If we are certain of the reading of letters missing in a word because of a torn or taped manuscript or tightly bound copy-book, we supply the letters silently.

If we cannot be sure of the word, or of how the author spelled it, but we can make a reasonable guess, we supply the missing letters in brackets.

When the writer has omitted a word absolutely required for clarity, we insert it in italics within brackets.

5. *Interlineations* by the author are silently incorporated into the text. If they are significant enough to require comment a footnote is provided.

Textual Conventions

/	denotes line break in addresses; separates multiple endorsements and notations.
⟨roman⟩	denotes a résumé of a letter or document.
[*italic*]	editorial insertion explaining something about the manuscript, as: [*one line illegible*]; or supplying a word to make the meaning clear, as: [*to*].
[roman]	editorial insertion clarifying the immediately preceding word or abbreviation; supplies letters missing because of a mutilated manuscript.
(?)	indicates a questionable reading.

Abbreviations and Short Titles

AAE	Archives du Ministère des affaires étrangères.
AD	Autograph document.
Adams Correspondence	Lyman H. Butterfield, Richard A. Ryerson *et al.*, eds., *Adams Family Correspondence* (9 vols. to date, Cambridge, Mass., 1963–).
Adams Papers	Robert J. Taylor, Gregg L. Lint *et al.*, eds., *Papers of John Adams* (15 vols. to date, Cambridge, Mass., 1977–).
ADB	*Allgemeine Deutsche Biographie* (56 vols., Berlin, 1967–71).
Adm.	Admiral.
ADS	Autograph document signed.
AL	Autograph letter.
Allen, *Mass. Privateers*	Gardner Weld Allen, ed., *Massachusetts Privateers of the Revolution* ([Cambridge, Mass.], 1927) (Massachusetts Historical Society *Collections*, LXXVII).
Almanach des marchands	*Almanach général des marchands, négocians, armateurs, et fabricans de France et de l'Europe et autres parties du monde . . .* (Paris, 1779).
Almanach royal	*Almanach royal* (91 vols., Paris, 1700–92). Cited by year.
Almanach de Versailles	*Almanach de Versailles* (Versailles, various years). Cited by year.
Alphabetical List of Escaped Prisoners	Alphabetical List of the Americans who having escap'd from the Prisons of England, were furnish'd with Money by the Commissrs. of the U.S. at the Court of France, to return to

	America. A manuscript in the APS, dated 1784, and covering the period January, 1777, to November, 1784.
ALS	Autograph letter signed.
Amiable, *Une Loge maçonnique*	Louis Amiable, *Une Loge maçonnique d'avant 1789* . . . (1897; reprint, followed by an introduction, commentary, and notes, separately paginated, by Charles Porset, Paris, 1989).
ANB	*American National Biography.*
APS	American Philosophical Society.
Archaeol.	Archaeological.
Assn.	Association.
Auphan, "Communications"	P. Auphan, "Les communications entre la France et ses colonies d'Amérique pendant la guerre de l'indépendance américaine," *Revue Maritime,* new series, no. LXIII and LXIV (1925), 331–48, 497–517.
Autobiog.	Leonard W. Labaree, Ralph L. Ketcham, Helen C. Boatfield, and Helene H. Fineman, eds., *The Autobiography of Benjamin Franklin* (New Haven, 1964).
Bachaumont, *Mémoires secrets*	[Louis Petit de Bachaumont *et al.*], *Mémoires secrets pour servir à l'histoire de la république des lettres en France, depuis MDCCLXII jusqu'à nos jours; ou, Journal d'un observateur* . . . (36 vols. in 12, London, 1784–89). Bachaumont died in 1771. The first six vols. (1762–71) are his; Mathieu-François Pidansat de Mairobert edited them and wrote the next nine (1771–79); the remainder (1779–87) are by Barthélemy-François Mouffle d'Angerville.

Balch, *French in America*

Thomas Balch, *The French in America during the War of Independence of the United States, 1777–1783* (trans. by Thomas Willing Balch *et al.;* 2 vols., Philadelphia, 1891–95).

BF

Benjamin Franklin.

BF's accounts as commissioner

Those described above, XXIII, 20.

BF's journal of the peace negotiations

Described in XXXVII, 291–346. This refers to the copy in Josiah Flagg's hand with corrections by BF, at the Library of Congress.

BFB

Benjamin Franklin Bache.

BFB's journal

Described above, XXXVII, 682n.

Bigelow, *Works*

John Bigelow, ed., *The Works of Benjamin Franklin* (12 vols., New York and London, 1887–88).

Biographie universelle

Biographie universelle, ancienne et moderne, ou histoire, par ordre alphabétique, de la vie publique et privée de tous les hommes qui se sont fait remarquer . . . (85 vols., Paris, 1811–62).

Bodinier

From information kindly furnished us by Cdt. Gilbert Bodinier, Section études, Service historique de l'Armée de Terre, Vincennes.

Bodinier, *Dictionnaire*

Gilbert Bodinier, *Dictionnaire des officiers de l'armée royale qui ont combattu aux Etats-Unis pendant la guerre d'Indépendance* (Château de Vincennes, 1982).

Bradford, *Jones Papers*

James C. Bradford, ed., *The Microfilm Edition of the Papers of John Paul Jones, 1747–1792* (10 reels of microfilm, Alexandria, Va., 1986).

xl

Burke's Peerage	Sir Bernard Burke, *Burke's Genealogical and Heraldic History of the Peerage Baronetage and Knightage with War Gazette and Corrigenda* (98th ed., London, 1940). References in exceptional cases to other editions are so indicated.
Burnett, *Letters*	Edmund C. Burnett, ed., *Letters of Members of the Continental Congress* (8 vols., Washington, 1921–36).
Butterfield, *John Adams Diary*	Lyman H. Butterfield *et al.*, eds., *Diary and Autobiography of John Adams* (4 vols., Cambridge, Mass., 1961).
Cash Book	BF's accounts described above, XXVI, 3.
Chron.	*Chronicle.*
Claghorn, *Naval Officers*	Charles E. Claghorn, *Naval Officers of the American Revolution: a Concise Biographical Dictionary* (Metuchen, N.J., and London, 1988).
Cobbett, *Parliamentary History*	William Cobbett and Thomas C. Hansard, eds., *The Parliamentary History of England from the Earliest Period to 1803* (36 vols., London, 1806–20).
Col.	Column.
Coll.	*Collections.*
comp.	compiler.
d.	*denier.*
D	Document unsigned.
DAB	*Dictionary of American Biography.*
DBF	*Dictionnaire de biographie française* (20 vols. to date, Paris, 1933–).
Dictionary of Scientific Biography	Charles C. Gillispie, ed., *Dictionary of Scientific Biography* (18 vols., New York, 1970–90).

Deane Papers	*The Deane Papers, 1774–90* (5 vols.; New-York Historical Society *Collections*, XIX–XXIII, New York, 1887–91).
DF	Deborah Franklin.
Dictionnaire de la noblesse	François-Alexandre Aubert de La Chesnaye-Dubois and M. Badier, *Dictionnaire de la noblesse contenant les généalogies, l'histoire & la chronologie des familles nobles de la France . . .* (3rd ed.; 19 vols., Paris, 1863–76).
Dictionnaire historique de la Suisse	*Dictionnaire historique & biographique de la Suisse* (7 vols. and supplement, Neuchâtel, 1921–34).
DNB	*Dictionary of National Biography.*
Doniol, *Histoire*	Henri Doniol, *Histoire de la participation de la France à l'établissement des États-Unis d'Amérique. Correspondance diplomatique et documents* (5 vols., Paris, 1886–99).
DS	Document signed.
Dubourg, *Œuvres*	Jacques Barbeu-Dubourg, ed., *Œuvres de M. Franklin . . .* (2 vols., Paris, 1773).
Ed.	Edition or editor.
Edler, *Dutch Republic*	Friedrich Edler, *The Dutch Republic and the American Revolution* (*Johns Hopkins University Studies in Historical and Political Science*, ser. XXIX, no. 2; Baltimore, 1911).
État militaire	*État militaire de France, pour l'année . . .* (36 vols., Paris, 1758–93). Cited by year.
Exper. and Obser.	*Experiments and Observations on Electricity, made at Philadelphia in America, by Mr. Benjamin Franklin . . .* (London, 1751). Revised and enlarged

	editions were published in 1754, 1760, 1769, and 1774 with slightly varying titles. In each case the edition cited will be indicated, *e.g., Exper. and Obser.* (1751).
f.	florins.
Ferguson, *Power of the Purse*	E. James Ferguson, *The Power of the Purse: a History of American Public Finance* . . . (Chapel Hill, N.C., 1961).
Fitzpatrick, *Writings of Washington*	John C. Fitzpatrick, ed., *The Writings of George Washington* . . . (39 vols., Washington, D.C., 1931–44).
Fortescue, *Correspondence of George Third*	Sir John William Fortescue, ed., *The Correspondence of King George the Third from 1760 to December 1783* . . . (6 vols., London, 1927–28).
France ecclésiastique	*La France ecclésiastique pour l'année* . . . (15 vols., Paris, 1774–90). Cited by year.
Freeman, *Washington*	Douglas S. Freeman (completed by John A. Carroll and Mary W. Ashworth), *George Washington: a Biography* (7 vols., New York, 1948–57).
Gaz.	*Gazette.*
Gaz. de Leyde	*Nouvelles extraordinaires de divers endroits,* commonly known as *Gazette de Leyde.* Each issue is in two parts; we indicate the second as "sup."
Gen.	General.
Geneal.	*Genealogical.*
Gent. Mag.	*The Gentleman's Magazine, and Historical Chronicle.*
Gillispie, *Montgolfier Brothers*	Charles C. Gillispie, *The Montgolfier Brothers and the Invention of Aviation, 1783–1784* (Princeton, 1983).

xliii

Giunta, *Emerging Nation*   Mary A. Giunta *et al.*, eds., *The Emerging Nation: a Documentary History of the Foreign Relations of the United States under the Articles of the Confederation, 1780–1789* (3 vols., Washington, D.C., 1996).

Harlow, *Second British Empire*   Vincent T. Harlow, *The Founding of the Second British Empire, 1763–1793* (2 vols., London and New York, 1952–64).

Hays, *Calendar*   I. Minis Hays, *Calendar of the Papers of Benjamin Franklin in the Library of the American Philosophical Society* (5 vols., Philadelphia, 1908).

Heitman, *Register of Officers*   Francis B. Heitman, *Historical Register of Officers in the War of the Revolution . . .* (Washington, D.C., 1893).

Hillairet, *Rues de Paris*   Jacques Hillairet, pseud. of Auguste A. Coussillan, *Dictionnaire historique des rues de Paris* (2nd ed.; 2 vols., [Paris, 1964]).

Hist.   Historic or Historical.

Hoffman and Albert, eds., *Peace and the Peacemakers*   Ronald Hoffman and Peter J. Albert, eds., *Peace and the Peacemakers: the Treaty of 1783* (Charlottesville, Va., 1986).

Idzerda, *Lafayette Papers*   Stanley J. Idzerda *et al.*, eds., *Lafayette in the Age of the American Revolution: Selected Letters and Papers, 1776–1790* (5 vols. to date, Ithaca, N.Y., and London, 1977–).

JA   John Adams.

JCC   Worthington Chauncey Ford *et al.*, eds., *Journals of the Continental Congress, 1744–1789* (37 vols., Washington, D.C., 1904–37).

Jefferson Papers	Julian P. Boyd, Charles T. Cullen, John Catanzariti, Barbara B. Oberg, *et al.*, eds., *The Papers of Thomas Jefferson* (37 vols. to date, Princeton, 1950–).
Jour.	*Journal.*
JQA	John Quincy Adams.
JW	Jonathan Williams, Jr.
Kaminkow, *Mariners*	Marion and Jack Kaminkow, *Mariners of the American Revolution* (Baltimore, 1967).
L	Letter unsigned.
Larousse	Pierre Larousse, *Grand dictionnaire universel du XIXe siècle* . . . (17 vols., Paris, [n.d.]).
Lasseray, *Les Français*	André Lasseray, *Les Français sous les treize étoiles, 1775–1783* (2 vols., Paris, 1935).
Laurens Papers	Philip M. Hamer, George C. Rogers, Jr., David R. Chestnutt, *et al.*, eds., *The Papers of Henry Laurens* (16 vols., Columbia, S.C., 1968–2002).
Le Bihan, *Francs-maçons parisiens*	Alain Le Bihan, *Francs-maçons parisiens du Grand Orient de France* . . . (Commission d'histoire économique et sociale de la révolution française, *Mémoires et documents*, XIX, Paris, 1966).
Lewis, *Walpole Correspondence*	Wilmarth S. Lewis *et al.*, eds., *The Yale Edition of Horace Walpole's Correspondence* (48 vols., New Haven, 1939–83).
Lopez, *Mon Cher Papa*	Claude-Anne Lopez, *Mon Cher Papa: Franklin and the Ladies of Paris* (rev. ed., New Haven and London, 1990).

xlv

Lopez and Herbert, *The Private Franklin*	Claude-Anne Lopez and Eugenia W. Herbert, *The Private Franklin: the* *Man and His Family* (New York, 1975).
LS	Letter or letters signed.
l.t.	*livres tournois.*
Lüthy, *Banque protestante*	Herbert Lüthy, *La Banque protestante en* *France de la Révocation de l'Edit de* *Nantes à la Révolution* (2 vols., Paris, 1959–61).
Mackesy, *War for America*	Piers Mackesy, *The War for America,* *1775–1783* (Cambridge, Mass., 1965).
Madariaga, *Harris's* *Mission*	Isabel de Madariaga, *Britain, Russia,* *and the Armed Neutrality of 1780:* *Sir James Harris's Mission to St.* *Petersburg during the American* *Revolution* (New Haven, 1962).
Mag.	*Magazine.*
Mass. Arch.	Massachusetts Archives, State House, Boston.
Mazas, *Ordre de* *Saint-Louis*	Alexandre Mazas and Théodore Anne, *Histoire de l'ordre royal et militaire de* *Saint-Louis depuis son institution en* *1693 jusqu'en 1830* (2nd ed.; 3 vols., Paris, 1860–61).
Medlin, *Morellet*	Dorothy Medlin, Jean-Claude David, Paul LeClerc, eds., *Lettres d'André* *Morellet* (3 vols., Oxford, 1991–96).
Métra, *Correspondance* *secrète*	[François Métra *et al.*], *Correspondance* *secrète, politique & littéraire, ou* *Mémoires pour servir à l'histoire des* *cours, des sociétés & de la littérature en* *France, depuis la mort de Louis XV* (18 vols., London, 1787–90).
Meyer, *Armement nantais*	Jean Meyer, *L'Armement nantais dans*

	la deuxième moitié du XVIIIe siècle (Paris, 1969).
Meyer, *Noblesse bretonne*	Jean Meyer, *La Noblesse bretonne au XVIIIe siècle* (2 vols., Paris, 1966).
Morison, *Jones*	Samuel E. Morison, *John Paul Jones: a Sailor's Biography* (Boston and Toronto, 1959).
Morris, *Jay: Peace*	Richard B. Morris *et al.*, eds., *John Jay, the Winning of the Peace: Unpublished Papers, 1780–1784* (New York, Cambridge, London, 1980).
Morris, *Jay: Revolutionary*	Richard B. Morris *et al.*, eds., *John Jay, the Making of a Revolutionary: Unpublished Papers, 1743–1780* (New York, Evanston, San Francisco, 1975).
Morris Papers	E. James Ferguson, John Catanzariti, Mary A. Gallagher, Elizabeth M. Nuxoll, *et al.*, eds., *The Papers of Robert Morris, 1781–1784* (9 vols., Pittsburgh, Pa., 1973–99).
Morton, *Beaumarchais Correspondance*	Brian N. Morton and Donald C. Spinelli, eds., *Beaumarchais Correspondance* (4 vols. to date, Paris, 1969–).
MS, MSS	Manuscript, manuscripts.
Namier and Brooke, *House of Commons*	Sir Lewis Namier and John Brooke, *The History of Parliament. The House of Commons, 1754–1790* (3 vols., London and New York, 1964).
NNBW	*Nieuw Nederlandsch Biografisch Woordenboek* (10 vols. and index, Amsterdam, 1974).
Nouvelle biographie	*Nouvelle biographie générale depuis les temps les plus reculés jusqu'à nos jours . . .* (46 vols., Paris, 1855–66).
ODNB	*Oxford Dictionary of National Biography.*

p.	pence.
Pa.	Pennsylvania.
Pa. Arch.	Samuel Hazard *et al.*, eds., *Pennsylvania Archives* (9 series, Philadelphia and Harrisburg, 1852–1935).
Palmer, *Loyalists*	Gregory Palmer, ed., *Biographical Sketches of Loyalists of the American Revolution* (Westport, Conn., 1984).
Parry, *Consolidated Treaty Series*	Clive Parry, comp., *The Consolidated Treaty Series* (243 vols., Dobbs Ferry, N.Y., 1969–86).
Phil. Trans.	The Royal Society, *Philosophical Transactions.*
PMHB	*Pennsylvania Magazine of History and Biography.*
Price, *France and the Chesapeake*	Jacob M. Price, *France and the Chesapeake: a History of the French Tobacco Monopoly, 1674–1791, and of Its Relationship to the British and American Tobacco Trade* (2 vols., Ann Arbor, Mich., 1973).
Proc.	*Proceedings.*
Pub.	*Publications.*
Quérard, *France littéraire*	Joseph Marie Quérard, *La France littéraire ou Dictionnaire bibliographique des savants, historiens, et gens de lettres de la France, ainsi que des littérateurs étrangers qui ont écrit en français, plus particulièrement pendant les XVIIIe et XIXe siècles . . .* (10 vols., Paris, 1827–64).
RB	Richard Bache.
Repertorium der diplomatischen Vertreter	Ludwig Bittner *et al.*, eds., *Repertorium der diplomatischen Vertreter aller Länder seit dem Westfälischen Frieden*

xlviii

	(1648) (3 vols., Oldenburg, etc., 1936–65).
Rev.	*Review.*
Rice and Brown, eds., *Rochambeau's Army*	Howard C. Rice, Jr., and Anne S. K. Brown, eds., *The American Campaigns of Rochambeau's Army, 1780, 1781, 1782, 1783* (2 vols., Princeton and Providence, 1972).
Roberts and Roberts, *Thomas Barclay*	Priscilla H. Roberts and Richard S. Roberts, *Thomas Barclay (1728– 1793): Consul in France, Diplomat in Barbary* (Bethlehem, Pa., 2008).
s.	*sou.*
s.	shilling.
Sabine, *Loyalists*	Lorenzo Sabine, *Biographical Sketches of Loyalists of the American Revolution . . .* (2 vols., Boston, 1864).
SB	Sarah Bache.
Schulte Nordholt, *Dutch Republic*	J. W. Schulte Nordholt, *The Dutch Republic and American Independence* (trans. Herbert M. Rowen; Chapel Hill, N.C., 1982).
Sellers, *Franklin in Portraiture*	Charles C. Sellers, *Benjamin Franklin in Portraiture* (New Haven and London, 1962).
Sibley's Harvard Graduates	John L. Sibley, *Biographical Sketches of Graduates of Harvard University* (18 vols. to date, Cambridge, Mass., 1873–). Continued from Volume IV by Clifford K. Shipton.
Six, *Dictionnaire biographique*	Georges Six, *Dictionnaire biographique des généraux et amiraux français de la Révolution et de l'Empire (1792–1814)* (2 vols., Paris, 1934).
Smith, *Letters*	Paul H. Smith *et al.*, eds., *Letters of*

	Delegates to Congress (26 vols., Washington, D.C., 1976–2000).
Smyth, *Writings*	Albert H. Smyth, ed., *The Writings of Benjamin Franklin* . . . (10 vols., New York, 1905–7).
Soc.	Society.
Sparks, *Works*	Jared Sparks, ed., *The Works of Benjamin Franklin* . . . (10 vols., Boston, 1836–40).
Taylor, *J. Q. Adams Diary*	Robert J. Taylor *et al.*, eds., *Diary of John Quincy Adams* (2 vols. to date, Cambridge, Mass., and London, 1981–).
Tourneux, *Correspondance littéraire*	Maurice Tourneux, *Correspondance littéraire, philosophique et critique par Grimm, Diderot, Raynal, Meister, etc. revue sur les textes originaux comprenant outre ce qui a été publié à diverses époques les fragments supprimés en 1813 par la censure les parties inédites conservées à la Bibliothèque Ducale de Gotha et l'Arsenal à Paris* (16 vols., Paris, 1877–82).
Trans.	Translator or translated.
Trans.	*Transactions.*
Van Doren, *Franklin*	Carl Van Doren, *Benjamin Franklin* (New York, 1938).
Van Doren, *Franklin-Mecom*	Carl Van Doren, ed., *The Letters of Benjamin Franklin & Jane Mecom* (American Philosophical Society *Memoirs,* XXVII, Princeton, 1950).
Villiers, *Commerce colonial*	Patrick Villiers, *Le Commerce colonial atlantique et la guerre d'indépendance des Etats-Unis d'Amérique, 1778–1783* (New York, 1977).

l

W&MQ	*William and Mary Quarterly*, first or third series as indicated.
Waste Book	BF's accounts described above, XXIII, 19.
WF	William Franklin.
Wharton, *Diplomatic Correspondence*	Francis Wharton, ed., *The Revolutionary Diplomatic Correspondence of the United States* (6 vols., Washington, D.C., 1889).
Wolf and Hayes, *Library of Benjamin Franklin*	Edwin Wolf 2nd and Kevin J. Hayes, eds., *The Library of Benjamin Franklin* (Philadelphia, 2006).
WTF	William Temple Franklin.
WTF, *Memoirs*	William Temple Franklin, ed., *Memoirs of the Life and Writings of Benjamin Franklin, L.L.D., F.R.S., &c* . . . (3 vols., 4to, London, 1817–18).
WTF's accounts	Those described above, XXIII, 19.

Note by the Editors and the Administrative Board

As we noted in volume 23 (pp. xlvi–xlviii), the period of Franklin's mission to France brings with it roughly two and a half times as many documents as those for the other seventy years of his life. In the present volume once again we summarize a portion of his incoming correspondence in collective descriptions; they appear in the index under the following headings: consulship seekers; emigrants, would-be; favor seekers; offerers of goods and schemes.

As we noted in volume 30 (p. lx), Franklin's French secretary Jean L'Air de Lamotte was responsible for keeping the official letterbook. Many of his copies are flawed, containing errors of spelling, punctuation, and syntax that could not have been present in Franklin's originals. Regrettably, these copies are the only extant versions of much of Franklin's official correspondence dating from this period, and we publish them as they stand, pointing out and correcting errors only when they threaten to obscure Franklin's meaning.

A revised statement of textual methodology appeared in volume 28 and is repeated here. The original statement of method is found in the Introduction to the first volume, pp. xxiv–xlvii. The various developments in policy are explained in xv, xxiv; XXI, xxxiv; XXIII, xlvi–xlviii.

As noted in volume 39 (p. liv), the digital edition of *The Papers of Benjamin Franklin,* conceived and sponsored by the Packard Humanities Institute, is freely accessible at www.franklinpapers.org. The Digital Franklin Papers contains texts of all the documents in our archive up to Franklin's death, including those that are only summarized or mentioned in the letterpress edition, as well as biographical sketches of Franklin's correspondents and an introduction by Edmund S. Morgan. Readers are advised that documents marked "unpublished" are preliminary transcriptions whose dates and attributions may change with further research. They will be replaced with verified texts as the letterpress edition proceeds.

Two editors left the project while this volume was in preparation. Senior Associate Editor Jonathan R. Dull retired in 2008 after thirty years. We are grateful for his long years of service and wish him well. We thank Assistant Editor Michael Sletcher, who left in 2009. Finally, we acknowledge with appreciation the assistance of Susanna Cover, who served as our Editorial Assistant in the early stages of the present volume.

Introduction

During the period covered by this volume, the United States of America completed its transformation into a fully recognized independent nation. Franklin, John Adams, John Jay, and Henry Laurens—the four Americans authorized to conclude a final peace treaty with Great Britain—commenced negotiations with their new British counterpart David Hartley on May 19, as the volume opens, after months of frustrating delays. Despite Hartley's goodwill, the intransigence of the new British ministry doomed their work. On September 3, the peace commissioners signed a definitive treaty that was essentially identical to the preliminary articles they had signed the previous November. While this marked the official end to the War for American Independence, the rest of Europe had long since recognized the United States. The interest of the present volume is not only in witnessing how the American peace commissioners concluded the war. It is in discovering how the United States of America took its place on the world stage.

Franklin had been elated at the signing of the preliminary treaty on November 30, 1782, and the subsequent cessation of hostilities, which he feared he would not live to see. When that preliminary treaty took effect on January 20, 1783, with the signing of the preliminary treaty between Great Britain and France, Franklin and his fellow peace commissioners expected to launch what they thought would be a quick round of negotiations for a definitive treaty. The fall of the Shelburne government in February caused the first major delay. It was not until April that Charles James Fox, the new secretary of state, sent Hartley to Paris to resume negotiations. The American commissioners' hopes for a speedy conclusion were again frustrated when they discovered that Hartley's credentials accorded him no particular powers. They refused to conduct any official discussions until his credentials were revised.

When Hartley's revised credentials arrived in mid-May, Franklin was anxiously awaiting from Congress the dismissal he had requested the previous December. He had been suffering from bouts of chronic and at times debilitating pain from gout and stones, and he longed to be at home with his family.[1] When he finally heard from Robert R. Livingston that Congress was not likely to act on his request for some time, he warned that "the Faults I may henceforth commit thro' the Infirmities of Age, will be rather theirs than mine."[2]

Franklin may have been infirm on occasion, but he had lost none of his acuity. Throughout the spring and summer, he and his fellow commissioners drafted proposals for new articles, reviewed Hartley's proposals, and waited endlessly for Fox to respond to both. Those responses, when they came, were generally negative and often duplicitous, and it soon became clear that Hartley did not himself enjoy the confidence of his government. The American commissioners' goodwill steadily devolved into resentment and suspicion. Not knowing how long the process would last, Laurens went to England to regain his health, and Adams went to Holland to settle financial affairs and meet his son, who was returning from St. Petersburg.

Franklin, meanwhile, continued to attend the weekly meetings of foreign ministers at Versailles and deftly navigated the approaches made to him by both official and unofficial representatives of foreign courts. Without the knowledge even of his fellow commissioners, he engaged in secret negotiations for commercial treaties with Portugal and Denmark, admitting that he had no specific powers to conclude such treaties but proposing drafts that were similar to what Congress had sent him for use with Sweden. Counterproposals from both governments arrived in time for him to include them in the diplomatic packet he sent to Congress with Joshua Barney at the end of July, without his colleagues' having read them. Franklin's extreme secrecy may have been a reaction to his experience of the previous

---

1. For his request to be dismissed, see XXXVIII, 416–17; XXXIX, 381, 397. BF told Thomas Barclay on May 25 how much he longed to return to Philadelphia; he wrote much the same thing to Capt. Falconer in June. For Barclay's report of the conversation see the annotation of WTF to Vergennes, May 28, below, and Butterfield, *John Adams Diary*, III, 135; see also BF to Falconer, June 18.

2. BF to Livingston, July 22[–26].

February, when Adams publicized the secret Swedish-American treaty long before Gustavus III gave permission for it to be signed, let alone announced. Although Adams in this case accused Franklin of assuming inappropriate power and being incompetent to negotiate commercial matters, Franklin was in fact carrying out the orders he had received from Congress the previous winter: to conclude treaties as quickly as possible for the credibility of the United States, regardless of whether additional terms would later be negotiated. Into the draft of the Portuguese treaty he quietly inserted the two humanitarian articles that Congress had not yet seen but that he had proposed for inclusion in the final treaty with Great Britain. The Portuguese counterproposal, which Franklin sent to Congress, retained both. Without realizing that he was the author of those articles, Congress in 1784 authorized Thomas Jefferson to bring them to France and include them in the treaty of commerce that he and a newly appointed set of co-commissioners were charged with proposing to some twenty European nations.

Other nations continued to ask Franklin for information on the state of American ports and commerce, and to argue the advantages of their local goods and manufactures. He assured them all that America intended to maintain a policy of open ports and free commerce. He pondered solutions to the problem of American vessels being harassed by the Barbary corsairs, and fielded a troubling overture to negotiate a treaty, at great cost, with the sultan of Morocco, who believed himself to be responding to an invitation made by the United States Congress. Franklin would eventually learn that the invitation had been extended by an American citizen who had dangerously overstepped his authority.

Ministers who did not officially approach Franklin in the spring were prevented by their courts from doing so until the American minister was recognized by the diplomatic corps. As soon as the peace seemed stable, they wondered why he did not observe the formality of presenting his card. Franklin explained that he would not do so until he received word that Congress had ratified the preliminary treaty. That news arrived with Captain Joshua Barney on July 2, and Franklin, Adams, and Jay immediately embarked on rounds of visits to ministers of countries that had not yet recognized the United States. At the next Tuesday gathering of ministers at Versailles, on July 7, the three Americans were greeted as members of the *corps diplomatique*. This finally allowed the papal nuncio to send Franklin the note concerning the future of American Catholics that he had been waiting to deliver since January.

As they contemplated how or even whether to approach the United States, diplomats wanted to know what kind of government they were dealing with. By July, Franklin could hand them the answer bound between boards. On July 18, Vergennes approved for publication the sheets of *Constitutions des treize États-Unis de l'Amérique*, a French translation of the state constitutions that Congress had published in 1781, along with the founding documents of the country and the treaties that America had signed to date. Franklin sent two copies to each member of the diplomatic corps, one for the diplomat and one for his monarch. The French royal family received deluxe copies printed on *papier vélin* and bound in gold-tooled moroccan leather. When sending a copy to Livingston on July 22[–26], Franklin described the volumes' reception: "They are much admired by the Politicians here, and it is thought will induce considerable Emigrations of substantial People from different Parts of Europe to America. It is particularly a Matter of Wonder, that in the Midst of a cruel War raging in the Bowels of our Country, our Sages should have the firmness of Mind to sit down calmly and form such compleat Plans of Government. They add considerably to the Reputation of the United States."

Diplomacy with Russia and Austria required particular delicacy. The day before the American commissioners received news of the ratification, Vergennes instructed them to pay official visits to the Russian and Austrian ministers who would be serving as mediators for the Anglo-French peace treaty, which had just been approved by the French court and was pending approval by the British. The Americans debated whether to invite Russian and Austrian mediation in their own treaty with Great Britain, as Vergennes had suggested that they consider. The issue was ultimately decided for them in the negative by Hartley, but their own willingness to accept mediation was regarded as a friendly overture to the Imperial courts and allowed Joseph II the opportunity he had been seeking to sound out the Americans on a trade agreement. It was this last issue—whether to allow mediators a ceremonial role in the signing of the Anglo-American peace treaty—that was the final delay in scheduling the signing ceremony. France and Spain had both declared that they would not sign their treaties with Great Britain until the American treaty was finalized; in fact, Vergennes counted on all three treaties being signed together at Versailles. When Hartley insisted on having the signing in Paris, Vergennes instructed Franklin to sign the American treaty early in the morning and immediately send word to Versailles; France and Spain would wait for the messenger before signing their own treaties. All was concluded by three o'clock in the afternoon, whereupon Vergennes hosted a dinner for all the negotiators and their secretaries. Hartley and the Americans traveled together to Versailles, none of them pleased that the past five months of negotiations had yielded no result. The Englishman assured the Americans that all their proposed articles, and any others that they wished to propose, would be considered during negotiations for a separate commercial agreement.

Franklin took comfort during these months from his family and intimate circle of friends. His grandson Benny returned from Geneva in the middle of July, a period that was fraught with challenges posed by diplomats from other nations as well as by dissensions within the American commission. Benny saw none of the strain. He found his grandfather "very different from other Old Persons." Whereas they were "fretful and complaining, and disatisfy'd," his grandfather was "laughing, & chearful, like a young person."[3] Around this time, Jay—who had moved into the Hôtel Valentinois with his family to escape the heat of Paris—prompted Franklin to reminisce about famous men he had known during his early life. Franklin would include some of these anecdotes in his autobiography, though the versions he told Jay were less guarded. On July 4 Franklin hosted his customary Independence Day banquet at Passy, for which a piano was borrowed from Madame Brillon. The abbé

3. See BF to Richard and Sarah Bache, July 27.

Morellet wrote a new song for the occasion, this one more serious than the flippant drinking song he had composed for the 1779 banquet. With the war finally over, Morellet celebrated the peace and declared himself a citizen of the United States as well as France. Later in July, the duchesse de Deux-Ponts sent Franklin a crabtree walking stick topped with a gold pommel in the shape of a liberty cap to replace the one Franklin had lost. This was the stick he bequeathed to George Washington; it is now at the Smithsonian Institution.

Franklin's other pleasure came from witnessing some remarkable scientific demonstrations and reestablishing his connection with the Royal Society. In May, Wolfgang von Kempelen invited him to see the chess-playing automaton he was touring throughout Europe as well as his more sophisticated experimental device, a speaking machine. Franklin considered him a "genius." In June, Franklin witnessed a demonstration of the extraordinary speaking machine invented by the abbé Mical: a walk-in cabinet featuring two "talking heads" that engaged in a dialogue. The most significant scientific development, however, was the Montgolfier brothers' invention of the hot-air balloon. As Etienne Montgolfier arrived in Paris to demonstrate his balloon to the Académie des sciences, and as Franklin learned that a group of competitors was bent on filling a globe with hydrogen, he promised Joseph Banks that he would keep him informed of the experiments. Indeed, the balloon demonstrations conducted in Paris during the summer and fall of 1783 provided Franklin with a means for reclaiming an active voice in the Royal Society, from which he had been estranged for eight years. His enthusiasm for the new technology became as famous throughout Europe as the balloons themselves. Of what use was this highly publicized, expensive invention, asked its detractors after a crowd of thousands witnessed a balloon ascend into the sky for the first time. *Well*, came Franklin's famous reply, *of what use is a newborn baby?*[4]

Of what use was the newborn nation? Franklin had no doubt that the infant Hercules who had shown superhuman strength

---

4. See the headnote to BF to Joseph Banks, Aug. 30[–Sept. 2].

in his cradle, as depicted on the *Libertas Americana* medal he designed, was rapidly approaching maturity. Underestimate us at your peril, he warned Fox three days after signing the definitive treaty. Rumors of dissension in America are exaggerated. The collective spirit of our people is as the "Sun's great Mass of Fire." Do not delay any longer the evacuation of New York; stop clinging to the desire to restrict our commerce. If you persist in your mischief, you will not achieve capitulation but only further alienation.[5]

Four days after writing those words, Franklin learned that rumors were gaining credence in America to the effect that Versailles had argued against America's gaining the fishing and territory rights granted by the treaty, and that he had supported the French. The rumors further asserted that those important rights had been obtained only through the efforts of John Adams, assisted by John Jay.

This was an accusation of treason that Franklin could not let stand while remedy was within his power. He fired off a letter to Adams, sending copies to their colleagues. "It is not my Purpose to dispute any Share of the Honour of that Treaty which the Friends of my Colleagues may be dispos'd to give them; but having now spent Fifty Years of my Life in public Offices and Trusts, and having still one Ambition left, that of carrying the Character of Fidelity at least, to the Grave with me, I cannot allow that I was behind any of them in Zeal and Faithfulness." He demanded certificates from all of them testifying to the falsity of the rumor. Jay composed his immediately, citing specific examples. Adams' lukewarm reply was composed several days later. In the meantime, he had sent a letter to America accusing Franklin of being secretive, conniving, vain, and "malicious to every Man and every Project, calculated for the public Good."[6]

To an old friend in Boston, who had alerted him some years earlier to similar rumors being spread against him in Congress, Franklin now poured out his heart with a freedom that he had never before allowed himself. He justified his actions even as he

5. BF to Hartley, Sept. 6.
6. See BF to JA, Sept. 10.

admitted knowing that his friend had never doubted him. "As to the two Charges of Age and Weakness," he wrote, "I must confess the first; but I am not quite so clear in the latter; and perhaps my Adversaries may find that they presum'd a little too much upon it when they ventur'd to attack me." Ultimately, however, he returned to the most important subject, and to an aphorism he never tired of quoting. "The Definitive Treaty was signed the third Instant. We are now Friends with England and with all Mankind. May we never see another War! for in my Opinion *there never was a good War, or a bad Peace.*"[7]

7. BF to Josiah Quincy, Sr., Sept. 11.

Chronology

May 16 through September 15, 1783

May 19: Hartley, American peace commissioners exchange powers; treaty negotiations recommence.

c. June 1: Jay and family move into the Hôtel Valentinois.

June 4: Congress accepts Livingston's resignation as secretary for foreign affairs; the Montgolfier brothers conduct first public experiment with hot-air balloon at Annonay.

June 7: Laurens travels to London.

June 17–20: Rochambeau's army lands at Brest.

June 21: Continental Army soldiers mutiny at Philadelphia; Congress removes to Princeton.

June 28: French Council of State establishes packet boat service between Port Louis and New York.

July 2: Barney arrives at Passy with congressional dispatches for the American peace commissioners; order in council denies American ships access to trade with British West Indies.

July 4: Franklin hosts Independence Day celebration at Passy.

July 18: Vergennes grants permission to distribute *Constitutions des treize États-Unis de l'Amérique.*

c. July 19: Benjamin Franklin Bache returns to Passy from Geneva.

July 19: Adams departs for Amsterdam.

July 23: Laurens returns to Paris.

July 24: Franklin sends elaborately bound copies of *Constitutions des treize États-Unis de l'Amérique* to Louis XVI, Marie Antoinette, Vergennes.

August 1: Laurens sails from Le Havre to England.

August 6: George III ratifies preliminary articles of peace.

August 9: Adams returns to Paris with John Quincy Adams.

August 13: Hartley, American peace commissioners exchange ratifications of preliminary articles of peace and agree to use them as definitive peace treaty.

August 27: Charles launches hydrogen balloon at the Champ de Mars.

September 2: Britain, Dutch Republic sign preliminary articles of peace at Paris.

September 3: Hartley, American peace commissioners sign definitive peace treaty at Paris; Britain, France, Spain sign definitive peace treaties at Versailles.

September 8: Hartley leaves Paris.

September 14: Thaxter leaves Paris to deliver definitive peace treaty to Congress.

THE PAPERS OF
BENJAMIN FRANKLIN

VOLUME 40

May 16 through September 15, 1783

Editorial Note on Franklin's Accounts

The following accounts, identified in previous volumes, continue to apply to the current period: VI and VII (xxiii, 21); XVII (xxvi, 3); XIX and XXII (xxviii, 3–4); XXV and XXVII (xxxii, 3–4); XXX (xxxvi, 3); and XXXI (xxxviii, 3). We offer here a summary of entries that have not found a place elsewhere in our annotation but provide insights into Franklin's private and public life.

Account XVII (Franklin's Private Accounts with Ferdinand Grand, xxvi, 3) reveals the usual mixture of personal and household expenses. A bill from Gabriel-Louis Marignac, Benjamin Franklin Bache's tutor, was paid on June 14. Franklin's secretary Jean L'Air de Lamotte received 268 *l.t.* on May 17, 221 *l.t.* on June 7, and 466 *l.t.* on September 12. Mlle Chaumont, who had been leasing a carriage to Franklin, was paid on June 20 and July 8. Two weeks later, on July 26, Franklin purchased a carriage of his own from a certain Louis Loiselle for 1,680 *l.t.* (Loiselle would later have dealings with William Temple Franklin, arranging to repair and sell for him a cabriolet.[1]) Franklin's carriage must have been the *diligence de campagne* that was thoroughly overhauled and refurbished in August by Veuve Fabre, master saddler, who charged such extraordinary prices to both Franklin and Temple that her bills were not honored until two years later, when Temple insisted on submitting her accounts to arbitration.[2] On August 9 Franklin was debited 6,000 *l.t.* for his

1. Loiselle's letters to wtf are at the APS.
2. Two versions of Veuve Fabre's "Memoire des Ouvrages faits et fournis Pour Monsieur Francklin," covering May 28 through Sept. 27, 1783, are at the APS. The first, 12 pages long and labeled by wtf "Fabre's 1st Acct," consists mostly of charges for the repair and refitting of a cabriolet and a whiskey (a light, two-wheeled carriage) that belonged to wtf. In addition, there are itemized charges posted on Aug. 16 and 27 for extensive work on a *diligence de campagne*. wtf marked these as bf's charges and must have asked her to separate them out. The revised "Memoire" contains only wtf's expenses; if she supplied a new account for bf alone, it has not been found. Prior to this time, wtf had used the services of the saddler Madlin; see xxxix, 521. For bf's previous carriages see xxxviii, 394n.

The *diligence de campagne* underwent a top-to-bottom restoration, including new hardware, harnesses, gun holsters, boxes, benches, windowpanes, upholstery, and elegant decorations, for a total of approximately 300 *l.t.* wtf's bill was 831 *l.t.* wtf evidently protested the charges as

draft of "4 Nbre" on Robert Morris; this surely refers to the draft of December 4, which Franklin described in a letter to Morris of December 14, 1782 (XXXVIII, 455).

Franklin was credited with two deposits on July 28. He received 14,583 *l.t.* 6 *s.* 8 *d.* as salary for the last quarter of 1782 and 40 shares of the *caisse d'escompte* worth 5,200 *l.t.*

Account XXV (Account of Postage and Errands, XXXII, 3), still being kept by L'Air de Lamotte during these months, reflects a steady flow of letters and packets sent and received, and the "commissions" or errands to Paris, Versailles, and Auteuil run by Jean-Nicolas Bonnefoÿ and, on occasion, Jacques Finck, the *maître d'hôtel.* Their monthly statements are filed with L'Air de Lamotte's summary sheets, as are the bills submitted by Berthelot the postman. In addition to letters for himself and the American commissioners, Franklin received mail for people identified as Bancroft, Miss Laurens, Mr. Vaughan, and, on August 22, Mr. Harrison.[3]

Account XXVII (Accounts of the Public Agents in Europe, XXXII, 4) lists monthly reimbursements to L'Air de Lamotte for postage and errands (the expenses he itemized in Account XXV) and his salary payment on August 9. On August 6 Grand transferred 2,005 *l.t.* 9 *s.* 8 *d.* to William Carmichael out of the public account. Fizeaux, Grand & Cie.'s bills were paid on May 22 and August 7.

Account XXXI (Jacques Finck's Accounts of Household Expenditures, XXXVIII, 3), with its daily tallies of groceries, shows a variety of fruits, vegetables, fish, poultry, and game, which grew more diverse as the season progressed. The cook was paid in May for three months' wages plus a wine allowance; that same month the cook's boy, Bouchet, received four months' wages plus wine. The *garçon de cuisine* received two months' salary in July; in August that same *garçon de cuisine* (we assume), now *malade,* was attended by a surgeon

---

excessive. The two members of the Saddlers' Company who conducted an "article by article" examination on May 5, 1785, agreed with him. The sieurs Tarn and Beau, serving as arbitrators, reduced WTF's bill by approximately 20 percent and BF's by nearly 30 percent. They wrote and signed their statements on the second version of Fabre's memoir, her account with WTF. Below their statements, L'Air de Lamotte drafted a receipt for Fabre, who signed on May 27, 1785, acknowledging that she had received the adjusted total from WTF, as well as 18 *l.t.* toward the arbitrators' fees.

3. Edward Bancroft, Martha Laurens, Samuel Vaughan, Jr., and the Harrison who brought BF an Aug. 19 letter from JW (below).

who charged 7 *l.t.* 10 *s.* for the house call. A dishwasher worked ten days in June, at the rate of 1 *l.t.* per day, and six days in July. In August, Mlle Chaumont supplied *herbage* of an unspecified nature and sold the household a wine press for 100 *l.t.* Two quarts of beer were purchased per month, on average. Bottles of wine from Frontignan and Málaga were bought, usually four at a time, and a dozen bottles of "vin de la cottes Rottie" (the côtes du Rhône). Finck also paid the entry duties on two bottles of Madeira and delivery charges on both the Madeira and a pannier of champagne. He purchased wood for the stove, pots for making pickles, four dozen jam jars, paper for the office, lard for greasing the carriages, and materials for assembling a mattress for "jaques." In August he bought couch grass (used for bladder and kidney stones, among other urinary tract disorders) and licorice.

Editorial Note on Promissory Notes

Although the hostilities had ceased and most prisoners had been exchanged, American seamen who had escaped from British jails continued to appear at Franklin's door seeking assistance. When they received it, they either signed or made their marks on triplicate promissory notes that Franklin had printed. Little is known about these men, as their notes were rarely filled in with anything other than their names and the amount.[4]

Seven men received 24 *l.t.* on May 20: Alexander Cox, Bannet and Stephen Jarboe, Barnard Limes, John White, John Wilson, and B. Youton. On May 24 William Carter, John Collins, William Harris, and William Morgan each received the same amount. The passport that Franklin issued to them still survives; signed the same day, it identified them as American sailors and allowed them to travel to Nantes.[5] Micel Benet signed a promissory note for 24 *l.t.* on May 29.

4. All the printed promissory notes described here are at the APS, and all the signatories are listed on the Alphabetical List of Escaped Prisoners. No promissory note has been located for William Herwins, whose name appears on the Alphabetical List of Escaped Prisoners as having received 36 *l.t.* on Aug. 1. That payment is confirmed by Grand's accounts (Account XXVII, xxxii, 4).

5. This passport (University of Pa. Archives) was printed with the large script type cut for BF by Fournier le jeune; see XXXVII, 283n and the facing page, where the earliest known example is shown. In this printing, BF reset

On July 10 William Pease and John Rush each signed notes for 15 *l.t.* Two days later, notes were issued for Robert Harrison, who received 24 *l.t.*, and for Ann Jamie, who received twice that amount. This was presumably for herself and her husband: Ferdinand Grand's accounts indicate that an Alexander "Jemmy" and his wife each received 24 *l.t.*[6] On July 16 John Smith, taken in the *Jack* of Salem, was granted 24 *l.t.*[7]

Two handwritten receipts survive from this period. On June 15, Franklin wrote a receipt for James Fife, who signed it: "Recd. of Mr Franklin One Guinea to bear my Expences to Nantes in my way home to Philadelphia, which I promise to repay on Demand." On July 6 William Temple Franklin wrote a receipt for three sailors whose names appear on the Alphabetical List of Escaped Prisoners: "Recd from B. Franklin Esqr fifteen Livres each to assist us in getting to America." It was signed by David Coleman, John Gray, and Thomas Howing.[8]

Editorial Note on Requests to Be Selected a Free Port

As soon as the preliminary peace was settled in January, Franklin began receiving appeals from Frenchmen who believed him capable of

---

the forms and altered certain elements. In the first line, for example, he capitalized "Franklin" instead of "Nous," and at the bottom of the form, beneath the space left for his signature, he used a smaller type which allowed him to spell out his title in full: Ellen R. Cohn, "The Printer at Passy," in Page Talbott, ed., *Benjamin Franklin: in Search of a Better World* (New Haven and London, 2005), p. 253.

6. Account XXVII (XXXII, 4). Ann Jamie is the only woman we have seen in this category. Her name (but not her husband's) was added to the Alphabetical List of Escaped Prisoners, perhaps on the basis of her signing their joint promissory note.

7. His was probably the Mass. ship commanded by David Ropes, which had been captured in 1782 off Nova Scotia. Some crew members were imprisoned at Kinsale: Allen, *Mass. Privateers*, pp. 189–90; *Royal Gaz.*, June 26, 1782; C. J. F. MacCarthy, "The American Prisoners at Kinsale," *Jour. of the Cork Hist. and Archaeol. Soc.*, 2nd ser., XCIV (1989), 46.

Smith must have landed at or near Calais, where five days earlier he received 24 *l.t.* from Jacques Leveux "pour se rendre chez le Docteur francklin." The certificate Leveux wrote for Smith, attesting to the loan and requesting that he be allowed to travel freely to Passy, is dated July 11, 1783 (APS).

8. Both sheets are at the APS.

influencing their government's selection of free ports for American goods. We summarized those appeals in volume 39,[9] and continue here to summarize the letters he received during the period of this volume.

On May 16 a lawyer named Denans from La Seyne sent an eight-page letter extolling the advantages of his city, a port on the Bay of Toulon. He also sent an undated eight-page "Mémoire Instructif" on the same subject.[1] Denans observed in his letter that Silas Deane had stayed in La Seyne rather than Toulon when returning to America in 1778.[2] The bay not only was a safe refuge from storms but also, because of the fortifications of Toulon, was well defended from any enemy incursion. Franklin wrote, "answd May 30," on the letter, but his response has not been located.

Writing as the mayor and consul of Saint-Nazaire, a few miles west of Toulon and La Seyne, the sieurs Icard and Monge praised their port in a letter of June 8 and forwarded a now-missing memoir.[3] Around the same time, Franklin received a letter referring to several previous communications about ports in the Saintonge region. The original was forwarded to Vergennes by William Temple Franklin; an undated copy in L'Air de Lamotte's hand survives among Franklin's papers, with Temple's draft of a note, written at Versailles on June 10, forwarding the letter. The writer was undoubtedly the chevalier Louis-Honoré Froger de La Rigaudière.[4] Finally, on July 22 the director and four syndics of the Chamber of Commerce of Aunis renewed their arguments of January 31 on behalf of La Rochelle.[5]

9. See XXXIX, 104–6.

1. Both are at the APS. The writer was probably Joseph-Romain Denans, an *avocat* from La Seyne who was killed by a mob in July, 1792: Louis Baudoin, *Histoire général de la Seyne-sur-Mer et de son port depuis les origines jusqu'à la fin du XIXe siècle* (n.p., 1965), pp. 315–16.

2. D'Estaing recommended that Deane and the four American ship captains who accompanied him stay there in order to preserve secrecy before they embarked on his flagship for their voyage: *Deane Papers*, II, 447–8; III, 184; V, 313.

3. Their names appear in Barthélemy Rotger, *De Saint-Nazaire à Sanary* ([Le Beausset, 1984]), pp. 259, 478. This letter is at the Hist. Soc. of Pa.

4. The chevalier's previous communications are summarized in XXXIX, 105–6. The copy of the present letter with WTF's draft note is at the APS.

5. Hist. Soc. of Pa. For their earlier letter see XXXIX, 107.

To Jan Ingenhousz

LS[6] and incomplete AL (draft):[7] Library of Congress

Dear Friend, Passy, May 16. 1783
I have before me your three Favours of Feby. 26, April 4. &
29.[8] the last delivered to me yesterday by Mr. Robertson to whom
I shall show the Respect due to your Recommendation.[9] I am
asham'd of being so long in Arrear in my Correspondence with
you, but I have too much Business. I will now endeavour to answer
your Letters, & hope I may be able to do it without Interruption.

I never receiv'd the Letter you mention, wherein you ask'd my
Leave to dedicate your Book to me.[1] I should immediately have
given my Consent, esteeming it a great honour to be so remembred by you, & handed down to Posterity as having your Friendship. The Cast of your Profile came safe to hand,[2] and gives me
Pleasure as I think it very like.— Pray what is the Composition?

My Journey to Italy and thence to Vienna, is yet an Uncertainty. I thank you however for your kind Advice respecting the
Conduct of it.[3]

I have long since been tired of the Acquaintance and Correspondence of Mr. V.[4] Having but a small Remnant left of Life,

6. In the hand of Jean L'Air de Lamotte.

7. The draft fills both sides of two folio sheets, the second of which is
missing the top and bottom portions.

8. XXXIX, 217–22, 444–6, 528–32. The date of the second letter was
actually April 8. BF corrected the date on his retained draft.

9. Ingenhousz introduced James Robertson in his April 29 letter.

1. Ingenhousz began his letter of Feb. 26 by referring to this request,
which he had made in his previous letter. That letter, dated Jan. 28, did
eventually arrive, as BF endorsed it and it remains among his papers:
XXXIX, 88–93. For the background on what would eventually be published
as *Nouvelles expériences et observations sur divers objets de physique* . . . see
XXXV, 548–50; XXXVI, 220–1; XXXVII, 211–12.

2. It was probably forwarded by Lebègue de Presle, who, in an undated
note, told BF that he was sending a letter from Ingenhousz "avec la figure"
and a letter from an unnamed traveler (APS). Ingenhousz began his letter
of April 8 by asking whether BF had received this portrait.

3. See XXXIX, 217–18.

4. In his letter of Jan. 28, which BF claimed not to have received (see
above), Ingenhousz described a recent visit by Valltravers during which the
unfortunate Swiss begged him to plead his case with BF.

I cannot afford to attend to his endless Discourse & numerous long Letters, and Visionary Projects. He wants to be employ'd in our affairs, but he manages his own so badly that one can have but little Confidence in his Prudence. I pity him however, tho' I see no possible means of serving him.

I thank you for your friendly Congratulations on the Peace and Cautions respecting our future Conduct; they are good & Wise.

Mr. Wharton's Treatment of you gives me pain. He never writes to me. I forget whether I have already sent you the Extract of his Letter to Dr. Bancroft, so I enclose a Copy.[5] I enclose also part of a Philadelphia Newspaper, by which you will see that your Name & Writings are already known in our Country. With regard to your Property in the Public Funds, I have no doubt of its being secure, according to the Value it had when it was plac'd there. But I can say nothing as to the Particulars of its Situation or Amount; Mr. Williams can better inform you. I have requested him to do it.[6]

It is long since I have seen M. le Begue. He is much in the Country. I have heard nothing of the Printing of your Book.[7]

Your Experiment of burning the Wire has been made here with the greatest Success. My Grandson had it try'd at Mr. Charles's Lecture,[8] where it gave great Satisfaction, and was much admired.

I have not yet found Leisure to explain the Fireplace, but hope for it, when I am quit of my present Station.

5. Ingenhousz' troubles with Samuel Wharton were a recurrent theme. In the postscript to his letter of April 29, Ingenhousz asked BF to forward a note on the matter to Bancroft and urge him to answer it. The extract of Wharton's letter to Bancroft has not been located, but it is discussed in XXXVIII, 366n.

6. JW was in Paris at this time: XXXIX, 503–4; JW to WTF, May 15, 1783 (APS).

7. Ingenhousz had asked BF to "rouse" Lebègue de Presle out of his "inaction," in the matter of overseeing the publication of *Nouvelles expériences . . . :* XXXIX, 89.

8. The previous fall, Ingenhousz sent BF a wire with which to perform this experiment, and on Jan. 28 he asked whether the experiment had been done: XXXVIII, 379–80; XXXIX, 88. The physicist Charles began a new lecture series on March 6: *Jour. de Paris*, issue of Feb. 26, 1783.

I have been, as you know, so little in America for these last 25 Years, that I am unqualified to answer the Request of M. Veinbrenner concerning the Names & Solidity of Houses there.[9] A new Set of Merchants have grown up into Business, of whom I know nothing; and the Circumstances of the old ones whom I formerly knew, may have been much altered by Time or by the War. It is besides an invidious & dangerous Thing for me, to give such a distinguishing List, if I were able to do it. My best Advice to your commercial People, is to send over a discreet, intelligent Person with Instructions to travel thro' the Country, observe the Nature of the Commerce, find out what of your Commodities are wanted there, and in what Quantities & Proportions; & what of the Produce of the Country can be purchased to make advantageous Returns. Such a Man on the Spot may obtain better Informations of Characters than I can possibly give, and may make the Connections desired with those that he finds to merit Confidence. If your People should think fit to take this Step, I will give Letters of Recommendation introductory of the Person, and which may be useful to their Design.[1] Please to acquaint M. Veinbrenner of this, presenting my Respects. I have already given such Letters at the Ambassador's Request, to a Person employ'd to make Collections of Natural History in America for the Emperor's Museum & Botanic Garden.[2] I have had a Number of Applications from Persons at Ostend, Trieste &c. solliciting to be appointed Consuls for America: But till the

9. See XXXIX, 444–5.
1. Beelen-Bertholff, who had already been selected for this mission, received his instructions in June (XXXIX, 445n) and arrived in Paris in July. There he presented his papers to Mercy-Argenteau, who was instructed to introduce him to the American commissioners. Beelen left France on Aug. 1, arriving in Philadelphia in early September (XXXIX, 491n). Though he was recalled in 1790, he remained in the United States and died there in 1805: H. van Houtte, "Contribution à l'histoire commerciale des Etats de l'empereur Joseph II (1780–1790)," *Vierteljahrschrift für Social-und Wirtschaftsgeschichte*, VIII (1910), 379–80, 393n; Hanns Schlitter, ed., *Die Berichte des ersten Agenten Österreichs in den Vereinigten Staaten von Amerika Baron de Beelen-Bertholff* . . . (Vienna, 1891), pp. 236–7n; "Notes and Queries," *PMHB*, LI (1927), 383–4.
2. Mercy-Argenteau had requested letters of introduction for Franz Joseph Märter in April, and BF obliged: XXXIX, 474–5, 490–1.

Trade is commenced, there can be no occasion for Consuls; and no such Magistrates can be nominated by either Government in the Dominions of the other, till such a Proceeding is authoriz'd by a Treaty of Commerce. I have receiv'd no Intimation except from you, that a Proposition for such a Treaty would be acceptable to his Imperial Majesty; I shall however venture to propose it to the Ambassador, when I request his forwarding to you this Letter. The Commodities you mention as Productions of the Emperor's Dominions are all wanted in America, and will sell there to Advantage.

I will send you another Piece of the Soap you mention,[3] when I can have a good Opportunity. I now send you one of the Medals I have caused to be struct here, which has the good Luck to be much approved.[4]

I am glad you have made the Experiments you mention,[5] and with Success. You will find that the holes are not made by the Impulse of the Fluid moving in certain Directions, but by Circumstances of Explosion of Parts of the matter; and I still think my Explanation of the Holes in the Vane probable, viz. that it was the Explosion of Tin against Parts of the Copper Plate, that were almost in a State of Fusion, and therefore easily burst thro', either on one Side or the other as it happened. The Bursting of the 12 Bottles all at once, I take to be owing to small Bubbles in the Substance of the Glass, or Grains of

3. XXXIX, 446. BF still had some of the two dozen cakes of crown soap that he had received from Jane Mecom c. March 5, 1780: XXX, 148–50, 480, 524–5; XXXII, 160–1; XXXIV, 200. On the verso of BF's Cash Book covering 1778 through 1780 (Account XVI, XXVI, 3), he drew up a list of intended recipients for the "Soap / 24 Cakes". Chaumont, at the head of the list, was to receive two cakes; the others would receive one. In order, they are: Ingenhousz, the abbé de La Roche, WTF, the abbés Chalut and Arnoux (who evidently were expected to share), "Myself", Holker, "M. Cayo" (probably Caillot, BF's neighbor), Le Veillard, and M. Brillon. BF placed an X next to all but the last three names.

Just before BF left France, Ingenhousz renewed his request for soap, as he had never received the promised second cake. By that time, however, the supply was exhausted: Ingenhousz to BF, June 11, 1785 (APS); BF to Ingenhousz, July 6, 1785 (Munson-Williams-Proctor Institute, 1955).

4. The *Libertas Americana* medal, for which see vol. 39.

5. In his letter of April 29.

Sand, into which a Quantity of the Electric Fluid had been forc'd & compress'd while the Bottles were charging; and when the Pressure was suddenly taken off by discharging the Bottles, that confin'd Portion by its elastic Force expanding caused the Breach. My Reasons for thinking that the Charge did not pass by those Holes you will find in a former Letter;[6] and I think you will always find that the Coating within & without is forced both ways by the Explosion of those Bubbles.—

With regard to the Statuary you mention,[7] I hardly think it can be worth his while at present to go to America in Expectation of being employ'd there. Private Persons are not rich enough to encourage sufficiently the fine Arts; and therefore our Geniuses all go to Europe. In England at present the best History-Painter, West; the best Portrait-Painter, Copely; and the best Landscape-Painter, Taylor at Bath, are all Americans.[8] And the Public being burthen'd by its War-Debts, will certainly think of paying them, before it goes into the Expence of Marble Monuments. He might indeed as you hint be easily paid in Land, but Land will produce him nothing without Labour; and he and his Workmen must subsist while they fashion their Figures. After a few Years, such an Artist may find Employment; and possibly we may discover a white Marble a little easier to work than that we have at present, which tho' it bears a fine Polish, is reckon'd too hard.

I have already spoke to Mr: Le Roy about taking Care of the Edition of your Work, which he very kindly & readily promis'd if you should have Occasion.—[9]

I will send your Note to Dr. Bancroft & engage him if I can to write to you.[1] But he confesses himself extreamly indolent

6. XXXVII, 504–12.

7. Giuseppe Ceracchi: XXXIX, 530–1.

8. Benjamin West (XXXVII, 236–7), John Singleton Copley, and John Taylor (XXXVIII, 394–6). West and Taylor were personal friends of BF's. For assessments of the latter's skill see Arthur S. Marks, "An Eighteenth-Century American Landscape Painter Rediscovered: John Taylor of Bath," *American Art Jour.*, X (1978), 81–96; William H. Gerdts, "American Landscape Painting: Critical Judgments, 1730–1845," *American Art Jour.*, XVII (1985), 29–31.

9. See XXXIX, 531.

1. Enclosed with his letter of April 29; see above.

and averse to writing; and I am not sure I shall prevail with him. Mr. Williams writes a few Lines which I enclose.

I thank you for your good Counsel respecting Physic,[2] I continue well, & live on without it; and while I do live I shall ever be with great & sincere Esteem, My dear Friend, Yours most affectionately   B Franklin

Dr. Ingenhauss.

Addressed:[3] A Monsieur / Monsieur Ingenhausz / à Vienne.

From Ann Ourry, with a Note from ———— Fagan

ALS: American Philosophical Society

Kinsale May 16th—1783—

Your Excellency After a Seperation of More than Twelve Years, And immersed as You have been in business of the highest Importance, deciding the Fate of Great and Mighty Kingdoms, Will doubtless find it difficult to recall to Your remembrance the Daughter of Your late sincere & Worthy friend Lewis Ourry: But even tho' You shou'd not, I well know the philanthropy of Your Nature, Studies No less the Felicity of Individuals, than the Happiness of Nations. If this shou'd be so fortunate as to reach Your Hands, it Will be accompanied by a Certificate, which will Make You Acquainted With My Dear Mothers, & My Situation And my Motive for troubling You with this.[4] I am certain You need no other inducements than the long Friendship that subsisted between Your Excellence, & My Dear &

2. In his letter of Jan. 28.

3. In BF's hand.

4. Capt. Lewis Ourry and his family, old friends of the Franklins (VII, 62–3n, and subsequent volumes), had moved from Scotland to Ireland in 1774. In 1778 Ourry was appointed commissary of prisoners at Kinsale; he died there of a fever in April, 1779: Donald Cornu, "Captain Lewis Ourry, Royal American Regiment of Foot," *Pa. Hist.*, XIX (1952), 261. The enclosed certificate is unlocated, but in a subsequent letter Ann Ourry—who had received no reply from BF—explained the circumstances of her father's death and related the financial difficulties that had befallen her and her mother: Ourry to BF, Jan. 27, 1785, University of Pa. Library.

ever Honor'd Father, & the impulse of Your own Humane disposition, to Serve his Injured, & Unfortunate Family. & there
are very Many, & some of the first Consequence in Paris, (to
Whome Were our Case known) Wou'd be Happy to second the
Grateful Wishes of the poor prisoners. Mrs. Ourry tenders You
her Most respectful Compliments. & I must beg Your Acceptance of those, of, Sir, Your Excellencies Most Obedient And
very Humble Servant   ANN OURRY

[*In Fagan's hand:*] M. Fagan who had been named Commissary
General for the French Prisoners on the breaking out of the war
takes the Liberty of Informing your Excellency that he has had
this poor womans memorial backed by his Excellency the Count
Adhemar and that he has certifyed the husband's humanity and
her distress. Lond June the 6th. 1783[5]

Addressed: To / His Excellency Benmn. Franklin / Paris

Notation: Aury 16 May 1783

From Reuben Harvey, with Franklin's Note for a Reply
ALS: American Philosophical Society

Respected Friend   Cork 17th. Ma[y, 1783][6]
I take the liberty to ask thy advice on the following Matter
[*faded:* and request(?)] an answer as soon as possible. A Mer-
chant(?) here named Stubbeman who has continued warmly

---

5. Fagan had been involved in the exchange of prisoners between France
and England since 1778: XXVII, 482, 485; XXXI, 354n. He may have known
Ourry during the latter's tenure at the Kinsale prison (also called the "French
prison"), which housed foreigners brought into Ireland: James Coleman,
"Antiquarian Remains and Historic Places in Kinsale District," *Jour. of the
Cork Hist. and Archaeol. Soc.*, 2nd ser., XVIII (1912), 133–6; C. J. F. Mac-
Carthy, "The American Prisoners at Kinsale," *ibid.*, XCIV (1989), 49–50.
    Jean Balthazar, comte d'Adhémar de Montfalcon (1731–1791), was ap-
pointed the French ambassador to the court of St. James's, *c.* May 14, 1783:
DBF; Repertorium der diplomatischen Vertreter, III, 118.
    6. The upper right-hand corner of the MS is torn. We base the date on the
April arrival of the *Enterprize*, mentioned in the postscript.

attach'd to America is now loading a Ship call'd the Ann Benjn. Edmonton Master for Philadelphia which will be ready to sail in 20 days; There are about 100 poor Tradesmen & Husbandmen offering to proceed on board this Ship in order to settle in America, but they have not Money to pay their Passage, & therefore propose to indent as Servants for a certain term, as has been the custom heretofore; but my friend Stubbeman is unwilling to accept them in this manner until he has thy opinion respecting the propriety of it, least Congress may disapprove of such Men being carried out to America; I own I think that those sort of useful laborious Men will be very acceptable in your Country, & I can assure thee there is not a Convict or Felon amongst them. Thy immediate Answer will be acknowledg'd a great favour, as the Vessel will only be delay'd until it comes.[7]

I am with the most respectful regard Thy sincere Friend

REUBEN HARVEY

I have had the pleasure to receive the first consignment that arrived from the United States; viz—The Enterprize Capt Garzia from Rhode Island, She was address'd to me by a Gentn. named Charles Green a Cousin Germain of Genl. Green.[8]

Benjamen Franklin Esqr.

Addressed: Benjamen Franklin Esqr. / Ambassador from the / United States of America / at / Paris

---

7. BF's answer has not survived, but Harvey acknowledged it in his letter of July 25. The *Ann* sailed in late June under Capt. Edmonstone's direction and arrived in Philadelphia in mid-August, when the various trades offered by these young men were immediately advertised: *Pa. Evening Post*, Aug. 14, 1783; *Pa. Gaz.*, Sept. 17, 1783.

8. Charles Greene (1753–1816), a shipowner from East Greenwich, R.I., was the son of Rufus Greene (x, 368n) and a first cousin of Gen. Nathanael Greene: Louise B. Clarke, comp., *The Greenes of Rhode Island* . . . (New York, 1903), pp. 129, 217–18. The *Enterprize*, said to be the first ship flying American colors to arrive in Ireland, entered Cork harbor on April 21 with a cargo of flaxseed and staves. Reuben Harvey was described as being "a gentleman well known for his firm and avowed principles in favour of the liberty and independence of America": *Boston Evening-Post and the Gen. Advertiser*, June 7, 1783.

Endorsed: They will go to a Country where People do not export their Beef & Linnen to import Claret, while the Poor at home live on Potatoes and wear Rags. Indeed America has not Beef & Linnen sufficient for Exportation, because every Man there, even the poorest, eats Beef and wears a Shirt.

From the Chevalier de Berruyer and Other Favor Seekers

ALS: American Philosophical Society

As usual, Franklin receives many unsolicited appeals from people, mostly unknown to him, who want to impose on his reputed benevolence. We summarize here those letters which produced no known response.[9] The first category includes people who seek help with financial matters or beg money outright. Others write for information or advice, ask him to forward letters, urge him to answer neglected correspondence, or plead with him to grant a personal interview. The chevalier de Berruyer, a former officer in the French army on Saint-Domingue, whose letter we print below as a sample, claims to be owed payment for services he performed in 1775 and 1776. Although he already has Sartine's support, he asks Franklin to write to Castries on his behalf to expedite matters.

Louis Frederic Stromeyer, a cloth merchant, and Straub, a master tailor, write on June 3 from Strasbourg to ask Franklin's help in collecting a debt. Baron von Steuben left them a promissory note, which they enclose, for 421 *l.t.* 14 *s.* They have sent Steuben several letters, one even forwarded by Franklin, without receiving a response. Might Congress help two French subjects by paying the general's debt out of his wages? Stromeyer and Straub reiterate their request on June 28 and enclose another copy of Steuben's promissory note.[1]

9. Unless otherwise specified, the following documents are in French and at the APS.
1. BF forwarded their June 3 letter to Charles Thomson on Sept. 13, below, and it remains among Thomson's papers at the Library of Congress. The June 28 letter and Steuben's promissory note (in German, dated June 10, 1777, and promising payment within six weeks) are at the APS. Steuben visited Strasbourg on his way to Paris (where he would meet BF: XXIV, 499–500) at a time when he was unemployed and already deeply in debt; see John M. Palmer, *General von Steuben* (New Haven, 1937), pp. 83–4.

On June 30 Madame Butler de Beaufort requests the return of the memoir she left for Franklin on May 20, on the ottoman in his apartment. (The memoir, addressed to Necker, the former director general of finances, concerns her effort to obtain the pension of her deceased husband, the sieur Boutin de Beaufort, a lieutenant colonel in the carabiniers with 30 years of service.)[2] M. de MacMahon, whom she saw the day before, told her that Franklin was unlikely to intervene. She would like the memoir returned before others see it.

The Paris bankers Bost, Horion & Cie.[3] ask Franklin on July 7 to honor a letter of exchange drawn on him for $60. They enclose it.

The baron de Perier, *colonel commandant d'infanterie* and *chevalier de Saint-Louis*,[4] writes from his estate, the château d'Ussau, on August 10. Three years earlier the *Jonathas* of Marseille had sailed from Cape François bound for Bordeaux with a load of sugar from his plantations on Saint-Domingue. A bad storm forced the ship into port at New London, where it was condemned and the sugar sold.[5] The captain deposited the receipts at the chancellery in Boston, as directed by the French consul M. de Valnais.[6] Perier, the father of a large family, would be grateful if Franklin could assist him in recovering his money.

Dr. Bry writes from Lorient on August 11, emboldened by the memory of the kind reception he received from Franklin in April, 1780. To whom should he direct his request for the prize money owed him for his service as medical officer on the *Vengeance* under John Paul Jones? Franklin had approved his medical certificate at that time; would he now grant a new certificate that would allow him to serve with a group of Americans about to establish themselves at Lorient?

2. Undated, Hist. Soc. of Pa.

3. They are listed among the "Banquiers pour les Traites & Remises de Place en Place" in the *Almanach royal* for 1783, p. 473.

4. Listed as Martin-Louis de Perrier, baron d'Ussau (b. 1745), in the *Dictionnaire de la noblesse*, XV, 687–8.

5. The incident took place in the fall of 1779. The *Jonathas* was convoyed by d'Estaing (XXX, 265n) and after the storm sailed into New London with the *Négresse*, which was unharmed. The *Négresse* carried the stranded crew back to France in May, 1780; among the other passengers was John Trumbull. The ship's captain later claimed that Trumbull introduced him to BF: XXXII, 245; Smith, *Letters*, XIV, 122; *Mémoires du capitaine Landolphe, contenant l'histoire de ses voyages pendant trente-six ans, aux côtes d'Afrique et aux deux Amériques*, ed. J. S. Quené (2 vols., Paris, 1823), I, 196–256.

6. XXXVIII, 473n.

Three days later M. Baron, now signing himself as a master tailor at Dunkirk, repeats his earlier request for Franklin's assistance in obtaining money owed him by Gognet and Colson, officers of the *Pallas* from John Paul Jones's squadron who had fled Dunkirk without paying their bills. An account of their debts was sent to the *commissaire* of Lorient in February, 1780, but Baron has heard nothing since that time.[7]

Three correspondents ask for money outright. On May 31 Cavelier de Macomble writes from Rouen seeking funds for an undescribed project which, eight years ago, he explained to Miromesnil. The expense of rearing, outfitting, and marrying three children has left him unwilling to risk the 25 *louis* necessary to execute his design. He would be overjoyed to explain it to Franklin and get his support.

Joseph Bouillot, identifying himself as a post boy, writes from Passy on June 3 conveying greetings from the abbé Rochon at Morlaix, whom he saw recently. Bouillot came to Paris hoping to find work at the *messagerie*, but as there are no vacancies, he is forced to return. If Franklin would give him assistance, he would never cease praying for his health and prosperity.

On July 26 John Dudley, an American, writes from Poultry Compter, a debtors' prison in London. He recounts his service in the Continental Army, first in the Second North Carolina regiment, then in Henry Lee's cavalry, and finally commanding 100 men stationed opposite the British lines in New York.[8] He was wounded for the thirteenth time in May, 1781, when he was also captured in an attack on Howbuck Island. Imprisoned and cruelly treated in New York, he was later sent to England, where his leg became so badly infected that it had to be amputated. After ten months in Deal Prison, he was released without any money. Unable to find help in London, he is now in jail for debt. Henry Laurens refused to advance him the £120 that he requested but offered to endorse his bills. As no one is willing to take bills drawn on America, his case is desperate.

7. Baron's previous letter, dated May 31, 1781, and written by a professional scribe, complained of three officers: Gognet, Colson, and Saillot. At the time of their offense, Baron was the keeper of a hotel: XXXV, 15. The *commissaire* of Lorient was La Grandville.

8. Dudley enlisted in the regiment in 1777: *Roster of Soldiers from North Carolina in the American Revolution* . . . (1932; reprint, Baltimore, 1967), pp. 60, 606. He wrote in English, and misaddressed this letter to "His Excellency W. Franklin."

C. E. Griffiths writes in English from Lisson Green near Padding-ton with a complicated tale of inheritance. Her late uncle May Bick-ley, attorney general of New York,[9] left a house and lands in New York and New Jersey which eventually descended to her mother, who is a widow. Several individuals pressed her mother to sell tracts for far less than their value. She hired an agent, who was of no help; the one promising sale, arranged through a friend in Connecticut, fell through when the war broke out. The New York lands and house are now occupied by a Mr. Livingston, who never received title. Griffiths, the sole heir, has now been told that she might "meet with redress" because "her heart was for America." She begs Franklin for his advice and assistance. Her undated letter is postmarked "17 JU," indicating either June or July, and assuming that she sought redress once the peace was declared, 1783 is the probable year.

Also counting on Franklin's far-reaching influence are two suppli-cants for letters of recommendation. The baron de Feriet, an infantry captain,[1] writes from Versailles on May 29 reminding Franklin that he had agreed the previous Saturday to provide a letter of recom-mendation for M. Berthier fils, a merchant from Nancy who wishes to establish a business in Philadelphia. Unable to find Temple to ask him to draft the letter, and not wishing to interrupt Franklin a sec-ond time, Feriet left with a servant the note he had shown Franklin.[2] The people on whose behalf he seeks this favor assure him that the Berthiers are esteemed merchants in Lorraine. The family hopes that the son, who is between 30 and 35 years of age, may be directed to someone in Philadelphia who can advise him on the execution of his project. Mme de Feriet joins in sending her respects.

On July 3 Stockar zur Sonnenbourg[3] writes from Schaffhausen to recommend a close relative, formerly in the service of Sardinia, to serve as a lieutenant in General Washington's army. He sends greet-ings to M. d'Alembert, should Franklin see him at a meeting of the Académie des sciences.

---

9. For May Bickley (d. 1724), who emigrated to New York from En-gland in 1701 and became attorney general in 1705, see William Smith, Jr., *The History of the Province of New-York*, ed. Michael Kammen (2 vols., Cambridge, Mass., 1972), II, 284.
1. Possibly a son or nephew of Joseph, baron de Fériet (1707–1779), *conseiller* at the court of Lorraine: English Showalter et al., eds., *Correspon-dance de Madame de Graffigny* (13 vols. to date, Oxford, 1985–), VIII, 180n.
2. This undated note, perhaps given to Feriet, asks that BF provide this recommendation. APS.
3. XXXVI, 204–5n.

The dowager M. E. de Platen, née Krassou, writes on August 30 from Garz, on the island of Rügen, begging Franklin for news of her son, Philip de Platen, who left home seven years ago to join the American army. He has not been heard from since then.[4]

Various people contact Franklin concerning letters that they want him to deliver, forward, or write. The widow Guillaume sends her request from Faÿ-les-Veneurs on July 7. When Franklin arrives in New York, would he be good enough to deliver the enclosed letter to her son Paul Guillaume, who lives in that city, and arrange for his return to France? He served as a *chasseur* in Lauzun's Legion,[5] was taken prisoner by the Indians, escaped, and made his way to New York after the peace. He has written seven letters to her but has not received any of her replies, which she sent by way of Lorient.

Also on July 7 the Paris banker Louis Tourton[6] forwards four letters he has received from Hamburg concerning an unscrupulous merchant named Borges, a "fripon insigne," who fled to Philadelphia on a ship he had outfitted leaving a trail of unpaid bills. Tourton asks Franklin to forward these letters to Philadelphia; two are from magistrates of Hamburg, and all are written in the hope that Borges's creditors will be compensated.

F. M. de Cabanes writes from Metz on September 12. Not knowing General Washington's address, he asks Franklin to forward the enclosed letter, which seeks information about one of his relatives who fought under the general at Yorktown.[7]

François Roi writes from Paris on July 9 and again on July 13 to remind Franklin that on June 28, when Roi delivered a letter from his father, Franklin had promised to answer it. He is about to return to Switzerland and would be honored to carry Franklin's response, which his father eagerly awaits.[8]

---

4. The son wrote BF for assistance in 1777: XXIV, 31.

5. The legion, created in March, 1780, as the "Volontaires étrangers de Lauzun," served in America with Rochambeau's army. Remaining there after most of the army had departed, it embarked for France in May, 1783: Rice and Brown, eds., *Rochambeau's Army*, I, 314–15; II, 182–3.

6. XXXIX, 304n.

7. Lt. Col. Cabanes had written almost two years earlier, hoping to settle in America with his family. In the same letter he mentioned no fewer than four relatives who fought at Yorktown: XXXVI, 314–15.

8. The father was probably J. J. Roi, the pastor from Neuchâtel who had offered to dedicate his work to BF and expressed a wish to emigrate to America: XXXVI, 314; XXXVIII, 390–1.

M. Dubois Martin, *avocat aux Conseils du Roi et de Monsieur*,[9] also offers to carry a response—this one to M. de Both, a lieutenant colonel in service to the emperor, who wrote to Franklin on February 24 and now wants to know whether he ever received the letter. Dubois Martin's letter is dated September 3 (a Wednesday); he offers to pick up Franklin's answer, and would like it to be ready by Sunday or Monday.

Some correspondents seek appointments to make their appeals in person. Although Franklin had suggested to the baronne d'Ahax that she explain in writing the matter she wished to discuss,[1] she insists in a letter of June 17 on speaking with him. She once again recommends M. Martin and his wife, and asks Franklin to forward her enclosed letter to them at the residence of M. de Gand.[2]

On August 2 Madame Loyer Deslande, writing from Versailles, requests an appointment to discuss certain business affairs which her husband has conducted in America since 1777.[3] She is staying at the home of M. Bretel, *premier commis* of the Marine, but will be leaving soon.

On August 1 the abbé Coquillot, who had presented his *Couplets sur la paix* to Franklin in April,[4] sends the manuscript of a fourteen-stanza "Ode a son Excellence Monsieur B. Franklin . . . en recevant de luy la Medaille frappée par les Americains en 1782" (the *Libertas Americana* medal). He requests permission to publish it as a mark of gratitude and admiration.

An unusual request comes on June 9 from a sieur Bousquetÿ, a lawyer in Beaumarchès, a fortified town west of Toulouse. He would like to know more about the illustrious doctor's discoveries and experiments and therefore asks for a collection of his writings on electricity in manuscript. Since he writes in the name of liberty and friendship, he hopes that Franklin will respond.

A. Laignier, a simple craftsman who has recently arrived in Paris knowing no one, writes on June 30 that he has made an important discovery about magnetism and electricity but does not know how to announce it. He submitted a letter to the *Journal de Paris* but has been

9. *Almanach royal* for 1783, pp. 130, 285.

1. See XXXIX, 597.

2. For the Martins see XXXIX, 373, 447, 455–7. De Gand (Degand) was Mme Martin's maiden name: Mme Martin to BF, March 10, 1784 (APS).

3. Her husband, a merchant, had aided an American prisoner on his way to America: XXV, 361n.

4. XXXIX, 241.

told that he should have had it reviewed first by a scientist. He hopes that Franklin will meet with him to discuss "Cette descouverte La plus importante pour Lumanite qui nait jamais parut."

Finally, in an undated letter, a certain Blanchard, who identifies himself as the person who recently sent Franklin a memorandum, begs on bended knee for a few minutes of his time, even if the doctor only expresses regret at being unable to help him. The 12-page memorandum, also undated, describes his misfortunes, including a nervous disorder that keeps him from doing anything more than giving a few language lessons. He has waited two years to send this appeal out of respect for Franklin's important occupations. Dr. Mac-Mahon, who recently saved his elderly wife from a serious illness, will doubtless vouch for him. His debts are many and his creditors merciless. Perhaps the United States, on the forthcoming announcement of peace, will authorize some largesse, in which he would of course be included. He requests that this appeal be kept confidential; he and Franklin have common acquaintances, and he does not want them to gossip. We can date these documents only as before September 3.

au chateau de st fromond par st lo
ce 18 may 1783. normendie

Je me croy fondé monsieur a reclammer au pres de vous pour vous prier d'ecrire au ministre de la marinne non pour me faire rendre la justice quil ne me paroit pas eloingué de me rendre mais pour en accelerer lexécution. Mon affaire est fort simple, monsieur le comte denry general de st domingue,[5] ma envoyé dans vottre pays en 1775 pour luy rendre des comptes de ce qui sy passoit et par consequent me rendre utille aux americains. En y passant avec ces pase ports sous des expeditions de st pierre de miquelon, je contrefesaisais le negotient en armant des navirs en marchandises. Ils ont eté pris en retour de Boston lun et les deux autres sortant de la martinique, messieurs du comitté de ports smuth ou j'ai armé pour aider le pays de poudre et canons vottre colonel lingdon[6] agent du congres en ce port en sonts les témoins j'ai en fin fait tout ce qui dependait de moy pour me rendre utille, cest moy qui me suis deplacé pour aller a gous Bray

---

5. Victor-Thérèse Charpentier d'Ennery was *commandant général* of Saint-Domingue from 1775 until his death at the end of 1776: *DBF.*

6. John Langdon: XXII, 323n.

[Goose Bay?] et a Kene Beck pour assurer les sauvages que la france s'alliait avec les americains, j'ai fait ce voyage a la sollicitation du comitté de port smuth avec un officier de Boston qui avoit des pouvoirs du congres. De ce moment il en a mesme embarqué 16 dont un corsaire de Boston armé par le congres de philadelphye.

Cest moy qui ai fait monter vos 90. pieces de cannon de fonte que vous aviez envoyee dans L'amphitrite capte fautrelle[7] vu que les officiers de la division de du coudray etoient partis pour l'armee et n'avoient l'aissé q'un officier qui ne parloit pas englois, j'ai egalement traduit touts les paquets du congres pour le capte: fautrel mesme lorsque ces messieurs luy envoyerent mr. paul jhoon [Jones] pour monter sa fregatte de moitié avec luy. J'ai mesme fait soingner du vin en Bouteilles que vous envoyiez a madame franklin j'ai eté notament le premier francais au commencement de vottre guerre qui a prouvai du zele sans coutter un sol aux americains il m'en reste les fatigues et 180000 *l.t.* de pertte malgré que j'aie le plus grand droit et en voila la preuve, j'ai Raporté chaque fois que j'ai ete depuis les sentences en englois de comdem nation vu que nous navions pas guere(?) de tortole, st christophe et antigua, monsieur le marquis de Bouillé generalle de la martinique et mr dar Baud[8] les onts viser onts renvoyai des parlementaires pour Reclammer mes navirs Ces generaux onts ecrits les lettres les plus instantes a mr de sartinne! Ce ministre ma mis vis avis de mr. chardon pour estre dedomagé sur les fonds des prises faittes sur les englois dans nos ports lors de la declaration de guerre, le Roy a disposé de ces fonds depuis, aujourdhuy lon ne peut me dire que j'ai tord et lon ma fait temporiser en me disant que j'ai Bon droit sans rien faire ny dire de décisif. Si j'étais sans fortunne il faudrait donc que je moureusse de faim. Je croy monsieur que vous ne pouvez me Refuser d'ecrire au ministre en luy faisant voire que ma demende est juste. J'ai un parent qui est mr. le Baron de chigny qui est directeur general des ports et arseneaux, qui a en main

7. Nicolas Fautrel: xxvi, 580.

8. Bache-Alexandre, comte d'Arbaud de Jouques, became governor of Guadeloupe in 1775 and served through the War for American Independence: *DBF.*

les certificats comme mr. de sartinne a Receut mes pieces, il sinteresse a moy et je suis seure de son amitié. Si vous voules bien y aider il fera le reste parceque il me la promis il y a un mois, mais il ne peut y mettre trop dinstance vu que cest mon parent, mr. de laporte ma promis aussi que rien n'arresterait de son costé et il trouve mon affaire juste. Comme vous voyes monsieur il ne faut que de l'aide pour reussire & avoire justice, je ne croy pas que vous vouluties me refuser celle d'ecrire une seulle lettre a mr. de castries. Vous voyes que j'ai aidé dans la nouvelle englettere de ce que j'ai peut tant de ma fortunne que de mon zele pour le service. Mr. William de Boston qui est vottre parent, a veut ma maniere honeste et discrette de me conduire dans ce pays la, il scait que j'ai manqué d'estre assaciné par des mauvais sujets de francais qui venoient de faire des coquineries dans le pays aux quels je fesais des Representations ils monts intercepté mes lettres pour le general. Mr. Baudoin[9] president du congres de Boston a eté obligai dinterposer son authorité, et ma maniére honeste de me conduire ma merité j'ause dire lestimme de ces messieurs.[1] Cest ce qui me fait esperer que vous ne me refuseres pas de m'accorder la vôttre./.

J'ai lhonneur d'estre avec Respect Monsieur vottre tres humble et tres obest serviteur

LE CHER. DE BERRUYER
encien offer des trouppes de st domingue

Notation: De Beruyer 18 May 1783.

9. James Bowdoin.

1. The chevalier wrote to Gen. Washington from Boston on Sept. 9, 1776, explaining that he was 36 years old and had come there from Saint-Domingue to recover his health. He requested permission to sail to France and asked Washington to forward an enclosed letter to Congress with the same request: W. W. Abbot *et al.*, eds., *The Papers of George Washington,* Revolutionary War Series (20 vols. to date, Charlottesville and London, 1985–), VI, 353n.

From ———— de Franck[2] and Other Offerers of Goods and Schemes

ALS: American Philosophical Society

With the general armistice in effect and peace virtually assured, merchants continue to come forward with offers of goods or requests for advice on how to establish commercial ventures. M. de Franck of Strasbourg, having heard that the new nation will be commissioning cannons in France, hastens to tell Franklin on May 18 that he will supply the best terms. His letter is printed below.[3]

G. Anquetil Brutiere,[4] writing from Saint-Malo on May 31, informs Franklin that he is expecting two of his cargo ships to arrive from La Rochelle any day now. He has no immediate plans for them, and would entertain advantageous proposals from either Franklin or his friends in America.

Frédéric-Robert Meuricoffre, Swiss by birth, has lived for the past 16 years in Naples, where more than 30 years ago he established a successful mercantile house. Writing from Paris on June 5, he offers the services of Meuricoffre-Scherb & Cie.[5] Asserting that Naples is perhaps the most important city in Europe for American trade, he encloses an annotated list of products that might be profitably exchanged. Naples would welcome American salt cod, tobacco, and sugar (but has no need for wood, wheat, or rice), and would export various oils, fabrics, wines, salt, licorice, and an infinity of other items that one could easily imagine.[6]

M. Urvoy, descended from an ancient Breton family, writes on June 6 telling Franklin to address his reply simply to the town of Saint-Brieuc, where he is known. He and a friend both love liberty

---

2. Undoubtedly one of the principals of the Strasbourg firm Franck frères; see XXIX, 343n.

3. Unless otherwise noted, the letters summarized in this headnote are in French, are at the APS, and elicited no known response.

4. The last extant communication between BF and Brutiere was in early 1779: XXVI, 597–8; XXVIII, 351–2, 583.

5. Meuricoffre (1740–1816) founded the Banque Meuricoffre & Cie. in Naples in 1760: *Dictionnaire historique de la Suisse*.

6. The only other letter from Meuricoffre is an undated request to be appointed consul general for the Kingdom of Naples. He names Girardot, Haller and Rilliet & Cie. as references (APS). This was evidently written around June, 1783, when Meuricoffre reportedly met with BF and made the request in person. BF told him that a treaty had to be negotiated before consuls could be appointed: Lefevbre de Revel père to Isidore Lefevbre de Revel, Aug. 28, 1783 (Hist. Soc. of Pa.).

and want to set up a commercial house for trade with America. He is 33 and retired from the military, but his friend, age 26, still serves. Once the friend has learned English and business management, he will establish himself in the United States; Urvoy will operate from one of the ports in his province. Between them, they have about 900,000 *l.t.* to invest, and while it may seem that they have little to offer, they share a love of work, goodwill, and the greatest probity. They request Franklin's advice, support, and a letter of recommendation for the younger partner to carry with him to America.

Writing from Paris on June 23, Walton & Stott of Ostend send a brief note requesting an interview. The merchants wish to discuss importing goods into America.

On July 7 the Liègeois arms manufacturer Jacques-Lambert Ransier writes about his hopes to go to America and sell arms of all kinds; a pistol of his manufacture is accurate at 300 paces. He is also thinking about establishing a factory there, for arms or perhaps even soap or perfume, or a distillery. He will be traveling with business associates who know these processes. The group will carry with them a selection of merchandise including cloth, silk, jewelry, and hardware. Franklin's answer should be sent care of Genefve & Cie. at Augsburg, where he is currently staying. Ransier writes again on August 12 from Fürth, near Nuremberg. He will be leaving for America in about five weeks with firearms and other merchandise, and asks for letters of recommendation and advice. He is staying with the merchant Pierre Lenoble.

John Gottfried Braumüller of Berlin writes in German on August 2. He has connections to manufacturers of silk, wool, linen, and other fabrics, and for a commission of 1½ percent will establish contacts with these firms on behalf of the United States. His trading partners include the house of Braunsberg Streckeisen & Cie. in Amsterdam, the silk merchant Doucet de Surini in Paris, Franz Sauvage in Dieppe, Boisselier Vogel & Cie. in Marseille, Smith Wienholt & Co. in London,[7] Paul Maistre & Cie. in Genoa, and Johann Michael Wagner in Venice. Braumüller's own trade is dry salting, and he asks for recommendations to American drysalters in Philadelphia and other respectable cities.

Two men offer to send to America products that they assume are needed. M. Delongueville, writing from Nancy on July 1, proposes to send grapevines, red and white potatoes, and large turnips that in-

7. Doucet de Surini and Smith Wienholt & Co. are in the *Almanach des marchands*, pp. 290, 376.

crease milk production in cows. Writing from Villentrode in Champagne on July 17, M. de Breuze has heard that America is setting up glass factories. They will need clay, and his is among the best available. Located 40 leagues from Paris, it could be shipped most conveniently from Rouen or Le Havre.

M. Sanherr, "Stättmeistre" of Colmar in Alsace,[8] asks Franklin's protection on August 3 for his plan of selling in the United States an exquisite *vin de paille* from his family vineyards. He encloses a printed price list. He would also be open to exchanging his wine for American products; once he receives a note detailing their cost when delivered to a French port, he will choose the ones best suited to his province.

Many writers seek Franklin's help in establishing commercial enterprises in America. The sieurs Duchesac and Clairval hope to establish a theater company in Philadelphia. Their first letter, unsigned and undated, was evidently written by Duchesac. He writes on behalf of himself and "Fauché de Clerval," who is the director of the "spectacle des Isles du Vent sous la domination du Roi." The second letter, signed "Clairval," is written from Paris on May 19. He has just learned that several American officials have arrived in Europe and will convene at Franklin's house. Because Franklin has approved the applicants' plan and afforded his protection, might he now be willing to grant Clairval a special audience? Lafayette, whom the actor saw a few days since, supports the project. He hopes Franklin will speak to the other Americans about it, and raise a subscription that would subsidize the troupe's passage.[9]

Charles Paleske, writing in English on May 27 from Hamburg, reminds Franklin of his previous letter of March 7, in which he had in-

---

8. Undoubtedly Jean-Mathias Sanherr (b. 1740), a merchant in Colmar, who held the post of *stettmestre* from 1777 to 1790 and was the eldest of three brothers: Jean-Pierre Kintz, ed., *Nouveau dictionnaire de biographie alsacienne* (40 vols. to date, Strasbourg, 1982–); Claude Muller, *Colmar au XVIIIe siècle* (Strasbourg, 2000), p. 147.

9. This is very likely the Parisian actor Fouchez, who performed under the name Clairval in a traveling theater troupe. During the French Revolution he became a lieutenant in the *armée révolutionnaire*, defected into Belgium, where he resumed acting, and was later court-martialed: Paul Friedland, *Political Actors: Representative Bodies and Theatricality in the Age of the French Revolution* (Ithaca, N.Y., and London, 2002), pp. 171–2. Though Clairval claims here that BF encouraged them, BF himself indicated the opposite when responding to a musician who wanted to join the theater company, saying that he doubted the project would be successful: Charles Stamitz to BF, with BF's Note for a Reply, Oct. 2, 1783 (APS).

quired about the incentives offered in America to new settlers.[1] Now he has decided to become himself "a partaker of American liberty & happiness." He is on his way to Amsterdam and London, from whence he and a clerk will embark in August to Philadelphia and there establish a merchant house under his own name. Having both money and connections in Europe, Paleske seeks only some recommendations from Franklin to his friends in Holland, England, and America. Paleske will await Franklin's answer at the Amsterdam firm Muilman & Sons,[2] which can also provide references for him.

From Karlsruhe on July 6 comes a letter from Michel Macklot, bookseller and printer to the Margrave of Baden, who hopes to establish one of his sons as a bookseller and printer in Philadelphia.[3] At the same time, he requests a *privilège* to send German language books to America. These would include the best German poets, works of the best foreign scholars, translations of the best Greek and Roman authors, moral tales and fables, and the finest plays. He has just printed Baron O'Cahill's work on new strategies for forming armies; the book is very interesting and might be used by American troops.[4] He begs to be allowed to send Franklin a copy.

François Truton de Sibery, a former navy recruiting officer, sends a note from Nantes on July 31 asking Franklin to consider the enclosed memorandum, which details his scheme: he hopes to establish a manufactory in New England to print designs in gold, silver, and other colors on all kinds of cloth. The fabric could be used for women's apparel, theatrical productions, funerals, interior decoration, and other applications too numerous to mention. This kind of printing has hitherto been reserved for court entertainments and the decoration of great halls. Truton and his uncle, who arranges the king's revels, are the only ones who know the secret formula. He hopes that Franklin will arrange free passage to Boston, Philadelphia, New York, or any other suitable place for his family and the two other people essential to the scheme.

1. See XXXIX, 50, where this Danzig merchant is identified.

2. XXXI, 136n.

3. Johann Michael Macklot (1728–1794) was the principality's foremost printer and bookseller. This is his only letter, and there is no indication that any of his three sons settled in America. The eldest two, Karl Friedrich (b. 1760) and Philipp (b. 1771), inherited the business after their mother's death in 1808: *Neue Deutsche Biographie* (23 vols. to date, Berlin, 1953–).

4. *Tacktischer Versuch über die Bildung einer guten Armee* (Karlsruhe, 1783).

28

François Giordana, writing from Turin on September 3, has all the skills necessary to establish a silk industry in the United States. He can teach the construction of large mills as well as small ones; both are simple and inexpensive, and the latter can be used in the home by women, children, and those with weak constitutions. The relationship of a small mill to a large one is like that of a harpsichord to an organ: mastering the former is excellent training for the latter.

Several correspondents want to shape the American system of government. Duboys de Lamoligniere, "Conseiller au Conseil Supérieur," writes from Port-au-Prince on July 27 enclosing a printed discourse on legislation (now missing) which is the product of seven years' work. He has sent copies to Washington, Hancock, and Charles Thomson.[5] The only other person who has received a copy is the head of his own family, Duboys de La Bernarde, a brigadier in the French army.[6]

Johannes Van der Hey writes voluminously to Franklin, Laurens, and Adams, beginning with a 14-page letter in English dated July 30 "Near Brussels." A 57-year-old member of the Reformed Church, born in Holland and fluent in most European languages, he was trained in commerce and is a specialist in financial administration, particularly the collection and distribution of tax revenue. He gives details about his writings on politics and finance and his service in various courts, and explains at length his recent misfortunes in trying to reclaim family property. He now wishes to emigrate to America with his unhappy family if he can secure employment there. He requests the permission of the American commissioners to send them a part of his work on finance, the first chapter of which outlines a plan whereby an integrated system of national and provincial taxes could be established by January 1, 1785. Under his scheme, five million dollars could be collected annually without placing an undue burden on manufacturers. This plan is based on the tax structure of Holland, the most reasonable and equitable one in Europe. As soon as he receives an answer, he will forward the first chapter of his work, written in French, to the desired address in Paris. He lists many Dutch officials as references. At the end of the letter, having just heard that John Adams is in Holland, he resolves to send this letter to him at

5. No copy of this work on legislation has been located. Washington acknowledged its receipt on Oct. 1, 1783: Fitzpatrick, *Writings of Washington*, XXVII, 173.

6. Jean-Elie Dubois-Labernarde (1716–1802): *DBF*. A duplicate of this ALS is also at the APS.

The Hague. In a postscript, he adds that he will send another copy to Franklin.[7]

That copy must be the memorandum which Van der Hey sent to the commissioners at Passy on August 1 under cover of a brief note. Nine dense pages in length, it repeats his account of his misfortunes and ends by offering to send the Americans copies of all relevant correspondence.[8] On August 5, this time writing in French, he alludes to the "Epitre" and memorandum previously sent, and encloses the first part of his work on finance, including a handwritten title page crammed with information. Another copy, including the first chapter, was sent on August 29,[9] along with copies in English and French of a two-page, fifteen-point "Outhlin'd Scheme of a Plan for a Nationnal Constitution and Permanent Gouvernement for the Thirteen United Provinces in North America."[1]

From Nantes, Coulougnac, who now adds "de Coste Belle" after his name and says he is of Franco-American origin, submits ten pages of detailed and wide-ranging reflections on how the United States should structure a strong federal government, judicial system, and military. His letter is dated September 10. He proposes a system of taxation that will support the public credit since at present all confidence is suspended not only in the government's ability to satisfy its liabilities but also in individual debtors. A representative federal assembly should pass bills on issues including term limits (he proposes no more than two ten-year terms), national academies, liberty of the press, arsenals and hospitals, and the settlement of Loyalist property disputes. If Coulougnac's reflections are of interest, he would be pleased to present an expanded version to Franklin. He closes by confiding that he plans to relocate to Philadelphia within the next year, whence he will establish trade with France and the colo-

7. Mass. Hist. Soc. This copy is endorsed by JA.

8. The note and memorandum, both in English, are at the Hist. Soc. of Pa. BF endorsed the latter "Van der Hey Propositions."

9. Laurens endorsed this, calling it Van der Hey's "project for Governing the U S of America." He noted that it was received on Sept. 10 and cost 4/8 in postage.

1. All of these documents are at the Hist. Soc. of Pa. Early in 1784 Van der Hey had two financial treatises published in London: *Observations politiques, morales & experimentees, sur les vrais principes de la finance* . . . and *Traité sur la finance: ouvrage utiles aux Anglais, Français, Autrichiens, Hollandais, aux Politiques, Négociants, & à tous autres Citoyens.* On the title page of the former, he is designated as *Conseiller Privé du Commerce* of the Prussian court.

nies. He ardently hopes to become a citizen, and asks if he can be so designated before he leaves.[2]

Four correspondents offer goods or schemes of a miscellaneous nature. M. Capion, a septuagenarian from Lyon, is a former army chaplain and doctor who traveled in French America between 1729 and 1731. He sends rambling thoughts studded with Latin quotations on July 19, praising Franklin and Washington and suggesting an allegorical design for a mural that should be placed in Congress' assembly hall. Capion ends by expressing disapproval of the immigration of Germans and Hessians, and especially the Irish, to America.

M. Gautier, from the rue Saintonge in the Marais, asks permission to dedicate to Franklin an onyx stone he has just engraved, set in a ring, which pays homage to the American's virtues. The bas-relief shows Liberty resting on a plinth, where she treads on a yoke. Her left hand indicates several ships, alluding to freedom of the seas and the abundance produced by peace. A device may be inscribed on the plinth. This letter, signed by Gautier, is in a secretarial hand. In a brief follow-up note, penned by Gautier himself, the sculptor and engraver wonders whether the stone pleased Franklin; he respectfully awaits the American's orders. Both letters are undated, but we place them after the signing of the definitive peace treaty on September 3.

On September 9, wanting to add his voice to the outpouring of congratulations on independence, M. de Bays, a lawyer from Nuits in Burgundy, sends a pannier of his best aged wine. He understands from Cabanis that Franklin has tasted it at Mme Helvétius' in Auteuil. He sends the same gift for Washington, and asks Franklin to forward it along with the cover letter. When the minister has a few minutes of leisure, de Bays would appreciate his reading a plan for the installation of lightning rods on the buildings of one of his country estates. The property includes a vineyard, which he also dreams of protect-

2. Hist. Soc. of Pa. Coulougnac was the principal in the firm of Coulougnac & Cie., which had long been supplying cloth to the American government and Virginia. In October, 1782, when Mercier, one of the firm's agents, was in Virginia sorting out difficulties with a tobacco contract and soliciting trade, BF wrote at Coulougnac's request to the governor: XXXI, 268, 289n; XXXII, 31–2; XXXVIII, 456n; ——— to George Mason, Sept. 30, 1782 (APS). Coulougnac did emigrate to America in 1784 and established John James Coulougnac & Co. (We therefore assume that his name was Jean-Jacques.) He died in Richmond, Va., on Feb. 2, 1786: Abraham P. Nasatir and Gary E. Monell, *French Consuls in the United States . . .* (Washington, D.C., 1967), pp. 89, 125, 308–10; *Pa. Packet*, June 24, 1784; *Daily Advertiser*, March 7, 1787.

ing from hail. He has sent this plan already to Abbé Bertholon[3] at Béziers, but above all he wants Franklin's advice. In a postscript he says he is attaching a printed slip that will give a more legible version of his address. It reads, "Avocat en Parlement & ancien Subdélégué de l'Intendance de Bourgogne."

The baron de Juilly Thomassin,[4] who describes himself as an *ancien sous lieutenant des gardes du corps du roi* and a superannuated student of the arts, dares to offer Franklin his admiration in a letter dated June 24 from Arc-en-Barois. He sends an eight-page homage to Louis XVI, the brave Americans, and Franco-American unity entitled "Le Cri d'un Cœur francois, aux Américains; sur Le Monument de leur indépendance, qu'ils consacrent au Roy." He knows that zeal is a poor substitute for talent but hopes that Franklin will not judge it harshly.

Monsieur! Strasbourg Le 18 May 1783

J'ignore si vous vous rapéllerez de moi, j'ai eû L'honneur de vous voir à différéntes reprises à Paris; et de passée dés journées dans votre societé; je desire ne pas être échapé de votre mémoire: mais si je l'etois M. de Reyneval, & M. Grand; ou bién M. de Beaumarchais, & même Mgr le Cte. de Vergennes pourroient vous donnér dés renseignemens satisfaisans sur mon compte; & la demande que je vais vous addréssér ne vous donnéra point de suspision. Le bruit s'est répandû ici que Lés Etats unis, êtoient dans l'intention de faire faire en france une grande quantité de Cannons de fonde on dit que le nombre est de 1500. Plusieurs Marchands & Négotians d'ici en ont parlé à notre chéf de La fonderie je crois, Monsieur, pouvoir vous assurér que rién ne pourra Se traittér mieux que par mon canal j'ai lés moyéns de vous arrangér le traitté si tot que vous voudrez en mains, mais j'ai l'honneur de vous prévenir que Si més offres peuvent vous être agréables, je n'entens traitter qu'avéc vous, Monsieur, et non

3. A scientist who shared BF's interest in electricity; he had sent his own work on lightning protection to BF in 1778: XXV, 668–9.

4. Bernard-Joseph, baron de Juilly de Thomassin (1723–1798), a former *mestre de camp* who was subsequently named governor of Nogent-le-roi. In retirement he devoted himself to the study of the military arts and history and wrote poetry. He was a member of the academies of Angers, Dijon, and Montauban: *Biographie universelle.* This letter is at the Hist. Soc. of Pa.

David Hartley

avéc dés Negotiants d'Amsterdam, tel qu'il parroit que l'affaire S'entame actuéllement.

Pour la remise dés fonds Mrs. Grand d'Amsterdam, ou de Paris, qui sont l'un & l'autre més bons amis me conviéndront parfaitement.

Il me sera trés agréable, Monsieur, de trouvér occasion pour faire une affaire qui intérrésse lés Etats, & avoir L'occasion d'entretenir une corréspondance avéc vous.

J'ai L'honneur d'être avéc lés sentiments lés plus distingués Monsieur Votre tres humble & tres Obeissant Serviteur

DE FRANCK

Notation: De Franck, 18 May 1783

David Hartley to the American Peace Commissioners: Memorial and Proposed Article

(I) Copies: Massachusetts Historical Society (four), William L. Clements Library, Library of Congress, National Archives (four); press copy of copy: National Archives; (II) Copies: Massachusetts Historical Society (four), Archives du Ministère des affaires étrangères, William L. Clements Library, Library of Congress, National Archives (four); press copy of copy: National Archives

Formal negotiations between the United States and Great Britain to establish a trade agreement and conclude the definitive peace treaty broke down almost immediately over the exchange of credentials. When Franklin, Adams, Jay, and Laurens met with British representative David Hartley on April 27 and discovered that he had not been granted any particular authority, they refused to negotiate formally until he received a commission under the Great Seal conferring full powers equivalent to their own. Hartley immediately wrote for such a commission, but in the meantime informal discussions continued. Hartley gave the American peace commissioners a document that he had sent to Franklin a month earlier—his proposed "Supplemental Treaty" regarding the opening of trade—and a memorandum explaining it. Two days later, on April 29, the Americans presented him with a set of three draft articles, the first of which concerned trade, which they asked him to forward to London. Regarding them as largely unobjectionable, Hartley forwarded them that same day to Charles James Fox, the new British secretary of state for foreign affairs, describing them as having been drawn up that morning "between the American Ministers and myself."[5]

Fox waited until May 15 to answer. He rejected outright the three draft articles, accusing Hartley of either having misunderstood his instructions or deliberately ignoring them. The most problematic article was the first one, which would have granted American ships full reciprocity in carrying goods into British ports. Hartley's instructions, Fox reminded him, specified that American ships would only be permitted to carry American produce. If the American commissioners entertained expectations of full reciprocity, it would be "an insuperable Obstacle." Fox enclosed an Order in Council of May 14 which specified that only oil or nonmanufactured goods or merchandise from America would be allowed to enter British ports on the same basis as formerly. He also enclosed a commission that the king signed on May 14, granting Hartley full powers to negotiate, conclude, and sign treaties, conventions, or any other instruments with ministers authorized by "our Good Friends the United States of America." Fox warned him, however, that he was not to sign any treaty without the king's approval, and emphasized that the king wanted this business concluded as soon as possible.[6]

On May 19 Hartley met with the American commissioners at Adams' residence, where they exchanged commissions. Hartley's was "very magnificent," according to Adams, having the Great Seal affixed to it in a silver box with gold tassels. Hartley expressed regret at the Order in Council, which he found unjust. The parties agreed to meet daily at six o'clock in the evening at Adams' lodgings until the work was finished. Their first session was held on Wednesday, May 21. On that day, Hartley gave the Americans the memorial and proposed article published below.[7]

The actual papers that Hartley handed to the Americans have been lost, though many contemporary copies survive. The variations among them have posed a challenge to the present editors. Hartley must not have dated the sheets, as none of the American legation copies is dated; they bear notations, however, indicating that Hartley delivered them

5. See XXXIX, 412–16, 510–16, 524–6.

6. Hartley's commission is in XXXIX, 605–7, where Fox's letter is discussed in annotation. On May 20 Hartley reported to Fox that the commissioners were "extremely pleased" by the king's referring to the United States as Britain's "good friends": Giunta, *Emerging Nation,* II, 123.

7. He also gave them a copy of the May 14 Order in Council: Butterfield, *John Adams Diary,* III, 120–1, 128.

on May 21. Hartley's own copies, made by his secretary as a record of what he sent to Fox, are dated May 19, but those texts are not identical to what the Americans received: the memorial differs slightly in its wording and the proposed article does not include the preamble.[8] Because Hartley refers to these documents by the date of May 19 in his subsequent correspondence with the American commissioners as well as with Fox we place them under that date, recognizing that he could have amended them at any time before the May 21 meeting. Regardless of when they assumed their final form, the texts published below are authoritative versions of what the Americans received, being endorsed by John Adams and retained as part of his official record of the negotiations. The memorial was copied by Franklin's secretary Jean L'Air de Lamotte, and its notation is in the hand of William Temple Franklin, the official legation secretary. The copy of the preamble and proposal was made by William Temple Franklin himself.

Hartley's memorial, while ostensibly addressed to the American peace commissioners, seems equally designed to placate Fox. The opening section hardly seems necessary for the Americans: it recapitulates events they knew well, and quotes back to them a text that they themselves had written. The heart of the memorial, in which Hartley explains why he is changing the terms of their previous agreement (paragraphs four through six), quotes nearly verbatim from Fox's letter to Hartley of April 10.[9] The British negotiator could no longer be accused of ignoring his instructions.[1]

[May 19, 1783]

I.

A Proposition having been offered by the American Ministers for the Consideration of his Britannic Majesty's Ministers, and of the British Nation, for an entire & reciprocal Freedom of Intercourse and Commerce between Great Britain and the American United States, in the following Words, viz,[2]

---

8. Hartley sent these to Fox on May 22, entitling the first "Memorial" and the second "Ulterior Article": Giunta, *Emerging Nation*, II, 124–30.

9. See XXXIX, 481–2n.

1. Hartley said as much in his cover letter to Fox of May 22. For that letter and a private one of May 23 see the annotation of WTF to Hartley, May 21.

2. The following extract is from the peace commissioners' first proposed article of April 29, which specified that the proposal was contingent upon a complete British evacuation of the United States: XXXIX, 524–5.

"That all Rivers, Harbours, Lakes, Ports & Places belonging to the United States, or any of them, shall be open and free to the Merchants and other Subjects of the Crown of Great Britain, and their trading Vessels, who shall be received, treated and protected, like the Merchants and trading Vessels of the State in which they may be, and be liable to no other Charges or Duties.

"And reciprocally that all Rivers, Harbours, Lakes, Ports and Places under the Dominion of his Britannic Majesty, shall be open and free to the Merchant & trading Vessels of the said United States, & of each and every of them, who shall be received, treated and protected, like the Merchants and trading Vessels of Great Britain & be liable to no other Charges and Duties, saving always to the chartered trading Companies of Great Britain such exclusive Use and Trade of their respective Ports and establishments, as neither the other Subjects of Great Britain, or any of the most favored Nation participate in." It is to be observed that this Proposition implies a more ample Participation of British Commerce than the American States possessed even under their former Connexion of Dependence upon Great Britain, so as to amount to an entire Abolition of the British Act of Navigation, in respect to the thirteen United States of America; and altho' proceeding on their part from the most conciliatory and liberal Principles of Amity and Reciprocity, nevertheless it comes from them as newly established States, & who in Consequence of their former Condition of Dependence have never yet had any established System of national commercial Laws, or of commercial Connexions by Treaties with other Nations, free and unembarassed of many weighty Considerations, which require the most scrupulous Attention, and Investigation on the Part of Great Britain, whose antient System of national and commercial Policy, is thus suddenly called upon to take a new Principle for its Foundation, and whose commercial Engagements with other ancient States, may be most materially affected thereby. For the Purpose therefore of giving sufficient time, for the Consideration and Discussion of so important a Proposition, respecting the present established System of the commercial Policy and Laws of Great Britain, and their subsisting commercial Engagements with foreign Powers,

It is proposed that a temporary Intercourse of Commerce shall be established between Great Britain and the American States, previously to the Conclusion of any final and perpetual Compact. In this intervening Period, as the strict Line & Measure of Reciprocity from various Circumstances cannot be absolutely and compleatly adhered to, it may be agreed that the Commerce between the two Countries shall revive, as nearly as can be upon the same footing and Terms as formerly subsisted between them; provided always that no Concession on either Side in the proposed temporary Convention, shall be argued hereafter in support of any future Demand or Claim. In the mean time the Proposition above stated may be transmitted to London, requesting (with his Majesty's Consent) that it may be laid before Parliament for their Consideration.

It is proposed therefore that the unmanufactured Produce of the United States shd. be admitted into Great Britain without any other Duties (those imposed during the War excepted) than those to which they were formerly liable.[3] And it is expected in return that the Produce and Manufactures of Great Britain shd. be admitted into the United States in like Manner. If there shd. appear any Want of reciprocity in this proposal, upon the Grounds of asking Admission for British Manufactures into America, while no such Indulgence is given to American Manufactures in Great Britain; The Answer is obvious, That the Admission of British Manufactures into America is an Object of great Importance and equally productive of Advantage to both Countries; while on the other hand, the Introduction of American manufactures into Great Britain, can be of no Service to either, and may be productive of innumerable Frauds, by enabling Persons so disposed, to pass foreign European Goods, either prohibited or liable to great Duties by the British Laws, for American Manufactures.

With regard to the west Indies, there is no Objection to the most free Intercourse between them and the United States. The only Restriction proposed to be laid upon that Intercourse, is

3. A summary of the May 14 Order in Council; JA's copy is in Butterfield, *John Adams Diary*, III, 128–30.

prohibiting American Ships carrying to those Colonies any other Merchandize than the Produce of their own Country. The same Observation may be made upon this Restriction as upon the former. It is not meant to affect the Interest of the United States, but it is highly necessary, least foreign Ships shd. make Use of the American Flag to carry on a Trade with the British west Indian Islands.

It is also proposed upon the same Principle to restrain the Ships that may trade to great Britain from America, from bringing foreign Merchandize into Great Britain. The Necessity of this Restriction is likewise evident, unless Great Britain meant to give up her whole Navigation Act. There is no Necessity of any Similar Restrictions on the Part of the American States, those States not having as yet any Acts of Navigation.—

Notations by William Temple Franklin: Mr. Hartley's Observations & Propositions, left with the American Ministers the 21 May 1783. / Mr. Hartley's, Observations, & Propositions 21. May 1783.

II.

Preamble to the following Agreement as proposed by Mr. Hartley

Whereas it is highly necessary that an Intercourse of Trade & Commerce should be open'd between the People & Territories belonging to the Crown of Great Britain and the People & Territories of the United States of America: And whereas it is highly expedient that the Intercourse between Great Britain and the said United States should be established on the most enlarged Principles of reciprocal Benefit to both Countries; but from the Distance between Great Britain & America, it must be a considerable time before any Convention or Treaty for establishing and regulating the Trade and Intercourse between Great Britain and the said United States of America, upon a permanent Foundation can be concluded: Now for the purpose of making a temporary Regulation of the Commerce and Intercourse between Great Britain and the said United States of America—It &ca.

Mr. Hartley's proposed Agreement.[4]

It is agreed that all the Citizens of the United States of America, shall be permitted to import into, and export from any Part of his Britannic Majesty's Dominions, in American Ships, any Goods, Wares & Merchandize, which have been so imported or exported by the Inhabitants of the British American Colonies, before the Commencement of the War, upon Payment of the same Duties & Charges, as the like sort of Goods or Merchandize are now or may be subject & liable to, if imported by British Subjects, in British Ships from any British Island or Plantation in America: And that all the Subjects of his Britannic Majesty shall be permitted to import and to export from any Part of the Territories of the thirteen United States of America, in British Ships, any Goods, Wares & Merchandize, which might have been so imported or exported by the Subjects of his Britannic Majesty, before the Commencement of the War upon Payment of the same Duties & Charges, as the like sort of Goods, Wares & Merchandize are now, or may be subject and liable to, if imported in American Ships, by any of the Citizens of the United States of America.

This Agreement to continue in force until [*blank*] Provided always that nothing contained in this Agreement, shall at any time hereafter, be argued on either side, in support of any future Demand or Claim.—

Notations: [*by John Adams*] Mr Hartleys Proposition of 21 May 1783 / [*by William Temple Franklin*] Mr. Hartley's proposed Agreement—deliver'd in the 21st. May 1783. for the Consideration of the American Ministers.—

---

4. This article in effect prohibits the export to Britain of American goods whose manufacture had been prohibited before the war. Such prohibition was part of the Navigation Acts' system by which colonial trade and economies had been regulated for the benefit of the British economy and the Royal Navy.

From Henry Laurens   AL: University of Pennsylvania Library

Monday Evening 19 May 1783.
Mr. Laurens presents his respectful Compliments to Doctor
Franklin & thanks the Doctor for his goodness in sending the
American News Papers, Mr. L. will convey them to Mr. Adams
to morrow.

Addressed: His Excellency / Doctor Franklin / Passy.

From Viscount Mountmorres[5]

AL: American Philosophical Society

Monday. [May 19, 1783?][6]
Lord Mountmorres has the honour to inform Dr Franklin that
he leaves Paris on Thursday morning & that if he has any commands for England he shall be happy to execute them.

5. This undated note is the only trace in BF's papers of Hervey Redmond
Morres, 2nd Viscount Mountmorres (1741/2–1797), a political writer and
member of the Irish House of Lords who met BF in London and dined
with him on at least one occasion in May, 1769. He later claimed to have
been an intimate acquaintance: *ODNB;* J. Bennett Nolan, *Benjamin Franklin in Scotland and Ireland, 1759 and 1771* (Philadelphia and London, 1938),
p. 132; [Mountmorres], *The Letters of Themistocles* (London, 1795), p. xxiv.
    Lord Mountmorres came to France by way of Brussels in December, 1782:
London Courant and Daily Advertiser, Dec. 30, 1782. We now realize that he,
and not Baron Mountnorris, was the Irish member of Parliament who attended Fitzherbert's dinner in Paris on Dec. 17: XXXVIII, 440. (In XXXVIII,
440n, we misidentified him based on JA's spelling of the name: Butterfield,
John Adams Diary, III, 96.) In a posthumous sketch of BF Mountmorres
mentioned spending a day at Passy in March, 1783, and noted how remarkable it was that BF "made no secret" of his humble origins. To illustrate this
point he recalled a conversation in Paris, in company with La Rochefoucauld and the conde de Aranda, during which BF admitted to having vast
knowledge about paper manufacturing in America since he "was originally
in the printing trade": *Letters of Themistocles,* pp. xxiv, 2–3 of Appendix.
    6. We do not know when Mountmorres left Paris, but he attended court
at St. James's on Thursday, May 29: *Gazetteer and New Daily Advertiser,*

Addressed: A Monsieur / Monsieur Le Docteur / Franklin A
Passy.——

From Richard Price ALS: American Philosophical Society

Dear Sir Newington-Green May 19th: 1783
This letter will be deliver'd to you by Mr Slaney,[7] a young
Gentleman of fortune who has been for some time on his travels
and is ambitious of the honour of being introduced to you. I
am not personally acquainted with him; but the account given
me of him by a friend of his and mine assures me, that he is a
Gentleman of the best principles and character. Any notice wch:
you may be pleased to take of him will, I believe, make him
very happy. Before this will be deliver'd to you the new Edition of my Treatise on Annuities, population, public credit &c.
will probably have reached you.[8] Encouraged by the favourable
reception wch: this work has met with I have in this edition en-

---

May 30, 1783. If the "Thursday morning" he left Paris was May 22, then
May 19 is the last possible Monday in 1783 that he could have written
this note. Another possibility, however, is February, 1785, when he was
back in Paris. He dined at BF's on Feb. 14 with a large company of family, friends, and notables. He was back in London by March 4, when he
presented himself at court: [Caroline A. Smith de Windt, ed.], *Journal and
Correspondence of Miss Adams, Daughter of John Adams* . . . (2 vols., New
York and London, 1841–42), I, 47–8; *Morning Post and Daily Advertiser,*
March 5, 1785.
 7. Probably Robert Slaney (1764–1834) of Hatton Grange, Shropshire,
who matriculated at Oxford in 1781. He seems to have been the Slaney who
set out for a Grand Tour of Italy in May, 1782, and stayed at least through
the following April: *ODNB,* under Robert Aglionby Slaney; John Burke
and John Bernard Burke, *A Genealogical and Heraldic History of the Landed
Gentry of Great Britain and Ireland* (2 vols., London, 1846), II, 1246; John
Ingamells, comp., *A Dictionary of British and Irish Travellers in Italy,
1701–1800* (New Haven and London, 1997), p. 864; Joseph Foster, *Alumni
Oxonienses: the Members of the University of Oxford, 1715–1886* . . . (4 vols.,
London, 1887–88), IV, 1306.
 8. It had not, as it was in one of the boxes shipped by Benjamin
Vaughan, which did not leave London until early June: Dessin to BF, June

larged it to two volumes, and taken great pains to make it as complete as possible. I reflect with pleasure that the part of it wch: is addressed to you will be the means of preserving some remembrance of our acquaintance and friendship. You will easily recollect the fact mentioned in the note P. 284, Vol. 1st: I have thot: there could be no impropriety in introducing it into this Edition.[9]

Wishing you all possible happiness, I am most affectionately Yours   RICHD: PRICE

To Samuel Cooper   LS:[1] Henry E. Huntington Library

Dear Sir,   Passy 20. May 1783.
The Bearer, M. de Bannes is exceedingly well recommended to me by Persons of the first Distinction in this Country.[2] He goes over to America with a View of seeing the Country, & of being serviceable to the Government here, who may here after probably confer on him one of the Counsulships. He appears to be a sensible Young Man, and will I doubt not, make himself agreable. Permit me to request for him your kind Notice and Civilities, & that you will favour him with your best Counsels, if he should at any time stand in need of them.

---

15. The work in question was the fourth edition of *Observations on Reversionary Payments* . . . , which Price had announced to BF the previous fall: XXXVIII, 320.

9. The part addressed to BF was "Observations on the Expectations of Lives . . ." (1769), an essay written in the form of a letter to BF and referencing BF's demographic works. While the essay had appeared in all previous editions, Price added a footnote on page 284 of the first volume, in which he explained the circumstances that had prevented a clause expressing sympathy with the American colonists from being published until now. For the full text of the footnote see XVI, 104n.

1. In L'Air de Lamotte's hand.

2. One of these persons was the comte de Maillebois, who introduced him to BF on May 15. BF noted on that letter that he intended to provide him with letters for Cooper, Gov. William Greene of Rhode Island, and

With great and sincere Esteem, I have the honour to be, Dear Sir, Your most obedient and most humble Servant.

B Franklin

Revd. Dr Cooper.—

From Pierre Chabrit[3]   ALS: American Philosophical Society

Monsieur le Docteur,   à Paris le 20 Mai 1783.
Permettés que J'offre à un homme qui doit donner des Loix au nouveau monde, le premier volume de l'histoire de celles d'un des grands peuples de l'ancien:[4] Je serois au comble de mes vœux, si le législateur de l'Amérique m'avoit Jugé digne de ses conseils.

Robert Livingston: xxxix, 608–9. The letter to Greene is essentially identical to this one (APS).

3. Chabrit (1747–1785), a *conseiller* in the *Conseil souverain de Bouillon* and an *avocat au Parlement,* had just completed the first volume of *De la Monarchie française, ou de ses loix* (2 vols., Bouillon, 1783–85), his study of the French legal system. He moved to Paris from Clermont-Ferrand after an unsuccessful attempt to establish a newspaper, the *Feuille hebdomadaire pour la province d'Auvergne.* In 1781 Diderot proposed him to Catherine II as an expert on legislation, forwarding a copy of his table of contents and first chapters. As there was no response, the jurist remained in France but continued to struggle financially. Despite the acclaim he received for his study (see the following note), he committed suicide shortly after the second volume was published, reportedly because of his mounting debt: *DBF;* Jean Sgard, *Dictionnaire des journaux, 1600–1789* (2 vols., Paris, 1991), I, 14–16; Denis Diderot, *Œuvres complètes,* ed. Roger Lewinter (15 vols., Paris, 1969–73), xiii, 1000–2; Tourneux, *Correspondance littéraire,* xiv, 196–7; Maurice Tourneux, *Diderot et Catherine II* (1899; reprint, Geneva, 1970), pp. 508–10.

4. *De la Monarchie française* was announced for sale on June 28 and favorably reviewed on Aug. 19 in the *Jour. de Paris.* The Académie française awarded Chabrit a prize "pour l'encouragement des Lettres" the following spring: Bachaumont, *Mémoires secrets,* xxv, 171; *Jour. de Paris,* March 17, 1784.

Je suis avec un profond respect, Monsieur le Docteur, Votre très humble et très obéïssant serviteur[5]   CHABRIT

Rue des fossés de M. le Prince.

Notation: Chabri 20 May 1783.

From Marie-Julie Rutledge d'Herbigny[6]

ALS: American Philosophical Society

Most honorable Sir,   reims ce 20 mai 1783

Give me leave to assure Your Excelence of my Gratitu'd Mr le Comte de Vergennes has been So good as to obtain me from his majesty a pension *Sur le fond des Eccossois* tho' the Some his very Smale I have the Same Obligasion to your Excelence, and beg youl Continue me the honnor of your protection, perhaps I am the only in france who has the honnor to be related to a member of Your Congress, I beg leave to Send you *a paquet* for Mr Rutledge.

Give me leave to assure Your Excelence of my gratitu'd wishs for you and your Countrys prosperity attachement and Respect.

I am with respect Most honorable Sir Your most humble and most oblidged Servante   RUTLEDGE DHERBIGNY

---

5. Among BF's papers at the Hist. Soc. of Pa. is a copy by Chabrit of two pieces he had given to the Musée de Paris, of which he was a member. The first is a text he had hoped to deliver at a meeting he knew BF would attend; it consisted of the introduction to *De la Monarchie française* prefaced by remarks alluding to the "Sage" in the audience who had worked so successfully for "la liberté du noveau monde." (The occasion was undoubtedly the March 6 celebration of the peace described in XXXIX, 342–3.) His reading was refused, however, on the pretext "qu'elle ne plairoit point aux femmes." The second piece is his response, which he hoped to read at a future assembly. It outlined his ideals for readings at the Musée: that they be serious rather than frivolous, designed to instruct as well as to please, and done without condescension.

6. The wife of a French army officer and relative of John Rutledge, member of Congress from South Carolina. Two months earlier, Rutledge d'Herbigny had asked BF to intercede with Vergennes on her behalf, in order to obtain a royal pension: XXXIX, 390, 392–3.

I beg youl excuse my bad english

my direction md dherbigny ché. Mr labbe Rutledge chanoine a
reims[7]

From the Comte de Vergennes: Proposal

Copies: Library of Congress, Massachusetts Historical Society; copy
and press copy of copy:[8] National Archives; L (draft): Archives du
Ministère des affaires étrangères

[May 20, 1783]

L'Intention de sa Majesté le Roi T. C. [Très Chrétien] et les
Etats Unis de L'Amerique Septentrionale en concluant entr'eux
un Traité d'Amitié et de Commerce, aiant été de faire jouir leurs
Sujets respectifs de tous les Avantages Privileges et Exemtions
dont jouissent ou pourront jouir les Nations les plus favorisées;
et sa dte. [dite] Mté. T. C. et les dits Etats Unis voulant prevenir
les mesentendus qui pourroient avoir lieu par une fausse application des Artes. 2. et 3 du Traité de Commerce du 6 fevrier 1778.[9]
ont cru devoir determiner d'une maniere precise les principes
qui devront etre suivis de part et d'autre sur la matiere dont il
est question. En consequence sa de. [dite] Majeste Le Roi T. C.
a nommé et constitué . . . .
Et le Congres des Etats Unis de l'Amerique Septentrionale
. . . . lesquels aprés s'etre communiqués . . . . sont convenus des Articles suivans.

Article 1er.

Pour interpréter en tant que besoin est l'Article 2 du Traité
d'Amitié et de Commerce conclû le 6 fevrier 1778 Les Etats
Unis declarent que tous les Avantages privileges et exemptions

---

7. One of her brothers: XXXIX, 392.
8. Marked as enclosure no. 9. These were sent with the commissioners'
Sept. 10 letter to Congress, mentioned below.
9. XXV, 598–9.

qui sont accordés ou pourront être accordés à l'avenir, sur le fait de la Navigation et du Commerce, a quelque Nation, Puissance ou Etat que ce puisse être, seront communs à la françoise et que celle ci en jouira conformement a l'article 3 du Traité susmentionné sans qu'en aucun cas ou sous quelque pretexte que ce soit les dits Etats puissent exiger de compensation de la Part de Sa Mté: T. C.

Article 2.

Sa Majesté Tres Chretien promêt et s'engage de son Côté, de faire jouir conformement a l'Article 3. mentionné ci-dessus, les Sujets des Etats Unis de tous les Avantages privileges et Exemtions dont jouissent ou pourront jouir a l'avenir les Nations les plus favorisées, et ce sans exiger de leur part aucune compensation.

Article 3.

La presente Convention sera ratifié par sa Majesté T. C. et par les Etats unis dans l'espace de trois mois à compter de ce jour, ou plustôt si faire se peut.

En foi de quoi, nous &ca. &ca. &ca.

Count de Vergenne's proposed new Articles, delivered to B Franklin the 20th. May 1783.[1]

---

1. BF did not send the articles to Congress until after the conclusion of negotiations with Britain. They were enclosed with the commissioners' Sept. 10 letter to President of Congress Boudinot. On May 11, 1784, after a long deliberative process, Congress ordered BF and his colleagues to assure France of its good intentions, but declined to take action on the proposal: *JCC*, XXV, 826, 828n; XXVII, 368–9.

From Ernst Frederik von Walterstorff[2]

AL: American Philosophical Society

Rue neuve St. Augustin, au coin de
La ruë Ste. Anne. May 20th. [1783]

M. de Walterstorff presents his respectfull compliments to Dr. Franklin, requesting the honour of his Company to dinner on monday next the 26th. instant at 3 o'Clock.—[3]

Addressed: The right honourable / Dr. Franklin / at / Passy.

2. The Danish courtier who was instructed by Danish Foreign Minister Rosencrone to approach BF about the possibility of negotiating a commercial treaty: XXXIX, 462, 467–8. Documents obtained from the National Archives of Denmark indicate that prior to his first extant letter of April 13, Walterstorff visited BF at Passy four times. Their first meeting, on March 22, was cut short by the arrival of other guests, but the following day Walterstorff showed BF his instructions from Rosencrone (XXXIX, 468n), and the two men began to discuss commercial relations. BF agreed to send Rosencrone a draft treaty (which he did on April 15: XXXIX, 473–4) and led Walterstorff to believe that he would send an American representative to Copenhagen to conclude the negotiations, as the court desired. These talks continued on March 28 and April 10.

A copy made in Rosencrone's office of BF's treaty proposal, entitled "Plan d'un Traité d'Amitié et de Commerce entre le Roi de Dannemark et les Etats Unis de l'Amerique," confirms that BF sent a French translation of Congress' proposed treaty with Sweden, as he told Livingston he had (XXXIX, 468). To those 18 articles, he appended two, numbered 19 and 20, stipulating that ratifications were to be exchanged within eight months and the treaty would be in effect for 15 years. These correspond to Article 27 and the unnumbered Separate Article of the Swedish-American treaty: XXXIX, 267–8.

The editors are indebted to Erik Gøbel of the Statens Arkiver, Rigsarkivet, for providing copies of documents relating to these negotiations. The information on Walterstorff's early meetings with BF is from his letters to Rosencrone of March 23 and 30 and April 10, 1783.

3. WTF ("Mr. Franklin") received his own invitation: APS. JA, Jay, and Laurens were also invited: Walterstorff to Rosencrone, May 25, 1783, Statens Arkiver, Rigsarkivet. This dinner may have been an attempt to smooth ruffled feathers. On May 18 Walterstorff had met with BF in the morning and dined, as part of a large company, at JA's in the afternoon. BF warned him that although he had told Jay about the negotiations, JA as yet knew nothing about them. JA was not pleased to learn about them, in general terms, from Walterstorff that afternoon. He insisted that Walterstorff tell the king that the only person in Europe authorized to conduct such

47

From John Viny and Family[4]

ALS:[5] American Philosophical Society

Wheel Manufactory Black Friars Road
Dr Sir   May the 21st. 1783
  I hope you will forgive my trespassing on your most valuable
moments, but I could not forego the Oppertunity by favor of
Mosr Du Chateau, to express my great pleasure in hearing of
your Health &c. O Sir, how happy shou'd I be, once more to
take you by the hand, but from a Line I read of yours at Cheam[6]
I have but little hopes as I am confind, but happy beyond Expression, having such Friends that have hitherto supported
me in the fulest degree possible, against the unnatural reverse
Conduct of the Jacobs.[7] Mrs V. and my dear Girls in No 3 are

---

negotiations was Francis Dana. When Walterstorff wrote his dispatch that
evening, he wondered at BF's never mentioning Dana and observed that "il
n'est pas impossible, qu'il ne regne un peu de jalousie entre quelques uns de
ces Messieurs": Walterstorff to Rosencrone, May 18, 1783, Statens Arkiver,
Rigsarkivet.

  4. Although the wheelwright John Viny and his family had known BF
for decades, this is their first extant letter to him. John was first identified
in XVII, 72n, and his wife, "R. W.," in XIX, 39n. Since then we have identified her as Rebecca Wilkinson Jacob, the sister of Viny's former business
partner (for whom see below); she and Viny were married in 1760. "R. J.,"
Rebecca Jacob, was the eldest daughter born in 1763, and Elizabeth ("E."),
known as Bess or, as BF once called her, "my little Patient *Bessum*," was
born the following year. Mary, the "pin Basket," was born in 1778: XXVIII,
366, 422; XXIX, 137–8; *London, England, Marriages and Banns, 1754–1921*
for John Viny, Joseph Jacob; *England & Wales Christening Records, 1530–
1906* for Rebecca and Elizabeth Viny (both databases accessed at Ancestry.
com).

  Evidence of BF's friendship with the couple may date to 1768, earlier
than we supposed, if (as we now think likely) the "Mr. Viney" mentioned
in XV, 237–8, was John Viny, who lived in London, rather than his brother
Thomas, who lived in Kent.

  5. According to a note on the enclosed list (see below), both it and this
letter were written by Viny's "Eldes Daughtr R. J. V."

  6. BF had just written to Mary Hewson that he would probably not visit
Cheam before returning to Philadelphia: XXXIX, 503.

  7. Following Viny's bankruptcy in 1778, BF pressed Mrs. Stevenson
and her daughter for details on the "break" between Viny and his partner

well, and most sincerely rejoice in your felicity. With the most hearty Affection permit us to subscribe ourselves most sincerely yours   JNO. VINY
R W VINY.
R. J. VINY
E VINY
R J VINY FOR PIN BASKET MARY

PS I have furnish'd Mr Du Chateau with a Set of Wheels I much wish you Cou'd see as I think you will say I have not forgot how to do the Buisness well[8]

Will my Friend honor me with a Sheet of Paper tho his Name alone should be thereon.

Joseph Jacob, and the nature of the wheel patent fueling their dispute. He had a strong personal interest in the matter, as the invention was based on his idea, which he had developed with Viny after Jacob rejected it: XX, 157–8; XXVIII, 165, 366, 422. The subsequent lawsuit had been settled in Viny's favor by the end of 1782, when Viny issued a public announcement claiming that he, "the original and sole Inventor of the Wheel, commonly called the *Patent* Wheel," had finally been "*restored* to the Merit of his Invention, and to the Right of reaping the Fruits of his laborious and expensive Experiments." Viny now advertised his wheel "in its highest Perfection of Beauty and Durability" and also offered his skills in carriage painting and repairs. He placed the announcement, dated "December, 1782," in various London papers in late January (*e.g., Parker's Gen. Advertiser and Morning Intelligencer,* Jan. 29, 1783) and had it issued separately as a broadside, where the date reads, "December, 1783" (surely a typographical error). BF's copy of that broadside is at the APS; it may have been sent with the present letter.

The announcement also thanked the generous patrons who had supported Viny "in the Days of his Oppression" and who, he hoped, would continue to assist him. Indeed, Viny's survival in the business had depended on the system of subscription that had been initiated at the time of his bankruptcy (see Viny to BF, [after Nov. 28, 1783], APS). Along with the current letter, Viny enclosed a separate sheet entitled "Subscribers for Seven Years" containing a list of some 17 men—including four dukes and a bishop—who had contributed a total of £1,800. At the bottom of the sheet he asserted: "In this Manner I have the happness to be Supported." APS.

8. BF would have seen them if Du Chateau, who carried the letter to Paris (see the address sheet), delivered it in person. Jacob & Viny had been soliciting French business since 1776, when the firm issued a three-page

Addressed: His Excellency Dr. B. Franklin / By favor of Monsr. Du Chateau

Notation: Viny 21 May 1783

William Temple Franklin to David Hartley

Copies: William L. Clements Library,[9] Library of Congress, Massachusetts Historical Society (two)

After Hartley gave his proposed article to the American peace commissioners on the evening of May 21 (see Hartley's memorial and proposed article, [May 19]), the Americans withdrew for discussion. Unsure of whether Hartley had the authority to sign it without consultation with his court, they decided to pose the question in writing. John Adams drafted a letter, and Franklin suggested that it be sent under Temple's signature. The present letter is Temple's adaptation of Adams' draft.[1]

The next morning, Adams drafted a formal proposal for a temporary trade agreement that adapted Hartley's proposal. He inserted an article calling for the ministers to be nominated and vested with full powers to conclude a permanent commercial treaty, and incorporated Hartley's article almost verbatim as Article 2.[2]

Around the same time, John Jay also drafted a provisional trade convention. While there is no evidence that Jay's three articles were ever presented to Hartley, the issues they raised were certainly discussed (see the annotation below), and the commissioners copied

---

French-language brochure that advertised their services and listed various coaches, diligences, and private carriages in England whose patent wheels had provided superior performance over time. The firm invited potential customers to talk directly with the owners, whose locations were specified. A copy of the brochure, entitled "Manufacture de Roues de Voitures, D'une nouvelle Construction, Etablie sur le Chemin de Black-Fryars, près du Pont-Neuf de Londres," is among BF's papers at the APS.

9. This copy, the only one that includes the complimentary close and signature, was made by Hartley's secretary George Hammond. The other copies are in the commissioners' legation letterbooks, and JA's letterbook.

1. For that draft see Butterfield, *John Adams Diary*, III, 124.

2. Butterfield, *John Adams Diary*, III, 125–7.

them into the legation letterbooks. The first article banned the British importation of slaves into America, "It being the Intention of the said States intirely to prohibit the Importation thereof." The second granted Ireland the right to negotiate its own trade agreements with the United States. The third emphasized the strictly temporary character of the convention, as "the Discussion of Questions respecting reciprocity has in forming of it been avoided."[3]

Sir   Paris May 21st 1783
    The American Ministers have done me the honour to direct me to present you their Compliments, and to desire to be informed, whether the Proposition you made them this Evening, is such as you can agree to & subscribe without further Instructions or Information from your Court?
    I have the honour to be Sir, Your most obedient & most humble Servt   W T FRANKLIN

His Excellency D Hartley Esqr

Notation by David Hartley: Answered in person—That I would write to London for special instructions[4]

---

3. The letterbook copies (Library of Congress, Mass. Hist. Soc.) are the only surviving versions, and they are undated. The text is in Morris, *Jay: Peace*, pp. 540–1, under the ascribed date of June 1.

4. Before replying to the commissioners, Hartley consulted the Duke of Manchester, the new British ambassador to the French court, who agreed that Hartley's instructions required him to write to London for an answer. Hartley called on JA the next morning (May 22) and so informed him. JA complained about the lack of reciprocity in Hartley's proposed article, and argued the importance of American participation in the British West Indies trade.

In his May 22 letter to Fox, Hartley speculated that the Americans might sign the proposed article with a few modifications. They had talked to him about excluding the importation of slaves as the first step in abolishing slavery; he hoped that this would not "meet with any difficulty on your side of the water." He predicted that "with a little management" the commissioners could be brought into agreement with the provisions about trade in manufactured goods, but that participation in the West Indies trade was "the rub." They had often asked him, "Why won't your nation come forward to meet us? What are they afraid of? We are ready to meet them upon any terms of liberality & reciprocity." Hartley followed this dispatch with

The American Peace Commissioners to Rodolphe-Ferdinand Grand

Copies:[5] Library of Congress (two), Massachusetts Historical Society; AL (draft): Massachusetts Historical Society[6]

Sir,   Paris May 22: 1783.

We have received the Letter you did us the honour to write us on the 10th. Day of this Month, containing a brief State of the affairs of the United States in your hands.[7]

We see the Difficulties you are in, and are sorry to say that it is not in our Power to afford you any Relief.

We have the Honour to be &c.

To Mr. Grand.

---

a private letter of May 23 appealing for concessions and emphasizing how impatient and mistrustful the Americans were. He begged Fox to send news about the evacuation of British troops from America, which was one of the commissioners' chief concerns: Giunta, *Emerging Nation*, II, 124–30, 131–2; Butterfield, *John Adams Diary*, III, 127–8.

In a June 18 letter to Fox (Clements Library), Hartley recalled that on May 21 the commissioners also asked whether the British-American commercial treaty would include Ireland. Two days later he wrote that the commissioners had inquired of the Shelburne ministry about the future terms of Irish-American trade in "a Memorandum upon the Margin of the Provisional Bill, which was sent to them for their opinion, about the time of its first appearance in the House of Commons": Giunta, *Emerging Nation*, II, 163. The ill-fated American Intercourse Bill (XXXIX, 296–7n, 352) had been presented to the commissioners by Fitzherbert in early March. The Americans much approved its "liberal spirit" and proposed to include an article in the definitive treaty guaranteeing reciprocal free trade, which they hoped would also include Ireland. However, Fitzherbert did not feel authorized to give them a response on this point: Morris, *Jay: Peace*, p. 539n; Fitzherbert to Lord Grantham, March 13, 1783, in Giunta, *Emerging Nation*, I, 784.

5. Official correspondence from this period was copied into three legation letterbooks, for which see below, pp. 437–8n.

6. JA drafted this letter before the commissioners' evening meeting on May 22; his draft is in Butterfield, *John Adams Diary*, III, 125.

7. XXXIX, 587–9.

The American Peace Commissioners to Wilhem & Jan Willink, Nicolaas & Jacob van Staphorst, and De la Lande & Fynje[8]

Copies: Library of Congress (two), Massachusetts Historical Society; AL (draft): Massachusetts Historical Society

Gentlemen,   Paris may 22. 1783

Mr. Grand, has laid before us, a State of the affairs of the United States under his Care,[9] and the Demands upon him for money to discharge the Bills drawn upon him, are such as to require some assistance from you, if the Demands upon you will admit of it. If therefore, the State of the Cash in your Hands compared with the Draughts made upon you, will allow of it, We advise you, to remit to Mr. Grand on account of the United States the Amount of five hundred Thousand Livres Tournois, and we doubt not that Congress and their Minister of Finances, will approve of it, although we have not in strictness Authority to give orders for it.

We have the honor to be, Gentlemen, &c

To Messrs. Wilhem & Jean Willink, Nicholas and Jacob Van Staphorst, & De La Lande & Fynge, Bankers of the United States of America at Amsterdam.

Letter in Support of Pierre-André Gargaz[1]

AL (draft): American Philosophical Society

Sir,   Passy, May 22. 1783

The Bearer Pierre André Gargaz is Author of a very humane Project for establishing a perpetual Peace. This has interested

---

8. The consortium of bankers who were underwriting JA's Dutch loan: XXXVIII, 433n.

9. XXXIX, 587–9.

1. Which Gargaz requested on March 2; see XXXIX, 238–9. This statement was evidently intended for Gargaz to present to the local magistrates. If a fair copy was sent, it did no good: Ferréol de Ferry, *Pierre-André Gargas (1728–1801), Galérien de Toulon* (Paris, 2000), pp. 92–3.

me much in his Behalf: He appears to me a very honest sensible Man, & worthy of better Fortune: For tho' his Project may appear in some respects chimerical, there is Merit in so good an Intention. He has serv'd faithfully 20 Years as a Gally-Slave, and now requests Letters of Rehabilitation, that he may enjoy for the Rest of his Life the Douceurs that State would be attended with. If this Request of his is not improper, & you can assist him in procuring such Letters You will do me a most sensible Pleasure. He will show you authentic Certificates of his good Conduct. With great Esteem, I have the honour to be, Sir,

To Vergennes   ALS: Archives du ministère des affaires étrangères

Sir   Passy, May 23. 1783—
    I beg leave to recommend earnestly to your Excellency's Attention the enclos'd Petition and Papers from Mr. Price,[2] an honest worthy American, who was to my Knowledge very serviceable to our Army in Canada, and much esteemed by the Congress.[3] I shall be very thankful if you can procure for him the Order he desires. With great Respect, I am, Sir, Your Excellency's most obedient & most humble Servant   B FRANKLIN

M. le Comte de Vergennes.

Endorsed: M. De R. [Rayneval]

Notation: Envoyé le memoire à m le garde des sceaux[4]

2. James Price was pursuing a lawsuit against his partners William Haywood and John Bondfield. (Their associations, and Price's trip to France, are mentioned in XXVIII, 413; XXIX, 330; XXXV, 338, 488; XXXVII, 40.) The enclosed papers have not been located, but they convinced both BF and Vergennes to intercede on his behalf; see Vergennes to BF, June 20 and June 26, below.
    3. See XXII, 360–1n; XXVI, 278n.
    4. The *garde des sceaux* was Armand-Thomas Hue de Miromesnil (XXI, 536n).

From the Baron de Monteil[5]

ALS: American Philosophical Society

paris rue st dominique chés le Vcte
[Vicomte] de monteil 23 may 1783

Jai lhonneur Monsieur, de vous remerçier de votre attention; flatté du mottif qui vous y a porté, jentrerai tres éxactement dans le désir que m'expliqua mr. votre fils, et au pais ou je vais voir des parents, je me contenterai de parler de vos vertus.

Jai lhonneur d'etre avec touts les sentiments de la consideration distinguée, et de Lattachement, Monsieur, Votre tres humble et tres obeissant Serviteur   LE CHEV. DE MONTEIL

a m. frankklin ministre plœnipotentiaire des états unnis.

Notation: Chever. de Monteil 23 May 1783 Paris

From ———— Moseley[6] and Jean-Joseph Sue fils[7]

AL: American Philosophical Society

Paris 23 May 1783

Mr. Moseley and Mr. Suë Junr. present their most respectful Compliments to his Excellency Doctor Franklin, and they will do themselves the honour of dining with him on Sunday the 25 Inst.—

---

5. One of de Grasse's chief subordinates. Sarsfield had warned BF a few weeks earlier of Monteil's desire for a *Libertas Americana* medal; see XXXIX, 548–9, where he is identified. Monteil was a chevalier de Saint Louis and a chevalier de Saint-Lazare.

6. Possibly the English surgeon Benjamin Moseley (1742–1819), who practiced for many years in Jamaica, was elected to the APS (1775), and returned to London in 1784 or 1785. Biographical accounts differ as to his whereabouts in the early 1780s. According to contemporary obituaries, he traveled through Europe before returning to London, visiting hospitals, meeting with physicians, and gaining an honorary medical degree at Leyden: *ODNB; Gent. Mag.,* LXXXIX (1819), 374–5; *Annual Biography and Obituary for the Year 1821,* V (London, 1821), 241.

7. We assume that the "Suë Junr." of this letter is Jean-Joseph Sue (1760–1830), son of the renowned anatomist of the same name (1710–1792), rath-

From John Allen

ALS: American Philosophical Society

Sir   Bordeaux May 24th. 1783

I had the Honnor of writing the 29th. of Last Month[8] to your Excellence, beging, you would be so good as to grant me a Register for the Brign Lovely Aglaé that I Purcheas'd at this Port, being without any Answer, I take the Liberty to request of your Excellence not to forget my just Demand, as my Brig is all Ready, and am only waiting for a favourable Answer, Which may be directed to Mr. Bondfield.

I have the Honnor to be with Due Respect, your Excellence's Most obeidient and most Humble Servant   JOHN ALLEN

---

er than his cousin Pierre, *dit* Sue le jeune (1739–1816), who was also a distinguished surgeon and the author of numerous works of medical history. Both Jean-Joseph and his father were known to BF and WTF (see below). Sue père was chief surgeon at the Hôpital de la Charité, professor of anatomy at the Académie royale de peinture et de sculpture, and a member of the Royal Society. Sue fils studied under his father, earned a doctorate at Edinburgh, and had a distinguished career as a surgeon and professor of anatomy, succeeding his father at the hospital and Académie and continuing his father's celebrated anatomical cabinet: *Nouvelle biographie;* Fernand Gillet, *L'Hôpital de la charité: Etude historique depuis sa fondation jusqu'en 1900* (Montévrain, 1900), p. 98; Louis Vitet, *L'Académie royale de peinture et de sculpture: Etude historique* (Paris, 1861), p. 405.

Though no letters survive between the father and BF, John Coakley Lettsom refers to Sue père as a mutual friend in his letter to BF of Jan. 28, 1784. John Foulke mentioned both father and son in a Jan. 12, 1782, letter to WTF, and in a note dated only "Saturday Morng.," George Fox invited WTF to a dinner with Foulke and Sue, whom he described as "a young Gentleman of Doct. Foulke's acquaintance." That dinner probably occurred between late fall, 1782, when Fox returned to Paris from various travels, and early May, 1783, when he left to sail for America (XXXIX, 563n). All three letters are at the APS.

8. Missing.

From the Duchesse de Deux-Ponts

ALS: American Philosophical Society

paris Samedis au soir 24 may [1783][9]

Je Vous envoye Mon cher amis de Nouvelle Lecture en Vous priant de me renvoyer Celle que je Vous ait Confiéz Si Vous Nen avéz plus besoin et en vous demandant toujours Le plus grand Secret Sur La Comunication que je Vous fait de Ces feuilles.

Je revient de Versaille ous il Ni a rien de Nouveau du moin de Ma Connessance et ous je retournerez a La fin de La semaine pour y aller attendre Mon grand garçons, quon Calcul qui pouras y arrivér dans Les 8 pier [premiers] jours de juin[1] votre belle ame exelant homme jugera facilement de La joye dont Cette esperence remplies La Mienne ditte moi si Vous dinez chez Vous un des jours de La semaine jirez Vous demander a dinee vous embrasser et Vous renouveller mon respectable amis ma tendre Veneration

FORBACH DOUAIRIERE DU SME DUC DE DEUXPONTS

From Elizabeth Holland[2]

ALS: American Philosophical Society

Great and Worthy Sir   London 25th May 1783

My Husband Thomas Holland Was an officer in the Congress Service and Was kild, he left me with three Children in

---

9. Dated by her reference to the return of her son. The only other year during BF's mission to France when May 24 fell on a Saturday was 1777.

1. Christian, her elder son, was colonel of the Royal-Deux-Ponts regiment, which returned to Brest from America and the West Indies on June 17, 1783. Upon landing he learned of his promotion to brigadier: Rice and Brown, eds., *Rochambeau's Army*, I, 180; Marc-Marie, marquis de Bombelles, *Journal*, ed. Jean Grassion and Frans Durif (7 vols. to date, Geneva, 1977–), I, 232. Her younger son, Guillaume, returned from America at the end of 1781: XXXVI, 77, 78n.

2. This is one of the many "little Affairs & Enquiries" concerning America with which BF was "pester'd continually" and which he forwarded to Charles Thomson for investigation: BF to Thomson, April 16, 1784 (Library of Congress). The only evidence we have of BF's having sent along this particular query is Thomson's reply a year later, summarized below.

the outmost Distress in boy [body] and mind your Well Knowing goodness will take my Cause into your Serious Consideration and Communicate it to the Congress that I might meet
with Such Relief as they Shall think most proper my Husband
and me was Nine years in New york and in that time he Con-
tractd So great a friendship for the American Cause, he was an
Officer in the King of great Brittain Servce maney years and
Quited that to go to america not to incrase his Rank or pay but
Puirly out of appoint of Concious Sake[3] I hope your goodness
will pardon this Freedom in take this Liberty in Writing to your
Honour I Shall be happey to have answer From this Letter and
you will much oblige your Humble Servant

ELIZABETH HOLLAND

I have inclosed my marriage Register[4]

Direct for Elizabeth Holland at Mr Beson oilman Smithfield
London[5]

Addressed: A Monsr / monsr Le Doctr Franklin / P P a Passey /
Proche De Paris

3. The only Thomas Holland known to have served in the British and
American armies and who died while fighting for the United States was a
captain in the Delaware regiment who was killed at Germantown in 1777.
This Capt. Holland married a Joanna Ross in Delaware in 1775, shortly after his arrival. The story he told a comrade was that he was forced to resign
from British service in 1775 under a threat from a superior officer. Being a
widower and having no money, he left his two young sons in the care of a
friend and sailed to Philadelphia: Christopher L. Ward, *The Delaware Continentals, 1776–1783* (Wilmington, Del., 1941), pp. 6, 7, 231, 287, 517–20;
Heitman, *Register of Officers*, p. 225; Joseph Jackson, "Notes and Queries,"
PMHB, LVI (1932), 286.
     The intelligence obtained by Charles Thomson corroborates the details
of this Capt. Holland's service, adding that his widow and children were
receiving a pension from the state of Delaware: Thomson to BF, Aug. 13,
1784 (APS). The Del. Council Minutes record a payment to Joanna Holland in 1781: Ward, *Delaware Continentals*, p. 520.
     4. Missing.
     5. Possibly the oilman Richard Benson at No. 3 Pye Corner: *Bailey's
British Directory* . . . (London, 1784); John Rocque, *The A to Z of Georgian
London* (London, 1982).

Notations in different hands: Elizabeth Holland 25 May 1783— /
London May 25th. 1784 Mrs. Elizabeth Benson to The Hone:
Doctor Franklin About the pay due her late Husband—

From Gabriel Johonnot[6]   ALS: American Philosophical Society

Sir,   Baltimore 25th. May. 1783.
Although I had the Honor of writing your Excellency a few
Days since,[7] I cannot omit Embracing the present Occasion,
least some Accident may prevent its reaching your Hands before this, of Recapitulating its Contents which Assured your
Excellency that Unforseen Circumstances, the Effects of the
Reports of the Approach of Peace for some Months before it
took place, Had been a Means of detaining Me much longer
than I expected, it Included Also my very particular request
supported by Doctr: Cooper.s Ardent Desires, that Your Excellency would be pleased to procure a passage for my Son,[8] recall
Him from Geneva, & direct His Embarkation for Boston to the
care of Mr: Williams or some other person whom your Excellency should think Proper. I informed your Excellency I could
not Get a single Bill or should have inclosed it. But that your
last Bill was paid as soon as it came to Hand,[9] and as your Excellency might still Have Occasion to lodge Monies in Boston
that you would be pleased to draw, and might be Assured your

6. This is his last known letter to BF. By 1784 he had moved to Maine,
where he died in 1820: Joseph W. Porter, *Memoir of Col. Jonathan Eddy, of
Eddington, Me.* . . . (Augusta, 1877), pp. 66–7.
7. Not found.
8. Samuel Cooper Johonnot. Earlier in May, Samuel Cooper had written
to BF about Gabriel Johonnot's plan to escort his son (Cooper's grandson)
back to America. In late June, after learning that his son-in-law would not
sail to Europe, Cooper wrote BF again, asking him and JW to arrange a
return passage for young Johonnot as soon as possible: Samuel Cooper to
Samuel Cooper Johonnot, June 23, 1783 (Yale University Library). Both
letters to BF are missing.
9. Possibly the bill for Samuel's schooling that BF sent on Dec. 20, 1782,
which still had not been paid by April: XXXVIII, 482; XXXIX, 534.

draughts would be punctually discharged. Permit me to Entreat Your Excellency.s Attention to Return My Son to the care of His Grand Father who is looking for it with no Small Anxiety. I Hope for some Future Occasion to testify to your Excellency the Gratefull Feelings of my Heart. For Your Paternal Attention to my Son, In the Interim please to Accept my Warmest Wishes for your Happiness—and Believe me with sentiments of the Most Sincere Respect & Esteem Your Excellency.s Most Obedient Most Humble Servant   G. JOHONNOT

P.S. Please to tender my Respectfull Compliments to your Nephew Mr. W. T. Franklin

Honble: Benja: Franklin Esqr:

Notation: Johonnot 25 May 1783.—

From the Chevalier de Kéralio[1]

ALS: American Philosophical Society

Dimanche, 25e. mai. 1783.
Notre Céleste amie[2] accepte avec le plus grand plaisir la proposition de son respectable ami pour jeudi prochain, si elle ne lui mene pas ses enfants, ce n'est pas sa faute; elle leur a mandé qu'il leur avoit fait l'honneur de les inviter; mais ils sont à forbach a 90 Lieues de paris, et elle doute qu'ils puissent arriver à temps pour diner; vous ne les attendrés pas: à leur place elle vous

1. Kéralio, who had been inspector of military schools, retired from military service on May 16: *DBF.* On May 21 he wrote to WTF requesting three *Libertas Americana* medals for the École militaire and its staff, "de la part de mr. Franklin". One was for the school's library, another for the marquis de Timbrune, its governor, and the third for the baron de Moyria, the commander of the battalion of students. The next day, May 22, Kéralio asked WTF to convey his thanks to BF for the medals. He added that the duchesse de Deux-Ponts would return from Versailles the next day. Both letters are at the APS.
2. The duchesse de Deux-Ponts.

60

amenera Mr. Le Baron de Wish[3] Capitaine au régiment Royal-Deux-ponts qui a combattu Bravement pour la liberté américaine. Vous permettés que le secretaire intime[4] accompagne sa bonne Dame et je me fais une fête nouvelle de vous assurer du Tendre Respect avec lequel je me ferai toujours gloire d'être, mon Digne ami, votre très humble et tres obéissant Serviteur.

LE CHR. DE KERALIO

Addressed: A Monsieur / Monsieur Franklin. / à Passy.

From Robert R. Livingston

ALS: American Philosophical Society; ALS (draft): New-York Historical Society

Sir   Philadelphia, 25th. May 1783

Not knowing when it may be convenient for Mr Bingham to deliver this I confine myself merely to introduce him to your acquaintance— I am persuaded I need not, as his character is known to you to bespeak your civilities for him.[5]

---

3. Jean-Christophe, baron de Wisch (b. 1739), who had been wounded at Yorktown: Bodinier, *Dictionnaire;* Rice and Brown, eds., *Rochambeau's Army,* I, 139, 144.

4. Kéralio himself.

5. BF had known William Bingham since at least 1774; most recently, he had helped pay the congressional agent's drafts: XXI, 403; XXII, 443n; XXXVI, 673. After returning in 1780 from his mission to Martinique, Bingham married Anne Willing and immersed himself in the political, financial, and social life of Philadelphia. He was a founder and director of the Bank of North America, formed two lucrative commercial ventures (a mercantile house with a branch in Amsterdam and a land-grant partnership in New York), speculated successfully in the money market, and helped finance Dickinson College. In the spring of 1783, after his accounts with Congress were settled, Bingham took his young family abroad, where he pursued business interests. They stayed for nearly three years, initially settling in London: Robert C. Alberts, *The Golden Voyage: the Life and Times of William Bingham, 1752–1804* (Boston, 1969), pp. 86–155; *Morris Papers,* VIII, 736. Bingham made his first trip to the Netherlands in August, and from there continued to Paris, when he presumably delivered this letter: Dumas

It may however be prudent if, (as he proposes) Mrs Bingham should accompany him to caution you against such attentions as may deprive us too long of the pleasure of seeing her here again.

I am sir with the greatest Esteem & regard Your most obedient humble servant   R R LIVINGSTON

Honble. Benjamin Franklin, Esqr.

From Charles-Etienne Gaucher

Printed invitation with MS insertions: American Philosophical Society

[before May 26, 1783]

VERITE.∴ UNION.∴ FORCE.∴

T.∴ C.∴ F.∴[6]

L.∴ R.∴ L.∴ des Neuf Sœurs, est convoquée pour le *lundy 26* du *3e.* mois D.∴ L.∴ D.∴ L.∴ V.∴ L.∴ 5783, en son local, rue Coquéron, à *4* heures précises. *Il y aura Reception au 1er. Grade et affiliation, l'on fera la Nomination des officiers, ensuite Banquet.*

Vous êtes prié d'y venir augmenter les douceurs de l'union Fraternelle.

Je suis par les N.∴ C.∴ D.∴ V.∴ M.∴ V.∴ T.∴ H.∴[7] & affectionné Frere.

GAUCHER
Secretaire de la R.∴ L.∴ des IX Sœurs.

---

to BF, Aug. 25 (below); BF to Richard Price, Sept. 16, 1783 (Library of Congress). One of his calling cards is among BF's papers at the APS.

6. Très Cher Frère. The two abbreviations in the next paragraph stand for La Respectable Loge and De L'année De La Vraie Lumière 5783. The masonic year began in March.

7. Nombres Connus Des Vénérables Maîtres Vôtre Très Humble.

BF received two other printed invitations during the months covered by this volume, both signed by Gaucher. The meeting of June 23 would celebrate the feast of St. John the Baptist; the new officers would be in-

L'adresse de la Loge est à M. GAUCHER, des Académies de Londres, &c. rue S. Jacques, porte cochére, vis-à-vis Saint-Yves

From ——— de Monteiro Bandeira

AL: American Philosophical Society

Lundi ce 26 May 1783.

Mr. de Monteiro Bandeira á L'honneur de faire bien des Compliments a Mr. Franklin, et Comm'il doit partir demain pour Lisbonne il prie Mr. Franklin de Lui envoyer Les Lettres qu'il Lui á dit vouloir Lui remetre: Mr. de Monteyro Bandeira á aussi L'honneur de faire rapeler Mr. Franklin de La part de Mr. L'Ambassadeur de Portugal[8] de Ce qu'il Lui a promis.

Addressed: A Monsieur / Mr. Franklin / Ministre Plenipotentiaire des Etats / Unis a La Cour de Versailles. / A Passi

---

stalled, followed by readings and a banquet. The July 21 meeting would include a "Reception au 1er. et 2d. Grade," a report by commissioners on a brother proposed for affiliation, a banquet, and readings by the following men: the comte de Milly, the new *vénérable* (XXIII, 128n); La Salle d'Offémont (XXXIV, 470n); François de Neufchâteau (XXXVI, 461n); Pastoret, the new *premier orateur* (XXXVIII, 486–7n); and "Le Blanc." This was *second secrétaire* Antoine Blanc, *dit* Le Blanc de Guillet (1730–1799), a man of letters, former Oratorian, and teacher of rhetoric: *DBF*, under Le Blanc de Guillet; Le Bihan, *Francs-maçons parisiens*, p. 297; Amiable, *Une Loge maçonnique*, pp. 323–4 of the 1st pagination and 186–7 of the 2nd; *Tableau des Frères . . . des Neuf Sœurs* for 1783 (Yale University Library).

8. The conde de Sousa Coutinho, with whom BF would soon exchange plans of a commercial treaty. BF's proposal has not been located; Sousa Coutinho delivered a counterproposal on June 4, which was amended after BF returned comments. BF's letter to Sousa Coutinho and the counterproposal are both below, under June 7.

From Robert Morris: Two Letters

(I) LS and copy: Archives du Ministère des affaires étrangères;[9] copy and press copy of copy:[1] American Philosophical Society; copy: Library of Congress; (II) LS: American Philosophical Society; copy: Library of Congress

I.

Sir　　　　　　　　　　　　Office of Finance 26th: May 1783.

By the enclosed Acts of the twenty eighth of April and second of May with the Copy of my Letter to Congress of the third of May you will perceive that I am to Continue somewhat longer in the Superintendance of our Finances.[2] Be assured Sir, that nothing but a clear View of our Distresses could have induced my Consent. I must at the same time acknowledge that the Distresses we experience arise from our own Misconduct. If the Resources of this Country were drawn forth they would be amply sufficient, but this is not the Case. Congress have not Authority equal to the Object, and their Influence is greatly lessened by their evident Incapacity to do Justice. This is but a melancholy Introduction to the Request contained in the Act of the second Instant.[3] But I shall not be guilty of Falsehood

9. A French notation on the LS indicates that it was sent to Vergennes by BF under cover of his letter of July 4. (The resolutions Morris enclosed remain among BF's papers at the APS.) The copy is in the hand of Morris' secretary and appears to have been sent to Vergennes by La Luzerne. It and its enclosures (all in the same hand) are filed with Morris' signed letter to La Luzerne of May 27 asking him to read the enclosed letter to BF and write a similar appeal to Vergennes; dispatches would go on the *General Washington*. La Luzerne informed Morris on June 3 that he had sent Morris' letters and enclosures to his court but could not give Morris the slightest hope of success: *Morris Papers*, VIII, 124–5, 157.

1. In the hand of L'Air de Lamotte with a notation by WTF. We presume that BF ordered this copy made before sending the LS to Vergennes.

2. The April 28 resolution extended Morris' service so that he could arrange to pay the army. The three acts of May 2 resolved that the states collect taxes to pay the army's expenses, an application be made to Louis XVI for an additional 3,000,000 *l.t.*, and Morris be authorized to carry out these directives: *JCC*, XXIV, 283–5, 325–6, 326. For Morris' reluctant decision to remain in office rather than resign at the end of May and his May 3 letter, see *Morris Papers*, VII, 767–81, 789–90.

3. For a new loan; see the preceding note.

nor will I intentionally Deceive you or put you in the Necessity of deceiving others. My Official Situation compels me to do things which I would certainly avoid under any other Circumstances. Nothing should Induce me in my private Character to make such Applications for Money, as I am obliged to in my Public Character. I know and feel that you must be in a disagreeable Situation on this Subject. I can anticipate the Answers to all your Requests. And I know you may be asked for Payment when you ask for Loans. Yet Sir I must desire you to repeat your Applications. My only Hope arises from the Belief that as the Kings Expences are much lessened he may be able to comply with his gracious Intentions towards America. And the only Inducement I can Offer is the Assurance that the Taxes already called for shall be appropriated as fast as other indispensible Services will admit to the Replacement of what the Court may advance.[4]

Our Situation is shortly this. The Army expect a Payment which will amount to about seven hundred thousand Dollars.[5] I am already above half a Million Dollars in Advance of our

---

4. When La Luzerne announced to Morris on March 15 that the king had granted a new loan of 6,000,000 *l.t.*, he also conveyed Vergennes' warning that it would surely be the last unless Congress demonstrated its ability to meet its obligations: *Morris Papers*, VII, 584–9. On April 18 Congress passed by majority vote a new plan to fund the national debt, pending unanimous ratification by the states, which called for the 5 percent impost on foreign imports that had long been discussed, as well as the appropriation of $1,500,000 annually in state revenues toward the payment of principal and interest. Ratification was so prolonged and contentious that the plan never went into effect: *JCC*, XXIV, 256–62; Ferguson, *Power of the Purse*, pp. 166–7, 221; Jack N. Rakove, *Beginnings of National Politics* (New York, 1979), pp. 337–9.

The plan was printed in the pamphlet that Livingston enclosed in his letter to BF of May 9. Livingston also enclosed a copy of the resolution seeking an additional loan that Morris enclosed in the present letter: XXXIX, 579–80. Both these letters—Livingston's and Morris'—were carried by Barney and delivered to BF on July 2.

5. The largest components of army expenses were rations and pay: *Morris Papers*, VIII, 58. Financial considerations influenced Congress on May 26 to order furloughs from the army: *JCC*, XXIV, 364; *Morris Papers*, VIII, 130–2.

Resources by Paper Anticipation.[6] I must increase this Anticipation immediately to pay Monies due on the Contracts for feeding our Army and I must make them the expected Payment by Notes to be discharged at a distant Day. Now Sir if these Notes are not satisfied when they become due, the little Credit which remains to this Country must fall and the little Authority dependent on it must fall too. Under such Circumstances it is that your are to ask Aid for the United States. If it can be obtained I shall consider the obligation as being in some degree personal to my self and I shall certainly exert my self for the Repayment. You will be so kind Sir as to Ship on Board the Washington[7] eighteen hundred thousand Livres, but if the Loan be not obtained I must intreat you will give me the earliest possible Information of the Refusal.

I shall communicate this Letter to the Minister of his Most Christian Majesty and request him to write to Mr. de Vergennes on the Subject of it.

Beleive me I pray With sincere & respectful Esteem & Regard Your Excellency's Most obedient & Humble Servt.

ROBT MORRIS

P.S. You have enclosed the Copy of a Letter which was sent with this to Monsr. de La Luzerne[8]

His Excellency Benjn Franklin Esqr.

II.

Sir   Office of Finance 26th: May 1783.

I have now before me your Letters of the fourteenth and twenty third of December which are the last I have received.[9] Enclosed you have a Letter from me to the Minister of France,

---

6. During the first four months of 1783, Continental Treasury expenditures exceeded receipts by an estimated $583,599.78: *Morris Papers*, VIII, 54.

7. The packet *General Washington*, commanded by Joshua Barney.

8. This postscript, not visible on the photostat of the LS supplied by the AAE, comes from the copy at the APS. For Morris' letter to La Luzerne see the first note, above.

9. XXXVIII, 453–6, 487–9.

with his Answer of the fourteenth of March on the Subject of the Delay which happened in transmitting his Dispatches. You will see by these that Lieutenant Barney was not to blame.[1]

Your Bills in Favor of Monsr: de Lauzun have not yet appeared or they should have been duly honoured. That Gentleman has since left the Country and therefore it is possible that the Bill may not come.[2]

The Reflections you make as well on the Nature of Public Credit as on the Inattention of the several States,[3] are just and unanswerable but in what Country of the World shall we find a Nation willing to Tax themselves. The Language of Panegyric has held forth the English as such a Nation, but certainly if our Legislatures were subject to like Influence with theirs we might preserve the Form, but we should already have lost the Substance of Freedom. Time, Reason, Argument and above all that kind of Conviction which arises from feeling are necessary to the Establishment of our Revenues and the Consolidation of our Union. Both of these appear to me essential to our public Happiness, but our Ideas (as you well know) are frequently the Result rather of habit than Reflection so that Numbers who might think justly upon these Subjects have been early estranged from the Modes and Means of considering them properly.

I am in the Hourly Wish and Expectation of hearing from You and sincerely hope that it may be soon.

Beleive me I pray with Esteem and Respect Your Excellency's Most obedient & Humble Servant   ROBT MORRIS

His Excellency Benjn: Franklin.

---

1. Morris' letter to La Luzerne, dated March 14, apologized for the news (contained in BF's Dec. 14 letter) that there had been an "extraordinary Delay" in Barney's delivering La Luzerne's dispatches to Vergennes and assured him that there would be an investigation. La Luzerne replied that none was necessary: *Morris Papers*, VII, 576, 576–7.

2. See XXXVIII, 455. The duc de Lauzun sailed for France from Wilmington, Del., on May 11: Rice and Brown, eds., *Rochambeau's Army*, I, 315.

3. XXXVIII, 488–9.

From Charles (Johann Karl Philipp) Spener

ALS: American Philosophical Society

Monsieur   Berlin ce 26. May 1783.

Ayant dessein de publier, vers la fin de Septembre, un Almanac américain en allemand pour l'année prochaine, & desirant le décorer de plusieurs Estampes y relatives, dont la composition ne doit point être idéale; c'est à Vous, Monsieur & à Votre portefeuille, qui doit être très riche en tout ce qui a rapport à l'histoire des Colonies anglo-americaines que j'ose recourir, bien que je n'aye point l'honneur de Vous être connû.[4]

Permettez Monsieur, que je Vous expose brievement, le plan de cet Almanac, & qu'ensuite je demande Votre gracieuse assistance, soit pour des renseignemens, soit pour les articles mêmes dont j'ai besoin & que certainement personne n'est mieux en état de me fournir que Vous Monsieur!

L'almanac contiendra en prémier lieu l'histoire de la Revolution d'après les meilleurs Auteurs & les avis les plus veridiques que l'on ait pû se procurer.[5] Ce sujet sera orné de gravures historiques, représentant les événemens les plus remarquables de cette guerre. *En second lieu:* Galerie des grands hommes de l'amérique avec un précis de leur carriere politique ou militaire decorée de leurs portraits, copiés sur ceux dessinés par du Simitier à Philadelphie[6] & sur d'autres qui ont parus en Angleterre.

---

4. Hilliard d'Auberteuil had already written to BF about Spener's project; see XXXIX, 458n, where the publisher is identified and *Historisch-genealogischer Calender oder Jahrbuch der merkwürdigsten neuen Welt-Begebenheiten* is described.

5. This history was written by Matthias Christian Sprengel (introduced below). It ran to some 180 pages, and its two-page bibliography included works in German, French, and English. Among them were BF's *Political, Miscellaneous, and Philosophical Pieces* (XXXI, 210–18), Hilliard d'Auberteuil's *Essais historiques et politiques sur les Anglo-Américains* (XXXVII, 132–3n), and Jackson's 1783 London edition of the American state constitutions (XXXVII, 20n). For a discussion of Sprengel's sources see Eugene E. Doll, "American History as Interpreted by German Historians from 1770 to 1815," APS *Trans.*, new series, XXXVIII (1948), 464.

6. For these engravings by Prevost, published in 1781, see XXXV, 4.

Come Vous tenez Monsieur un si haut rang parmi les grands hommes de l'Amérique, souffrez que je Vous demande, si votre Portrait, tel qu'il a été gravé en 1782. par Pélicier pour l'Essai sur les Anglo-Américains est assez ressemblant pour pouvoir me servir de modèle?[7]

Pour rendre cette Galerie plus complette, je passerois des grands hommes aux hommes celebres de l'Amérique & c'est là où je suis en peine pour les portraits suivans:

Portrait de John Adams
_____ du Sr. Payne, Auteur du *Common Sense*
_____ du Dr. Warren, tué à Bunkers-Hill
_____ du Genl. Montgomery tué à Quebec
_____ du Sr. Paul Jones Commodore au Service des 13 Etats unis.

A ces portraits je désirerois de pouvoir joindre les morceaux suivans:

Mausolée érigé par Ordre du Congrès au Dr. Warren.
_____ dit _____ à la memoire du Genl. Montgomery.
Medaille frappée par Ordre du Congrès à l'occasion de la prise du Major *André*.
_____ dite _____ à l'occasion de la paix pour eterniser l'histe. de la Revolution.
Forme du Pappier-monnoye
Espèces monnoyées aux Armes des 13 Etats
Les Armes des Treize Etats.
Le Pavillon des Treize Etats *coloré*

---

7. The portrait of BF used by Hilliard d'Auberteuil (*Essais historique* . . . , II, facing p. 60) was a 1782 engraving by J. Pélicier which excerpted the framed portrait of BF held by Diogenes in a 1781 engraving published by Bligny (XXXIII, frontispiece and XXVII), itself derived from the Cathelin engraving after Filleul (XXIX, frontispiece). Spener's instincts were correct; the likeness had not improved with successive iterations. In the end, his artist adapted the ubiquitous "fur cap" engraving by Saint-Aubin (XXIV, frontispiece).

Uniforme des Troupes américaines, nommément des Regiments de Washington et de Gates, *colorée*[8]

La partie historique de cet Almanac étant confiée à un de nos meilleurs historiens, le Sr. Sprengel, Professeur d'histoire à l'université de halle, qui possède à fond l'anglois & toutes les connoissances & qualités qui constituent le bon historien, j'ose me flatter, que Son Ouvrage méritera Votre approbation.[9] Aussi me réserve-je l'honneur de Vous le présenter Monsieur & même, par Votre entremise aux honorables Membres du Congrès auxquels je desire d'en faire l'hommage.

Pardonnez moi, Monsieur, en faveur de cette idée, de ce que j'ose interrompre Vos graves occupations par un hors d'oeuvre

---

8. *Historisch-genealogischer Calender* was published with black-and-white engravings of 12 scenes of the Revolution, the *Libertas Americana* medal, the design for a Continental coin, and portraits (crowded into a single plate) of Generals Washington and Gates, John Paul Jones, Henry Laurens, and BF. Three colored plates were included at the end: the American flag and a pennant, the uniforms of Washington's troops, and the uniforms of regular infantry troops from Pennsylvania. There was also a German re-engraving of William Faden's 1783 map of the United States. There is no evidence that BF assisted in this project and contrary evidence to suggest that he did not: in the explanation of the plates, for example, Sprengel based his description of the *Libertas Americana* medal on published news accounts rather than BF's own explanation (for which see XXXIX, 549–55). In his biographical sketch of BF, however, Sprengel reported a rumor of particular interest: he had heard "credibly" that BF would be writing an account of his early life and intellectual development. *Historisch-genealogischer Calender,* pp. 174, 179.

9. Sprengel was already a published authority on the history of North America. This history of the American Revolution was the first comprehensive German study of the subject and was republished separately the following year as *Allgemeines historisches Taschenbuch* and in later editions as *Geschichte der Revolution von Nord-Amerika.* By 1788 it had gone through five editions, making it the most successful German book on North America of the late eighteenth century. Sprengel was the son-in-law of naturalist Johann Reinhold Forster (XV, 147–8), whose influence might be reflected in his pro-American attitude: Doll, "American History," pp. 461–4; Horst Dippel, *Germany and the American Revolution, 1770–1800 . . . ,* trans. Bernhard A. Uhlendorf (Chapel Hill, N.C., 1977), pp. 52–3.

de cette espece & faites moi la grace de déférer à ma très humble demande.

Enfin, permettez moi d'ajouter, que, le temps d'icy à la fin de Séptembre terme fixé pour la publication des Almanacs de notre pays, n'étant guères eloigné, & l'exécution des differentes gravures exigeant un temps considérable, en me fournissant le plutôt possible les matériaux qui me manquent, Vous ajouterez infiniment au prix du bienfait que je sollicite, *Bis dat, qui cito dat.*—[1]

Qu'il me soit permis Monsieur, de Vous témoigner icy la vénération & le respect les plus vivement sentis, dont je suis pénétré pour le Philosophe & l'homme d'état que les deux hémisphères ré[vèrent(?)] en Vous!

C'est dans ces sentimens que j'ai l'honneur d'être Monsieur Votre très soumis & obeissant Servt   CHARLES SPENER
Libraire du Roy.

Notation: Charles Spener 26 May 1783

From Louise-Geneviève Du Ponceau

ALS: American Philosophical Society

Monsieur—   a st martin ce 27 mai 1783

Pardonnéz Monsieur a linquiétude d'unne soeur qui étan obligeè devivre è loigneè dun frére que jaisme ausi tantdrement [tendrement] ne peut supporter les riguer de la panse que par les nouvelle frécante quelle peut avoir en ètant privèe depuis 8 mois josse vous suplier monsieur de vouloir bien avoir la bontez de lui faire tenir la lètre que je pren la libertez dinsèrer dans la votre jes [j'ai] deja resantie tandefois les èfes de votre bienfésanse par

---

1. A Latin proverb: "He gives twice who gives quickly." The work may not have been ready until the end of the year. Sprengel's preface is dated Oct. 30, 1783, and BF was sent his copy in January (Treuttel to BF, Jan. 15, 1784, APS).

71

selle que vous avez deja fait tenir tan a lun qua lostre[2] que je me flatte encorre que si vous saviez de mon frère duponceau qui est sousècrétairre détat au dèpartement des afairre ètranjérre a philadelphie quelque nouvelle bonne ou mauvaisse[3] votre charitez sétandrèt jus que en fairre donner a selle dont la reconnoisanse è Galle le profon respect avec lequell jés lonneur destre monsieur votre aubeisante servante   LOÜISE GÉNEVIEVE DUPONCEAU

Addressed: pour monsieur de franklin

From Robert Morris

LS: American Philosophical Society; copy: Library of Congress

Sir   Office of Finance 27th. May 1783
   It was my earnest Desire from the first Moment when it was known that the Troops of his most Christian Majesty were intended for this Continent to promote his Service and forward the Views and Interests of his faithful Servants— It would appear like an empty Boast to say that I was early and frequently useful to them nor would I hint any thing of that kind or of the improper Returns I have met with. My present Object is meerly to possess you of facts as far as they relate to the Kings Service. Shortly after the Commencement of my Administration I proposed supplying the Kings Troops by Contract but found Obstacles were raised and objections were made by such as I was induced to suppose were interested in opposing œconomi-

2. In 1782 BF had promised to forward letters between Mlle Du Ponceau and her brother Pierre-Etienne, who was serving in Philadelphia as an undersecretary for foreign affairs: XXXVI, 581–2. She subsequently entrusted to BF a letter dated Jan. 16, 1783, to her older brother Jean-Michel, chevalier Du Ponceau, who was serving under Rochambeau. That letter remains among BF's papers at the APS. For the chevalier see his letter of Sept. 6.
3. Pierre-Etienne Du Ponceau left the office of foreign affairs around June 4, when Livingston's resignation was accepted (for which see Boudinot to BF, June 16): *DAB; ANB.*

cal Arrangements and therefore I desisted—[4] Very slight enquiry will determine whether the Expences of this Army have been Moderate or excessive— The enclosed Letter from me to the Intendant will explain one Transaction—[5] I shall add to it only that the Intendant having refused to pay, a Suit was commenced against Mr. DeMars by Solomons the Broker for all the Bills which he sold to DeMars and to Debrassine. On the Trial it appeared not only that Mr. Debrassine was employed by Mr. De Mars in public and private Business but that the Monies obtained by Sale of all those Bills of Exchange were applied to private Purposes— The Jury were but a few Minutes out of Court and brought in their Verdict for the Principal Interest &ca.[6] Indeed had the Intendant thought proper to enquire into the facts stated in my Letter to him I have no Doubt but that they and others of equal Importance would have appeared— Enclosed you have the Copy of a Letter which has fallen into my Hands and which will shew you Something of the Business which has been transacted by the French Administration—[7] The original of this Letter is now in my Hands and can (at any Time) be delivered if necessary to the Minister or Consul of France here—

I am to request Sir that you will have a Conference on the Subject of this Letter with General de Chattelleux. That Gen-

4. See *Morris Papers*, II, 7–9, 77–9, 82–3; III, 519–20. Morris also had been unable to comply with BF's plan for furnishing supplies to Rochambeau's army: XXXIV, 36–8, 97–9; XXXV, 301–2; XXXVI, 139, 149–50.

5. The enclosed letter, dated March 12, was addressed to pay commissioner Benoît-Joseph de Tarlé (1735–1797), who served as intendant of Rochambeau's army: *Etat militaire* for 1783, p. 17; Bodinier, *Dictionnaire*. Morris appealed to Tarlé for justice, detailing a complicated story of bills of exchange obtained from him under false pretences by Jean-Baptiste de Mars (Demars de Grandpré), *directeur des hôpitaux* for Rochambeau's army, and his agent Fontaine de Brassine, *garde-magasin des hôpitaux*. This letter is published in *Morris Papers*, VII, 564–9; see the text and annotation there. De Mars's full name is given in Howard G. Brown, *War, Revolution, and the Bureaucratic State: Politics and Army Administration in France, 1791–1799* (Oxford, 1995), pp. 292, 294.

6. Morris' broker Haym Salomon (*ANB*) won the suit on April 26: *Morris Papers*, VII, 568, 603–5, 755; VIII, 124n.

7. Not found.

tleman always appeared to me extremely Zealous and attentive to the King's Interest, desirous of introducing Œconomy and opposed to Plans which entailed a profuse Expence— Should you after a Consultation with him think it would at all conduce to the Kings Interests I shall be glad that you would bring the Matter regularly before his Ministers who will I perswade my-self cause the proper Investigations by which means the Crown will be better served on Subsequent Occasions.

With perfect Respect I have the Honor to be Sir Your Excellency's most obedient & humble Servant ROBT MORRIS

His Excellency Benjamin Franklin Esqr.

From ——— Foucher, Chevalier d'Obsonville[8]

ALS: American Philosophical Society

a paris ce 27e. may [1783]—f.B. St. denys no. 18.
Monsieur
Je n'ay point L'honneur d'etre Connu de votre excellence; mais en qualité d'homme pensant j'ay Crû vous devoir L'hommage d'un ecrit qui Semble offrir quelques points de vuë d'utilité generalle.[9] Mde. La mqse. de Boisserolles soeur de Mr Law de lau-

---

8. An adventurer turned naturalist and orientalist, Foucher d'Obsonville (1734–1802) left France when he was only 19 years old for what would become a 20-year sojourn in India and parts of the Middle East. He served various French officials on military and diplomatic missions, barely survived the plague and a near-shipwreck, escaped his share of wild beasts, and was a close observer of the local customs and fauna he encountered. Upon his return to Paris around 1774, he was examined by eminent physicians from the Invalides and the Faculty of Medicine, who confirmed that plague and guinea worm were the cause of his scarring. In 1783, at Buffon's urging, he published the book enclosed with the present letter (from which many of these biographical details are drawn). His later publications included a translation of the Indian Vedas: *DBF; Nouvelle biographie.*

9. *Essais philosophiques sur les mœurs de divers animaux étrangers, avec des observations relatives aux principes & usages de plusieurs peuples* . . . (Paris, 1783). Published anonymously and dedicated to Buffon, the work was arranged by animal; the accounts were based on Foucher's own observations and experiences as recorded in his journals. It was announced in the

riston[1] et amie de Madame de Chaumont, avoit bien voulu me promettre de vous presenter elle même Cet exemplaire, mais un rhume Considerable Continuant à La retenir chez elle, je prens la liberté de vous l'envoyer directement.

Comme l'ouvrage a eté imprimé pendant que j'etois en province, il a besoin de beaucoup d'indulgence pour la partie typographique, et des negligences de Stile. Les Suffrages que j'ose ambitionner Sont ceux de personnes qui telles que votre excellence recherchent et appretient dans un voyageur non des formes, mais des faits et des observations.

Je desire garder l'anonyme vis à vis du public, cependant Je Saisis avec empressement cette occation de me dire avec une Consideration profondement Sentie et un profond respect De votre excellence Monsieur Le tres humble Et tres obeissant Serviteur   CHER D'OBSONVILLE

Robert R. Livingston to the American Peace Commissioners

Copies: Massachusetts Historical Society, South Carolina Historical Society; AL (draft): New-York Historical Society; transcript:[2] National Archives

Gentlemen,   Philadelphia. 28th. May. 1783.

By the direction of Congress, contained in the enclosed resolutions, I have the honor to transmit you the Correspondence between General Washington & Sir Guy Carlton, together with

---

Jour. de Paris on May 26 and extensively described on June 25. In 1784 an English translation by Thomas Holcroft was published in London, made with Foucher's cooperation and identifying him as the author.

1. Elizabeth-Jeanne Law, marquise de Boisserolles, was the sister of Jean Law, baron de Lauriston, whom Foucher served under and knew well. Law de Lauriston was the governor and commandant general of the French settlements in India, and was promoted to a *maréchal de camp* upon his return to Paris in 1780: *DBF*. For the marquise see the *Dictionnaire de la noblesse*, XI, 814.

2. A notation on the transcript indicates that three copies were sent, the first one by the *General Washington*.

minutes of their Conference, when, in pursuance of the invitation of the first, they met in Orange County.[3] Nothing can be a more direct violation of the 7th: Article of the Provisional Treaty,[4] than sending off the Slaves, under pretence that their Proclamation had set them free, as if a British General had, either by their laws, or those of nations, a right by Proclamation to deprive any man whatever of property: They may with much more propriety pretend to re-establish every of their Adherents in all the Rights they had before the war, since they have engaged so to do, and the People, with whom they made these engagements, were capable of entering into them, which Slaves were not—or even, if they were, the promise made to them must be under the same limitations with those made to their other Adherents in this Country, & amounts to nothing more than this, make yourselves free, and we will protect you in that freedom as long as we can. The Articles imply that they were no longer able to protect them. You will be pleased to remonstrate on this Subject, and inform Congress of the Effect of your Representations— We have been much embarassed by our not having a line

3. For background see xxxix, 579. Congress passed a resolution on May 26 directing that the American peace commissioners should "remonstrate" with the British court about Britain's harboring escaped American slaves, and should be sent copies of the correspondence that passed between Gen. Washington and British Army Commander Sir Guy Carleton on the subject: *JCC*, xxiv, 363–4. Carleton, who had met with Washington on May 6, claimed that only free blacks had been permitted to accompany departing British soldiers, but agreed to have American commissioners inspect future embarkations: Washington to Carleton, April 21; Substance of a Conference between George Washington and Sir Guy Carleton, May 6; Washington to Carleton, May 6; Washington to President of Congress Boudinot, May 8; Washington to Egbert Benson *et al.*, May 8 (Fitzpatrick, *Writings of Washington*, xxvi, 345–8, 402–6, 408–9, 410–12, 412–14, copies of the final four being among BF's papers at the APS); Carleton to Washington, May 12 (Giunta, *Emerging Nation*, I, 855–8); Simon Schama, *Rough Crossings: Britain, the Slaves and the American Revolution* (London, 2005), pp. 129–55. Carleton ultimately prevailed since Congress did not want to risk the renewal of hostilities over the issue.

4. Which forbade the British from "carrying away any Negroes, or other Property of the American inhabitants," when they evacuated their forces from the United States: xxxviii, 386.

from you since the Provisional Articles took effect, nor being at all acquainted with the progress of the Definitive Treaty, tho' the earliest information on this Subject becomes very important. Congress, after some hesitation, have ventured to hope, that it will meet with no obstructions, & have accordingly discharged, by the enclosed Resolutions, a very considerable part of their army upon those principles of Œconomy which extreme necessity dictated—[5] As scarce a week passes without several arrivals from France, Congress complain, with some reason of your Silence: for my own part, I could wish that you would, severally, impose upon yourselves the task of writing weekly, & sending your letters to Mr: Barclay— As you are possessed of Cyphers there can be no hazard in this where the Subject of your Correspondence requires Secrecy—

I am, Gentlemen, with the greatest respect & Esteem, Your Most Obedt: humle: servant,   (signed) R. R. LIVINGSTON.

The Honourable John Adams, Benja: Franklin, John Jay, & Henry Laurens. Esquires.

No: 3.

(Copy)

Notation by John Adams: Mr Livingstone to the Ministers for Peace 28. May. 1783.

From Joseph Banks   ALS: University of Pennsylvania Library

Dear Sir   Soho Square May 28 1783
I cannot Miss the opportunity of Our Mutual Assistant in the Experiment of Pouring Whale Oil on the surface of the Sea Dr. Blagden who no doubt you remember Stationd on shore to mark the Effect of our process,[6] I cannot I say Miss the opportunity of his Journey to Paris to present to you my sincere

5. See the annotation of Morris to BF, May 26, letter (I).
6. This 1773 experiment, born of BF's observing the effect of oil poured on the pond at Clapham Common, was an unsuccessful attempt to quiet

congratulations on the return of peace which in whatever form she is worshipd bad peace or good Peace never fails to prove herself the Faithfull nurse of Science. Dr. Blagden has now for some years Servd as Physician to the Army both in America & at home with no small degree of reputation but the principal reason why I have requested him to wait upon you is that he is master of the present state of Science in this Countrey & will I am sure have great satisfaction in Amusing as well as instructing your leisure hours by ample information of what we pacific ones have been doing here during the past times of turbulency.[7]

You will find I hope that we have not been idle a new Planet & a new periodical Phenomenon happening to a fixd star mark the progress of Active astronomy.[8] The point of Congelation of

---

the ocean surf on a blustery day in October. It involved several boats and numerous assistants: xx, 472–4.

7. Charles Blagden (xx, 474n) served as an army surgeon on a hospital ship off the American coast for the first three years of the war. After his return to England he renewed contacts with Banks and the greater London scientific community while working in the military hospital in Plymouth. In late 1782 or early 1783 he became the assistant of the celebrated chemist Henry Cavendish and moved to London: *ODNB;* Christa Jungnickel and Russell McCormmach, *Cavendish* (Philadelphia, 1996), pp. 212–15.

Blagden arrived in Paris on June 4 and stayed through the end of July, meeting with as many scientists as possible and trying to establish more fluent communication between the Royal Society and the Académie des sciences. His trip sparked the so-called water controversy. On June 21 he read to Lavoisier and others an unpublished paper of Priestley's describing work that revealed the chemical composition of water, based on an experiment by Cavendish. (Priestley had sent the manuscript to Banks in April, but Banks did not present it to the Royal Society until June 26: *Phil. Trans.,* LXXIII [1783], 398–434.) Two days later Blagden dictated it to Le Roy and helped him translate it into French. On June 24, with Blagden at his side, Lavoisier repeated the experiment; the next day he presented the results to the Académie des sciences. Lavoisier's subsequent publication of the discovery claimed primacy, sparking a long-lasting debate.

Blagden delivered the present letter to BF on June 6, but did not dine at Passy until the 26th; see his letter of June 22. Details of his trip are from his 1783 journal at the Yale University Library.

8. Both the discovery of what is now called Uranus and the theory of the solar system's movements were the work of William Herschel (1738–1822). Herschel received the Copley medal in 1781 for the former, though

Mercury the Dr. himself has written largely about[9] many many more are the things he will inform you of which hitherto I suppose you only to have heard in the press & I trust that the Politician has not so entirely devourd the Philosophical part of your Character but that you will wish to hear them in detail.

To lengthen this letter would be only to waste your time in unnecessary employment Dr. Blagden who is my mouth on this occasion will tell you every thing which you want to know & I could write.

May then your Philosophy revive & shine as high in the Annals of Literature as your Politicks will & do in those of America is the sincere wish of You Faithfull & Obedient Servant

Jos: BANKS

Dr. Franklin

---

he initially thought it a comet. On Nov. 7, 1782, he announced to the Royal Society that the "star" was actually a "Primary Planet of our Solar System" and submitted a paper entitled "On the Diameter and Magnitude of the Georgium Sidus; With a Description of the Dark and Lucid Disk and Periphery Micrometers." The following spring he submitted "On the proper Motion of the Sun and Solar System; with an Account of several Changes that have happened among the fixed Stars since the Time of Mr. Flamstead": *Phil. Trans.*, LXXIII (1783), 1–3, 4–14, 247–83.

9. During the winter of 1781/82, Thomas Hutchins, stationed in Hudson's Bay, performed a series of experiments for the Royal Society that determined the freezing point of mercury; these were based on Cavendish's detailed instructions and apparatus. Hutchins' paper was read to the Royal Society on April 10, 1783. Cavendish submitted his own "Observations" on Hutchins' results on May 1. Blagden's contribution was to write a lengthy history of all previous attempts, entitled "History of the Congelation of Quicksilver." This was read to the Society on June 5, shortly after he left London; upon his return, he inserted additional information gleaned in Paris. His final version, and the other two papers mentioned above, are in *Phil. Trans.*, LXXIII (1783), *303–*370, 303–28, 329–97.

From Wolfgang von Kempelen[1]

ALS: American Philosophical Society

Monsieur   A Paris ce 28 Mai 783
Si je ne vous ai averti plutot de mon retour de Versaille, et
renouvellè ma priere d'assister a une representation de mon
automate joueur d'échec,[2] ce n'etoit que pour gagner encore
quelques jours, qui m'etoient necessaires pour avancer une
autre machine très interessante,[3] que j'ai a l'ouvrage, et que je
voudrois vous faire voir en même tems. Ayez donc Monsieur la
bontè pour moi, de fixer le jour et l'heure, dans la quelle je pour-
rai avoir l'honneur de vous recevoir chez moi. Ma demeure est a
l'hôtel d'Aligre rûe d'Orleans St Honorè. J'ai l'honneur d'être
avec le Respect, et l'estime la plus parfaite Monsieur votre très
humble et très obeissant Serviteur   DE KEMPEL

Addressed: a Monsieur / Monsieur Franklin / a Passy

Notation: De Kempel Paris 28 May 1783

---

1. The inventor who had arrived in Paris from Vienna the previous
month with a chess-playing "mechanical Turk," a hoax which he claimed
to be an automaton; see XXXVIII, 495–6.

2. The "Turk" was first exhibited to great acclaim at Versailles before
moving to Paris in early May, where it played a number of well-attended
exhibition matches. By June 12, according to a journalist, it had mystified
all the members of the Académie des sciences and all the best mechani-
cians of Paris: Bachaumont, *Mémoires secrets*, XXIII, 3–5. The top-ranked
players defeated it but commended its performance; most notable among
them was François-André Danican Philidor, the champion of all Europe,
who supposedly played a match shortly before Kempelen left for England,
c. September: Tom Standage, *The Mechanical Turk: the True Story of the
Chess-Playing Machine That Fooled the World* (London, 2002), pp. 43, 45,
49–54.

3. This was the elaborate speaking machine on which he had been working for over a decade; see XXXVIII, 496, and the references cited there.
While touring Europe in 1783–84, Kempelen demonstrated the device to
select audiences and sought the advice of scientists on how to improve it:
Alice Reininger, *Wolfgang von Kempelen: eine Biografie* (Vienna, 2007),
pp. 325–35. We have no record of when BF saw it, but he was sufficiently
impressed that he recommended Kempelen as a "Genius": BF to Brühl,
Vaughan, and Whitehurst, all dated Aug. 22.
    BF's interest in speaking machines dates back to at least 1772, when

From Pierre Richard[4]

ALS: American Philosophical Society

Monsieur   Paris Le 28e. mai 1783.

La maniere honnete & affable avec laquelle, Son Excellence, a bien voulu m'accueillir, se charger de mes paquets pour l'amérique, & recommander mes intérêts au Président du congrès & à M. Bingham, m'enhardit á lui adresser une lettre pour ce dernier, avec priere de la lui faire passer: je continue á ne point avoir de ses nouvelles, & l'on me mande de la martinique, qu'il a obtenu du Congrès une Mission pour une Cour d'Europe; ce qui me feroit desirer plus fortement que jamais de terminer les affres. [affaires] qu'il a avec moi avant son départ.[5] J'ose prier, Son Excellence, de vouloir me pardonner ces détails, qu'il est peut être nécessaire qu'elle sache.

Je Suis avec un profond respect Monsieur Votre très humble & très obeissant serviteur   RICHARD

rue de menars No. 9.

William Temple Franklin to Vergennes

Reprinted from John Bigelow, ed., *The Works of Benjamin Franklin* (12 vols., New York and London, 1904), X, 120.

Sir: Passy, 28 May, 1783.

By direction of my grandfather, I have the honor to send your Excellency a copy of the proposition Mr. Hartley lately made to the American ministers, and which he has wrote to his court

---

he told Erasmus Darwin about a mechanical clock whose wooden sentry announced the hour of 12. Darwin himself had invented a speaking machine by 1770, which BF may have seen: XIX, 210–11; BF to Darwin, July 22–Aug. 1, 1772, published in Desmond King-Hele, ed., *The Letters of Erasmus Darwin* (Cambridge, 1981), pp. 64–5.

4. For Richard and his relationship to William Bingham see XXXII, 112–13. There we noted that he described himself as an editor of the *Gaz.de la Martinique*. In fact, he was its founder: Jean Sgard, ed., *Dictionnaire des journalistes, 1600–1789* (2 vols., Oxford, 1999), I, 143–4.

5. For Bingham's "mission" see Livingston to BF, May 25.

for permission to sign, provided the same is agreed to on our part.[6] With great respect, I am sir, your Excellency's most obedient and most humble servant, W. T. FRANKLIN.

Wilhem & Jan Willink, Nicolaas & Jacob van Staphorst, and De la Lande & Fynje to the American Peace Commissioners

LS and copy: Massachusetts Historical Society; copy and incomplete copy: Library of Congress

Gentlemen Amsterdam 29 May 1783.

We observe by the favour of your Excellencies most honour'd letter of 22 Inst. that Mr. Grand has laid before your Excs. a state of the Affairs of the United States under his Care; and that the Dispositions made upon him are Such, that therefore your Excs. advise us to remit to Mr. Grand on account of Said States a sum of half a Million Livres Tournois, if the Cash in our hands, compared with the Drafts made upon us will allow it.

We take the liberty in answer to this, to assure your Excs. that we would be very Sorry to observe, that the Drafts for Congres might Suffer a disappointment any where, and that we would gladly contribute to prevent such a misfortune, but we are obliged in the present Case to represent to your Excs.

6. He enclosed a copy of the preamble and proposed article of [May 19], on which he added a brief note of explanation (AAE).

The person who sent these documents to Congress was JA, whose colleagues viewed him as "first in the Commission" (according to his diary). Under cover of a May 24 letter to Livingston, he enclosed copies of everything Hartley had presented to the commissioners on May 21, as well as the commissioners' proposed articles of April 29: Butterfield, *John Adams Diary*, III, 124; *Adams Papers*, XIV, 490–2. On Sunday, May 25, Barclay visited both BF and JA, reporting to the latter that BF did not expect to live long and was "greatly disappointed in not having received Letters from Congress, containing his Dismission": Butterfield, *John Adams Diary*, III, 135.

that it is impossible for us to make the Comparison which your Excs. mention, because we know that there are at least running 22 bills from Mr. Morris upon us, of which we don't know the Amount, Since we got not his advise, and Since the letters are not offered for acceptance. This we know by the numbers of the bills which we already accepted, being from No. 1 till 27 together $f.$ 150000. and No. 50 of $f.$ 100,000——. We want also to know the Amount of the No. 28 till 49, which may be presented every moment, and as soon as we will be informed about it, we promise to make that Comparison, and to write again to your Excellencies, if the State of the Cash in our hands will permit us to comply with your advise. For we beg your Excs. to observe, by the Amount of the bill No. 50, that there is sometimes opportunity for large bills, and consequently it is quite impossible to make any Supposition upon the whole Amount of 22 bills,[7] and we should be sorry in case by paying out a Sum of £500/m [500,000 $l.t.$], for which we have no proper authority, we should be in want for the payment of those Drafts, as may be made upon us in consequence of the informations, which Congress might have received about the Success of the Loan. We beg to consider this and to let us know in answer to this your advise, how in such a case we should do, without displeasing our principals?

We hope that, after having considered what we have mentioned, your Excellencies will justify us, if we Should wish to be excused from complying with their advise.

However since it comes from so respectable a society, we think we could do it either for the whole Sum of £500,000 or part of it upon the following two Conditions.

1°. That your Excs. in your respective Qualities should properly Authorize us to furnish that Sum to Mr. Grand, out of the Stock of Money of the United States in our hands, and be guarant for the approbation of Congres. It is our humble opinion

---

7. The 50 sets of bills of exchange drawn by Morris upon the consortium of Dutch bankers were worth a total of 300,706 $f.$: *Morris Papers*, VII, 124, 383, 700, 758–60.

that your Excs. can better do this, then we, who are not so good informed about the particulars of the Affairs of the United States, and of their concerns as your Excellencies.

2°. That Mr. Grand should give his Engagement to us, that in case the Dispositions of Congress upon us should exceed the Amount of the Cash in our hands, and we also should want a restitution of the money remitted to him, he in that case will pay our drafts upon him for that purpose, on account of the United states.

If your Excellencies think it convenient to do the matter upon this footing, we beg to let us know in answer to this your resolution, and against what time Mr. Grand should wish to receive the remittances.

With much respect, we have the honour to be Gentlemen of your Excellencies, the most humble and obedt. Servts[8]

WILHEM & JAN WILLINK
NICS. & JACOB VAN STAPHORST.
DE LA LANDE & FYNJE

To Their Excellencÿs Mr. John Adams Esqr. Mr. B Franklin Esqr. Mr. John Jay Esqr. Mr. Henry Laurens Esqr. Ministers Plenipotentiares of the United States of America Paris

Endorsed by John Adams: Messrs Willinks & Co to the Ministers for Peace.

---

8. Having received no reply, the consortium wrote again on June 12, enclosing a duplicate of the present document. They had received no letters from Morris in the interim, and asked the commissioners to reply as soon as possible (Library of Congress; Mass. Hist. Soc.).

84

From David Hartley

ALS: Library of Congress

My Dear friend   August [*i.e.*, May?][9] 29 1783

Will you be so good as to send me Mr Maddison's pamphlet,[1] the time is come for me to return. Be so good as to send me the memorials of the merchants trading to Carolina & Georgia.[2] I must take copies in case of any future correspondence upon the Subject— Can you & Mr Franklin do me the favour to dine with me on Saturday next at 3 o'clock   D H

London Chronicle page 484 Sad Stuff—[3]

Addressed: A Son Excellence / Monsr Monsr Franklin / &c &c &c / Passy

Endorsed: By his insisting so much on the *Impolicy* of the Writings he proposes to refute, his Reader may be led to suspect *Policy* in his Refutation; and not give his State of Affairs all the Credit it deserves—

9. Hartley's dateline is both unmistakable and inexplicable. Immediately beneath it BF wrote, "recd May 29. 83." The month of May is confirmed by Hartley's references to the merchants' memorials Fox had sent him in May and a newspaper article published later that month.

1. We cannot identify this pamphlet. George Maddison (XIII, 545n), the newly appointed secretary to the British embassy in Paris, may have brought it with him when he accompanied Manchester to France at the end of April: XXXIX, 547, 566; *General Evening Post*, April 26–29, 1783. The comments BF wrote on the address sheet (see the endorsement) probably pertain to it.

2. Which Fox forwarded to Hartley on May 9 to show the American commissioners; see our annotation of their July 27 letter to Livingston.

3. That page, in the May 20–22 issue, contained a lengthy extract of an April 11 letter from New York which criticized the terms of the provisional peace treaty and predicted the downfall of the United States.

From Benjamin Franklin Bache

ALS: American Philosophical Society[4]

My Dear Grand Papa   Geneva 30 May 1783
I have receiv'd the 24 May your kind letter dated the 2[5] and Mme Montgomery's which was inclosed in it, By Mr Ridley Conductor of the young Morris's as well as the medal you please to Send me you Refuse me a wacth I dont Insist on asking it no more.[6] I thought that I could obtain one for 2 reasons 1° Every Boy of my Society has one or gold or at lest Silver they ar of my age Me. Cramer's Son that is not as old as me[7] has a gold one I talk to Mr Marignac about it he told me I did Very well Because I would find Very good watch's at Geneva but si [if] you Beleive one would not serve me I have nothing more to say having had the fever and not being yet very well I pray you to excuse the schortness of my letter.

Beleive me for ever Your most Dutiful and affectionate Grand Son   B. FRANKLIN B

Mr Marignac's Family & Johonnot present their Respects.

Addressed: Dr. Benjamin Franklin / Passy

Notation: B. F. B. to Dr. Franklin Geneva, May 30—'83

---

4. Castle-Bache Collection, available on microfilm.
5. XXXIX, 542–3.
6. BFB had requested *Libertas Americana* medals as well as a gold watch on March 30: XXXIX, 410. For the journey of Robert Morris, Jr., and his brother Thomas, who traveled under Matthew Ridley's care, see XXXIX, 543n.
7. Gabriel (XXX, 248n) was a year younger than BFB. He was born on Oct. 14, 1770: Lucien Cramer, *Une Famille genevoise: Les Cramer . . .* (Geneva, 1952), p. 73.

From Robert Morris

LS: American Philosophical Society

Dear Sir   Philadelphia 30th. May 1783.

I have received your private Letter of the twenty third of December.[8] When I informed you of what was said by your Enemies[9] I did not mean to insinuate any Doubt of your Exertions in my own mind. With Respect to your Resignation[1] I personally lament it, and more so on the Part of the United States. But I shall readily agree that you will more consult your own Ease and Happiness by abandoning public Life and it will be almost impossible to add to your Reputation. I cannot however take a Part in procuring your Dismission for this would be an Injury to the Public. In whatever Situation and Character Believe me always with sincere Esteem & Respect Your Most Obedient & humble Servant   ROBT MORRIS

His Excellency Benjamin Franklin Esqr.

Robert R. Livingston to the American Peace Commissioners

Copy: Massachusetts Historical Society; AL (draft): New-York Historical Society; transcript: National Archives

Gentlemen,   Philadelphia. 31st: May. 83.

Congress were yesterday pleased to pass the enclosed Resolutions on the subject of the payment of British Debts— The language they speak requires no Comment—[2] I complained

---

8. Not found. BF wrote an official letter to Morris on that date (XXXVIII, 487–9) dealing with subjects other than the one discussed here.

9. On Sept. 28, 1782: XXXVIII, 155.

1. Which BF requested in December: XXXVIII, 416–17.

2. On May 30 Congress passed a resolution instructing the commissioners to press for an amendment to the preliminary peace agreement giving American debtors at least three years to pay their British creditors and excusing them from any demands of interest accrued during the war. They were further instructed to negotiate for the definitive treaty a settlement

in my last[3] of your long Silence, or rather laid before you the Complaint of Congress. These I think receive additional force from Intelligence I have since had, that the Negotiations are still going on, and that important Propositions have been made you from Holland.[4] As Congress have adjourned for two Days, & the Packet sails tomorrow,[5] I cannot procure their Instructions on this Subject, tho' I think I may venture to say, that they will not, without reluctance, go one step further than their honor requires of them, in making new engagements which may involve them in the disputes of Europe, from which they wish to be totally disengaged—

I make no observations on these Propositions, or your power to accede to them, being well persuaded that you will take no Steps in this business without a full persuasion that important Advantages will result therefrom to these States.— The second Proposition, in case France & Spain should decline acceding to the first, is more peculiarly delicate from the inability of the contracting Powers to enforce them, if, which is hardly to be supposed, they should unite in wishing it. I cannot help lamenting, since so much time has elapsed before any Conclusion is formed, that you had not thought it adviseable to write to me on this

---

of charges incurred for the subsistence of prisoners of war. Congress also passed a resolution calling on the states to abide by Articles 4 and 6 of the preliminary peace agreement and "take into serious consideration" Article 5 (XXXVIII, 385–6), which related to the rights of creditors and former Loyalists: *JCC*, XXIV, 369–72, 374–6.

3. Above, May 28.

4. The propositions, put forward by Engelbert François van Berckel at the request of Pieter van Bleiswijk, were that (1) the United States should join the League of Armed Neutrality, or (2) it should contract similar engagements with France, Spain, and the Netherlands, or (3) if France and Spain declined such engagements, it should make a separate convention with the Netherlands. The commissioners (through JA) replied that if possible Minister Designate to Russia Francis Dana should be the one to negotiate any such agreement: *Adams Papers*, XIV, 208–11, 217–19; XV, 513–14n. On June 12 Congress instructed the peace commissioners to avoid any engagement to support by arms the rights of neutrals; see Boudinot's letters of June 16 and 18, below.

5. The packet *General Washington*. According to the transcript, it carried the first copy of the present letter.

subject, explaining the advantages & disadvantages of the measure and ennabling me to take the Sense of Congress thereon: for tho' they have the highest Confidence in your judgement, & knowledge of the true Interests of this Country, yet, I am persuaded, that they think it a duty to see with their own eyes & to form their own Conclusions on great national Objects, where there is a possibility of so doing. The experience of the last war has shewn that the Propositions of the Empress of Russia[6] were little more than a dead letter—those whom England dared to offend derived no advantage from them. Our Engagements therefore on this head will, in my opinion, add little weight to them, unless the great Maritime Powers of Europe agree to support them, and they may involve us in disagreable discussions. These howr: are only my Sentiments: those of Congress I am ignorant of—

The 5th: & 6th. Articles of the Provisional Treaty excite much ferment here, for, tho' the most dissatisfied Spirits acknowledge the whole Treaty taken together to answer their highest expectations, yet they wish to take only what they like, & leave out what they disapprove, and such is the relaxation of Governmt: so great the disorders & licentiousness[7] introduced by the war, that it will be found very difficult to bridle the just resentments of some, and the unfounded apprehensions that others entertain of re-imbursements, that may affect their particular Interests.[8]

I have the honor to be, Gentlemen, with the greatest esteem & respect, Yr: Most Obedt: humle: servt:

(signed) Robt: R. Livingston

The Honble, John Adams, Benja: Franklin, John Jay, & Henry Laurens. Esquires.

6. The League of Armed Neutrality.
7. The transcript has "uneasiness".
8. American mistreatment of Loyalists eventually helped provide Britain with an excuse not to evacuate the military posts it still occupied in the American interior: Charles R. Ritcheson, *Aftermath of Revolution: British Policy Toward the United States, 1783–1795* (Dallas, 1969), pp. 59–63.

No: 4.

(Copy)

Notation by John Adams: Mr Livingstone to the Ministers for Peace 31. May. 1783.

From Richard Bache

ALS: Musée de Blérancourt

Dear & Hond: Sir Philadelphia May 31, 1783.

I have wrote repeatedly to you since the receipt of your last favor of 26 Decr.—[9] I hope the Bills I sent you have reached you—[1] There appears very little disposition in some of the States, to pass the necessary Laws for establishing a fund for the payment of the interest of the national Debt, notwithstanding the repeated recommendations of Congress for this good and salutary purpose;[2] hence there is no judging when any more Interest will be paid; as soon as it shall come to my hands, it shall be punctually remited you—[3] We had the pleasure yesterday of

9. Since receiving that letter on March 12, RB wrote once on March 13 and twice on April 30: XXXIX, 325–6, 537. While only a brief extract of BF's Dec. 26, 1782, letter is extant (XXXVIII, 503), it appears from the following paragraph that BF had inquired again about the interest accrued on his loan office certificates (XXIII, 280–1n). RB had not forwarded any interest since 1780, citing his own financial difficulties; see XXXVII, 664, and the references there.

1. RB had sent five sets, beginning on July 3, 1782; see XXXVII, 576–7, and XXXIX, 24, 325. BF evidently did receive one of them: XXXVIII, 237.

2. On April 18, by a majority vote, Congress passed a new plan for funding the national debt that was subject to unanimous ratification. For details on the plan see the annotation to the first of Robert Morris' letters of May 26, above.

3. RB failed to mention that the Pa. Assembly, anticipating a long delay before Congress would be able to collect revenue, had passed its own bill on March 21 assuming for one year all interest payments on Continental loan office certificates held by state citizens: *Morris Papers*, VII, 145–8;

hearing from Mrs. Mecom, she is lately recovered from a severe
indisposition, which she has labored under, the greatest part of
last Winter; & which, as she writes us, she was apprehensive
would have carried her off— She was going to spend her Summer in the State of Rhode Island—[4]
Inclosed is a Letter for Ben[5]—I have the pleasure to tell you
that Sally and the Children are well, the two youngest have just
got thro' the Meazles— Betty is up at Mount Airy with Miss
Beckwith, whose School increases fast.[6]
Be pleased to accept our joint Love & Duty & be assured I
remain ever Dear sir Your dutifull & affece. Son RICH: BACHE

Dr. Franklin

From Bache & Shee   ALS:[7] American Philosophical Society

Sir   Philadelphia May 31st: 1783.
We were honored yesterday by your recommendatory Letter
of 22d. February last, of Torris & Wante's house of Dunkirk;[8]
their Brig Franklin with a supercargo on board, is safe arrived;
but to a bad Market, as our Port is glutted with every species

---

James T. Mitchell and Henry Flanders, comps., *The Statutes at Large of
Pennsylvania from 1682 to 1801* (17 vols., [Harrisburg], 1896–1915), XI, 81–
91. See RB's letter of July 27, where he acknowledges receiving this year's
interest.
4. Jane Mecom to RB, April 11, and to SB, May 18, 1783: Van Doren,
Franklin-Mecom, pp. 218–19, 222–3.
5. Not found, but BFB answered it on July 27; see the annotation of BF to
RB and SB, July 27.
6. Sally Beckwith had shared a bed with "Miss Betsy" while staying
with the Baches, and was much taken with the girl's intelligence. She had
established her boarding school at Mount Airy only recently: XXXIX, 44,
325, 345.
7. In RB's hand.
8. Not found, but BF had promised J. Torris & Wante that he would send
it: XXXIX, 174–6.

of Goods;[9] we shall however do every thing in our power to serve the interest of this House, and we trust, not discredit your recommendation of us to them—
Please to accept our thanks for your so kindly interresting yourself in our behalf, and believe us to be with respect Sir Your most Obedt. & very Humble servts.   BACHE & SHEE
The Honble. Dr. Franklin

From William Barton[1]   ALS: American Philosophical Society

Sir,   Philada. May 31st. 1783
Altho' I am, personally, an entire Stranger to your Excellency, you may perhaps recollect the late Revd. Mr. Barton,[2] a Clergyman of Lancaster in this State, whose Son I am.
Permit me, Sir, to introduce to your Notice as an American, the Bearer of this, my Brother Matthias Barton; who has resided some Time at L'Orient, as a Merchant, in Copartnership with a Nephew of Mr. Macarty of the House of Cuming and Macarty.[3]

9. Caused by a dramatic increase in the number of ships arriving at Philadelphia in May, many of them from the Netherlands, France, and Portugal: Richard Buel, Jr., *In Irons: Britain's Naval Supremacy and the American Revolutionary Economy* (New Haven and London, 1998), p. 246.

1. Barton (1754–1817), a lawyer in Lancaster, Pa., was an advocate for the revitalization of paper money and the author of *Observations on the Nature and Use of Paper-Credit; and the Peculiar Advantages to be derived from it, in North America* . . . (Philadelphia, 1781). He assisted Charles Thomson in designing the Great Seal of the United States in 1782 (XXXVIII, 152n), was elected to the APS in 1787, and published a biography of his uncle David Rittenhouse in 1813: Milton Rubincam, "A Memoir of the Life of William Barton, A.M. (1754–1817)," *Pa. History*, XII (1945), 179–93; *Morris Papers*, IV, 38n; VI, 46; Maeva Marcus and James R. Perry *et al.*, eds., *The Documentary History of the Supreme Court of the United States, 1789–1800* (8 vols., New York, 1985–2007), I, 188n.

2. Thomas Barton: VI, 24n.

3. Matthias Barton (1762–1809) eventually returned to Lancaster County, where he was admitted to the bar and served in both the Pa.

I beg your Excelly. will pardon this Liberty, which I should not take, if my Brother's Character would not bear the strictest Scrutiny: My own Name is, I beleive, not unknown to some Americans at Paris.

I have the Honor to be, With the highest Respect, sir, Your Excelly's. most obedt. hble. servt.   W. BARTON

Dr. Franklin.

Addressed: His Excelly. / Benjn. Franklin, Esqr. L.L.D. / Minister &c. &c. / Versailles. / Mr. M. Barton

Notation: Barton May 31. 1783

From Robert R. Livingston

LS: University of Pennsylvania Library; AL (draft): New-York Historical Society; transcript:[4] National Archives

Sir,   Philadelphia 31st. May 1783

I informed you some time since, that I had written to the Court of Appeals on the subject of the Nostra Signora da Soledade Saint Miguel e Almas, and lay'd before them the papers you sent me, the cause has since been determined in such way as I hope will be satisfactory to her Portuguese Majesty— I enclose the copy of a Letter from the first Judge of the Court of Appeals upon that subject[5]—nothing has yet been done as to

---

legislature and the State Senate: Daniel K. Cassel, *The Family Record of David Rittenhouse* . . . (Norristown, Pa., 1896), pp. 19–20; *Biographical Annals of Lancaster County, Pennsylvania* . . . ([Chicago], 1903), p. 187. For Cuming & Macarty see XXXVII, 53n.

4. The transcript indicates that the LS was carried by the packet *General Washington.*

5. The now-missing enclosure must have been a copy of Cyrus Griffin's letter to him of May 31 announcing the judgment for the Portuguese shipowner (National Archives). Griffin, George Read, and John Lowell were the three judges of the court: Henry J. Bourguignon, *The First Federal Court: the Federal Appellate Prize Court of the American Revolution, 1775–1787* (Philadelphia, 1977), pp. 117–21. For background see XXXVIII, 185; XXXIX, 395.

the acceptance of your resignation,[6] nor will as I beleive any thing be done very hastily—many think your task will not be very burthensome now, and that you may enjoy in peace the fruit of your passed labours, As this will probably be the last Letter, which I shall have the pleasure of writing to you in my public Character[7]—I beg leave to remind you of the Affairs of the Alliance and the Bon Homme Richard, which are still unsettled—[8] I must also pray you not to loose sight of the Vessels detained by his Danish Majesty, this will be a favorable opportunity to press for their restitution—[9] I do not see how they can decently refuse to pay for them— Great Britain is bound in honor to make them whole again— Preparations for the evacuation of New York still go on very slowly, while the distress of our finances have compelled us to grant furloughs to the greater part of our Army, If it was possible to procure any addition to the last six Millions[1] it would be extremely useful to us at present.

An entire new arrangement with respect to our foreign Department is under consideration, what its fate will be I know not—

I am Sir with the greatest Regard and Esteem your most obedt. humble servt   R R LIVINGSTON

Honble Benjn: Franklin Esq.

No. 28.

6. BF renewed his request to resign after the preliminary articles were signed: XXXVIII, 416–17.

7. Livingston's resignation was accepted four days later; see Boudinot to BF, June 16. This is his last known letter to BF.

8. Livingston had ordered Barclay to secure this unpaid prize money in May, 1782: XXXVII, 430.

9. BF did so, in his negotiations with the Danish minister for a commercial treaty; see his letter to Livingston, July 22[–26].

1. The most recent French loan of 6,000,000 *l.t.*

From Jonathan Williams, Jr.

ALS: University of Pennsylvania Library

Dear & hond Sir. Nantes May 31 1783.
With this you will receive a Letter from Capt Alexander He-
guye(?) inclosing a Memoire to the Marquis de Castries.— The
Favour requested is highly merited and is in itself such as ministers have frequently granted on Slight pretentions— It is only
to have *Lettres de Capitaine* which in this Country is necessary
to have, before a man (however he may be qualified) can command a Ship.—
Mr de la Ville² the Proprietor of the Ship for which this Request is made is one of the first Characters in this Town & a
Gentleman for whom I have a particular Respect & Esteem,
more especialy as I have experienced Acts of Friendship from
him which lay me under great Obligations.—
You will oblige me very highly by Sending the Memoire to
the Marquis de Castries, who I am Sure will grant the Request
contained in it; A Note from you on the Subject will make it
Certain.³
I am as ever most dutifully & Affectionately Yours.

JONA WILLIAMS J

His Excellcy Dr Franklin.

Addressed: His Excellency / Doctor Franklin.

---

2. Amand (Armand)-François Delaville (b. 1734) was from a prominent
Nantes family of outfitters and merchants. By 1783 he was sole proprietor
of his firm, which specialized in the slave trade: Meyer, *Armement Nantais,* pp. 199–200, 278, 373; Dieudonné Rinchon, *Les Armements négriers
au XVIIIe siècle, d'après la correspondance et la comptabilité des armateurs et
des capitaines nantais* (Bruxelles, 1956), pp. 27–76.
3. JW wrote to WTF on June 18, alerting him to the present document
and asking him to make sure BF forwarded the memoir and accompanying papers to Castries, with a good word for the captain. He also asked
WTF to notify Delaville when it had been done (University of Pa. Library). On July 8, annoyed that nothing had happened, JW asked WTF to
return the papers; the ship was about to sail, and the captain, not having
received his authority, had been obliged to transfer command to another
(APS).

To Ingenhousz

ALS: American Philosophical Society

Dear Sir, Passy, June 1. 1783—
This will be delivered to you by an ingenious young Friend
of mine, Mr. S. Vaughan, who travels with a View of improving
himself in Mineralogy.[4] He will be much oblig'd by the Informations & Counsels that you can give him; and as I have a great
Regard for him, and for his Family, I earnestly recommend him
to those Civilities which you are accustomed to show to Strangers of Merit. With sincere Esteem I am, my dear Friend, Yours
most affectionately B FRANKLIN

Dr Ingenhauss.

4. Samuel Vaughan, Jr., had written to WTF on May 30 (APS), requesting a passport from BF for Germany by way of Strasbourg; he would have
asked the English ambassador except that he had not yet called on him. BF
could not have issued such a pass without Vaughan's swearing an oath of
allegiance to the United States. Whichever minister eventually issued the
passport, at least BF provided this letter. After spending a week in Strasbourg, during which he met various scientists, Vaughan sought WTF's help
in obtaining a bill of exchange from Ferdinand Grand. He also reported
what he had learned about François Hoffmann, a native of that city: Hoffmann had amassed a fortune in growing and exporting madder but had lost
everything during the war and was now bankrupt. Samuel Vaughan, Jr., to
WTF, June, 1783, APS. Vaughan and WTF had visited Hoffmann in Paris:
XXXIX, 438.

David Hartley to the American Peace Commissioners: Memorial[5]

Copies:[6] National Archives (two), Library of Congress, Massachusetts Historical Society, Public Record Office; transcript: National Archives

June. 1st: 1783.

Memorial.

The proposition which has been made for an universal & unlimited reciprocity of Intercourse & Commerce, between Great-Britain and the American United-States,[7] requires a very serious Consideration on the part of Great-Britain, for the reasons already stated in a Memorial, dated 19th: May. 1783, and for many other reasons, which, in the future discussion of the proposition, will appear. To the American States, likewise, it is a matter of the deepest importance, not only as a proposition of Commercial Intercourse, which is the least part, but most principally as a political basis & Guarantee for their newly established Constitutions. The introduction of British Interests, into a communion of Intercourse, will bring forward an universal Guarantee on the part of Great-Britain, in the future progress of political events, which may affect the United-States of America in their national Capacity. The Proposition is fertile in future prospects to Great-Britain, & America may also wisely see in it a solid foundation for herself.

All Circumstances are most fortunately disposed, between Great-Britain & the American States, to render them usefull friends & Allies to each other, with a higher degree of

---

5. Drafted while waiting for Fox to comment on his memorial and proposed article of [May 19]; see that document and WTF to Hartley, May 21. Hartley sent this new draft of a memorial to Fox on June 2, before showing it to the American commissioners (Giunta, *Emerging Nation*, II, 141–2). Responding to the Americans' growing impatience, however, he soon told them of its contents and by June 5 had read it to them. He did not give them a copy until June 14; see Hartley to the commissioners of that date.

6. We publish the one with the fewest abbreviations and obvious copying errors, made by JA's secretary Charles Storer. We have corrected one erroneous word, noted below, and silently corrected one slip of the pen.

7. Proposed by the commissioners on April 29: XXXIX, 524–5.

suitableness between themselves than any other nations can pretend to. France cannot interchange Reciprocities with the American States, by reason of numberless impediments in her System of Government, in her Monopolies, & in her system of Commerce. France has the great dis-ability of difference in Language to contend with, and the institution of the present French Manufactures has never, at any time heretofore, been trained or adapted to American Commerce. The only particular & specific facility, which France ever possessed for American Intercourse, has for many years been transferred into the British Scale, by the Cession of Canada to Great-Britain. The future Commerce between France & America will chiefly be regulated by such Conveniences as France can draw to herself from America, without much aptitude, on the part of France, to accommodate her manufactures & Commerce to American Demands. In short, an Interchange of reciprocities between France & America, would run against the stream on both sides, and all established habits manners, language, together with the principles of Government and Commerce, would militate against such a System.—[8]

Conformably to this Reasoning it appears that France has not, at any time, entertained any systematical design of forming any union or consolidation of Interests with America. She took up the American Cause as instrumental to her political views in Europe. America likewise accepted the Alliance with France for her seperate views, vizt. for the establishment of her Independance. The Alliance therefore is completed & terminated without leaving behind it any political principle of future, permanent Connection between them. Occasional Circumstances produced a temporary alliance. Similar Circumstances may, on any future occasion, produce a similar event of a temporary Compact. Dissimilar Circumstances, arising from any future

---

8. Hartley's analysis is very perceptive. For a variety of economic and cultural reasons, including those listed by Hartley, French businessmen failed to capture a substantial portion of the American market after the war: Claude Fohlen, "The Commercial Failure of France in America," in Nancy L. Roelker and Charles K. Warner, eds., *Two Hundred Years of Franco-American Relations* . . . ([Worcester, Mass., 1983]), pp. 93–119.

political views of the Court of France in Europe, may, without any inconsistence of principle, throw the power of that Kingdom into a scale adverse to the future Interests of the American States. In such Case, therefore, where there cannot exist any permanent political Connection, between France & America, and where the commercial Attachments can be but feeble, it would be in vain to expect in the French nation any such Ally as newly established States ought to look out for, to give maturity and firmness to their Constitutions.—

As to Spain, every argument which has been stated, respecting diversity of language, manners, government, system of Commerce & monopolies, from those which prevail in the United-States of America, obtains in a superior degree: And much more to add besides, for Spain is not only incompetent to interchange reciprocities with the American States, but likewise her own situation in America will, at all times, render her extremely jealous of her neighbors. The only activity which Spain has exerted in the war, has been to procure a barrier against the American States, by annexing West-Florida to her former acquisition of New-Orleans; thereby embracing the mouth of the Mississippi, &, by means of that river, jointly with her landed possessions, establishing a strong & jealous boundary against any future progress of the American States in those parts.— Spain therefore cannot be looked upon by the American States as a suitable object of their election, to become a permanent Ally & friend to them. Portugal likewise labours under all the disabilities of language, manners, monopolies, Government & System of Commerce. Her national Power & Importance would be likewise insufficient to constitute a strong and permanent Ally to the American States. All these Nations will undoubtedly be found to have many commodious Qualities for participation in Commerce; but the pre-eminent faculties, necessary to constitute a firm & permanent Ally to the American States, will be found deficient in them.— As to the Italian States, or any other Powers in the Mediterranean, they are certainly not adequate to any Competition of political Alliance with the rising States of America. They will also constitute very commodious links & Connections in the general Circuit of Commerce; but, beyond these Considerations, they have no share in the present Question. The several States in the Germanic Body are in the same predicament.—

As to the Northern Powers, vizt: those in the Baltic, they are not favoured,[9] either by vicinity or Climate, for a frequent or facile Intercourse of Commerce with America: and even, respecting several material Articles of Commerce, jealousies & Competitions might arise. As to political Alliances there are no such in prospect from them towards the American States. Even if there were any superfluity of force in any of them, beyond the necessities of their respective domestic situations, the extreme distance would be conclusive against any possible application of such power, as a political Alliance, favorable to the establishment & confirmation of the American States.—

The only maritime State on the Continent of Europe, remaining to be discussed, as a competent Candidate for Commerce or Connection with America is the Republic of the United-Netherlands, commonly called Holland. In respect to American Commerce, the Dutch have among themselves every facility, combined, which the seperate States of Europe possess distinctively, in their own Concerns, or nearly. Their Industry, frugality & habits of Commerce may even carry them so far as to make them rivals to the Americans themselves, in the transportation of European Merchandize to America— These faculties of Commerce would have been of infinite Importance to the American States, if the war had continued between Great-Britain & them: But upon the event of Peace it becomes a matter of the most perfect Indifference to America, whether each European State navigates its own Commerce into the Ports of America, which will be open to all, or whether the commercial faculties of Holland ennable her to exceed in rivalship her European Neighbours, & thereby to navigate European Goods to America, beyond the proportion of her national share. The faculties of a nation of Carriers may be fortunate for the Marine of that nation, but, considered in themselves & with respect to other nations, they are but secondaries in Commerce. They

---

9. We substitute this word, present in all other copies (including the one Hartley sent to Fox), for what Storer wrote: "formed".

give no ground of reciprocity or participation. That one nation should say to another, you shall navigate all our rivers, harbors, Lakes, ports & places, if we may do the same in yours[1] is a proposition of reciprocity: but that Holland should say to America, we will bring European Goods to you, or you may be your own Carriers, is neither Concession or Reciprocity. Holland is not a nation of Rivers, Harbors, Lakes, Ports & Places for the distribution of Goods & manufactures for internal Consumption, and therefore her reciprocities must be very scanty. Holland is the market-place of Europe & the Dutch Seaman are the Carriers, appertaining to that Market-Place. The admission of American Ships to that market-place, freely to import & export, is an act of reciprocity undoubtedly, on the part of Holland, as far as it goes, but in no degree adequate to the unlimited participation of the Commerce of America, thro'out all the Rivers, Harbours, Lakes, Ports & Places of that vast Continent. The Commercial Reciprocities of Holland, therefore, being inferior on her part towards America, the next point of view, in which Holland is to be considered, as relevant to this Question, is, as a nation of Power capable of becoming an effectual & permanent Ally & Guarantee to the American States; for that is the great Object, which America, as a wise nation, recently arisen into Independence, ought to keep in view. Holland has undoubtedly been a nation of great & celebrated naval force. She remains so still, but having, for many years, suspended her exertions of force & having directed the faculties of her people into the commercial line, she seems not to have any superfluity of force, beyond the necessity of providing for her own Security, & certainly no such redundance of power, as to extend to the protection of distant nations, as Allies or Guarantees. It appears therefore, upon the whole of this argument, that Holland, tho' a commercial nation, cannot even interchange commercial reciprocities with America, upon an equal footing, and that her faculties of force are inadequate to those, which America ought to expect in the permanent Allies & Guarantees of her Country.—

The Independence of the American States, being established,

---

1. A paraphrase of the commissioners' Article 1: XXXIX, 524–5.

their first Consideration ought to be, to determine with what friendships and Alliances they will enter into the new world of nations. They will look round them & cast about for some natural, permanent & powerfull Ally, with whom they may interchange all cementing reciprocities, both commercial & political. If such an Ally is to be found anywhere for them, it is still in Great-Britain—at least it is certain, that, in looking round Europe, no other is to be found. There is no inherent impossibility to prevent such a Connection from taking place—it must depend upon the free will & common Interest of the parties. There are all possible faculties, on both sides, to give & to receive all adequate & beneficial reciprocities, which are practicable & more likely to be permanent, between Independant parties, than between two parties, where one is dependant upon the other. Great-Britain is undoubtedly the first of European nations in riches, credit, faculties, Industry, Commerce, manufactures, internal Consumption & foreign export, together with civil liberty, which is the source of all, and naval Power, which is the support of all. The Dominions appertaining to the Crown of Great-Britain are large & fertile—its Colonies still extensive, & in close vicinity to the American States—Great-Britain herself, being an American, as well as an European power, and all her Empire connected by her naval force— The Territories of the American States, from the Atlantic Ocean to the Missisippi, contain an inexhaustible source of riches, industry & future power— These will be the foundation of great events in the new page of life. Infinite good or infinite evil may arise, according to the principles, upon which this Intercourse between Great-Britain & America shall be arranged in its foundation. Great-Britain & America must be still inseperable, either as friends or Foes.[2] This is an awful & important truth—these are Considerations not to be thought of slightly, not to be prejudged in passion, nor the arrangements of them to be hastily foreclosed. Time given for Consideration may have excellent

2. As Hartley put it to Fox on June 5, "for their own security, they [the commissioners] must desire the alliance & friendship of the only power who can in any degree be a terror or restraint to them": Giunta, *Emerging Nation*, 1, 860.

effects on both sides. The pause of peace, with friendly intercourse, returning affection & dispassionate enquiry can alone
decide these important events, or do justice to the anxious expectations of Great-Britain & America.

Notation: No. 8. Mr. Hartley's Memorial 1st. June 1783.

From Sarah Bache ALS: American Philosophical Society

Dear & Honoured Sir Philad. June 1st. 1783
 Our worthy Friend Mr Oster[3] just now called to let me know
he goes on board Ship amediately, as there is seldom a week
passes, but he sees the Family two or three times, he will tell
you how we all look, he caught me to day playing with the
Children and rabbits, I see Betsy the day before yesterday she
is with Miss Beckwith[4] who is like to do extreamly well, has
already ten young Ladies, and I take her up another tomorrow,
she will I make no doubt be quite independant in a few Years,
Mrs Brodeau who was recommended to you when you were last
at home,[5] has made a handsome fortune, Mr Bache wrote to you
yesterday and notwithstanding I write to day I am not without
hopes this letter will miss you and that you will be on your way
home. I never wished for any thing more in my whole life than
to see you— Aunt Mecom was well about two weeks ago, I just
receiv'd a long letter from her—remember me afectionately to
Temple and Benny, I am as ever Your dutiful daughter—
 S BACHE

Addressed: Dr: Franklin / Mr Oster

3. Martin Oster, the French vice-consul (XXXIX, 571n).
4. At Mount Airy; see RB's letter of May 31.
5. BF had in fact publicly endorsed Mrs. Brodeau's character and her
plan to open a boarding school for girls in Philadelphia: XXII, 282–3; XXIII,
254n.

From the Chevalier de Chastellux

ALS: American Philosophical Society

1er juin 1783

Monsieur coste[6] qui vous remettra cette lettre est mon cher docteur, un trés habile medecin et un excellent homme. Il étoit premier medecin de notre petite armée americaine. Il a souvent eté dans le cas de traitter vos soldats et il l'a fait avec zele et avec succès. Il aime vos compatriotes et en est aimé. L'ouvrage qu'il vous presente prouve l'estime qu'ils ont eue pour lui.[7] Je vous prie donc de le bien recevoir au nom de notre chere amerique, dont mon cœur sera toujours citoyen

LE CHER DE CHASTELLUX

Addressed: A Monsieur / Monsieur franklin &

Notation: le chevr de chatellux

From John Sargent

ALS: American Philosophical Society

My Dear Friend   Halsted Place 1 June 1783.

It must seem strange to You, that You should not have had an answer from me to a Letter that You favourd me with

---

6. Jean-François Coste (1741–1819), first physician of Rochambeau's army, who after the Battle of Yorktown treated American as well as French wounded. Chastellux, who fell seriously ill in America, credited Coste with saving his life. In 1782 both men received honorary degrees from the University of the State of Pennsylvania and the College of William and Mary. *DBF;* Maurice Bouvet, *Le Service de santé français pendant la guerre d'indépendance des Etats-Unis, 1777–1782* (Paris, 1933), pp. 34–5, 96–7; Marquis de Chastellux, *Travels in North America in the Years 1780, 1781 and 1782,* ed. and trans. Howard C. Rice, Jr. (2 vols., Chapel Hill, N.C., 1963), I, 309–10n; II, 366, 563n, 605–6n.

7. The Latin oration that Coste delivered upon receiving his honorary doctorate in medicine from William and Mary was published in Leyden in 1783: *De Antiqua Medico-philosophia orbi novo adaptanda: Oratio habita in capitolio Gulielmopolitano in comitiis universitatis Virginae, die xii junii M.DCC.LXXXII.* For a description see Chastellux, *Travels,* II, 605n. BF's copy is at the Hist. Soc. of Pa.

so long agoe as the 27th of Jany last—[8] But it is owing to a
strange Concurrence of unlucky Incidents— In the first place,
the Post master of 7 Oaks,[9] the most negligent in his Line of
Christendom,—it coming in my Absence,—let it lay in his
Office, & did not convey it to me in Town till near a Month
after—from that Time to This, We have been daily thinking
of You, and talking of You, & I proposing to reply, if I had not
heard from an intimate Friend of Dr. Price's, for *Two* Months,
that You were expected here *weekly*, in a private, if not a Publick
Character—the same Thing was for a long Time confirmed
to me by that worthy Man Mr. West,[1] The King's Painter,—
but; at last, I hear I have been misled, and for a fortnight past,
I have been looking out for a safe private hand to convey these
trifling Lines, which are no longer Penal here,[2] & it would not
matter if were published upon the Pont Neuf, and yet I do not
know how, a certain delicacy,—not knowing what Effusions
of Heart might take place in Them,—restrained me from addressing You, unless I could secure Them from the Curiosity,
& Enquiry, that I thought Your Name on the Superscription of
a Letter would for some time naturally excite—

 If You have any Channel of Confidence, do me the Favour,
in answer to This, to let me know how I shall use it, and how
direct to You. Our Post Master is removed by Death, & a better
succeeds[3]—a Letter to me may come hither, or be addressed to
Great Ormond Street Queen's Square, where having given my
House in Downing Street to my Younger Son on Marriage,[4] We
have lived for these Three Years in a House built on the Site

 8. xxxix, 68–70.
 9. Sevenoaks, Kent.
 1. Benjamin West.
 2. Sargent had earlier alluded to the suspension of the Habeas Corpus
Act; see xxxviii, 547.
 3. Thomas Foley, second Baron Foley, succeeded Charles Bennett,
fourth Earl of Tankerville, as joint postmaster general on May 1, 1783:
C. F. Dendy Marshall, *The British Post Office from Its Beginnings to the End
of 1925* (London, 1926), pp. 155, 171.
 4. John Sargent was married in 1778. For him and the family members
mentioned below see xxxviii, 547–8.

of Powis House, a very airey Situation looking out to Hampsted, & agreeing with my Wife better than the lower Situation of Westminster, altho' We had the Opening to the Park.

It gives us the greatest Pleasure that You are so well at Your Age, & We most ardently hope that the same Providence & all ruling Power, which has made You the Instrument of effecting such great Things, will continue Your Life, Health & Vigour of Mind for some Years, to perfect Them, & crown them with Order, Counsel, & Stability—

My Wife & Mother are full of Esteem & affection for You— much concerned to be disappointed of the proposed pleasure of seeing You—and so is all my Family— My Sons desire me to convey every Mark of Respect from Them—

Poor Mrs. Deane dyed at this place Three Years agoe— Her Grief for the Loss of Her Husband The General soon caused Her to follow Him—[5]

Mr. Chambers and The Younger Ladies His Sisters[6] are all well & happy—and often joyn Us in affectionate, & honourable Mention of You—

Your Reflections on Matrimony are true and just— You'll be pleased to find We think as You do on the Subject, & that my Eldest Son has, within this Fortnight, enterd into the State in a manner quite to my Mind,—with a Young Lady whom He had known, & thought favorably of for some Years,[7] a Match of Reason neither produced by Interest & the Love of Money nor by sudden Youthful Passion—so that nothing can bid fairer for a reasonable Share of the Comforts that Union affords—

5. William and Elizabeth Deane died in 1775 and 1779, respectively: VII, 321n; XXXIX, 70n.

6. Christopher Chambers' sisters were Sophia and Frances: Thomas Belsham, *Memoirs of the Late Reverend Theophilus Lindsey* . . . (2nd ed., London, 1820), pp. 62n, 306–7; G. M. Ditchfield, "The Revd. William Chambers, D.D. (*c.* 1724–1777)," *Enlightenment and Dissent*, IV (1985), 6.

7. George Arnold Sargent married Marianne Langston in May: Henry Wagner, "Pedigree of Sargent, Afterwards Arnold, and Sargent," *Genealogist*, 2nd ser., XXXIII (1917), 189; David Hancock, *Citizens of the World: London Merchants and the Integration of the British Atlantic Community, 1735–1785* (Cambridge, New York, and Melbourne, 1995), p. 403.

I have the Comfort, in having finished this Business, to have wound up all the Great Concerns of my Family—

If America pays me any part of my Debt, as I think from the many good Characters I know among Them, She will, I will celebrate Their Justice & Fidelity—if not, I am too old, & far advanced on my Journey to let Those Concerns make me uneasy, I will forgive Them with all my Heart & content myself with what is left, which I hope is quite enough for the rest of my Road—

I shall never think of new Enterprizes, & compensating myself for the past, but by endeavouring to gain, in *Æquanimity*, what I have lost in Money, & calmly wynding up my Bottoms— Tho my Relations & Partners Mr. Chambers & Mr. Rolleston,[8] from their difference of Age & Situation, may take a different Course & act another part— If You should see the Comte De la Touche[9] please to make my Compliments to Him, & let Him know I remember Him with great Respect— I am as all my Circle is Dear Sir Your most affectionate & devoted

J SARGENT

PS. You are remembred with great respect by My Neighbour Lord Stanhope—[1]

I hear from that Family, that Your Friend Ld. Chatham's Son has just declared His Intention of what You would wish every hopeful Young Man of Good Family to do,—not to give into the Libertinism of the present Times, and as Solomon expresses it,—I think—*give His Strength unto a Stranger,—but take unto Him a fair Possession*— He has made known his Wish in favour of Miss Mary Townsend, (Lord Sidney, late Tommey Townsend's Daughter)[2] a Family much connected with His

---

8. Robert Rolleston (1747–1826): Hancock, *Citizens of the World*, pp. 11, 74–5, 107–8, 218, 405.

9. The comte had been released from an English prison around the time the preliminary peace was signed, and wrote BF from Paris on Jan. 24: XXXIX, 25–6.

1. When BF stayed with Sargent in 1774, Stanhope introduced him to Chatham: XXI, 547.

2. John Pitt, second Earl of Chatham (XXI, 518), married Mary Elizabeth Townshend on July 10: *ODNB*.

own, & made all Parties happy by it— There is a small Fortune, but correct Education, & good Example in her Family to recommend Her. which is every Thing— His Brother Mr. William[3] is a Prodigy—! Calumny itself knows not how to fasten on Him—adieu Dear Sir—

Dr. Franklin

Addressed: A Monsieur / Monsr. Le Dr. Franklin / a / Paris

From Jean-Georges Treuttel[4]

ALS: American Philosophical Society

Monsieur   strasbourg le 1. Juin 1783.

A la priere, que mon ami à Berlin au quel je suis attaché prend la liberté de Vous adresser,[5] je n'ajoute que, s'il y a des frais, je constitue le Sr. Durand Neveu[6] Libraire rue Gallande à Paris pour y satisfaire & en même temps pour recevoir & m'expédier tout ce qu'il plairoit à Votre Excellence d'envoyer à M. Spener.

Je profite de l'occasion, Monsieur, pour rendre mes hommages à Votre Excellence & l'assurer du zele respectueux avec lequel j'ai l'honneur d'être Monsieur De Votre Excellence Le très humble & très-obéissant serviteur

TREUTTEL
Libraire cidevant Bauer & Treuttel

Notation: Treuttel 1. Juin 1783

3. William Pitt the Younger.
4. Treuttel (1744–1826) established himself in Strasbourg about 1770 in association with Jean-Geoffrey Bauer: Jean-Dominique Mellot and Elisabeth Queval, comps., *Répertoire d'imprimeurs/libraires* . . . (Paris, 1997), pp. 63–4, 578.
5. Spener's letter is above, May 26.
6. Pierre-Etienne-Germain Durand (1728–179?): Mellot and Queval, *Répertoire d'imprimeurs/libraires*, p. 248.

Ferdinand Grand to the American Peace Commissioners

LS:[7] Historical Society of Pennsylvania

Messieurs   Paris le 2 Juin 1783

Quoique la lettre que vous m'aves fait l'honneur de m'écrire le 22e du mois passé, ne me flattat pas de recevoir les Secours dont les Finances du Congrès avoient besoin; Néantmoins, l'Espérance du Succès des Soins que j'étois bien assuré que vous donneriès, Messieurs, à un objet aussi intéressant, m'a fait parvenir à Satisfaire à tous les payemens qui se sont présentés, jusqu'à ce moment; qui me fait voir avec douleur le terme fatal de cesser d'honorer les Traittes de Mr Morris, si vous ne pouvès, Messieurs, me procurer les moiens de l'éviter:

Je regrette infiniment que les miens Soient insuffisans pour Sauver un Eclat, Sur les suites duquel je n'ose pas Seulement réflechir, mais ma fortune ne me le permet pas, comme vous en jugerés, Messieurs, par la Somme des besoins, ainsi que de la nécessité de prendre un parti Sur cet objet.

L'on m'a prèsenté depuis quelques jours pour Quatre cens vingt trois mille Livres de Traittes que je dois rendre acceptées, ou non acceptées; Depuis la publication des Lettres de Monsieur Morris au Congrès Sur Sa retraitte future,[8] les porteurs de Ses Traittes Sont extrémement pressés de les faire accepter: Cette Somme n'est malheureusement qu'une foible partie de celles qui existent, puisqu'il y en a encore pour Neuf cens vingt un mille Livres dont j'ai depuis assès longtems l'avis, & qui vont paroitre Sucessivement, ce qui fait près de Quatorze cens mille Livres auxquelles il faut pourvoir, sans compter les Loan Offices, & les autres Dépenses courrantes ou Imprévues.

L'Idée de laisser retourner à protes les Traittes de Monsieur Morris me paroit si revoltante, que je ne puis m'y déterminer à moins que je ne voie par la réponse que vous voudrés bien, Messieurs, me faire, qu'il ne me reste plus d'autre parti à prendre.

---

7. In the hand of his son Henry.

8. The *Gaz. de Leyde*, in its supplement of May 13, published translations of Morris' Jan. 24 and Feb. 26 letters to President of Congress Boudinot announcing his intention to retire on May 31 if adequate measures were not taken to fund the public debt (*Morris Papers*, VII, 361–71, 462–74).

Je Suis avec un Respect Sincère Messieurs votre très humble & très obéissant Serviteur   GRAND

Leurs Excellences Messieurs John Adams Benjamin Franklin John Jay Ministres Plénipotentiaires des Etats-Unis d'Amérique

Endorsed by Franklin: Lettre de M. Grand

From Elias Boudinot   ALS: American Philosophical Society

Dear Sir   Philadelphia June 2d 1783.

The Bearer Dr. Waring⁹ a Gentleman of exceeding good Connections in South Carolina, having served his Country very faithfully & honorably during the War, is about making a Voyage to Europe for his advancement in medical Science—

At his earnest Request, I must beg leave to introduce him to your Excellency, and to request your Notice of him, as one who has deserved so well of his Country, as to entitle him to the respect, of all its well wishers—

I have the honor to be with every Sentiment of Respect & Esteem Your Excellency's Most Obedt & very Hble Servt

ELIAS BOUDINOT

His Excellency Benjamin Franklin Esqr

Notation: Elias Boudinot June 2 1783.—

9. Dr. Richard Waring (1760–1814): Joseph Ioor Waring, comp., "Waring Family," *S.C. Hist. and Geneal. Mag.*, XXIV (1923), 85, 91. He also carried a May 27 letter of recommendation from John Ross to WTF, which describes him as "a Gentleman of a very Genteel fortune and good connections in Carolina" (APS).

To John Vaughan[1] ALS: American Philosophical Society

Dear Sir Passy June. 3. 1783

I received a Pacquet you were so good as to bring for me from Philadelphia; but it contains no Letters later than the 13th. of January. As the Ministry here received Letters at the same time, & I believe brought also by you, that are as late as the 4th of April, I cannot but be surpriz'd that we have no fresh Letters by the same Ship that you came in.— Can you give me any Light on this Subject? You were acquainted with Mr Morris, & perhaps may have heard him say something of his having written, or intending to write by some other Vessel: or of giving his Letters to some other Passenger. I beg a Line from you on this Matter. My Love to the Family. I am ever Affectionately yours

B Franklin

Mr Jno Vaughan

Addressed: To / Mr John Vaughan / at Samuel Vaughan's Esqe / Mercht / London

Endorsed: Dr. Franklin Passy June 3. 1783 Recd. 9 June ansd. 10th.

1. Vaughan had recently returned from Philadelphia, where he had gone in the spring of 1782, hoping to establish himself and purchase land for his family. On March 20, 1783, he entered into a land speculation agreement with Robert Morris and Gouverneur Morris. The contract specified that Vaughan would "proceed with all convenient Speed to Europe" in order to borrow the necessary funds. He sailed for Ostend on April 12 and was in London by May 15, when he forwarded dispatches to Paris. Two days later he scrawled a hasty letter to WTF, telling him of the dispatches for BF and giving him news of the Baches: XXXVI, 450, 657–8; XXXVII, 391; *Morris Papers*, VII, 616–17, 690–1, 697; John Vaughan to WTF, May 17, 1783 (APS). Vaughan's fundraising efforts were unsuccessful, and on June 2 he explained to Robert Morris why he was abandoning them: *Morris Papers*, VIII, 145–7.

To Vergennes

ALS: Archives du Ministère des affaires étrangères; AL (draft): American Philosophical Society

Sir, Passy, June 3. 1783.
Having long known Mr Williams to be a very just Man in all his Transactions, I hope the Favour he requests of a Surséance may be granted to him, being confident that it will be employed to the compleat Satisfaction of his Creditors. I therefore earnestly pray your Excellency to obtain it for him.[2] With great Respect, I am, Sir, Your Excellency's most obedient & most humble Servant   B FRANKLIN

M. le Comte de Vergennes.

2. BF enclosed the petition JW had written at Passy that same day, June 3, addressed to Vergennes, seeking an *arrêt de surséance* (protection from creditors) for his own firm in Nantes and his Lorient firm, Williams, Moore & Co. Asserting that in the past six years he had shipped more than 10,000,000 *l.t.* of French fabric to America, he explained that his present cash-flow problem stemmed from the bankruptcy of Parisian banker Vincens (XXXVIII, 158) and the delayed arrival from America of remittances that would cover his present debts. If granted temporary protection, he promised not to engage in any further speculations until these debts were paid.

On June 5 JW sent Vergennes a second letter along with a detailed financial statement of Williams, Moore & Co., begging the minister to save his reputation. BF had known him since infancy and would never protect him if he had the slightest doubt of his probity. JW sent these under cover of a solicitous letter to Rayneval, also dated June 5. The following day, June 6, he was granted an *arrêt* that was good for three months: notation on [Vergennes] to Louis XVI, [*c.* June 5, 1783]. All documents cited in this note are at the AAE.

From James Walsh[3]   ALS: American Philosophical Society

June, the 4th 1783 dunkirkque
To His Excellency Benjamin Franklin Esqr.—
The Humble Case and petition of James Walsh Moast hum-
bley sheweth that he as Been a prisoner in England since the 4th
Day of April 81 until the 1st. of Last Month I Got My Liberty &
Made the Best of My way over to Calais, wheare the American
Agent[4] was good a nough upon Examanation to give Me a pass
and 2 Livers 16 sous and when yr. Excellencys petitioner arived
in Dunkirk, he Made his adress to Mr. Cofine,[5] he told him to
Do for himself, as he seen petitioner in a Deasent Aperl [apparel]
and 2 or 3 Crowns in his pocket, which was sent poor petitioner
from Ireland when sick in the English Hospital, I belive Mr. Cofine Helps Run a way English sailors By a great ads. and preference, before Americans, yr. Excellencys petitioner was taken
in the Luzerne Letter Marque Belonging to Mr. Morris and
Mr. Englsh[6] in phillidelphia, and Commanded By Captn. Thos.
Bell from Do. Bound For phillidelphia, from Leorent, and taken
of the Wester Island By the Old Interprise Frigate and Brout
Into Limrick in Ireland and from thence on Board the Lynox
guardship at the Cove of Cork, and, then Carrid to England
and sent on Board the Dunkirk guardship at plymouth[7] wheare
4 more and yr. Excellencys Petitioner Cut a way the jolly Boat,

3. This is the second of two petitions from a man who claims to be an
escaped American prisoner. The first, written on May 20 (APS), covers the
same ground but in less detail; the one difference is his mention in the first
petition of being married in Bedford County. Neither appeal received a
response, to the best of our knowledge.
4. Probably Jacques Leveux: XXVI, 515; XXIX, 172–3.
5. Francis Coffyn.
6. The *Chevalier de La Luzerne* was owned by Robert Morris and William Bingham & Co.: Charles H. Lincoln, comp., *Naval Records of the
American Revolution, 1775–1788* (Washington, D.C., 1906), p. 253.
7. The privateer may have been the *Enterprize;* the guardships were the
Lenox and *Dunkirk:* David Lyon, *The Sailing Navy List: All the Ships of
the Royal Navy Built, Purchased and Captured, 1688–1860* (London, 1993),
pp. 67, 76, 86.

and after Cut out a sloop in Coasten Bay with Intent to run Into france But the wind failing was taken a gain a Brought Back and kept in Irons for 3 months and after wards sent to Millprison, wheare petitioner took a Sevare fit of Sickness, and Missed of Geting Hoame a long with the rest of his shipmates,[8] yr. Excellencys. Petitioner has Been out 4 times a gainst the Indians this War: Viz once with Collonell Daniel Broadhead from fortpit to the Shaneytowns and 2 along with Captn Bready to the Shaneytowns, once a long with Collonell gebson from Carlisle to the standing stoane frankstown, & Led Mines[9] &c: &: the is the second petition yr. Excellencys Petitioner has wrote, and Moast humbley hopes, of some relief yr. Excellencys Petitioner, Diets and Lodges along with some of the rest of the americans, and Moast Humble hoapes that yr. Excellency will order the same allowance with rest for petitioner per Day and order some allowance for him to travil to Leorint from Hear or if yr. Excellency pleases He will go to paris or any wheare Else that hes orderd as thers no american ships hear, But Leorint is the surest port in france for them, and would wish to Be orderd there and yr. Excellency Does Not Relive yr. Poor petitioner, he will Sertainly Be Laid in Prison for his Diete and Lodging He humbly hopes yr. Excellency will pardon his Boldness in posumeing to writ to you, But hes is reduced to the lowest Extremity and has No other Recourese in the world, But to Lay His Case Before yr. Excellincy in hopes of some aid and assistance from the Chief governer and Commander of His Country Hear and Being Well Convinced of yr. Excellencys Humanity will rest Content until the Next return of poast after the rect. of this, when yr. Excellencys poor petitioner will Expect relief, from yr. hand, and a line or two Derected to him at Mr. Frances Hutchings in

8. Except for those too ill to travel, the American prisoners held in British jails were released and embarked for the United States in June, 1782: XXXVII, 447.

9. For Daniel Brodhead (*ANB*), Capt. Samuel Brady, and John Gibson (*DAB*) see John B. B. Trussell, Jr., *The Pennsylvania Line: Regimental Organization and Operations, 1776–1783* (Harrisburg, Pa., 1977), pp. 15, 63–4, 103, 105–6, 109; Heitman, *Register of Officers*, pp. 96, 100, 190. "Lead Mines" referred to Fort Roberdeau, outside present-day Altoona, Pa.

rutelet street, By one of yr. Excellencys Clarks, and will as in Duty Bound For Ever Pray   JAMES WALSH
petitioner

N:B: petitioner is Hear since the 11th May

Dunkirkque June the 4th. 1783

Addressed in another hand: A Monsieur / Monsieur de franquelin / ministre plenipotentiaire de / La Nouvelle amérique / En La Couer

Notation: James Walch, June 4. 1783—

From Lewis R. Morris[1]

ALS: University of Pennsylvania Library

Sir   Office for foreign affairs June 5th. 1783
     I had the Honor to remit by the Packet Washington the first Number of the enclosed Bills,[2] with a particular State of your

1. Congress had just accepted Robert Livingston's resignation as secretary for foreign affairs; his last official letter was written on June 5. (BF would not be informed until Boudinot wrote on June 16.) Because Congress had not been able to agree on a successor, Lewis Morris, one of the undersecretaries (XXXVIII, 299n), took charge; he left soon afterward, dissatisfied with his salary. Congress functioned without a foreign affairs office until March 2, 1784, when they elected Henry Remsen, Jr., as undersecretary. Two months later, upon learning that John Jay would soon return to America, they elected him secretary for foreign affairs without his knowledge: Samuel F. Bemis, ed., *The American Secretaries of State and their Diplomacy* (10 vols., New York, 1928; reprint, 1958), I, 182–3, 193; *JCC*, XXIV, 382; XXVI, 122, 355.
2. The enclosures are missing, but they were undoubtedly bills of exchange to pay salaries, as in November, 1782 (XXXVIII, 299). He consulted with Robert Morris about "Bills for foreign Ministers" on May 20 and probably sent them on May 31, the day he inquired of Robert Morris when the *General Washington* was sailing: *Morris Papers*, VIII, 102, 136. On July 27, several weeks after Capt. Barney of the *General Washington* arrived in Paris, Grand advanced a quarter's salary (14,583 *l.t.* 6 *s.* 8 *d.*) to BF: Account XXVII (XXXII, 4).

Account with the United States—[3] Copies also went by the Ship Hope— These being such good Conveyances I am perswaded they will reach you safe—

I have the Honor to be Sir with great Respect and Esteem your most obedient humble servant   L R MORRIS

N.B. I have enclosed also a Bill of Exchange for your Grandson to the Amount of 1811 *l.t.* 5 *s.* Tournois   L. R. M

Hon'ble Mr. Franklin

Endorsed: Letters from Secry of Foreign Affairs

Notation: R. Livingston.

From John Adams   L: American Philosophical Society

Hotel du Roi: June. 6th. 1783.
Mr: Adams' Compliments wait on Dr: Franklin, in return to his polite Invitation for Sunday the 8th. inst:—[4]

Mr: Adams will do himself the honor of waiting on Dr: Franklin.

Addressed: Monsieur / Monsr: Franklin. / Passy.

3. Conceivably a May 12 account of bills of exchange drawn on BF (*Morris Papers*, VIII, 34–5).

4. Charles Storer, who penned this letter, received a similar invitation from BF. He wrote his own note on June 6 accepting on behalf of himself and John Thaxter, Jr. (APS).

From François Bernier[5]   ALS: American Philosophical Society

Monsieur   Paris 6. Juin 1783
Lorsque j'eus hier l'honneur de rendre mes hommages a votre
Excellence, avec Mr. le Marquis de la Salle,[6] en vous engageant a
venir voir nos travaux, j'eus celui de vous dire qu'il serait assés
tôt sur les unze heures, mais aiant fait reflexions qu'il y a tres
peu d'especes a fraper, nos opérations Effigiaires pourraient
être finiës dés les huit heures, Jai crû devoir vous en prevenir
pour vous eviter une démarche en vain; si cette heure prenait
Sur vos precieux instants ce qui nous priverait de l'honneur de
votre présence, je me ferai un vrai devoir de vous informer du
jour et d'une heure plus analogues a votre commodité, Lorsque
nous recommencerons de nouvelles opérations; Je souhaitte,
cependant, que cela n'arrive pas, et que l'heure prematurée que
je vous annonce ne nous prive pas de l'honneur de vous voir
demain.
      Je suis avec un tres profond respect de votre Excellence Le
tres humble et tres obeissant serviteur   F. BERNIER

Notation: Bernier 6 Juin 1783.

5. A member and sometime officer of the Loge des Neuf Sœurs (1778–
83) who was a *graveur de la Chancellerie et de la Monnaie* and lived at the
Royal Mint: *Tableau des Frères . . . des Neuf Sœurs* for 1783 (Yale University
Library); Le Bihan, *Francs-maçons parisiens*, p. 69; Amiable, *Une Loge maçonnique*, pp. 131, 334 of the first pagination and 194 of the second. Bernier
designed the *jeton* featuring BF's profile that was issued at the lodge's May
10 *fête académique:* XXXIX, 584. We identified him there as "Jean-François,"
following the commonly accepted entry in Sellers, *Franklin in Portraiture*,
pp. 193–4. We now suspect that Sellers may have conflated two artists with
similar names, as we have found no evidence that the engraver was also (as
Sellers says) the sculptor Jean-François Bernier, who was a member of the
Académie de Saint-Luc. We therefore identify the engraver as the masonic
sources list him, and as he indicated in his signature.

6. La Salle's term as *vénérable* of the Nine Sisters had just expired; see the
invitation from Gaucher, [before May 26].

From Bon-Joseph Dacier *et al.*

AL: American Philosophical Society

Le Vendredi 6 juin 1783.

M. M. Dacier, Le Roi, Désormeaux et Dusaulx sont venus, en qualité de Députés de l'Académie des inscriptions et Belles-Lettres,[7] pour remercier Monsieur Frankelin de la Médaille dont il a gratifié la Compagnie:[8] Médaille où l'on regrette de ne point voir le nom du premier et véritable Auteur de la plus grande, de la plus belle révolution des tems modernes; mais qui n'en rappelera pas moins ce nom glorieux à la posterité la plus reculée.

Addressed: Pour son Excellence / Monsieur Franckelin, / Ministre plénipotentiaire / des Etats-unis de / L'Amérique

From the Marquis de Lafayette

Printed invitation with MS insertions: American Philosophical Society

Paris *the 6e June 1783*.

The Marquis de la Fayette has the Honor to present his Compliments to *Mr. Franklin* and begs the Favor of *His* Company at Dinner on *Monday* next[9]

An Answer is desired

7. Bon-Joseph Dacier (*DBF*) was the perpetual secretary of the academy, while Julien-David Le Roy (XXIX, 634n), Joseph-Louis Ripault Désormeaux (*DBF*), and Jean-Joseph Dusaulx (XXIX, 123n) were associate members: *Almanach royal* for 1783, p. 505.

8. On May 4 Sarsfield apologized to BF for having asked him in front of one of the members of the academy whether he had already given them a *Libertas Americana* medal: XXXIX, 548. BF then made the gift, which Dacier presented on his behalf at the academy's June 6 meeting: Lester C. Olson, *Benjamin Franklin's Vision of American Community: a Study in Rhetorical Iconology* (Columbia, S.C., 2004), p. 165.

9. June 9. BF was a frequent guest at the Monday dinners held at Lafayette's magnificent new home: XXXIX, 520–1n; Louis Gottschalk, *Lafayette between the American and the French Revolution (1783–1789)* (Chicago, 1950), pp. 14–15. At the APS are similar printed invitations of June 26, 1783 (for Monday, June 30), and of Aug. 28, 1783 (for Saturday, Aug. 30).

From Antonio Francesco Salucci & fils[1]

ALS: American Philosophical Society

Votre Excellence   Livourne 6e Juin 1783

Nous prenons la liberté de presenter a Votre Excellence nos tres humbles respects, et de Luy rendre compte que depuis le comencement du mois passé, nous avons fait partir directement pour Philadelphie notre propre Vaisseau du port de 150 Tx [tonneaux] portant Pavillon Toscan et chargé de Vin, huille, Chapeaux, Bas, Drogues, Soyeries, et autres produits et Manufactures de notre Paÿs ce qui forme la premiere expedition de Toscanne pour ces Contreés la jusque icy sans imitateurs. Ce Vaisseau S'appelle Le Diligent.

L'envie de former des Liaisons agreables de Comerce avec ce Nouvel Empire, nous a determiné a nous livrer en pleine confiance aux encouragements de nos bons Amis Ameriquains, lesquels par leur Lettre du 7. Avril passé nous annoncent des dispositions egallement favorables pour nous expedier icy quelque Vaisseau Chargè de leur denrëes. Un seul obstacle Sembloit le Retenir encore; Celuy cy regarde uniquement le Danger des Corsaires de la Barbarie, avec les quels vos Etats auront bientôt pris quelque Arrangements.[2]

Nous Serions enchantes d'apprendre de la part de V. E. [Votre Excellence] l'approbation de Nos Speculations avec l'Amerique

1. Who had proposed sending two more ships to the United States, now that the peace had been declared: XXXIX, 302–3.

2. The United States would have to convoy its own ships trading with Livorno (Leghorn) because in 1778 the Grand Duchy of Tuscany had abolished most of its navy: Jan Glete, *Navies and Nations: Warships, Navies and State Building in Europe and America, 1500–1860* (2 vols., Stockholm, 1993), I, 308. The United States, however, hardly was in a position to offer protection. Congress as yet had taken no steps to negotiate with the Barbary States, and in July, 1783, they made the decision to sell two frigates (*Morris Papers*, VIII, 265, 325, 397, 415), leaving the *Alliance* as the only remaining American frigate.

The *Diligent*, Capt. Teorentine, did complete its voyage, arriving in Philadelphia around Aug. 19 and departing on Sept. 25 after selling her cargo: *Pa. Evening Post*, Aug. 19 and Sept. 25, 1783; *Pa. Packet*, Aug. 23, 1783.

Septentrionalle, et la Certitude que l'entrave des Barbaresques puisse cesser, pour en entretenir agreablement nos Amis de Philadelphie.

Que V. E. daigne accepter les humbles temoignage de notre devouement, et accepter les Offres Sinceres de nos Services; Tandis que nous sommes avec le plus profond Respect. De Votre Excellence Les Tres humb & o. serviteurs

ANTE. FRANS. SALUCCI & FS:

Monsr. Benjamin Francklin Ministre Plenipotentiaire des 13. Etât Unis/ Paris/.

Notation: Saluci 6 Juin 1783.

From Henry Harford[3] ALS: American Philosophical Society

Sir   [before June 7, 1783][4]

Being as your Excellency must know, very deeply interested in the welfare of America, permit me to congratulace the Congress in General and the state of Maryland in particular, thro your Excellency on the approaching acknowledgement of that independance that has been so Gloriously Struggled for, which

---

3. This is the only extant letter from the last proprietor of Maryland, the illegitimate son of Frederick Calvert, sixth Lord Baltimore. Upon Lord Baltimore's death in 1771, when Harford was only 12 years old, the latter inherited a large portion of his father's estate, including the proprietorship. Challenges to the will kept this inheritance in litigation until Parliament confirmed it in the Estate Act of 1781: *ANB*. The last of the lawsuits was finally resolved in July, 1782, according to Harford's later testimony: Vera Foster Rollo, *The Proprietorship of Maryland: a Documented Account* (Lanham, Md., 1989), p. 254. In August, 1782, John Shuttleworth evidently discussed Harford's Md. land claims with BF: XXXVII, 745n.

4. The day Harford sailed for America aboard the ship *Harford*, accompanied by former Md. governor Sir Robert Eden. They arrived on Aug. 11: Rollo, *Proprietorship of Maryland*, pp. 248, 270n. This letter may have been written as early as December, however. The allusion to poor sailing conditions suggests the winter, and his mention of the "approaching acknowledgement" of independence may signal a date soon after news arrived in London of the Nov. 30, 1782, preliminary articles.

cannot fail giving to the United States the wished for prosperity, that their commerce, Consequence, Situation, and indeed every thing entitle them to, and will I most cordially hope eventually when past hostilities shall be forgotten closely ally them in the strongest bonds of union with this Kingdom, an union that nature dictates and must in the end give laws to the whole world—

Your Excellencys known Candour will do justice on the other side the Atlantic to my past situation and present sentiments— My intention is to Embark for America as soon as the weather will permit. I wish to become a Citizen (if I may be allowed the expression) of that country which was not in my power till lately or I undoubtedly shoud have sought the honor sooner—[5]

I beg your Excellency to accept my most gratefull acknowledgements for your polite attention to Doctr Shuttleworth and for the letter and pasport you were so obliging to furnish him with[6] and I request you to believe me to be with the highest respect for your Carecter Sr Your Excellencys most obedient and obliged humble Sert   HENRY HARFORD

Endorsed: Mr Smith[7] who brought this Letter informs me that Mr Harford is Proprietary of Maryland

Notation: Henry Hartford

5. There is no indication that Harford ever intended to pursue American citizenship. Carrying deeds and other documents that attested to his land claims, he seemed chiefly concerned with seeking compensation from the Md. General Assembly. That body did not take up his case until November, 1785, and in January, 1786, rejected it. Harford returned to England shortly thereafter and pursued his compensation claim with the British government, where he was relatively successful: Rollo, *Proprietorship of Maryland,* pp. 245–74.

6. See XXXVII, 745–6; XXXVIII, 15.

7. Presumably Harford's agent Robert Smith, former secretary to Robert Eden, who accompanied the two men to Maryland: *Mass. Spy: or, Worcester Gaz.,* Sept. 4, 1783; *London Chron.,* Oct. 30, 1783; *Morning Post and Daily Advertiser,* July 8, 1786.

To [the Conde de Sousa Coutinho][8]

LS[9] and transcript: Library of Congress

Sir,   Passy, June 7. 1783

I have perused carefully the Plan of a Treaty which your Excellency did me the honour to leave with me on Wednesday.[1] I shall transmit it to my Sovereign as it is, to avoid delay; but in the meantime would make a few Remarks for your Consideration.

1. I apprehend the Words at the End of the first Article [*que celles dèja établies avec les Puissances les plus favorisées*][2] are not necessary in that Place, as the Article relates merely to Peace or Friendship, and not at all to Commerce.

2. The 4th. and 5th. Articles promising Protection to each others Ships, only against Injuries done by the Subjects of the Government where they are, leaves it open to other Nations who may happen to be at War with either of the contracting Parties, to attack and take in the Harbours of one the Ships of the other, which ought not to be suffered, and certainly is not intended to be suffered: Some farther Words therefore seem to be necessary.

3. I should be glad to have a Copy to send to Congress of the *Reglements dèja établis*, mentioned in the 6th. Article. It is the more necessary as the 7th. Article engages us to observe them.

4. I approve much of the 9th. & 10th. Articles which your Excellency has added. They are reasonable and just.

---

8. The Portuguese ambassador to the French court. This letter is the earliest evidence of BF's ongoing negotiations for a commercial treaty between the United States and Portugal. BF comments here on Sousa Coutinho's counterproposal to the now-missing plan for a treaty that BF had supplied at the ambassador's invitation. The counterproposal as sent to Congress, with BF's suggested changes marked, is published immediately below; see the headnote there for background on the negotiations.

9. In L'Air de Lamotte's hand, with BF adding the final portion of the complimentary close. Located among BF's papers, this seems to be his retained copy.

1. June 4.

2. Here and below, the brackets and underlining are BF's.

5. In Article 12. It seems to me that it would be well to omit the Words [*que seront*] in the 6th. and 7th. Lines;[3] and to add, after the Word [*respectifs*] in the 9th. Line, the following Words of Explanation [*c'est à dire les Armes et Munitions de Guerre de toute Espece*].[4]

I submit these Remarks to your Excellency's Judgment, and I am with great Respect, Sir, Your most obedient & most humble Servant   B FRANKLIN

Portuguese Counterproposal for a Treaty of Amity and Commerce
Copy[5] and transcript: National Archives

The initial negotiations for a commercial treaty between the United States and Portugal, conducted between Franklin and the conde de Sousa Coutinho, took place without the knowledge of the other American commissioners[6] and have left no written trace. Whether Sousa Coutinho had pressed for secrecy is not known; neither do we know when discussions began in earnest.[7] After the present draft

3. Article 12, which had to have been supplied by BF, closely resembles Article 5 of the American commissioners' June 29 proposals to Hartley, with the exception of the phrase on which BF is here commenting, beginning with "que seront" and ending with "leurs Traités respectifs". Sousa Coutinho must have added this phrase.

4. A general definition of contraband had to be included because Sousa Coutinho had removed Congress' Article XVI, which defined it specifically.

5. In the hand of L'Air de Lamotte and enclosed in BF to Livingston, July 22[–26]. The English translation prepared for Congress by John Pintard (National Archives) is published in Wharton, *Diplomatic Correspondence*, VI, 588–91.

6. JA complained to Livingston on July 12 that he and Jay had only recently learned about the negotiations, which he believed to be ongoing. In that and subsequent letters, he warned Congress of BF's ignorance in commercial matters, cautioned the members against signing whatever BF sent, and recommended that the treaty be negotiated by knowledgeable ministers in either Philadelphia or Lisbon. He similarly criticized BF's negotiations with Denmark. See, for example, *Adams Papers*, XVI, 105–6, 195–6, 223–5, 229.

7. The comte de Creutz heard a rumor at the beginning of February that Portuguese-American negotiations were ongoing, with the full knowledge of England: XXXIX, 252. This is unlikely, as it was not until Feb. 15

was agreed upon, Franklin informed Robert R. Livingston only that Sousa Coutinho had urged him to propose a plan for a treaty and that he had done so (acknowledging that he had no authority to sign), offering a text that was "nearly the same" as what Congress had sent him to use in the negotiations with Sweden.[8] Franklin's proposal has not been located. Judging by the available documentation, as explained in the following paragraph, we believe that it consisted of the articles proposed by Congress (*mutatis mutandis*), two articles of his own composition, and two final articles on ratification and duration taken from the Swedish-American treaty. Sousa Coutinho returned to him a counterproposal on June 4, and after reading Franklin's response of June 7 (immediately above), he agreed to the changes Franklin suggested to Article 12. The present text, incorporating those changes, is what Franklin sent to Philadelphia and Sousa Coutinho sent to Lisbon for comment.

The congressional draft treaty contained a preamble and 18 articles.[9] The preamble and 11 of the articles appear in the counterproposal, in their original order and with variations as noted. Interspersed among them are eight others. As Franklin's June 7 letter indicates, Sousa Coutinho inserted Article 6 and the reciprocal Article 7, general guidelines which may have been intended to substitute for the specific situations covered in the congressional articles that were deleted.[1] Of the remaining six "new" articles, four of them (Articles 9, 10, 18, and 19) were derived from the final Swedish-American treaty.[2] Sousa Coutinho added Articles 9 and 10; Franklin noted this with pleasure in his June 7 response. Franklin probably added Articles 18 and 19, as he had included them in the proposal he had given Denmark in April.[3] Articles 11 and 12 could only have

---

that Portugal recognized American independence and lifted the ban on American shipping: José Calvet de Magalhães, *História das relações diplomáticas entre Portugal e os Estados Unidos da América (1776–1911)* (Mem Martins, 1991), pp. 23, 338. The royal edict (misdated Feb. 5) was reprinted in the *Gaz. de Leyde*, March 18, 1783.

8. BF to Livingston, June 12 and July 22[–26]. For the Swedish-American treaty see XXXIX, 250–85.

9. *JCC*, XXIII, 610–21.

1. The articles deleted from the congressional draft were Articles 7, 8, 9, 11, 12, 16, and 17.

2. Some appear in previous treaties as well, but only the Swedish-American treaty contains all four.

3. See the annotation of Walterstorff to BF, May 20.

come from Franklin and had to have been present in his initial proposal. Both were articles that he had long hoped would be included in the definitive peace treaty with Great Britain, and they are among the articles that the American commissioners proposed to David Hartley on June 29 (below).

[*c.* June 7, 1783]

Plan d'un Traité d'Amitié et de Commerce entre Sa Majesté Très Fidelle la Reine de Portugal et des Algarves: Et les Etats Unis de l'Amerique Septentrionale.

Sa Majesté Très Fidelle la Reine de Portugal et des Algarves,[4] Et les Etats Unis de l'Amerique Septentrionale, Voulant établir d'une maniere équitable et permanente les Regles qui devront être suivies relativement au Commerce qu'ils desirent d'établir entre leurs Pays respectifs, ont jugé ne pouvoir mieux atteindre à ce but qu'en prenant pour base de leur arrangement l'Egalité et la Reciprocité la plus parfaite; laisant à chaque Partie la Liberté de faire relativement au Commerce et à la Navigation les Reglements interieurs qui seront à sa convenance, et ne fondant les avantages du Commerce que sur son utilité reciproque et sur les Loix d'une Juste Concurrence: C'est d'après ces Principes et en consequence d'une mûre Déliberation que Sa Majesté très Fidelle et les Etats Unis ont arrêté les Articles suivants.

Art: 1er.

Il y aura une Paix ferme, inviolable et universelle, et une Amitié sincere entre Sa Majesté très Fidelle la Reine de Portugal, ses Heritiers et Successeurs et les Etats Unis de l'Amerique Septentrionale, ainsi qu'entre les Citoyens et sujets des dittes deux Parties, comme aussi entre leurs Peuples, Isles, Villes et Lieux situés sous leurs Jurisdictions respectives, et entre leurs Peuples et Habitans de toutes les Classes sans aucune exception de Personnes et de lieux[5] que celles dèja établies avec les Puissances les plus favorisées.

---

4. Queen Maria I.

5. Article I of the congressional draft ends here. In his June 7 letter to Sousa Coutinho, BF suggested that the following phrase, added by the Portuguese, was unnecessary.

Art: 2d.

Les Sujets de Sa Majesté T.F. pourront librement frequenter et resider dans les Etats Unis et trafiquer de toute Sorte d'Effets et marchandises, dont l'Importation ou l'Exportation n'est point ou ne sera point prohibée, et ils ne payeront dans les Ports, Havres, Rades, Contrées, Isles, Cités et Lieux des Etats Unis, d'autres ni plus grands Droits ou Impôts, de quelque nature qu'ils puissent être, que ceux que les Nations les plus favorisées sont ou seront tenues de payer; Et ils Jouiront de tous les Droits, Libertés, Privileges, Immunités et Exemptions en fait de Négoce, Navigation et Commerce, soit en passant d'un Port des dits Etats à un autre soit en y allant ou en revenant de quelque Partie ou pour quelque Partie du monde que ce soit, dont les dites Nations jouissent ou jouiront.

Art: 3e.

Pareillement les Citoyens et Habitants des Etats Unis de l'Amerique Septle. pourront librement frequenter et resider dans les Etats de Sa Majesté T.F. en Europe, ainsi qu'à Madére et aux Açores, et y trafiquer de toute Sorte d'Effets et marchandises, dont l'Importation ou l'Exportation n'est point on ne sera point prohibée, Et ils ne payeront dans les Ports, Havres, Rades, Contrées, Isles, Cités, et lieux des Etats de la Reine de Portugal d'autres ni plus grands Droits, de quelque nature qu'ils puissent être, que ceux que les Nations les plus favorisées sont ou seront tenues de payer; et ils jouiront de tous les Droits, Libertés, Privileges, Immunites et Exemptions en fait de Négoce, Navigation et Commerce soit en passant d'un Port des Etats de Sa Majesté T.F. à un autre, soit en y allant on en revenant de quelque Partie ou pour quelque Partie du monde que ce soit dont, les dites Nations Jouissent ou Jouiront.

Art: 4.[6]

Sa Majesté T.F. fera usage de tous les Moyens qui sont en son pouvoir pour proteger et deffendre tous les Vaisseaux et Effets

---

6. Articles 4 and 5 (corresponding to the same articles of the congressional draft) were substantially truncated by Sousa Coutinho, thereby

appartenants aux Sujets, Peuples et Habitants des dits Etats Unis qui seront dans les Ports, Havres ou Rades, contre quelque Violence qui puisse être commise par les Sujets de sa dite Majesté, en faisant punir ceux qui porteront atteinte à ces Principes.

Art: 5.

L'Article précedent sera par la même reciprocité exactement observé en côté des Etats Unis par rapport aux Vaisseaux et éffets appartenants aux Sujets de sa dite Majesté qui se trouveront dans leurs Ports, Havres, ou Rades, contre quelque Violence qui puisse être commise par les Sujets des Etats Unis.

Art: 6.[7]

Si quelques Escadres ou Batiments de guerre touchent dans les Ports ou entrent dans les Mers voisines des Etats de Sa M.T.F. on s'y conformera aux Reglements deja établis vis à vis des autres Puissances maritimes les plus favorisées.

Art: 7.

Les Etats Unis de l'Amerique s'obligent aussi par reciprocité d'observer exactement tout ce qui est stipulé dans l'Article ci dessus.

Art: 8.

Il est également convenu et arrêté que tous les Marchands, Capitaines de Navires marchands ou autre Sujets de Sa Majesté T.F. auront l'entiere Liberté dans toutes les Places de la Domination ou Jurisdiction des Etats Unis de l'Amerique, de conduire eux mêmes leurs propres affaires, et d'y employer qui il

---

restricting the protection offered to shipping in the two countries' ports. BF voiced his objection in his June 7 response. The articles as proposed by Congress were identical (*mutatis mutandis*) to Articles 6 and 7 of the Franco-American treaty: XXV, 601–2.

7. As noted in the headnote, Articles 6 and 7 were added by the Portuguese. In his response to Sousa Coutinho, BF asked for the rules to which Article 6 alluded so that he could forward them to Congress. Because they are not presently filed with the treaty proposal, we cannot say whether BF received them.

leur plaira pour les conduire, et qu'ils ne seront point obligés de
se servir d'aucun Interprete ou Courtier ni de leur payer aucun
Honoraire à moins qu'ils ne s'en servent: En outre les maitres
des Navires ne seront point obligés, chargeant ou dechargeant
leurs Navires de se servir d'ouvriers établis pour cet éffet par
l'Autorité publique, mais ils seront entierement libres de charger
ou de decharger eux mêmes leurs Vaisseaux, et d'employer pour
charger et decharger ceux qu'ils croiront propres pour cet éffet,
sans payer aucuns Honoraires à titre de Salaire à aucune autre
Personne que ce soit, et ils ne pourront être forcés de verser aucune Espece de Marchandises dans d'autres Vaisseaux, ou de les
recevoir à leur bord, et d'attendre pour être chargés, plus long
tems qu'il ne leur plaira, et tous et un chacun des Citoyens, Peuples et Habitants des Etats Unis de l'Amerique auront et jouiront
reciproquement des mêmes Privileges et Libertés dans toutes les
Places susdites de la Jurisdiction de sa Mté. T.F.[8] en Europe:
Et pour ce qui concerne les Marchandises de Contrebande qui
peuvent s'introduire dans les Vaisseaux marchands de l'une ou
de l'autre Nation; ils seront obligés de subir la Visite des Employés destinés dans les deux Etats à empecher les mêmes Con-
trebandes, et de se conformer à cet éffet aux Reglements établis,
ou qui s'établiront dans les Etats respectifs.

Art: 9.

Il sera accordé une pleine et entiere Liberté de Conscience
aux Habitants et Sujets de chaque Partie, et personne ne sera
molesté à l'égard de son Culte, moyennant qu'il se soumette,
quant à la demonstration publique aux Loix du Pays. Il sera
permis aux Habitants et Sujets de chaque Partie qui decederont
dans le territoire de l'autre Partie, d'être enterrés dans des en-
droits convenables et décens qui seront assignés à cet effet, et
les deux Puissances contractantes pourvoiront chacun dans sa
Jurisdiction à ce que les Sujets et Habitants respectifs puissent

---

8. What follows must have been added by the Portuguese, as it does not
appear in any previous version of this article. It is a shortened and general-
ized version of Article 8 of the American draft treaty (Article 15 of the
Franco-American treaty: XXV, 608–10).

obtenir les Certificats de Mort, en cas qu'ils soient requis de les livrer.

Art: 10.

Les Sujets des Parties contractantes pourront dans les Etats respectifs disposer librement de leurs fonds, Biens meubles et immeubles, soit par Testament, donàtion ou autrement, en faveur de telles Personnes que bon leur semblera; et leurs Heritiers, dans quelque endroit où ils demeureront pourront recevoir ces Successions, même abintestate, soit en personne, soit par son Procureur sans qu'ils aïent besoin d'obtenir des Lettres de naturalisation. Ces Heritages aussi bien que les capitaux et fonds que les Sujets des deux Parties, en changeant de demeure, voudrant faire sortir de l'endroit de leur domicile, seront exempts de tout droit de détraction de la part du Gouvernement des deux Etats respectifs. Le Contenu de cet article ne derogera en aucune maniere aux ordonnances promulguées contre les émigrations ou qui pourront par la suite être promulguées dans les Etats des deux Puissances, dont elles se reservent l'exercice.

Art: 11.[9]

Si par la suite il survenoit une Guerre entre le Portugal et les Etats Unis, ce qu'à Dieu ne plaise, il sera accordé un terme de neuf mois aux Marchands de chaque Pays residant alors dans l'autre, pour recueillir leurs Dettes et mettre ordre à leurs affaires et ils pourront en sortir librement avec tous leurs effets sans quils puissent en être empêchés ou molestés. Tous les Pêcheurs, Cultivateurs, et tous les artisans ou manufacturiers sans armes et habitant des Villes Places ou Villages non fortifiés, qui travaillent pour la Subsistance et le bien commun du Genre humain, et qui exercent paisblement leurs emplois respectifs, pourront continuer leurs occupations, sans qu'ils puissent être molestés par la Force armée de l'Ennemi ou pouvoir du quel ils pourroient tomber par les évenements de la Guerre; mais que,

---

9. BF wrote this article in December, 1782: XXXVIII, 444–5, and see BF's sketch of articles of peace on pp. 433–5. It is the fourth article proposed by the American commissioners to Hartley on June 29.

s'il est nécessaire de leur prendre quelque chose pour l'usage de la force armée, ou le leur payera à un prix raisonable. Il sera permis à tous les Marchands et Commerçants dont les Vaisseaux ne seront point armés en guerre, mais employés dans le Commerce à échanger les Produits des different Pays, et rendant par là les Besoins, les Commodités et les douceurs de la vie plus aisés à obtenir et plus universels, de passer librement et sans être molestés. Aucune des Puissances contractantes ne pourra accorder aucune Commission à aucun Corsaire, l'autorisant à prendre ou detruire de tels Vaisseaux marchands ou à interrompre un tel Commerce.

Art: 12.[1]

Afin d'écarter et de prevenir a part et d'autre toutes les Difficultés et mésintelligences qui s'élevent ordinairement concernant les Marchandises appellées cidevant Contrebande et [*qui seront*] jugées telles par les Puissances de l'Europe dans leurs Traités respectifs;[2] c'est à dire les Armes & Munitions de guerre il a été convenu que dans le cas où l'une des Parties contractantes se trouveroit engagée dans une Guerre contre quelque autre Nation, aucun de ces articles portés dans les Vaisseaux ou par les Sujets de l'une des Parties aux Ennemis de l'autre, ne sera reputé Contrebande sous quelque Pretexte que ce soit, ni confisqué et enlevé comme tel à aucun Individu: Il sera néanmoins permis d'arrêter de tels Vaisseaux et de les retenir aussi longtems que les Capteurs le jugeront necessaire pour prevenir les inconvenients ou domages qui pourroient resulter de la Continuation de leur Voyage, en payant toutefois aux Proprietaires une

---

1. This is the first known instance of this article's appearing in complete form; the English version was proposed to Hartley on June 29 as Article 5. BF included these ideas in his sketch of articles of peace, drawn up in December, 1782 (XXXVIII, 435).

2. In his June 7 letter to Sousa Coutinho, BF suggested omitting the words that are bracketed, above, and adding the phrase that immediately follows, ending with "guerre." These changes were made after L'Air de Lamotte prepared this copy: brackets were inserted and the phrase was added in the margin by an unknown hand.

Compensation raisonable pour la perte qu'une telle Detention pourra leur occasionner: Et en outre il sera permis aux Capteurs de se servir en tout ou en partie des munitions de Guerre ainsi detenues, pourvû qu'ils en payent l'entiere Valeur aux Proprietaires.

Art: 13.

Tous Vaisseaux et marchandises de quelque nature que ce puisse être, lorsqu'ils auront été enlevés des mains de quelque Pirate en pleine mer, seront amenés dans quelque Port de l'un des deux États et seront remis à la garde des officiers du dit Port, afin d'être rendus en entier à leur veritable Proprietaire, aussitôt qu'il aura duement et sufisament fait conster de sa Propieté.

Art: 14.

Aucun Sujet de sa Majesté très Fidelle ne prendra de commissions ou de Lettres de marque pour armer quelque Vaisseau ou Vaisseaux à l'éffet d'agir comme Corsaires contre les Etats Unis ou quelqu'un d'entre eux, ou contre les Sujets, Peuples ou Habitants d'iceux, ou contre leur proprieté ou celle des Habitants d'aucun d'entre eux, de quel Prince que ce soit avec lequel les dits Etats Unis seront en guerre. De même aucun Citoyen, Sujet ou Habitant des Susdits États Unis et de quelqu'un d'entre eux ne demandera ni n'acceptera aucune Commission ou Lettres de marque pour armer quelque Vaisseau ou Vaisseaux pour courre sus aux Sujets de la Reine T.F. ou quelques uns d'entre eux ou leur Propriete, de quelque Prince ou Etat que ce soit avec qui la dite Reine se trouvera en guerre, et si quelqun de l'une ou de l'autre Nation prenoit de pareilles Commissions ou Lettres de marque, il sera puni comme Pirate.

Art: 15.

Dans le cas où les Vaisseaux des Sujets et Habitants de l'une des deux Parties contractantes approcheroient des côtes de l'autre, sans cependant avoir le Dessein d'entrer dans le Port, ou, après être entré, sans avoir le dessein de decharger leur Cargaison, ou rompre leur Charge, ils auront la Liberté de partir, ou de poursuivre leur Voyage sans être molestés.

Art: 16.[3]

Il est stipulé par le present Traité que les Bâtiments libres assureront la Liberté des Personnes qui se trouveront à leur bord, quand même elles seroient Ennemies de l'une des deux Parties contractantes, et elles ne pourront être enlevées des dits Navires, a moins qu'elles ne soient militaires et actuellement au Service de l'Ennemi.

Art: 17.

Les deux Parties contractantes se sont accordées mutuellement la Faculté de tenir dans leurs Ports respectifs des Consuls; Vice-Consuls, Agents et Commissaires dont les fonctions seront reglées par une Convention particuliere, lorsqu'il plaira à l'une ou l'autre des Parties d'en établir.

Art: 18.[4]

Le present Traité sera ratifié de part et d'autre et les Ratifications seront échangées dans l'espace de huit mois, ou plustôt si faire se peut à compter du Jour de la Signature.

Art: 19.[5]

Sa Majesté T.F. la Reine de Portugal et des Algarves et les Etats Unis de l'Amerique Septentrionale sont convenus que le present Traité aura son plein effet à compter du Jour de sa Ratification du quel les deux Parties contractantes se promettent reciproquement l'observance la plus exacte.

Notations by Franklin: 2d Copy. / Plan of a treaty with Portugal

---

3. This article comprises only the second half of Article 15 of the congressional draft. The first sentence had expressed the concept of "free ships, free goods."

4. This article repeats the first half of Article 27 of the Swedish-American treaty, dropping the second sentence about the plenipotentiaries signing: xxxix, 267.

5. Adapted from the Separate Article of the Swedish-American treaty: xxxix, 268.

From Nathaniel Falconer

ALS: American Philosophical Society

My Dear Sir   London June the 7. 1783

I inclose a Book that Came out yesterday hear and is Like to make Some Noise hear[6] I Recd Letters yesterday from philadla via Newyork as Late as the 24 of April one Ship had arrivd from Irland and omitted to Land there Goods an order to the Collecter to Enter all vessells from Grait Britton[7] I wrote you Sir on my First arrivall hear[8] but as I have not heard from you am fearfull it has not Reacht your hand I then mentioned my intention of Bying a ship hear and Going out to philadla I Expect to Sail from hear about the 15 of July if there is aney thing that I Can do hear for my old frend I beg he will Lay his Commands on me I Dined yesterday at the post office at mr Jacksons your old frend mr watley was with us[9] whe had much Talk about old times they Both Desier to be Rememberd to you I have been once to our old frends mr Strawns[1] and find him jest the Same man belives Every Ly he hears against the united States the French armey and our army have been killing Each other and that whe Shall be Glad to Come to this Countrey again Let thees Gentelmen

6. [John Baker Holroyd, Baron Sheffield], *Observations on the Commerce of the American States with Europe and the West Indies,* an attack on the prospect of Britain's granting the United States reciprocal trade privileges. The first edition was published anonymously and seems to have been first announced for sale on June 5: *General Evening Post.* In the preface to the second edition, written on June 21, Sheffield revealed himself to be the author. For the pamphlet and its influence see Harlow, *Second British Empire,* I, 221–2, 454.

7. We cannot be certain of Falconer's meaning, but around this time John Vaughan heard from an unnamed American merchant in London that on April 24 Congress had opened ports to British ships. The rumor was false; see Vaughan to BF, June 10.

8. On May 15: XXXIX, 607–8.

9. BF had known Charles Jackson, comptroller of the Foreign Office in the General Post Office, since at least 1767, and had sent regards to Jackson and his wife shortly before the outbreak of the war; see XIV, 301n; XXII, 393. BF's old friend George Whatley had written to him on May 6: XXXIX, 565–7.

1. William Strahan.

belive all this for am very Shure I Do not my best Compliments mr wm T Franklin and mr hartley if he is with you I am Dear Sir your most obident Sr   NATH FALCONER

Notation: Falconer June 7. 1783.

From ———— Gauthier   ALS: American Philosophical Society

Monsieur   Du College de Bayeux,[2] le 7 Juin 1783.
J'ai l'honneur de vous donner avis, qu'il vous manque encore, pour completter votre Exemplaire du Dictionnaire des Sciences Morale, Politique, &c.[3] les Tomes 26 & 27. Les derniers que Votre Excellence a reçus étoient les Tomes 24 & 25.[4]
Je suis avec respect Monsieur De Votre Excellence Le très humble & trés obéissant serviteur   GAUTHIER

Notation: Gauthier 7 Juin 1783

2. The *Dictionnaire universel* that Gauthier represented was ostensibly published in London, but the title page gives as the publisher's address in Paris the rue de la Harpe, in the quarters of the former Collège de Bayeux.

3. *Dictionnaire universel des sciences morale, économique, politique et diplomatique; ou Bibliothèque de l'homme-d'état et du citoyen* (30 vols., London [*i.e.*, Paris], 1777–83) was written and compiled under the direction of Jean-Baptiste-René Robinet (1733–1820), who also worked on *Les Affaires de l'Angleterre et de l'Amérique*, to which BF contributed several anonymous pieces (XXVIII, 256–9). The *Dictionnaire universel* focused on diplomacy, administration, agriculture, and political economy, and was explicitly designed to educate royal administrators on the necessity and practical means of reform: Terence Murphy, "Jean Baptiste René Robinet: the career of a man of letters," *Studies on Voltaire and the Eighteenth Century,* CL (1976), 183–8, 223–31; Jean Sgard, ed., *Dictionnaire des journaux, 1600–1789* (2 vols., Paris, 1991), I, 7.

4. Volume 25 was announced and described in the February, 1783, issue of the *Jour. des sçavans,* pp. 373–4.

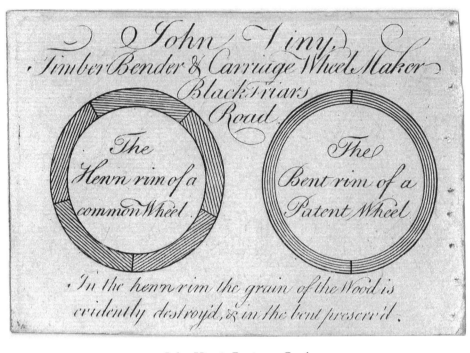

John Viny's Business Card

From William James
ALS: American Philosophical Society

Grand Hotel de Russie, Rue Richlieu,
Sr—   June 7th. 1783—
Since I had the honor of waiting upon you I have gained no
Intelligence of Mr Sayre,[5] for which Reason I have thoughts of
Returning Immediately to England. But before I quitted Paris
I was desirous of Informing you, that I am the person, that for
near twenty years, wrote in the English Newspapers upon public Improvements, many of which in Consequence have taken
place.— My Objects were Roads, Rivers, Bridges, pavements,
Carriages, Copper Sheathing Line of Battle ships, Roman Oval
sewers, Rounding off the Angles of narrow streets, levelling
the Ground And Iron Railing Churchyards &ca &ca—[6] When
I was in Paris six years ago, Monsr Le Roy of the Academy at
the Louvre, Invited me to his Apartments to Consult me upon
a Vareity of Matters but many Things that we Agreed upon

5. Stephen Sayre's final extant letter to BF was written in June, 1782:
XXXVII, 469–70. By December he was in Bordeaux, preparing to return to
America aboard the *Minerva* and vainly hoping that he would be entrusted
with official dispatches from the American commissioners. He directed his
request for a passport to Jay because he did not expect BF to reply: Sayre to
Jay, Dec. 10, 1782, Columbia University Library; John R. Alden, *Stephen
Sayre: American Revolutionary Adventurer* (Baton Rouge, La., and London,
1983), pp. 135–6. The *Minerva* did not sail until mid-March and arrived
in Philadelphia on April 22: *Pa. Packet or the Gen. Advertiser*, April 24,
1783.
6. James had been peppering London newspapers with these articles
since the 1750s. Most appeared in the *Public Advertiser*, and almost all
were published anonymously. Occasionally James signed with his initials, writing from Garraway's Coffeehouse. More often, if he signed at
all, he employed pseudonyms such as "A Friend to Broad Wheels" (*Gen.
Advertiser and Morning Intelligencer*, Feb. 21, 1778) and "An Enemy to
Locks and Shoals" (*Public Advertiser*, Aug. 21, 1781), reflections of his
two primary missions: to improve roads through the use of proportional
broad wheels, and to better inland waterways through ballast work instead of locks. These projects, he argued, would dramatically reduce
British debt.

have not been Carried into Execution, by which Neglect Paris is secondary to London in many Circumstances.—[7] As I think your Influence would have the desired effect, if not out of the line of your Amusement, I have taken the liberty of sending you my Opinion.— Every street in Paris should have Trottoires, or Footways of *broad Stones.*— Such as have not width Enough for 2 footways, And two Carriages, should Admit of One Carriage Only. And where not wide Enough for One Carriage with footways paved with flat stones like Cranbourne Ally Liecester Fields, Change Ally &ca— The streets of London never became Magnificent, nor the shops elegant until Enginiers gave the level, And formed the footways upon their present principle, And the Carriageways upon a small Convex.— In this Improvement I include the footways of the Boulevards, to make them Equally perfect in wet weather.— The next Thing I would Recommend is the upright Roman Oval sewer, As now Carrying on in London six feet high, which Receives the filth of all the Houses, And Conveys it to the Thames.— It would likewise be of great Advantage to France, to pass an Edict, that all Carriages should have a proportional broad wheel According to their several Classes, those with four wheels to Roll double surfaces— The preservation of the Roads, And pavements, in this great Monarchy, would be an Immense saving, As would the lessening the Number of Horses.— I Could Save the State some hundred thousand pounds a year, in Reforming these Kind of Abuses, having spent at least One Thousand pounds On Carriages in Experiments.— The best wheels Ever Invented Are the Hoop Fellies.— I have tried them many years, And Know their Merit.— You have the Reputation of the

7. James had, in fact, used his meeting with Le Roy to leverage public improvements in England. In 1778 he warned Parliament that the French ministry meant "to improve upon the English" not only by adopting a nationwide plan for proportional broad wheels but also by establishing manufactories for British hoop fellies (mentioned below) in every province, reforms expressly "under the Care of the ingenious Mons. le Roy": *Gen. Advertiser and Morning Intelligencer*, Feb. 21, 1778; *St. James's Chron. or the British Evening Post*, Sept. 12, 1778.

Invention.—[8] The destruction of the pavements in paris is Owing intirely to narrow wheels— In time the flat square, becomes Round headed, great weights Are moved with difficulty, Cruelty Ensues, and all Carriages are shook to pieces.— In London I have drawn 29 Sacks of Coals with 2 Horses, which is 2 Chaldron And 5 sacks.—[9] 4 Chaldron with six Horses, And 5 Chaldrons Or 63 sacks 15 Miles with Eight Horses.— In a Chariot, Mr Viny that makes the hoop Felly wheels, has Run 28 Miles with One Horse in 3 Hours with two people in it—[1] Before I left London, I Compleated for a Family of your Acquaintance, a post Chariot with the front wheels 4 feet 10 Inches high, with a Strait perch.— It is As short As Another Carriage, And locks As Easy, the perch bolt being Advanced in front of the Axle.— I Judge Also, that making the natural Rivers of Any Kingdom navigable without Locks, by Improved ballast Work, a most Advantageous Improvement.— I tried the Experiment On the Thames, And supplied the Roads with ballast.— With a Wheel of 15 feet diameter I Could Raise 100 Tun in 4 Hours.— For want of this being Carried into Execution the Thames is Unnavigable several Months in the year.— By a Calculation I found that 300 Tuns from Staines to London of a day Made a saving Against Land Carriage of

8. BF had suggested the method of using steam to bend single-piece hoop felly wheels to Joseph Jacob and John Viny in the early 1770s; see XX, 157–8, and the letter from John Viny and Family, May 21, above. James had advocated these wheels from the beginning, claiming that they outlasted common wheels, would lessen the consumption of timber by four-fifths, and would save the public hundreds of thousands of pounds sterling annually in horses and road repairs. He urged Parliament to abolish "all but the bent felly wheels" and to "buy out this patent, and throw the improvement open to all the ingenious wheelwrights in general": *Public Advertiser*, April 17 and Dec. 1, 1772; *Morning Chron. and London Advertiser*, Jan. 20, 1773, and Feb. 14, 1774.

9. One chaldron is the equivalent of 12 sacks or 36 bushels.

1. James also praised John Viny's stagecoach design and in 1784 argued that it be the model for the next government "mail-machine," as it was the "most expeditious carriage in the kingdom": *Public Advertiser*, April 30, 1777; July 28 and Aug. 26, 1784.

£25000 a year—[2] Judge then What pains should be taken to Abolish All Lock work on natural Rivers And to Avoid them when possible On Artificial Canals.— I have taken the liberty of sending what Width I think would aggrandize France.—[3]

	Inches	Inches	
waggons	9 to roll	16	12 Horses not less than 2 abreast.
	6 to roll	12	8
	3 to roll	6	4
carts	9	6	
	6	4	
	3	1	
Double Stagecoaches }	4 to roll	8	6 Horses— No Luggage
private Coaches Chariotts &ca }	2½ to roll	5	6 Horses
Light Carriages with One horse }	2½		

If I have trespassed a Moment upon your Time Improperly, I beg to Apologize, And to Assure you that I am with great Respect, Sr, your most, Obedt Hum Servt,   WM JAMES.

P.S. Is it not a pity that all France does not Employ Hoop Felly Wheels.—

To Dr Franklin—

Notation: William James Paris June 7. 1783

2. James had repeatedly announced the findings of both experiments in the London press, with varying levels of detail. See, for example, the *St. James's Chron. or the British Evening Post* of Oct. 29, 1782, for the first, and the *Public Advertiser* of Oct. 23, 1780, for the second.

3. The following plan for proportional broad wheels had appeared repeatedly in the London papers, in various forms, for over a decade. See, for example, the *Morning Chron. and London Advertiser,* Jan. 20, 1773.

From Philippe-Denis Pierres

ALS: American Philosophical Society

Monsieur,   Paris le 7. Juin 1783.

J'ai l'honneur de vous adresser un Exemplaire Complet de tout ce qui est imprimé des Constitutions de l'amerique.[4] Vous voudrez bien avoir la bonté de me faire part de votre détermination derniere. Je vous prie aussi de me faire savoir si vous avez écrit à Mr Le Garde des sceaux,[5] & de m'envoyer la note des Exemplaires brochés ou reliés que vous desirerez.

Je suis avec un respect infini, Monsieur, Votre très humble & très obeissant serviteur   PIERRES

J'ai l'honneur de presenter mes très humbles Civilités à monsieur franklin.

M. Franklin.

Endorsed:[6] 50 relie en Veau & titrés
50 en demi Relieure
6 des in 4° en maroc.

4. Pierres had received authorization to begin printing *Constitutions des treize Etats-Unis de l'Amérique* in early April. For background on the edition and its printing see, in particular, XXXIX, 376–8, 434–5, 477, 568.

5. Armand-Thomas Hue de Miromesnil, whose permission was needed both to print and to sell the work; see the references cited above.

6. These decisions about bindings were spelled out in BF's response to Pierres, June 11.

From Joseph Salvador[7]   ALS: American Philosophical Society

Sir   Nantes 7th. June 1783
I had the Honour to acquaint your Excellency from London
of my Intention of proceeding to America by the first Opportunity I have so far carried my design into Execution as to be
on the point of Settling my Passage with Captain Cunningham
who is going to Philadelphia and hope to Sail in less than a Fortnight[8] your Excellencys Commands will be a favour to me if
directed to Mr. Dobree here they will be forwarded to me wishing your Excellency Health and happiness I have the Honour
to Subscribe my Self Sir Your Excellencys most Devoted and
Obedient Humble Servant   JOSEPH SALVADOR

Addressed: A Son / Excellence Monsieur le Docteur / Franklin
Ambassadeur Extra / Ordinaire et Plenipotentaire / des Etats
Unis de LAmerique / A La Cour de France &ca &ca / &ca A
Paris

7. Joseph Salvador (1716–1786), F.R.S., a once-wealthy London merchant and prominent member of that city's Jewish community, had lost the
bulk of his fortune by the early 1770s. In 1773 he dispatched his son-in-
law Francis Salvador to manage his extensive plantation in South Carolina;
Francis was elected to the S.C. legislature, supported independence, and
died in 1776 fighting British-allied Cherokees. Joseph Salvador immigrated
to South Carolina in 1783 and took control of the plantation: *ODNB*. His
earlier letter, mentioned in the first sentence, has not been located.

8. The *Hannibal*, Capt. Gustavus Conyngham, did not sail until July 13:
XXXV, 182n; JW to Thomas Barclay, July 15, 1783 (Yale University Library).

From William James   ALS: American Philosophical Society

Grand Hotel de Russie Rue Richlieu
Sr—   Sunday Morning. [after June 7, 1783]⁹

I meant soon after I had the Honor of dining with you at passy, to have Returned to England, but meeting with an English Phyzician, he has made Paris so agreable to me, that I think of Staying Until the Middle of September, without I Can gain An Establishment in France Or America.—

Having taken, in my leisure Hours, An Active part in the Improvements in England, I was equally desirous of not being Idle in Paris.— My Communicant has been daily surveying this great City, And Communicating by Letters my Remarks to Monsr Le Roy.— A few weeks ago, I made a Tour with my Friend into Normandy, And sent him likewise my Observations on what I thought most Momentous.— I discover many Things Right in France.— Their Roads Are Magnificent, And well Conducted— The Arts flourish in Architecture, Ship building, painting, sculpture &ca yet I think them deficient in many Essential Circumstances.— Their Modern Bridges Are fine, but Unhappily Are Over Uncorrected Rivers— There is not a City Or Town in France Conducted on a Regular survey like London And Windsor. Neither is there One Carriage of Any Sort Upon a Mechanic principle.— Paris is Unreformed— It wants a better supply of water, And Oval sewers to Carry off the Filth.— The English seldom Revisit paris— The Reason is they Can neither Ride, drive Or walk About the City.— The plantations without Are however Very grand, pleasant, And Agreable.— If Rome, by the Remains of its Ancient Magnificence, brings in by the Resort of Foreigners more than London gains by its Trade, what would not France do, if all the Cities, And Towns, were

9. The date of James's only other letter, in which he introduces himself more fully (he had already waited on BF) and reveals his connections with two men BF knew well: Le Roy and John Viny. The dinner James mentions in the first sentence, below, probably took place after that letter. His allusion to a subsequent trip to Normandy and a mid-September departure also suggest a date later in the summer.

Conducted upon the principle of London And Westminster?—
I have but poor Abilities, And yet I think the Hints I have given
Mr Le Roy, would Advantage France many Million a year.—[1]
I Judge Improved Carriages would save nearly half the draft
Horses.— That Roads, And pavements, in their Repairs, might
be decreased One half, by a proportional Broad wheel— The
same in the wear and Tear of Carriages of Every denomina-
tion.— In the preservation of Goods 10 per Ct.— Hoop Fellies
would save ⅘ths of the Timber now wasted, And last as long
again.— In Barge work 100 per Ct may be gained, by Creating deeper upper Levels.— The Ingenious Mr Peronetts Books
being published, his Art of Bridge Building is now Universally
Known.—[2] If in the Reform of Rivers, Any Even of his Own
Bridges Should prove Unsafe, they may be Rebuilt On the
same Construction.— The present structures of that sort Are
not Equal to a deepened Navigation.— I have walked under
An Intire dry Arch of pont Neuilly— This proves the River
defective, not the Bridge.— The navigation of the Thames is
Ruined. The Corporation of London want to Regain it by Lock
work.— I Recommend Improved Ballast work.

Although I Intend to Return to England in a few Days, yet
I had Rather spend the Remainder of my Days in France, Or
America.— I was used Ill by the Bank Directors in the year

---

1. James had met with Le Roy years earlier; see his June 7 letter. Once
he returned home, he filled the London press with rumors of France's remarkable progress, as he had done after his earlier meeting. The French had
"already begun upon improving their internal Navigations," and they were
"ambitious of imitating the English" by adopting a national plan for proportional broad wheels and spearheading the cause across Europe: *Public
Advertiser*, Feb. 28, April 14, and July 5, 1784. By the end of 1785, however,
James was still pressing Le Roy on road reform in France, the lack of which
had kept the French postal service far behind that of England and even
America: "I address you to take the lead in this great post improvement,"
he wrote in a public letter, "and Germany will soon imitate France." *Gen.
Advertiser*, Oct. 25, 1785.

2. Engineer Jean-Rodolphe Perronet (XXVII, 249) had recently published *Description des projets et de la construction des ponts de Neuilly, de Man-
tes, d'Orléans et autres . . .* (2 vols., Paris, 1782–83).

1772, Or Rather by Mr Payne the Governor[3] who Ruined me to save himself.— After I had paid Away Twenty thousand pounds in supporting a Million of Stock against Sr George Colebrooke,[4] who gave false Dividends On India stock, they Supported him, And Others in July 1772 to the Amount of 8 Millions of Money—by which Means, Instead of Recovering £50,000 which I Should have done, I was forced to pay £10,000 More.— I was then a Tenant of the Bank— I Resented their treatment, but they were too powerfull to Contend with.— I then took up the American Cause very Warmly, And Sent them Letters to the proprietors, which they Smuggled, that if Ever America was lost to England, it would be thro' the Bank parlor, And that [*torn:* all(?)] their political Discounts were paper swords Issued to destroy the Innocent Americans, but that they would not succeed, for the Inglorious Conduct of England would End in a happy Independency to America.—[5] Now sir, As you have done Numberless great Things in your Life, I Should not be Ungratefull, if through your Consequence, you Could Establish me in France, Or America, in any Employ I am Equal to.— I had Rather Remain Abroad On 200 per Annum, than Return to England on £500.—

I am, Sr, your Most, Obedt And Obliged Hum Servt.—

WM JAMES.

P.S.— If it is Necessarry for Me to quit France I intend taking the Liberty of waiting upon your Excellency to take my

---

3. Edward Payne, governor of the Bank of England: *The Royal Kalendar . . . for the Year 1772* (London, [1772]), p. 215.

4. The banker and speculator Sir George Colebrooke was a director of the East India Company from 1767 to 1773. He served as its chairman in 1769, 1770, and 1772; during his final year he was accused of stockjobbing and was heavily in debt. His own bank failed in 1773, and four years later he was declared bankrupt: *ODNB;* Namier and Brooke, *House of Commons,* II, 235–6.

5. James had integrated his pro-American sentiments into his pleas to the British government for road and canal reform: "Small Sums are grudged by Administration for any commendable National Improvement, but we don't mind Millions in Support of an Army to demolish the innocent Subjects of America." *Public Advertiser,* July 9, 1777.

Leave, And to thank you for the several Civilities I have Received.—[6]

To his Excellency Dr Franklin

Notation: Wm. James

From the Comtesse d'Houdetot

LS: American Philosophical Society

a Sanois Le 8. juin 1783

Vous M'avés promis Mon Cher Et Venerable Docteur une petite Visitte pour Sanois. Voicy Le Moment De Vous En Rapeller
Le Souvenir; nôtre Vallée Et Mon jardin sont Dans toutte Leur
Bauté Et touttes nos fleurs vous apellent s'il Vous Convenait De
Venir; Vendredy, Samedy, Dimanche ou tel autre jour De La
Semaine. Souvenés Vous que Vous M'avés promis D'Estre tout
a fait mon hôte Et D'habiter Sous mon toît. Vous n'en trouverés
pas ou lon se fasse un plus grand honneur Et un plus grand plaisir De Vous y Voir Ce Sera un Monument De plus, qui Embel-
lira Et honnorera ma petite Retraite Champêstre ou je Conserve
Avec Soin Le Souvenir, De tout Ce qui a Attiré mon Admiration Et touché Mon Cœur;[7] Combien Mon Cher Docteur avés
Vous De Droits a Ces titres La. Vous ferés Vôtre Reponse a Mon

---

6. James was back in London by Nov. 3, agitating to be awarded the position of Water Bailiff, for which he had been recruited two years earlier by
"some of the Heads of the City" but which was still vacant and evidently
contested: James to the Corporation of London, published in the *Public
Advertiser*, Nov. 11, 1783. After BF left Europe, James began invoking the
American's name in his newspaper articles urging reform. According to
these accounts, BF had recommended to the French ministers that they issue an edict mandating proportional broad wheels, urged the French to use
hoop felly wheels exclusively in order to improve carriages, and advised
them on how to make rivers navigable without locks: *Morning Herald*,
Nov. 30, 1786; *Public Advertiser*, Dec. 7, 1786, and March 12, 1790.

7. An allusion perhaps to the Virginia locust tree BF planted in the gardens of Mme d'Houdetot's country estate during the *fête champêtre* she
staged in the spring of 1781: XXXIV, 544.

frere qui Vous Verra Mardy.[8] J'Espere Qu'elle Sera favorable Et que Monsieur Votre petit fils Vous Suivra je Le prie D'agréer mon invitation Et Mes Complimens, Agrées Mon Cher Docteur L'assurance De Mon tendre attachement

LA CTESSE. DHOUDETOT

Si Mon frere n'avait pas L'honneur De Vous Remettre Luy même Cette Lettre je Vous prirais D'Envoyer Votre Reponse Chez moy a paris Le plutot possible Et S'il se peut jeudy matin.

Notation: La Comtesse D'houdetot A Sanois 8 Juin 1783

From Edward Bridgen

ALS: American Philosophical Society

My Dear Sir   London June 9 1783
Your kind favour of the 22nd past[9] reached my hands the 4th. Currant and I thank you for it, because it ordered the payment of arrears to the Society of Antiquaries, of which you were one of the first who has paid his arrears, after a *general call* ordered for the Secretary[1] to make; but I undertook that office to you as some had doubted your honour.

There are several prints your due, and I think 3 or 4 Vol: of the Archiologia—also would you chuse to have the 2 or 3 Volumes preceeding purchased to make them compleat.[2]

8. Alexis-Janvier La Live de La Briche (XXXV, 105), who as *introducteur des ambassadeurs* would be present at the king's Tuesday reception for foreign ambassadors at Versailles.

9. Neither this letter nor the one that must have elicited it has been located.

1. The society had two secretaries, William Norris and Thomas Morell. Bridgen was the treasurer: *A List of the Society of Antiquaries of London, April 23, MDCCLXXXIII* ([London], [1783]), p. 1.

2. BF joined the Society of Antiquaries on May 13, 1773: *A List of the Members of the Society of Antiquaries of London . . .* (London, 1798), p. 26. The first two volumes of its journal, *Archaeologia: or Miscellaneous Tracts, Relating to Antiquity,* were published in 1770 and 1773, respectively. Volumes 3 through 6 had been published since BF left England in 1775.

Mr Hodgson paid me the 16 Guineas, & I have given him an Official receipt for the same.[3]

If My Worthy Friend Mr. Laurens is still with you pray Say all that is kind for me, and that I don't answer his last as I expect to hear from him *in person* daily. God Bless & protect you and give you long life, & every comfort your advanced age can admit of, and be assured that I am unalterably My Dear Sir Most respectfully and Affecty. your ev hub st   EDWD: BRIDGEN

The Honbl Benj Franklin

Notation: E. Bridgen 9th June 1783

Henry Laurens to the Other American Peace Commissioners[4]

Copies: Massachusetts Historical Society, Library of Congress

Gentlemen,   Tuesday Morning, 4 oClock 10. June 1783. This Moment landed—[5] As a Boat is going over to Calais, the inclosed Proclamation may *possibly* arrive new to you. To me it wears the Aspect of one Part of a commercial Treaty.[6] I

3. William Hodgson paid Bridgen £16 16 s. on BF's account in June: Hodgson's account of Oct. 24, 1783, described in XXXVII, 31n.

4. Laurens was on his way to London in the vain hope of raising a private loan for the United States, a venture he proposed after the commissioners received Ferdinand Grand's May 10 warning about the dire state of American finances (XXXIX, 587–9). He delayed his departure on account of the stalled negotiations with Hartley but finally left Paris on June 7 with the consent of his colleagues: *Laurens Papers*, XVI, 207n, 210–11.

5. At Dover; see his next letter of June 17.

6. Laurens enclosed a copy of the king's Order in Council of June 6. This permitted importation into Britain of American masts, naval stores, and indigo carried aboard British or American ships. It also restored the American tobacco trade to its former footing, with only a small duty being due on American tobacco being re-exported. The latter part of this order was not merely a concession to America but also served British plans to recapture the American tobacco trade from France: Harlow, *Second British Empire*, I, 472n; Price, *France and the Chesapeake*, II, 732–3.

146

shall not wonder, should I see our Friend, D. H. in London this Week.[7] I purpose Lodging there to night. There & every where, I shall be as I am, Your faithful However feeble Aid & obedient Servant.   (signed) HENRY LAURENS

To His Exy. Dr. Franklin, &c.

From John Vaughan[8]   ALS: American Philosophical Society

Dear Sir   London June 10. 1783
    I am Somewhat Surprised to find your letters are of So early a date; I have recd a letter from Mr Jay to Same purport;—all I can say upon the Subject is that the Genl. letters given me, were those intended to go by Mr Jefferson two months before;[9] Mr Morris gave me Some letters the morning I came away, directed If I recollect right, to Mess. Grand, Le Coulteux, & Barclay.[1] I was bound *to Ostend*; & there were two merchant Vessels & three french frigates bound *to France* lying in the river, & perhaps Mr Morris reserved his letters of Intelligence for what he esteemed a *Shorter* conveyance. Mr Livingston *did so*; I received no dispatches from *him*. I shall be very uneasy 'till I learn from Mr Morris, wr. [whether] he did give me any letters for you pos-

7. On May 26 the London press announced that Hartley had completed a commercial treaty and would soon return home: the *Morning Post and Daily Advertiser, Public Advertiser,* and *Parker's General Advertiser* of that date. On June 3 *Parker's* reported that Laurens was expected and would probably travel with Hartley.

8. In answer to BF's of June 3. As noted below, Benjamin Vaughan added to the postscript.

9. After Jefferson's mission was canceled on April 1, he returned to Robert Morris the letters and dispatches he had planned to carry to Paris: XXX-VIII, 537, 545, 558–9n; *Morris Papers,* VII, 263n, 673.

1. Morris' diary confirms that on April 12 he gave Vaughan the dispatches Jefferson had returned: *Morris Papers,* VII, 697. For an April 12 letter to Le Couteulx & Cie., and an April 10 letter to Ferdinand Grand, see *Morris Papers,* VII, 698–9, 831.

terior to the date mentioned by you.—[2] This I am certain of, every thing he gave me, was put in a bag in my trunk Seperate from my other papers, & were immediately on my arrival enclosed to you by my brother Benjn. in my presence, & by him Sent to the person who carried them to Paris. As I left Philadelphia the morning after the declaration of peace,[3] nothing material could have been done by Congress. The family present their most affectionate respects; they expect to Sail in a fortnight, & I propose Setting off tomorrow, in order to be there before them.[4] I remain with the most unfeigned respect & esteem, Dear Sir, Your affectionate & much obliged friend & servant,

JN VAUGHAN

I must beg leave to refer you to Mr Jay for what little intelligence I am master of, which I have sent (in answer to his letter) with some Newspapers.

Congress Resolved 24 April, that British Vessels should be admitted to an entry,[5] as I am told by one of the Com: of American Merchants[6] at this place. Ld. Daer goes on Monday next &

2. Vaughan did check and reported that Morris had indeed sent the later letters by a "more expeditious" conveyance: John Vaughan to WTF, Sept. 6, 1783, APS.

3. Congress proclaimed a cessation of hostilities on April 11: XXXIX, 485n.

4. See Samuel Vaughan to BF, June 14. John Vaughan's sailing was delayed; see Falconer to BF, June 24.

5. We find no such resolution. On April 16, the day after Congress ratified the preliminary articles, Dickinson ordered Pennsylvanians to forbear acts of hostility against the British. Port officials in Philadelphia soon wondered whether they could admit British ships, and this question was quickly put to Congress. On April 22 a congressional committee recommended against Congress' taking any formal decision. The lack of action on Congress' part was seen as tacit permission, and on April 26 a British ship at Philadelphia was unloaded: William T. Hutchinson *et al.*, eds., *The Papers of James Madison*, First Series (17 vols., Chicago, London, and Charlottesville, 1962–91), VI, 471–2n.

6. John Vaughan ended his letter here. His brother Benjamin, whose handwriting is unmistakable, added "at this place" and squeezed in the rest of the postscript.

will bring my brother's letters & a long *Bystander,*[7] with new Pamphlets.

Mr Spalding & his attendant have been suffocated in a diving bell off Dublin, in an attempt to recover some things out of a wreck there (the Belgioso.) He had before succeeded in getting up some of the cannon of the Royal George, on which vessel they are about making a second attempt.[8]

B. Franklin Esqr—

Addressed: His Excellency B. Franklin Esqr / &c: &c: / Passy / near Paris

Notation: Vaughan June 10. 1783

To Pierres   AL (draft): American Philosophical Society

Sir,   Passy, June 11. 1783—
I received the Exemplaire of the Constitutions.[9] I intended to have waited on M. le Garde des Sceaux yesterday at Versailles, but was prevented.— I shall write to him today.—[1] The Ratification of the Swedish Treaty is arrived,[2] so that there is no farther Obstruction to the Publication. I desire to have 50 of the 8vos [octavos] bound in Calf, & Letter'd, and 50 half bound,

7. Benjamin Vaughan's article signed "A By-Stander" was so long, in fact, that it had to be serialized; see his letter (II) of June 16. He had already mentioned it in a letter to WTF of June 6, promising that "My next will inclose a Bystander" (APS).

Basil William Douglas, Lord Daer (1763–1794), was the eldest surviving son of Dunbar Douglas, fourth Earl of Selkirk: *ODNB,* under London Corresponding Society.

8. Charles Spalding of Edinburgh and his assistant Eben. Watson were accidentally killed in Dublin Harbor on June 2. Earlier, Spalding had brought up 17 cannon from the submerged wreck of the *Royal George* (for whose sinking see XXXVIII, 65–6n): *Gent. Mag.,* LIII (1783), 541–2.

9. Which Pierres sent on June 7, above.

1. He did so; see Miromesnil to BF, June 16.

2. BF must have learned this from Staël von Holstein at Versailles the day before; see that minister's letter to BF, June 13.

that is, between Pasteboards, with a Sheepskin Back & Letter'd, but not cut. I desire also 6 of the 4tos [quartos] bound in Morocco.[3] I am with great Esteem, Sir,

M. Pierres

To Robert R. Livingston   ALS and transcript: National Archives

Sir   Passy, June 12. 1783
    I write to you fully by a Vessel from Nantes, which I hope will reach you before this.[4] If not, this may inform you, That the Ratification of the Treaty with Sweden is come, & ready to be exchang'd when I shall receive that from Congress;[5] That the Treaty with Denmark is going on, and will probably be ready before the Commission for signing it arrives from Congress; it is on the Plan of that propos'd by Congress for Sweden:[6] That Portugal has likewise propos'd to treat with us, and the Ambassador has earnestly urg'd me to give him a Plan for the Consideration of his Court, which I have accordingly done, and he has forwarded it:[7] The Congress will send Commissions &

3. Pierres printed the quarto edition first, identifying the paper as either "Papier d'Annonay, de la Fabrique de MM. Johannot" or "Papier-Vélin, de la Fabrique de M. Réveillon, à Courtalin, en Brie." For the octavo edition, printed on ordinary paper, he reset the title page and corrected certain typographical errors including the spelling of New Hampshire on the half-title: Durand Echeverria, "French Publications of the Declaration of Independence and the American Constitutions, 1776–1783," Bibliographical Soc. of America *Papers*, XLVII (1953), 318–19.
    4. No record of it survives.
    5. BF had just learned of Sweden's ratification; see BF to Pierres, June 11. Two months earlier, when sending a duplicate copy of the treaty to Livingston, BF hoped that Congress had already received the original and ratified it: XXXIX, 467. They did not ratify until July 29; see Boudinot to BF, Aug. 15.
    6. See the annotation of Walterstorff to BF, May 20.
    7. BF and the Portuguese ambassador in fact agreed upon a modified version of that draft; see BF to Sousa Coutinho, June 7, and the Portuguese counterproposal immediately following.

Instructions for concluding these Treaties to whom they may think proper; it is only upon the old Authority given (by a Resolution) to myself with Messrs Deane and Lee, to treat with any European Powers, that I have ventured to begin these Treaties in consequence of Overtures from those Crowns.[8] The Definitive Treaty with England is not yet concluded, their Ministry being unsettled in their Minds as to the Terms of the Commercial Part; nor is any other definitive Treaty yet compleated here, nor even the Preliminaries signed of one between Holland and England.

It is now near 5 Months since we have had a Line from you, the last being dated the 13th of January:[9] Of course we know nothing of the Reception of the Preliminary Articles, or of the Opinion of Congress respecting them:[1] We hop'd to have receiv'd before this time such Instructions as might have been thought proper to be sent us for rendring more perfect the definitive Treaty. We know nothing of what has been approv'd or disapprov'd. We are totally in the dark, and therefore less pressing to conclude, being still (as we have long been) in daily Expectation of hearing from you.— By chance only we learn that Barney is arriv'd; by whom went the Dispatches of the Commissioners, and a considerable Sum of Money:[2] No Acknowledgment of the Receipt of that Money is yet come to hand, either to me or Mr Grand. I make no doubt that both you and Mr Morris have written; and I cannot imagine what is become of your Letters.—

With great Esteem, I have the honour to be, Sir, Your most obedient & most humble Servant   B FRANKLIN

8. XXII, 629–30; XXXVII, 204.

9. Though Robert Morris wrote on Jan. 13 (XXXVIII, 580–2), no letter of that date from Livingston has been found. His letters of Jan. 2 and 6 are in XXXVIII, 537–8, 552–6.

1. Livingston informed the American commissioners of the ratification in a letter of April 21: XXXIX, 486.

2. Capt. Barney arrived in Philadelphia on March 12 with specie from the French government and a copy of the Nov. 30 preliminary agreement: XXXVIII, 560n; XXXIX, 380.

P.S. I beg leave to recommend to your Civilities the Bearer of this, Dr Bancroft; whom you will find a very intelligent sensible Man, well acquainted with the State of Affairs here, and who has heretofore been employ'd in the Service of Congress. I have long known him, and esteem him highly.

honble. R. R. Livingston Esqe

Notation: Letter June 12. 1783 Doct Franklin Read 30 Sept 1783 Referred to Mr. Huntington Mr Lee Mr Duane Answered by the Instruc. to our foreign Ministers[3]

From Alleyne Fitzherbert

AL: Library of Congress

Paris Thursday morning. [June 12, 1783] Mr Fitz-Herbert presents his best Compliments to Dr Franklin; — he purposes leaving Paris this afternoon and will be exceedingly happy to take charge of any commissions that he or Mr Franklin may have for Brussels or England.[4]

Addressed: A Monsieur / Monsieur Franklin / &c— &c— &c— / a Passy

Endorsed: June 12. 83

---

3. A congressional committee of Samuel Huntington, Arthur Lee, and James Duane drafted instructions for American ministers abroad which were approved on Oct. 29: *JCC*, XXV, 631, 637, 753–7.

4. Fitzherbert, whose temporary mission to the French court had ended, seems to have been returning home by way of Brussels, where he had been posted as minister for the six years prior to this assignment. He would soon be sent as envoy plenipotentiary to the Russian court and would spend 20 more years in the diplomatic service: *ODNB*.

From Peter Green and Timothy Parmele[5]

ALS:[6] American Philosophical Society

Sur,   Nance [Nantes] June 12th D 1783.
You will Excuse my Boldnes but it is In A Case of distress
to Let yo now the Circumstance That we two are in with many
others.

We have taken all opertunitys to meet with Mr Williams the
American Agent but we Cannot finde Him we go day after day
to his Clerks they Always tell us He is Coming home[7] when we
Show our pass and Lets Them now how we ware prisoners to
the English they Tell us they Can do Nothing For us.

We have had one Shift of Clothes From the Clerks. The man
that we have boarded with will Keep us No Longer and keeps
our Clothes they Will not pay our Board For tim paste nor to
Come So we Expect to Starve In the Streets, we Can get No
Ship atall, nor work.

The other prisoners Are on board Cap Cuningham Ship[8] we
have Spoke With him but he will not take Any More For he Says
hes got Somany that he Does Not Know what to do with them.

So I Remain Your most Humble Servant

> PETER GREEN
> TIMOTHY PARMELE

Addressed: To Passe / Benjamin Franklin / Esr Minister of the
/ Eunited States of America / pour M. francklin—à Paris

Notation: Timothy Parmele 12 June 1783

---

5. American sailors who had escaped from British prisons and received
assistance from BF on April 27: XXXIX, 5.

6. In the hand of Parmele, who signed for Green.

7. JW made two long trips to Paris between early April and June 17. He
was only back in Nantes between May 24 and *c.* June 1: XXXIX, 503, 504n;
JW to Thomas Jenkins, April 10, 1783, and to James Moore, May 25 and
June 17, 1783 (Yale University Library); BF to Vergennes, June 3, above.

8. The *Hannibal,* Capt. Conyngham (XXIII, 585n). For JW's role in sending home former prisoners of war, who flooded into Nantes during the
summer of 1783, see our annotation of JW to BF, July 29. Both Parmele and
Green are listed on JW's account of those who received support in May: Account XXVII (XXXII, 4).

From Richard Price AL: American Philosophical Society

June 12th: 1783

Dr Price presents his best respects to Dr Franklin and desires his acceptance of one of these Pamphlets.[9] The other he desires Dr Franklin would be so good as to present to Mr Laurens if at Paris. If not, he wishes it may be presented to Mr Adams.

Addressed: To / Dr Franklin

From John Wheelock[1] ALS: American Philosophical Society

Sir, Hague 12th June 1783

I should long before this time have done myself the honor to write—but the situation of my affair has been such, that a letter might have been impertinent, as it could have communicated nothing with precision.

Their Serene & Royal Highnesses, the Prince and Princess of Orange have manifested great approbation of the design, and have munificently favored it.— As the proposal has not been encouraged by the gentlemen of influence at Amsterdam, nothing has been obtained from that city.— But it has succeeded well at Haarlem; and many gentlemen in other places have been disposed to promote it.

I should be particularly obliged to your Excellency for the favor of a letter, in behalf of the affair, to Dr Price. We shall likely leave this country in a fortnight, and go to England, (agreeable to your advice) and may wait on him, within three

9. Price may have been sending more copies of *The State of the Public Debts and Finances at Signing the Preliminary Articles of Peace in January 1783: with a Plan for Raising Money by Public Loans, and for Redeeming the Public Debts.* The pamphlet was issued soon after the publication of the fourth edition of *Observations on Reversionary Payments.* Copies of the pamphlet as well as the book had been among a miscellany of items shipped earlier in June; see the annotation of Dessin to BF, June 15.

1. Wheelock and his brother James were in Europe trying to raise funds for Dartmouth College. BF suggested they go to England and Holland; see XXXVIII, 134–5; XXXIX, 176–7, 333.

154

or four weeks—[2] I should be happy, Sir, to hear, whether any thing has appeared within your particular acquaintance in favor of the plan, could I be honored with a letter directed to the care of the Dr.

Please to accept my most grateful acknowledgments for your kindness and attention, and esteem me as being with the greatest respect, Sir, Your Excellency's, much obliged, & very Obedt servt   JOHN WHEELOCK

His Excellency Dr Franklin &c. &c. &c.

Notation: Weelock 12 June 1783.

From Gijsbert Karel van Hogendorp

ALS: American Philosophical Society

Monsieur!   La Haie Ce 13 Juin 1783.

Les lettres dont Votre Excellence a eu la bonté de me charger pour Messieurs Washington Levingston et Morris,[3] m'assurent une reception dans votre patrie, telle que je la désirois ardemment, afin de m'instruire à fond de tout ce qui regarde un païs aussi intéressant que la nouvelle République des treize Provinces uniës de l'Amérique. Recevez en Monsieur mes très sincères remercimens avec le témoignage ingénu de mon admiration pour un Si grand-homme.

J'ai l'honneur avec un très profond respêct Monsieur de Vôtre Excellence le très humble et très obéïssant Serviteur

CHARLES DE HOGENDORP

2. They left for England on July 5: Leon B. Richardson, *History of Dartmouth College* (2 vols., Hanover, N.H., 1932), I, 206–7.

3. See BF to Livingston, May 10 (XXXIX, 586–7), where Hogendorp is identified. He sailed on the ship of the line *Den Erfprins*, part of the squadron taking Dutch Minister Plenipotentiary Pieter Johan van Berckel to the United States, and barely escaped a shipwreck off the Massachusetts coast: *Morris Papers*, VIII, 622n; Schulte Nordholt, *Dutch Republic*, pp. 252–3; *Adams Papers*, XIV, 497n.

From the Comte de Hülsen[4]

ALS: American Philosophical Society

Monsieur,   Passy, Ce 13. Juin 1783./.
Je suis au despoir de ne Vous avoir pas trouvé ayant quelque
chose d'important à Vous dire.
J'ay cherché des Connoissances avec M. le Marquis de
Condorcet, & M. Le Cte de Milly. J'ay appris que le premier
n'etoit pas (?)çon,[5] et qu'il ne Cultivoit pas les Connoissances
dont j'avois besoin. Quant au 2d. il promet de me guerir dans
quelques Semaines me proposant une Cure fort austere.[6] Son
premier remede que je dois d'abord prendre, et que j'ay es-
sayé hier, m'a donné la Colique pendant toute la nuit. Daignez
m'instruire Charitablement Si je dois m'abbandonner entierement à ses soins, Et permettez moy encore une seule fois de
venir Vous trouver en particulier, et de profiter de Vos Leçons

---

4. Former governor of Minsk and Mstislavl (then part of the Polish-
Lithuanian Commonwealth), Józef Jerzy Hylzen (Hülsen in German;
1736–1786) was a prominent political reformer and freemason. He was instrumental in constituting the lodge Catherine of the North Star, and served
as its Grand Master in 1781. He devoted the last years of his life to travel
and study; while in Paris in 1783, he read his *Mémoire sur le caractère du roi
de Pologne* at a session of the Musée de Paris: Władysław Konopczyński
et al., eds., *Polski słownik biograficzny* (46 vols. to date, Krakow, 1935–),
under Hylzen; J. G. Findel, *Histoire de la franc-maçonnerie depuis son origine
jusqu'à nos jours*, trans. E. Tandel (2 vols., Paris, 1866; reprint, Bologna,
1976), I, 402–3; Jean Fabre, *Stanislas-Auguste Poniatowski et l'Europe des
Lumières: étude de cosmopolitisme* (2nd ed., Paris, 1984), pp. 499, 673. In
addition to this letter, he left an elaborately engraved calling card (APS).
5. This may be an abbreviation for "franc maçon." Although Condorcet
was rumored to be a member of the Neuf Sœurs, his name does not appear
on the *Tableau des Frères . . . des Neuf Sœurs* for 1783 (Yale University Library). See Daniel Ligou, ed., *Dictionnaire de la franc-maçonnerie* (rev. ed.,
Paris, 1991), pp. 291–2.
6. The comte de Milly, now *vénérable* of the Neuf Sœurs, was a devoted
follower of the Pythagorean regime, a strict vegetarian diet popularized
earlier in the century by Antonio Cocchi, who claimed that it could treat a
variety of physical and mental diseases. Milly was also known for seeking
out new remedies and testing them on himself, which is said to have contributed to his untimely death the following year at the age of 56: Marquis
de Condorcet, "Eloge de M. le comte de Milly," in *Œuvres*, ed. A. Condorcet O'Connor and M. F. Arago (12 vols., Paris, 1847–49), III, 180–7.

sages et Humaines. Le G. A.[7] rendra dans les Benedictions qu'il repandra sur Vous et Votre Digne famille le secours genereux de Lumieres que Vous accorderez à un F∴[8] qui cherche a apprendre, et qui a le merite de la bonne Volonté.— Si Vous daignez me reppondre, Vous aurez la bonté d'adresser Votre Lettre à l'Hotel de Tours, ruë du Paôn, Fauxbourg St Germain.

J'ay l'honneur d'etre avec une Consideration tres distinguée, Monsieur, Votre trés humble, & très Obeissant Serviteur

CTE DE HÜLSEN
Palatin de Mscislavie

From Jean Rousseau[9]

ALS and copy:[1] American Philosophical Society

Monsieur   Londres le 13. Juin 1783.

Depuis la Suisse oû je demeurois, j'eus l'honneur d'envoier à Vôtre Excellence, la copie d'un manuscrit sur l'indépendance du Nord de l'Amerique: au commencement de cette mémorable levée de boucliers, j'en avois déja envoié des Copies à la Cour de France & notamment à feu Mr: Le Comte de Maurepas, Mr: Le Comte de Vergennes Mr: Necker &c.

On avoit eu Soin dans ce tems la, de leurer le public, en voulant lui persuader que cette indépendance, Seroit d'un mauvais exemple pour les autres Colonies, & Surtout pour celles de la Monarchie Espagnole. Ce manuscrit dont je ne crains pas à présent de me nommer l'Autheur, non seulement prouvoit le contraire, mais demontroit aussi, que c'etoit le vrai intérêt de toutes les Puissances qui avoient des possessions en Amerique, de favoriser l'indépendance des treize Provinces unies.

7. Grand Architecte.
8. Frère.
9. This is Rousseau's first communication since the spring of 1780, when he sent the manuscript he here inquires about: XXXII, 152–3.
1. In an unknown French hand, which marked it as a copy. L'Air de Lamotte wrote a notation misidentifying the writer as "Cornhill."

Il a plut enfin à la Divine Providence de benir vos genereux efforts; l'Empire Ameriquain est au comble de sa gloire: Dieu veuille le regarder toujours d'un œuil favorable & le faire prosperer à jamais.

Forcé de quitter Genève ma Patrie, je suis revenu à Londres, où cy devant, j'avois demeuré pendant nombre d'années. S'il plaisoit au Congrès, de ranimer par un de Ses rayons, un homme marié de Soixante ans, il feroit Sans cesse des vœux au Ciel pour la Majesté du nouvel Empire, & pour le bonheur de Vôtre Excellence en particulier.

Je suis avec respect Monsieur, De Vôtre Excellence Le très humble & très obeissant Serviteur   JEAN ROUSSEAU

mon adresse est No. 87 Cornhill.

Mon Neveu Rousseau² chez Mess: Isaac LeMaitre & Compe. Banquiers à Paris rue Montmorency aura l'honneur de vous remettre, la présente.

From ——— Saint-Martin

ALS: American Philosophical Society

Monsieur   par tonnein, a verteuil, En agenois
                                      le 13e. juin 1783.

Il y a Bien des jours que J'ai Eu L'honneur de vous Ecrire vous priant davoir la bonté de minstruire de quelle fasson Les officiers françois qui ont Esté Employé au servisse des Etats unis de lamerique seront treté, il faut sans doute que ma lettre ne vous soit pas parvenue;³ agrées que je vous suplie De macorder Cette faveur, veu que si les Etat ne veulle pas me Continuer

---

2. Jean-François Rousseau, son of his brother Théodore: R. A. Leigh, ed., *Correspondance complète de Jean Jacques Rousseau* (52 vols., Geneva, Banbury, and Oxford, 1965–98), XVIII, 82, 83n; XLV, 313–16; XLVII, 202n.

3. The letter, dated Feb. 27, did arrive; see XXXIX, 224–5, where Saint-Martin's service under Washington is described. BF evidently did not answer the present letter either; Saint-Martin repeated his query on Sept. 25, 1783 (APS).

au moins dans les memes Grades, je tacherois de me pourvoir ailleur, je suis venu avec Eun Congé d'un an pour Retablir ma santé est aller aux Eaux de Barege, Lorsque je suis parti il netoit nullement question de paix, insi je panse qu'il se fera un grand changement. Je ne voudrois pas Repartir sans savoir a quoi ment tenir, Esperant Cette Grace de vous, je L'honneur dettre avec Respects Monsieur Votre tres humble est tres obeissant serviteur

ST MARTIN

Notation: St. Martin 13 Juin 1783.

From Erik Magnus Staël von Holstein[4]

LS,[5] copy, and transcript: National Archives

Monsieur,   Paris le 13 Juin 1783
   Je viens de reçevoir la ratification de Sa Majesté du Traité de Commerce conclu avec les Etats Unis, la quelle j'aurai l'honneur de vous remettre aussitot qu'elle pourra être echangée contre

4. Baron Staël von Holstein (1749–1802) had been an attaché to the Swedish delegation in France since 1778. The king chose him to succeed the comte de Creutz as minister plenipotentiary when he recalled Creutz in early February, 1783, to become head of the office of foreign affairs. Creutz left Paris in May. Staël von Holstein was initially elevated to chargé d'affaires and was received as minister plenipotentiary at the end of July; see his letter to BF, July 30. A friend of the Necker family and favored by Marie-Antoinette, he would eventually marry the Neckers' daughter Anne-Louise-Germaine (XXXIV, 480n). The match was already being discussed in the French and Swedish courts at the time of this appointment. The wedding took place at the beginning of 1786; thereafter the fame of Mme de Staël (as she became known) would outshine that of her husband. Gunnar von Proschwitz, ed., *Gustave III par ses lettres* (Stockholm and Paris, 1986), pp. 229–30, 284n; *Repertorium der diplomatischen Vertreter*, III, 408; *Svenska män och kvinnor: Biografisk uppslagsbok* (8 vols., Stockholm, 1942–55).

5. BF sent the LS to Livingston with his letter of July 22[–26]. The English translation made for Congress by John Pintard is on the same sheet; a translation is also published in Wharton, *Diplomatic Correspondence*, VI, 483.

celle du Congré.[6] Permettez Monsieur que je vous repette à cette ocassion la demande que Monsieur l'Ambassadeur[7] vous a faite au sujet de Monsieur franklin votre petit fils. Il a eu l'honneur de vous dire que le Roi veroit avec plaisir resider auprès de lui en qualité de Ministre du Congrés une personne qui porte votre nom et y joint des qualités aussi estimables que le jeune monsieur franklin. Avant de partir S. E. m'a chargé de vous repeter la Même assurance et vous me permettrez d'y ajouter les voeux que je fais en mon particulier pour la reuissite de cette affaire.

J'ai l'honneur d'être avec l'estime et l'attachement les plus parfaits et inviolables Monsieur votre très humble et très obeissant serviteur   LE BARON DE STAEL

Endorsed:[8] Letter from the Ambass. of Sweden to BF— June 13. 83. Ratification arriv'd—

Notation by William Temple Franklin: The Original Letter from the Swedish Ambassador to the American Minister at the Court of Versailles dated 13 June 83—

6. Gustavus III ratified the Swedish-American Treaty of Amity and Commerce (XXXIX, 250–85) on May 23. BF knew this by June 11 (see his letter of that date to Pierres); he probably learned the news at Versailles the day before, undoubtedly from Staël von Holstein himself. In what sense, therefore, had the Swedish minister-designate "just" received the ratification on June 13? We suspect that this letter may have been written at BF's request, after the two men conversed on June 10, and that its chief purpose was to document the topic that follows: the king's wish that WTF be made minister to Sweden. When BF wrote to Livingston on July 22 that he was enclosing the present letter, it was in the context of discussing WTF's candidacy. Sweden's ratification of the treaty, by contrast, was never mentioned. See also the curious reply to Staël von Holstein that WTF prepared on June 16, below.

Congress' ratification of the treaty did not arrive until *c.* Nov. 1, and it would be another four months, approximately, before the exchange took place. BF sent the Swedish ratification to Congress on March 9, 1784: Wharton, *Diplomatic Correspondence*, VI, 721, 786.

7. Creutz, as was specified in BF's purported reply to Staël von Holstein, June 16, and in his letter to Livingston, July 22[–26].

8. Both this statement and the notation by WTF must have been added when BF sent the MS to Livingston.

From Edward Bancroft[9] ALS: American Philosophical Society

Dr. Sir   [before June 14, 1783][1]
  I have done myself the honor to call to inform you of my intention of setting out on the Journey which has been explained
to you, on Sunday Evening— I had intended to have Left this
sooner, but as I could not possibly be ready to *day*, it would be to
no purpose— If you should think of any thing in which I can
be useful to you, I shall be happy to be employed—
  I am with the utmost respect & Affection Your Excellency's
most Humble & Devoted Servant[2]   EDWD BANCROFT

9. This undated letter appears to have been written in the days before
Bancroft left for London, from whence he intended to sail to America. He
had been planning this voyage since at least May 1, when Matthew Ridley
(who was about to leave Paris) provided him with a letter of recommendation to Robert Morris: *Morris Papers*, VII, 786–7. Lafayette and Jay wrote
letters of recommendation on June 10 and 11, and BF entrusted him with
a June 12 letter to Livingston (above), adding a few lines of introduction
in the postscript: *Morris Papers*, VIII, 706–7; Idzerda, *Lafayette Papers*, V,
132–3; Morris, *Jay: Peace*, p. 526.
  Bancroft's missions were various: he had financial interests as a member
of the Vandalia Company and was eager to collect the North American
barks whose dye properties he had discovered in the early 1770s and for
which, just before the war broke out, he had been awarded patent rights
to import and market. He also agreed to serve as agent for Silas Deane
and, at Ferdinand Grand's request, for the chevalier de Montmorency-
Luxembourg, the outfitter of the frigate *South Carolina* (XXXV, 653n):
ODNB; Julian P. Boyd, "Silas Deane: Death by a Kindly Teacher of Treason?," *W&MQ*, 3rd ser., XVI (1959), 534–7; Edward Bancroft, *Facts and
Observations, Briefly Stated, in Support of an Intended Application to Parliament* ([London], 1798), pp. 2–4; *Morris Papers*, VII, 787n; VIII, 21, 317–18;
James A. Lewis, *Neptune's Militia: the Frigate* South Carolina *during the
American Revolution* (Kent, Ohio, and London, 1999), p. 113.
  1. The day Bancroft left Paris with his family: Thomas J. Schaeper,
Edward Bancroft: Scientist, Author, Spy (New Haven and London, 2011),
p. 194.
  2. Also among BF's papers at the APS is a letter from Bancroft to WTF
dated only "Saturday noon," which asks two favors. First, he encloses "another Power of attorney to be Legalised & returned by the Bearer." If WTF
and BF are not at home, they should please forward it to London care of
William Hodgson, along with any other mail. Second, Bancroft encloses a
letter he had just received from John Paul Jones, addressed to a third party;

Addressed: A Son Excellence / Son Excellence M. Franklin / Ministre Plenipotentiaire / des Etats Unis &c

Notation: Bancroft

From the Duc de Deux-Ponts[3]

L or AL: American Philosophical Society

Paris Le 14. juin 1783.

Memoire

M. Le Prince des Deuxponts S'est déja adressé a monsieur Franklin pour Savoir Si LElectorat Palatin et Le Duché de Baviére pourroient entrer en Liaisons de Commerce avec Les treize Etats unis de Lamérique. Mais n'en ayant obtenu qu'une Réponse trop vague pour etre transmise a Ses Commettans, il Le prie tres instamment de vouloir bien Lui spécifier par écrit qu'elles Seroient Les productions et Les objets d'industrie qui pourroient Le plus aisément donner de la Consistance a ce projet et Le Faire prosperer. Il insiste Sur cette Réponse parce qu'on La Lui demande, et il se Flatte que monsieur Franklin verra d'un Oeil favorable L'Empressement que témoignent plusieurs Etats de L'allemagne davoir des raports avec une nouvelle Puissance qui est en tres grande partie Son ouvrage.

Notation: Le Prince de Deuxponts.

---

as that person was known to WTF, Bancroft asks him to deliver it. APS. This letter was probably written before Bancroft left Paris on June 14, a Saturday.

3. The nephew of the duchesse de Deux-Ponts' late husband and heir to his title (XXXIX, 489n). He was also the nephew and heir of Karl Theodor, elector of both the Palatinate and Bavaria, who had evidently asked him to approach BF about a potential commercial arrangement. The duchesse introduced him to BF in late April, referring to him as the "prince" de Deux-Ponts, as he himself does in the present letter: XXXIX, 489, 509, 517.

To [the Duc de Deux-Ponts]

AL (draft):[4] American Philosophical Society

[on or after June 14, 1783][5]

Reponse

Without Information what are the Productions & Manufactures of the Palatinate & of Bavaria and their Prices, of which Mr Franklin is totally ignorant, it is impossible for him to say what of them will be proper for a Commerce with the United States of America. He can only answer in general, that America purchases from Europe all kinds of Woollens & Linnens coarse & fine, proper for Clothing of Men & Women; with a variety of Iron & Steele Manufactures. And she pays in Tobacco, Rice, Indigo, Bills of Exchange or Money. If the Electorates abovementioned can furnish any of these Manufactures cheaper than France, Holland, or England, they may thereby obtain a Share of the American Commerce. But it will be prudent for the Merchants to send a discreet intelligent Man with a small Cargo of Samples of all their Kinds of Goods, in order to obtain a thorough Knowledge of the Nature of the Commerce in that Country, and of the Kinds of Goods & Proportions of their Quantities, that are most in demand there, before they hazard the making of large Adventures.— There is no doubt but that the Commerce of the German States will be favourably receiv'd in America, where a great many People of that Nation are establish'd. Mr F. will give it all the Encouragement that can be expected of him: but he cannot take upon him to point out and name as he has been desired the most Solid Houses of Commerce there, having been long absent from that Country, and the War having probably made a Change in the Circumstances of many.

4. Written in pencil on the verso of the preceding document.

5. Whenever BF drafted this answer, he had not sent it by June 25. On that date, the duchesse de Deux-Ponts' brother Fontenet (XXXII, 151n) wrote WTF to remind him of his promise to send the "prince" a reply about commerce with the German states. He also requested an answer for the consul at Civitavecchia, who sought a position for his son. APS. This was Vidaú père, whose most recent letter in a long campaign was dated May 12; see XXXIX, 79–80.

To [Gaspard-Bonaventure-Timothée Ferry][6]

AL (draft) and copy:[7] Library of Congress

Sir,   Passy June 14th, 1783

I received some time since the Letter you honour'd me with, containing your Hypothesis for explaining the Shock given by the electric Bottle, on which you seem to desire my Opinion. It is many Years since I was engag'd in those pleasing Studies, and my Mind is at present too much occupied with other and more important Affairs to permit my returning to them.— I cannot therefore examine your ingenious Hypothesis with the Attention it appears to merit.— You will find in a Letter of mine to Dr. Lining dated March 18. 1755,[8] that I abandoned my Hypothesis of the greater Density of Glass in the Middle than near its Surfaces, as contributing to produce the Effect; because I found the Effect to be the same after I had ground that part away. And I think you might likewise try yours by an easy Experiment. Take a Plate of Lead 12 Inches square, cover one of its sides with a Coat of Bees Wax about one Line thick; upon that apply closely a thin Plate of Lead 8 Inches square, so as to leave a Margin of two Inches all round.— Electrify this Composition of Lead & Wax, and try if you can receive a Shock from it; if not, you may draw from thence a farther Argument to support your Hypothesis, because the Wax tho' a Non Conductor is not elastic, any more than pure Lead. I see you are endow'd with a Genius for the Study of Nature and I would recommend it to you to employ your time rather in making Experiments than in making Hypotheses & forming imaginary Systems, which

6. In answer to Ferry's 18-page treatise of March 28: XXXIX, 402–4. On June 8 the man who had delivered it, M. Parraud, wrote from Paris to remind BF of his promise to answer, advising him to address his response to the abbé Baudet, *chez* the comte de Vergennes; they would take care of forwarding it to Marseille. APS.

7. The copy is in the hand of Josiah Flagg and was therefore made in 1786: XXXVII, 291n.

8. Published in *Exper. and Obser.* (1769). The section to which BF refers is the fourth paragraph; for that text see V, 522–3, where we refer to the present letter as addressed to an unknown recipient.

we are all too apt to please ourselves with till some Experiment comes, & unluckily destroys them.— Wishing you Success in your Enquiries, I have the Honour to be, Sir,[9]

David Hartley to the American Peace Commissioners

Copies:[1] Library of Congress, William L. Clements Library, Massachusetts Historical Society; two incomplete copies and incomplete transcript: National Archives

The American peace commissioners grew increasingly suspicious as they waited for Fox to respond to the article that Hartley had presented to them without prior approval on May 21.[2] Hartley drafted another memorial for them on June 1, but this time he sent it to Fox for review before discussing it with the commissioners.[3] As the days wore on, however, Hartley complained to Fox that he and the commissioners were expecting an answer hourly and were growing impatient. The Americans were also expressing "some degree of discontent, as if their business was neglected in England, or that there were rubs & difficulties." On June 5 Hartley let Fox know that he had finally read to the commissioners his June 1 memorial along with sections of his June 2 cover letter to Fox.[4] The secretary of state finally answered on June 10. Fox approved of the memorial as "cogent and convincing"—a phrase Hartley repeats in the present letter, which encloses a copy of it.

9. Ferry answered on Oct. 12. Calling BF one of the most sublime geniuses the universe had ever produced and thanking him effusively, he enclosed a verse of his own composition, a prize-winning poem in praise of BF that was published in the Sept. 6 issue of the *Jour. de Provence*. Finally, he mentions that he performed the experiment BF suggested and it seems to confirm his hypothesis; not wanting to impose on BF's time, he will not report any details. APS.

1. All these copies (the first and third from the commissioners' legation letterbooks, the second by Hartley's secretary George Hammond) contain obvious errors and display occasional variations in wording. We publish the best of them, written by BFB, and silently correct a few slips of the pen.

2. Hartley sent it to Fox on May 22. See Hartley's memorial and proposed article, [May 19], and the annotation of WTF to Hartley, May 21.

3. See Hartley's June 1 memorial, above.

4. Giunta, *Emerging Nation*, 1, 860–1.

Fox informed Hartley that the king was pleased by his reports of the commissioners' goodwill. The king now wanted Hartley to tell them about the concessions he had made, including his order for the immediate evacuation of British troops from the United States. (In a private letter of June 10, Fox explained that he had delayed writing until that order was given.) The king approved the idea of a temporary convention, as this would delay a decision on whether to loosen the trade restrictions of the Navigation Acts. Fox warned, however, that Britain would not permit the importation of West Indian products on American ships into Britain, and he drafted an explanation that Hartley could offer the Americans. (Hartley quotes it here.) As for the United States' prohibiting the importation of slaves, Britain would abide by such a policy as long as it applied equally to all countries. Finally, Fox stressed the importance of obtaining a temporary convention as soon as possible, hoping that its duration might extend beyond May or June, 1784, as the commissioners had suggested.[5]

Hartley drafted the beginning of the present letter before he received Fox's dispatch. He finished it once Fox's letter arrived. The portion beginning "I am ordered to inform you" follows Fox's letter closely, quoting large sections and paraphrasing the rest. Hartley explained to Fox that he did this deliberately and with the commissioners' knowledge.[6]

Gentlemen   Paris June 14th. 1783.

Permitt me to address the inclosed Memorial to your Excellencies, & to explain to you my Reasons for so doing. It is because many consequences now at a great Distance and unforeseen by us, may arise between our two Countries, perhaps from very minute and incidental Transactions which in their Beginnings may be imperceptible and unsuspected as to their future Effects. Our respective Territories are in vicinity, & therefore we must be inseparable. Great Britain with the British Power in America is the only Nation with whom by absolute Necessity you must have the most intimate Concerns, ether of Friendship or Hostility. All other Nations are 3000 Miles distant from you. You may have Political Connexions with any of these distant

---

5. Giunta, *Emerging Nation*, II, 127, 146–9, 150.
6. Hartley to Fox, June 18, 1783, Clements Library.

Nations but with regard to Great Britain it must be so, Political Intercourse and Interests will obtrude themselves between our two Countries because they are the two Great Powers dividing the Continent of North America. These Matters are not to come into Discussion between us now. They are of too much Importance either to be involved or even glanced at in any present Transaction.

Let every eventual principle be kept untoucht, until the two Nations shall have recover'd from the animosities of the War. Let them have a pacific Interval to consider deliberately of their mutual and combined Interests & of their Engagements with other Nations. Let us not at the outset of a temporary Convention, adopt the severe Principle of reducing every transaction between the two Countries to the footing of exact Reciprocity alone.[7] Such a Principle would cast a Gloom upon conciliatory Prospects. America is not restrained from any conciliation with Great Britain by any Treaty with any other Power. The Principles of Conciliation would be most desireable between Great Britain and America and forbearance is the Road to Conciliation. After a War of Animosities, time should be allowed for recollection. There are all reasonable Appearances of conciliatory Dispositions on all sides, which may be perfected in time. Let us not therefore at such a moment as this and without the most urgent Necessity establish a morose Principle between us. If it were a decided Point against Amity and Conciliation it would be time enought to talk of Partition & strict Reciprocity. To presume in favour of Conciliation may help it forward, to presume against it may destroy that Conciliation which might otherwise have taken Place.

But in the present Case there is more than reason to presume Conciliation. I think myself happy that I have it in my Power to assure you from Authority that it is the fundamental Prin-

7. Hartley was taking his cue from Fox but could have had little optimism about such an appeal. On May 20 he had reported to Fox that "precise reciprocity is the line imposed upon [the peace commissioners] by their constituents" and that the American states, hitherto "restrained & crampt" by the Navigation Acts, "have now no other object of negotiation, but absolute reciprocity": Giunta, *Emerging Nation*, II, 122.

ciple of the British Councils to establish Amity and confidence between G Britain and the American States as a Succedaneum for the Relation in which they formerly stood one to the other. The Proof of this consists not in Words but in substantial Facts. His Britannick Majesty has been graciously pleas'd to send orders to his Commanders in North America for the speedy and complete evacuation of all the Territories of the United States. His Majesty has given Orders in Council, on the 14th of the last Month, for the Admission of American Ships and Cargoes into G. Britain; & on the 6th Inst. he has given farther Orders permitting the Importation from America of several Articles which have been usually considered as Manufactures. He has likewise provided for the Convenience of American Merchants who may wish to land Tobacco in Great Britain for Re-exportation.[8] Upon the same Principle Mr. Fox the Secy. of State corresponding with America, has moved for and received the leave of the House of Commons, (nem. con)[9] to bring in a Bill that any American Merchants importing Rice into Great Britain, may upon Re-exportation drawback the whole duty paid on its first Importation. All these Circumstances put together, undoubtedly form the most indisputable Evidence of the Disposition which prevails in the British Councils to give every facility to the Establishment of that Intercourse which must be so beneficial to both Nations.

I am ordered to inform you that his Majesty entirely approves of the Plan of making a temporary Convention, for the Purpose of restoring immediate Intercourse & Commerce; & more particularly for the purpose of putting off for a time, the decision of that important question, how far the British Acts of Navigation ought to be sacrificed to Commercial Considerations, drawn from the peculiar Circumstances of the present Crisis; a question which will require much deliberation and very much Enquiry before it can be determined. I am sure, Gentlemen, you will see and admitt the reasonableness of our proceeding

8. For these two Orders in Council see Hartley's memorial and proposed article, [May 19], and Laurens' letter to the other commissioners, June 10.

9. *Nemine contradicente*, "no one objecting."

in such a Case with Deliberation and Discretion, more especially when these Acts of Prudence, do not proceed from any motives of Coolness or reserve towards you. In the mean time the temporary convention may proceed, upon principles of real and accommodating Reciprocity. For instance we agree to put you upon a more favourable footing than any other Nation. We do not ask a rigid Reciprocity for this because We know by your present subsisting Treaties it is not in your Power to give it to us. We desire only to be put upon the footing of other Nations with you and yet we consent that you shall be upon a better footing with us than any other Nation.

Thus far we must be allowed to be giving something more than reciprocity and this we do as I said before because we are unwilling to ask what you are unable to give. Surely it is not unreasonable, nor more than from Principles of Reciprocity, we have a Right to expect that you should imitate our Conduct in this particular and that you should abstain from asking things under the Title of exact and literal Reciprocity, which upon the Consideration of our Case you must know that we cannot give. Virtual and substantial Reciprocity we are willing to give; literal Reciprocity is impossible as much from your Engagements as from our System of Navigation.

If we can agree upon an Article of Intercourse & Commerce, in the nature of a temporary Convention, on the Basis of the Memorial which I had the honour of giving lately to you bearing date 19th of May 1783, no time need be lost, in finishing this business; but with this Explanation that altho' it is proposed that the Commerce between the United States and the British West Indies should be free with regard to their respective Productions, yet that we are not bound to admit the Importation of West Indian Commodities into Great Britain in American Vessels.[1] Believe me, Gentlemen, that this Restriction does not

1. This restriction was added to a revised copy of the [May 19] memorial that Hartley gave the commissioners; see the annotation of the document immediately below. He was aware of its difficulties. When sending his initial proposal to Fox on May 22, Hartley warned that the commissioners had "declared in the most absolute terms" that the temporary convention must acknowledge an American right to share in the trade between Britain

proceed from any invideous Disposition towards the American States. It is imposed by indispensable Prudence and Necessity upon the British Ministers, who in the present State of things, could not be justified to their own Country to go hastily to a larger extent of Concession. This point is not to be looked upon merely as Commercial, but as affecting fundamentally the great political System of British Navigation, And you are to consider, that the principle upon which the whole of our proposed temporary Convention is to stand, is, that the *Commerce* between the two Countries is to be revived nearly upon the old footing; but that each Nation is to keep in its own Hands, the Power of making such regulations respecting *Navigation*, as shall seem fit. I assure you that this point has been discussed by the Ministers of the British Cabinet, with infinite Candour, and with every possible disposition of Amity & favour towards your Country; but the more they have enquired upon this subject the more they are overborne by conviction that the prejudices upon this Matter (if that be the name these opinions deserve) are so strong, that such a measure as a relaxation of the Act of Navigation in this instance, never can be taken, but upon such a full and solemn Parliamentary Enquiry, as it is impossible to go into at this time of the year, & in this Stage of the Sessions. I cannot therefore Gentlemen help flattering myself that you are so well acquainted with the Difficulties which must embarass an English Administration, in a business of this sort will rather endeavour to remove them, than to encrease them; and I am sure that such a plan on your part would ultimately be most conducive to your own Objects. When an amicable Intercourse is once opened and when conciliatory Confidence comes to take place of those Jealousies which have lately subsisted, you may easily conceive in how different a manner the whole of this matter will be considered. I am confident that this will be the Case; but if it is not the Provisions being only temporary, it will be in the Power of the United States to take up any hostile mode of proceeding by restraints and prohibitions &ca. whenever they may think fit.

---

and the West Indies. "I am assured," he wrote, "that no persuasion in the world would prevail without this point explicitly secured to them": Giunta, *Emerging Nation*, II, 125.

I have made use above of the word *Prejudices*, in speaking of the principles of the British Act of Navigation. I hope you will accept that term from me as proceeding so far in compliance towards the consideration of the points now between us, as to keep the question open and free for discussion. If G. Britain should in any Case throw down the Barriers of Act of Navigation towards America, she should be very secure against the possible Case of future Enmity, or Alliance against her. Such Considerations as these lead to Objects far beyond our present Scope or Powers. But I must still add one word more upon this Article of *Prejudices*. Such *prejudices* (if they are so) are not confined to Great Britain. By your Commercial Treaty with France Article 4th[2] you are only intitled to an European Trade with that Kingdom and not even by that Treaty, to any direct Commerce between their west Indian Islands and the Ports of the American States much less to the Immediate Communication between the French Islands and the Dominions of the Crown of France in Europe.

Every public proceeding in England since the Commencement of our present negotiation for opening Intercourse and Commerce between our two Countries will I am sure support me in saying that we have very liberally taken the lead, that we have not waited for any assurance of reciprocity but have given Orders for almost an universal admission of American Articles before we even know that any Vessel of Great Britain will find admission into American Ports. What do we ask in return? No more than this; That while we gratuitously and without stipulation, give advantages to the American States which we deny to all other nations they would so far justify our liberal way of proceeding as to receive us in the same Manner as other Nations which are foreign and to permitt us to carry to North America what it is evidently for their Interest that we should carry thither.

I need hardly add that it is of infinite Importance, that some temporary Convention should be finished without loss of time. I hope and trust that we shall not find much more difficulty in this

2. An article which BF had tried unsuccessfully to alter: xxv, 599n.

Business. You must see the Advantage of an immediate renewal of Intercourse and from the Candour of your Dispositions, I am sure you must likewise be convinced, that to give us some facility in the outset is the sure road to such an equitable Arrangement for the future as you must have at Heart. The reasons which I have given in the Memorial dated the 1st. June inst. appear to me to be cogent and convincing upon the natural Alliance between our two Countries and when the Intercourse has once begun every thing will go in its natural road. It is therefore of infinite Consequence to begin that Intercourse. Great Britain by all public proceedings of repeals Proclamations &ca &ca. has made the first Advances with warmth and Confidence and therefore I conclude with the fullest assurance, that you will meet those Advances with Cordial reciprocity—

I have the Honour to be Gentlemen, with the greatest respect & Consideration Your most obedient humble Servant

D HARTLEY.

To the Commissioners of the United States of America for negotiating Peace.

David Hartley to the American Peace Commissioners: Revised Article[3]

Copies: Library of Congress (two), William L. Clements Library, Massachusetts Historical Society, National Archives; press copy of copy: National Archives

June [14–18,] 1783
It is agreed, that the Citizens of the United States of America shall be permitted to import into and to export from any Port or

---

3. On June 14, when delivering the letter immediately above, Hartley also gave the commissioners a revision (now missing) of his [May 19] proposed article, which added one sentence prohibiting American ships from carrying West Indian produce into Great Britain. This change, based on Fox's June 10 instructions, was fully explained in his June 14 letter.

We know this from a subsequent exchange between the two men. On the night of June 17, Hartley received a private note from Fox instructing

Place of the Territories belonging to the Crown of Great Britain in American Ships, any Goods, Wares & Merchandize, which might have been so imported or exported by the Inhabitants of the British American Colonies, before the Commencement of the late War upon Payment of the same duties and Charges as the like sort of goods or Merchandize, are now or may be Subject & Liable to if imported or exported by British Subjects in British Ships into or from any Port or Place of the Territories belonging to the Crown of Great Britain— Provided however that the Citizens of the United States shall not have any Right or Claim under this Convention to carry on any direct Intercourse of Commerce between the British West Indian Islands, and the Ports of Great Britain.

It is agreed likewise that the Subjects of Great Britain, shall be permitted to import into and to export from any part of the Territories of the United States of America, in British Ships,

---

him to make sure that nothing in the convention would "bind us to let the produce of the W Indies go even to America in American bottoms." This restriction "need not be mentioned," Fox added; Hartley should simply describe general terms under which American ships would be admitted into Britain and vice versa: Giunta, *Emerging Nation*, II, 154–5.

Hartley replied the next day, also in a private letter. Surely, Fox could not mean that "when American Ships bring lumber to the West Indies, they should not carry West Indian produce home for their own use"? This would be inconsistent with all Fox's previous instructions, the provisional bills debated in the House of Commons, and "practicability." Hartley would therefore assume that by "America," Fox meant "British America." Having already given the commissioners a revised article that conformed to Fox's June 10 guidelines, he would simply "superadd" a phrase to that text, replacing "Great Britain" with the phrase "any Ports or Places within the territories belonging to the Crown of Great Britain." He then begged Fox to "send me specifically an article that I may sign," as his knowledge of legal language was limited. For example, the Americans had asked whether Ireland was considered a territory belonging to the crown: Hartley to Fox, June 18, 1783, Clements Library.

The change Hartley promised to make is in the present text, which is the version copied into the commissioners' legation letterbooks. There it is dated simply "June 1783," but we assume he made the alteration on June 18, the day after receiving Fox's instructions. When writing his official letter to Fox on June 20, Hartley referred to this document as the "proposed Agreement June 14th 1783": Giunta, *Emerging Nation*, II, 162.

any Goods Wares and Merchandize, which might have been so imported or exported by the Subjects of Great Britain, before the Commencement of the late War, upon Payment of the same Duties and Charges as the like sort of Goods Wares and Merchandize are now or may be liable to, if imported or exported in American Ships, by the Citizens of the United States of America.

Mr. Hartley's proposed agreement

From Girardot, Haller & Cie.

LS: American Philosophical Society

Monsieur   Paris le 14 Juin 1783
   Nous avons l'honneur de Vous presenter Monsieur Volmers, associé de la maison la plus solide & la plus riche de Breme sous la raison de Pundsack & Volmers.[4]
   Les Etats unis ne pourraient etre en de meilleures mains pour tout ce qui peut les Interesser dans cette Ville, & nous rendons ce temoignage plus encore comme un homage a la Verité qu'a l'amitié.
   Nous vous demandons la grâce monsieur d'entendre Monsr. Volmers & de le recevoir avec cette bonté qui caracterise touttes Vos actions.
   Nous Sommes avec respect Monsieur Vos tres humbles & trés obts   GIRARDOT HALLER & CO

Addressed: monsieur / monsieur Francklin / Passy.

Notation: Girardo Haller & Co. 14 Juin 1783.—

4. Johann Vollmers (1753–1818) joined the firm of Thomas Pundsack (1733–1813) in 1779 and made it into one of the most prominent houses in the Bremen-American trade: Karl H. Schwebel, *Bremer Kaufleute in den Freihäfen der Karibik: von den Anfängen des Bremer Überseehandels bis 1815* (Bremen, 1995), p. 195n.

From Samuel Vaughan ALS: American Philosophical Society

My dear Sir, London 14th. June 1783

Well knowing Your engagements, I have hitherto declined encroaching upon Your important time, but as I shortly embark with my family for Philadelphia,[5] I could not refrain returning You my very sincere and affectionate thanks, for your repeated friendly & affectionate attention to each of my sons when on the continent, and which (if possible) has added to that respect affection, and I may say reverence I have retained for You, ever since I have had the pleasure of Your acquaintance, and I rest with pleasing expectation of renewing and perpetuating an intercourse with You in America, which I shall esteem as the most valuable of the many advantages I expect to derive in that new World, being with perfect regard, My dear Sir, Your affectionate and obliged hble Servt. SAML VAUGHAN

Honble. Benjn. Franklin Esqr.

5. Vaughan began making preparations to emigrate as soon as the peace was declared. By March, 1783, his household effects were packed, his country home was for sale, and he anticipated a departure in April or May: XXXIX, 293. His son John had gone to Philadelphia to look for property the previous year, and after a brief return to England was sailing back to Philadelphia in advance of the family: BF to John Vaughan, June 3; John Vaughan to BF, June 10. The youngest son, Samuel, Jr. (21 years old), was on his way to Germany: BF to Ingenhousz, June 1. Benjamin and William, the two eldest, stayed in London. The remaining children were Ann (1757–1847), Charles (1759–1839), Sarah (1761–1818), Barbara (b. 1764), and Rebecca (1766–1851): John H. Sheppard, "Reminiscences and Genealogy of the Vaughan Family," *New England Hist. & Geneal. Register*, XIX (1865), 355. The family sailed on July 9: William Vaughan to WTF, Aug. 8, 1783 (APS). For this final chapter in Vaughan's life see Sarah P. Stetson, "The Philadelphia Sojourn of Samuel Vaughan," *PMHB*, LXXIII (1949), 459–74.

From Pierre Dessin[6]

LS: American Philosophical Society

Monsieur   Calais le 15. Juin 1783.

M. Benjin. Vaughan par sa lettre de Londres du 6 de ce mois m'annonçoit qu'il venoit de me faire adresser 4 Boëtes à l'adresse de votre Excellence.[7] Ces boëtes sont effectivement arrivées ce matin par le Paquebot du Capne. Bagster, mais l'une d'elles, la plus forte, paroissant être beaucoup endommagée, on l'a retira du Vaisseau, et elle fut portée à la Douane avec tout le soin possible.[8]

Ne pouvant me resoudre, Monsieur, a faire suivre cette boëte, sans préalablement avoir pris connoissance de l'état des choses qu'elle renfermoit, je la fis ouvrir et vis avec autant de peine que de surprise, que le tout étoit entierement brisé ou endommagé.

---

6. This is the first extant letter from the keeper of the Hôtel d'Angleterre at Calais, whom BF had known since at least 1771: XVIII, 107.

7. For background on this shipment, which included items ordered by BF and WTF, see XXXIX, 212, 437. The boxes had left the port of London around June 4 or 5 aboard the *Diligence*, Capt. Hall, addressed to Mr. Hervey (Harvy) of the Ship Inn, Dover, who was to forward them to Dessin at Calais. Once in Paris they were to be consigned to Ridley's clerk Darcel, who was to distribute the contents. The first and largest box contained WTF's order of glassware from William Parker & Sons. Another large box marked as glass contained Nairne's "patent electrical machine" for BF and a MS description of it, the imprint of Blagden and Nairne's account of the Heckingham lightning strike (BF received another copy from Blagden; see his letter of July 10), and two packets for other friends. The third box contained miscellaneous items for a host of people in and around Paris. For BF there were shoes, four of Woodmason's damping presses with two phials for holding the water, "three or four small packages of books" including BF's Bible, Richard Price's *Observations on Reversionary Payments* . . . and *The State of the Public Debts and Finances* . . . (Jay and JA received copies as well), and a quantity of red Peruvian bark, a superior form of cinchona bark recently introduced into England: William Saunders, *Observations on the Superior Efficacy of the Red Peruvian Bark, in the Cure of Agues and other Fevers* . . . (3rd ed., enl., London, 1783), pp. 18–20. The fourth and smallest box contained Wedgwood figurines for the duc de Chaulnes. Benjamin Vaughan to WTF, June 6; to Nicolas Darcel, June 10; to ——— Harvy, June 20, 1783, all at the APS.

8. The damaged box was the one containing Nairne's electrical machine; see Benjamin Vaughan to BF, June 24.

Le peu d'objets qui reste ne pouvant aller plus loin sans encourir le risque d'être aussi cassé, j'ai pris le parti de laisser cette boëte en lieu de sureté à la Douane, pour y rester jusqu'a ce qu'il vous plaise me donner ordre de faire arranger les choses pour vous l'envoyer, ou pour la retourner en angleterre.

Quant aux trois autres boëtes, Monsieur, elles sont en bon état, et je viens de vous les expedier sous plomb, avec acquit à Caution, par le Carosse du Casuel qui partira demain Lundi, pour arriver le samedi suivant à Paris. J'espere qu'elles vous parviendront en bonne condition, les ayant fortement recommandées aux soins du conducteur de la voiture.[9]

Enchanté de trouver cette occasion pour vous faire l'offre entiere de mes services, j'ai l'honneur de me protester avec respect Monsieur Votre tres humble & tres obeissant Serviteur

PIERRE DESSIN

Notation: Dessin 15 Juin 1783.

To Staël von Holstein[1]   L: American Philosophical Society

Monsieur,   Passy, le 16 Juin 1783.

J'ai reçu la Lettre que votre Excellence m'a fait l'honneur de m'ecrire le 13 de ce Mois, pour me faire Part que vous avez reçu

---

9. The boxes reached Paris on June 25: Darcel to WTF, June 26 (APS).

1. We have found no evidence that this response to Staël von Holstein's letter of June 13 was sent, and we suspect that WTF may have drafted it. It is a fair copy ready for BF's signature, entirely in WTF's hand, and its main subject (notwithstanding the first sentence) is the desirability of WTF's appointment as minister to Sweden. The language does not seem subtle enough to be BF's: in large measure it mimics the prose of the Swedish minister while needlessly clarifying his references. It seems unlikely that BF would choose to echo so literally the king's desire to have at court someone "who bears my name." Moreover, the strong implication that Congress' compliance is certain seems diplomatically inept for so public a letter, especially considering BF's relationship with his colleagues.

When next writing to Livingston (July 22[–26]), BF enclosed Staël von Holstein's June 13 letter as evidence of Sweden's request, setting it in context and emphasizing that he himself was not soliciting a position for his

de votre Cour la Ratification du Traité conclu entre nos deux Nations: J'attens de Jour en Jour la Ratification du Congrès, & dès que je l'aurai reçue je m'empresserai de vous en faire Part, afin que nous puissions faire les Echanges reciproques.

Le Desir que temoigne sa Majesté Suedoise, (et dont Mr. le Cte. de Creutz votre Predecesseur, m'avez instruit avant son depart) d'avoir pour resider auprès d'Elle, de la Part des Etats-Unis, quelqu'un qui porte mon Nom, m'honore et me flatte infiniement; ainsi que les Termes obligeants dont vous vous êtes servis pour me rapeller cet desir.— Je m'empresserai de le faire connoitre au Congrès, et je ne doute pas que ce Corps ne se prete a faire tous ce qui peut etre agreable a un Souverain pour qui ils ont tant d'estime, & qui a eté le premier de l'Europe a nous offrir son Amitié.

J'ai l'honneur d'etre, avec une respectueuse Considération et un sincere Attachement, De votre Excellence, Le très humble et très obeissant Serviteur.

Son Exe. le Baron de Stael

Elias Boudinot to the American Peace Commissioners

Copies: Library of Congress (two), Massachusetts Historical Society, National Archives

This letter from Elias Boudinot, president of Congress, not only announces the resignation of Minister for Foreign Affairs Robert R. Livingston, it also encloses a resolution of great importance to the peace commissioners. On February 5 John Adams had written to Congress that there no longer was a reason to delay making a commercial treaty with Great Britain or sending a minister there to negotiate it.[2] That letter prompted the appointment of a congressional committee, which on May 1 reported that although the peace commissioners had an implied power to include commercial provisions in the final peace treaty, they had no direct authority to make a separate commercial treaty with Britain. Congress immediately passed the

---

grandson. In preparing this response, WTF may have assumed that it, too, would be sent to Congress. In the end, BF did not enclose it, but explained the situation in his own words.

2. *Adams Papers*, XIV, 238–45.

resolution enclosed with the present letter, ordering that a commission be prepared for Adams, Franklin, and Jay to enter into a commercial treaty with Great Britain, subject to revision by Congress and the British government, and meanwhile to make a commercial convention good for one year. Congress also ordered Livingston to draft a commercial treaty and relevant instructions.[3] Livingston presented them to Congress five days later, and they were referred to a new committee,[4] whose report was finally submitted on June 19, long after Livingston had resigned and three days after Boudinot wrote the present letter. Ignoring Livingston's draft, the committee simply recommended that the commissioners be authorized to make both a commercial convention and a treaty, subject to congressional revision.[5] Congress failed to act on the recommendation. After the signing of the peace treaty, Congress resolved to negotiate with *all* the commercial powers of Europe. In May, 1784, with Jay and Laurens returning to America, Congress appointed a new commission consisting of Franklin, Adams, and Thomas Jefferson to negotiate comercial treaties with twenty nations including Great Britain.

Gentn.   Philadelphia June 16. 1783.
I am sorry to inform you, that by the Resignation of M. Livingston, as Minister for foreign affairs,[7] it has become necessary, that you should receive the Resolutions of Congress relative to your Mission, through my Hands. The disadvantage arising from this Necessity, until a Successor to that worthy Gentleman is appointed, will be yours, as it is impossible for me to do more than barely to transmit the Acts of Congress, necessary for your Information.

3. *JCC*, XXIV, 320–1. The question of the commissioners' powers to make a commercial treaty had already been discussed by Congress: William T. Hutchinson et al., eds., *The Papers of James Madison*, First Series (17 vols., Chicago, London, and Charlottesville, 1962–91), VI, 452.
    4. Giunta, *Emerging Nation*, II, 108–9, 110–12; Hutchinson, *Papers of James Madison*, VII, 15.
    5. *JCC*, XXIV, 404–5.
    6. *JCC*, XXVII, 372–4; *Jefferson Papers*, VII, 262–6.
    7. Livingston had actually submitted his resignation in December, 1782, claiming that his salary did not cover the expenses of office, but agreed to remain until the following spring. He submitted a new letter of resignation on May 9, 1783, which Congress accepted on June 4, passing a resolution thanking him: XXXVIII, 405–6n; *JCC*, XXIV, 336–7, 382. For the difficulties this caused see our annotation of Lewis R. Morris to BF, June 5.

Enclosed you have one of the 1st. May last,[8] and another of the 12th. Instant,[9] which I hope will get safe to hand, time enough for your Government. The Commission & Instructions referred to in the first, not being ready, it was thought best to forward the Resolution without delay, that you might know what was intended in the present important Period of your Negotiation. We have been much surprized that we have not received any Communications from you, since the Cessation of Hostilities, except a Letter of the 5 April from M. Laurens.[1]

I have the honor to be with the most perfect Consideration & Esteem, Gentlemen, your most obedt. and very hble Servt.

(signed) ELIAS BOUDINOT.

To the American Ministers.

Lafayette to Franklin and John Jay[2]

AL: Columbia University Library

Paris June the 16th 1783

Mquis. de Lafayette's Compliments waït upon Mr. Franklin and Mr. Jay, and Has the Honour to Acquaint them He Had letters

---

8. The resolution discussed in the headnote.

9. For this June 12 resolution (*JCC*, XXIV, 392–4) see our annotation of Livingston to the Commissioners, May 31. It was copied into the commissioners' legation letterbooks, and BF noted on the copy that he retained, "Resolution of Congress June 12. 83 relating to Holland &c" (APS). For additional background see Livingston's Report to Congress, June 3, 1783 (Giunta, *Emerging Nation*, II, 143–5); Hutchinson, *Papers of James Madison*, VII, 127–33, 137–41.

1. *Laurens Papers*, XVI, 174–9.

2. At BF's suggestion, the Jays left Paris in early June and came to live with him in the country, where the air was more wholesome. John and his daughter had been ill, and Sarah was seven months pregnant. The family was installed by June 10, the day Jay wrote his first letter from Passy. He left for England on Oct. 9; his family stayed until the beginning of November, when they moved to the neighboring village of Chaillot: Morris, *Jay: Peace*, pp. 607–9, 619, 636n; John Jay to Robert R. Livingston, June 10, 1783 (N.-Y.

from America down to the first of May— On Many points He is Referred to the letters those Gentlemen Must Have Received— The Mquis. de Lafayette Intends paying them His Respects to Morrow at Breakfast time, and will Communicate what Intelligence is Come to His knowledge.[3]

Count de Vergennes was yesterday Expressing a Desire to know if Mr. Hartley's last Dispatches were as Satisfactory as they are Said to be by the Duke of Manchester.

Endorsed by John Jay: Marqs. Fayette 16 June 1783 ansd. same morng[4]

From Barthélemy Faujas de Saint-Fond

ALS: American Philosophical Society

Monsieur   a paris le 16. juin 1783

Sachant Combien les arts vous sont agreables, j'ai l'honneur de vous faire part q'un de mes Compatriotes, homme de Condition de ma province, vient de finir un ouvrage en mécanique que je regarde Comme tres etonnant.[5]

Hist. Soc.); Sarah Jay to Catharine Livingston, June 11, 1783, and to Lady Juliana Penn, Oct. 8, 1783 (both at the Columbia University Library).

3. On June 21 Lafayette wrote a one-sentence note to BF and Jay, sending American newspapers. APS.

4. Jay answered in BF's absence: neither he nor BF had received any recent letters from America, though JA had received one mentioning that Congress had ratified the preliminary articles and released British prisoners. Lafayette was welcome to breakfast with them the next morning: Jay to Lafayette, June 16, 1783, Columbia University Library. The letter JA received (an April 14 dispatch from Livingston) had arrived the previous day: JA to Livingston, June 16, 1783, in *Adams Papers*, XV, 34.

5. The inventor, named at the end of this letter, was Honoré-Nicolas Mical (b. 1727), and his invention—the culmination of 30 years' work—was a mechanical speaking machine with which two "têtes parlantes" conversed. Triggered by the same kind of cylinder mechanism used in music boxes, this was the first programmable speech synthesizer. It was also the first machine to simulate the physiology of the human vocal tract, forcing air through artificial glottises whose sounds were modified in various resonating cavities. The mechanism was encased behind an elaborate stage framed by col-

Ce sont deux têtes dorées qui prononcent les paroles suivantes *le roi donne la paix a leurope.* La 2de tête repond. *la paix Couronne le roi de gloire* la 1ere replique *et la paix fait le Bonheur des peuples.*[6] Jai vu et entendu moimême ces deux têtes, qui n'ont encore êté vues par personne; et je puis vous assurer que Cest un ouvrage Bien etonnant, qui n'est peut être pas encore à son dernier degré de perfection, mais dont la mécanique est faite sur les plus Scavants principes. Je puis vous assurer quon entend tres Bien les paroles, et que les dipthongues qui sont d'une si grande difficultés à pronnoncer Sont Ce quil y a de mieux dans Ces deux machines parlantes.

Comme mon Compatriote est un homme fort modeste, et quil n'a pas l'honneur d'etre Connu de vous, il ma demandé en grace, de vous prier de venir voir Ces deux Belles pieces de mécanique mercredy prochain, 18 de Ce mois. Cest a dire apres demain matin vers les deux heures, vous priant de lui faire l'honneur

---

umns resting on plinths, which created an acoustically defined space wide enough for two people to enter. Viewers found themselves face-to-face with a pair of large (one observer called them "colossal") carved heads perched on a podium—mature men with full beards, one of whom wore a crown. A banner suspended beneath them displayed the text of their dialogue; this helped listeners recognize the indistinct sounds produced by the machinery. See Thomas L. Hankins and Robert J. Silverman, "*Vox Mechanica:* the History of Speaking Machines," in *Instruments and the Imagination* (Princeton, N.J., 1995), pp. 186–7, where an engraving of the "Têtes parlantes" is reproduced; Antoine Rivarol, *Lettre à Monsieur le président de ****. Sur le globe airostatique, sur les têtes parlantes . . .* (London, 1783), pp. 20–4. The editors express particular gratitude to Gordon Ramsay, Haskins Laboratories and Yale University, for sharing his expertise on Mical and his invention.

6. In addition to this dialogue, the first head made a short speech. Addressing Louis XVI, it declaimed, "O Roi adorable! Père de vos Peuples! leur bonheur fait voir à l'Europe la gloire de votre Trône." These lines, also printed on the banner, were quoted with the rest of the dialogue in an extensive article about Mical's achievement in the *Jour. de Paris,* July 6, 1783, written after the reporter witnessed the June 18 demonstration to which BF is here invited. For the demonstration see Faujas de Saint-Fond's letter of June 18.

de dinner ches lui, ou vous trouverés quelques académiciens de votre Connoissance, ne refusés pas Cette faveur à ce galant homme. qui se nomme *mr mical chanoine de Saint maurice de vienne en dauphiné* et qui loge *rue du temple enface de la rue de montmorenci maison du Commissaire.* Jaurai l'honneur de vous y attendre vous et monsieur votre petit fils.[7] mercredy a deux heures. Jai lhonneur d'etre avec le plus respectueux attachement Monsieur votre très humble et très obeissant serviteur

FAUJAS DE SAINT FOND

Notation: Faujas de Saint Fond Paris 16 Juin 1783

From Armand-Thomas Hue de Miromesnil

Copy: Archives du Ministère des affaires étrangères

A Versailles, ce 16 Juin 1783.

M. Le Garde des Sceaux a communiqué à M. de Neville, Maître des Requêtes, Directeur Général de la Librairie, la Lettre que Monsieur Franklin a pris la peine de lui adresser le 11 de ce mois: il lui envoie copie de la reponse de ce Magistrat.[8]

Monsieur Franklin verra que rien ne S'oppose à la permission telle qu'elle a été accordée dès le 11 du mois de Mai dernier: il est bon qu'il charge quelqu'un d'en Suivre l'effet.

M. Le Garde des Sceaux prie Monsieur Franklin d'être persuadé de la sincerité de ses sentimens.   signé MIROMENIL.

M. Franklin.

---

7. Faujas de Saint-Fond wrote a separate invitation to WTF on the same date. APS.
8. BF's letter has not been located. Néville, whose role was explained to BF by Vergennes on April 5 (XXXIX, 434–5), wrote to Miromesnil on June 15 that the censor had granted permission on May 11. As long as Vergennes approved the sheets before publication, they could proceed. AAE.

From Benjamin Vaughan: Two Letters

(I) and (II) ALS: American Philosophical Society

I.

My dearest sir,   London, June 16, 1783.

I beg permission to introduce to your warm civilities, Lord Daer, son of the Earl of Selkirk. He was introduced to me lately as a very valuable & philosophical acquaintance, & my short intercourse with him has confirmed every report I had heard of him. His political principles are well known, & very friendly to us. He means to stay some time at Paris for his instruction & amusement.— As I have no small persuasion that he will be remarkable in life, I have a pleasure in making him known to you, and to my excellent friend your son, to whom he will prove a companion often.

I am, my dearest sir, Your ever affectionate, respectful & grateful,   BENJN. VAUGHAN

Dr. Franklin.

II.

My dearest sir,   London, June 16, 1783.

I inclose you a paper, which must be in part my apology for not writing to you; and if Ld. Daer stays a day longer, I shall be able to send the *sequel*.—[9] A farther reason why neither Mr Oswald nor myself have written to you, was that

---

9. On Monday, June 16, the *Public Advertiser* carried the first part of a pamphlet-length article arguing for free trade entitled "Upon the American Commerce, and Commerce in General" and signed "A By-Stander." The paper had announced on June 14 that the piece would appear that Monday, and several days earlier Vaughan himself had alerted BF to the fact that he would soon send a "Bystander"; see his unsigned postscript to John Vaughan's letter of June 10. It seems that Vaughan had not yet finished the article at the time of writing the present letter. When the continuation was published on June 18, the editor appended a note explaining that he could not follow the writer's directions and publish the entire conclusion in that issue because the last part of the copy had been "withheld to so late an Hour." The third and final installment appeared on June 19.

we saw no good we could do, and therefore we avoided doing harm.— A third reason was, that there was a personage at
Paris concerning whom there were *difficulties*; which reason if
you do not understand by these few words, I must let it rest till
we meet.

I have no news to send you. I believe ministers have at last
got over the idea of the loyal colonies being sufficient to supply the West Indies; and have prepared an act for an intercourse
with the other colonies.— I make no remarks, *because they can
do no good*; and I love the public too well to think of serving my
friends in your opinion, at *its* expence.

Had not my hands been tied by these circumstances, I should
much oftener have written, & even sent you expresses, had there
been occasion.

My father's departure, and hourly consultations with me,
and the solicitations I make by person or letter for my brother
John, with the above letter, & my own concerns, have worne
me down so much, that I have not spirits to write you a long
letter, and yet I have abundance of matter.— I must therefore
again *beg* a respite till the next opportunity.— After this week,
& some time in the course of the next, the family embark;[1] and
then I shall be myself again.

I am every day however thinking of something or other we
shall do together, when you come to London with your son.

I am, my dearest sir, Your most devoted affectionate &
grateful   BENJN. VAUGHAN

I send your son a pair of buckles & a whimsical purse; and
Mr Jay a watch chain, by Ld. Daer.

There is a pocket globe & a pocket glass in the box containing the miscellaneous articles for different persons, which
globe & glass are directed to Mr Whitefoord, but are a present
from Mr Oswald to Mr Faujas de St. Fond; & are to be forwarded to the Duke of Chaulnes, after stripping off the cover
to Mr Whitefoord.[2]

1. See Samuel Vaughan to BF, June 14.

2. For the four boxes that had just arrived at Calais see Dessin to BF,
June 15. Oswald believed the articles to have been shipped long before

You will receive a pamphlet of Mr Sinclairs; another relative to the Colony trade & the Loyal colonies (said by some to be written by Lord Sheffield & Mr Eden;) and Sr. John Pringle's discourses before the Royal Society.—[3] When I asked Dr. Priestley after *other* things to send you, he named our Coalition prints,[4] with which the shops swarm. Though I dislike the subject, I have desired my brother John to choose some prints of a political nature, of which I dare say these will make a part.

Henry Laurens to the Other American Peace Commissioners

LS and copy: Massachusetts Historical Society; copies: Library of Congress, South Carolina Historical Society

Gentlemen, London 17th. June 1783
I had the honor of addressing you the 10th. immediately after my landing at Dover— As early as possible after my arrival here I obtained an Interview with Mr. Secretary Fox, who was pleased to read to me part of his latest Dispatches to Mr. Hartley which he supposed would reach Paris on the 14th[5] tis probable therefore that before this time, as much of the Contents as is proper for your Knowledge, has been communicated.

---

this: on April 5 he wrote Whitefoord that he had sent a "small Globe and Lunette for Monsr Fuzas" a month earlier, by way of a friend of Vaughan's: W. A. S. Hewins, ed., *The Whitefoord Papers* . . . (Oxford, 1898), p. 186.

3. The first two pamphlets are Sir John Sinclair, *Lucubrations During a Short Recess* (London, 1782), and John Baker Holroyd, Baron Sheffield, *Observations on the Commerce of the American States* . . . (London, 1783). The third work was compiled by Andrew Kippis, to whom Pringle had given permission to publish a collection of his discourses after his death. Kippis added to these a hundred-page biography of his friend in *Six Discourses, Delivered by Sir John Pringle, Bart. When President of the Royal Society; . . . To Which Is Prefixed the Life of the Author* (London, 1783).

4. Which doubtless commented on the coalition between Fox and North.

5. Fox's letter of June 10 did reach Hartley by the 14th; see Hartley to the Commissioners of that date.

"Reciprocity" since the 10th of April[6] has undergone a certain Degree of Refinement; the definition of that term appears now to be, Possession of advantages on one side, and Restrictions on the other. "The Navigation Act is the vital of Great Britain, too delicate to bear a Touch"—the sudden and unexpected, perhaps illicit arrival of Ships and Cargoes from America may have caused this change of Tone.[7] But you have heard in detail & are more competent to Judge.

From a desire of forming an opinion I asked Mr. Fox whether he thought, I might venture for a few days to take the benefit of Bath, and yet be time enough at Paris for the intended commercial Agreement? He replied, "I rather think you may." One need not be a Conjurer to draw an inference— You will either have finished the Business before I could travel to Paris; or without being missed there, I may go to Bath and repair my nerves.

In this state of uncertainty, when 'tis easy to percieve affections are not as We could wish them, nor quite so warm as We have been taught to believe, it would not be wise to commit the United States, wherefore I shall rest the Business till I hear from you, or until a more favorable prospect, flattering myself with hopes of your surmounting the late seeming Difficulties; an inconvenience on your side is preferable to the hazard of a disgrace.

I am with great Regard and Respect, Gentlemen, Your most obedient, and most humble servant,   HENRY LAURENS

Their Excellencies. The Ministers Plenepotentiary from the United States of America at Paris.

6. When he last talked with Fox: *Laurens Papers*, XVI, 183.
7. Laurens wrote the same thing to Livingston on June 17, adding that the British minister at Paris had told him "candidly" that he was of this opinion: *Laurens Papers*, XVI, 211.

From the Comte de Ségur   AL:[8] American Philosophical Society

[after June 17, 1783][9]

Le Cte de ségur est venu pour avoir l'honneur de Voir Monsieur franklin, et pour lui remettre deux lettres, l'une de Madame Green, Et l'autre du Docteur Cooper.[1] Il les lui rapportera un autre jour, ces lettres ne Sont que dès Reponses aux lettres de Recommandation que Mr. franklin avoit eu la bonté de donner au Cte de ségur à Son depart pour l'Amerique.[2]

Il auroit eu plustost l'honneur de r[endre] visite à Monsieur franklin mais dep[uis] Son arrivée il a prèsque toujours été à S[on] Regiment, et n'en est revenu que depuis peu de jours; il desire fort trouver bient[ôt] l'occasion de Causer avec lui d'un pays qu'il est impossible de voir Sans Emotion, et de quitter Sans Regret.

To Nathaniel Falconer

Transcript:[3] Historical Society of Pennsylvania

Dear Friend   Passy, June 18. 1783.

I received your kind Letters of May 15. and June 7. and was glad to hear of your Welfare and safe Arrival in England.— I wish you much Success in entring again upon your old Occupation, and should be happy if I could be ready to return in a Ship

---

8. The MS is badly mutilated, with the right margin torn away. The only affected portion is the second paragraph, for which we supply missing text in brackets.

9. The date on which Ségur's squadron arrived at Brest from the Caribbean: *Courier de l'Europe,* XIV (1783), 18; Rice and Brown, eds., *Rochambeau's Army,* I, 99–100, 179–80, 327; Louis-Philippe, comte de Ségur, *Mémoires ou souvenirs et anecdotes* (3 vols., Paris, 1827), I, 472–3. His family welcomed him home on June 22: Marc-Marie, marquis de Bombelles, *Journal,* ed. Jean Grassion *et al.* (7 vols. to date, Geneva, 1977–), I, 231–2.

1. They both thank BF for having introduced the count: XXXVIII, 417–18, 484–5.

2. XXXVII, 105–6, 107.

3. A note on the verso indicates that it was "Copied from the Originals in possession of Peter Thompson of Philada."

188

under your Care. But I have not yet receiv'd the Permission I requested from Congress, nor do I know any thing of their Intentions respecting me or my Grandson, having no Letter later than the 13th. of January. I am surpriz'd they did not take the Opportunity of writing by you. We are here totally in the Dark as to their Opinion of the Preliminary Articles of the Peace, which we sent by Capt. Barney in the Washington; who sail'd from L'Orient the 17th. of January, and carried with our Dispatches a large Sum of Money; we have not so much as heard with Certainty of his Arrival. I beg you will give me what Information you can of these Particulars and any others that you may think interesting, either respecting Public Affairs, or relating to me and mine. Is it true that Mr. Morris has resigned his Office; and that the Constitution of Pensilvania is to be altered in October? Was any one appointed to succeed me here, or who was intended? I never long'd so much to be at home, and am afraid that if my Discharge is delay'd I shall be oblig'd to stay here another Winter.—

I am glad to hear from you of the Welfare of my old Friends Mr. Jackson and Mr. Watley. If you see them again, please to present my best Respects to them. I have still a regard for Mr. Strahan in remembrance of our ancient Friendship, tho' he has as a Member of Parliament dipt his Hands in our Blood. He was always as credulous as you find him: He told me a little before I left London that there was News of a Scotch Sergeant's having alone met a party of 40 American Soldiers, disarm'd them, and brought them Prisoners into Boston. This he appear'd to believe, and may therefore well believe the Lie you mention of the French Troops & our Army killing each other. His believing such Falshoods would be of Less consequence, if he did not propagate them by his Chronicle; in the last of which that I have seen there are two lying Letters said to be from New York of April 13. but actually fabricated in London.[4] In refutation of his Story of our quarrelling & fighting with the French Troops,

4. These letters accused the Americans of conspiring to violate the terms of the peace agreement and of murdering Loyalists who returned to their homes in New Jersey: *London Chron.*, issue of June 7–10, 1783.

I send you enclos'd part of a Pennsylvania Journal of May 7.[5] which I wish you would give to him, and I doubt not but he will have the Candour to publish it. It will there appear authentically that the most perfect harmony subsisted between them to the last. My Grandson presents his Respects to you, as does Mr. Hartley. We are all (Thanks to God) well & hearty: But I am uneasy about Barney, fearing he may be lost, and therefore beg you would as soon as possible inform me if you know any thing of his Arrival. With great and sincere Esteem, I am ever, my dear Friend, Yours most affectionately   B. FRANKLIN.

Tell me every thing you know about the Arrival & Reception of the News respecting the Peace, and whether it is true that the Articles were kept some time secret, & why;[6] for we have received no Intelligence from Government, & know not what to believe or think

Capt. Falconer

5. On May 7 the *Pa. Jour. and Weekly Advertiser* printed an address from the merchants of Baltimore to the commander of the French troops still in that city, expressing their gratitude and best wishes for a safe return voyage. The address was dated April 30.

6. We do not know the source of this rumor, but it may have stemmed from the debate in Congress about communicating to France the secret article in the preliminary agreement. Livingston explained this to the American commissioners on March 25 when acknowledging receipt of the preliminary treaty from Capt. Barney: XXXIX, 380–5.

From Elias Boudinot

Copies:[7] Massachusetts Historical Society, Library of Congress (two), National Archives; AL (draft): Library of Congress

Sir,   Philadelphia, June 18. 1783
I have the honor of enclosing you an official Letter, directed to our Ministers Plenipotentiary at Paris.[8]

The Resignation of the late Secretary for foreign affairs, (occasioned by his Preference of the Chancellorship of the State of New-York, which he could not hold longer, & retain his Secretaryship,)[9] has cast the Business of his office on me, till a Successor is elected, which I hope will speedily take Place.

As Part of the Resolution of Congress of the 12. Inst. enclosed in that Letter, is of a secret Nature, I have wrote it in Cyphers, but not having that of Mr. Livingston, I thought it best to use Mr. Morris' to you, which he has obligingly supplied me with; so that the Ministers will be indebted for your deciphering of it.

Your Letter to Mr. Livingston of the 15. April, enclosing the two Medals, came to hand this Morning.[1] I am sorry to find, that you have cause for similar Complaints, to those we have been making two Months past, on the Subject of want of Intelligence. We have not heard from any of our Commissioners at Paris, since February, excepting a Letter from Mr. Laurens, tho' our Anxiety & Expectations have been wound up to the highest Pitch.

I feel myself much indebted for your polite Compliment of the Medal; it is thought very elegant and the Device & work-

7. The copies at the Mass. Hist. Soc. and Library of Congress, from the peace commissioners' letterbooks, were made from the now-missing original. The National Archives copy (published in Smith, *Letters*, XX, 339–40) may have been made from Boudinot's draft, which differs slightly in wording from what he eventually sent.

8. Above, June 16.

9. A faction in New York State who resented his absences had been scheming for months to remove him as chancellor: George Dangerfield, *Chancellor Robert R. Livingston of New York, 1746–1813* (New York, 1960), p. 177.

1. XXXIX, 467–72.

manship much admired. You will be pleased, Sir, to accept of my Acknowledgments on this occasion. As I doubt not but the Copper one was designed for Mr. Livingston personally, I shall send it to him by the first convenient Opportunity. He is a worthy deserving Character, and the United States will suffer greatly by his Resignation, tho' I think him justified in attending to the Calls of his private affairs.

You will receive herewith a Number of our late News-Papers, in which are inserted many resolves, Associations &c from all Parts of the Country, which I earnestly wish could be kept out of Sight— But the Truth is, that the Cruelties, Ravages & Barbarisms of the Refugees & Loyalists have left the People so sore, that it is not yet time for them, to exercise their good Sense & cooler Judgment—[2] And that cannot take Place while the Citizens of New-York are kept out of their City, and despoiled daily of their Property, by the sending off their Negroes, by hundreds, in the Face of the Treaty. It has been exceedingly ill judged in the British to retain New-York so long, and to persist in sending away the Negroes, as it has irritated the Citizens of America to an alarming Degree.—[3]

I have the honor to be, with the greatest Respect & Esteem, Sir, Your most obedt. & very hble Servt.

(signed) ELIAS BOUDINOT

private

From Daniele Andrea Dolfin

ʟ: American Philosophical Society

Mercredi Ce 18. Juin. 1783.
L'Ambassadeur de Venise Prie Monsieur Francklin de lui faire L'honneur De Diner Chez lui Mercredi Le 25. de Ce mois.

2. That very day, a set of anti-Loyalist resolutions from Germantown was printed in the *Pa. Gaz.*

3. As a result of the war, an estimated 80,000–100,000 slaves had fled or been taken from their owners, leading to a severe labor shortage in the American South: Sylvia R. Frey, *Water from the Rock: Black Resistance in a Revolutionary Age* (Princeton, 1991), p. 211.

Réponse S'il vous Plait

Addressed: A Monsieur / Monsieur Francklin

From Faujas de Saint-Fond

ALS: American Philosophical Society

Monsieur   a paris le mercredi 18. juin 1783.
J'eu l'honneur de vous écrire[4] pour vous engager a venir
voir deux morceaux de mècanique tres intéressants et de faire
l'honneur à la personne qui les à inventés et de venir dinner
ches elle, que vous y trouveriés des académiciens de votre
Connoissance.[5]
      J'envoyai un exprés pour vous porter ma lettre, et Comme
vous etiés allé à la Campagne, elle fut remise à un de vos
secretaires.
      J'envoie un Second exprés pour m'assurer Si le Commis-
sionaire S'est acquitté exactement de Ce que je lavois chargè de
faire, et s'il à remis ma lettre chés vous. Dans Cette incertitude

---

4. Above, June 16.
      5. According to the press the guests were BF and the comte de Milly, of
the Académie des sciences, and Charles Blagden and Faujas de Saint-Fond,
of the Royal Society. (Faujas was not, in fact, a member.) These men appeared to be "aussi satisfaits qu'étonnés": Bachaumont, *Mémoires secrets*,
XXIII, 37–8; *Jour. de Paris*, July 6, 1783. Blagden's private view was that
the machine's speech was "a little articulate, but not much." The mechanism consisted of "a bellow, valves, tubes, cavities," but the sound did "not
seem to come from the mouth, but from an instrument inside: too much
like [*a*] trumpet": Charles Blagden's Journal, entry of June 18, 1783 (Yale
University Library).
      On July 2 the abbé Mical petitioned the Académie des sciences to exam-
ine his invention. A committee was appointed that same day, consisting of
the comte de Milly, Le Roy, Lavoisier, Vicq d'Azyr, Jacques-Constantin
Périer, and the mathematician Laplace. Their Sept. 3 report was favorable
overall, recognizing that the sound reproduction was imperfect: Académie
des sciences, *Procès-verbaux*, CII (1783), 150, 202. Mical was inducted into
the Loge des Neuf Sœurs on July 21, with a speech praising the genius of
his achievement: Charles Porset, *Mirabeau franc-maçon* . . . (La Rochelle,
1996), pp. 106–7.

je prend la liberté de vous en envoyer une seconde, pour vous reiterer la même priere, et vous engager a venir voir les deux *têtes parlantes* dont je vous ai entretenu dans ma lettre, en vous priant de faire l'honneur à l'inventeur de venir dinner chès lui aujourd'hui avec monsieur votre fils. Il se nomme mr l'abbé mical chanoine de Saint maurice rue du temple, en face de Celle de montmorency maison du Commissaire.

Jai l'honneur d'etre avec les sentiments les plus respectueux Monsieur votre trés humble et trés obeissant serviteur

FAUJAS DE SAINT FOND

ches mr girard rue des Bon enfants no 33.

From Henry Grand

ALS: American Philosophical Society

Sir   Wednesday Morn. [June 18, 1783?][6]

I was thinking you might perhaps be desirous to see la Procession du Bon Dieu, a most magnificent Shew, with an excellent Band of Martial Musik & as they are to make a full Stop at St. Joseph our house is the very best place to enjoy that Sight.[7] Not Knowing precisely what time they'll begin their March between 11 & 1 o.Clock, I think the first is the hour for coming.

That will not prevent your being back at Passy at ½ past one or 2 at latest.

6. Though this invitation may well date from an earlier year, it is unlikely that it is later. We place it in 1783 because of Grand's comment about his convalescence, which possibly relates to his only other mention in these papers of an indisposition, which occurred *c.* May, 1783; see our annotation of Francis Dana to BF, June [20]. The feast of Corpus Christi (*la Fête-Dieu*), which always takes place on a Thursday, fell on June 19 in 1783: *Almanach royal* for 1783, p. 5.

7. JA attended the procession but reported that the stormy weather rendered it "less brilliant than ordinary": Butterfield, *John Adams Diary*, III, 139. The cemetery and chapel of St. Joseph were located at the intersection of the rue du Temps-Perdu (now St. Joseph) and rue Montmartre, where the Grand family lived: XXXIII, 321; Hillairet, *Rues de Paris*, II, 154.

I Should have done my self the honour of waiting upon you personally were it not that I just begin to be convalessent & that am not Strong enough yet.

I crave to be Kindly remembered to your grand Son & that you will believe me with due Respect Sir Your most obedt. & most humble servt.   HY. GRAND

To morrow Thursday is the Fête & Procession du bon Dieu.

Addressed: The Honourable / Doctor Franklin / Passy.

Notation: Henry Grand.

David Hartley to the American Peace Commissioners: Propositions for the Definitive Treaty

Copies:[8] Massachusetts Historical Society (two), William L. Clements Library, Library of Congress, National Archives (two); transcript: National Archives

When the American peace commissioners saw David Hartley at Versailles on Tuesday, June 17, they told him that Congress had issued an order on April 24 opening American ports to British vessels—or so they understood from credible private sources.[9] They were expecting official confirmation in the dispatches from America that were due to arrive any day. In reporting this to Fox, Hartley observed that if it were true, it would obviate the need for a commercial convention. As the Americans had responded to his proposed article of June [14–18] with silence, a reaction he considered "very significant," Hartley believed that they should focus on concluding the definitive treaty. Indeed, he told Fox, he and the commissioners had arranged to meet on June 19 "to draw up a project of the definitive treaty."[1]

8. We publish the one in JA's hand.

9. One source of this false rumor was John Vaughan; see his letter of June 10 and Giunta, *Emerging Nation*, II, 166.

1. When congressional confirmation of the rumor had still not arrived by June 26, the commissioners began to doubt its veracity: Hartley to the Duke of Portland, June 26, 1783, Clements Library. For the commissioners' conversation with Hartley see his letter to Fox, June 18, 1783, Clements Library; Butterfield, *John Adams Diary*, III, 138. That same day at

At the June 19 meeting, held at Franklin's residence, the parties agreed to suspend negotiations for a temporary commercial convention "upon the presumption of the American Ports being actually open to British Ships." Hartley then presented the commissioners with this set of propositions, calling them "Memorandums for consideration" since they were subject to Fox's approval.[2] They were prompted by the complaints of Quebec fur traders, who had lost access to American furs. Fox had forwarded these complaints to Hartley in April, along with instructions on what to propose by way of regulations.[3]

[June 19, 1783]

Mr Hartleys Propositions for the definitive Treaty.

1. That Lands belonging to Persons of any Description, which have not actually been sold, Shall be restored to the old Possessors without Price.

2. That an equal and free Participation of the different carrying Places, and the Navigation of all the Lakes and Rivers of that Country, through which the Water Line of Division passes, between Canada and the United States Shall be enjoyed fully and uninterruptedly by both Parties.[4]

3. That in any Such Places, within the Boundaries assigned, generally to the American States as are adjoining to the Water

Versailles, Vergennes also counseled the Americans to postpone commercial discussions until a future time, given the inequity of the recent British proposal: Butterfield, *John Adams Diary*, III, 138.

2. Butterfield, *John Adams Diary*, III, 139; Hartley to Fox, June 20, 1783, in Giunta, *Emerging Nation*, II, 165.

3. Hartley to Fox, May 3 and June 20, 1783: Giunta, *Emerging Nation*, II, 106, 165–6. In the June 20 letter just cited, Hartley said that he had in fact exceeded his instructions in some respects, and that memoranda 2, 5, and 6 were taken from the Quebec merchants' memorial. See also Harlow, *Second British Empire*, I, 463–5.

4. This was a restriction of what the American peace commissioners had proposed on April 29, which gave American merchants access to all lakes and rivers under British dominion: XXXIX, 525.

Line of Division and which are not Specifically under the Dominion of any one State, all Persons at present resident, or having Possessions or Occupations as Merchants or otherwise may remain in peaceable Enjoyment of all civil Rights and in Pursuit of their respective Occupations.

4. That in any Such Places adjoining to the Water Line of Division, as may be under the Specific Dominion of any particular State, all Persons at present resident, or having Possessions or Occupations, as Merchants or otherwise, may remain in the peaceable Enjoyment of all civil Rights, and in pursuit of their Occupations untill they Shall receive Notice of Removal from the State to which any Such Place may appertain; and that upon any Such Notice of Removal a Term of three Years Shall be allowed for Selling or withdrawing their valuable Effects, and for Settling their Affairs.

5. That his Britannic Majestys Forces not exceeding [*blank*] in Number, may continue in the Posts now occupied by them contiguous to the Water Line, for the Term of Three Years, for the Purpose of Securing the Lives, Property and Peace of any Persons Settled in that Country, against the Invasion or Ravages of the neighbouring Indian Nations, who may be Suspected of retaining Resentments in Consequence of the late War.

6. That no Tax or Impost whatsoever Shall be laid on any Articles of Commerce, passing or repassing through the Country, but that the Trade may be left entirely open for the Benefit of all Parties interested therein.

From Patience Wright

ALS: American Philosophical Society

Honred Sir   London June 19th 1783
   Mr Mascall is on his Way to Settel in Philadelphia—he was amongst the first men who wrote against the American War, and one of the first in the London association &ce—his Stedy behavour against the Wicked Medlars of the Ministry—and he

faithful in the Cause of THE RIGHTS OF THE PEOPLE[5]—Brott on a Suffering and percecution—from Lords Mansfield and other Men in Power which has deservedly Recomended him to the favour of America—

Mr Mascall has a Knowledge of Phisick, Brot up an appotacary—Cymistt &ce has a Strong understanding, Knows the laws of England has Read Men and Books, and been usefull in the Cause of America and Intends Spending the Remainder of his Days in that Contry of Peace and Liberty—

I am Sir with the higest Esteem your faithful friend and humbl Servnt   PATIENCE WRIGHT

To Doct Franklin

Addressed: To / His Exelency Doctr Franklin

Notation: Wright 19 June 1783.

Henry Laurens to the Other American Peace Commissioners

Copies: Massachusetts Historical Society, Library of Congress, South Carolina Historical Society

Gentlemen,   London 20 June 1783.

Permit me to refer to what I had the honor of writing to you the 17th. You will recollect my Suggestions, as soon as we perceived the falling off, from those warm Assurances which had been pressed in March and April, they were not ill founded; I dalayed a Week in hopes of Intelligence & left you with Reluctance; the temper of the times forbids even an essay. What a happy Country is this, where every thing pertaining to the Public, is rendred to them in public Newspapers; see the inclosed, containing nearly as accurate an Account of certain recent Occurrences, as if it had been penned by one of the Parties. It might indeed have been made a little stronger. Modest Men

5. Mascall criticized the North administration at a Sept. 25, 1775, meeting of the freeholders of Middlesex: Peter Force, ed., *American Archives . . .*, Fourth Series (6 vols., Washington, D.C., 1837–46), III, 785.

are sometimes restrained from attempting a public good, from a dread of the Effects of Envy, of being held up in an invidious Light. It would be cruel to disturb them. I have learned nothing from America, save what you may have read in the Prints. To-morrow I shall proceed to Bath and be waiting for Intelligence as well from Your selves as from Congress. Some Consolation arises from reflecting that while I am endeavouring to mend my Health, you suffer no Inconvenience from my Absence. With sincere Regard & respect, I have the honour to be, Gentlemen, Your obedient & most humble Servant

(signed) HENRY LAURENS

To their Excellencies the Ministers Plenipoy. from the United States of America, at Paris.

From Benjamin Franklin Bache

ALS: American Philosophical Society[6]

My dear grand Papa   Geneva June 20th 1783
    I write you to informe you that I reciev'd the books you mentioned in your letter of the 7th of June[7] I have obtain'd another prize the same as my last but one rank more advanc'd[8] I told you in my last letter that I was well,[9] but I had the fever again and Mr Marignac went with me into the country for few holidays upon my arrival in Town the Fever left me but not being well I still take physic for that excuse my dear grand Papa the schortness of my letter and Beleive me for ever Your most obidien and Dutiful son   B. FRANKLIN BACHE

6. Castle-Bache Collection, available on microfilm.
    7. The word is unmistakable; either a June 7 letter is missing, or BFB intended to write "Jany." On Jan. 7 BF wrote to BFB that he had sent a parcel of books. Ever since, BFB had been reporting that the parcel had not yet arrived: XXXVIII, 557; XXXIX, 101, 206, 410.
    8. For BFB's last prize see XXXVIII, 533, 557.
    9. BFB must have written a now-missing letter after May 30, when he reported himself "not being yet very well." According to BF's reply of June 23, that letter also enclosed a drawing.

I am a Scolar of the 1st classe

Mr and Mrs Marignac present you their respects as well as Johonnot who incloses a Word or two.[1] My compliments to my Cousin

Addressed: A Monsieur / Monsieur Franklin ministre / Plenipotentiaire des etats unis / de L'Amerique aupres de sa majèsté / tres chretiènne / a Passy près Paris

Notation: B. F. B. to Dr. Franklin Geneva, June 20 — '83

From Edward Bancroft ALS: American Philosophical Society

Dear Sir Dunkerque 20th. June 1783.

Inclosed I send you an Extract of a Letter, from our friend Commodore Jones, which came to my hands a few hours before my Departure from Paris[2] & which I had not time to Communicate, whilst there.

I arived here on tuesday afternoon[3] with Mr. Coffyn & my family all well, though the journey was rendered unpleasant by almost incessant rains the whole way. & Since my arival the Winds have been Contrary, & still remain so; I think however that we shall warp out of the Harbour this afternoon if Practicable.

---

1. Missing.
2. For his departure see Bancroft to BF, [before June 14]. Jones's letter, dated Feb. 28, was written aboard the French ship of the line *Triomphant* at Puerto Cabello in the West Indies. The portion Bancroft copied, two pages in length, told of Jones's disappointment at not receiving command of the *America,* which instead had been presented by congressional resolution to the king of France. He refused to be insulted, however, and was now volunteering aboard the marquis de Vaudreuil's ship. He sent his regards to BF and WTF. (The full letter is in Bradford, *Jones Papers,* reel 7, no. 1450.) For Congress' promise to give Jones command of the *America* and its resolution of Sept. 3, 1782, see, in particular, XXXVI, 245; XXXVIII, 70.
3. June 17.

Since my Stay here I have been again a Witness to the troublesome importunity & interruption which Mr. Coffyn dailey receives from American Seamen discharged out of Prison in England & resorting here for the means & opportunities of returning to our Country not being able to Procure employment on board English Vessels.— It is really difficult for you to Conceive the waste of time & trouble to which Mr. Coffyn has been exposed since the begining of the War, by the Applications of these distressed but generally unreasonable People, & the Enquiries & Precautions necessary to prevent impositions &c. & you will I hope permit me again to express my hope, that on this acct. as well as in Consideration of his Merit, & Superior Ability to Serve the United States here, he will be appointed their Consul or Agent at this Port whenever Powers to make such an appointment shall arive— You were pleased a few days before my Departure to express the like Sentiments and good Wishes towards Mr. Coffyn, and an intention to interfere in his behalf with Barclay &c;[4] My great regard However for Mr. Coffyn has impeled me once more to mention the Subject to you though I am perswaded your own dispositions towards him render it unnecessary. There are Vessels going from Hence in about ten days both for Boston & Philadelphia & Mr. Coffyn will carefully forward any Letters which you or Mr. Jay may wish to send by them. I beg you will make my respectful Compliments to him, his Lady, your Grandson &c. I shall have the honor of writing to you & them from London meantime beleive me with great Respect Dear Sir Your most affectionate & Devoted Humble servant   EDWD. BANCROFT

Addressed: A Monsieur / Monsieur Franklin / Ministre Plenipotentiaire des / Etats Unis &c &c &c / a Passy / pres de Paris.

Notation: Bancroft 20 Juin 1783

4. Coffyn had met with BF on June 7 to argue for Dunkirk's being made a free port. He met with Vergennes a few days later: Eric Leroy, "Calonne, Dunkerque et la mer," *Revue du nord*, LXXVIII (1996), 475, 480–2.

From Francis Dana   Copy:[5] Massachusetts Historical Society

St. Petersbourg June 9th. 1783. O.S.
Sir   [*i.e.*, June 20, 1783][6]
Having occasion to write to Mr: Grand on the 21st. of February last to enclose to him a bill of Exchange for 6666„13. Liv: T:
drawn by Mr: Robert Morris upon him, in my favour in part of
my salary, I acquainted him that the Credit he had given me here,
wou'd be out on the next[7] March, and that I shou'd stand in need
of another in a short time; and referred him to you for particular
information upon the subject. I have not yet been honoured with
an answer to my Letter;[8] nor has any further Credit been opened
here for me. This omission will soon oblige me to have recourse
to the Credit of £2500. which was given for another purpose.[9]
I hope however you will be pleased to give directions to Mr:
Grand for another years Credit,[1] as no bills have since come to

5. In Dana's own hand.
6. As is our practice, we print this letter under its date in the Gregorian
(New Style) calendar, which differed by 11 days from the Julian (Old Style)
calendar used in Russia.
7. This word was interlined to substitute for "15th.", which Dana crossed
out.
8. Grand had received it, however. In a letter dated only Tuesday noon,
which had to have been written on or before May 13 (for reasons explained
below), Henry Grand informed WTF of its contents and proposed sending
Morris' bill of exchange back to Morris, if BF had no objections. Grand
also urged BF to settle his own accounts, the sooner the better. Finally, he
complained of a sore heel, which had confined him to bed for most of the
month: APS. BF settled his account with Ferdinand Grand on May 16, 1783
(Account XVII, xxvi, 3), making Tuesday, May 13, the last possible date
for Grand's letter. May 13 is also the day JA wrote to the Dutch banking
consortium to extend Dana credit: Mass. Hist. Soc., and see *Adams Papers*,
XIV, 487n.
9. It was to be used to pay Russian government officials: XXXVIII, 372–3.
On March 24 JA answered a letter from Dana, telling him that £5,000
was too high a sum and adding that BF wondered "whether you had not
been imposed upon, and told of a Custom, which never existed." Dana responded on May 21/June 1 that he was absolutely certain of the custom:
Adams Papers, XIV, 358; XV, 1.
1. Ferdinand Grand made no more payments to Dana, probably because
JA arranged credit through the Dutch consortium; see the annotation above.

hand, and I am totally destitute of money except that I break in upon the above particular Credit, the whole of which I expect soon to have occasion for, as the main difficulties, which were raised here, have been removed, and an audience will be granted to me the moment the Definitive Treaty shall be concluded.[2]

I have the honour to be with much respect and esteam, Sir, Your most obedient & most hble Servant

His Excellency Benjamin Franklin Esqr: Minister Plenipotentiary &c

From Charles-Guillaume Le Normant d'Etioles[3]

ALS: American Philosophical Society; copy: Archives du Ministère des affaires étrangères

Neuïlly sur Seine ce 20e. Juin 1783.

Monsieur Le Docteur,

N'ayant pas été assés heureux pour rencontrer votre excèllence,[4] Je crois devoir vous rendre compte de mes dernieres

2. On July 27 Dana learned that Congress had refused his request for funds to pay Russian negotiators and had authorized his return to America, provided he was not engaged in negotiating a commercial treaty. He left St. Petersburg on Sept. 4 without having had an audience with the empress: Dana to Livingston, July 16/27 (Giunta, *Emerging Nation*, I, 900–1); *Adams Papers*, XV, 179–82; W. P. Cresson, *Francis Dana: a Puritan Diplomat at the Court of Catherine the Great* (New York and Toronto, 1930), pp. 303, 317.

3. Le Normant d'Etioles (1717–1799), a farmer general and *directeur de la ferme des postes*, is remembered primarily as the first husband of Jeanne-Antoinette Poisson, the future marquise de Pompadour. They separated in 1745, when she became Louis XV's mistress: Yves Durand, *Les Fermiers généraux au XVIIIe siècle* (Paris, 1971), pp. 67–8; H. Thirion, *La Vie privée des financiers au XVIIIe siècle* (Paris, 1895), p. 162. He remarried 20 years later, though the identity of his second wife is uncertain. It was rumored that she was his mistress Mlle Rem (or Raime), a *fille d'opéra:* Bachaumont, *Mémoires secrets*, II, 155. The family genealogy lists him marrying Marie-Anne Martha, dame de Baillon, with whom he had a son and a daughter: Emile Campardon, *Madame de Pompadour et la cour de Louis XV au milieu du dix-huitième siècle* (Paris, 1867), p. 308. Whether either woman was the mother of the sons he discusses here is unknown.

4. Le Normant d'Etioles had written an earlier letter dated only "ce Dimanche matin" (probably the preceding Sunday, June 15) to express his

démarches auprès de M. le Comte de vergennes. J'ai eû l'honneur de le voir Dimanche dernier, et il m'a parû toujours dans les dispôsitions les plus favorables en faveur de Mrs. d'Eberstein[5] dont les malheurs et les miens, non mérités, ont affecté Sensiblement Son ame paternelle. Je n'ay pas vû avec moins de Sensibilité que MM. de Rayneval et hénin Sont affectés des mêmes Sentimens et qu'ils S'empressent de concourir au même bût, c'est à dire, à celuy de ne pas les envoyer en amérique les mains vuides.

Je Suis assés instruit des Circonstances et M. le Cher. de Chatelux ne m'a point caché que dans ce moment cy il y a peû d'espérance de fortune dans la partie du commerce, tous les magazins du Pays etant combles de marchandises arrivées de toutes parts depuis la Signature de la Paix. Il ne reste donc de ressource dans ce moment que celle des Concèssions plus ou moins nombreuses et plus ou moins avantageusement placées que par votre crédit et celui de M. de vergennes vous voudrés bien demander pour eux au Congrés. Mais que leur Servira pour le moment cet avantage 1°. si elles ne Sont compôsées d'un assés grand nombre d'acres pour que nos Jeunes gens qui n'ont aucune ressource du Côté de la fortune puissent en Sacrifier une partie pour faire cultiver l'autre et 2e. si on ne les obtient gratuitement. En vain objecteroit-on qu'ils Sont fils d'un bon Pere. M. de vergennes n'ignore pas que ma fortune quoique brillante en apparence, mais toute viagère, á Souffert depuis quelque tems de tels échecs que je ne puis y porter de nouveaux Coups Sans injustice envers mes autres Enfans. Quoique le Ministre Sache et approuve toutes mes raisons, il est trop discret et trop

---

disappointment at not seeing BF at Passy the previous afternoon. He had come with M. Bougon (XXXI, 317), who was charged by Vergennes to intercede with BF in the writer's "affaire très intéressante." He asked BF to set a day and time before next Tuesday when he might call again. APS.

5. Charles-Marie and Charles de Neuilly, both called baron d'Eberstein, were Le Normant d'Etioles' sons. They had returned from Holland, where they worked for their father's purchasing agents. In late May and early June, Le Normant d'Etioles had written to Vergennes and the farmers general, seeking positions for them in America. If they could not obtain consulships, he hoped they might be appointed as tobacco agents: Price, *France and the Chesapeake*, II, 741, 1086n.

réservé pour demander que les concèssions qui Seront accordées Soyent gratuites. Mais Je crois pouvoir vous assurer que Mr. de vergennes verroit ce Sacrifice de la part du Congrés comme une marque de Reconnoissance des Services essentiels qu'il luy á rendûs ainsi qu'a votre Patrie. Votre excèllence conviendra que c'est un petit Sacrifice en comparaison de ceux que ce Ministre á obtenûs du Roy en faveur des americains. Je crois cependant qu'il Seroit indiscret de lui en parler parcequ'il est de Sa façon de penser de ne vouloir en aucune circonstance être éxigeant. Mais Je crois que Si vous consultés á Cet Egard M.M. de Rayneval et hénin, ils ne vous dissimuleront pas tout l'interêt que prend M. de vergennes á Cette affaire. Daignés donc Servir de Second Pere á Mrs. d'Eberstein. Ils Sont au moment d'arriver icy pour se rendre en Amérique et Je compte incèssament être en état de vous faire voir en vous les présentant qu'ils ne Sont point indignes de vos bontés.

J'ay l'honneur d'être avec Respect de votre excellence, Monsieur Le Docteur, Le très humble et très obeissant Serviteur

LENORMANT DETIOLES

From Sir Edward Newenham

ALS: Historical Society of Pennsylvania

My Dear Sir—   Leige 20 June 1783—
Hearing that the Irish Parliament will immediatly be dissolved,[6] I am obliged to return to Dublin without having the pleasure of paying my respects to you, & Congratulating you, upon the final completion of your Glorious Cause—

I am now at the house of William Augustus Miles Esqr: whose writings have rendered Essential services to the Cause of Liberty; he Early & warmly Supported the rights and Privi-

6. Parliament was dissolved on July 25, and the general election in County Dublin was held from Aug. 13 to Aug. 16: *Dublin Evening Post,* July 26, 1783; James Kelly, *Sir Edward Newenham MP, 1734–1814: Defender of the Protestant Constitution* (Dublin, 2004), pp. 193–5.

ledges of your Excellencys fellow-Subjects in america;[7] he intends to Visit Paris before he returns to England, therefore I beg leave to Introduce him to your Excellency, & shall consider any Civilities you or your Amiable & Virtuous Grandson Shew him, as *personaly* conferred upon me—
Wishing you Every happiness that this Life can bestow—I have the Honor to remain, My Dr: Sir with the most Sincere Respect & Esteem your Excellencys Most obliged & Humble Sert
EDWARD NEWENHAM

PS Lady Newenham & my Son have charged me to present their best Respects to your Excellency & your Grandson—

Addressed: To / His Excellency Doctr: Benj: Franklin / Minister Plenipotentiary from / the United States of America / Passy / Paris—

From Vergennes: Three Letters

(I) L (draft):[8] Archives du Ministère des affaires étrangères; (II) LS: Historical Society of Pennsylvania; L (draft): Archives du Ministère des affaires étrangères; (III) L (draft): Archives du Ministère des affaires étrangères

I.

Mr Franklin   A Vlles. Le 20. Juin 1783.
J'ai reçu, M, la lettre que vous m'avez fait l'honneur de mecrire en faveur du Sr. James Price;[9] je l'ai communiquèe à

---

7. Miles (1753/4–1817) was a political journalist and pamphleteer. In 1779, while serving in the Royal Navy, he published anonymously *A Political Mirror; or, a Summary Review of the Present Reign* . . . (London, 1779), a critique of the British war in America as well as the government under George III. The following year he issued a second edition under his name and dedicated it to Newenham. In early 1783 Miles moved to Seraing, near Liège, from whence he sent articles to the *Morning Post* in 1784–85 defending the Pitt ministry: *ODNB;* Charles P. Miles, ed., *The Correspondence of William Augustus Miles on the French Revolution, 1789–1817* (2 vols., London, 1890), I, 13–16.
8. Drafts of all three letters are in Gérard de Rayneval's hand.
9. Above, May 23.

Mr. le garde des Sceaux, et ce chef de la magistrature vient de me répondre. Vous avez la réponse ci-jointe; vous y verrez les mesures qui seront prises [que][1] pour mettre le Sr. Price en etat de Suivre, Son procès contre les Srs. Bonfield et Haiwood. Il alloit lui faire expédier un sauf-conduit pour un an et qu'il chargeoit M. le procureur général de Bordeaux[2] de le prévenir dans le cas où le Sr. la framboise traduiroit le Sr. Price pardevant les Consuls de Bordeaux.

II.

à Versailles Le 20. Juin 1783.

Je ne puis me dispenser, Monsieur, de vous envoyer les piéces cy-jointes. Vous y verrés que le Sr. Pauli, négociant à Paris, se trouve Créancier d'une somme considérable du Sr. Penet, agent de L'Etat de Virginie.[3] Je ne doute pas, Monsieur, que vous ne vous portiès á solliciter en faveur de ce particulier, et que L'Etat de Virginie ne se fasse un devoir de remplir des engagements contractés en son nom et pour Son compte.

J'ai L'honneur d'être trés parfaitement, Monsieur, vôtre trés humble et très obéissant serviteur   De Vergennes

M. franklin

III.

A Vlles le 20. Juin 1783.

J'ai communiqué à Mr. le Mis. de Castries, M, vos nouvelles reclamations au sujet de la saisie faite par les Srs. forster Sur le produit des prises faites par la frégate américaine l'alliance; Ce

---

1. The draft is difficult to read and heavily revised in this section. The word "que" is interlined, but a vertical line stemming from it suggests that the writer thought about striking the entire sentence instead of revising it further.

2. The procurator general of the Parlement of Bordeaux was Jean-Baptiste-Pierre-Jules Dudon: *DBF;* William Doyle, *The Parlement of Bordeaux at the End of the Old Regime, 1771–1790* (New York, 1974), pp. 192, 318, and *passim.* The *sauf-conduit* was granted; see Vergennes to BF, June 26.

3. For Penet's difficulties with his creditors and eventual fate see XXXVII, 640–1, 683–4; XXXVIII, 234–6, 328–9, 455–6, 485.

Ministre vient de me répondre Que cette affaire a été évoquée au Conseil, et qu'elle ne tardera pas à y ètre jugée aussitôt Que les formalités requises auront été remplies.[4]

Mr franklin

4. The Bordeaux firm of Forster frères had attached the proceeds from a recent sale of prizes made by the *Alliance* as retribution for its having illegally seized (under a different captain) one of their ships three years earlier. After BF protested, Castries had the attachment lifted: XXX, 173–4; XXXIX, 308, 367. Castries' order was promptly appealed by Forster frères in concert with another Bordeaux firm and Puchelberg & Cie. of Lorient. BF complained to Vergennes at their weekly meeting on April 8; Barclay also complained, sending copies of these appeals to Vergennes three days later. Vergennes forwarded the documents to Castries on April 19. After six weeks of silence, Barclay—acting on BF's advice—wrote to Rayneval asking for news, conveying the urgency of the situation, and requesting that a reply be sent to either him or BF. On June 17 Vergennes (who had learned from Castries' office that the appeal might have had legal merit) received official notification of the king's June 6 *arrêt* annulling all previous actions and ordering that the case be tried by the *conseil des finances pour les prises en mer:* Barclay to Vergennes, April 11, 1783; Barclay to Rayneval, April 12 and [end of May], 1783; Vergennes to Castries, April 19 and May 30, 1783; Chardon to Vergennes, June 14 and 17, 1783; Castries to Vergennes, Aug. 31, 1783 (all at the AAE); Barclay to WTF, May 9, 1783 (APS). Our thanks to Priscilla M. Roberts for her assistance.

From François-Marie-des-Neiges-Emmanuel de Rohan-Poulduc[5]

LS and press copy of copy: American Philosophical Society; draft: Royal Library of Malta; copy and transcript: National Archives

Monsieur,   A Malte le 21. Juin 1783.

J'ai reçu avec la plus vive sensibilité la médaille que Votre Excellence m'a fait parvenir, et le prix que je mets à cette acquisition ne laisse pas de bornes à ma reconnaissance. Ce monument de la liberté Américaine, d'un événement que Votre Excellence a eu la gloire de préparer et de conduire, tient une place distinguée dans mon Cabinet comme votre nom, Monsieur, mérite d'occuper la première dans la liste des grands-hommes.[6]

Lorsque le hazard ou le commerce ameneront dans les Ports de mon Isle quelques-uns de vos Concitoyens ou de leurs bâtimens, Je serai empressé de les accueillir, ils trouveront auprès de moi tous les secours qu'ils pourront réclamer, et Je verrais avec un plaisir infini naître quelque liaison entre cette nation intéressante et mes Sujets, surtout si elle pouvait servir à convaincre Votre Excellence des sentimens distingués avec lesquels Je suis Monsieur, De Votre Excellence, Très affectionné serviteur,

Le Grand Maître,

ROHAN

S. Exc. Mr. Franklin

---

5. The grand master of the Knights of Malta, answering BF's letter of April 6: XXXIX, 436.

6. In the copy of this letter that BF enclosed in his to Boudinot of Sept. 13, this sentence was shortened to: "Ce monument de la Liberté Américaine tient une place distinguée dans mon Cabinet."

From Michel-Guillaume St. John de Crèvecœur

ALS: American Philosophical Society

Sir, [before June 22, 1783][7]
The Marquis de Castries Shew'd me Yesterday the Model of the Edict which he proposes obtaining for the Establishment of the 5. Pacquets boats.[1] I desired him to Send it you, Ere he had presented it, which he will Shortly do, I beg You'd Read it attentively & Send him back all your observations thereon,— Woud you be Kind Enough to Inform the Countesse de Houdetot, in what part of the Town that big Wire is to be had, that She may place a Second Electical Rod.

I am With Respect Sir Your Very Humble Servt. ST. JOHN

Addressed: a Son Excellence / Monsieur Benjamin Franklin / ambassadeur des Etats unis de Lamèrique / a Passy

Notation: de Crevecœur

7. This letter has to have been written before June 28, when the edict it discusses was signed into law. From its tone, it also appears to have been written before June 22, the day Crèvecœur learned of his appointment as French consul in New York and began making preparations to leave. (For that appointment see his letter of [June 24 or July 1].) One biographer believed that it dated from before April 2, and that the note from the comtesse d'Houdetot of that date (XXXIX, 421–2) was urging BF to answer it: Julia P. Mitchell, *St. Jean de Crèvecoeur* (New York, 1916), pp. 179–80. That seems unlikely, since the comtesse's note reminds BF to review a report that Crèvecœur needed to deliver to Castries, whereas the present letter concerns an edict that BF would soon receive from Castries himself.

1. Crèvecœur had recommended a service at an annual cost of less than 300,000 *l.t.* and later expressed regret at Castries' decision to use more luxurious vessels: Mitchell, *St. Jean de Crèvecoeur,* pp. 82–3, 178–9.

From Charles Blagden[2]

AL: American Philosophical Society

Hotel d'Espagne Rue Guénégaud June 22, 1783
Dr. Blagden will do himself the honour of dining with
Dr. Franklin next thursday.

Addressed: A Monsieur / M. Le Docteur Franklin &c / à Passy.

To Benjamin Franklin Bache

ALS: University of Pennsylvania Library

My dear Child,   Passy, June 23. 1783.
I received your late Letter,[3] and am pleas'd to see that you
improve in your Writing. I have also receiv'd the little Drawing of a Country-house, which seems to be prettily done, and

---

2. For Blagden's visit to Paris see Joseph Banks to BF, May 28. According
to his journal, the June 26 dinner included WTF, John Jay, Mme Helvétius,
and Mrs. Barclay. Blagden commented of BF: "He is become very reserved
& cautious. eyed me much." Jay, he wrote, was "evidently not quiet." WTF
was "much more like his father than his grandfather: voice wonderfully
like." BF asked Blagden to procure the volumes of *Phil. Trans.* due him,
which the latter promised to do: Charles Blagden's Journal, entry of June
26, 1783 (Yale University Library). When writing to Banks on July 1,
Blagden observed that although BF had "neglected Science for politics" and
was not as well-informed as others on "new discoveries," he "still retains
the same soundness of understanding": Neil Chambers, ed., *Scientific Correspondence of Sir Joseph Banks* (6 vols., London, 2007), II, 98.

BF had tried at least twice before to obtain his copies of *Phil. Trans.* In
May, 1779, he asked Ingenhousz to apply for them, and the Royal Society
approved the measure: XXIX, 428, 544. A letter from Edward Bridgen, undated as to year but which we now realize belongs to 1779, indicates that
BF made the same request of John Paradise around the same time. Bridgen
claimed that Paradise had requested the volumes but that they had been delivered to Magellan, who in turn gave them to one of the secretaries of the
Spanish embassy in London for delivery to Passy: Bridgen to BF, June 18,
[1779], APS.

3. Missing. It must have been written between BFB's of May 30 and
June 20.

shows that you advance also in that Art. I write by this Post to Mr. Marignac, requesting that he would permit you to come and see me and stay with me during the Vacation of the Schools.[4] I hear you have been sick,[5] but I hope you are recover'd and strong enough to undertake the Journey; and then it may do you good, and help to confirm your Health. Your Cousin remembers his Love to you, and I am ever your affectionate Grandfather,

B FRANKLIN

My Love to Johonnot I have lately heard from his Friends and yours who are all well.

4. Not found.

5. BF undoubtedly heard this from Matthew Ridley, who had just seen BFB in Geneva and had wanted to bring the child back to Paris with him; see BFB to BF, May 30, and Robert Pigott to BF, June 27. Ridley arrived in Paris on June 13: Matthew Ridley's Journal, entry of June 13, 1783 (Mass. Hist. Soc.).

On June 2, in Ridley's absence, his clerk Nicolas Darcel sent BF three bills for acceptance: no. 1902 for 300 *l.t.* and nos. 551 and 552 for 60 *l.t.* each. On July 15 Darcel sent nos. 1960, 1961, 1963, and 1964, listed at 90 *l.t.* each. (Both letters are at the APS.) According to the ledger of loan office bills accepted by BF (XXXVII, 439n), a set of the former group had been paid on Feb. 11. A notation on Ridley's letterbook copy of the June 2 letter confirms this (Mass. Hist. Soc.). As for the latter bills, no. 1960 had been paid on Jan. 20, 1783, and the other three on Sept. 30, 1782; all four were for 60 *l.t.*

From Thomas and Mary Barclay[6]

L:[7] American Philosophical Society

Auteuil 23rd June 1783./.
Mr. & Mrs. Barclay presents their Complimts. to Doctor Frank-
lin, and will have the Honor of Waiting on him at Dinner on
Thursday.[8]

Addressed: His Excellency Benjamin Franklin Esqr. / Passy

From Nathaniel Falconer   ALS: American Philosophical Society

My Dear Frend   London June the 23 1783
I Recived yours of the 18 this month this Day which Give
me Great Joy to hear of your helth but much Surprised you
have had no Letters Latter than you mentiond for a Mr Vaughan
that Came in the Same vessell Told us he had Dispaches for
you as Soon as I had Determined on my imbarcation I waited
on Mr Charles Thomson to Let him know that if Congress
had aney Dispaches I would Take Care off them but this Said
Mr Vaughan I belived plaged Mr Morris and Told him he Should

---

6. This is one of three extant dinner acceptances from the Barclays, all
written from Auteuil in a hand we now recognize as Henry Champion's
(for whom see the following footnote). Another, dated July 1, 1783, accepts BF's invitation for an Independence Day dinner the following Friday
(APS). The third, written on an unspecified "Thursday evening" and including Matthew Ridley, was published in December, 1781, at what we er-
roneously believed was the earliest possible time that Mary Barclay might
have been with her husband in Paris: XXXVI, 201. She and her children did
not leave Lorient until mid-June, 1783, moving into the spacious house at
Auteuil that he leased from May 1, 1783, to April 30, 1784. The Ridley family joined them there in July, 1783, staying through the end of the year. A
Thursday between July and December is therefore the most likely time for
the acceptance: Roberts and Roberts, *Thomas Barclay*, pp. 117–19, 121–3,
126, 137–9.
7. In the hand of Henry Champion, who served as Barclay's clerk from
February, 1783, to July, 1784: Account XXVII (XXXII, 4).
8. June 26.

Go to France⁹ the Last part is Conjecter from his owne Conversation I must Confes I was not well pleased if there was aney Dispaches that a stranger Should be Trusted with them in preference to my Self Sir the preliminary articles of peace was Recived with Great Joy and was not kept back as you have been informd but was Given out to the publick as Soon as possable¹ General Mifflin who is in Congress² and makes his home at my house and is your most Steedey frend hass keep back nothing from me that past about you I understood from him that your Request was admitted in part for to Come home but keep it in Such amaner that if they Could not Carrey aproper person that they might Still keep you there another year there is asertain A Lee in Congress has Tried to make aparty again Mr Morris and your Self but has not been able to accomplish aney thing³ when I Came away nor I hope will never be able to Carrey his point for belive if he Did it would Be to Come Back under the Brish yoake again whe have Great Reason to belive Some among us have been in pay from this Countrey most of the war Sir the washington was Sauef arrived Long before I Saild and also Capt Barney Last from the havanah at Road Island with alarge Sum of money aboard all which was Sauef Lodgd in the Bank at philadla which Bank is in as Good Credit as the Bank of Ingland the procklamation of peace Came out from Congress the morning I Came away which was the 12 of april⁴ on my arrivall

9. See John Vaughan to BF, June 10.
1. The preliminary articles were printed in the newspapers as if they were unconditional, even before the news of a general armistice arrived, and were greeted by cannon salutes and general celebrations: William C. Stinchcombe, *The American Revolution and the French Alliance* (Syracuse, 1969), pp. 198–9.
2. Thomas Mifflin was elected to Congress as a delegate from Pennsylvania on Nov. 12, 1782: Smith, *Letters*, XX, xxi.
3. Arthur Lee was part of a bloc of delegates opposed to government centralization: H. James Henderson, *Party Politics in the Continental Congress* (New York, St. Louis, and San Francisco, 1974), pp. 318–21. For his recent criticism of BF see XXXIX, 381.
4. The proclamation (*JCC*, XXIV, 238–40) was approved on April 11 and published that day as a supplement to the *Pa. Evening Post*. It was is-

hear I found that they Did not no the peace had Reacht the Congress I Directly Sent one to the post office to Mr Tod[5] to Send up to adminstration but it has Never apeard in aney paper hear tho they print Every Lie they Can Git hold off as to the Constitution of pensilvania being alterd Next October is the year for Chuesing the Councell of Cencors and then it must be two years before it is alterd[6] I hope youl be blest with your health to Reach home Long before that time but Should be Glad of your oppion on that point as I no it will have Great wait I understood from Generall Mifflin that asalrey was Fixt on your Grand Son but what Sum I Cannot Recollect[7] I Expect to hear from Mr Mifflin Every Day by aship was to Sail the 25 of May from our place aney information I Git Shall write you Directly as to Mr Morris Resing his office Depended on Congress Funding the publick Debts if they Did that I think he will Stay in another year which I thing they will notwithstanding the it is oposed So by Mr A L and his frends I Shall Call on Mr Strahan with the paper inclosed and Git him to print it if posable I Send you by this Convance aCoppy of the Duteys intend to be Layd by Congress which I Should have Sent before had I not thought you had Recd them mr mifflin Got them out of Congress for me[8] I wrote to your Grand Son to Solicte your intrest to Send me over a mittretain(?) for the Ship olive Branch 225 Tons Britsh Built Nath Falconer master Carring 15 hands americaian Bottom[9] if it Cant

sued the next day as a broadside: Charles Evans *et al.*, *American Bibliography* . . . (14 vols., Chicago and Worcester, Mass., 1903–59), VI, 254.

5. Secretary of the Post Office Anthony Todd, who wrote BF on June 25.

6. For the duties of the council of censors see XXXIX, 608n.

7. In December, Congress had approved the salary BF was paying WTF as his secretary: XXXVIII, 59–60, 538.

8. The list of duties was part of the long-debated plan to fund the debt that was finally approved by Congress on April 18, subject to ratification; for that plan see Morris to BF, May 26, letter (I). A copy of the April 18 resolution in Charles Thomson's hand is among BF's papers at the APS. Falconer, as he reminds BF above, left Philadelphia on April 12.

9. Falconer explained to WTF that after he had purchased a ship, he discovered that passes were granted only to British subjects. He hoped that BF could obtain a pass for him to sail as an American. The letter is undated (APS).

be obtaind by you Shall be obliged to make my Ship an Inglish
Bottom hear and Goe under Inglish Coulars from hear till I Git
to phild which will mortify me verey much I beg your answer
as Soon as posable on this matter I will Redley Remitt or pay to
your order all Expences I am my Dear frend with Great Respect
your most Hbl Sr   NATH FALCONER

My Compliments to your Grand Son and to Mr Hartley

Addressed: Docter Franklin

Notation: Falconer June 23 1783

From Ingenhousz   ALS: American Philosophical Society

Dear Friend   Vienna juin 23 1783.
This is only to accompany the adjoin'd lettre of mr. Weinbrenner, who, as you see, does not loose time to make use of
your kind proposition of giving some introductory letters to
his agent, who is mr. *Donath.* This gentleman will set out in a
few weeks for Philadelphia New york & Boston, where he will
spend two years. He will carry with him various productions of
this Country. I hope you will as soon, as Convenient for you,
grant the request of Mr. Weinbrenner.[1]
    Your original lettre with the medal inclosed is not yet come

1. Weinbrenner's letter is missing, but see BF to Ingenhousz, May 16.
Joseph Donath (1751–1829) arrived in Philadelphia in December, 1783, and
lived there for the rest of his life. He initially brought with him samples
of cloth but later imported shoes, boots, slippers, and Bohemian glass.
In 1795 he supplied Thomas Jefferson with window glass for Monticello:
John J. Maitland, "St. Mary's Graveyard, Fourth and Spruce Streets,
Philadelphia. Records and Extracts from Inscriptions on Tombstones,"
American Catholic Hist. Soc. of Philadelphia *Records,* III (1888–91),
293; Hanns Schlitter, ed., *Die Berichte des ersten Agenten Österreichs in den
Vereinigten Staaten von Amerika Baron de Beelen-Bertholff* . . . (Vienna,
1891), pp. 326, 327–8, 382, 525, 818; *Jefferson Papers,* XXVIII, 259, 284,
436, 469.

to hand,[2] neither the Philadelphia Almanach, you was so good as to send me a year ago.[3]

The Cast of my profil, I send you, is made in the usual manner of gypse or plaster of Paris; which being dryed is smeared over with parchment glue or glue of ising glas warmed. When this kind of varnish is thereabout dry, the whol is covered, by means of a very fine brush or pencil, which silver dust, called *silver bronze*, to be got every where in Colour Shops. The parts of the cast thus finish'd, which aught to be polishd, are rubbed with a polish'd piece of steel.

Your advise about the statuary was thankfully recieved and much approved of. I recieved at last from mr. le Begue the first 5 sheats of my book under the press at Paris. I did not find one Single typographical error in them.

I hope still to see you here with your grandson before you set out for your beloved America.

I am with the greatest estime Your most obedient Serv and affectionate friend   J. INGEN HOUSZ

to Benj Franklin Passy

Endorsed: June 23. 83—

From José de Arriaga Brum da Silveyra[4] and Other Consulship Seekers   ALS: Historical Society of Pennsylvania

Throughout the summer, Franklin continued to receive applications for American consulships from Portugal, Spain, Italy, France, and

2. According to his next letter, of Aug. 15, Ingenhousz received a copy of BF's May 16 letter before the original arrived, enclosing the medal. The rest of the present letter largely addresses issues BF raised on May 16; see that letter and its annotation.

3. In a letter he began writing in 1781, BF told Ingenhousz he was sending a German almanac. He did not finish the letter until June, 1782, and may not have enclosed it: XXXV, 547.

4. The Arriagas were an important aristocratic family in the Azores: Joel Serrão, ed., *Dicionário de história de Portugal* (9 vols., Porto, [1992?]–2000), I, 207.

Germany. Their number is smaller than in the spring, when news of the preliminary peace had raised expectations of an immediate burst of commercial activity between Europe and the United States.[5] The current applicants use the familiar strategies of highlighting their ideological affinity to the new republic, their port's strategic importance to American commerce, or their previous service to the United States. Several also approach Franklin under the auspices of prominent figures in Paris.

As an expression of his deep admiration for the American republic, José de Arriaga Brum da Silveyra, whose letter is printed below, offers the services of his son as American consul general in the Azores. Arriaga's letter is forwarded by the Paris banker Jean Dupont père.

Several applications arrive from the Mediterranean. Brothers Roch and François de Manescau recommend themselves as American consuls in Málaga on July 1. Málaga, being the premier port in the Mediterranean, is an ideal place for Americans to gather intelligence about the markets. As partners in the firm Joseph Manescau, Maury & Cie., they have already done business with American merchants since the return of peace; they now wish to become even more useful to the new republic. Though French, one of them speaks English fairly well, having spent several years in England. For more information, Franklin may consult either the French consul in Málaga, Monsieur Humbourg,[6] or the Spanish ambassador to France, the conde de Aranda.[7]

On an unspecified day in July, the Loge du Patriotisme forwards an extract of a memoir by French merchant and fellow mason John Guy Gautier in Barcelona, who has asked them to forward it along with their recommendation. Gautier wishes to become the American consul in Barcelona.[8] Monsieur Le Guay has promised to support his

5. See XXXIX, 76–87. Unless otherwise noted, all letters cited in this headnote are in French, are at the APS, and elicited no known response.

6. Antoine-François-Armand Humbourg de Fillières was named consul at Málaga in 1767: Anne Mézin, *Les Consuls de France au siècle des lumières (1715–1792)* ([Paris, 1998]), pp. 351–2. François Manescau's association with Juan Bautista Maury in transatlantic trade is mentioned in Aurora Gamez Amian, *Málaga y el comercio colonial con América (1765–1820)* (Málaga, 1994), p. 130.

7. Their letter is at the Hist. Soc. of Pa.

8. This was Gautier's second approach to BF. Five years earlier, he applied for the position of consul general for Catalonia: XXVI, 210–11. In 1782 he asked John Jay for help in obtaining the consulship in Barcelona, and Jay forwarded his petition to Congress: *JCC*, XXIII, 468n.

application to Congress, but Gautier believes that Franklin's approval is necessary and hopes that this channel will be effective. The Loge assures Franklin that it has no other motive than the masonic injunction to do good. In a postscript, Nogaret (who wrote the letter) adds that if Franklin wants to respond, he can send his reply to Nogaret's address, which he knows well.[9]

Tournachon, signing himself "Député de Lyon au conseil Royal de commerce,"[1] writes from Paris on August 25 on behalf of Aimé Bonnaffons, a Lyon merchant residing in Genoa, where he is partner in the firm of Regny père & fils. Anticipating that the United States will soon appoint consuls in Mediterranean ports, Bonnaffons seeks the consulship in Genoa. Tournachon regrets that illness prevents him from discussing the matter with Franklin in person. He assures the American minister, however, that Bonnaffons is industrious, honest, very intelligent, and associated with an old firm that has always enjoyed the highest reputation. Since neither he nor Bonnaffons has the honor of being acquainted with Franklin, Tournachon puts his trust in Franklin's reputation for fairness.

From Naples on August 30 comes another application for the much-coveted prospective consulship there. Jean Vieusseux is a partner in the Neopolitan firm of Vieusseux, Reymond & Cie., renowned for its wealth and connections to the French ministry as well as the

9. For the Loge du Patriotisme, which had recently invited BF to a meeting, see XXXIX, 577–8. This letter was signed by twelve *frères*, six of whom had signed the earlier invitation: Vauchelle, the *vénérable*, Nogaret, now serving as second *surveillant*, Terrasse, Simon, Louis, and Cuillié. The other six, all listed in Le Bihan, *Francs-maçons parisiens,* are: Jacques-Nicolas Mottet, a *commis principal de la guerre;* Etienne-Marie Desnois, a *commis de la guerre,* then *commis principal des finances;* sieur Beccard, *greffier en chef du Port Dauphin* in Saint-Domingue; sieur Pelloux, *chef du gobelet de la comtesse d'Artois;* and Antoine-Jean Georgette-Dubuisson, sieur de La Boullaye, *huissier de la chambre du Roi et gouverneur des pages de la chambre du Roi.* The first *surveillant,* "Dutillet de Villars," is either Jean-Joseph du Tillet de Villars père, *ancien valet de chambre du Roi et ancien gouverneur des pages de la chambre du Roi,* or Léonard-Antoine du Tillet de Villars, *valet de chambre du Roi et commis de la marine, officier des ordres du Roi,* and *subdélégué de l'Intendant de Paris.*

1. Tournachon is listed in the *Almanach royal* for 1783, p. 270; he is identified as François Tournachon in Louis Trénard, *Lyon: de l'Encyclopédie au préromantisme* (2 vols., Paris, 1958), I, 21. He probably was a partner in the firm of Tournachon, Zenon & Cie., cloth merchants in Lyon: *Almanach des marchands* for 1779, p. 309.

House of Bourbon. He has just received a long-awaited letter from the Paris banker Louis Julien,[2] reassuring him that Franklin spoke encouragingly when the banker recommended Vieusseux as a consul a few months ago. Vieusseux now writes directly, presenting a catalog of potential objects of trade. The Kingdom of the Two Sicilies can offer silk, oil, wool, hemp, wood, wine, dried fruits, manna, tartar, and soda ash, which it would trade for American indigo, leather, and especially salt provisions. Once commercial relations are established, the United States will want to appoint a consul. Born in Geneva, Vieusseux was raised on republican principles and would be honored to serve a state that fought so gloriously and successfully for its liberty.[3]

A man whose name was known to Franklin, John Diot, writes from Morlaix on July 18. He summarizes his services to the American republic over the previous four years, ranging from outfitting privateers to helping destitute seamen upon their return from British prisons.[4] These efforts, made at his own expense, now embolden him to request the position of vice-consul at Morlaix. He speaks and writes English fluently, having lived in Ireland, whereas the person currently serving as commercial agent[5] does not speak English and is merely the representative of a man who fled town three years ago because of bankruptcy. Since the office of vice-consul is "plus honorifique que lucrative," Diot hopes that it is obvious that he is not pursuing his own financial interests but only seeking new opportunities to be useful to America.

Dominque-François Belletti sends his sixth and final entreaty for the American consulship in Trieste on September 15.[6] He begins by announcing that Monsieur Bertrand, the French consul in Trieste,[7] has promised to remind Franklin about him. Belletti also knows that Franklin promised Monsieur Le Roi that he would respond. He once again points to the substantial commerce with America that could flourish in Trieste and reiterates that he would gladly serve without pay. A duplicate of this letter, marked "Copie," is at the Historical

2. Identified in xxv, 394n.
3. The letter is at the Hist. Soc. of Pa.
4. Diot's first services to the United States were in 1779; see xxx, 155n.
5. Pitot Duhellés, who in fact applied for the position of consul or vice-consul on Jan. 28: xxxix, 76, 86–7.
6. His five previous applications, written between February and April, are summarized in xxxix, 82–3.
7. Abbé Antoine-Madeleine Bertrand, a former professor of mathematics at the Ecole militaire, was named consul in Trieste in 1781: Mézin, *Consuls de France*, pp. 143–4.

Society of Pennsylvania, where there is also an undated and un-signed letter of recommendation from Bertrand. He attests that Bel-letti, who wrote to Franklin three months ago, is one of the best-respected merchants in Trieste: honest, intelligent, and experienced in all aspects of commerce.

On September 2 Jean-Baptiste-Artur de Vermonnet, a French of-ficer who had served for three years in the Continental Army, writes a letter in excellent English from Saint-Domingue, where he has been stranded with his wife and children ever since the ship carrying them back to France was forced into that port. He asks Franklin to inter-cede with Castries in support of his application for the position of French vice-consul in the United States, a country in which he "ar-dently desires to live." He also encloses a letter that he had hoped to be able to deliver in person.[8]

Finally, from Germany comes a letter recommending an unnamed person as a commercial agent or chargé d'affaires. Colonel Charle de Qureille writes in German from Giessen in Hesse-Darmstadt on July 30. Inspired by the victorious American struggle on behalf of all mankind, he wants to help the new republic to increase its standing in Germany. Since Americans are unfamiliar with the principal com-mercial towns on the Rhine and Main rivers, which could supply the United States with products like linen, sailcloth, and yarn, Qureille's friend could be of great assistance. He has served for 17 years as a lo-cal government official and has knowledge of politics, history, geog-raphy, mathematics, astronomy, and physics. Moreover, he has long been a fervent admirer of the American cause.[9]

8. That letter, from Elizabeth Partridge, was written from Boston in December, 1781, and recommends Vermonnet, the bearer, to BF. We pub-lished it in its chronological place, explaining the delay in its delivery and identifying Vermonnet in annotation: xxxvi, 202–4. His memoir to Cas-tries, in French and in a secretarial hand, was also enclosed with the present letter and remains filed with it at the APS.

Two more letters from Vermonnet survive. He writes again from Saint-Domingue on Dec. 10, 1783, providing further details about his family and mentioning his intention to return to Boston in May. On March 15, 1785, he writes from Saint-Germain, outside Paris. Reminding BF of his previous correspondence, he now asks for an audience. Both letters, in French, are at the APS.

9. Qureille enclosed a small sheet on which he wrote his address and identified himself as a knight of the Order of the Brandenburg Red Eagle and a judge in Itzbach and Bünau. A French translation of his letter, in a hand we do not recognize, is also at the APS.

Monsieur Franklin   a Lisbonne Le 24 de Juin de 1783
Le desir de pouvoir contribuer á lavantage d'une Republique, que par tant de faits eclatants á merite l'admiration de l'Univers m'a fait prendre la resulution de vouloir aussi temoigner ma singulièr'estime, en lui offrant mon fils Jose de Arriaga habitant dans lIsle de Fayal pour lui servir de Consul General dans les Assores, et pour l'aider a renouveller par cette voie l'ancien commerce, q'il y avai entre ces Isles et lAmerique.
L'accuillement, que le Sieur Dupont a merité ches vous raport a celá,[1] me rend tres sensiblement obligé, et encore que je suis icy occupé au Parlement de la Justice je fairai tous les oforts possibles pour que le dit mon fils se puisse acquitter de son devoir avec le zele, et efficace correspondants a l'honeur que lui plaira lui accorder, et en vous assurant l'haute consideration que j'ai pour vous je vous prie de me croire avec le plus profond respect Monsieur Votre tres Humble e tres Obeissant Serviteur

JOSE DE ARRIAGA BRUM DA SILVEYRA

Addressed: a Monsieur / Monsieur Dr. Franklin / Charge des affaires des Etats unis de / lAmerique a / Paris

From the Baron de Borde Duchatelet,[2] with Franklin's Note for a Reply, and Other Applicants for Emigration

ALS: Historical Society of Pennsylvania

The cessation of hostilities and Franklin's reputation as a philanthropist continue to inspire the hopes of prospective emigrants. During the

---

1. Jean Dupont père, "Banquier à Paris," forwarded this letter to BF on July 13, reminding him that they had spoken about this applicant some two months earlier. If BF wants to respond directly, Dupont will be glad to forward the letter; otherwise, BF should inform Dupont of his decision and he will pass it along (Hist. Soc. of Pa.). BF knew of the Paris banking firm Dupont & fils as early as 1777 (XXV, 255), and we presume that the writer of this letter was its principal. The man we believe to be his son, born in Lisbon and also named Jean, formed his own banking firm in 1780 and made a considerable fortune: *DBF*.

2. Possibly Jean-Pierre-Louis de Bordes du Chatelet, baron du Châtelet (1752–1796), or one of his brothers. They were members of an old family

five months covered by this volume, letters come from France, Italy, the Austrian Netherlands, Germany, and England. Petitioners appeal either to American national interest by detailing the essential skills they will bring to the new republic or to Franklin's sentiments through heartrending tales of misfortune and thwarted ambition. The baron de Borde Duchatelet, whose letter is printed as a sample, does both.[3]

Paillet, a 24-year-old from Versailles, lists three reasons for writing to Franklin on May 17: the gratitude he feels toward his parents who have made sacrifices for his education, continue to support him, and wish to see him placed in a good position; his desire for travel, which was the path to wisdom for Lycurgus, Solon, Thales, and Plato; and the difficulty of securing a post at Versailles. It would be to Franklin's glory if he were to provide Paillet with the means of fulfilling his obligation toward his parents and to secure him a job, presumably in America.[4]

Louis Terrier,[5] having practiced surgery for six years in Guadeloupe, is now a professor at the *collège de chirurgie* of Marseille. Although he is unknown to Franklin, as he writes on May 21, he is nonetheless confident that the American minister will help him establish himself in America as a surgeon. He details his own training and explains the importance of his art. By contrast, Pietro Maggi of Milan, who writes in Italian on May 26, covers himself in humility, addressing his letter to the immortal Franklin, whose name is the glory of the century and who will be the object of admiration throughout the ages. The young man (he is not yet 24) explains that he received his law degree from the University of Pavia three years earlier, but his family's poverty and an unspecified cabal have prevented him from finding work. He asks only for the privilege of serving Franklin and his country on any terms Franklin may decide.

---

from the Bresse region: Henri de Jouvencel, *L'Assemblée de la noblesse de la Sénéchaussée de Lyon en 1789: étude historique et généalogique* (2 vols., Lyon, 1907; reprint, 1999), I, 228; *Dictionnaire de la noblesse*, III, 558–9.

3. Unless otherwise noted, all letters described in this headnote are in French, are at the APS, and produced no known response.

4. He may be the François-Hippolyte Paillet who became librarian of the city of Versailles and a professor at the *lycée* there, who published a study of Virgil's *Aeneid:* J. Hippolyte Daniel, *Biographie des hommes remarquables de Seine-et-Oise . . .* (Paris, 1837), pp. 91–2, 229.

5. He signs with only his first initial but is identified in Augustin Fabre, *Histoire des hôpitaux et des institutions de bienfaisance de Marseille* (2 vols., Marseille, 1854), I, 369–70.

Another story of persecution and injustice comes from Germany. Herr Greyer explains in German on May 28 that he is a former court secretary and cashier from Minden an der Weser in Westphalia. He has been embroiled in a legal battle with his former superior, Hofmeister Albrecht, who accused him of embezzling money from the court treasury. Greyer fears that he will not be vindicated because Albrecht has friends more powerful than his own. Prevented from working in his homeland, he asks Franklin to help him make a new start in America. He has worked as a court secretary since he was 13 years old, in the provinces as well as Berlin, and is willing to bring this experience to bear at the American "Hof" (court). In particular, the American government might consider revising its court constitution along Prussian lines. If required, Greyer can provide references, but he is convinced that Franklin's well-known altruism will cause the American minister to come to his aid.

L. J. Lahaÿe, an arms manufacturer writing on May 31 from Nessonvaux Sous Olne, also seeks to escape local constraints on his ambition. He has been anxiously waiting for the United States to gain its independence so that he can settle there with his family and work in a firearms factory. His long, confused letter is full of bitter complaints about the low pay and lack of support for his trade in the Liège province. His skill (as we understand it) is in forging iron for gun barrels, and he hopes to bring with him to America the machine required for this work. He requests a large loan from Franklin and the other American commissioners, an investment that will be repaid many times over. He closes with a request for a meeting to discuss his ideas more fully.

In a letter from Paris dated June 4, Mme Fournier la jeune introduces an unnamed relative who ardently wishes to go to Boston. The 26-year-old has apprenticed with a notary and has received an excellent education. As he comes from a large family, he must provide for himself, and he has asked for his father's permission to go to the United States. Once there, he would try to distinguish himself in whatever field Franklin deemed suitable. His father consented on condition that Franklin look favorably on the plan. Mme Fournier and her entire family would be infinitely obliged if Franklin took an interest in this virtuous and commendable young man. In a postscript she sends the compliments of her husband.[6]

God willing, writes Owen Owen in English on June 11, he intends to go to America at the end of this summer or the beginning

---

6. Typefounder Simon-Pierre Fournier le jeune (xxx, 346).

of the next. Does he need to apply to Congress for permission to settle there? A clergyman in the Church of England, and currently a curate in Stoke near Coventry in Warwickshire, he has no hope of advancement in the church as he cannot buy a benefice and refuses to flatter the powerful. His brother Edward, from North Wales, lived in Virginia and was in France about five years ago; if he is still alive, he should contact Owen or their brother Richard, a vicar in Carnarvonshire, to "hear of something to his advantage."

J. Gaupin is one of a group of three men in Brussels who desire to emigrate; he writes on their behalf on June 17. Two of them are capable of establishing a factory that could print wallpaper, playing cards, and calico: one, an expert woodblock engraver, manages one of the foremost wallpaper factories in Brussels, and the other is skilled in color printing as well as constructing wind- and watermills. The third man, son of an artillery officer, is a good engineer and mathematician, has worked as a land surveyor and builder, and speaks German, French, Latin, and Flemish. Before their departure, the first two each want an advance of a hundred *louis* and Franklin's promise that Congress will sponsor their factory. The third demands the same advance and Franklin's assurance that he will immediately obtain a job suitable to his talents.

On June 26 Graf von Graevenitz writes in German from Vienna. As the youngest of 18 children of a large aristocratic family, he has little hope of inheriting more than his name.[7] After a career as privy councilor, Graevenitz' health has deteriorated, and he dreams of retiring in the United States. He would prefer to rent or own a small estate in either Georgia, the Carolinas, or Virginia, not too far from other settlements. If money should be required, his only source of wealth is a small collection of paintings, which he would be willing to sell. A new country needs experienced and accomplished men like him, so Graevenitz is hopeful that Franklin, who has bestowed contentment, quiet, and peace on an entire country, will do the same for a single individual.

Two days later, Delisle-Pierrugues sends a desperate plea from Draguignan in Provence. Although he inherited a considerable fortune, the events of the war have ruined him just as he was about to be made a judge at the *cour des comptes*. His education is all he has left. He was born in American climes and wants to return there to

---

7. The Graevenitz family was an old noble family from the Altmark region in northern Germany: *Neue Deutsche Biographie* (24 vols. to date, Berlin, 1953–).

bury his bad luck. He will forget his downfall if he can obtain some employment in the service of the United States, be it in the army or somewhere else. He offers to provide letters of recommendation from prominent residents of Aix.

Johann Philipp Breidenstein of Giessen writes on July 15 in Latin, disappointed that he has received no response to his letter of February 1.[8] Franklin's silence has not diminished his desire to emigrate and serve the American people, especially German immigrants, with useful knowledge. He begs Franklin to answer a fellow scholar.

Another petition in Latin, dated July 19, comes from Jacob Augustus Hoppe in Bochnia, Galicia.[9] He too is a scholar versed in many subjects and several languages, but in America he would be happy just tilling the fields. Hoppe asks Franklin for a recommendation and the assurance of a position. Moreover, before sailing, he needs a place to stay in Paris while he works on improving his English; he would gladly share the food of Franklin's servants.

To whom can the most unfortunate patriot turn for help but the most illustrious patriot of the universe? asks the sieur Tonon from Paris on July 25. He has been the victim of persecution but will not tire Franklin with the details of his ordeal. His chief passion and talent is agriculture, which he wants to pursue in America; his treatise, *Détail des usages, indication des abus, et idées de réforme pour l'agriculture*, was based on ten years' observation.[1] In the four years since he has been forced to abandon his profession, he has traveled through many countries and observed the lackluster state of European agriculture. America would benefit from someone who combines theoretical principles with practical knowledge, and with Franklin's approval Tonon will raise the rural economy to a hitherto unknown degree of perfection. If he can be useful to another country after his own has rejected him, he will have suffered for a reason. He asks for a meet-

8. The letter is described and its author identified in xxxix, 27–8.

9. Hoppe served as principal of the district school in Bochnia and later wrote *Ältere und neuere Geschichte der Königreiche Gallizien und Ludomerien* (Vienna, 1792): George Christoph Hamberger and Johann Georg Meusel, *Das gelehrte Teutschland, oder Lexikon der jetzt lebenden teutschen Schriftsteller* (5th ed., Lemgo, 1801); Peter Geils and Willi Gorzny, eds., *Gesamtverzeichnis des deutschsprachigen Schrifttums, 1700–1910* (160 vols. and sup., Munich, New York, and London, 1979–87), LXIV, 220.

1. Tonon left off the last two words of the title: "*en Béarn.*" It was published in Pau in 1778: Christian Desplat, *Pau et le Béarn au XVIIIe siècle* (2 vols., [Pau], 1992), II, 1360.

ing with Franklin during which he will provide more details. Tonon signs himself as deputy of the Société Patriotique de Béarn.[2]

Granier de Pollier in Paris writes on July 26 on behalf of a friend, a man of quality living in the provinces, whose company of royal grenadiers has been disbanded, leaving him penniless and unemployed. He hopes to settle with his wife in Franklin's republic and would like to know whether former French officers can find employment and at what salary, if Congress is offering land grants and assistance with cultivation, and whether he would be free to settle wherever he wants.

Two young mathematicians, J. Chrétien Remmel and Jean Houba, who are well instructed in geometry and algebra, ask Franklin on August 9 for recommendations and free passage to America, where they hope to be usefully employed. They write from the château d'Issum.

The chevalier de La Combe, writing from Tulle on August 20, has heard that Congress gives land grants to those who wish to come to America. He would like to know more about what kind of reception he might expect. Although well born, he currently serves as cadet lieutenant of the colonial troops in the Limousin region and does not have any money. He will not hesitate to emigrate if it gives him an opportunity to make his fortune in far-off lands.

In Tournay, Joseph Maroteau, who addresses Franklin on August 22, is the head of a family that has fallen on hard times and would like to settle in the United States provided they receive support and protection from the American government. They are Roman Catholics but ardent supporters of civil and social order as well as religious tolerance. The family unites an astonishing array of talents: its members are experienced in commerce, accounting, agriculture, and mathematics, can write in French and English, and know how to

2. A lawyer and viticulturist of Saint-Faust in the province of Béarn, Tonon founded the Compagnie (Société) Patriotique pour le commerce des vins du Béarn in 1779 and was named director the following year. The war with Britain, tensions with the company's chief trading partner, and his idiosyncratic leadership were said to be the causes of the company's failure at the end of 1782. The shareholders revoked his powers and liquidated the company in January, 1783: Pierre Dejean, "L'Exportation des vins béarnais dans le pays du nord au XVIIIe siècle: La 'Compagnie Patriotique pour le commerce des vins du Béarn,'" *Revue d'histoire moderne*, new ser., XI (1936), 225–34; Christian Desplat, "La Politique viticole des états de Béarn au XVIIIe siècle," in Fédération Historique du Sud-Ouest, *Vignes, vins et vignerons de Saint-Emilion et d'ailleurs* (Talence, 2000), pp. 159–66.

make a great variety of fabrics. The father has invented a new kind of mill. Despite their gifts, they have had an undeserved and unforeseeable string of bad luck in all their endeavors. If Franklin knows of a business in the United States that could use their abilities, would he please extend his protection to an honest family?

Misfortune has also befallen a relative of Mme Briant, a young man not yet 40 years old. She appeals to Franklin on his behalf on September 2 from Aix-la-Chapelle. In the past three years he has lost all his money and a great part of his family, and he has been abandoned by his best friends. He is honest and industrious, if perhaps too sensitive and delicate for this evil world. He and his wife want Franklin's help and protection to settle in America. They have asked Mme Briant to approach Franklin, but she hesitates to arrive without an appointment. As she does not live in Paris at the moment, Franklin should respond to M. Debernieres, *administrateur des hôpitaux*, whose address she provides.[3]

A sieur Briaud, who writes from Caen on September 4, has been assured that Franklin helps workers to emigrate to America, where liberty favors all men of talent. He knows carpentry and turning and makes netting of all kinds, fly-whisks, and English-style fishhooks. A friend of his who also wants to emigrate has a grasp of experimental physics and chemistry and knows how to dye, starch, make gunpowder, and construct pendulum clocks. They will submit to both practical and theoretical examinations.

From Göttingen comes a more specific business proposal in German, dated September 8. Johann Christoph Bauer is a glass and brick manufacturer who read in the *Dantziger Zeitung* that conditions for glassblowers are favorable in the United States. He offers a detailed account of how he would establish an American factory producing Flemish and mirror glass. Of course, this would require a substantial advance from Congress, which Bauer offers to repay in yearly installments.

---

3. N. de Bernières, an engineer, author, and inventor, had been serving as *contrôleur général* of the ponts et chaussées since 1751. He won a prize in 1779 for designing the most effective machine to draw water from the well at Bicêtre, which he improved in 1782: *Almanach royal* for 1783, p. 116; *Nouvelle biographie;* Bachaumont, *Mémoires secrets*, XX, 270.

paris à L'hotel de Bresse cul de sac des

Monsieur   quatre vents ce 24e. juin. 1783.

M'etant rendu a passy pour avoir L'honneur de vous y faire ma Cour, et vous entretenir d'objets qui m'interessent, permettè que je vous detaille par lettre mes motifs, ayant etè icommodè depuis lors jusqu'a ce jour par une varietè de chaud et de froid qui me saisit a mon arrivèe.

Les malheurs excessifs que j'ay eprouvès, bien plus sensibles que ceux dont belisaire se plaignoit,[4] m'ont determinè à quitter dècidement une ingrate patrie ne desirant d'autre vengeur que les reproches que mes ennemis auront à se faire eternellement. La providence m'ayant dèpartis des Connoissances dans L'agriculture; ainsi que vous en pourrés juger Monsieur, par le double du diplôme dont le feu Roy m'avoit honnoré, et que vous trouverès ci inclus;[5] Comme je n'ignore pas que L'homme est fait pour se voüer au travail pendant sa vie, je desirerois m'occuper utilement le peu qui me reste à vivre a des deffrichés qui en faisant mon bonheur put faire par suite celui de mes successeurs dans la patrie que j'adopterai. Comme les moeurs pures et tranquiles sont celles que j'adopte, je pense avec raison que je ne puis arriver a ce but qu'en me transplantant dans un pays où la corruption n'a pas pris encore heureusement racine, celui de votre patrie me semble le plus propre à remplir mes vües, et Comme je regarde tous les hommes de bien, egaux entre eux, ma naissance ne doit point faire un obstacle à ce qu'on me regarde avec cet oeuil de fraternité doû nait la concorde generale; je vous prie donc Monsieur, d'apres la sinceritè de mon avoeu de me mander si je puis esperer une reponse favorable de votre part, ou si vous preferè de M'indiquer un jour pour conferer avec vous sur les moyens que vous voudrè bien me procurer, et ma reconnoissance sera aussi etendue que les sentimens sinceres et

---

4. Flavius Belisarius (c. 505–565), a celebrated general of the Byzantine Empire. His supposed travails as a blind beggar after he was condemned by Emperor Justinian were the subject of Jean-François Marmontel's novel *Bélisaire* (Paris, 1767).

5. Not found.

respectueux avec lesquels j'ay L'honneur d'etre Monsieur Votre
tres humble et tres obeissant serviteur

LE BON. DE BORDE DUCHATELET

Endorsed: That America is open to all the French, who have
Permission of their Government to go there. That Strangers of
good Character are receiv'd there with open Arms. That if he
desires to confer with me on the Subject, he will find me at home
every Morning except Tuesdays & ready to give him every Information he may desire.

From Crèvecœur   ALS: American Philosophical Society

Sir   Paris Tuesday Night— [June 24 or July 1, 1783][6]
I forgot the other day To Inquire of you where I cou'd procure Two of Your Medals,[7] which I have Imprudentely promised
in Normandy—after Fruitless Inquirys, I find myself obliged to
ask you that Question, being Anxious To procure them Ere I
Leave the Capital which will be on Saturday—
I am with unfeigned Respect Sir Your Very Humble Servt.

ST. JEAN DE CRÈVECŒUR

Addressed: a Son Excellence / Benjamin Franklin Ecuyer /
Plènypotentiaire des Etats unis de Lamérique / Passy

---

6. The two most likely Tuesdays. Crèvecœur's appointment as consul,
conferred in recognition of his report on the United States (see XXXIX,
421–2n), was signed on June 22. Anticipating a quick departure, he hastened to Normandy to bid farewell to his family and friends and was there
by at least July 9. On Aug. 24 he was named consul to New York, and in
September he sailed on the first of the packets in the newly created service
to North America: Anne Mézin, *Les Consuls de France au siècle des lumières
(1715–1792)* (Paris, 1998), pp. 542–4; Robert de Crèvecœur, *Saint John
de Crèvecoeur: sa vie et ses ouvrages (1735–1813)* (Paris, 1883), pp. 79–80,
82, 85.

7. The *Libertas Americana* medal, an illustration of which was used on
the title page of the 2nd ed. of Crèvecœur's *Lettres d'un cultivateur américain* (Paris, 1787).

From Nathaniel Falconer als: American Philosophical Society

My Dear Frend London June the 24 1783
I Recd your kind Letter of the 18 June yesterday and wrote the Same Evening by a Mr Heptenstall[8] and inclosed you Some papers which I Refer you too I Shall Send you by the Next privet hand Some pamplets and Some more News papers Least that Should not Come to hand as Soon as this beg to inform you that the washington and Capt Barney where Both Sauef arrived and there money in the Bank before I Sailed pray writ Mr Morris to know weather or no there was aney Letters Sent by the Gentelman I mentiond[9] for I Fear there has been Some Foul play the Said Gentelman has with this two or three Days gone to Falmouth to Sail in the packet for philadla my Compliments to your Grandson and Mr hartley I am my Dear Sir your most Sincerly
NATH FALCONER

Addressed: To / Docter Franklin / at the Court / of parris

Notation: Falconer June 23. 1783.—

From William Hodgson als: American Philosophical Society

Dear sir London 24 June 1783
I beg leave to introduce to your Notice & Civilities the Bearer Seward Esqr & his Friend Mr Graves, they are Gentlemen of Fortune & Letters going to France for their Pleasure, not the least of which will be that of paying their respects to you.[1]

---

8. Perhaps R. D. or H. Heptinstall, haberdashers of 6 Ludgate Hill: *Kent's Directory for the Year 1783* (London, 1783), p. 83.
9. John Vaughan.
1. William Seward, F.R.S., who circulated among London's literary elites and is best known for the anecdotes he collected, was traveling on the Continent with his friend Richard Graves the younger (*DNB*, under both names). This seems to be their only appearance in BF's papers. Seward later published the following anecdote: "The sagacious Dr. Franklin used to

Mr Seward is a Member of our old Club[2] & well known to most of your Friends here, every attention you shall pay him will be pleasing to them & particularly so, to Dear sir Your much obliged Hble Servt WILLIAM HODGSON

To His Excellency Benj Franklin Esqr

From the Loge des Commandeurs du Temple[3]

LS: American Philosophical Society

A L'o∴[4] de Carcassonne, d'un lieu éclairé ou régnent la paix, le Silence et la Charité, Le 24e. du 4me. mois de l'an 5783. de la V∴ L∴ et de l'ere vulgaire Le 24 Juin 1783./.

A la Gloire du Grand Architecte de L'Univers

La R∴ L∴[5] Saint Jean Sous Le Titre distinctif des Commandeurs du Temple A L'O∴ de Carcassonne
Au trés digne trés Vertueux, & très Respectable frére Docteur Franklin, Ministre, Plenipotentiaire des Etats unis de L'Amérique auprés de la Cour de france à L'O∴ de Paris
S∴ F∴ V∴[6]
T∴ T∴ C∴ & T∴ R∴ f∴[7]

---

say, that the purest and most useful friend a man could possibly procure, was a Frenchwoman of a certain age who had no designs upon his person; 'they are,' added he, 'so ready to do you service, and from their knowledge of the world know so well how to serve you wisely.'" [William Seward], *Anecdotes of Distinguished Persons* . . . (4th ed., 4 vols., London, 1798), IV, 223n.

2. The Club of Thirteen (XXI, 119–20). Both Hodgson and Seward were members: J. Dybikowski, *On Burning Ground: an Examination of the Ideas, Projects and Life of David Williams* (Oxford, 1993), pp. 273, 275.

3. In answer to BF's May 1 acceptance of their invitation of membership; see XXXIX, 541.

4. L'orient.

5. La Respectable Loge.

6. Salut Force Union.

7. Très Très Cher & Très Respectable frère.

A La reception de vôtre planche[8] en datte du 1er. du 3me. mois là Loge fut extraordinairement assemblée; a peine eumes nous fait Lécture de ce que vous nous faites la faveur de nous Ecrire, que vôtre admission fut celebrée avec tous les transports de la Joye la plus vive.[9] Il etoit impossible de Contenir nos freres. Les applaudissements et les Vivats les plus rédoublés retentissoint de L'orient à L'occident. Cépendant voulant donner à vôtre agrégation tout L'eclat dont elle est Susceptible, la fête Sollemnelle en fut renvoyée a la st. Jean.[1] Nous ne vous en donames pas avis parceque nous respectons trop vos occupations. Ce jour est enfin venû aprés avoir été bien desiré, vous trouverés cy joint le detail de nos travaux mais vous ni [n'y] verrés pas quoique on aye pû dire, Cette Joye et ces transports dont nous etions penétrés, en vain tenteroit-on de les peindre.

Le Comte de Caux[2] absent n'a point eû L'honneur de vous répresenter et vous l'avès fait vous meme. Un peintre excellent Italien et Maçon a Copié votre portrait daprès Veilles peintre en mignature Sur L'Email à Paris.[3] Ceux qui ont eû le bonheur de vous voir ne peuvent Se méprendre à Ses traits.[4] C'est cette image qui a été apportée en Triomphe Le Jour de votre

8. Any piece of writing sent by a lodge or brother: xxxiii, 305n.

9. BF was admitted on June 15: Alain Le Bihan, *Loges et chapitres de la Grande Loge et du Grand Orient de France*, Mémoires et documents (Commission d'histoire économique et sociale de la Révolution française) (39 vols., Paris, 1930–81), xx, 58.

1. The lodge celebrated the feast of St. John the Baptist on June 24: Daniel Ligou, ed., *Dictionnaire de la franc-maçonnerie* (rev. ed., Paris, 1991), pp. 1084–6.

2. Louis-Gaspard de Roger de Cahusac, comte de Caux (1736–1827), was chevalier de Saint-Louis and *capitaine des vaisseaux du roi:* [Alphonse-Jacques] Mahul, *Cartulaire et archives des communes de l'ancien diocèse et de l'arrondissement administratif de Carcassonne* (8 vols., 1857–82; reprint, Rennes-le-Château and Nîmes, 1980–2004), I, 63.

3. The copy has not been located. Charles Sellers suggested that by "Veilles," the writer may have meant the celebrated French miniaturist Jean-Baptiste Weyler: Sellers, *Franklin in Portraiture*, pp. 171–3, 404–6, frontispiece, plates 34 and 36.

4. Among whom, the baron de La Courtette: xxxiv, 482–3.

affiliation. Une deliberation de la L'oge ordonne quelle restera perpetuelement dans notre Temple./.

Quoique eloigné de nous par ce moyen vous serès toujours present à nos assemblées. C'est la que vous recevrés nos homages et que vous Serés témoin de ces vœux ardents que nous formons pour la Conservation des jours d'un homme d'un Sage et d'un Savant qui n'a pas dedaigné de sunir plus étroitement à nous.

Nous avons la faveur d'etre par les N.∴ M.∴ A.∴ N.∴ C.∴⁵ T.∴ C.∴ T.∴ D.∴ & T.∴ R.∴ f.∴⁶ Vos trés affectionnès freres

VIDAL DE ST MARTIAL vble. en exce: [vénérable en exercice]

par Mandement de La R.∴ L.∴ f.∴ THORON sre [secrétaire]

Sêlé et timbré par nous garde des sceaux timbres et archives DAVID⁷ p.∴ t.∴

Notation: Les francs Maçons de Carcassone. 24 Juin 1783.

From Benjamin Vaughan ALS: American Philosophical Society

My dearest sir, London, June 24, 1783.

Having an opportunity of writing you by the Dutch envoy from London, I cannot omit sending you a line to tell you that I see nothing more that is amiss here than you know of, notwithstanding Mr Knox & two or three people pretend that the Loyal Colonies are to have the trade to the islands.⁸ If you keep firm, & good humored, I hope you will in the end lose nothing. From

5. Nombres Mystérieux A Nous Connus.
6. Très Cher Très Dévoué & Très Respectable frère.
7. For Vidal and David see XXXVII, 647. Thoron, a merchant, is on the *tableau des officiers* for 1785–86, reprinted in Julius Friedrich Sachse, comp., *Benjamin Franklin as a Free Mason* (Philadelphia, 1906), p. 109.
8. In May, North had turned to William Knox (XV, 94n) for advice on trade regulations with the United States. Knox was largely responsible for

what I know however of this & of the last ministry, things will
go down better, if put them upon the footing of reasonableness
and kindness, & the necessity & concordance of circumstances,
rather than upon any other footing. John Bull has been fed a
long time upon dainty food of his *own* dressing, and he does
not like to see other people *prescribing* to him.— Your former
proceedings have been successful, principally because you had
people of better sense at home than you now have. At least I,
who am a timid conciliating man, am apt to think so. You may
be wiser at Paris however than I am, but I wish you may not
push the *manner* of conducting the thing too far, for we are on
the whole *irritable*.

There are strong symptoms that the king does not relish the
present ministry, and if he were to change, it is likely enough he
would think of our friends. He has gained, & the ministers have
lost credit, by the disputes about the Prince of Wales's establishment;[9] to whom the king has been very liberal hitherto, as to
money.— Lord Shelburne is gone to Spa, with Lady Shelburne;
but Mr. Pitt stays at home.— The prince is very far from being
pleased, they tell me.

I am very sorry for the accident to your electrical machine, the box containing which, appears to be damaged;[1] but
I have ordered a new one to be forwarded immediately.— I
am sorry that so much of the summer slips away without
your coming here. If you do not come with your son, it will

---

the July 2 Order in Council that denied American ships access to the trade
between Britain and its West Indian colonies. Vaughan is wrong here; Knox
(unlike other advocates of the order such as Baron Sheffield) did not feel
that Canada was adequate for supplying these colonies: Harlow, *Second
British Empire*, I, 478–81.

9. George, Prince of Wales, was due to come of age in August. His
father balked at granting him an establishment of £100,000 per year, as
the Cabinet had recommended: John Brooke, *King George III* (New York,
St. Louis, and San Francisco, 1972), pp. 247–9.

1. See Dessin to BF, June 15. Dessin must have written to Vaughan about
the damage around the same time, as Vaughan acknowledged it in his letter
to Darcel of June 20 (APS).

be the very *deepest* disappointment of my life; of which be assured.

I am soon going to be relieved from the troublesome state I am in with my family. They embark this week. My time will then be my own again; and, unless I see an honest *reason* why I should not write, or these *Bystanders* should occupy me, you & Mr Jay will often hear from me probably, if matter occurs.

I remember some time ago I was desired to enumerate the virtues of castor oil, & the mode of taking it.[2] Its first virtues arise from its being an *innocent* evacuant, & which gives no *pain* when it operates. The West Indians add a thousand others; as for the gravel, & so on.— The mode of taking it is putting a *table* spoonful, more or less according to constitution or use, into a little cold water, or into milk or brandy or rum. I use the former method; and when the oil is *good*, that is, not rancid, it is not unpleasant altogether in point of taste.

I am keeping open my letter to learn news for you, without missing however my opportunity.

NB. My friends not returning in time I close this letter, with my usual assurances that I am, my dearest sir, your ever devoted, most affectionate & grateful,   BENJN: VAUGHAN

P.S. In speaking above, I wish to convey, that it will not be wholly well taken to be cavalier-like & cold about the English connection. I do not indeed see how sensible men here could help themselves upon this subject, but men who have not sense may feel less embarrassed on the subject;—and though they may be forced to come to, at last, yet they will first try to get many other methods of putting an end to the business.

2. XXXIX, 371.

From the Abbé Girault de Kéroudou[3]

ALS: American Philosophical Society

Monsieur, Paris Le 25. Juin 1783./.
Votre excellence verra que L'ouvrage Cy joint â été imprimé
par ordre du Bureau d'administration du College de Louis
Legrand;[4] C'est à Ce titre que Je prends La Liberté de vous
L'adresser pour La societé de Philadelphie, persuadé de son utilité
pour L'education publique dans Les etats Americains Comme
dans La france; dumoins M. Le President Rolland, autheur de
Ce recueil n'â Jamais Eû d'autres Vües. Il y â plus de vingt ans
que Ce respectable magistrat Consacre avec un Zele infatigale

3. Apart from his duties at the Collège Louis-le-Grand (the affiliation
he mentions here), Georges Girault de Kéroudou taught mathematics and
physics at the Collège de Navarre, where in the early 1770s he inspired
and became a mentor to the young Condorcet. Condorcet in turn helped
his former professor obtain an appointment as professor of mechanics at
the Collège royal de France, which he held until 1786. The abbé published
several works on mathematics and physics as well as a textbook on calculus:
M. Lacoarret and ―――― Ter-Menassian, "Les Universités," in *Enseigne-
ment et diffusion des sciences en France au XVIIIe siècle*, ed. René Taton *et al.*
(Paris, 1964), pp. 147–8, 156; Charles C. Gillispie, *Science and Polity in
France at the End of the Old Regime* (Princeton, 1980), pp. 138, 143; Keith
Michael Baker, *Condorcet: from Natural Philosophy to Social Mathematics*
(Chicago and London, 1975), pp. 4–5, 399; Quérard, *France littéraire*.
    4. *Recueil de plusieurs des ouvrages de Monsieur le Président Rolland*, im-
*primé en exécution des délibérations du Bureau d'administration du Collège de
Louis-le-Grand, des 17 janvier et 18 avril 1782* (Paris, 1783), a collection of
writings on education by Barthélémy-Gabriel Rolland d'Erceville. Rolland, himself a member of the *bureau d'administration* of Louis-le-Grand,
was a magistrate and president of the *chambre des requêtes* of the Parlement
de Paris and a member of the academies of Amiens and Orléans and the
Musée de Paris. Following the expulsion of the Jesuits, who had been in
charge of most French *collèges*, Rolland became a pioneer in the movement
for universal education in state-run public schools, although his proposals maintained a strict social hierarchy. He also advocated separating the
teaching of mathematics and physics from general philosophy, a reform
that was instituted at Louis-le-Grand in 1784: Larousse; *Almanach royal* for
1783, p. 488; Santo L. Arico, "Elitism versus popularism in the education
treatises of La Chalotais, Morveau and Rolland," *Studies on Voltaire and
the Eighteenth Century*, CCLXXVIII (1990), 401, 410–14; Lacoarret and Ter-
Menassian, "Les Universités," pp. 137–9, 149.

tous Ses moments Libres à travailler pour L'education publique, et notre maison Luy â des obligations qui Surpassent tous Les efforts de notre reconnaissance. Permettez moy de vous presenter Le respect Le plus profond avec Lequel J'ay L'honneur detre, Monsieur, Votre trés hble et trés obt. serviteur

GIRAULT DE KEROUDOU,
grand-maitre-adjoint du College de Louis Legrand./
M. frankelin./.

Notation: Girault de Keroudon 25 Juin 1783

From Alexander Lermonth

ALS: American Philosophical Society

Honoured Sir,   Paris 25th June 1783
Please to pardon this Address from an American Gentleman that has not the agreeable pleasure of Your Acquaintance, but from the Amaible Character you bear in life and in the World in General by that you are Well known to be a Gentleman of a most humane Temper and dispossition and one who a Heart that feels for every Man brought up in that Line and Capasity and thro. Unhappy Misfortunes is under the disagreeable necessity to let his Case be made known to so worthy a Gentleman as you are, permit me to inform you that I Traded from Edinton North Carolina to the Island of Saint Eustatua for Sixteen Years, in the Cource of that time I reallized by Trade a Fortune of Eight Thousand Pounds Sterling— This was all taken from me by Admiral Rodney when he took that Island. I with many more American Gentlemen had every thing taken from us we had in the World,[5] I was then reduced from Living in Afflue-

5. Adm. Rodney seized St. Eustatius on Feb. 3, 1781, confiscating more than 150 merchant ships and their cargoes. Americans were allowed to leave with only their household goods: XXXIV, 465n; J. Franklin Jameson, "St. Eustatius in the American Revolution," *American Hist. Rev.*, VIII (1902–3), 704.

ence and plenty to a State of Want and distress. I went from Saint Eustatua to a Neighbouring Island called Saint Thomases from thence I got a Passage to Ostend in Flanders, having a Correspondant there that owed me Money but upon my Arrivall found he was dead by that means lost the debt he contracted with me, when in Saint Eustatua, I came to Paris from Flanders in hopes to meet with a Gentleman that owed me some Money but can hear nothing of him, by that means I am disappointed in my Expectations, permit me to Inform you that my Misfortunes and disappointments has reduced my present Circumstances to a much lower Eb than ever I was before, its true I am a Stranger in a manner to you, notwithstanding I have had the pleasure to see you in Philadelphia a good many Years ago, I was acquainted with a Good many Merchants there permit me to say that I always Lived in Affluence & plenty before my Misfortunes, I am here a Stranger in a Strange Country not having Money at present to enable me to pay for the Common Necessarys Life requires, from my distressed Situation I hope it may prevail upon your heart so far to pitty me, so that you may be pleased to assist me with a little Money. You may depend its like death to me to be reduced to the disagreeable necessity to ask a Favour at your hands, depend its far from my heart my Principles or dispossition to do a thing of the kind was it not real distress' obliges me at present to it, your kind Compliance to my request will for ever oblige with due Esteem and Regard Your Excellencys Most Obedt. very humble Servt.   ALEXR. LERMONTH

His Excellency Benjamin Franklin Esqr.

Addressed: His Excellency Benjamin Franklin Esqr. / Ambassador Plenepotentiary from the / United States of America to the Court / of France at Passy / near Paris

Endorsed: Cost a Guinea[6]

6. On the same sheet as a June 15 receipt of payment to James Fife (see the Editorial Note on Promissory Notes), BF added: "Another Guinea to one Alexr Lermenth who had been a mercht in N. Carolina / without Receipt". APS.

From Anthony Todd[7]

LS: American Philosophical Society; copies: Public Record Office, Royal Mail Archive

Dear Sir,   General post Office June 25. 1783

I must confess I have taken a long time to acknowlege the last Letter you were pleased to write me the 24th. of March 1776 from New York.[8] I am happy however to learn from my Nephew Mr. George Maddison[9] that you enjoy good health and that as the French were about to establish five Packet Boats at L'Orient for the purpose of a Monthly Correspondence between that Port and New York,[1] you were desirous of knowing the Intentions of England on that Subject.

I am going out of Town for a few days and do not write to you quite officially at present, but I can venture to assure you, it is the Wish of His Majesty's Post Master General[2] to continue the Communication with New York by the Packet Boats, and that the Mails should be dispatched both to and from that place, the first Wednesday in every Month as at present, and to appoint an Agent to reside at New York, for the management of the Business there.

If this should meet your Ideas, very little Regulation will be necessary for carrying on the Correspondence with the United States, after New York has been evacuated, as the Packet Postage of 1 sh [shilling] for single Letters and so in proportion, as settled by Act of Parliament, must be continued, but I do not know how far it might be of Advantage to both Countries, to

---

7. Secretary of the General Post Office: x, 217n; *ODNB*. BF mislaid this letter, and Todd sent a duplicate on Aug. 22 (below).

8. Actually, March 29: XXII, 392–4.

9. Who wrote to Todd on June 18: Kenneth Ellis, *The Post Office in the Eighteenth Century: a Study in Administrative History* (London, New York, Toronto, 1958), p. 94n.

1. The decision would not become official until June 28; see BF to Morris, July 27.

2. There were two joint postmasters general: Henry Frederick Thynne, who in 1776 had taken the name Carteret, and Thomas Foley, Baron Foley. Todd, however, ran the daily operations of the post office: Namier and Brooke, *House of Commons*, II, 446; III, 531; Ellis, *Post Office*, pp. 12, 91–3.

leave it, as at present, to the option of the Writer to pay or not the Postage beforehand, and keep accounts on both sides of the internal Postage up to London and to New York, and therefore I should be glad to be favoured with your Sentiments fully upon this point, or upon any other, not doubting from my long experience of your Candour and Abilities, that every thing will be easily adjusted to the reciprocal Advantage of both Countries.

When any Arrangement may be settled, it will be necessary to apprise the public by Advertisement, that Letters to and from any parts of the Continent of Europe, must of necessity be inclosed to some Correspondent in London to avoid a variety of difficulties on account of the Postage.

I send you herewith in a seperate Packet, at Mr. Maddison's Request, a Collection of the Post Office Statutes with some other papers, and should be glad for my own curiosity to know what kind of Packets the French propose to employ, Ours are about 200 Tons, coppered, and thirty Men Officers included.[3]

I am, Dear Sir, with the greatest Truth and Respect, Your most obedient and most humble Servant ANTH TODD Secy

Dr. Franklin Paris

From Job Bunker   ALS: American Philosophical Society

Sir.   St Malo June the 26th. 1783—

I Take the freedom in wrighting unto your honour baging for your Assistance to Enable me to Guit out of this Cuntry into my one which is Amarica & was born in the Iseland of Nantucket & have fought two yrs in the first of the warr untill I had

3. Among BF's papers at the APS is a copy of *General Instructions for Deputy Postmasters* (London, 1782), a 19-page pamphlet issued by the General Post Office. This may have been one of the items Todd enclosed. As for the British packets, they are elsewhere described as 170 tons each, carrying a crew of 28, with six passenger cabins: Brian Lavery, *Nelson's Navy: the Ships, Men and Organisation, 1793–1815* (London and Annapolis, 1989), p. 277. The packet service itself is discussed in Ellis, *Post Office*, pp. 34–7; for BF's recollection see XXXIX, 425–6.

the misforten to be taking & Carried in England & After made
my Ascape in france & Ever Since have ben fighting for them
whare as I have ben un Sucksesfull, & at this Presant time am
So Dreand of money that am not Able to Clear my Self of my
Boarding. After Seling All the Clothing that I Could Spare am
in want of 300 hundred Livers. Also I have made A Request
unto mr Dessagray[4] for A Passague on Board of his Vessell that
is Bound for Amarica & will Saill within 20 Days from this &
he Refuses me without I Give him 400 hundred Livers in Hand
before I Sail which is not in my Power at Presant & If yr honour
will Consider my Situation & Assist me in this Dark & mallon-
coully Situation I will Endavour to Reinbust the Same unto yr
honour by yr honour in Amarica. I Pray yr honour to Consider
my Situation at this Presant time & Request the favour of yr
Answer to me by the Next Post & in Ending I Subcribing my
Self unto you yr humble Servant to Serve   JOB BUNKER

Pscript

I have Saild in the Station of 2d. Lutenant Ever Since I have
ben in their Employ & have made my first Cruse with Monsieur
Guidlo in the Duches of Paling Nack[5] & have hed A high Recommendation of my Bravery & qualification, in Every Point
from him in this town

Addressed: A Son Excellence / Monsieur Benjamin Franklin /
Ambassadeur des Etats Unis de LAmericque / a Passy pres /
Paris

Notation: Bunker June 26. 1783

4. Desegray was the unofficial American agent in Saint-Malo, and a
merchant of that town: XXIII, 588.
5. The *Duchesse-de-Polignac,* Capt. Guidelou: Anatole, marquis de
Granges de Surgères, *Prises des corsaires français pendant la guerre de
l'indépendance (1778–1783)* . . . (Paris and Nantes, 1900), p. 41.

From Jean-Baptiste Pecquet: Memorial[6]

DS and transcript: National Archives

Excellence,   [*c*. June 26, 1783][7]

Jean Bapte. Pecquet agent interprete de la Nation françoise à Lisbonne à l'honneur d'exposer à votre Excellence, qu'il a été assez heureux pour rendre, depuis le Commencement de la rupture entre les États unis de l'amerique et L'angleterre, des Services essentiels aux differents matelots américains que les hazards de la guerre ont amenés dans ce port, principalement, avant que la france Se fut declarée en faveur de l'amérique, et bien avant que le Congrés eût dans cette ville une personne pour pourvoir à leurs besoins.[8]

Le zele et le desinteressement qu'il y a mis, lui font esperer que votre Excellence ne trouvera point de disproportion entre l'importance de ces mêmes Services, et la nature des recompenses qu'il prendra la liberté de lui indiquer.

Dès l'année 1775. il retira du bord de plusieurs fregattes angloises une grande quantité de matelots américains. Le parti que les Anglois avoient pris de les garder constamment prisonniers à leurs Bords, le fit recourir à plusieurs artifices pour les delivrer. Ils lui ont toujours reussi; et jusqu'à l'epoque de la declaration de la france, il a eu le bonheur d'en Embarquer au moins quatre cent. Sur les vaisseaux negriers de sa Majesté très Chretienne, qui en differents tems avoient relaché dans ce port. Il joint ici une note de tous ces vaisseaux et du nombre a peu près de matelots dont chacun à été chargé, moins pour reclamer un remboursement qu'il n'a jamais eu l'intention de demander, que

---

6. One of several Frenchmen who assisted American sailors in Portugal: xxxvi, 628n. Pecquet sent this memorial to Jacques-Bernard O'Dunne, the French ambassador to the Portuguese court (xxxi, 316n; *Repertorium der diplomatischen Vertreter*, iii, 130), who forwarded it to Vergennes along with Pecquet's cover letter to him. Vergennes forwarded both documents to BF on July 31. BF in turn sent them to Congress with his Sept. 13 letter to Boudinot. In 1785 Congress would order the American ministers in France to compensate Pecquet for his service.

7. The date of Pecquet's cover letter to O'Dunne.

8. Congress appointed Arnold Henry Dohrman as its agent in June, 1780: xxvi, 211n.

pour donner à votre Excellence une idée juste de la nature des Services qu'il a rendus au Congrés.[9]

Lorsque Sa Majesté très Chretienne Jugea à propos de se declarer ouvertement en faveur des états unis, l'Exposant fut nommé agent interprete de la nation françoise à Lisbonne, par un brevet du Consul general, et avec l'agrément de la Cour. C'est en cette qualité qu'il a continué à rendre ses Soins aux infortunés matelots qui se trouvoient à Bord des vaisseaux anglois qui entroient dans ce port. C'est pour lors que prevenu que le sieur Dohrman etoit chargé de pourvoir aux besoins des Américains, il lui conduisit tous ceux que sa vigilance put lui procurer, et c'est de cet instant que le dit Sieur Dohrman lui a remboursé les comptes de fraix qu'il lui a produits.

C'est aussi a cette epoque qu'il engagea Monsieur Le Chevallier de Montaigu capitaine du vaisseau de guerre anglois Le Ramilies,[1] a lui delivrer Sur le reçu du Consul general de france, cinq prisonniers américains qu'il avoit à Son bord.

Malgré le Secrét que l'Exposant a toujours taché de mettre dans toutes Ses demarches, il n'a pu cependant eviter de devenir Suspect au Ministre anglois. Il avoit été plusieurs fois reconnu dans les courses nocturnes qu'il faisoit autour des vaisseaux anglois pour recueillir des matelots que sa presence engageoit à se jetter à la nage; plusieurs fois l'on avoit fait feu Sur lui. Mais ce qui le decouvrit entierement fut l'enlevement public du capitaine Benjamin Wikés,[2] qu'il retira du milieu de plus de vingt anglois par lesquels il avoit été surpris à terre. Dès cet instant le Sr. Walpole[3] ne menagea plus rien, il se plaignit au gouverne-

9. The attached list names one ship in 1776, 13 in 1777, and seven in 1778; others were put aboard a Spanish squadron bound for South America and ships bound for Le Havre and Cadiz.

1. The commander of the *Ramillies* from March, 1779, to January, 1781, was John Moutray: *ODNB*.

2. Probably Benjamin Weeks or Wickes of Baltimore: Claghorn, *Naval Officers*, p. 330.

3. The Hon. Robert Walpole (1736–1810), Horace Walpole's cousin, who served as the British minister in Lisbon from 1772 to 1800: *Repertorium der diplomatischen Vertreter*, III, 169; Lewis, *Walpole Correspondence*, IV, 133n.

ment, et presenta Son zele à Secourir les américains, comme une infraction à la neutralité que la cour de Portugal avoit adopteé. En consequence il lui fut ordonné de se retirer du Royaume.[4] Il instruisit Monsieur Le chargé des affaires de la Cour de france, et Mr. Le Consul de cet incident.[5] Tous deux de concert firent connoître la pureté de ses demarches. Bientot ce premier fut autorisé par la Cour de france à demander l'abolition du decret qui ordonnoit sa retraite; en Sorte qu'au bout de quelques mois, il eut la Satisfaction d'être rendu à sa famille, et à ses fonctions d'agent interprete de la nation françoise.

Ce desagrement n'a été que personnel à l'Exposant; les américains n'en ont point Souffert. Un fils qu'il a auprès de lui, et quelques personnes qu'il avoit preposées leur rendirent tous les Secours dont ils avoient besoin, pendant tout le tems qu'il lui fut impossible de le faire lui même. Mais une fois libre il les a secourus plus ouvertement; la liberté même qu'eut de le faire peu de tems après au nom de la france, en écartant tous les risques ne fit que redoubler son zele.

Le certificat ci-joint de son Excellence Monsieur L'ambassadeur de france, celui de son Excellence Monsieur L'ambassadeur d'Espagne, ceux de Monsr. Le Consul general de france, et du vice-consul chargé des affaires du Consulat, celui enfin de Mr. Dohrman negociant de cette ville, et agent du congrés, que l'Exposant prend la liberté d'envoyer à votre Excellence, lui Seront un Sur garant de la verité de ce qu'il vient d'avoir l'honneur de lui exposer.[6] Il ose Se flater en conséquence, que votre Ex-

---

4. This happened in 1780: Waldo G. Leland, ed., *Guide to Materials for American History in the Libraries and Archives of Paris* (2 vols., Washington, D.C., 1932–43), II, 775.

5. In 1780 the French chargé d'affaires to Portugal was the abbé d'Ognac and the French consul in Lisbon was François-Philippe Brochier: *Repertorium der diplomatischen Vertreter*, III, 130; Anne Mézin, *Les Consuls de France au siècle des lumières (1715–1792)* ([Paris, 1998]), p. 698.

6. He enclosed certificates of April 10 from Ambassador O'Dunne; of April 14 from Spanish Ambassador Fernán-Núñez (*Repertorium der diplomatischen Vertreter*, III, 438); of April 19 from French Consul General Meyronnet de Saint-Marc (XXXIX, 103); and of March 20 from French Vice-Consul d'Hermand (*Repertorium der diplomatischen Vertreter*, III, 140): National Archives. Dohrman's certificate has not survived.

cellence representera Ses Services au congrés des Etats unis, et qu'elle en obtiendra une gratification proportionnée aux depenses excessives qu'il a faites, et aux peines qu'il s'est données pendant le tems des hostilités entre les Etats unis de l'amérique, et L'angleterre. Dans cet espoir il prie votre Excellence d'agréer les vœux qu'il fait au Ciel pour votre conservation, et les assurances du profond respect avec lequel il a l'honneur d'être, de votre Excellence Le très humble, et très obéissant Serviteur

JAN BAPTIS PECQUET

A Son Excellence Monsieur Franklin, Ministre Plenipotentiaire des Etats-unis de l'Amerique, près de Sa Majesté Très Chrétienne.

From Vergennes

L (draft):[7] Archives du Ministère des affaires étrangères

Vlles. le 26. Juin 1783

Vous trouverez ci-joint, M, le sauf-conduit que le Roi a bien voulu accorder au Sr. Price; cette pièce mettra ce particulier en état de Suivre tranquilement et sûrement ses affaires. Mr. Dudon, procureur-général du parlement de Bordeaux, préviendra M. le garde des sceaux dans le cas où le Sr. laframboise ou autres feroient des poursuites contre le Sieur Price.[8]

Mr. franklin

7. In the hand of Gérard de Rayneval.
8. On Sept. 13 James Price sent word to BF that he had "Compleatly gained his Suit at Parliament against Mr. John Bondfield with all Costs, damages &c. All the Voices were Unanimous in Mr. Price's favr.": V. & P. French & Nephew to WTF, Sept. 13, 1783, APS. Bondfield, Haywood & Co. evidently refused to accept the verdict, prompting Price to petition the Parlement for an affirmation of judgment and a citation against his adversaries for contempt of court. Price's appeal was published: Durand Echeverria and Everett C. Wilkie, Jr., comps., *The French Image of America . . .* (2 vols., Metuchen, N.J., and London, 1994), I, 534.

To the Chevalier de Cambray-Digny[9]

Reprinted from Valentine Giamatti, "Le Chevalier de Cambray in America, 1778–1783" (unpublished doctoral dissertation, Harvard University, 1940), p. 149.[1]

[before June 27, 1783][2]

Dr. Franklin requests the honour of Mr. Cambray's Company at dinner on Sunday the 29th inst.

Passy, June 1783

The favour of an Answer is desired

From Ferdinand Grand: Memorandum

Copy:[3] Historical Society of Pennsylvania

Paris 27 Juin 1783

Etat de Situation actuelle

Pour satisfaire aux payemens qui restent à faire, & liquider & payer tout ce que je connais d'Engagemens pour le Congréss, il faudrait les Sommes suivantes aux Epoques ci-après, sçavoir

---

9. A military engineer who served with distinction in the American army and spent two years as a British prisoner. He was finally exchanged in the fall of 1782 and granted a one-year leave of absence from the American army. Cambray was in Paris by mid-June, 1783, and carried letters to BF: XXXVIII, 535n and the references there; Harold E. Selesky, ed., *Encyclopedia of the American Revolution* (3 vols., Detroit, 2006), I, 146; *Laurens Papers*, XV, 234–5n; Morris, *Jay: Peace*, p. 607.

1. Giamatti transcribed the text from a copy made by an Italian archivist. The original must have been one of BF's printed dinner invitations, the first known example of which is reproduced in XXXIX, facing p. 409.

2. Cambray answered on a "Friday morning," which had to have been June 27. He was "extremely Sorry" that a previous engagement prevented him from attending. APS.

3. In BF's hand. The American commissioners sent the original to Vergennes the next day.

£ 400,000 en Juillet[4]
500,000 en Août.
500,000 en Septembre
500,000 en Octobre
_____
1,900,000 en tout

Si Monsieur Franklin ne voit pas jour à se procurer cette Somme, il faudrait forcement, comme j'ai déja eu l'honneur de l'en prévenir, cesser des aujourd'hui tout payement, puisqu'il m'a été signifié des Sommations pour rendre acceptées, ou non, les Lettres qui sont à l'acceptation chès moi.   Signée GRAND.

Copy—

Notation by Franklin: Etat de nos Besoins 1783

From [John] Hunt[5]

AL: American Philosophical Society

Rue de Clery Friday Evening June 27th: 1783

J. Hunt has the Honor to present his most respectful compliments to his Excellency Dr. Franklin, and will do himself the pleasure; agreeable to his Excellency's kind invitation, to dine with him on Sunday next.

Addressed: His Excellency Dr. Franklin / Passy

4. Grand customarily used the symbol "£" for *l.t.*
5. Hunt, who was related to Matthew Ridley by marriage, had dined with BF in February: XXXIX, 136. He sailed to America on the *General Washington* at the end of the summer to settle some of Ridley's business affairs: *Morris Papers*, VIII, 313–14; IX, 469.

From Pierres ALS: American Philosophical Society

Monsieur,   Paris, le 27 Juin 1783.

Vous devez être étonné sans doute de ne point recevoir de ma part les Exemplaires des Constitutions de l'amérique que je vous ai promis le 20 du courant, jour que j'ai eu l'honneur de vous voir.

En vous quittant j'ai été chez M. de Néville. On m'a montré le nouvel Embargo mis sur cet Ouvrage; c'est une Note que M. le Garde des Sceaux a écrite à côté de la permission, la voici: *à condition que l'ouvrage passera encore sous les yeux de M. le Comte de Vergennes avant d'être distribué.* On m'a dit qu'il étoit à propos que j'en envoyasse un Exemplaire à M. le Comte de Vergennes, c'est ce que j'ai fait en rentrant chez moi: j'y ai joint la Lettre dont je vous envoie copie.[6] J'attends la réponse de ce Ministre pour la faire passer aussitôt à M. le Garde des Sceaux qui l'enverra à M. de Néville, pour enfin après tout cela m'autoriser à faire la distribution.

Vous voyez, Monsieur, que Paris ne ressemble point dutout à Philadelphie, & qu'il nous faudroit ici un second Franklin, s'il pouvoit en exister deux, pour nous délivrer de toutes ces entraves, entraves que je ne puis ni ne dois condamner, puisque je suis citoyen.

Cela ne m'empêche pas, Monsieur, de faire en attendant relier & brocher, & je serois en état actuellement de vous livrer tous vos Exemplaires, si les Reglemens auxquels je suis assujetti m'en donnoient la liberté. Aussitôt que je serai dégagé de toutes les entraves que je viens de vous détailler, j'aurai l'honneur de vous en faire part.

Je suis avec un profond respect, Monsieur, Votre très-humble & très-obeissant Serviteur   PIERRES

M. Franklin.

---

6. Pierres' letter to Vergennes of June 20, sending a copy of *Constitutions des treize Etats-Unis de l'Amérique,* also enclosed a copy of Miromesnil's June 16 letter to BF (above) and its enclosure, Néville's June 15 letter to Miromesnil, which contained the injunction Pierres quotes here. APS.

From Robert Pigott

ALS: American Philosophical Society

Hond: Sir   Pent[7] near Geneva 27 June 1783.

I have a long time intended to address you this Letter concerning the Situation of your Grandson at Geneva as being such which I am persuaded would not receive your approbation if you was acquainted with the necessary circumstances. It is now some weeks that He had a Fever, the cause of which may be reasonably attributed to his unhealthy dwelling improper diet & ignorance on the part of his Rulers. His apartment in no respects betters than that of a Prisoner, it is so confined with Walls, included in a little Alley & crowded with other Cotemporarys who sleep in the same Chamber that it would be Almost a miracle that He should escape some Pestilential Disorder. I am so sensible of the very urgent Necessity for him to change his abode that I have taken the liberty of going to Mr Mariniac, & desiring He might come to Pent for the benefit of the Air till his Health was established. Altho' I have gone myself & have frequently sent Mr Webb[8] who is equally sensible of the necessity & propriety of the measure from unknown reasons we have not been able to obtain the desired End. I propose going again this day but much doubt if I shall succeed, as I understand some such request was refused Mr Ridley, whom otherwise proposed conducting him to Paris.

Your Grandson demonstrates many *very* estimable qualitys which exclusive of other circumstances entitles him to very different management than he experiences. If Mr Ridley is now returned to Paris, He will probably strengthen the Evidence which I have given.[9] In regard to his Learning I wish It be of such quality & degree as to answer your expectations, persuaded at the same Time that It originates not on the part of the young Man, whom is neither wanting in disposition or natural abilitys, but every Telemachus has need of a Mentor.[1] It is

7. Penthes, Pigott's estate: XXXVI, 321n, 322n.
8. Benjamin Webb. When he last wrote BF, he was living with Pigott: XXXVI, 321–2.
9. See the annotation of BF to BFB, June 23.
1. In Homer's *Odyssey*, Odysseus placed his son Telemachus in the care of Mentor when he left for the Trojan War.

with reluctance that I find myself called upon to represent Objects as striking to my Senses & so little agreeable as when they have a tendency to [*torn*:² do ot]hers detriment, but my Zeal for America [my pers]onal respect for You & my regar[d for your] Grandson makes it a needfull Duty. Be assured Sir I have none, nor can have any other Motive. I think Sir no time should be lost in coming to some resolution either of removing him from this country, or of placing Him in a more advantageous manner.

The little prospect of any Amendment in the Politicks of England has almost brougt: me to a determination of going to America in the following Spring which I hope will prove another *promised* Land. I have the Honour to be with the most sincere respect and Regard Hond: Sir Your very faithfull & obedt Sert   ROBERT PIGOTT

Mrs Pigott desires me to present her most respectfull compliments. Since writing the above I have brought away your Grandson who presents you his duty & is greatly better.

Addressed: A Monsieur / Monsieur Franklin / Ministre Plenipotentiare / des Etats Unis de l'Amerique / a Passy / pres Paris

Franklin and John Jay to Vergennes

LS:³ Archives du Ministère des affaires étrangères; copies: Library of Congress, Massachusetts Historical Society, National Archives

Sir,   Passy, June 28th., 1783

Mr Grand, Banker to the Congress, having laid before us the annexed State of their Affairs in his Hands,⁴ we conceive ourselves indispensably obliged to communicate the same to your Excellency, as some important Interests of both Countries are concerned.

---

2. A section of the MS is torn; our guesses as to the missing letters are in brackets.
3. In WTF's hand.
4. Grand's memorandum of June 27, above, as confirmed by the docketing in the margin.

Before the Peace was known in America, and while Mr Morris had hopes of obtaining the Five per Cent Duty,[5] and a larger Loan from his Majesty, the immediate urgent Necessities of the Army obliged him to draw Bills, and sell them to the Merchants, to raise Money for the Purchase of Provisions, to prevent their starving or disbanding.

The Merchants have thereupon formed their Plans of Business and remitted those Bills to their Correspondents here, to pay Debts, and purchase Goods in this Kingdom to be carried home in the Ships that are come or coming to France, thus to open a larger Commerce with this Nation.

If those Bills cannot be paid the Creditors of America will be disappointed and greatly hurt, & the Commerce will be deranged & discouraged in its first Operations, of which the Numerous ill Consequences are more easily imagined than described.

Our Loan in Holland is going on, and with such Prospect of Success, that the Bankers who have the Care of it, have lately sent by express to Mr. Adams all the Blank Obligations necessary to complete it, for him to sign, that they might have them ready to deliver as demanded,[6] his Return thither being delayed.

This Loan will therefore probably answer the Bills Mr Morris has drawn on those Bankers.

But the protesting any of his Bills here would occasion such an Alarm there as must probably entirely stop any further progress of that Loan, and thereby increase the Mischief.

The Government of the Congress would also be enfeebled by it.

We apprehend too, that in the present unsettled Situation of our Affairs with England, such a Failure might have very ill Effects, with respect to our Negociations.

We therefore request your Counsel, hoping your Wisdom,

---

5. See the annotation of Morris to BF, May 26, letter (I). In December, 1782, BF reported to Morris that the states' refusal to go along with this plan hurt American credit in Europe: XXXVIII, 488–9.

6. The bankers sent 2,000 obligations plus three as spares: *Adams Papers*, XV, 42–3. On July 22 Grand paid 1,027 *l.t.* 13 *s.* for the shipment back to Amsterdam and the courier's return: Account XXVII (XXXII, 4).

which has so often befriended our Nation, may point out some Way by which we may be extricated from this Distress.

And as the King has hitherto so generously assisted us, we hope that if it is any way practicable, his Majesty will crown the glorious Work by affording us this Help at the different Periods when it will be wanted, and which is absolutely the last that will be asked.

We are with great and sincere Respect, Sir, Your Excellency's most obedient & most humble Servants   B Franklin
                                                                        John Jay

His Exy Ct. de Vergennes.

Notation: rep [répondu]

From Joseph-Jérôme Le Français de Lalande

ALS: Harvard University Library

Monsieur et illustre confrere   a Paris le 28 juin 1783.

J'ai été chargè par m. le President Rolland de vous prier de vouloir bien faire passer au Congrès un ouvrage relatif a l'education et a l'instruction publique.[7] On n'en a tiré que 200 exemplaires, et il les a voulu placer de la maniere la plus utile pour l'objet du bien public, il est convenable qu'il y en ait un Sous les yeux des administrateurs d'une republique ou l'on ne négligera pas l'education, et j'espere que vous voudrés bien Seconder les desirs de l'auteur qui est un magistrat distingué et digne de votre consideration. Ce motif me fait esperer que vous voudrés bien avoir la bonté de me faire ècrire que vous l'avés reçu et que vous le ferés parvenir. Je ne vous demanderois pas la peine et la faveur d'une reponse Si l'objet n'etoit digne de quelque attention et Si la personne que je Sers ne meritoit des egards beaucoup plus que moi. Je Suis avec un profond respect Monsieur et illustre docteur de votre Excellence Le tres humble et tres obeissant Serviteur   De la Lande
                                        de l'academie des Sciences au College royal

---

7. BF had already received a copy to forward to the APS; see Girault de Kéroudou to BF, June 25.

The American Peace Commissioners to David Hartley: Answers to Propositions[8]

Copies: William L. Clements Library,[9] Library of Congress, Massachusetts Historical Society (two), National Archives (two), Archives du Ministère des affaires étrangères; transcript: National Archives

[June 29, 1783]

Answers to Mr Hartleys six Propositions
for the definitive Treaty—

To the 1st This matter has been already regulated in the 5th & 6th Articles of the Provisional Treaty[1] to the utmost extent of our Powers: The Rest must be left to the several States.

2d All the Lakes, Rivers and Waters, divided by the Boundary Line or Lines, between the United States and his Britannic Majesty's Territories shall be freely used & navigated by both Parties during the whole extent of such Division. Regulations concerning Roads, Carrying Places and any Land Communications between said Waters, whether within the Line of the United States or that of his Majesty, together with the Navigation of all

8. After receiving Hartley's six propositions on June 19, BF, JA, and Jay met frequently to craft their answers and to complete their own proposals (immediately below). An unannounced visit by Hartley on June 25 found them all together, "in great agitation" over what he surmised were letters from London warning them against trusting the British: Hartley to the Duke of Portland, June 26, 1783 (Clements Library). On June 27 JA wrote to Livingston that they had made so much progress in preparing a definitive treaty that they expected to be able to give it to Hartley the next day: *Adams Papers*, XV, 61. They presented this and the following documents to him on June 29, according to Hammond's notations on each.

9. Hartley's retained copy, in the hand of his secretary George Hammond. We publish it for two reasons: it is the only extant copy that is dated, and it incorporates the numbering changes that the commissioners made after they had prepared the now-missing holograph and made their own copies. (They drafted only five answers and originally numbered them 1–5. They later added the number "4" to their third answer, and renumbered the rest. WTF made these changes in one of the copies sent to Congress, now at the National Archives.) Hartley forwarded a copy to Fox on July 1, indicating that it was a duplicate (Giunta, *Emerging Nation*, 1, 866–70); we have not located the first copy, which was presumably dated June 29.

1. XXXVIII, 385–6.

Waters and Rivers in America belonging to either Party, may be made in the Negotiation of a Treaty of Commerce.

3d & 4th That in all Places belonging to the United States in the Country adjoining to the Water Line of Division, and which, during the War were in his Majesty's Possession, all Persons at present resident, or having Possessions or Occupations, as Merchants or otherwise, may remain in the peaceable Enjoyment of all civil Rights, and in pursuit of their Occupations, until they shall receive Notice of Removal from Congress, or the State, to which any such Place may appertain, and that, upon any such Notice of Removal, a Term of two Years shall be allowed for selling or withdrawing their Effects, and for settling their Affairs—

5th That his Britannic Majesty's Forces not exceeding [*blank*] in number, may continue in the Posts now occupied by them, contiguous to the Water Line, until Congress shall give them Notice to evacuate the said Posts; and Garrisons of their own shall arrive at said Posts, for the purpose of securing the Lives, Property and Peace of any Persons settled in that Country, against the Invasion or Ravages of the Neighbouring Indian Nations, who may be suspected of retaining Resentments in consequence of the late War.

6th The Consideration of this Proposition may be left to the Treaty of Commerce.

Passy 29 June 1783

The American Peace Commissioners to David Hartley: Proposals[2]

Copies: William L. Clements Library,[3] Massachusetts Historical Society, National Archives, Archives du Ministère des affaires étrangères; press copy of copy and transcript: National Archives

[June 29, 1783]

Propositions made to Mr Hartley for the definitive Treaty—

1st To omit in the Definitive Treaty the Exception at the End of the 2d Article of the Provisional Treaty: Viz: these Words "Excepting such Islands as now are, or heretofore have been within the Limits of the said Province of Nova Scotia."[4]

Article[5]

2dly The Prisoners made respectively by the arms of his Britannic Majesty & the United States, by Sea and by Land,[6] not already set at Liberty, shall be restored reciprocally and bonâ fide immediately after the Ratification of the definitive Treaty, without Ransom, and on paying the Debts they may have contracted during their Captivity; and each Party shall respectively reimburse the Sums which shall have been advanced for the

---

2. Hartley sent Fox a copy of these proposals on July 1, with a lengthy cover letter: Giunta, *Emerging Nation*, 1, 866–70.

3. Hartley's retained copy, in the hand of his secretary George Hammond. This is the only copy that includes a date, and it has the fewest number of obvious errors.

4. XXXVIII, 384. The main effect of this alteration would have been to transfer Deer, Campobello, and Grand Manan Islands, now part of New Brunswick, to the United States. The intervening waters, seabed, and subsoil were the object of subsequent litigation, though they still remain under American control; see Richard B. Morris, "The Durable Significance of the Treaty of 1783," in Hoffman and Albert, eds., *Peace and the Peacemakers*, pp. 245–6.

5. This article had been among the three presented by the commissioners to Hartley on April 29: XXXIX, 526. It was adapted from Article 21 of the British-French provisional treaty of Jan. 20, 1783 (published in the Jan. 31 issue of the *Courier de l'Europe*).

6. We have corrected this phrase (from "by Land and by Sea") to conform with all other copies and the language of Article 21, cited above.

Subsistence & Maintenance of the Prisoners, by the Sovereign of the Country where they shall have been detained, according to the Receipts and attested Accounts, and other authentic Titles which shall be produced on each side.

Article[7]

3dly His Britannic Majesty shall employ his good Offices and Interposition with the King or Emperor of Morocco or Fez, the Regencies of Algier, Tunis & Tripoli, or with any of them, and also with every other Prince, State or Power of the Coast of Barbary in Africa, and the Subjects of the said King, Emperor, States & Powers, & each of them, in order to provide as fully and efficaciously as possible for the Benefit, Conveniency and Safety of the said United States, and each of them, their Subjects, People and Inhabitants, and their Vessels and Effects against all violence, insults, attacks or depredations on the Part of the said Princes & States of Barbary, or their Subjects.

Article[8]

4thly If War should hereafter arise between Great Britain and the United States, which God forbid, the Merchants of either Country, then residing in the other, shall be allowed to remain nine Months, to collect their Debts & settle their affairs, and

---

7. Adapted from Article 8 of the Franco-American Treaty of Amity and Commerce: XXV, 602–3.

8. The article BF composed in December, 1782 (XXXVIII, 444–5), and inserted into the proposed commercial treaty he had recently given Portugal; see Article 11 of the Portuguese Counterproposal for a Treaty of Amity and Commerce, [c. June 7], above.

When Hartley sent these proposals to Fox on July 1, he enclosed "some explanatory Papers from Dr. Franklin upon the subject of the 4th. Article," which he said he had known about for some time. BF had sent him the article on May 8, with copies of "Thoughts on Privateering," "Thoughts concerning the Sugar Colonies," and an excerpt of his July 10, 1782, letter to Benjamin Vaughan: XXXIX, 569–70. Hartley urged Fox to delay responding to this article, which he described as unprecedented, "beyond the scope of a Treaty," and leading to such "deep and important consequences" that it demanded serious consideration. Fox, in his Aug. 4 reply, called it "highly exceptionable": Giunta, *Emerging Nation*, I, 867, 903.

may depart freely, carrying off all their Effects without Molestation or Hindrance. And all Fishermen, all Cultivators of the Earth, and all Artisans & Manufacturers, unarmed & inhabiting unfortified Towns, Villages, or Places, who labour for the common Subsistence and Benefit of Mankind, and peaceably follow their respective Employments, shall be allowed to continue the same, and shall not be molested by the armed force of the Enemy, in whose Power by the Events of War they may happen to fall; but if any thing is necessary to be taken from them for the use of such armed Force, the same shall be paid for at a reasonable price. And all Merchants or Traders with their unarmed Vessels employed in Commerce, exchanging the Products of different Places, and thereby rendering the Necessaries, Conveniences & Comforts of Human Life more easy to obtain and more general, shall be allowed to pass freely unmolested. And neither of the Powers, Parties to this Treaty, shall grant or issue any Commission to any private armed Vessels empowering them to take or destroy such trading-Ships or interrupt such Commerce.

Article[9]

5thly And in Case either of the contracting Parties shall happen to be engaged in War with any other Nation, it is farther agreed in order to prevent all the Difficulties & misunderstandings that usually arise, respecting the Merchandize heretofore called Contraband, such as Arms, Ammunition & Military Stores of all Kinds, that no such Articles carrying by the Ships or Subjects of one of the Parties to the Enemies of the other, shall on any Account be deemed Contraband so as to induce Confiscation & a loss of Property to Individuals: Nevertheless it shall be lawful to stop such Ships, and detain them for such length of Time as the Captors may think necessary to prevent the Inconvenience or Damage that might ensue from their proceeding on their Voyage, paying however a reasonable Compensation for the Loss such Arrest shall occasion to the Proprietors. And it shall farther be allowed to use in the Service of the Captors, the

9. This corresponds to Article 12 of the Portuguese counterproposal, cited above.

whole or any Part of the Military Stores, so detained paying to the Owners the full Value of the same.

Article[1]

6thly The Citizens & Inhabitants of the said United States, or any of them, may take and hold real Estates in Great Britain, Ireland or any other of his Majesty's Dominions, and dispose by Testament, Donation or otherwise, of their Property, real or personal, in favour of such Persons, as to them shall seem fit; and their Heirs, Citizens of the United States or any of them, residing in the British Dominions or elsewhere, may succeed them Ab intestato, without being obliged to obtain Letters of Naturalization.

The Subjects of his Britannic Majesty, shall enjoy on their Part, in all the Dominions of the said United States, an entire & perfect Reciprocity relative to the Stipulations contained in the present Article.

Article

7thly The Ratification of the Definitive Treaty shall be expedited in good & due form, and exchanged in the Space of five Months (or sooner if it can be done) to be computed from the Day of the Signature.

8thly Query Whether the King of Great Britain will admit the Citizens of the United States to cut Logwood on the District allotted to his Majesty by Spain,[2] and on what Terms?—

Passy 29th June 1783—[3]

1. A variation of Article 13 of the Franco-American treaty: xxv, 606. Hartley believed it to be a modification of Article 10 of the supplemental treaty he sent BF on March 31 and proposed to the commissioners in April (xxxix, 415, 510–11). For his analysis of it see his July 1 letter to Fox, cited above.

2. The British right to cut logwood in specified districts of central America was guaranteed by Article 4 of the British-Spanish provisional treaty of Jan. 20, 1783.

3. In his July 1 letter to Fox, Hartley commented only on Articles 4 and 6, as noted above. While expressing general optimism about the spirit of

From Bethia Alexander

ALS: American Philosophical Society

St. Germain ce 29 Juin [1783][4]
Je suis chargée d'une invitation pour vous mon cher Docteur, qu'il faudroit bien que vous acceptiez. Madame la Comtesse de la Mark[5] a été desolée de ne vous avoir pas vu avant hier, pour se dedommager elle veut absolument que vous veniez passer une Journée chez elle ici et pour eviter un refus elle vous donne a choisir tous les Jours du mois prochain Jusqu'au vingt et un— Vous n'aurez point d'escaliers a monter comme vous savez, et vous n'y trouverez que Madame de la Mark et nous— Fixé bien vite le Jour Je vous prie, et mandez le moi. Mes complimens au petit cousin—qui est prié aussi dites lui que demain Je commence ses Noix— Adieu mon cher Docteur Je vous embrasse mille fois, et Je vous promets pour le Jour que vous viendrez un baiser longue d'une aune— Votre   B: ALEXANDER

Addressed: A Son Excellence / Son Excellence Monsieur Franklin / Embassadeur des Etats unis de L'amerique / a / Passy

Notation: Alexander 29 Juin

---

the proposals, he nonetheless told Fox that there were sentiments he could not commit to paper. He would therefore return to England for a personal conversation, once he had settled the temporary commercial convention (for which he awaited Fox's final instructions).

Fox did not respond for almost a month. On July 2, however, he wrote a private letter to Hartley instructing him to assure the peace commissioners that their suspicions were "ill founded" and that the British would "adhere to the principles we set out with": Giunta, *Emerging Nation,* II, 175. That last statement was false the day Fox wrote it. On July 2 the king issued an Order in Council denying American ships access to the British West Indies (see Falconer to BF, July 8). Hartley was never informed of this order. He learned of it from the American commissioners on July 16; see the annotation of their letter to him, July 17.

4. The year is established by William Alexander's follow-up letter of July 8, below.

5. We assume that Bethia is writing on behalf of the elder comtesse de la Marck, who resided at Saint-Germain: XXXVII, 208n.

From John Hancock LS: Historical Society of Pennsylvania

Dear Sir   Boston June 30. 1783
I beg leave to introduce to your Excellcy Mr. DeValnais the bearer, late Consul of France, here; who is going home wth his lady.[6] I take the Freedom to refer your Excellcy, to this Gentleman, for the particulars relative to the present Scituation of Affairs in America after so advantagious a Settlement of Peace, with which, I in the most cordial manner take this opportunity to Congratulate you.

Mrs. DeValnais is nearly connected wth my family, and Mr DeValnais his Conduct, during his residence among us, and in the Office of Consul as far as I have had any knowledge of the Same, entitles him, I think, justly to the favor of the court & ministry of France.

As I rely much upon the honor of my former acquaintance wth your Excellcy, permit me to ask an interest in your Friendship, influence & credit, in behalf of Mr DeValnais, in order to his more effectually accomplishing the business he is going upon wth the Court and Ministry of France—

I have the honor to be with peculiar esteem & regard (tho. at present much afflicted with the gout) Dear Sir Your most Obedient and very Hble Servt   JOHN HANCOCK

His Excellcy, Doctr Franklin

Addressed: His Excellcy / Doctr. Franklin / Minister Plenipotentiary from the U. States / of No. America to the Court of / France / at Versailles / per favor of Mr DeValnais

---

6. Valnais married Hancock's niece Eunice Quincy in 1781; see XXXVIII, 473n, where he is identified. His consulship was revoked without pension at the end of 1781 because of irregularities concerning the sale of a French merchant ship. His finances and reputation ruined, he returned to France in 1783 with his family, hoping to restore his good name and obtain a continuation of his pension. They were in Paris by Sept. 13, when Valnais began petitioning the court: Anne Mézin, *Les Consuls de France au siècle des lumières (1715–1792)* (Paris, 1998), p. 577; Abraham P. Nasatir and Gary E. Monell, *French Consuls in the United States . . .* (Washington, D.C., 1967), p. 308.

From the Duchesse de Deux-Ponts

ALS: American Philosophical Society

Versaille Mardis 1er juillet 1783.
Me Voici Mon respectable ami embasadeur de deux americains
francois bien empresséz de Vous rendre homage chez Vous,
Lun est Mon grand garçon[7] et L'autre son Colonel en second,
M le Comte de fersen[8] ils Me chargent de Negogiér pour eux
pres de vous la permission d'aller Vous demander a dinée jeudis
ous Vendredis Vue quils reviennent ici Le samedis si Vous La
Leur accordez exelant home jespere que vous Ne refuserez pas a
Votre vieille et tendre amie Lavantage de Les accompagner vous
scavez que Cest un bonheur pour moi de Vous Voir de Vous entendre et de Vous embrasser aussi tendrement que je Vous aime
bon soir Mon respectable et cher amis

M F DOUAIRIERE DU DUC DE DEUXPONT

Mille amitie a votre Aimable fils

From Andrew Limozin[9]

ALS: American Philosophical Society

Sir   Havre de Grace 1rst July 1783.
I have the honor to inform your Excellency of the Safe ar-
rivall of the Continental Frigate the General Washington
Captn Barny which left Philadelphia on the 7th. Ulto in the

---

7. Her son Christian, colonel of the regiment of Royal-Deux-Ponts,
which recently had returned to France; see the duchesse's letter of May 24.
8. Hans Axel von Fersen (1755–1810) had been appointed *colonel en second*
of the Deux-Ponts regiment the previous September. He was now seeking
the proprietorship of another French infantry regiment, Royal-Suédois,
which he obtained with the assistance of Queen Marie-Antoinette. He left
for Sweden in September, not returning to France until June, 1784: H. Arnold Barton, *Count Hans Axel von Fersen: Aristocrat in an Age of Revolution*
(Boston, 1975), pp. 29, 38–9, 46–7, 64–5.
9. The Le Havre merchant who was appointed American agent there in
1778. Only one previous letter from him is extant: XXVI, 60; XXXVI, 91–2.

Evening.[1] She is consign'd to my care being apointed Agent for the United States of America for the Port of Havre.

I take the freedom to annex to this Severall Letters directed for your Excellency & arrivd by the Said Packet.

I have the Honor to Subscribe my self with a great regard Sir of your Excellency The most obedt. & very Humble Servt.

ANDW LIMOZIN

Captn Barny setts of just now with his dispatches for the Court.[2]

His Excellency Dr Ben: Franklin Esqe. Minister Plenipotentiary of the United States of America Passy

Notation: Limozin 1er. Juillet 1783

From Philip Schuyler[3]

ALS: American Philosophical Society

Dear Sir   Albany July 1st. 1783
Permit me to introduce to your Excellencys attention John Carter Esqr. my son-in-law and Colo: Wadsworth of Hartford[4] they have been joint agents for supplying the french troops who have served in America. Count Rochambeau, General Chatlus[5] and other of the General Officers have afforded me the pleasure of signifying to me, how well the Army was served, and how

1. Despite his instructions to proceed without delay to Le Havre, Joshua Barney spent six days in Plymouth before continuing to France: Hulbert Footner, *Sailor of Fortune: the Life and Adventures of Commodore Barney, U.S.N.* (New York and London, 1940), pp. 143–6.
2. Barney went first to BF's residence, arriving on July 2: BF to Laurens, July 6. He carried dispatches from La Luzerne, which BF evidently forwarded to Vergennes; see Vergennes' note of July 3.
3. BF had stayed with the general and his family on his way to Canada in the spring of 1776; see vol. 22.
4. For Jeremiah Wadsworth and his business partner John "Carter" (an alias for Church), who had married Schuyler's daughter Angelica in 1777, see XXXVIII, 546n.
5. Probably the comte de Charlus (XXXVI, 133n).

perfectly contented they were with the conduct of those two Gentlemen. They are going to sollicit in France, payment of the bills which have been drawn in their favor by the intendant of the Army.[6] It is probable that you may able efficiently to intervene in their behalf, and permit me to intreat Your assistance to them.—[7]

Accept Sir of my best congratulations on the prospect of a speedy peace, and the perfect establishment of our independance. America is so much indebted to your exertions, on these important occasions, that I am persuaded every one of her honest citizens is pervaded with those sentiments of Gratitude, regard and esteem which I have the happiness intimately to feel.—

I have the honor to be with unfeigned Sincerity Dr. Sir Your Excellency's Most Obedient Servant   PH: SCHUYLER

His Excellency Benjamin Franklin Esqr &c

6. Benoît-Joseph de Tarlé, for whom see Morris to BF, May 27.

7. Wadsworth, Carter, and Carter's wife and children sailed on July 27, arriving in France one month later. John and Angelica Carter were already known to the Jays and Matthew Ridley: *Morris Papers*, VIII, 342, 566n, 598, 599. Several brief notes from the Carters to BF, written during their stay in Paris, suggest a comfortable friendship. Only one is altogether undated: "Mrs. Carter" sent word to BF on "Monday morning" that she would call on him accompanied by "the young Gentlemen" (APS). Her two eldest children were sons Philip and John, Jr., who would have been around five and four years old in the fall of 1783: Don R. Gerlach, *Proud Patriot: Philip Schuyler and the War of Independence, 1775–1783* (Syracuse, 1987), p. 446.

It is not known when Angelica Carter discovered her husband's true name, but BF learned of it, in confidence, in late October: John Jay to Sarah Livingston Jay, Oct. 26, 1783 (Columbia University Library). The couple were still writing to BF as Mr. and Mrs. Carter as late as Feb. 10, 1784 (APS), but by the time they left for England, Carter had reclaimed the name Church: Wadsworth and Church to BF, June 24, 1784 (APS).

The American Peace Commissioners to Prince Bariatinskii

Retranslation: reprinted from Nina N. Bashkina *et al.*, eds., *The United States and Russia: the Beginning of Relations, 1765–1815* ([Washington, D.C., 1980]), p. 199.[8]

On Tuesday, July 1, at the weekly gathering of ministers at Versailles, Vergennes informed the American peace commissioners that the Anglo-French treaty had been settled, pending British approval, and the time had come for them to pay official visits to the Russian and Austrian ministers who would be signing the treaty as mediators. The commissioners did so the next day, calling first on the comte de Mercy-Argenteau, who was not at home, and then on Prince Bariatinskii, who received them "very politely." Arkadii Markov, who had been sent to Paris in April to join Bariatinskii as a co-mediator, arrived during their visit and warmly acknowledged their intention of calling at his residence later that day. (He was not at home when they did.) Before the summer heat became unbearable, they also called on the ministers of the Netherlands, Sweden, and Denmark, leaving their cards.[9]

Because neither Russia nor Austria had yet recognized the United States, John Adams wondered whether those ministers would need to consult with their courts before returning the visits.[1] He need not have worried. Austrian representatives had been wondering since January how they could lure Franklin into making an official overture, allowing Joseph II to confer recognition and launch trade negotiations.[2] When Mercy-Argenteau received notification in April that he would be receiving full powers and instructions for serving as a mediator in the treaties of France and Spain, he observed to the emperor that signing the Anglo-American treaty as well would provide the opportunity for establishing the trade relations they had been seeking.[3] By the end of April, he and the Russian ministers had agreed that

8. It is likely that the original was written in French, as Bariatinskii did not speak English. He translated it into Russian before forwarding a copy to Catherine II on July 6. The present text was translated from that Russian copy: Bashkina, *United States and Russia*, pp. 198–9, 219.

9. *Adams Papers*, xv, 76–7. For Markov see the commissioners' draft letter to the Russian mediators, [before July 15].

1. *Adams Papers*, xv, 76–7.

2. See xxxix, 188n.

3. Alfred d'Arneth and Jules Flammermont, eds., *Correspondance secrète du comte de Mercy-Argenteau avec l'empereur Joseph II et le prince de Kaunitz* (2 vols., Paris, 1889–91), I, 175, 181.

they would participate in the signing of the Anglo-American treaty if asked.[4] This must have been what prompted Vergennes in May to sound out the American commissioners quietly as to whether they would "prefer" to invite mediation. They did not.[5]

As the time for signing the treaties approached, however, Vergennes must have known that the mediators would still welcome a role in the Anglo-American treaty and were prepared to recognize the American commissioners. Protocol required that the Americans pay the first visit. The imperial ambassadors returned those visits the next day, leaving cards.[6]

[July 2, 1783]
Mr. Adams, Mr. Franklin, and Mr. Jay, Ministers Plenipotentiary of the United States of America to treat of peace, have called to have the honor of visiting His Excellency the Minister Plenipotentiary of Russia.

To Le Couteulx & Cie.

AL (draft): Historical Society of Pennsylvania

Gentlemen, Passy, July 2. 1783
I have the honour of sending you enclos'd a Letter I have just receiv'd for you from Mr Morris.—[7] I find that from a Mistake in his Expectations of the Funds I should be able to furnish, he has drawn on Mr Grand to a larger Amount than I can possibly supply.[8] Mr Grand will therefore be obliged to protest some of those Bills unless Means can be found to prevent that Misfortune, which may be attended with very mischievous Consequences. As I understand that Mr Morris has Cash in your Hands,[9] waiting his Orders, permit me to suggest to you my Opinion, that it

4. Bashkina, *United States and Russia*, p. 209n.
5. See XXXIX, 596.
6. Bashkina, *United States and Russia*, p. 198; *Adams Papers*, XV, 78–9.
7. Dated May 31 and brought to France by Joshua Barney. It enclosed 18 bills of exchange totaling 506,204 *l.t.: Morris Papers*, VIII, 136–7n, 141.
8. See Morris to BF, May 26, letter (I), and Grand's letters of June 2 and 27.
9. In April, Morris estimated that the firm had about 1,800,000 *l.t.: Morris Papers*, VII, 698.

will be doing a very acceptable Service to him and to our States, if you should consider his Drafts as Orders, and either pay them for his Honour, or furnish Mr Grand with Money to pay them as they arrive, as to you may seem most proper and convenient. I have the honour to be Gentlemen,

Messrs Couteulx & Co

Letter to Messrs le Couteulx

From Benjamin Franklin Bache

ALS: American Philosophical Society[1]

My dear grandpapa,— Pente[2] July 2. 1783—
I received your kind Letter of the 23 June the 29 of the same mounth I was very glad when I read that you desir'd me to come at Passy during the Vacation of the School to See you, I have been Sick, but I Am now recover'd and Strong enough to undertake the Jorney.[3] By the Complasance of Mr Pigott I went I great many times beffor my sickness to dine to his house with Johonnot when he heard that I was sick He made me come to his country house where I recover'd my health. Remember my Love to my cousin, I only expect an occassion to undertake the agreable Jorney to See you.
I am You most obedient and dutiful Grand Son
B Franklin B.

Be So good as to render the inclos'd to his addess

Addressed: A Monsieur / Monsieur Franklin Ministre Plenipotentiare / des etats Unis de L'Amerique auprès / de Sa Majesté trés Chretienne / A Passy / Pres Paris.

Notation: B. F. B. to Dr. Franklin July 2— '83

1. Castle-Bache Collection.
2. Robert Pigott's estate; see his letter of June 27.
3. BFB left Geneva on July 9, carrying Webb's letter to BF of July 7. He arrived at Passy on either July 18, according to John Jay's recollection two days later (Morris, *Jay: Peace*, p. 566), or July 19, the date BFB told his father that he "saw my Dear Grandpapa" (BFB to RB, July 27, 1783, APS).

From ——— Fabre Dubosquet[4]

ALS: American Philosophical Society

Monsieur   Paris le 2. jeuillet. 1783

Il ÿ a Pres de trois ans que Présenté chez Vous Par Mr. paul jones Commodore des états unis de lamérique, Nous Dissértames un peu de temps Sur les qualités D'un Métal pour le Doublage Des Vaisseaux Dont Mr. Paul jones Vous avoit remis un échantillon. Ce nouveau Doublage Monsieur, est aujourdhuÿ a sa perfection; ainsi que les Cloux de fer Vernissés, qui doivent l'assujetir au Vaisseau. Les lames ont cinq Pieds De longueur sur 18 pouces de hauteur, Si elles etoint Moins ambarrassantes, je les ferois Porter a Passÿ; Cependant Comme il seroit tres intérréssant que Vous les Vissies si lorsque Vous Viendres a paris Vous Voulies Me faire lhonneur de passer ches Moÿ, et de Me prevenir du jour ou je Devrois attendre Vostre èxcelence, Nous confererions sur tous les points dont cet objet est suscéptible; elle trouvera cÿ joint, les lettres patentes, que jaÿ obtenu et des observations qui aideront a la Mettre au fait De ce Doublage.

Je suis avec beaucoup de respect Monsieur Vostre tres humble Et tres obeissant serviteur   FABRE DUBOSQUET

Pr. [Premier] gentilhomme de la grande fauconerie De france, rue poissonière, apres la bariére ste anne.[5]

From Le Couteulx & Cie. LS: Historical Society of Pennsylvania

Monsieur   Paris 2. Juillet 1783

Nous Sommes Vraiment embarrassées pour repondre à la Lettre que vous nous avez fait l'honneur de nous écrire le 2. Juillet nous Sentons Toute l'Importance pour le bien des Etats

---

4. Fabre Dubosquet (du Bosquet) was an entrepreneur and inventor who in 1780 had shown BF the prototype of a new metal alloy for the sheathing of ships' hulls. It was now available for purchase, and Faujas de Saint-Fond had given BF a sample in January; see XXXVIII, 603n.

5. This appears to be his address. The grand falconer was Joseph-François de Paule, comte de Vaudreuil: *Almanach royal* for 1783, p. 122; Larousse, under Vaudreuil.

unis de Laisser retourner Sans payement aucunes des Traittes que Mr. Morris peut avoir fourni Sur Monsieur Grand en Sa qualité de Sur-Intendant des finances & le mauvais Effet qui pourroit en resulter. Nous avons remis à Mr. Morris la notte exacte des fonds qui Sont entre nos mains et Il nous à Expressement ordonné de les Tenir à Sa disposition.[6] Par consequent nous ne pouvons Sans aucune raison quelconque nous dispenser d'acquitter ces memes dispositions lorsqu'elles pourront nous etre présentés. Dans cette position des choses Monsieur nous Croyons ne pouvoir prendre aucun Engagement positif, mais Lorsque l'Echeance des Traittes Sur Mr. Grand aura Lieu S'il se Trouvoit forcé d'en Laisser protester quelq'une nous le prierons de nous renvoyer les porteurs et nous les payerons pour l'honneur de Mr. Morris Si ses dispositions Subsequentes nous le permetent.

Nous avons l'honneur d'Etre avec Respect Monsieur Vos trés humbles et très obt. Serviteurs   Le Couteulx & Comp

P.S. Depuis cette Lettre écritte nous devons vous prevenir que le Capitaine Barney arrivé aujourd'huy nous á apporté l'avis d'Environ Sept cents mille Livres[7] Traittes de Monsieur Morris et que nous devons Croire par consequent que les dispositions dudit Sieur pour le Surplus des fonds entre nos mains ne Tardera pas à parroitre./.

6. In his letter of April 12: *Morris Papers*, VII, 698–9.

7. Barney is known to have carried only one letter from Morris to the Paris firm, that of May 31, which evidently went under cover of BF; see our annotation of BF to Le Couteulx & Cie. of this date, above. If he also carried Morris' letter of April 30, enclosing eight sets of bills of exchange worth 50,224 *l.t.*, the total is still only 556,428 *l.t.*: *Morris Papers*, VII, 765–6; VIII, 141.

From Charles-Henri Titius[8]

ALS: American Philosophical Society

Monsieur!   à Dresde le 3me. Juillet 1783.

Je meriterois le titre d'ingrat si je laissois passer l'occasion qui se presente de Vous assurer de mon estime parfaite et de la plus vive réconnoissance que je Vous ai, pour toutes les marques de bienveillance et d'amitié que Vous daignates m'accorder pendant mon séjour à Paris, ou j'avois l'honneur de Vous voir souvent chès Msr. le Comte de Buffon, nôtre vénérable ami:[9] acceptés donc l'hommage que Vos vertus meritent d'un homme réconnoissant, qui fait gloire de les publier à ses concitoyens.

J'ose en même tems Monsieur, recommander à Vos bonnes graces celui qui a l'honneur de Vous remettre les présentes, c'est le Sr. Thieriot, Marchand, qui va en amérique:[1] daignés Monsieur lui accorder Vos recommandations pour ce pays; la connoissance parfaite que j'ai de Vôtre caractère élévé, me promet en avance que Vous daignerés condescendre à mes sollicitations; si j'occupois un rang plus haut, je Vous offrirois Monsieur mes foibles services, cependant je me flatte que Vous aurès la bonté de m'honorer de Vos commandemens, si Vous m'en croyés digne, et la plus exacte exécution Vous fera voir combien j'en sais faire cas.

Non content Monsieur de Vous avoir demandé une grace, j'y joints encore une autre, mais je me vois obligé d'entrer premierement au détail du fait: Il y a plus de cinquante ans qu'un certain

---

8. Carl (Karl) Heinrich Titius (1744–1813) was a German physician and naturalist. He practiced and taught medicine in Dresden and in 1778 became the supervisor of the Electorate of Saxony's natural history collection: Christoph Johann Gottfried Haymann, *Dresdens theils neuerlich verstorbne theils jetzt lebende Schriftsteller und Künstler* (Dresden, 1809); Georg Christoph Hamberger et al., eds., *Das gelehrte Teutschland oder Lexikon der jetzt lebenden teutschen Schrifftsteller* (5th ed., rev., Lemgo, 1827). This is the second of two letters from Titius. The previous day, without identifying himself, he wrote to recommend an unnamed friend, a poor but honest former cavalry captain who spoke French, German, and English. A good man, he wished to serve the United States and would leave immediately for Paris if BF could promise him employment. APS.

9. BF met the comte de Buffon soon after his arrival in France in 1776: XXV, 138–9n.

1. Philipp Thieriot; see Schönfeld to BF, July 20.

270

Médécin içi, nommé Oehme[2] inventa des médécines efficaces contre beaucoup de maladies, il gagna par ce moien un bien très considerable dans ce pays çi; je ne puis pas dire si ces remedes ont toutes les proprietés que l'inventeur leur attribue, car leur composition est un secret, cependant comme leur credit s'est soutenu jusqu'içi et que leur débit bien considérable s'etend presque sur toute l'Europe, l'on doit pourtant croire qu'ils meritent quelque attention: L'inventeur laissa après sa mort leur composition aux mains de son fils unique, qui fut aussi Docteur en Medécine; ce dernier étant mort au commencement de l'année courante,[3] les laissa par Testament à l'école des pauvres de cette capitale, institut fondé sur la générosité des vénérables freres maçons, le profit qui en revient est donc pour cette école, ou l'on éleve actuellement cent et sept orphelins garçons et filles: c'est donc pour l'amour de ceux que je Vous prie très humblement de vouloir instruire le Sr. Thieriot si l'entrée des medécines inconnues est libre en amèrique, et de lui accorder Vôtre assistance pour y faire quelque debit. Vous voyés bien Monsieur que c'est un oeuvre de charité, soutenés le, je Vous en sollicite, les prieres de ces pauvres enfants pour Vous, seront agréables à nôtre maître suprème et sa grace Vous recompensera. Pardonnés ma hardiesse de Vous être à charge par une priere de ce genre, considerés seulement que c'est le sort des ames grandes et généreuses d'être attaquées de tous cotés de la multitude qui implore leur sécours. Au reste Monsieur soutenés moi aussi en avénir Vos bonnes graces, et soyés persuadé que rien n'égale à l'estime et à la vénération sublime avec laquelle j'ai l'honneur de me nommer Monsieur Vôtre très humble et très obéissant Serviteur

CHARLES HENRI TITIUS,
Docteur en Medécine et Inspecteur du Cabinet de l'histoire naturelle de S. A. Erale [Son Altesse Electorale] de Saxe

2. The Dresden physician Johann August Oehme (c. 1692–1754): Christian Gottlieb Jöcher, *Allgemeines Gelehrten-Lexicon* . . . (11 vols., Leipzig, 1750–1819, 1897), IX, 952.
3. Carl Joseph Oehme (1752–1783), who also practiced medicine in Dresden, died on Jan. 26: *ibid*. The entry for Johann August states that his son bequeathed his recipes to the Friedrichstädter Armenschule, but gives the son's name as Johann August.

JULY 3, 1783

M. de Francklin

Notation: Charles Henri Titius Dresde 3 Juillet 1783

From Vergennes

L: Library of Congress

Versailles le 3 Juillet 1783.
M. De Vergennes a reçu avec le billet que Monsieur Francklin lui a fait l'honneur de lui ecrire hier les paquets qui y etoient joints.[4] Il le prie d'en recevoir ses sinceres remercimens, ainsi que l'assurance de son fidelle et inviolable attachement.

To Vergennes

LS:[5] Archives du Ministère des affaires étrangères; AL (draft): Library of Congress; copies: Library of Congress, National Archives

Sir,   Passy July 4. 1783.
I have the honour to communicate to your Excellency, by Order of Congress, their Resolution of the 2d of May.[6] It will explain itself; and I can add no Arguments to enforce the Request it contains, which I have not already urged with an Importunity that nothing but a Sense of Duty could oblige me to use, when I see so clearly that it is painful to you as well as to me. I confide also much more in the Representation M. de la Luzerne has probably made to you on the Affair. I will only say, that

---

4. BF's note is missing, but it doubtless forwarded dispatches from La Luzerne that had just arrived on the packet *General Washington;* see Limozin to BF, July 1. La Luzerne had corresponded with Morris about the date of the ship's sailing: *Morris Papers,* VIII, 70–1.

5. In WTF's hand.

6. Requesting an additional loan of 3,000,000 *l.t.* It was enclosed with Morris' first letter of May 26 (above), which was carried by Joshua Barney: *Morris Papers,* VIII, 120n. The commissioners themselves had just asked Vergennes for assistance in meeting 1,900,000 *l.t.* of debts: above, June 28.

from a perfect Knowledge I have of their present Situation, no Favour of the Kind from his Majesty could ever be more essentially serviceable to the United States, or make a more lasting Impression.

I send withal an Address the Congress has just made to the several States,[7] wherein you will see the Steps they are taking to procure the necessary Funds, for answering all Engagements; in which I have no doubt they will succeed. Your Excellency will also see there, the Manner in which I have written on the Subject;[8] and you will find that the Contract of July last was ratified, and with Expressions of Gratitude, in January last,[9] tho' the Original Ratification is not yet come to hand. With great Respect, I am, Sir, Your Excellency's most obedient & most humble Servant.   B FRANKLIN

His Exy Ct. de Vergennes

Endorsed: M de R[1]

Notation: Rep. le 18 Juillet

The Abbé Morellet's Song in Honor of Independence Day

D:[2] American Philosophical Society

The Fourth of July in 1783 was the first Independence Day since the United States of America had been recognized by Great Britain and hostilities had ceased. Although the terms of the definitive peace

---

7. *Address and Recommendations to the States, by the United States in Congress assembled,* which Livingston sent on May 9; for a description see XXXIX, 579n.

8. An excerpt of BF to Morris, Dec. 23, 1782 (XXXVIII, 487–9).

9. The July 16, 1782, contract (XXXVII, 633–9) was ratified on Jan. 22: *JCC,* XXIV, 50–64. The expressions of gratitude are in the address to the states and are immediately followed by a reference to the fifth enclosure, the ratification: *JCC,* XXIV, 282, 290.

1. Rayneval.

2. Mostly in the hand of Morellet's secretary Poullard, with additions and corrections by Morellet. The last two stanzas are in Morellet's hand.

treaty had not yet been settled, the preliminaries had been ratified and the French troops had returned home. To celebrate the occasion, Franklin hosted a banquet at Passy whose guests of honor, according to the *London Morning Post and Daily Advertiser* of July 28, were the comte d'Estaing, the comte de Rochambeau, and the marquis de Lafayette, who wore their military uniforms. Also present were ambassadors Aranda and Berkenrode, the duc de Lauzun, and "a great number of other noblemen and ladies of the first distinction." It was, according to the newspaper, a "most brilliant entertainment."

Franklin had hosted an Independence Day celebration in 1779, his first as sole minister plenipotentiary, for which he printed invitations on his newly established press.[3] If he printed invitations for this occasion, no example has been located. What we believe to be a partial guest list, written by William Temple Franklin on the address sheet of an unrelated letter,[4] contains twenty-one names. Heading it are d'Estaing, Rochambeau, Rochambeau's son the vicomte de Rochambeau, Chastellux,[5] the marquis and marquise de Lafayette, Lewis Littlepage, who had recently accompanied Lafayette to Paris,[6] and Michel Capitaine de Chesnoy, one of Lafayette's aides-de-camp.[7] Next are a series of Americans: John Adams and his secretaries Charles Storer and John Thaxter, Jr., Matthew and Anne Ridley and Anne's cousin John Hunt, Thomas and Mary Barclay, Dorcas Montgomery, Joseph Mayo,[8] and William Vernon, Jr.[9] Finally, Temple wrote the

3. See XXIX, 726–7; XXX, 44–6.

4. The list is written on Elkanah Watson, Jr., to WTF, June 24, 1783 (APS).

5. He and Rochambeau returned on the same ship; see XXXIX, 200n.

6. See Littlepage to BF, Sept. 1.

7. Capitaine had maintained a friendship with WTF since 1779; their correspondence is at the APS.

8. The peripatetic friend of WTF's (XXXV, 375n; XXXVIII, 198) who was back in Paris by at least April 30, when he wrote WTF about an opportunity to send mail to America (APS).

9. The son of a Rhode Island merchant who had sailed to France in 1778 with JA, carrying a letter of introduction to BF from John Hancock. His father asked BF to look out for his welfare: XXV, 641; XXVIII, 204–5. Vernon worked for John Bondfield in Bordeaux until March, 1782, when he left for Paris, planning to "pass a few Days" there before returning to America: XXXVII, 46. By December of that year, when he had still not sailed, Bondfield wrote JA of his concern that the young man might fall into "habits of Disipation": *Adams Papers*, XIV, 151–2. He did, and turned to BF in 1784 and 1785 for help in paying his debts.

names "Grand" (Franklin's banker and neighbor) and "Price," undoubtedly the merchant currently in Paris pursuing a lawsuit and petitioning the French government.[1] John and Sarah Jay, who were then living in Franklin's residence, also attended.[2]

Only three responses to Franklin's invitations survive.[3] The Barclays accepted on July 1.[4] Capitaine sent heartfelt regrets to Temple on July 3; he was too busy assisting Lafayette, who was about to depart for his family estate.[5] The abbé Morellet, also addressing his response to Temple, accepted with pleasure. His letter, dated only "Mercredy" (July 2), requested that a piano rather than a harpsichord be available; surely Madame Brillon would lend one of hers. The abbé proposed to arrive before one o'clock and have music before dinner. In that case, he teased, Madame Brillon would be more likely to come, as Fridays were one of the two mornings she customarily entertained Franklin.[6]

The accounts kept by Franklin's maître d'hôtel Jacques Finck hint at a sumptuous banquet. The guests dined on fattened hens, duck, quail, a turkey, chickens ("communs" and otherwise), six pigeons *à la Gautier*, a wild boar, rabbit, and hare. There were six mackerel, a ray, carp, eels, cod, flounder, sole, and one hundred crayfish. From the grocer, Finck ordered peas, carrots, turnips, romaine lettuce, chicory, onions, lemons, cabbage, cauliflower, cucumbers, white and green string beans ("aricots"), shallots, and 1,112 eggs. Six baskets of strawberries were delivered, as well as two varieties of cherries, one hundred apricots, pears, melons, and red and white currants. Some of that fruit was doused in the twelve pints of *eau de vie* ordered for the purpose. Additional stores included oil for the lamps, firewood

1. For James Price, a partner of John Bondfield in Bordeaux (XXXVII, 40), see BF to Vergennes, May 23, Vergennes' answer of June 20, and Price to BF, July 11.

2. Sarah Jay mentioned the celebration in a letter to her sister, though she did not describe it. She did, however, enclose a list of toasts written by her husband and the text of Morellet's song: Sarah Jay to Catharine Livingston, July 16, 1783; List of thirteen toasts, [1783] (Columbia University Library).

3. All three, described here, are at the APS.

4. See the annotation of their June 23 letter.

5. The château de Chavaniac, in the Auvergne, where he spent the remainder of July, at least: Idzerda, *Lafayette Papers*, V, 142–7.

6. Mme Brillon owned an English and German piano as well as a harpsichord: Bruce Gustafson, "The Music of Madame Brillon: a Unified Manuscript Collection from Benjamin Franklin's Circle," *Notes*, XLIII (1987), 529; and see Medlin, *Morellet*, I, 490, where the letter to WTF is published.

for the kitchen, coffee, spices, salt, parmesan cheese, six pounds of chocolate, fifty pounds of candles, and two quarter-casks of *bière de paris*. A large order of flowers cost 6 *l.t.* Whatever the table decorations consisted of,[7] it took a porter several trips to deliver them. Either before or after the banquet (the accounts are not clear on this point), Finck bought six carafes and three dozen goblets.[8]

The only known description of the event is the paragraph published in the *London Morning Post and Daily Advertiser*, based on an unknown source in Paris. According to this account, "an allegorical representation was given of the military prowess of every one of those who had in any material degree contributed to effect that great revolution; this naturally leading the attention of the company to the great merits and signal services performed by the Doctor himself, they bestowed on him those praises which both his public and private character so well deserved; to which he replied by the following couplet, no less polite à propos: 'Des Chevaliers François, tel est le caractere, / Leur Noblesse en tout temp nous fut utile et chere.'"

No trace has survived of that "allegorical representation." Morellet's song, however, has been preserved among Franklin's papers. Set to the same tune as the drinking song he composed for Franklin in 1779,[9] this series of patriotic stanzas is more serious and heartfelt than its predecessor. Here, Morellet proclaims himself an American and pays homage to the heroes of the war. The manuscript makes clear that he originally ended the song after twenty-one stanzas. The afterthought, which he marked for insertion as the penultimate stanza, was a toast to Adams and Jay.

le 4 juillet. 1783.

Chanson

pour la fête de l'anniversaire de l'indépendance
et de la paix de l'Amérique célébrée chés
M. franklin le 4 juillet. 1783.

---

7. In 1779 BF had rented porcelain figurines: XXX, 44.

8. Account XXXI (XXXVIII, 3). One entry for July, 1783—36 *l.t.* "pour les cuissiniers"—may indicate that extra cooks were employed for the occasion.

9. XXX, 47–50.

I. Enfin il brille à nos yeux
Ce jour objet de nos vœux,
Jour où la liberté fonde
Le bonheur du nouveau monde,
Où le destin
Se déclare Américain.

II Je ne me plaindrai jamais
Du Sort qui m'a fait françois.
Mais en ce moment j'envie
Encore une autre patrie.
Dans ce festin,
Je me fais américain.

III Vous voyés qu'un très grand Roi,
Louis, a fait comme moi;
Quand Sa noble politique
A protégé l'Amérique,
Son cœur humain
S'est bien fait Américain.

IV De nos guerriers valeureux
je suis les pas glorieux
je serai le camarade
du vainqueur de la Grenade
Avec d'Etaing
Je me fais Américain.

V Je veux aux champs de Trenton
Rendre hommage à Washington,
Ce fabius d'Amérique
Qu'eut préféré Rome antique
A Son Romain.
Je me fais Américain.

VI. Je veux cueillir un rameau
Du laurier de Rochambeau,

Et pour aider ma mémoire
Voir Sa route à la victoire
    Sur le terrain.
Je me fais américain.

VII Je veux voir ce champ d'honneur
Si digne d'un noble cœur,
Où la liberté répete
Le beau nom de la fayette
    La palme en main
Je me fais Américain.

VIII Je verrai le magazin
Et la presse de franklin
Nobles titres de Sa gloire
Que consacrera l'histoire
    Malgré Cherin.
Je me fais Américain.

IX Dieu nous fit un vrai cadeau
Créant ce monde nouveau.
j'en dirai tout bas La cause
Le vieux ne vaut plus grand-chose.
    A Son déclin
Je me fais Américain.

X Bonnes mœurs et loyauté
Raison et Simplicité,
Tels Sont les biens que recele
Cette terre encor nouvelle
    Dans Son beau Sein.
Je me fais Américain.

XI. Chés nous il est bien encor
Quelques gens de l'âge d'or,
Mais les cieux toujours avares

Nous les y montrent plus rares
    Qu'un jour Serein.
Je me fais Américain.

XII On nous dit que le bon ton
    n'est pas encore à Boston,
    Mais vivre à l'ancienne mode
    Est selon moi plus commode
        Et bien plus Sain.
    Je me fais Américain.

XIII Je n'y retrouverai pas
    Nos grands et beaux operas,
    Mais autant vaut, quand on l'aime,
    Danser et chanter soi-même
        Sans tant de train.
    Je me fais Américain.

XIV Les belles de moins d'apprêts
    Y rélevent leurs attraits,
    Mais la coquette nature
    Entend l'art de la parure
        Mieux que Bertin.
    Je me fais Américain.

XV Elles ont à tous les jours
    De bien moins couteux atours,
    Encore un peu d'innocence
    Et beaucoup plus de constance
        C'est double gain.
    Je me fais Américain.

XVI Qu'à jamais il Soit tosté
    Cet admirable traité,
    Et qu'à ma voix tout réponde,
    De l'ancien au nouveau monde,

Le verre en main,
françois comme Américain.

XVII Pour Louis de ce nectar
Nous boirons un coup à part.
Au Roi dont la bienfaisance
S'étend plus que Sa puissance
honneur Sans fin
françois comme Américains.

XVIII Il a bien droit à nos vœux,
Son ministre vertueux,
A la Sagesse profonde
Qui rend le repos au monde
Buvons tout plein,
françois comme américains.

XIX Dans nos bachiques Souhaits
Rendons hommage au Congrès.
Gloire à la rare prudence,
Qui Secondant la vaillance,
Assure enfin
Le triomphe Américain.

XX Nous tosterons bien aussi
Celui qui nous traite ici.
Puissent couler fortunées
Encor de longues années
Pour Benjamin
Le Solon Américain.

XXI buvons aux heureux succés
de ces deux anges de paix*   [*in the margin:* mrs adams
qui portent à leur patrie   et jay]
l'olive en leurs mains fleurie

gage certain
du bonheur americain

XXIIe[1] Que les deux peuples unis
soient à jamais bons amis
et que l'Anglois fier et brave
libre sans avoir d'esclave
traite en voisin
francois comme americain

Vergennes to Franklin and John Jay

Press copy of copy:[2] American Philosophical Society; L (draft): Archives
du Ministère des affaires étrangères; copy: National Archives

[July 5, 1783]

J'ai reçu, Messieurs, la Lettre que vous m'avez fait l'honneur de m'ecrire le 29 du Mois dernier[3] et par laquelle vous demandez, au Nom des Etats Unis un Secours extraordinaire de 1900/m *l.t.*

Le Roi se seroit fait un Plaisir, Messieurs, de prendre votre Demande en Consideration: mais l'Etat de ses Finances lui fait la Loi a cet Egard:[4] bien loin que sa Majesté ait les Fonds necessaires pour solder les Depenses enormes de la dere. Guerre, Elle se trouve dans la Necessité de s'en procurer pour cet Effet par

1. After he had added the new stanza XXI, Morellet renumbered this one and added the words, "et dernier."
2. In the hand of WTF.
3. The letter was actually dated June 28 (above).
4. The monarchy estimated its debts as of Jan. 1, 1782, at more than 3,300,000,000 *l.t.*, with an annual interest cost of more than 165,000,000: Robert D. Harris, "French Finances and the American War, 1777–1783," *Jour. of Modern Hist.*, XLVIII (1976), 248–9. Subsequent mismanagement compounded the problem; by 1787 the debt was about 5,000,000,000 *l.t.* and the annual interest cost 318,000,000: J. F. Bosher, *French Finances, 1770–1795: from Business to Bureaucracy* (Cambridge, 1970), pp. 23–4.

la Voye de l'Emprunt.[5] Vous pourez juger par là que le Roi est dans l'impossibilité absoluë de vous accorder la somme qui fait l'objet de votre Demande; vous ne devez pas douter, Messieurs, du Regret qu'eprouve sa Majesté de ne pouvoir dans cette Occasion donner aux Etats Unis une nouvelle Preuve de son Affection; je n'en ai pas moins de m'etre trouvé hors d'etat de seconder votre Zêle en concourrant au Succès de vos Sollicitations.[6]

J'ai l'honneur d'etre tres sincerement, Messieurs, votre tres humble et très obeissant Serviteur. (signé) DE VERGENNES

Notation by William Temple Franklin: Copy of Letter from his Excellency Count de Vergennes, to Messrs: Franklin & Jay. dated at Versailles the 5. July 1783.

From Ferdinand Grand

L:[7] Historical Society of Pennsylvania

Monsieur Paris le 5 Juillet 1783.

La rèponse de Mrs. Le couteulx[8] que vous avez bien voulu me communiquer n'est pas satisfaisante, en ce qu'ils ne s'expliquent point sur l'objet des fonds qu'ils ont à Monsieur Morris; ils se contentent de laisser entrevoir qu'ils en ont en disant qu'ils ne peuvent en faire d'autre employ que celui de les tenir à la disposition de Monsieur Morris Suivant ses ordres; mais ce qui me

---

5. Loans to the monarchy were obtained only at increasingly higher interest rates: George V. Taylor, "The Paris Bourse on the Eve of the Revolution, 1781–1789," *American Hist. Rev.,* LXVII (1961–62), 958.

6. Vergennes sent a copy of this letter to La Luzerne on July 21. He treated the commissioners' request as being for an advance on the 3,000,000 *l.t.* requested by Congress (for which see BF to Vergennes, July 4) and pointed out that Morris' bills alone exceeded the 6,000,000 *l.t.* being provided by France during 1783. He argued that the costs of disarmament and settling accounts made 1783 more costly than a year of war: Giunta, *Emerging Nation,* I, 889–90. Naval expenditures for 1783 exceeded those of 1781: Jonathan R. Dull, *The French Navy and American Independence* (Princeton, 1975), p. 349.

7. Written and signed on Grand's behalf by his eldest son, Jean-François-Paul (XXIX, 424n). Grand himself added the postscript.

8. Above, July 2.

paroit le plus clair dans leur lettre c'est qu'ils veulent proffiter de l'avis que vous leur avez donné[9] & se rèserver ces fonds pour avoir l'honneur d'intervenir & payer les traittes sur un protest, ce que l'on veut èviter. Il me semble que ces Messieurs pourroient & devroient concourir à èviter une façon de payer aussi humiliante que deshonorante à tous ègards; encore se font ils peut être illusion; J'ai eu l'honneur de vous faire voir un Etat par le quel les traittes qui rèstent à payer pour Monsieur Morris s'elèvent à £1,519,528. [*l.t.*] 17. *s.* 3. *d.*[1] Peut être que ces Messieurs ne s'attendroient point à cela ni à avancer cette Somme à Monsieur Morris s'ils n'en avoient pas les fonds, & alors il auroit mieux valu qu'ils n'intervinssent à rien qu'à une partie. Quant à moi il ne m'en rèste plus; Mr. Barklay ne pense pas que ceux qu'il aura à me remettre suivant les ordres de Monsieur Morris, Quand il les aura recouvré, l'Epoque n'en etant pas encore certaine, ne fissent au delà de cent mille livres; Le vaisseau Le Duc de Lauzun n'etant pas encore vendu, son produit ainsi que le tems de cette rentrée est incertain;[2] mais quand ces deux objets seroient reçus ils ne feroient pas deux cent mille livres & quest ce que cette Somme vis à vis de nos besoins? Je ne vois donc que les fonds qui sont en hollande capables de nous aider, Mrs. Le couteulx ne voulant pas en donner & comme nous sommes depuis dix jours dans le besoin le plus préssant & qu'il auroit dèja èclaté sans mes soins, je crois qu'il n'y a pas un instant à perdre de faire partir un courrier pour Mrs. Willinck, Staphorst, & De la lande d'amsterdam, aux quels il seroit important que Monsieur adams eut la bonté de confirmer l'ordre que leur donne Monsieur Morris de tenir à ma disposition les fonds qu'ils ont à lui, en leur demandant de lui marquer ainsi qu'à moi en rèponse sur quelle somme je puis positivement compter. On pourroit peut être leur demander en même tems s'il ne leur Seroit pas possible de trouver à emprunter une Somme sur les obligations nouvelles

9. In BF's letter to the firm of July 2.

1. The enclosure has not been located.

2. Barclay finally sold the ship in October. Morris had purchased it for the United States but in April, 1783, recommended selling it: *Morris Papers*, VII, 708–10; VIII, 660.

qu'on leur envoye dans le cas qu'ils ne prèvoyent pas pouvoir les placer dans ce mois & le Suivant. Il me paroit important d'avoir tous Ces renseignements pour pouvoir nous diriger ici & règler nos opèrations. Si l'on ne prenoit pas ce seul parti qui nous rèste il en rèsulteroit les effets les plus cruels puisque comme j'ai dèja eu l'honneur de vous le dire n'ayant plus de fonds à Monsieur Morris les miens propres ne suffiront pas pour lui sauver un affront que je ressens au point que si l'Etat ou ceci me met depuis quelques tems devoit durer encore, ma Santé s'en altèreroit ainsi je vous suplie de m'en tirer de façon ou d'autre & d'agrèer les Sentimens Respectueux avec les quels Je Suis Monsieur vôtre très humble & très obeissant serviteur   GRAND

Mr. adams à pris comunication de cette lettre & en à Ecrit une en consequence aux Banquiers d'amsterdam à qui je lai envoyée avec la miene par un Courrier.[3] Ainsy celle cy ne sert plus que pour ce qui regarde MM. LeCouteulx

Endorsed: Lettre de M. Grand sur la Lettre de Messrs le Couteulx

To Henry Laurens   ALS: Historical Society of Pennsylvania

Dear Sir,   Passy, July 6. 1783.

We have been honoured with several of your Letters, and we have talk'd of writing to you, but it has been delayed. I will therefore write a few Lines in my private Capacity.

Our Negociations go on slowly, every Proposition being sent to England, & Answers not returning very speedily.

Capt. Barney arrived here last Wednesday,[4] & brought Dispatches for us as late as the first of June. The Preliminary Articles are ratified. But General Carleton, in Violation of those Articles, has sent away a great Number of Negroes, alledging that

---

3. JA's July 5 letter to the banking consortium is in *Adams Papers*, XV, 83–4. He enclosed Grand's letter as well as one from Robert Morris to them of May 8 (*Morris Papers*, VIII, 17–18, 316), ordering them to furnish Grand with all possible assistance.

4. July 2.

Freedom having been promised them by a Proclamation, the Honour of the Nation was concern'd, &c.[5] Probably another Reason may be, that if they had been restor'd to their Masters, Britain could not have hop'd anything from such another Proclamation hereafter.—

Mr Hartley call'd yesterday to tell us, that he had receiv'd a Letter from Mr Fox, assuring him that our Suspicions of affected Delays or Change of System on their Side were groundless; & that they were sincerely desirous to finish as soon as possible.[6] If this be so, and your Health will permit the Journey, I could wish your Return as soon as possible. I want you here on many Accounts, and should be glad of your Assistance in considering and answering our public Letters. There are Matters in them of which I cannot conveniently give you an Account at present.—

Nothing could be more seasonable than Success in the Project you proposed,[7] but we have now very little Expectation.

Please to give my Love to your valuable & amiable Son & Daughter,[8] and believe me with sincere Esteem and Affection, Dear Sir, Your most obedient & most humble Servant

B Franklin

Henry Laurens Esqr

Endorsed: Doctr Franklin 6th July 1783 Recd. & Answd 17th

Baron de Thun to Franklin and John Jay

AL: Library of Congress

Since at least March, when independence seemed assured, certain members of the diplomatic corps had wondered when Franklin would present his card, which would allow them to recognize him officially.

5. See Livingston's letters of April 21, May 9 (XXXIX, 485–8, 578–80), and May 28.
6. Fox's letter was dated July 2; see the final footnote to the commissioners' June 29 proposals.
7. Raising a loan; see Laurens to the other commissioners, June 10.
8. Henry Laurens, Jr., and Martha Laurens.

Franklin explained that he would do no such thing until news of the ratification arrived.[9] On July 2, prompted by Vergennes, the three American commissioners paid their first official visits to the ministers of Russia and Austria, calling also on the ministers of the Netherlands and Sweden (with whom they had treaties) and the minister of Denmark (with whom Franklin was negotiating one).[1] That day Captain Barney arrived with news of the ratification, sparking a new round of diplomatic visits on the following Monday and Wednesday, July 7 and 9.[2] Though the present note is the only extant acknowledgment of such a visit, other ambassadors reported to their courts that they had returned visits by the American ministers, signaling the beginning of diplomatic relations.[3]

Between these two days of visits, the American commissioners went to Versailles for the weekly gathering of foreign ministers. There they were received by the diplomatic corps for the first time. Adams noted the occasion in a letter to Congress: "Yesterday at Court all the foreign Ministers behaved towards us, without reserve, as Members of the Corps Diplomatique—so that we shall no longer see those lowering Countenances, solemn looks, distant Bows, & other peculiarities, which have been sometimes diverting & sometimes provoking, for so many years."[4]

ce 7 Juillet 1783

Le Baron de Thun, Ministre Plénipre. de Wirtemberg, êtant empeché par une indisposition de rendre sa visite en personne, fait ses remercimens a Messieurs franklin et a Monsieur Jay de l'honneur qu'ils ont bien voulu lui faire.

9. Antonio Pace, *Benjamin Franklin and Italy* (Philadelphia, 1958), pp. 98–9, 113–15.

1. See the American Commissioners to Bariatinskii, [July 2].

2. *Adams Papers*, XV, 94. For Barney's arrival see BF to Laurens, July 6.

3. Those of Venice and Genoa are mentioned in Pace, *Benjamin Franklin and Italy*, p. 114.

4. *Adams Papers*, XV, 94–5.

From Benjamin Webb

ALS: American Philosophical Society

Dear Sir   Geneva July 7th: 1783.

So peculiarly a good Opportunity as by the hands of your amiable Grandson, I could not let slip, without thanking you for the Favour of your Letter[5] by Mr. Pigot. I am much obliged by those Terms of respect & Sentiments of Good-will you are so Kind to express relative to Me & Mine. I still wait the happy Issue. No material Alteration has yet happen'd in the health of my dear little Woman.[6]

Your Taste for the enjoyment of Retirement and Leisure in the decline of Life, has certainly met with an Interuption—But, of important Magnitude—and Providence has crown'd It with a Success the Glory of which will never die. Distant Ages will immortalize the Negociations of your latter days by perpetual Commemmoration. I heartily congratulate you my dear Sir on these great Events—and hope my native Country will yet learn the Wisdom to be good—and thereby still continue to be one Asylum for the Sons of Liberty. A defection in the Quantum of real Worth, I take to be at the Foundation of all the Evils as a Nation we have suffer'd, & are but too surely still threatned with. Pray God avert them!

It is not the least Compliment to the Bearer of this to say that his Sweetness of Temper & amiableness of Manners has render'd him here as universally beloved as Known, & promises fair to be his portion under whatever Climate his Lott is cast. I was rejoiced that you had Sent for him, on many Accounts, particularly on that of a seeming present Delicacy of Health, which by being properly attended to now, may make him rich as is his Grandfather in this respect, at a very distant Period. I heartily wish It. Being with the greatest Respect Dear Sir Yr. much obliged & most Obedient hble Servt   B: WEBB.

---

5. Missing.
6. Webb and Pigott were close friends; see Pigott's letter of June 27, above, and Webb's previous letter to BF, which was conveyed by Pigott (XXXVI, 321–2). In the latter, Webb lamented that his wife had been in poor health ever since giving birth seven years earlier.

Mr. Pigot gave me hopes we had some Chance of the pleasure to See you in this part of the World. Have you laid aside all thoughts of It?—or rather, does not the Termination of your great Negociation afford the Opportunity, as well as point out the propriety of relaxing a little with the calm Scenes of Nature in this fine Country?

Notation: B Webb

William Alexander to Franklin and William Temple Franklin

ALS: American Philosophical Society

Dear Sir   Tuesday 8 July 1783

   Betsey[7] wrote you last week to ask a day when you & your son Can dine wt Madme de la Marke any time before the 20th— We have no Answer— You will oblige me by desiring your son to write— On recolection I address this to Him & beg He will drop me a line to st Germains—

   I am most faithfully Your & His Most obt hble s

W ALEXANDER

Addressed: A Monsieur / Monsieur Franklin Fils / a Passy

Notations: W Alexander 8 July 83 / W Alexander 8 July 1783

From Nathaniel Falconer   ALS: American Philosophical Society

My Dear Friend   London July the 8. 1783

   I inclose you a gazzet that Came out on the 5 day of this month which Surprised me much after hearing So much Taulk about Giveing the amerricans Everey thing but Bringing the Shugers Directley from the west indies that they Should issue

---

7. Bethia, who wrote on June 29, above.

an order of Councel for there owen Ships onley.[8] I have taken Care to Send two of the Gazetts one by Each Ship Bound to philadelphia as Soon as they apear to our friend Mifflin who is in Congress. I hope this will meet with your approbation. Yesterday on Change I taulkt to Some of the Committee of Merchants about it they all Seemd Surprised I told them they might be Shure Congress as Soon as it Got to hand would prevent aney of there Ships Loading in the united States for the west indies. I Shall take Care while I am hear to Give you Everey information in my power am Glad to inform you that our friend Mr Bingham is arrived and his Lady will make a stay hear for Some time he will also Give Everey information I am Dr Sir your Sincer friend
NATH FALCONER

Addressed: For / Docter Franklin / at the / Court of / parris

Notation: Falconet July 8. 1783

From Marcus Gerhard Rosencrone

LS: National Archives; press copy of copy:[9] American Philosophical Society; press copy of copy: Library of Congress; transcript: National Archives

Monsieur!   a Copenhague Le 8. Juillet 1783./.
Je n'ai rien eû de plus pressé monsieur, que de mettre sous Les yeux du Roi la Lettre que Vous m'aves fait L'honneur de m'ecrire ainsi que Le Projêt pour un Traité d'amitié et de Com-

---

8. The king's Order in Council of July 2, published in the *London Gaz.* of July 5, restricted trade between the United States and the British West Indies to British subjects using British-built, British-owned, and British-manned ships. This marked a complete reversal of British policy toward the United States and doomed the commercial negotiations. See Harlow, *Second British Empire*, I, 476–7; see also the annotation of the commissioners' proposals to Hartley, [June 29], and their letter to Hartley, July 17.

9. In the hand of L'Air de Lamotte. The press copy at the Library of Congress was made from a text transcribed by William Short for Thomas Jefferson.

merce qui L'accompagnoit.[1] Le Roi a appris avec la plus parfaite Satisfaction les assûrances que cette Lettre contenoit des bonnes Dispositions du Congrês de contracter des Liaisons d'amitié et de Commerce avec ses Royaumes, ces Liens etant egalement conformes aux Interêts des deux Etats et aux Desirs sincêres de Sa Majesté, qui tendent à cimenter par tous Les moyens possibles L'harmonie, L'union et La Confiance qu'Elle souhaite d'etablir à perpetuité entre sa Couronne et les Etats-unis.

Le Contre-Projet ci joint ne diffère en rien d'essentiel du Projet envoye, etant dressé entièrement sur les mêmes Principes, et Vous en serés certainement convaincû monsieur, par La Notte qui explique Les Raisons, qui ont fait ajouter quelques articles et donner seulement une Tournûre differente à d'autres, de sorte que je me flatte d'apprendre dans peu, que Vous en aurés eté entièrement satisfait, ayant trouvé La reciprocité La plus parfaite soigneusement etablie par tout.[2]

Quant au second Objêt dont il est parlé dans La Lettre dont Vous m'aves honoré,[3] Vous connoissés deja monsieur, les Intentions genereuses de Sa Majesté envers les particuliers dont il est question,[4] et Sa Majesté s'est plû d'autant d'avantage à saisir

1. BF to Rosencrone, April 15: XXXIX, 473–4.
2. BF received these documents—the Danish counterproposal and Rosencrone's explanation—on July 25, just in time to give the originals to Barney for delivery to Congress; see BF to Livingston, July 22[–26]. English translations made from those originals are in Wharton, *Diplomatic Correspondence*, VI, 519–25, 525–7. The counterproposal, containing 26 articles, is heavily influenced by the Dutch-American commercial treaty which Rosencrone had suggested as the model (XXXIX, 468n). It retained the 20 articles BF had proposed, modifying them as necessary, and interspersed six more adapted from Articles 4, 6, 13, 16, 17, and 25 of the Dutch-American treaty.
3. The three prizes brought into Bergen under American colors in 1779 and returned by the Danish government to Great Britain. Livingston had instructed BF in May, 1782, to continue pursuing restitution, and BF, when informing Livingston of Denmark's interest in a commercial treaty, urged Congress to make restitution a precondition for signing such a treaty: XXXVII, 430–1; XXXIX, 468, 473–4.
4. Walterstorff told BF on May 29 that Christian VII was offering £10,000 sterling in compensation. Although BF rejected the offer and they debated it at some length, as BF describes in his letter to Livingston of July 22[–26], Walterstorff reported to Rosencrone only that BF was pleased by this mark of the king's friendship and promised to communicate

Le premier moment de manifester ces Intentions, qu'Elle a crû pouvoir esperer avec raison, que le Congrês les envisageroit en même Tems, comme une Preuve marquée de son Amitié et de son Estime pour ce Corps respectable. Il ne me reste ainsi rien à ajouter, si non, que Le Roi se prêtera avec Plaisir à La manière la plus propre à accelerer La Conclusion du Traité que nous venons d'ebaucher. Ce sera pour moi une partie des plus agreables de mes fonctions, monsieur, de travailler à La Confection de ces heureuses Liaisons avec un Ministre d'une reputation aussi universelle que La Vôtre, et c'est avec Les Sentiments de La Consideration La plus distinguée que j'ai L'honneur d'être, Monsieur! Votre três humble et três obeissant Serviteur.

ROSENCRONE

à Mr. Francklin, Ministre des Etats unis de L'amerique, à Paris.

From Thomas Lloyd[5]   ALS: American Philosophical Society

Hond. Sir   Rouen 9 July 1783

You'll please to let my situation beg your excuse for this trouble, the Gentleman to whom the enclosed is addressed I know not how to direct to, because my baggage is gone on for Calais & with it his instructions on this head. It being of moment to him, & your polite disposition will be a early conveyance—

Had I it in my power to have reached Paris I was order'd to

---

the offer to Congress: Walterstorff to Rosencrone, May 29, 1783, Statens Arkiver, Rigsarkivet.

5. London-born Thomas Lloyd (1756–1827) had been settled in Maryland for several years when the American Revolution broke out. He served in the Md. militia, surviving a gunshot wound and capture by the British, and after his discharge in 1779 was hired to superintend the printing of the *Journals* of the Continental Congress. He later became clerk to Michael Hillegas, treasurer of the United States. We know little about this trip to France, other than that he later claimed to have carried dispatches to the American peace commissioners: Marion Tinling, "Thomas Lloyd's Reports of the First Federal Congress," *W&MQ*, 3rd ser., XVIII (1961), 521–3, 543.

Make Mr & Mrs. Hillegas's respects to you and the Young Ladies who are all well.[6] Permit me to have the honor of assuring
I am with respect Hond Sir Yours   THOMAS LLOYD

honble docr. Benj Fraklin

Addressed: the honble / Doctor Benjamin Franklin / a Passey

Notation: Thomas Lloyd Rouen 9 July 1783

The American Peace Commissioners to Vergennes

AL:[7] Archives du Ministère des affaires étrangères

Paris, July 10. 1783—
Messieurs Adams, Franklin & Jay, Ministers of the United States
for treating of Peace, present their Respects to Mr le Comte de
Vergennes, & request he would be pleased to favour them with
a Copy of the Offer made by the two Imperial Courts of their
Mediation.[8]

Notations: juillet 10 / rep. le 31 Juillet 1783.

6. Michael and Henrietta Hillegas and their daughters Margaret, Henrietta, Deborah, and Mary Ann: Emma St. Clair Whitney, *Michael Hillegas and His Descendants* (Pottsville, Pa., 1891), p. 35; William Henry
Egle, "Michael Hillegas. First Treasurer of the United States," *PMHB*, XI
(1887), 408.

7. Written by BF.

8. At Versailles on Tuesday, July 8, Vergennes asked BF and JA whether
they had made the visits to the Russian and Austrian ministers that he had
suggested to them the week before (for which see the Commissioners to
Bariatinskii, [July 2]). Upon learning that the visits had been made and returned, he asked the commissioners to consider again whether they wanted
those ministers to be involved in the Anglo-American treaty. If so, they
should write a letter of invitation. JA allowed that he "did not know what
a mediation meant." Vergennes responded with an enigmatic smile. The
commissioners promised to consider the matter, though they remained uncertain as to how to make the decision: *Adams Papers*, XV, 92. Judging from
the present letter, they reasoned that the first step would be to review the
terms to which France had agreed. Vergennes did not answer this request
until July 31, long after the commissioners had decided in the affirmative;
see their draft letter to Bariatinskii and Markov, [before July 15].

From Charles Blagden

AL: American Philosophical Society

Thursday July 10. [1783]

Dr. Blagden presents his Compliments to Dr Franklin, & begs He will do him the honour of accepting two papers printed in the Philosophical Transactions since the time Dr Franklin has received any of the volumes. That part which contains the Report upon the accident at Heckingham is not yet published.[9] Dr B. has not forgot the commission he undertook to procure all the volumes due to Dr Franklin, & will make it his first business upon his return to London

Addressed: Dr. Franklin.

From Jonathan Williams, Jr.

ALS: American Philosophical Society; copy: E. Marie Lorimer, Melrose, Pennsylvania (1957)

Dear & hond Sir.   Nantes July 10. 1783.

I am sorry to trouble you with my Difficulties, I know you have Friendship enough for me to be afflicted at my misfortunes, & I am doubly distressed by being the Cause of any uneasiness of mind to you; but I cannot avoid telling you myself what you must hear from others, because you might have a partial Account & I might Suffer in your Esteem.— All my Misfor-

---

9. Blagden's journal entry for July 10 notes that he sent to Le Roy "Gulf Stream and Heckingham for Dr. Franklin" (Yale University Library). Le Roy must have delivered the present cover letter along with the two papers. The first was Blagden's "On the Heat of the Water in the Gulf Stream . . . ," published in *Phil. Trans.*, LXXI (1781), 334–44. The second was an account of a lightning strike co-written for the Royal Society by Blagden and Nairne, the latter of whom had already sent BF a detailed account in MS (see XXXVII, 150–1n). "Proceedings Relative to the Accident by Lightning at Heckingham" appeared in Part II of the *Phil. Trans.* for 1782, which was not published until the end of 1783: *Critical Rev.*, LVI (1783), 410. The imprint Blagden sent to BF was a pamphlet of the same title published by J. Nichols; BF's copies of it and the Gulf Stream article are at the Hist. Soc. of Pa.

tunes proceed from other People, for had I in my own hands the Funds my Confidence in others has drawn out I should not now be distressed as I am, and had the War continued I do Suppose these Funds would have returned to me; At present I cannot promise myself relief untill I can have answers from my Several Applications to America, which will necessarily take up Several months[1]—in the mean Time I think it abusing the Confidence of any Friend to draw them in to go on paying without a certaintity of getting through, I have therefore written to Mr Grand & after mentioning the Extent of what Succors I want, I have proposed the Alternative, and if he cannot assist me so far, I had better Stop at once & let all my Creditors fare alike. I am sure I shall eventualy not only pay all but have Something left, but I plainly See I cannot do it very Soon.— The Loss of any Credit affects me ten Times more than the Loss of all I am worth would do, but I hope at least I shall not Suffer in the Esteem of my Friends who know me, give me leave to Hope you will not deprive me of the Same Share of your Affection you have hitherto honoured me with, and I shall bear all my misfortunes with becoming Fortitude.

I am as ever most dutifully and affectionately Yours.

JONA WILLIAMS J

My Father in Law[2] who delivers this will Show you my Letter to Mr Grand. JWJ

Doctor Franklin.

Addressed: Doctor Franklin / Passy.

1. JW's remittances from America were overdue, and the recent failures of Cuming & Macarty in Lorient (XXXV, 482n) and their Paris banker, Vincens, had caused a run on JW's businesses. In early June he had been granted bankruptcy protection for three months; see our annotation of BF to Vergennes, June 3; JW to John and Andrew Cabot, July 6, 1783 (Yale University Library).

2. William Alexander.

From James Price

ALS: American Philosophical Society

Sir   Paris 11 July 1783

Having lately sent a Memorial to the controuler General of finance, praying that he would permit me to sell 180 Hogds. of Jamaica prize sugars, which is now stored at Bordeaux, on paying the same duties that french sugars pay, which memorial the farmers Genl. acquaint me must be recommended by your Excellency before it can be taken notice of. If therefore it would not be thought too presuming, I would ask the favour of a line from you to the Minister on this subject,[3] & have the honor to be very respectfuly Sir your most huml. Servt.   JAMES PRICE

Doctor Franklin

Addressed: A Monsieur / Monsieur Franklin / Minister des Estats uni a / son hotel a / Passy

From Charles Churchill[4]

ALS: American Philosophical Society

Bennet St: (No: 5.) Westr: [Westminster]

Sir—   July 14th: 1783.

Singular as this address may appear at first sight, I am sanguine to beleive it will not pass unnoticed by you: Though I have not at present the *long-wish'd-for* honor to be personally known (to a Gentleman, whose well-known abilities, and incorruptible integrity of character, recommended him to the confidence of the noblest association ever formed to stem the

3. We have no record of a response or of any letter on the subject sent to Lefèvre d'Ormesson, Controller General of Finance.

4. The elder of the two known sons of the poet Charles Churchill (1732–1764). Charles (b. 1754) was educated at the expense of a family friend, and what portion he inherited of his father's estate was dissipated by the time he wrote the present letter. He wrote begging letters to John Wilkes, a friend of his father's, until 1786: Douglas Grant, ed., *The Poetical Works of Charles Churchill* (Oxford, 1956), p. xiiin; *DNB* and *ODNB*, under the poet.

tide of corruption & Tyranny, & once more erect the too long over-borne standard of American freedom) I am well assured the Name must have been rendered rather familiar to you, from the Poetical Works of a deceased father, whose Pen, like your own, was uniformly exerted in the cause of Liberty and truth.

You will I hope Sir, excuse me for avoiding a studied form of words and every hackneyed art of insinuation to apologize for this address.

An obscure Stranger is about to implore your kind assistance—it is his duty—& he feels it a pleasure to explain his business with candour & without reserve.

My Father, the late Charles Churchill, whose literary Productions you cannot be unacquainted with,[5] resolved at every disadvantage to cultivate some seeds of genius which his Paternal fondness alone inclined him to fancy he had discovered in me. Thus entered did I pursue a course of studies till his death, when the want of every necessary means put a stop to the prosecution of them.

Full of the romantic ideas with which so ill-adapted an education served to fill my mind, I rambled through England, France & the West Indies, without friends to procure, or discretion to continue in any necessary employment:

One time Assistant in a Grammar-School, next Edidor of a News-Paper; soon after dependent on the profits of some Satyrical Squibs, next a Lecturer on Elocution &c. &c., stranger as I was to the virtues of moderation, as well as to the Arts of knavery, I attempted too many things to have succeeded in any.

I am too sensible, Sir, of the value of your time to think of taking it up with any further detail of my chimerical pursuits.

Cured of castle-building, I could now profit by a favourable opportunity which presents itself of forming an Academical Es-

---

5. BF was in London in 1761 when Churchill's first published poem, *The Rosciad* . . . , became an immediate success and established his reputation: *ODNB*. BF owned both that work (4th ed., London, 1761) and the harsh critique it inspired: *The Churchiliad: or, a Few Modest Questions Proposed to the Reverend Author of the Rosciad* (London, 1761). His copies are at the Hist. Soc. of Pa.: Wolf and Hayes, *Library of Benjamin Franklin*, p. 197.

tablishment in America, but tho' I have always supported the character & appearances of a Gentleman, I am really from an increase of family, & a variety of misfortunes, destitute of the means necessary to provide me with a passage and procure some few Articles.— 50 £. or 60 £ would complete my wishes— If Sir! You will vouchsafe to aid an unhappy Stranger, (without friends, or power) with that sum; I shall deem myself bound in Gratitude to acknowledge with chearfulness, & remember Eternally the Benevolent Deed.

In short, Sir! if this artless statement of my situation serves in any sort to recommend me to your kind regard; I flatter myself neither my ingratitude, nor indeserts will ever make you repent having favored me with your assistance.

I have the honor to be, Sir, with the sincerest respect Yr. most humble servant, CHARLES CHURCHILL.

PS. The favor of an immediate answer is most earnestly requested.[6]

From Gaetano Filangieri

Translation of ALS in Italian:[7] Historical Society of Pennsylvania

Sir,   Naples, July 14, 1784 [*i.e.*, 1783][8]
In order to keep the promise I made you, I am sending through the mail the third volume of my Works, and within a

---

6. Churchill wrote again on July 31 and Aug. 25, begging BF for a reply (APS). There is no evidence that he received one, or that he ever emigrated. In 1789 he was still in London, acknowledged as a "notorious swindler": *The [London] Times*, Sept. 9, 1789.

7. Prepared by Claude A. Lopez. The Italian original is published in Antonio Pace, *Benjamin Franklin and Italy* (Philadelphia, 1958), p. 402, and Eugenio Lo Sardo, ed., *Il Mondo nuovo e le virtù civili: l'epistolario di Gaetano Filangieri, 1772–1788* (Naples, 1999), pp. 242–3.

8. The incorrect year was obviously a slip of the pen. Filangieri's marriage to Charlotte (Carolina) Frendel, mentioned here as imminent, occurred in the summer of 1783: XXXVIII, 399n. Luigi Pio forwarded this letter and the enclosed volume to BF on Aug. 10; see his letter of that date.

few days I shall send you the fourth. I beg you not to judge one without having read the other. Both those volumes make up the third book of my Works, whose subject is the criminal part of legislative science.[9] Please do not attribute to a vain display of erudition the use I make of the content of ancient and modern legislations. I felt it necessary to provide the analysis of what has been done in the past, in order to illuminate what should be done now. By reading that part of my work, you shall understand the reasons that led me to the adoption of this method.

I don't want to keep from you the reasons for my withdrawal in the solitary countryside[1] where my literary output will be accelerated by the quiet and the silence. Six days from now, I shall be married to Mademoiselle Frendel whose mere presence will suffice to fill the void that the distance from my friends, relatives, and society as a whole might affect my spirits. The only circumstance that could take me away from this solitude would be the offer of a Minister's post in America that you alluded to.[2] When I hear that my Court has decided to send a Minister to the United Provinces of America, I shall do all in my power to be nominated. My greatest pleasure in such a case would be to be able to tell you *viva voce* the feelings of veneration and respect with which I proclaim myself your most devoted and obedient servant,   Gaetano Filangieri

9. See XXXVIII, 37–8, 400–1. According to Marcello Maestro, the second part of Book III of *La scienza della legislazione* was published in the autumn of 1783: *Gaetano Filangieri and His* Science of Legislation (Philadelphia, 1976), p. 28.

1. During the summer of 1783, Filangieri moved to the town of Cava dei Tirreni, 25 miles from Naples: *ibid.*

2. XXXVIII, 571–3.

Draft Letter from the American Peace Commissioners to Bariatinskii and Arkadii Markov[3]

AL (draft): American Philosophical Society

Around July 13, the American commissioners had been given to understand that mediation by the imperial courts was "a mere formality—a mere Compliment, consisting wholly in the Imperial Ministers putting their names & Seals to the parchment, & can have no ill effect."[4] On that basis, and believing that Vergennes was in favor of it, Adams drafted the present letter accepting the offer of mediation. Two French versions were then prepared: a translation of the draft, which was addressed to the Russian mediators, and a similar translation addressed to Mercy-Argenteau, the Austrian mediator. The commissioners took the former to Versailles on Tuesday, July 15, for Vergennes' approval. The latter remains among Franklin's papers at the American Philosophical Society.[5]

Vergennes did approve the letter. The commissioners asked him directly whether engaging mediators might not expose them to unwelcome interference, perhaps instigated by the British. Vergennes explained that they were free to do as he had done, tell the ministers that their mediation would be "accepted" only after the major points were settled—in other words, consign them to a ceremonial function. He also pointed out how awkward it might be if, during the signing ceremony, the mediators were permitted to sign all the

3. Markov (Morkov) (1747–1827) had served as the Russian special envoy at The Hague since 1782. In April, 1783, he was appointed joint minister plenipotentiary to France to assist Bariatinskii in mediating the Anglo-French and Anglo-Spanish definitive treaties: Nina N. Bashkina *et al.*, eds., *The United States and Russia: the Beginning of Relations, 1765–1815* ([Washington, D.C., 1980]), p. 1135; *Repertorium der diplomatischen Vertreter*, III, 354, 359; Giunta, *Emerging Nation*, I, 827.

4. JA to Livingston, July 13, 1783, in *Adams Papers*, XV, 106–7. Unbeknownst to the commissioners, this is what France and Britain had intended all along. Before reviving the idea of mediation with the imperial courts in February, 1783, Vergennes and Manchester agreed that they would not allow the mediators to play any substantive role in the negotiations: Madariaga, *Harris's Mission*, p. 432.

5. It is in the hand of L'Air de Lamotte. As explained below, the unsigned letter taken to Versailles was left there. It was never retrieved, to our knowledge, and is now missing.

treaties but theirs. Involving Russia and Austria, moreover, would be a significant public acknowledgment of the United States. Satisfied that accepting mediation could be to their advantage, the American commissioners left their unsigned letter with Vergennes to be shown to the Russian and Austrian ministers.[6] In the meantime, they waited for Fox to respond to their treaty proposals.

Passy July [*blank; i.e.*, before July 15,] 1783
To their Excellencies The Prince Bariatinskoy, and Mr De Markoff Ministers Plenipotentiary from her Majesty the Empress of all the Russias.

The Subscribers, Ministers Plenipotentiary, from the United States of America, for making Peace with Great Britain, have the Honour to inform the Ministers from Her Majesty the Empress of Russia, that the United States of America, on the fifteenth day of June 1781 having been informed by his most Christian Majesty, that their Imperial Majesties the Emperor of Germany, and the Empress of Russia, actuated by Sentiments of Humanity, and a desire to put a Stop to the Calamities of War, had offered their Mediation to the belligerent Powers, in order to promote Peace, constituted the Subscribers together with the Honourable Henry Laurens and Thomas Jefferson Esquires, their Ministers Plenipotentiary, giving and granting to them, or Such of them as Should assemble, or in Case of Death, Absence, Indisposition or other Impediment of the others to any one of them, full Power and Authority in their Name and on their Behalf, in Concurrence with his Most Christian Majesty to accept in due Form the Mediation of their Imperial Majesties the Emperor of Germany and the Empress of Russia.[7]

The Subscribers have also been informed by his Excellency the Comte de Vergennes, that his Most Christian Majesty and his Britannic Majesty, have accepted the Mediation of their Imperial Majesties in the definitive Treaty of Peace about to be concluded between those Powers.

6. JA to Livingston, July 16, 1783, in *Adams Papers*, XV, 122–3.
7. XXXV, 161–3, 166, 173.

The Subscribers therefore in the absence of the Honourable Henry Laurens and Thomas Jefferson, have the Honour to inform your Excellencies that by Virtue of their Commission aforesaid Copy of which is inclosed, they are ready in Behalf of the Said United States of America to accept the Mediation of their Imperial Majesties in the definitive Treaty of Peace to be concluded between his Britannic Majesty and the Said States.
Signed.

Elias Boudinot to the American Peace Commissioners

Copy:[8] National Archives

Gentlemen,   Princeton 15. July 1783
   As Congress have not yet elected any Minister for Foreign Affairs, and knowing the importance of your Being fully informed of every public transaction relative to these States, I have concluded that you would not think it amiss to hear from me on the subject of the removal of Congress to this place, tho' I cannot consider this communication as official but merely for your information in my Individual capacity.
   The State of our Finances making it indispensably necessary to abridge the public expences in every instance that would not endanger the union, we concluded to reduce the army by discharging all the Soldiers enlisted for the War, with a proportionate number of Officers, on condition that the discharge should operate no otherwise than as a furlough, until the rati-

---

8. Though the original of this letter and enclosures did not arrive, BF acknowledged the duplicate on Nov. 1 (National Archives). The duplicate of Boudinot's letter is now lost, but many of its enclosures, as noted below, remain among BF's papers at the APS. The letter, enclosures, and supplemental documents are published in *The Diplomatic Correspondence of the United States of America, from the Signing of the Definitive Treaty of Peace, 10th September, 1783, to the Adoption of the Constitution, March 4, 1789* . . . (7 vols., Washington, D.C., 1833–34), I, 8–39.

fication of the Definitive Treaty. This not only eased us of a heavy disbursement of ready Cash for subsistence money and Rations, but gratified many of the army who wished to be at home in the early part of the Summer, to provide for the following Winter. Three months pay was ordered, which could no otherwise be complied with, but by a paper anticipation of the Taxes, payable in six months.

By an inevitable accident, the Notes did not arrive at the army till six days after the Soldiers were discharged and had left the camp. This, together with some difficulty in settling their accounts, created an uneasiness among the Troops; but by the General's Address and the good conduct of the Officers, they all retired peaceably to their different States, tho' without a single farthing of cash to buy themselves a meal of Victuals.

In the Barracks in Philadelphia and at Lancaster, in the State of Pennsylvania, there were a number of new Recruits, who had been enlisted since the months of December and January last, and who had not yet taken the field; these Soldiers having not been brought under any regular discipline, made many objections against accepting their discharges and gave their Officers reason to fear some difficulty in getting rid of them; but the Secretary at War thought he had satisfied them by assuring them of the like pay with the rest of the army. On the 15th. of June a petition was received from the Serjeants, requiring a Redress of their grievances, in a very turbulent and indecent Style, of which no notice was taken;[9] but on the 18th. we received the letters No. 1 and 2.[1] A Committee was immediately appointed

9. Secretary at War Benjamin Lincoln had failed to tell the Pa. troops that the furloughs were optional. He also had not informed them that they were to receive a month's pay in cash and three months' pay in notes issued by Robert Morris. No copy of the sergeants' petition is extant: *Morris Papers*, VIII, 215–16. For a detailed account of the mutiny see *Morris Papers*, VIII, 215–38.

1. The copyist either identified or gave archival locations for all the enclosures in the left margin. Here the note reads: "letters from Colo. Butler & Colo. Henry, on the files of Congress." Both letters were written on June 17 to John Dickinson, president of the Pa. Supreme Executive Council. Col. Richard Butler of the Third Pa. regiment was

to confer with the Executive Council of Pennsylvania, and to endeavour to get them to call out the Militia to stop the Mutineers; but to no purpose;[2] the Council thinking that the Citizens would not choose to risque themselves when fair means might do. The first Report of the Committee, contained in No. 3 will shew their proceedings.[3] On the 19th. the troops arrived and joined those at the Barracks in the City, who had been encreased in number by a few companies of old Soldiers arrived the day before from Charles Town. The whole being very orderly and quiet, Congress adjourned on Friday the 20th., as usual, till Monday morning. On the 21st. one of the Committee called on me and informed, that the Soldiers at the Barracks were very disorderly and had cast off the authority of their Officers—that it was suspected they had a design, the following night, against the Bank; and advised me to call Congress without delay. This I did, to meet in half an hour. The Soldiers by accident hearing of it, very fortunately hastened their designs a day or two sooner than was intended. The Members of Congress had just got together, except one, when the State House (in which also The President and Supreme Executive Council were then sitting) was surrounded by about three hundred armed Men with fixed Bayonets under the command of seven Serjeants. Congress immediately sent for Genl. St. Clair[4] and demanded the reason of

---

commander of the post at Lancaster; Col. William Henry was treasurer of Lancaster County. They warned that 80 soldiers had left to join the soldiers who refused to leave their barracks in Philadelphia. Butler also sent a copy of the orders he had issued, urging the men to return: *Morris Papers*, VIII, 218–19; *JCC*, XXIV, 405n.

2. Alexander Hamilton was a member of this committee, and on June 19 he issued orders to Maj. William Jackson to meet the mutineers and bring them back. The effort was unsuccessful: Harold C. Syrett *et al.*, eds., *The Papers of Alexander Hamilton* (27 vols., New York and London, 1961–87), III, 397–8, 399–401.

3. Note: "See Journals of Congress July 1, 1783." This is the first of two reports published on that day, with a copy of Hamilton's June 19 orders (mentioned in the previous note): *JCC*, XXIV, 413–16.

4. Maj. Gen. Arthur St. Clair, commander of the troops of the American army in Pennsylvania: *Morris Papers*, VIII, 216.

this hostile appearance, who informed of his having just arrived in Town from his seat in the Country in obedience to the orders of Congress of the day preceding; that he had received information from the Commanding Officer of the mutinous disposition of the Troops, who had marched from the Barracks contrary to the orders of their Officers; and that the Veteran Troops from Charles Town had been unwillingly forced into the measure. The President of the State then appeared, and produced the insolent paper of which No. 4[5] is a copy, which had been sent into him by the Serjeants.

Congress determined they would enter on no deliberations while thus surrounded; but ordered Genl. St. Clair immediately to endeavour to march the Mutineers back to the Barracks by such means as were in his power.

After several prudent and wise measures the General prevailed on the Serjeants to return to their Barracks, convincing them that if they were aggrieved they had a right to make it known in a decent manner, thro' any persons they might think proper to appoint. But previous to this, after waiting surrounded by this armed force for near three hours, Congress broke up and we passed thro' the files of the Mutineers without the least opposition, tho' at times before our adjournment, the Soldiers, many of whom were very drunk, threatened Congress by name.

The Mutineers had taken possession of the powder House and several public Arsenals in this City, with some Field pieces from the public Yard.

In the evening Congress met and made a House and came to the resolutions contained in No. 5.[6] and broke up without ad-

---

5. Note: "Message to Council by the Serjeants." Enclosure no. 4 (APS) is entitled "Copy of the Message from the Mutineers to the Supreme Executive Council" and is unsigned. It threatens violent action if commissioned officers are not appointed to redress the mutineers' grievances in the next 20 minutes. Not enclosed, evidently, were the more respectful letters from Sgt. James Bennett to President Dickinson, justifying their actions and listing seven "requests," and apologizing for "any irregularities": *Diplomatic Correspondence*, 1, 22–5.

6. Note: "Resolutions of Sat. 21. June." Enclosure no. 5 (APS) listed the three resolutions adopted on June 21. Informing the president and Supreme Executive Council of Pennsylvania of the day's events, Congress

journment. The Committee not being able to meet the Council till Sunday morning were then prevailed on to wait for an answer till Monday morning and then received the answer contained in the 2d. Report No. 6.[7] However hoping that the Council would change their sentiments, the Committee did not think proper to give me their advice till Tuesday at two O'Clock in the Afternoon. In the mean time the Mutineers kept in arms, refusing all obedience to their Officers, and in possession of the powder House and Magazines of Military Stores. On Tuesday morning the Officers reported to me that the preceding evening the Serjeants, notwithstanding some talk of a submission and return to their duty, had presented six Officers with a commission each as in No. 7.;[8] and on one refusing to accept it they threatened him with immediate death—and that, at the time of the Report, they were getting very drunk and in a very riotous state. By the second Report of the Committee you will be acquainted with the particulars of the transaction, with the addition that the behaviour of the six Officers was very mysterious and unaccount-

---

asked them to take action, warned that otherwise Congress would move to Princeton or Trenton, and ordered that the incident be reported to Gen. Washington so he could send troops: *JCC*, XXIV, 410; Syrett, *Papers of Hamilton*, III, 401–2.

7. Note: "See Journals July 1." Enclosure no. 6 (APS), the comprehensive second report issued by the committee appointed to confer with the Supreme Executive Council, combined its previous written report with verbal accounts. It is dated June 24 but was delivered on June 30 and entered into the record the next day: *JCC*, XXIV, 416–21; Syrett, *Papers of Hamilton*, III, 403–7. The Council's answer was verbal. The councillors declined to act and pointed out that Gen. St. Clair (with the approval of members of Congress and the Council) had declared in writing that the mutineers could choose a committee of commissioned officers. They had heard that the mutineers were showing signs of accommodation, and recommended negotiation rather than "coercive means" to deal with them.

8. Enclosure no. 7 (APS) was a commission written on June 23 by James Bennett, signing himself as secretary of the mutineers, to Capt. James Christie, president of the committee of officers. It appointed Christie to a committee of six commissioned officers that would rule on their grievances. The penalty for non-cooperation would be death. See also *Morris Papers*, VIII, 221–2.

able.[9] At two O'Clock agreeably to the advice of the Committee, I summoned Congress to meet at this place on Thursday the 26th. of June, issued the Proclamation No. 8[1] and left the City. As soon as it was known that Congress was going, the Council were informed, that there was great reason to expect a serious attack on the Bank the night following, on which the President of the State collected about One hundred Soldiers and kept Guard all night. On Wednesday it was reported that Congress had sent for the Commander in Chief with the whole Northern Army, and the Militia of New-Jersey, who were to be joined by the Pennsylvania Militia, in order to quell the mutiny; which was no otherwise true than ordering a detachment of a few hundred men from the North River. The Serjeants being alarmed, soon proposed a submission, and the whole came in a Body to the President of the State, making a most submissive acknowledgement of their misconduct, and charging the whole on two of the Officers, whom they had commissioned to represent their grievances, A Capt. Carbery and Lieutenant Sullivan, who were to have headed them, as soon as they should have proceeded to violences. These Officers immediately escaped to Chester and there got on board of a Vessel bound to London. The Serjeants describe the plan laid by these Officers as of the most irrational and diabolical nature, not only against Congress and the Council, but also against the City and Bank. They were to be joined by straggling parties from different parts of the Country, and after executing their horrid purposes were to have gone off with their plunder to the East Indies. However incredible this may appear the letters No. 9 & 10 from Sullivan to Colo. Moyland, his Commanding Officer, from Chester and the Capes clearly

9. Christie's June 24 letter to John Dickinson, enclosing Bennett's June 23 commission, stated that the mutineers had admitted that their conduct had been disorderly and had made satisfactory concessions: *Diplomatic Correspondence*, I, 35–6.

1. A June 24 proclamation that Congress would convene at Princeton on June 26 to take measures to suppress the revolt: Smith, *Letters*, XX, 360–1. Enclosure no. 8, a newspaper clipping from an unnamed publication, is the proclamation reprinted from the *Pa. Packet* (APS).

shew that it was a deep laid scheme.[2] It appears clearly to me that next to the continued care of divine Providence, the miscarriage of this plan is owing to the unexpected meeting of Congress on Saturday, and their decided conduct in leaving the City, until they could support the federal Government with dignity. It is also said that two of the Citizens have been concerned in this wicked plot, but they are not yet ascertained. They were certainly encouraged by some of the lower class as well as by the general supineness in not quelling the first movement. Some very suspicious circumstances attending the conduct of the other four Officers, who were commissioned by the Serjeants have caused them to be arrested. The whole matter has so far subsided. The detachment under Genl. Howe from the Northern Army[3] has arrived in the vicinity of the City and a Court of enquiry is endeavouring to develope the whole affair.

The Citizens are greatly chagrined at the predicament in which they stand and endeavour to lay the blame on the Council

2. Enclosure no. 9 (APS) is a summary written from memory of Lt. John Sullivan's June 26 letter to Col. Stephen Moylan, written from Chester; a note indicates that the original was in the hands of Gen. St. Clair. Sullivan asks Moylan not to blame him, pointing out that had they not been betrayed, they would have either been victorious or "perished in the attempt," and asks him to pay an outstanding debt. Enclosure no. 10 is Sullivan's letter to Moylan of June 30, written from Cape Henlopen, enclosing a banknote. He explains his actions, says that he and Capt. Henry Carbery are bound for London, and states that while they both would fight again for the United States, neither regrets his recent actions.

Sullivan was an officer in the Fourth Continental Dragoons, and Carbery (or Carberry) was an officer of the Eleventh Pennsylvania regiment. Neither was convicted. Carbery returned to the United States in 1784, eventually was rehabilitated, and served again as an army officer in 1791–94 and 1813–15. Sullivan returned in 1785 and was later ordered arrested for planning to attack Spanish settlements along the western frontier: Smith, *Letters*, XXIII, 376–7; XXV, 77; *Morris Papers*, VIII, 216; W. W. Abbot et al., eds., *The Papers of George Washington*, Presidential Series (16 vols. to date, Charlottesville and London, 1987–), III, 310–12n.

3. On June 21 Boudinot asked George Washington to bring forces into Pennsylvania. Washington answered on June 24 that he had dispatched Maj. Gen. Robert Howe. Howe brought 1,500 troops and two cannon from West Point: *Diplomatic Correspondence*, I, 40–5; Freeman, *Washington*, V, 447.

for not calling on them and proving them, while the Council justify themselves by the advice of the Militia Officers, whom they called together for that purpose. The Citizens are universally petitioning Congress to return to the City, assuring us of their constant protection.

You will excuse me for tiring you with so circumstantial an account, which nothing but the necessity of preventing the many falsehoods that are generally propagated on these occasions and the propriety of your being well informed, would ever have justified me in.

I do myself the honor to send herewith the News-papers, and particularly a Circular Letter of Genl. Washington to the different States, which in my opinion gives the finishing stroke to his inimitable Character.[4]

I have committed this letter to the care of my younger Brother, who is bound for London, having been in the Merchant service at that port for several years, but who, I have the best evidence is well attached to the interests of this Country, and who can inform you of many particulars relating to the State of things here.[5]

I have the honor to be &c.   E. B

The Honorable The Ministers Plenipotentiary of the United States &c. at Paris.

From John Butler   ALS: American Philosophical Society

May it Please Your Excellency.   Amsterdam July 15th 1783

In behalf of myself and other American Sailors who have been prisoners in England, I make bold to petition your Excellency, whose humanity and beneficence is known to all the World. There are three of us here who were taken on board

---

4. He enclosed the July 15 issue of the *Pa. Packet* containing Washington's June 12 letter to Governor of Virginia Benjamin Harrison (APS). For Washington's circular letter to the state governors announcing his retirement see Fitzpatrick, *Writings of Washington*, XXVI, 483–96.

5. See Lewis Boudinot to BF, Sept. 29, 1783 (APS).

the Congress Ship the Confederacy Captain Hardinge.[6] We have been discharged some time, and after attempting to get a passage from London to our own Country, in which it was impossible to succeed went from thence to Dunkirk; where the difficulty was still as great; after staying some time at Dunkirk without obtaining what we so much wished for we applied to Mr Coffin Your Excellency's agent to supply us that we might be enabled to go to Amsterdam, where we were told we were sure of obtaining our desire; Mr Coffyn supplied us, but so small the sum, 15 Livres, that by the time we got to Amsterdam we had nothing left, which made one of our Companions who has but little patience to enter on board an East India Ship. Upon our Arrival at Amsterdam we applied to those who we were told would supply us till we embarked, when to our great surprise we were told Mr Adams had left no order concerning such supply, therefore could not give us any. This answer rather amazed, more so as we were informed that several had before received such relief.[7] We therefore determined to apply to Your Excellency, and unless your Excellency can invent some means or other to extricate us from our difficulties, our state will not be altogether desirable. After adventuring our lives in defence of our Country, and being prisoners several months it is peculiarly hard to be thus neglected, that Country, I say who thus abandons us, cannot be worthy of our future services. To leave brave men without any provision certainly merits not esteem. We know your Excellency has made ample provision for those in your province (France). Why should not the same be made in Holland. We live here upon Credit, and we are at the mercy of our Landlords, whither our liberty (which to us is precious) shall last for another hour. Where we not Confident our Petition would be answered we would not have applied to Your Excellency.

If your Excellency should deign to answer the petition of your Humble Servants, they will always, bear such an instance

6. The *Confederacy*, Capt. Seth Harding, was captured on April 14, 1781: XXX, 357n; XXXVI, 687n.

7. While in the Netherlands, JA had supplied escaped prisoners with his own private funds: XXXV, 604.

of generosity for ever in their Breast. Your Excellency by giving an order upon your Excellencie's Correspondent in this City will give us great satisfaction.

I am Sir Your Excellencies Most willing Servant.

JOHN BUTLER

at Mrs. Margrath's the Sign of the Ship Warmer Street Amsterdam

Notation: John Butler July 15. 1783.—

From Giacomo Francisco Crocco[8]

LS and press copy of copy: American Philosophical Society; three copies and transcript: National Archives

Sir,   Cadiz 15th. July 1783—

His Imperial Majesty the Emperor of Morroco[9] did me the honour to appoint me to be the bearer of his Answer to the United Provinces of North America with whom he is willing

8. Crocco, a Genoan, had been the secretary of Etienne d'Audibert Caille, a French merchant living in Morocco who in 1779 (not 1778, as we stated in XXVI, 285n) was named consul for unrepresented foreign nationals. Caille wrote BF in 1778 volunteering to negotiate a treaty between America and the sultan of Morocco. In 1779 he wrote directly to Congress, this time in an official capacity, extending the sultan's offer of friendship. BF had reason to distrust Caille and did not respond to either overture. Caille fell out of favor at court in April, 1782, and left the country; his whereabouts in 1783 are unknown, but he was back in Morocco as consul for various countries in 1784 and visited BF in July of that year. Crocco, meanwhile, performed commissions for the sultan in 1783: XXVI, 285–6; XXIX, 558; XXXIV, 84; XXXVIII, 293; Priscilla H. Roberts and James N. Tull, "Moroccan Sultan Sidi Muhammad Ibn Abdallah's Diplomatic Initiatives Toward the United States, 1777–1786," APS *Proc.*, CXLIII (1999), 233–65.

9. Sidi Muhammad ibn Abdallah. Since assuming the throne in 1757, he had reorganized the army, developed a navy, and negotiated commercial treaties with Britain, France, and at least 11 other European countries: Roberts and Tull, "Moroccan Sultan," pp. 234–5; Roberts and Roberts, *Thomas Barclay*, pp. 197–8.

to sign a Treaty of Peace & Commerce,[1] & in conseqce. has already given orders to his captains of Men of Warr not to molest on the open Seas the American Vessells, which agreable News I have already given to Richard Harrison Esqr.[2] According to my instructions I am to accompany to the Court of Morroco the Embassador that will be appointed to conclude the Treaty of Peace. I presume that your Excellency is already acquainted that the travelling expences & other charges of Embassadors or Envoys Sent to Europe by the Emperor of Morroco, are to be paid by the Court or Republick that demands his friendship. In a few days I intend to sett out for Madrid where I will remain till I receive your Excellency answer to this letter directed to the Honorable William Carmichael Esqr. The United States Chargé d'Affaires at the Court of Spain, who I make no doubt shall receive orders to supply me the Money I may want on the occasion. As soon as I arrive at Paris I will have the Satisfaction to entertain at large your Excellency on the present negociation,

1. The sultan was responding to an unauthorized letter of Jan. 4, 1783, from Robert Montgomery, an American merchant at Alicante (XXVI, 242n; XXIX, 746n), who claimed to be writing on behalf of Congress, "sovereign" of a nation that was "now declared independent by the Great & Principle Powers of Europe." Presuming that the "several letters" Congress had written to the sultan had miscarried, Montgomery had been ordered to repeat Congress' offer to send an ambassador to Morocco to negotiate a treaty of amity and commerce (National Archives). This unauthorized overture and the puzzling references it contained angered and embarrassed the American commissioners: *Adams Papers*, XIV, 502n; BF to Crocco and to Carmichael, both of Dec. 15, 1783 (National Archives).

The sultan sent word to Montgomery on April 23 that he was ordering the protection of American ships, would welcome an American ambassador, and was dispatching Crocco (who was already in Spain on another commission) to deliver his message to the American commissioners at Paris. He acknowledged having received one previous letter on the part of Congress: Secretary to the Sultan Eliahu Levy to Montgomery, April 23 and July 6, 1783 (National Archives).

2. The American agent at Cadiz: XXII, 447n; XXXVI, 247n. In April, 1782, when Caille was in Cadiz, he told Harrison about the letter he had sent to Congress on behalf of the sultan. He wondered whether it had miscarried, as they had received no reply: Harrison to Robert R. Livingston, April 24, 1782, National Archives.

not doubting it will be soon concluded to the advantage of both Courts, in the mean while I remain most truly Sir, Your most obedient & humble Servant   GIACOMO FRANCO: CROCCO

I was obliged to value on a friend to write you this letter in English otherwise I could only do it in the Italian Language.

From John Coakley Lettsom

ALS: American Philosophical Society

Esteemed Friend   London July 15. 1783
John Lister,[3] a respectable Friend (Quaker) has just informed me that he sets off for Paris tomorrow; and I embrace the opportunity of acknowledging the favour of thy Letter, inclosing one of Dr. Fothergills herein returned,[4] tho' I regret that I have not time by his sudden departure, of writing more fully in answer to thine.

My Friend Lister will spend about a week in Paris, & will convey any thing for England thou may wish to entrust him with. He is kind enough to take my Acct. of Dr. Fothergill; the use I have made of thy Letter, will, I hope meet with thy approbation, as well as my political ideas.[5]

I am respectfully   J. C. LETTSOM

Addressed: Benjamin Franklin / at Passey / near Paris

3. Possibly the former watchmaker, who was now a wine merchant in Lothbury: *ODNB*, under Joseph Jackson Lister; *Bailey's Western and Midland Directory . . . For the Year 1783* (Birmingham, 1783), p. 97.
4. XXXIX, 294–5.
5. *Some Account of the Late John Fothergill . . .* had just been published: XXXIX, 294n.

From the Abbé Nolin[6]

ALS: American Philosophical Society

Monsieur   a Paris Le 15 Juillet 1783

Mr. De marbois Secretaire de L'ambassade de france en Amerique, me mande que mr Le cher. de La Luzerne désire des Graines potageres et me prie de Luy en envoyer un assortiment de choix. Il m'ajouté que Le Vaisseau le Vashington Caine. Barcley aborde au havre, que Ce navire est à vôtre disposition que Son Séjour ne Sera pas Long.[7] Et que C'est une occasion tres favorable pour ce Transport. J'ay en Consequence rassemblé Les graines qu'on desire. Je prends La Liberté de vous Les adresser, en vous Supliant d'avoir La bonté de Les faïre passer á philadelphie, a Leur destination, J'ose attendre Cette Grace de votre Complaisance.

J'ay L'honneur d'être avec Respect Monsieur Vôtre tres humble et tres obeissant Serviteur

L'ABBE NOLIN,
Directeur gal des pepinieres du
Roy au Roule faubourg st honorë

Notation: Nolin 15 Juillet 1783

6. The director of a royal nursery that specialized in foreign plants: xxx, 285n.

7. The packet *General Washington*, Capt. Barney, scheduled to depart around July 21, sailed from Le Havre on Aug. 1: Henry Laurens to the Other American Peace Commissioners, Aug. 9; *Morris Papers*, VIII, 394n.

To the Farmers General: Memorandum[8]

Press copy of AD[9] and transcript: University of Pennsylvania Library

[before July 17, 1783]

Copy of [Note given] to the Farmers General

Mr Robert Morris, Merchant, of Philadelphia, is Superintendant des Finances of the United States.

It belongs to him to make Provision for the [Payment of the Debt due from the States to the Farmers General].

Mr Morris is a Man of S[kill][1] in Business, great Activity, great Exactness, & Integrity, in whom the most perfect Confidence may be placed.

Mr Franklin therefore advises, that a Letter be written by Messrs. the Farmers General to Mr. Morris,* mentioning the Sum due & their Desire of being paid, and requesting that he would in part send them a Cargo of Tobacco, purchased by him for them, he being allow'd a Commission of [*blank*] per Cent. that they may judge from the Experiment whether it will be advantageous for them to give Orders for a Continuation of the Payment of the Debt in this Manner, [& in future] [*illegible*]

*they chose to [write it to Mr Franklin]

8. At some time before July 17, the farmers general approached BF to request that the United States repay its debt. The present document is BF's retained and annotated copy of the note he gave them, advising them to write to Robert Morris. They wrote instead to him (below, July 17). See also BF to Morris, July 27.

9. The press copy is impossible to read in places where the ink has blurred or dissolved the tissue paper. The transcript was obviously made from this press copy—it does not even attempt a reading of the final phrase, which is all blurred—but it does render words and phrases that are missing now. We supply those readings in brackets.

1. "Spirit" in the transcript, but we can see enough letters in the copy to suggest an alternate reading.

The American Peace Commissioners to David Hartley[2]

LS:[3] Public Record Office; AL (drafts):[4] American Philosophical Society, Massachusetts Historical Society; copies: William L. Clements Library, Library of Congress, Massachusetts Historical Society, National Archives

Sir,   Passy, July 17th. 1783.

We have the honour to inform you that we have just received from Congress their Ratification in due Form of the Provisional Articles of the 30th. of November 1782,[5] and we are ready to exchange Ratifications with his Britannic Majesty's Ministers as soon as may be.

By the same Articles it is stipulated, that his Britannic Majesty shall with all convenient Speed, and without causing any Destruction or carrying away Negroes or other Property of the American Inhabitants, withdraw all his Armies, Garrisons and Fleets from the United States and from every Port, Place &

---

2. This letter was drafted over the course of a week during which the commissioners received the king's Order in Council of July 2; this, in Hartley's words, "produced a convulsion in our negotiation." (For the Order in Council see Falconer to BF, July 8.) The Americans had received it by Monday, July 14, when JA made a copy. The next day at Versailles, they ascertained that Vergennes had also read it; this prompted a discussion about American trade with the French West Indies. Hartley learned of it only on July 16 during a meeting with JA; his inability to answer for his government further eroded what little remained of the commissioners' trust. Hartley complained to Fox, warning him of the damage this had caused and repeating his desire to return to England to discuss these issues in person. *Adams Papers*, XV, 111–14, 122–6; Hartley to Fox, July 17, 1783, Clements Library; Hartley to Fox, July 24, 1783, in Giunta, *Emerging Nation*, II, 202–5.

3. In the hand of L'Air de Lamotte.

4. This document was drafted in multiple stages. JA wrote a first draft on July 11, to which BF made two suggestions for wording changes (APS). WTF made a fair copy, which JA signed; this then went to Jay for review. Jay crossed out a sentence and interlined a substitute. The three commissioners obviously conferred at that point; two new sections were drafted (one by Jay, the other by JA) and marked for insertion, with BF altering one phrase. The date was also changed to July 17 (Mass. Hist. Soc.). Part of the final draft is published in Morris, *Jay: Peace*, pp. 546–8, where Jay's contributions are identified.

5. Joshua Barney had brought the ratification on July 2; see BF to Laurens, July 6, and the Commissioners to Livingston, July 18.

Harbour within the same.[6] But, by Intelligence lately received from America, and by the inclosed Copies of Letters and Conferences between General Washington and Sir Guy Carleton,[7] it appears that a considerable Number of Negroes belonging to the Citizens of the United States, have been carried off from New-York contrary to the express Stipulation contained in the said Article.[8] We have received from Congress their Instructions to represent this Matter to you, and to request that speedy and effectual Measures be taken to render that Justice to the Parties interested which the true Intent and Meaning of the Article in Question plainly dictates.

We are also instructed to represent to you,[9] that many of the British Debtors in America have in the Course of the War sustained such considerable and heavy Losses by the Operation of the British Arms in that Country, that a great Number of them have been rendered incapable of immediately satisfying those Debts: we refer it to the Justice and Equity of Great Britain, so far to amend the Article on this Subject, as that no Execu-

6. Article 7 of the preliminary articles: XXXVIII, 386.

7. Hartley forwarded these enclosures "without any Comment" to Fox on July 25, along with the present letter. (His copy of the entire packet is at the Clements Library.) The enclosures were Thomas Walke's May 3 letter to the Va. delegates to Congress about Britain's refusal to return slaves; Congress' May 8 resolution transmitting Walke's letter to George Washington; Washington's May 8 letter to President of Congress Boudinot; a report of the May 6 conference between Washington and Carleton; Washington's May 6 letter to Carleton; and Washington's May 8 commission to Egbert Benson, William S. Smith, and Daniel Parker to supervise the British embarkation from New York. For these see William T. Hutchinson et al., eds., The Papers of James Madison, First Series (17 vols., Chicago, London, and Charlottesville, 1962–91), VII, 5–7; JCC, XXIV, 333; Fitzpatrick, Writings of Washington, XXVI, 410–14; Giunta, Emerging Nation, I, 848–52. In his Aug. 9 response, Fox defended Carleton but promised to make inquiries: Giunta, Emerging Nation, I, 916.

8. Livingston reported this in his letters of May 9 (XXXIX, 578–80) and May 28, above. BF informed Laurens about the complaints on July 6, above.

9. This paragraph was drafted by Jay and concerns the May 30 congressional resolutions that Livingston sent to the commissioners on May 31 (above).

tion shall be issued on a Judgment to be obtained in any such Case but after the Expiration of three Years from the Date of the definitive Treaty of Peace. Congress also think it reasonable that such Part of the Interest which may have accrued on such Debts during the War shall not be payable, because all Intercourse between the two Countries, had, during that Period, become impracticable as well as improper, it does not appear just that Individuals in America should pay for Delays in payment which were occasioned by the civil and military Measures of Great Britain. In our Opinion the Interest of the Creditors as well as the Debitors requires that some Tenderness be shewn to the Latter, and that they should be allowed a little Time to acquire the Means of discharging Debts which in many Instances exceed the whole Amount of their Property.

As it is necessary to ascertain an Epocha, for the Restitutions and Evacuations to be made, we propose that it be agreed, that his Britannic Majesty, shall cause to be evacuated the Posts of New-York, Penobscot and their Dependences, with all other Posts and Places in Possession of his Majesty's Arms, within the United States, in the Space of three Months after the Signature of this definitive Treaty, or sooner if possible, excepting those Posts contiguous to the Water Line, mentioned in the fourth Proposition,[1] and these shall be evacuated, when Congress shall give the Notice therein mentioned.

We do ourselves the honour of making these Communications to you, Sir, that you may transmit them and the Papers accompanying them to your Court, and inform us of their Answer.

We have the honour to be, Sir, Your most obedient and most humble Servants
                                        JOHN ADAMS.
                                        B FRANKLIN
                                        JOHN JAY

Dd. Hartley Esqr.

1. Actually, the fifth of Hartley's six propositions of [June 19], above; see also the commissioners' response of June 29.

From William Alexander ALS: American Philosophical Society

My Dear Sir   Paris 17 Julliet 1783

In case our friend Williams[2] shoud not provide for Some bills drawn by Mr Bache of Philadelphia will You not think it proper to do it? They can hardly exceed 1000— If you think this proper—You shoud Write Williams to address the holders to you—[3] My meaning in this is that you woud probably Chuse to save Mr Bache the dishonor & loss which is very Considerable on the return of Bills— I have written to Williams & am going to set out for St Germains.[4] I beg my respects to Your Son & am wt greatest Esteem Dear Sir Your most obt hble S

W ALEXANDER

If You write to Williams desire him to tell You the precise amount that You may know Exactly the Extent.

Addressed: A Son Excellence / Monsieur Le Docteur Franklin / Ministre Plenipotentiaire des / Etats Unis d'Ame à la Cour de France / à Passy

2. JW.
3. BF did so the next day: JW to BF, July 29.
4. Alexander's country estate in Saint-Germain-en-Laye: XXX, 153n, 263n.

From the Farmers General[5]

Press copy of copy:[6] American Philosophical Society

Monsieur,   [July 17, 1783]

Suivant le compte arrêté entre vous et nous, le 17. Novembre 1781,[7] Il reste du à la Ferme Générale, sous le nom de David,[8] une Somme de huit cent quarante Six mille Sept cent soixante dix livres quatorze Sols cinq deniers, et ce Debit, comme vous sçavés, est le restant d'un million que nous avons prêté aux Etats Unis, pour la valeur du quel ils devoient nous fournir des Tabacs à quarante Livres le quintal, rendu dans nos Ports, ce qui n'a été exécuté que pour la Somme mentionnée dans le Compte que nous avons l'honneur de vous rapeller.

Le Bail de David est expiré depuis trois ans, et nous sommes occupés, Monsieur, à terminer les Liquidations relatives à ce Bail; Nous desirons beaucoup, en consequence, que vous veuillés bien acquitter l'engagement que vous avez contracté avec nous; Nous ne vous en avons point parlé pendant la durée de la Guerre, Nous ne reclamons point les Intérêts de la Somme prêtée, mais le Retour de la paix, et l'Expiration, déja ancienne du Bail de David, seront sans doute pour vous, comme pour nous, des motifs pressans de terminer cette affaire.

Sa Conclusion naturelle seroit l'acquitement du Solde du Compte, le traité n'ayant point été executé, et le Bail de David étant expiré, mais nous pensons, Monsieur, qu'elle pourroit finir dans les mêmes Principes qui l'ont fait naitre, et que les Etats Unis pourroient acquiter la Somme qui nous reste dûe, en nous fournissant sa Valeur en Tabac, et nous vous prions d'en faire la

---

5. Written after the farmers called on BF to discuss how America might begin to repay its debt. BF recommended that they write to Robert Morris, but they addressed their letter to him instead; see BF's memorandum to the farmers general, [before July 17].

6. Made from the copy by L'Air de Lamotte that BF sent Morris on July 27. An English translation is published in *Morris Papers*, VIII, 347–8.

7. XXXVI, 145n.

8. Laurent David held the lease of the farmers general from 1774 to 1780: Price, *France and the Chesapeake*, I, 370.

proposition au Congrès, en lui rappellant tout ce qui s'est passé entre vous et nous, au sujet de cette Affaire.

Si elle est acceptée, comme nous l'esperons, il conviendroit, Monsieur, que M. Morris, chargé du Département des finances, nous expédiat à compte, une Cargaison de Tabac pour le port du Havre; Nous repartirions les matieres dans les Manufactures du Havre, Dieppe et Paris, au moyen de quoi nous serions en état de faire connoitre promptement à M. Morris, l'Opinion que nous aurions de son Envoy, quant à la Qualité; il nous adresseroit une facture qui nous indiqueroit les Prix d'achats, et tous les frais faits en amerique, et y joindrait un connoissement qui nous annonceroit le Prix du Fret.

Nous ne fixons aucuns Limites à M. Morris, pour l'objet du Chargement, et naturellement il doit être reglé suivant le Port du Bâtiment qu'il aura occasion de freter; nous demandons quant au prix du Tabac, qu'il soit combiné, de maniere que celui d'achat, tous les frais d'Amerique, La Commission, et le fret, reünis ensemble, n'en portent point la Valeur, à l'arrivée au port du havre, audessus des quarante livres par quintal, rendu dans nos ports, qui avoient été convenus entre vous et nous, lors du prêt dont nous sollicitons le Remboursement; Nous ne déterminons pas le Tau de la Commission qui doit entrer dans le prix combiné, et, pour le chargement en question, nous nous en rapportons à ce que fera M. Morris; nous observons seulement qu'elle est de deux pour cent dans les opérations ordinaires du Commerce, et qu'elle doit naturellement diminuer, suivant l'importance des objets.

Nous Sommes persuadés, Monsieur, que l'Essay dont il s'agit nous mettra dans le Cas de souhaiter que toute la Somme qui nous est due soit [acqui]ttée par la même voye; Nous verrons avec plaisir que ce soit l'occasion d'une Correspondance entre M. Morris et nous; ses lettres alors devront être adressés à Mrs. les Fermiers Généraux du Bureau des achats du Tabac, à l'hotel des Fermes à Paris.

Cette correspondance peut avoir des Suites beaucoup plus interessantes que l'objet qui nous occupe, dans le moment; Cette perspective, sans doute, n'échapera point à M. Morris, et s[achant(?)] que vous avez la bonté de nous dire de ses Principes et de ses Talents, nous verrions avec plaisir que nos Relations avec lui se multipliassent; Nous vous serions très redavables, Monsieur, de lui recommander nos Intérets et nous reclamons vos bons offices pour la Conclusion de l'affaire qui donne lieu à la présente.

Nous sommes avec Respect, Monsieur, Vos tres humbles et très obeissants Serviteurs.

(signé) DeLaage. de la Hante. Pignon. St. Amand.[9]

Copie d'une Lettre de Messrs. les Fermiers Généraux à Mr. Franklin, datée de Paris le 17. Juillet 1783.

From Henry Laurens

ls:[1] Library of Congress; copy: South Carolina Historical Society

Dear Sir,   Bath 17th July 1783.

I have but this moment 1 0 Clock PM been honored with your Letter of the 6th. Instant, it has been long in its Passage, I must endeavour to make more Expedition in complying with your wish to return as soon as possible to Paris. I had flattered myself with hopes of being free.

As tis possible nay probable that I shall be with you as soon as this, tis unnecessary to enlarge, indeed I have not time for I mean to begin my Journey to morrow morning. I purpose to go from St Dennis to Passy where I hope to have the honor on the 24th or 25th. of repeating how truly I am, Sir, your most obedient and most humble Servant,[2]   Henry Laurens.

9. Clément de Laage, Jacques de la Hante, Michel Pignon, and Alexandre-Victor de Saint-Amand, for whom see *Morris Papers*, VIII, 348n, and Yves Durand, *Les Fermiers Généraux au XVIIIe siècle* (Paris, 1971).

1. In the hand of Henry Laurens, Jr., who was serving as secretary to his ailing father: *Laurens Papers*, XVI, 224n.

2. Laurens arrived in Paris on July 23, but the trip left him ill: *Laurens Papers*, XVI, 241–2.

We, meaning this little family, present most respectful Salutes to yourself Mr. & Mrs. Jay and our good friend Mr. Franklin Junr: and also to Miss Maria[3]

His Excellency Benjamin Franklin Esqr: Paris.

Addressed: His Excellency / Benjamin Franklin Esquire / &c &c / Passy.

From John Wheelock   ALS: American Philosophical Society

Sir,   St James' Street No. 40 London 17 July 1783

I wrote to your Excellency from the Hague, requesting a letter to Dr Price, & the favor to be informed, whether any thing had appeared in the circle of your acquaintance conducive to the furtherance of the Object of my attention.[4] But likely my letter has not reached you, as I have heard nothing since.

I beg, Sir, the honor to be informed whether or no, in your opinion, any thing can be done to effect in any part of His Christian Majestys dominions— A compliance, so soon as you might think it convenient, would be very obliging, as we shall not stay long in this country, unless something should turn up more favorable to success than now appears.[5]

I am with the greatest respect, Sir, your Excellencys most obedient & very humble servant   JN WHEELOCK

3. John and Sarah Jay's 17-month-old daughter (Morris, *Jay: Peace,* p. 218n).

4. The letter is above, June 12.

5. The brothers sailed for America on Oct. 20 aboard the *Peace and Plenty,* which ran aground off Cape Cod on Jan. 2, 1784. No lives were lost, but Wheelock lost a strongbox containing all his papers and donations for the college: Leon B. Richardson, *History of Dartmouth College* (2 vols., Hanover, N.H., 1932), I, 207–8; Dick Hoefnagel, "Benjamin Franklin and the Wheelocks," Dartmouth College Library *Bulletin,* new ser., XXXI (1990), 24–5.

Addressed: His Excellency / Benjamin Franklin LLD / Minister plenipotentiary &c / Passey / near Paris

Notation: Wheelock 17 July 1783.

To John Jay[6]

Copies:[7] Massachusetts Historical Society, Library of Congress

[before July 18, 1783][8]

Mr. F. submits it to the Consideration of Mr. Jay, whether it may not be adviseable to forbear, at present, the Justification

6. These are BF's comments on Jay's draft of an official response to Livingston. The final version of the commissioners' letter is immediately below; see the annotation there for background. The portion of Jay's draft to which BF here objects, and which was removed, is published in Morris, *Jay: Peace*, pp. 550–3. Jay sent a revised version of it in a personal letter to Livingston of July 19: Morris, *Jay: Peace*, pp. 558–64.

7. From the commissioners' letterbooks.

8. It is not known when Jay produced his draft. Livingston's March 25 letter reporting on the debates in Congress and criticizing the commissioners for signing the preliminaries without notifying France (XXXIX, 380–5), which the commissioners received on July 3, struck such a nerve that JA lost no time in firing back private letters justifying their conduct. (He wrote to Robert Morris on July 5, and to Livingston on July 9, 10, and 11: *Adams Papers*, XV, 81–3, 92–7, 99–100.) Meanwhile, the commissioners were expecting Henry Laurens to return from England, as BF had asked him to do on July 6 (above). We believe that BF, Jay, and JA had decided to wait for Laurens' return before composing an official response to Livingston. Laurens, however, did not receive BF's letter until July 17 (see his answer of that date). By that time, Barney must have informed the commissioners of his imminent departure (for which see the annotation of the following document). The pressure of having to send some response with Barney makes it likely that Jay produced his version shortly before July 18. BF's last argument, after all, was that Laurens was not in Paris, and he wondered what harm would be done if the contested section were postponed.

Thirty years later, JA recalled how he had asked Jay to draft their answer because he thought it more likely that BF would "subscribe" to something Jay wrote, and furthermore, he did not trust himself to be objective. He found Jay's draft "a great consolation and a high gratification," as it agreed with "everything [he] had ever said or written" about the French: *Boston Patriot*, Feb. 15 and 19, 1812. See *Adams Papers*, XV, 140–3, where these reminiscences are quoted and an alternate interpretation of events is proposed.

of ourselves, respecting the Signature of the Preliminaries; because

That matter is, at present, quiet here;

No Letter sent to the Congress is ever kept secret;

The Justification contains some Charges of unfavourable Dispositions in the Ministers here towards us, that will give offense & will be deny'd;

Our Situation is still critical with respect to the two Nations, and the most perfect good Understanding should be maintained with this;

The Congress do not call upon us for an Account of our Conduct, or its Justification. They have not by any Resolution blamed us. What Censure we have received is only the private Opinion of Mr. L.

Mr. Laurens is not here, who is concern'd with us, Will it be attended with any Inconvenience, if that Part of the Letter, which relates to the Signature be reserved to a future Occasion?

B. Franklin's Observations on Mr Jay's Draft of a Letter to Mr Livingston, which occasioned the foregoing Part to be left out.

The American Peace Commissioners to Robert R. Livingston[9]

LS:[1] National Archives; press copy of LS: Massachusetts Historical Society; copies: Library of Congress, Massachusetts Historical Society, Yale University Library; transcript: National Archives

Sir,   Passy, 18th. July 1783

We have had the honour of receiving by Capt. Barney your two Letters of the 25th. of March & 21st of April,[2] with the Papers referred to in them.

We are happy to find that the Provisional Articles have been approved & ratified by Congress, and we regret that the Manner in which that Business was conducted, does not coincide with your Ideas of Propriety. We are persuaded however that this is principally owing to your being necessarily unacquainted with a Number of Circumstances, known to us who

---

9. The commissioners differed on how to respond to the letters from Livingston that Barney delivered to them at the beginning of July. Each of them answered privately, justifying the way the preliminary articles were concluded; JA did so long before the present letter, Jay the day after, and BF on July 22[–26]. (See the annotation of the preceding document.) The present letter, the product of much discussion, is their official response. That they wanted to preserve a record of their individual contributions is evidenced by the fact that various drafts, comments, and deleted sections were copied into the legation letterbooks, with the authors identified. From these, it emerges that Jay drafted the first version. BF thought it imprudent in many respects; we publish his remarks above, [before July 18]. A large section of Jay's original was eliminated as a consequence.

This final version was signed on July 18 by the three commissioners then at Paris, who had been told that Barney (who would carry their letters to America) would be leaving on July 21: Morris, *Jay: Peace*, p. 558. JA left for Holland the next day, July 19 (*Adams Papers*, XV, 165). Laurens, whom BF had called back from England on July 6 (in part to help draft this response), did not arrive in Paris until July 23, which, as it happened, was several days before Barney actually left. The last version of the present document in the commissioners' letterbooks is an undated text by Laurens, which must have been written at this time. It revises the present letter substantially, justifying the commissioners' actions in ways that BF had cautioned against in Jay's draft.

1. In WTF's hand.

2. XXXIX, 380–5, 485–8.

were on the Spot, and which will be particularly explained to you hereafter, and, we trust, to your Satisfaction & that of the Congress.

Your Doubts respecting the Separate Article[3] we think are capable of being removed, but as a full State of the Reasons and Circumstances which prompted that Measure would be very prolix, we shall content ourselves with giving you the general Outlines.

Mr Oswald was desirous to cover as much of the Eastern Shores of the Missisippi with British Claims as possible and for this purpose we were told a great deal about the ancient Bounds of Canada & Louisiana &ca &ca &ca. The British Court who had probably not yet adopted the Idea of relinquishing the Floridas,[4] seemed desirous of anexing as much Territory to them as possible, even up to the Mouth of the Ohio— Mr. Oswald adhered strongly to that Object as well to render the British Countries there of sufficient Extent to be, (as he express'd it) worth keeping & protecting; as to afford a convenient Retreat to the Tories for whom it would be difficult otherwise to provide; and among other Arguments he finally urged his being willing to yield to our Demands to the East, North and West, as a further Reason for our gratifying him on the Point in Question. He also produced the Commission of Govr Johnson extending the Bounds of his Government of W. Florida up to the River Yassous [Yazoo][5] and contended for that Extent as a Matter of Right upon various Principles which however we did not admit.

We were of Opinion that the Country in Contest was of great Value both on Account of its natural Fertility, and of its Posi-

---

3. Enlarging the borders of West Florida, should it be awarded to Britain in the peace treaty: XXXVIII, 388.

4. See XXXIX, 383–4.

5. George Johnstone (*DNB*), a member of the 1778 Carlisle Commission (XXVI, 108n), had been appointed in 1763 as the first British governor of West Florida. In 1764 he persuaded the government to extend the colony by moving its northern border to "a Line drawn from the Mouth of the River Yasons [Yazoo], where it unites with the Mississippi due East to the River Apalachicola," the same boundary specified in the separate article cited above: Lawrence H. Gipson, *The British Empire Before the American Revolution* (15 vols., Caldwell, Idaho, and New York, 1936–70), IX, 203.

tion, it being in our Opinion the Interest of America to extend as far down the Mouth of the Missisippi as we possibly could.[6] We also thought it adviseable to impress Britain with a strong Sense of the Importance of the Navigation of that River, to their future Commerce on the interior Waters from the Mouth of the River St Lawrens to that of the Missisippi, and thereby render that Court averse to any Stipulations with Spain to relinquish it. These two objects militated against each other; because to inhance the Value of the Navigation was also to inhance the Value of the Countries contiguous to it, and thereby disincline Britain to the Dereliction of them. We thought therefore that the surest Way to reconcile & obtain both Objects would be by a Composition beneficial to both Parties. We therefore proposed that Britain should withdraw her Pretensions to all the Country above the Yassous and that we would cede all below it to her in Case she should have the Floridas at the End of the War, and at all Events that she should have a Right to navigate the River throughout its whole Extent. This Proposition was accepted, and we agreed to insert the contingent Part of it in a separate Article, for the express purpose of keeping it secret for the present. That Article ought not therefore to be consider'd as a mere Matter of Favour to Britain, but as the Result of a Bargain in which that Article was a "quid pro quo." It was in our Opinion both necessary & justifiable to keep this Article secret. The Negotiations between Spain France & Britain were then in full Vigour, and embarrass'd by a Variety of clashing Demands. The Publication of this Article would have irritated Spain, and retarded if not have prevented her coming to an Agreement with Britain. Had we mentioned it to the French Minister, he must have not only informed Spain of it, but also been obliged to act a Part respecting it that would probably have been disagreable to America, and he certainly has reason to rejoice that our Silence saved him that delicate and disagreable Task. This was an Article in which France had not the smallest Interest, nor is there any thing in her Treaty with us, that restrains us from making what Bargain we pleased with Britain about those or any other Lands, without rendering Account of such Transaction to her

6. For BF's views on the importance of the Mississippi see XXXIII, 357.

or any other Power whatever. The same Observation applies with still greater Force to Spain, and neither Justice or Honour forbid us to dispose as we pleased of our own Lands, without her Knowledge or Consent. Spain at that very time extended her Pretensions and Claim of Dominion not only over the Tract in Question, but over the Vast Region lying between the Floridas and Lake Superior; and this Court was also at that very Time soothing & nursing of those Pretensions by a proposed conciliatory Line for splitting the Difference. Suppose therefore we had offer'd this Tract to Spain in Case She retained the Floridas, should we even have had Thanks for it? or would it have abated the Chagrin she experienc'd from being disappointed in her extravagant and improper Designs on that whole Country? we think not.—

We perfectly concur with you in Sentiment, Sir, *"That Honesty is the best Policy"*[7] but untill it be shown that we have tresspass'd on the Rights of any Man or Body of men, you must excuse our thinking that this Remark as applied to our Proceedings was unnecessary.

Should any Explanations either with France or Spain become necessary on this Subject, we hope & expect to meet with no Embarrassments. We shall neither amuse them nor perplex ourselves with ostensible and flimsy Exuses, but tell them plainly that as it was not our Duty to give them the Information, we consider'd ourselves at Liberty to withhold it, and we shall remind the French Minister that he has more Reason to be pleased than displeased with our Silence. Since we have assumed a Place in the Political System of the World let us move like a Primary & not like a Secondary Planet.

We are persuaded, Sir, that your Remarks on these Subjects resulted from real Opinion, and were made with all Candour and Sincerity. The Best Men will view Objects of this Kind in different Lights even when standing on the same Ground: and

---

7. Livingston used this expression in a March 18 letter to President of Congress Boudinot discussing the separate article, which he enclosed in his letter to the commissioners of March 25: XXXIX, 384n.

it is not to be wonder'd at that we who are on the Spot and have
the whole Transaction under our Eyes should see many Parts of
it in a stronger Point of Light than Persons at a Distance, who
can only view it through the dull Medium of Representation.

It would give us great Pain if any thing we have written or
now write respecting this Court, should be construed to im-
peach the Friendship of the King & Nation for us. We also believe that the Minister is so far our Friend, and is disposed so
far to do us Good Offices, as may correspond with, and be dictated by his System of Policy for Promoting the Power, Riches
and Glory of France. God forbid that we should ever sacrifice
our Faith, our Gratitude, or our Honour, to any Consideration
of Convenience; and may he also forbid that we should ever be
unmindful of the Dignity and independant Spirit which should
always characterize a free and generous People.

We shall immediately propose an Article to be inserted in the
Definitive Treaty for postponing the Payment of British Debts
for the Time mentioned by Congress.[8]

There are, no doubt, certain Ambiguities in our Articles, but
it is not to be wonder'd at when it is consider'd how exceedingly
averse Britain was to Expressions which explicitly wounded
the Tories; and how disinclined we were to use any that should
amount to absolute Stipulations in their Favour.

The Words for restoring the Property of *Real British Subjects* were well understood and explained between us not to
mean or comprehend American Refugees. Mr. Oswald and
Mr. Fitz-Herbert know this to have been the Case, and will readily confess and admit it. This mode of Expression was preferr'd
by them as a more delicate Mode of excluding those Refugees,
and of making a proper Distinction between them and the Subjects of Britain whose only *particular* Interest in America consisted in holding Lands or Property there.

The 6th. Article vizt. where it declares that no *future Confiscations* shall be made &ca ought to have fixed the Time with
greater Accuracy: We think the most fair and true Construc-

8. They had already proposed this to Hartley; above, July 17.

tion is, that it relates to the Date of the Cessation of Hostilities. That is the Time when Peace in Fact took Place, in consequence of Prior unformal tho' binding Contracts to terminate the War. We consider the Definitive Treaties as only giving the Dress of Form to those Contracts, and not as constituting the Obligation of them. Had the Cessation of Hostilities been the Effect of a Truce, & consequently nothing more than a temporary Suspension of War, another Construction would have been the true one.

We are Officially assured by Mr. Hartley that positive Orders for the Evacuation of New-York have been dispatched; and that no avoidable Delay will retard that Event. Had we proposed to fix a Time for it, the British Court would have conte nded that it should be a Time posterior to the Date of the definitive Treaty and that would have been probably more disadvantageous to us than as that Article now stands.

We are surprized to hear that any Doubts have arisen in America respecting the Time when the Cessation of Hostilities took Place there. It most certainly took Place at the Expiration of one Month after the Date of that Declaration in all Parts of the World whether Land or Sea that lay North of the Latitude of the Canaries.

The Ships afterwards taken from us in the more Northerly Latitudes ought to be reclaimed and given up: We shall apply to Mr. Hartley on this Subject, and also on that of the Transportation of Negroes from New York contrary to the Words and Intention of the Provisional Articles.

With great Esteem, we have the honour to be, Sir, Your most obedient & most humble Servants JOHN ADAMS.
                B. FRANKLIN
                JOHN JAY

The honble: Robt. R. Livingston Esqr

Notation: Joint Commissioners July 18. 1783.

From Nathaniel Falconer

ALS: American Philosophical Society

My Dear Frend   London July the 18. 1783

The time Draws near for my Leaveing this place I Expect whe Shall be at Graves End about the Second of august[9] I find Capt Barney is arived in France and hope he has Brought Dispatchs for you Mr Bingham I understand has wrote you[1] the Gazet I Sent you hope Got sauef to hand Mr Silas Dean is hear[2] he paid me a viset and I find from him Self that he wrote Some part of the phamlet I Sent you but he Says he Did not write the Conclusion in Short from his being So much with arnold and Lord Shefeld I Cannot Esteem Mr Dean as before[3] Docter Bancroft is also hear and appling to Go to phila[4] with I Shall be obliged to you for your opinion of thees two Gentelmen for Sir there is but few men beside your Self that I Dont Suspect of Desines agains our Countrey Mr Strahan I have not Seen to Shew him the paper you was So kind as to inclose[5] but he is Expected in Town Every Day when I hope to See him yesterday I Dined with your old Friend Mr Sergent he Disierd if I wrote to Remember him kindley to you my Dear Sir I beg you will Give an accot of publick matters as far as you thing you Can Trust me for it will be Thought Strange by maney of our friends the

9. Gravesend is downriver from London. Falconer's ship, the *Olive Branch*, did not reach Philadelphia until November: *Pa. Gaz.*, Nov. 12 and Nov. 19.

1. If so, Bingham's letter is no longer extant.

2. He arrived in London at the end of March; see our annotation of Deane to BF, July 20.

3. For Sheffield's pamphlet arguing against liberal trade relations with the United States see Falconer to BF, June 7. On Oct. 19, after having heard that rumors about his collaborating with Sheffield were circulating in Paris, Deane wrote to BF denying any participation in the pamphlet and claiming only limited contact with Benedict Arnold: *Deane Papers*, V, 212–15.

4. Bancroft wrote to WTF on July 11 that he had not yet found a conveyance to Philadelphia. Capt. Falconer's ship was the first scheduled to leave, but Falconer might not be able to accommodate him: APS. Bancroft sailed on Aug. 13 aboard the *Commerce*, Capt. Truxton: Morris, *Jay: Peace*, p. 572. The ship arrived on Sept. 24: *Pa. Evening Post*, Sept. 25, 1783.

5. In his letter of June 18.

other Side if I Can Give no account of matters in France My Best Compliments to Mr W T Franklin and Mr Hartley if Still with you. I am my Dear Sir your Sincer friend and Hb Sr

NATH FALCONER

Addressed: Docter Franklin / at / the Court of France / parris

Notation: Falconet July 18 1783.

From Vergennes

Copies: Archives du Ministère des affaires étrangères, National Archives

A Vlles. le 18. Juillet 1783.

J'ai recu M. la lettre que vous m'avez fait l'honneur de m'ecrire le 4 de ce mois ainsy que les pieces dont vous l'avez accompagnée, relativement au Secours extraordinaire que vous etes chargé par le Congrès de demander au Roi.

Ma lettre du 5 de ce mois vous a deja instruit de l'impossibilité où etoit S.M. de deferer a cette requisition.[6] J'ai mis encore Sous Ses yeux vos nouvelles instances à cet egard, et c'est avec regret que je Suis dans la necessité de vous mander que le Roi n'a pas cru possible de rien changer à Sa premiere determination.[7]

M. franklin

6. Vergennes' letter of July 5 answered a June 28 appeal for funds from BF and Jay based on what they had just learned from Grand, whereas BF's appeal of July 4 was ordered by Congress.

7. Vergennes' next letter to La Luzerne, written on July 21, enclosed copies of BF's July 4 letter, this response, and his earlier response of July 5 (Giunta, *Emerging Nation*, 1, 889–93). He seems to have entrusted these dispatches to BF at their weekly meeting on Tuesday, July 22, presumably to send to America with Capt. Barney. The next day, July 23, the *commis principal* in the foreign affairs office sent BF an additional packet from Rayneval to add to what was being forwarded to La Luzerne. It was inadvertently omitted from what BF had been given the day before: Jean-Jacques Le Goüeslier de Montcarel to BF, July 23, 1783, APS.

The enclosure from Rayneval may have been the memoir on fixing the boundaries between Spain and the United States that La Luzerne acknowledged receiving. It was so impartial, he observed, that even Jay would not be able to fault it. La Luzerne predicted that JA's criticisms of BF would have

From Jonathan Loring Austin[8]

ALS: American Philosophical Society

Sir   Boston 19th July 1783
   Give me leave respected Sir to introduce to you my Brother
Mr Benjamin Austin jr. & Mr Oliver Brewster (a young Gentleman of this Town who accompanys him on a Tour to Europe)[9]
who wish to have an Opportunity of paying their Respects to
your Excellency & see that Country which has so generously
exerted herself in behalf of America; & permit me to congratulate your Excellency on the glorious Event of Peace so honorable to America & beneficial to Mankind; & to assure you it is
with sensible pleasure I felicitate you on this glorious Era, in
the Accomplishment of which your Excellency has taken so
distinguish'd a part, the Recollection must cause the most pleasing Reflections, & more than compensate for the many anxious
hours when Hope & Fear for the fate of your Country ruled
alternate; thus in the Eve of Life to see an Empire rising in this
Western World, acknowledged free & independant by Euro-

---

no effect on Congress (whose members did not think BF had "sold himself"
to the French), and reassured Vergennes that Jay—though independent
minded—would not knowingly prejudice France or the alliance. Jay's letters were full of praise for BF and solicitations for WTF to be given a diplomatic post. La Luzerne doubted that Congress would confer this honor on
WTF because of his father, though people regretted BF's insistence on being
recalled: La Luzerne to Vergennes, Sept. 26, 1783, in Giunta, *Emerging
Nation*, I, 943–5.
   8. This appears to be Austin's first letter since 1781, when he was last in
France: XXXV, 297–8.
   9. Thirty-one-year-old Benjamin Austin, Jr., Jonathan's younger
brother, and 27-year-old Oliver Brewster were merchants on their way to
England and then France; see Cooper's letters of recommendation imme-
diately below. While they were in London, we believe they were among the
Bostonians tricked into presenting their letters of introduction to Elkanah
Watson's dummy "Franklin": XXXIX, 482–3n. After returning to America,
Austin formed a business partnership with his brother Jonathan, became
an outspoken political reformer, and served in the state Senate: *ANB*.
Brewster died in Boston in 1812: American Antiquarian Society, *Index of
Obituaries in* Massachusetts Centinel *and* Columbian Centinel, *1784 to 1840*
(5 vols., Boston, 1961), I, 577.

pean Powers, is a grand Epoch to your former acquired Fame. May our internal police be as wisely regulated continue respectable, & terminate as gloriously, for the Benefit of Mankind in general—

Requesting you will honor my Brother & his Friend with your Notice Advice & usual Civilities, I remain with the highest Respect Your Excellency's, Most Obedient & Very huml Servant JON L AUSTIN

Please to make my Compliments agreable to Mr Franklin—

His Excellency Dr Franklin—

Notation: Austin Mr. John 3. July 1783.—

From Samuel Cooper: Two Letters[1]

(I) and (II) ALS: American Philosophical Society

I.

Sir, Boston July 19th. 1783.

Having wrote you at large by the America that has lately sailed from Portsmouth, you will give me Leave to write this merely as an Introduction to my Friend Benjn. Austin junr. Brother to Mr Austin who carried to France the News of Burgoigne's Surrender.[2] He is a worthy Branch of a respectable Family; a young Gentleman of much good Sense, highly esteemed by all his Acquaintance, and of good Reputation in the Mercantile World. I most sincerely wish him Success in his Plans of Business. He means to pass from England to France, and will not fail to do himself the Honor of waiting on the American Ambassador at the Court of that Nation. I hope he will find your Excellency in good Health, and surrounded with every Blessing.

I have the Honor to be most respectfully and with the most constant Friendship Your most obedient humble Servant

 SAML. COOPER.

1. For the men Cooper introduces see the preceding letter.
2. XXV, 102–3, 218, 234–5.

His Excellency Bn. Franklin Esqr.

Notation: Cooper Mr. Saml. July 19. 1783.

II.

Sir,   Boston July 19th. 1783.
Mr Brewster, a young Gentleman with whom I have long been acquainted, and for whom I have conceived a particular Regard, who is much esteemed here for his Modesty, his Assiduity and fair Character in Business will deliver this to you. He goes for England in Company with Mr Austin, and from thence to France upon Mercantile Affairs; and will not fail to pay his Respects to our Ambassador at the Court of Versailles. I could not omit to give you that favorable Idea which I have formed of him. Renewing my Wishes for the Continuance of your Excellency's Health and great Usefulness, I am with unceasing Respect and Friendship Your most obedient and most humble Servant   SAML. COOPER.

His Excellency B. Franklin Esqr.

Notation: Cooper Mr. Saml. July 19. 1783.

From Sousa Coutinho

L: American Philosophical Society

Paris ce 19 Juillet 1783

L'Ambassadeur de Portugal a l'honneur de faire part a Monsieur Francklin que l'Assemblée[3] que devoit etre chez lui sera tenue dorenavant chez l'Ambassadeur d'Espagne.[4]

Addressed: A Monsieur / Monsieur Francklin / Ministre Plenre. des Etats unis / de l'Amerique Septentrionale / en son Hotel / a Passy. / de sousa./.

---

3. Based on four similar notifications among BF's papers at the APS, the "Assemblée" seems to have been a regular, informal Sunday gathering of diplomats assigned to the French court. It always met at the residence of one of the ambassadors. BF had been included since at least 1781. In a note that had to have been written that year, dated only June 16, the ambassador of Malta informed BF that due to the death of his mother, he would not be able to receive the "Assemblée" the following day. The Dutch ambassador (Berkenrode) would host it instead. The ambassador of the Order of Saint John, or Malta, was Jacques-Laure Le Tonnelier, bailli de Breteuil (1723–1785). His mother, Laure O'Brien de Clare, died on June 10, 1781: *Dictionnaire de la noblesse*, XIX, 36; *Repertorium der diplomatischen Vertreter*, III, 213.

The ambassador of Malta sent two additional notices. On "28 avril" he apprises BF that because he has to leave Paris for a month, he will not be able to welcome the assembly next Sunday; it will be hosted by the Venetian ambassador (Dolfin). On Oct. 29, 1784, he notifies BF that his illness prevents him from receiving the assembly next Sunday; it will meet instead at the British ambassador's residence. The British ambassador was the Duke of Dorset; he wrote on Aug. 5, 1784, notifying BF that he would host next Sunday's assembly.

For a discussion of the importance to diplomats of such informal social gatherings see Hamish Scott, "Diplomatic Culture in Old Regime Europe," in *Cultures of Power in Europe during the Long Eighteenth Century*, ed. Hamish Scott and Brendan Simms (Cambridge, Eng., and New York, 2007), pp. 72–82.

4. The conde de Aranda.

From the Ulster Volunteer Corps Committee of Correspondence[5]

ALS:[6] American Philosophical Society

[July 19, 1783]

At a meeting of the Comittee of Correspondence appointed by the Delagates of Forty five Volunteer Corps, assembled at Lisburn on the 1st. July Inst., held at Belfast 19 July 1783— Present—

5. In 1782 the Volunteers (for whom see XXIX, 265n; XXXVIII, 187n) and their allies in the Irish Parliament successfully pressured the British government to grant Ireland legislative independence. Many reformers believed that this autonomy would be meaningful only if it was followed by a change in the system of political representation within Ireland. On July 1 delegates representing 45 Ulster Volunteer corps met at Lisburn and resolved to call a general meeting of Ulster Volunteers at Dungannon for Sept. 8 to debate parliamentary reform. In preparation for this meeting, the Lisburn delegates established a committee of correspondence charged with gathering "the best authorities and informations on the subject of parliamentary reform": Patrick Rogers, *The Irish Volunteers and Catholic Emancipation (1778–1793)* . . . (London, 1934), pp. 80–94.

The present text was adapted from the committee's "Circular Letter for England." That letter was published, along with responses from seven prominent English reformers, in *Proceedings Relative to the Ulster Assembly of Volunteer Delegates* . . . (Belfast, 1783). One of them, John Cartwright, credited Henry Laurens with having convinced him of the advantages of ballot voting.

According to one of the committee members, circular letters were also sent to reformers within Ireland and to two men in France: BF and the abbé Raynal. Neither one had responded by the time the Sept. 8 meeting approached: Jean Agnew and Maria Luddy, eds., *The Drennan-McTier Letters* (3 vols., [Dublin], 1998–99), I, 129–30. BF did rejoice at the unanimous resolves taken at the Dungannon meeting, however. Writing to Sir Edward Newenham on Oct. 2, he observed that "liberty, which some years since appeared in danger of extinction, is now regaining the ground she had lost": WTF, *Memoirs*, II, 226–7.

6. The final paragraph was added by Henry Joy, Jr., who signed. The body of the letter is in another hand.

Leiut. Col. Sharman,[7] in the Chair
Major Burden—[8] Captain Cunningham[9]
Captain Prentice Captain Moore
Captain Crawford[1] Leiut. Tomb
and Mr. Robert Thompson,[2]

Ordered, that the following Letter, signed by the Secretary in
the Name of this Comittee,[3] be forwarded to his Excellency
Benjamin Franklin Inclosing a Copy of the Resolutions of the
Provincial meeting of Volunteers of Munster, & of the proceedings of the forty five Volunteer Delagates assembled at Lisburn on the 1st. Inst. respecting a Parlimentary Reform, as also
a Copy of the Circular Letter written this day by this Comittee
to the several Volunteer Corps of this Province—[4]

7. William Sharman (1730–1803) served as the collector of the revenue
for Lisburn until 1783, when he was elected as M.P. for the town: Edith M.
Johnston-Liik, ed., *History of the Irish Parliament, 1692–1800* . . . (6 vols.,
Belfast, 2002), VI, 261–2.

8. Maj. Robert Burden of the Ulster regiment: Rogers, *Irish Volunteers
and Catholic Emancipation*, p. 154.

9. Born in Ireland, Waddell Cunningham (1729–1797) rose to great
wealth and prominence as a merchant in New York in the 1750s before
returning to Belfast in 1764. During the Revolution he traded both with
American insurgents and with Loyalists in New York. In 1783 Cunningham retired from business and ran successfully for a seat in the Irish Parliament: *ODNB*.

1. John Crawford, a justice of the peace: Agnew and Luddy, eds.,
Drennan-McTier Letters, I, 126n.

2. A merchant and sugar refiner: Agnew and Luddy, eds., *Drennan-Mc-
Tier Letters*, I, 81n.

3. Henry Joy, Jr. (1754–1835), worked as a journalist for his family's
newspaper, the *Belfast News-Letter*, before taking over as editor in 1789:
John Bradbury, *Celebrated Citizens of Belfast* (Belfast, 2002), p. 47.

4. The enclosures are missing. Delegates of the Volunteers of Munster
met on March 1 and passed resolutions calling for parliamentary reform:
Rogers, *Irish Volunteers and Catholic Emancipation*, p. 89. The resolutions
of the Volunteer delegates at Lisburn and the committee's circular letter to
the Volunteer Army of the Province of Ulster are in *Proceedings Relative to
the Ulster Assembly of Volunteer Delegates*, pp. 3–7.

Sir   Belfast 19 July 1783
   Your attachment to the rights of mankind,[5] induce us to address you on the present great and momentous occasion—
   The Spirit of freedom, which pervades all ranks of people
in Ireland, with the Justice & wise policy of the British Nation,
having forever removed all possible cause of Jealousy between
the Sister Kingdoms, and united us to Britain on the basis of
equal liberty & similar Constitution; it becomes the Duty, as
it is the interest of each Kingdom to assist the other in their endeavours to restore to its ancient purity & vigour, a decayed,
enfeebled & sickly Constitution.
   In both nations it is now generally acknowledged that this
great object can be obtained by *no* other means, but by a reform
of the representation in Parliament— In England, the measure has for the present miscarried, tho' supported by so many
wise, honest, great & independent men—[6] We trust however
it has misscarried only for a Season, & that the next attempt
will prove successfull— Ireland has now taken up the Idea, and
if we shall be so happy as to see success crown our efforts, we
think considerable weight will be thereby added to the endeavours of the freinds of the People in England. The People of the
two nations united in pursuit of the same important object, must
be not only powerfull but irrisistable.
   The inclosed papers, which we request you may peruse, will
show how far this Country has already gone in determining
to procure a more equal Representation; the unanimous resolutions of about fifteen thousand Volunteers, already declared
in a very few weeks, assure us the resolves of the Delagates
of Ulster, who are to assemble at Dungannon on the 8th Sepr.
next, will be no less unanimous and we will know that what the

   5. This word was substituted for "the people, and to the general prosperity of the British empire" in the circular for England.
   6. On May 7 William Pitt had introduced a motion for moderate parliamentary reform in the House of Commons. Although it was defeated, with
only one-third of the members voting in favor, reformers like Christopher
Wyvill were encouraged by the tone of the debate: John Ehrman, *The
Younger Pitt* (3 vols., New York and Stanford, Calif., 1969–96), I, 73–6.

Volunteers (vast numbers of whom are freeholders) shall determine on, the other freeholders and people in general, who are
not Volunteers, will adopt & Support by every means in their
power—the aged fathers cannot differ from their Sons, respecting a matter on which depends every thing, that either holds
dear for themselves, or their Posterity—

That you may see the very depraved state of our representation it is necessary to observe, that out of three hundred Members, of which our House of Commons consists, two hundred
& twenty are returned by Boroughs. Those one hundred & ten
Bouroughs are divided into three Classes— 1st. Those where
the right of Election is vested in the Protestant Inhabitants at
large— 2d Those where the right of Election is vested, in the
Chief Majestrate Burgesses & Freemen— 3d Those where
the right of Election is confined to the Chief Majestrate &
Burgesses— frequently not exceeding five or Six in number &
seldom above ten or twelve—

Almost all the Boroughs are venal & Corrupt, or implicitly
obedient to the arbitary will of their respective Land lords, who
dictate to the Electors in the most absolute manner, those Land
lords, claim by prescription a kind of property in those Boroughs, which they transfer by sale, like an Estate, & receive
from eight thousand to Nine thousand pounds for a Borough.
And a seat for a Bourough is generally sold for Two thousand
pounds, so that every Seven or Eight Years, the borough brings
In Four thousand pounds to the Patron— Unhappily for Ireland our Counties are also too much governed by our Peers—&
great men, whose influence over many of their respective ten-
ants is very great, & this consideration has given rise here, to a
doubt in the minds of many well meaning men, as to the propriety of adding to the Number of knights of the Shire—as generally now two great families endeavour to divide between them
the Seats for the County, the others remain Neuter or join the
independent interest, it is alledged were there Six Seats for the
County—*six* great families woud divide them, and against such
a junction, the independent freeholders woud not be able to
make any effectual opposition—

May we now intreat as a most important favour conferred on
not only us, but on this Kingdom, that you may be pleased to

favour us with your sentiments & advice, as to the best, most eligible & most practicable mode of destroying, restraining, or counteracting this Hydra of Corruption, Borough Influence; that we may be enabled to lay yr. opinion before the Provincial assembly of Delagates at Dungannon; and as our last meeting for arranging buisness previous thereunto, is fixed to be on the twentieth of August, we hope you will be obliging enough, to forward your reply so as to be with us about that time—

Many apologies are due for this long address & for the very great trouble we have requested you to take, but we are Young in Politicks, & wish for information from men of more wisdom—experience—& abilities. This however we may venture to assert, that if we can only be directed to the best mode, The mass of the inhabitants of Ireland is at this moment so compleatly alive & sensible to the necessity of a well digested Reform—that there cannot remain a doubt, that what it attempts in conjunction with the Virtuous part of England, must be effectual—

The several matters on which we have requested your opinion are thrown into one Veiw in the following Queries— In order to the purity of Parliament & to restore that constitutional controul, which the constituent body shoud have over the Representative—

1st. Is it necessary that the Boroughs, when the right of election is vested in a few, and which in general are at the absolute disposal of one or two persons—should be disfranchised, and in their place the County Representatives increased—

2d The protestant inhabitants consist of near one million who return three hundred members, woud it be wise to encrease the Number of Representatives of the Nation at large?

3d A plausible objection (mentioned above) has been raised against an increase of County Representatives, has that argument much weight, and if it has—is it remediable—

4th. Should the right of suffrage be extended, and if it should, who are the proper objects of such extension—?[7]

5th. In order to gaurd against undue influence woud it be wise to have the Members returned by Ballot?

7. An oblique reference to the potential extension of the franchise to Irish Catholics: Rogers, *Irish Volunteers and Catholic Emancipation*, p. 90.

6th. Woud not a limitation of the duration of Parliaments to a shorter term then eight Years have excellent effects, & shd. it be less then triennial?

7th. If the abolition of the enslaved Boroughs is necessary, woud it be equitable or expedient, that they be purchased by the Nation—

8th. What specific mode of Reform, in the representation of Ireland best suits your own Ideas—considering the situation of this Country and what are the Steps which you conceive best adapted to effect the Reform—

You will be so obliging as to direct your reply to our Chairman Leiut. Col. Sharman at Lisburn—[8]

The long Connexion that has subsisted between America & this Country, and the ties of Nature which must ever hold that Country dear to this—must plead our apology for this Address.

Signed by order.   HENRY JOY. JUNR
                                             Secry of the 45 Corps

John Jay: Account of Conversations with Franklin

AD: Columbia University Library

On July 19, the day after the American peace commissioners finalized their letter to Livingston, John Adams left for Holland, and Franklin and Jay, to judge by the present document, indulged in some moments of relaxed conversation. The thirty-eight-year-old Jay had been living at the Hôtel Valentinois with his family for more than a month, and Franklin seemed comfortable enough with him by this time to reminisce in an unguarded way about prominent people he had met as a young man, in many cases before Jay was born. Jay recorded these stories in a small quire reserved for occasional anecdotes about people, which he began in 1781 and continued through the spring of 1784. In addition to the two entries presented here, Jay also recorded anecdotes Franklin told him on unspecified days in September, 1783, and March, 1784, which will be published in

---

8. The original circular letter for England ended here.

John Jay

our next volume.⁹ Franklin would eventually include some of these stories in his autobiography, but most of what he told Jay remained private. Both of the reminiscences recorded on July 19 begin with anecdotes about New York attorneys, leading us to suspect that Jay had prompted them.

19 July 1783
Dr. Franklin told me that not long after the elder Lewis Morris (who was once chief Justice of N York) came to the Governmt. of N Jersey, he involved himself in a Dispute with the Assembly of that Province—¹ The Doctr. (who was then a printer at Pha.) went to Burlington while the Assembly was sitting there, & were engaged in the Dispute with their Govr.— The House had referred his Message to a Committee, consisting of some of their principal Members, Jos. Cooper was one of them—but tho they were Men of good Understanding & respectable, yet there was not one among them capable of writing a proper ansr. to the Message—and Cooper who was acquaintd with the Dr. prevailed upon him to undertake it.— He did and went thro the Business much to their Satisfaction.— In Consideration of the Aid he gave them in that Way then & afterwards, they made him their Printer (this shews the then State of Literature in Jersey).²
Robert Hunter Morris, the Son of the former, and who for about a Year was Govr. of Pennsylvania, the Dr. knew very well— It seems that the Dr. was at New York on His Way to

9. All of Jay's entries are in Morris, *Jay: Peace*, pp. 712–19.
1. One of many during Morris' tenure as governor of New Jersey (1738–46): *ANB*.
2. J. A. Leo Lemay identified the "ghostwritten" speech mentioned here as the N.J. Assembly's reply of April 25, 1740, to a message the governor delivered on April 18, the same day the Assembly appointed BF to print the legislature's *Votes and Proceedings*. If this is the case, as Lemay points out, then BF's appointment as printer predated his composing the Assembly's answer: J. A. Leo Lemay, *The Life of Benjamin Franklin* (3 vols., Philadelphia, 2006–08), II, 504–9.
Although BF had intended to write about this incident in his autobiography ("Writing for Jersey Assembly" is the last entry of the outline Abel James discovered and sent to him at the end of 1782), he never did so. For the outline entry see *Autobiog.*, p. 271; for James's cover letter urging BF to finish the autobiography see XXXVIII, 425–9.

Boston when Morris arrived there from England— He asked
the Dr. many Questions abt. Pennsylvania, abt. the Temper of
the People, and whether he thought it difficult for him to pass
his Time agreable among them— The Dr. told him nothing wd
be more easy if he avoided Disputes with the Assembly—but
replied he laughingly, *why wd. you have me deprive myself of one
of my greatest pleasures*— He was fond of disputing and thought
he had Talents for it— However added he I will take your advice— On Franklin's Return from Boston to Pha, he found the
Govr. and Assembly in warm Altercations— The Dr. was a
Member of the Assembly, and was appointed to Draw up their
answrs. Morris after having sent a Message to the Assembly,
met Saml. Rhodes and asked him what he thought of it—
Rhodes said he thought it very smart— Ah sd. Morris I thought
so too when I had finished it—but tomorrow we shall see Benj.
Franklin's Answer and then I suspect we shall both change our
Minds— Altho he knew that Franklin conducted the Dispute
agt. him—yet they were always good Friends, and frequently
dined together &c—[3] When the Dr.'s Son was many Years afterwards made Govr of Jersey, & was going to take upon him
the Govt. Morris came to meet him on the Road, and behaved
kindly & in a friendly Manner— He was a very good natured
Man—had Talents & Learning but his Imagination was too
strong & he was not deep in any thing—
   The elder Lewis Morris was brought up by an Uncle— When
young he was very wild— His Uncle sent him to the W. Indies
with a Vessel and Cargo, which he spent— On his Return he
married—[4] His Uncle observed to him on that occasion "that

---

3. Morris (v, 527–8n) appears throughout vols. 5 and 6. The version of
this story and the account of their friendship that BF eventually included
in part 3 of his autobiography is more detailed in certain aspects but does
not include the conversation between Morris and Samuel Rhoads (11, 406n):
Autobiog., pp. 212–14, 239.
   4. The uncle was the merchant and sugar planter Lewis Morris, Sr.,
who raised Lewis Morris after his parents' death in 1672. Young Morris' trip to the West Indies was not sponsored by his uncle, however; he
ran away from home. Lewis Morris, Sr., died only days after bringing his
nephew back to New York in 1691, leaving him a substantial inheritance
and having arranged his marriage into the prominent Graham family:

now when he wanted every thing he got himself a Wife". He replied "that now he did not want every thing"— His Uncle asked him What it was that he did not want.— He answered that *now he did not want a Wife*— Dr. Franklin was told this by some of Morris's Cotemporaries—

19 July 1783
Dr. Franklin says he was very well and long acquainted With Andw. Hamilton the Lawyer who distinguished himself on Zengers Tryal at New York—[5] He was a Scotchman who came young into Pensylvania, some said he came a Servant— Mr Brooks who in those Days was an old Man told Dr. Franklin that he had seen Hamilton who then lived at Lewis Town studying the Law in an Osnabrigs Shirt and Trowsers, that he observed him often, and that from his great application he predicted that he wd. one Day make a Figure in that Proffession— He was a Man of exceeding good Talents & ready Elocution— Wm. Allen then one of the most Wealthy Men in Pensa. & afterwards Chf. Justice—married Hamilton's Daughter—[6] That Event gave Hamilton more Weight & Consideration— He practiced generously, & took no Fees in the Cause of Zenger. The City of New York presented him with the Freedom of the City in a Gold Box with handsome Inscriptions—
He left a good Estate, made by laying out his Money as he acquired it in Lotts & Lands wh. rose daily in Value—
His Son[7] was afterwards Govr of Pensylv.—sustained a

Eugene R. Sheridan, *Lewis Morris, 1671–1746: a Study in Early American Politics* (Syracuse, 1981), pp. 1–8.

5. The prominent Philadelphia lawyer and politician Andrew Hamilton (*c.* 1676–1741), whose origins remain obscure, became famous for his precedent-setting defense of publisher John Peter Zenger, who was tried for seditious libel in New York in 1735: I, 333; *ANB.* BF met Hamilton on his first voyage to England in 1724. He had already written in part 1 of the autobiography about how he had cultivated that friendship and how useful it was but did not include any of the personal details mentioned here: *Autobiog.*, pp. 93–4.

6. William Allen (III, 296–7n) married Margaret Hamilton in 1734: *ANB.*

7. James Hamilton: III, 327–8n.

good Character, had a decent Share of Talents but not much
improved—

Poem on Presenting Franklin with a Walking Stick from the Duchesse de Deux-Ponts

Printed by Didot l'aîné (1783): Yale University Library, University
of Pennsylvania Library, Library of Congress

This undated poem and Kéralio's letter of July 20 written on behalf
of the duchesse de Deux-Ponts (below), concern the gift reproduced
on the facing page: a walking stick topped with a gold pommel in
the shape of a liberty cap. The duchesse sent it to replace the walking stick she had given to Franklin in 1779, which he had lost.[8] The
author of this poem is unknown, and no manuscript copy has been
found.[9] Because Kéralio probably delivered the gift, he also may have
written the lines.

In a codicil to his will, Franklin bequeathed his "fine Crabtree
Walking Stick with a Gold Head curiously wrought in the Form
of the Cap of Liberty" to his "Friend and the Friend of Mankind,
General Washington." He added that "If it were a Sceptre he has
merited it, and would become it. It was a present to me from that excellent Woman Madame de Forbach, the Dowager Duchess of Deux
Ponts, connected with some Verses which should go with it."[1] If a
copy of the verses did accompany the bequest, it has not survived
among Washington's papers.[2]

8. For the original gift see XXIX, 710, 748.
9. Three examples of the imprint have been located to date, as listed in
our source note. It is discussed and reproduced in Luther S. Livingston,
Franklin and His Press at Passy . . . (New York, 1914), pp. 190–2. Livingston conjectures that BF must have received the verses in handwritten form
and commissioned the imprint. We are skeptical of the latter claim, given
the poem's extravagant hyperbole.
1. Codicil to BF's Will, July 17, 1788 (APS).
2. See W. W. Abbot *et al.*, eds., *The Papers of George Washington*, Presidential Series (16 vols. to date, Charlottesville and London, 1987–), V,
388–90.

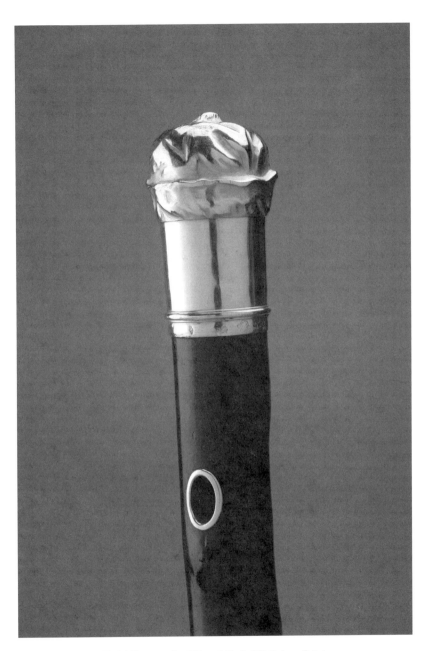

Gold Pommel of Franklin's Walking Stick

[before July 20, 1783]

A Mr. FRANKLIN,

En lui présentant, de la part de Madame la Comtesse Douairiere de Deux Ponts, un bâton d'épine surmonté d'une pomme d'or, figurant le chapeau de la liberté.

Dans les plaines de Marathon,
Où l'insolence Musulmane
A d'éternels affronts condamne
La postérité de Solon;
Parmi la ronce et les épines
Qui couvrent ces bords malheureux,
Et cachent les cendres divines
Des sages, des héros fameux,
La Liberté, votre déesse,
Avant d'abandonner la Grece,
Arracha ce bâton noueux:
On le vit aux Alpes Pennines,
Pour terrasser l'Autrichien,
Briller entre les javelines
Du valeureux Helvétien;[3]
Elle en fit depuis une lance,
Lorsque dans les champs de Trenton
Elle dirigeoit la vaillance
Et l'audace de Washington.
   Ce symbole de la victoire
Qu'orne aujourd'hui le chapeau du grand Tell,
   Ce ferme appui que votre gloire
   Rendra désormais immortel,
Assurera vos pas au Temple de Mémoire.

DE L'IMPRIMERIE DE DIDOT L'AÎNÉ, 1783.

---

3. William Tell, the hero of Swiss legend and title character in Antoine-Marin Lemierre's 1767 tragedy, which established him as a symbol of national liberation; see XXXIV, 543n.

From Silas Deane[4]

ALS: University of Pennsylvania Library

Sir   London 20th July 1783

I have been very credibly informed that The Count De Vergennes, & others at Versailles have lately expressed, great resentment against Me personally, which gives Me the greatest
uneasiness, on Account of my personal Safety at Paris, where
I wish To be, To adjust & Settle my Accts.,[5] the best foundation, for me to expect Justice from in other respects. I therefore

4. As soon as the preliminaries were signed in January, Deane, in desperate financial difficulties and living in Ghent, asked Bancroft (in a now-
missing letter) to sound out the American commissioners about his intention to go immediately to London in order to recover the balance due him
from a private venture. Bancroft reported on Feb. 4 that Jay had objected.
Deane wrote an angry letter to Jay, to which the latter responded that he
had never said "it would be taken ill" but rather cautioned Deane to consider the further risks to his reputation if he should make such a journey so
soon. Deane answered on Feb. 28: now that he understood that there was
no objection to his trip, he would leave very shortly. In fact, he did not arrive in London until late March. The date is impossible to pinpoint, as his
reports of his arrival varied according to correspondent: *Deane Papers*, v,
122–4, 128, 131–2, 135–8, 142–4, 145–6, 148–50.

 5. Deane had been waiting for years to resolve his outstanding accounts
with Congress (see XXXVII, 43–4, 76–7), a situation to which BF was sympathetic: XXXVIII, 455. Deane communicated his desperation in many of
the letters cited in the note above. The fear of coming to Paris, however,
was hardly new. He had wanted to stop in Paris to settle certain financial
affairs before going to London, but, as he wrote on Feb. 28 in letters to Jay,
Bancroft, and Chaumont, he had heard that his "person . . . would be in
danger" if he set foot in that city, and that a "wicked and malicious" man
in Brussels had written "a long letter to the Count de Vergennes, abusing
me in the most outrageous manner": *Deane Papers*, v, 133–4, 140, 143–4.

 Thomas Barclay informed Deane on March 3 that he had received a congressional commission to settle all U.S. accounts in Europe, and recommended that they review Deane's accounts when he returned to France.
Throughout the spring, however, illness and the pressure of other affairs
prevented Barclay from setting a meeting date. In July, Deane expressed to
Barclay the concerns about coming to Paris that he writes here to BF (and
reiterated to Barclay on Aug. 28). He may have proposed coming to Paris in
the fall, as he told his brother on July 25 that he hoped to do: *Deane Papers*,
v, 144–5, 154–7, 161–2, 179–80, 187–8.

request of You, to inform Me, by a Letter, if I may rely on being personally safe, & unmolested in France, and at Paris, whilst necessarily detained there, on the Settlement of my Accompts, I shall dispatch the Business, as soon as possible, & hope it will be without my giving the least Offence, to any one; I am extremely sorry to have cause to Trouble You, on this Occasion, but with strong prejudices against Me both in America, and in France, and without protectors, or patrons, to apply to, I am obliged to do it, & presume that You will see the propriety of my precaution, & request.

I have the honor to be with the most Sinere Respect & Esteem Your most Obedt. & Very humle servt.   S DEANE

His Excelly. B. Franklin Esqr.

Addressed: A Monsr. / Monsr: Franklin / Minister plenipo. des / Etats Unies de L'Amerique / en France / à Passy pres de / Paris

From Kéralio

ALS: American Philosophical Society

Paris, le 20e. juillet. 1783.

Nôtre excellente Douairiere, mon respectable ami, Espere que vous aurés reçu avec votre bonté ordinaire la petite marque d'amitié qu'elle a cru devoir vous donner, après la perte que vous aviés faite de sa premiere canne.⁶ Plaignés la de n'avoir pu vous aller voir depuis long-temps; mais vous concevés toutes les affaires tous les embarras dont elle est accablée en ce moment-ci: elle vient de partir pour Versailles d'ou elle reviendra lundi, et à son retour elle se propose bien de vous aller chercher; en attendant elle me charge de vous mander que vous lui devés Une

6. For background on this "petite marque d'amitié" see the Poem on Presenting Franklin with a Walking Stick from the Duchesse de Deux-Ponts, [before July 20].

médaille pour remplacer celle qu'elle a cédée à mr. de Vauban.[7] Ce monument lui est trop cher pour ne pas desirer d'en avoir un en sa possession: elle vous prie encore de lui renvoyer les nouvelles Littéraires qu'elle vous a prêtées.

Recevés, mon respectable ami, l'hommage de ma profonde et tendre Vénération,   LE CHR. DE KERALIO

Mille et mille amitiés, S.V.P. à mr. votre petit-fils.

Notation: Keralio 20 Juillet 1780.—

From Graf von Schönfeld[8]

ALS: American Philosophical Society

Monsieur   a Paris ce 20 Juillet 1783
    Ayant ordre de ma Cour de Vous presenter Mr. Thieriot de Leipsic et qui va se rendre à Philadelphie en qualité de Commissionaire du Commerce de Saxe,[9] je Vous prie Monsieur, de

---

7. BF had sent her a *Libertas Americana* medal in April: XXXIX, 460. The comte de Vauban had served in America as one of Rochambeau's aides-de-camp: XXXIII, 158n; Bodinier, *Dictionnaire,* under Le Prestre.

8. In the four months since he had last written (XXXIX, 311–12), the Saxon minister had puzzled over why he had been unable to engage BF in establishing formal commercial relations, attributing BF's reticence to such reasons as his own perceived errors of protocol and the influence of France, a commercial rival of Saxony. By June, he had realized that Saxony's proposals were "vague et générale" by comparison with the maritime nations: William E. Lingelbach, "Saxon-American Relations, 1778–1828," *American Hist. Rev.,* XVII (1911–12), 521–3.

9. Philipp Thieriot was selected for this position on June 24 and awarded an annual salary of 1,500 thalers. His mission was to establish mercantile relations between the two countries and assist his fellow Saxon merchants. He also intended to establish his own business in Philadelphia. When informing Carmichael of the appointment, the Saxon minister to Spain described Thieriot as a "merchant of Bordeaux" born in Leipzig, and characterized him as honest and intelligent: Lingelbach, "Saxon-American Relations," pp. 524–5; Horst Dippel, *Germany and the American Revolution, 1770–1800* ..., trans. Bernhard A. Uhlendorf (Chapel Hill, N.C., 1977), p. 270; Wharton, *Diplomatic Correspondence,* VI, 609–10.

JULY 21, 1783

vouloir bien me faire Savoir si je ne Vous generois point en me rendant chés Vous avec lui demain Lundy ou Mercredy dans la matinée.[1]
Agrées je Vous en prie Monsieur l'assurance des Sentimens respectueux avec les quels j'ai l'honneur d'être Monsieur Votre très hûmble et très obeissant Serviteur   DE SCHÖNFELD

Notation: Schonfeld: 20 Juillet 1783

From Elkanah Watson, Jr.   LS: American Philosophical Society

Sir   London[2] 21st. July 1783
    I beg leave to crave the Liberty of introduceing to your acquaintance Griffin Green Esqr. who has lately arrivd from America, & is nearly related to that Ilustrious Character Genl: Green—[3] The respectibility of this Gentlemans character together with the information you may collect from him respecting the present state of affairs in America, will I presume sufficiently plead my excuse for the Liberty I have taken.—
    I am, most respectfully Your Excellencys, Very hhble Servt
                                                            E. WATSON JR.

His Excellency Doctor Franklin Passy

1. They may have come on Wednesday. On that day, BF wrote three letters of introduction for Thieriot and sent them to Schönfeld, as requested. See BF to Schönfeld and to Livingston, July 23.
    2. In a July 11 letter to WTF, Watson gave his return address as Watson, Coussoul & Co., No. 2 Billiter Square. He needed WTF's help with two commissions, asking him to procure an elegant miniature of BF for the bracelet of "one of the most accomplish'd Lady's in the City," made to the dimensions he sketched, and to send a "handsome watch" for another lady. APS.
    3. Griffin Greene (1749–1804) was the first cousin of Gen. Nathanael Greene. He sailed from Newport for France on the brigantine *Minerva* on May 21 and remained in Europe until 1785: Richard K. Showman *et al.*, eds., *The Papers of General Nathanael Greene* (13 vols., Chapel Hill, N.C., 1976–2005), I, 107n; XII, 677–8; XIII, 132–3.

Addressed: His Excellency Dtor. Franklin— / Passy

Notation: Watson 21 Juillet 1783

Franklin's Responses to the Maréchale de Beauvau's Questions on Lightning Rods

D:[4] American Philosophical Society

On July 21, 1783, Bethia Alexander wrote to William Temple Franklin with a request from the maréchale de Beauvau, who was desperate for Franklin's advice on installing a lightning rod at her residence, the château du Val.[5] Temple was to place before his grandfather the paper she enclosed. "Une reponse tres exacte" was to be written in the margin beside each question, and the paper returned to Alexander "bien vite." Do hurry, she repeated, because if you delay, and if a lightning bolt should lack the decency to wait until the answers arrive, you will be filled with remorse.

Lightning rods were still relatively new to Paris. When the first two were installed in December, 1782, under the supervision of the abbé Bertholon (who had installed several in his native Lyon and elsewhere), the *Mercure de France* published their locations and dimensions, praised the abbé, and announced, with obvious relief, that Paris no longer lagged behind the countryside in this important development.[6] Any lingering doubts about the safety of these devices must

4. We surmise that this text, written in labored French by WTF on a torn sheet of paper, is his translation of responses that BF drafted in English. The French answers were doubtless copied onto Mme de Beauvau's sheet of questions and returned in accordance with Bethia Alexander's letter to WTF described in the headnote. This sheet is filed with Alexander's letter.

5. The château was in the forest of Saint-Germain, not far from the Alexanders' estate. Marie-Charlotte-Sylvie (Elisabeth-Charlotte) de Rohan-Chabot, princesse de Beauvau-Craon (1729–1807), was the wife of Charles-Just, maréchal prince de Beauvau-Craon, a distinguished military man and member of the Académie française and the Accademia della Crusca: *DBF,* under Beauvau; *Dictionnaire de la noblesse,* II, 740, 742; Georges Poull, *Fléville: son histoire et ses seigneurs, XIIIe s.–XIXe s.* (Rupt sur Moselle, 1988), pp. 122–6; Julia P. Mitchell, *St. Jean de Crèvecoeur* (New York, 1916), p. 81.

6. *Mercure de France (Jour. politique de Bruxelles),* Dec. 28, 1782, pp. 188–9. In vol. 38 we stated that the first lightning rods in Paris were

have been allayed when, in a highly anticipated ruling of May 31, the appeals court at Artois ordered Vyssery de Bois-Valée's lightning rod reinstated in Saint-Omer.[7] The urgency in this request from the maréchale de Beauvau, however, was surely due to the terrifying storms that had been sweeping across France, causing widespread destruction and loss of life. "Extraordinary lightning" was reported in the Paris region on July 2 and 3—14 strikes in one area, with four people killed—and again on July 15. Reports were also published of lightning strikes, ground tremors (were they subterranean thunder?), high winds, and torrential rains in the provinces. Adding to the general disquietude was the fact that since June the temperature had been unusually hot and the atmosphere clouded by a mysterious, smoke-like "dry fog" that obscured the sun's rays. La Lande and others wrote articles for the *Journal de Paris* attempting to reassure the frightened population that these conditions did not presage a major earthquake, like the recent one in Calabria. In the months and years to come, scientists throughout Europe would publish theories on the cause of this dry fog. Franklin himself speculated on possible causes in May, 1784.[8]

At the château du Val, it was the maréchale's husband who made the first inquiries about lightning rods, seeking advice from St. John

installed in December, 1783, citing an otherwise scrupulous work that misreported the year of this article in the *Mercure* and a personal letter written the same month by Bertholon: XXXVIII, 436n.

7. For the case see XXXVIII, 435–8; XXXIX, 237–8. The extensive brief published in November, 1782, by Buissart, the chief lawyer, was much discussed in Paris throughout the following spring: Jessica Riskin, *Science in the Age of Sensibility: the Sentimental Empiricists of the French Enlightenment* (Chicago and London, 2002), p. 175. Buissart left the oral arguments in May, 1783, to his junior colleague, Maximilien Robespierre; they are discussed in *ibid.*, pp. 176–84. The court's decision was announced in the *Mercure de France (Jour. politique de Bruxelles)*, June 21, 1783, pp. 135–7, where Robespierre was described as a young lawyer "d'un mérite rare" who had displayed "une éloquence & une sagacité qui donne la plus haute idée de ses connoissances."

8. For reports on the extreme weather conditions see the *Jour. de Paris* of July 1, 2, 9, 16, 21 (supp.), and 22, 1783; *Mercure de France (Jour. politique de Bruxelles)*, July 12 and 26, 1783, pp. 77–8, 175–6. In "Meteorological Imaginations and Conjectures," BF speculated that the fog of the previous summer might have been caused by burning celestial bodies whose smoke was trapped in the atmosphere or by volcanic dust from the recent eruptions in Iceland: Smyth, *Writings*, IX, 215–18.

de Crèvecœur, who was a regular guest at the family's Sunday dinners during the spring and early summer of 1783. Crèvecœur, according to his later account, recommended that a lightning rod be mounted atop a very tall mast in the middle of the courtyard—a plan, he claimed, that Franklin approved. In spite of the answers printed here that Franklin evidently returned to the maréchale, which hardly recommended it as a first choice, a mast was indeed constructed. Made from two poplar trunks grafted together, the pole, raised before a large crowd of friends, elevated the tip of a 12-foot lightning rod 89 feet into the sky. According to Crèvecœur, the structure created a sensation and caused many other "grands seigneurs" to protect their properties.[9]

[after July 21, 1783]

1

Avant de placer un Conducteur ou Paratonnere il est nécessaire que quelqu'un qui s'y entend bien, voye le Batiment qui est destiné a etre garanti de la foudre.

Dans un étendu aussi considerable que celle de 45 Toises, on croit qu'il sera bien d'eriger 4 Conducteurs à égale distance les uns des Autres, & communiquants ensemble par un barre de Fer sur le Toit du Batiment.

2

Il doit etre environ dix a douze Pieds plus haut que la partie la plus elevée du Batiment. 3. Il doit etre appliqué immediatement à la muraille.

4 Un Mât n'est pas necessaire pour le Soutient du Conducteur.

On trouvera cette Matiere très detaillé dans l'Ouvrage de M. Franklin sur l'Electricité.— Et on fera bien d'employer un des Ouvriers de Versailles ou de Paris, qui ont deja construit des Conducteurs.

9. Robert de Crèvecœur, *Saint John de Crèvecoeur, sa vie et ses ouvrages (1735–1813)* (Paris, 1883), pp. 72–3. After a July 10 electrical storm in Normandy, where he then was staying, Crèvecœur also convinced more than 20 people to install lightning rods on their homes, and insisted that a lightning rod be installed on the ship that carried him back to New York, the *Courrier de l'Europe;* see Mitchell, *St. Jean de Crèvecoeur,* pp. 81–4.

From the Princesse de Chimay[1]

L: American Philosophical Society

[before July 22, 1783]

Made. la Psse. de Chimay prie monsieur Francklin de diner au traitement que la Reine donne à Madame l'Ambassadrice d'Angleterre, chez Mr. le Marquis de Talaru Premier Maitre d'hôtel de Sa Majesté, mardi 22 juillet[2]

Addressed: A Monsieur / Monsieur Francklin, ministre Plénipotentiaire / des Etats unis de L'Amérique Septentrionale / A Passy

To Robert R. Livingston

LS,[3] press copy of LS, and transcript: National Archives; AL (draft): Library of Congress

Sir,   Passy, July 22d.[–26] 1783.

You have complained sometimes with reason of not hearing often[4] from your foreign Ministers; we have had cause to make

1. Laure-Auguste de Fitz-James (b. 1744) was the wife of the prince de Chimay et d'Empire and Grand d'Espagne. As *dame d'honneur* to Marie-Antoinette her duties included sending out invitations for the queen and presenting the guests to her on these occasions: *Dictionnaire de la noblesse,* I, 388; VIII, 73; Marie Cornaz, *Les Princes de Chimay et la musique: une famille de mélomanes . . .* (Brussels and Tournai, 2002), p. 36.

2. The Duke of Manchester had presented his credentials at court on May 6: XXXIX, 568. Elizabeth Dashwood, his wife, was presented to the queen and royal princesses on July 22, with the king himself making a brief appearance. The *traitement,* a dinner of high ceremony which followed, was overseen by César-Marie de Talaru, marquis de Chalmazel, the queen's *premier maître d'hôtel* (*Dictionnaire de la noblesse,* XVIII, 763–4). It was served in the *salle des ambassadeurs* at Versailles, and was attended by all the court officers, ladies-in-waiting to the queen and royal princesses, ministers of state, and foreign ambassadors: Marc-Marie, marquis de Bombelles, *Journal,* ed. Jean Grassion and Frans Durif (7 vols. to date, Geneva, 1977–), I, 245–6; *Gaz. de Leyde,* Aug. 1. For the Duke and Duchess of Manchester see the *ODNB,* under Montagu.

3. In WTF's hand, with minor corrections by BF.

4. In his draft, BF interlined "with reason" and "often."

the same Complaint, six full Months having intervened between the latest Date of your preceeding Letters, and the receipt of those per Capt. Barney.[5] During all this Time we were ignorant of the Reception of the Provisional Treaty, and the Sentiments of Congress upon it, which if we had recd. sooner, might have forwarded the Proceedings on the Definitive Treaty, and perhaps brought them to a Conclusion at a time more favourable than the present. But these occasional Interruptions of Correspondence are the inevitable Consequences of a State of War & of such remote Situations.

Barney had a short Passage, and arrived some Days before Col. Ogden, who also brought Dispatches from you,[6] all of which are come safe to hand.

We, the Commissioners, have in our joint Capacity written a Letter to you, which you will receive with this.[7] I shall now answer yours of March 26. May 9 & May 31st. It gave me great Pleasure to learn by the first, that the News of the Peace diffused general Satisfaction. I will not now take upon me to justify the apparent Reserve respecting this Court at the Signature, which you disapprove. We have touch'd upon it in our general Letter. I do not see, however, that they have much Reason to complain of that Transaction. Nothing was stipulated to their Prejudice, and none of the Stipulations were to have force, but by a subsequent Act of their own. I suppose indeed that they have not complained of it, or you would have sent us a Copy of the Complaint, that we might have answer'd it. I long since satisfy'd Count de V. about it here.[8] We did what appear'd to all of us best at the time, and if we have done Wrong, the Congress will do right, after hearing us, to censure us. Their Nomination of five Persons to the Service, seems to mark that they had some Dependance on our joint Judgment; since one alone could have made a Treaty by Direction of the French Ministry, as well as

5. As BF had written to Livingston on June 12, above.
6. For Matthias Ogden and the letters he carried see XXXIX, 518–19, 535–6. He arrived in Paris on July 12: *Adams Papers*, XV, 106.
7. Above, July 18.
8. For BF's dealings with Vergennes on this matter see XXXVIII, 461–2, 464–6, 487–8n.

twenty. I will only add, that with respect to myself, neither the Letter from M. Marbois handed to us thro' the British Negocia-tors, (a suspicious Channel) nor the Conversations respecting the Fishery, the Boundaries, the Royalists &ca. recommending Moderation in our Demands, are of Weight sufficient in my Mind to fix an Opinion that this Court wish'd to restrain us in obtaining any Degree of Advantage we could prevail on our Enemies to accord; since those Discourses are fairly resolvable, by supposing a very natural Apprehension, that we, relying too much on the Ability of France to continue the War in our Fa-vour, & supply us constantly with Money, might insist on more Advantages than the English would be willing to grant, and thereby lose the Opportunity of making Peace so necessary to all our Friends.[9]

I ought not however to conceal from you that one of my Col-leagues[1] is of a very different Opinion from me in these Mat-ters. He thinks the French Minister one of the greatest Enemies of our Country, that he would have straitned our Boundaries to prevent the Growth of our People, contracted our Fishery to obstruct the Increase of our Seamen, & retained the Royal-ists among us to keep us divided; that he privately opposes all our Negociations with foreign Courts, and afforded us during the War the Assistance we received, only to keep it alive, that we might be so much the more weaken'd by it: That to think of Gratitude to France is the greatest of Follies, and that to be influenc'd by it, would ruin us. He makes no Secret of his hav-ing these Opinions, expresses them publickly, sometimes in presence of the English Ministers;[2] and speaks of hundreds of

9. For the intercepted letter and Vergennes' view of the negotiations see XXXVIII, 220n, 504.

1. JA. Because Livingston was no longer in office when this letter arrived, it was referred to a congressional committee. Elbridge Gerry copied this entire paragraph and sent it to Abigail Adams. She sent it to her husband, who received it on May 5, 1784: *Adams Correspondence*, V, 250–2, 280–2.

2. BF had complained similarly to Robert Morris in March: XXXIX, 301–2. In May, Samuel Cooper alerted BF to the accusations against him and the French that JA had written to correspondents in America. That letter seems to have arrived in September: XXXIX, 561–2.

Instances which he could produce in Proof of them, none however have yet appear'd to me, unless the Conversations & Letter abovementioned are reckoned such. If I were not convinced of the real Inability of this Court to furnish the farther Supply's we asked,[3] I should suspect these Discourses of a Person in his Station, might have influenced the Refusal; but I think they have gone no farther than to occasion a Suspicion, that we have a considerable Party of Antigallicans in America, who are not Tories, and consequently to produce some Doubts of the continuance of our Friendship. As such Doubts may hereafter have a bad Effect, I think we cannot take too much Care to remove them; and it is therefore I write this to put you on your guard, (believing it my Duty, tho' I know that I hazard by it a mortal Enmity) and to caution you respecting the Insinuations of this Gentleman against this Court, & the Instances he supposes of their Ill-Will to us, which I take to be as imaginary as I know his Fancies to be, that Count de V. and myself are continually plotting against him & employing the News Writers of Europe to depreciate his Character, &ca. but as Shakespear says, "Trifles light as Air, &ca."[4] I am persuaded however that he means well for his Country, is always an honest Man, often a Wise One, but sometimes and in some things, absolutely[5] out of his Senses.

When the Commercial Article, mentioned in yours of the 26th.[6] was struck out of our proposed Preliminaries by the British Ministry, the Reason given was that sundry Acts of Parliament still in force were against it, and must be first repealed, which I believe was really their Intention; and sundry Bills were accordingly brought in for that purpose: But new Ministers with

3. See Vergennes to the Commissioners, July 5.
4. "Trifles light as air / Are to the jealous confirmations strong / As proofs of holy writ": *Othello*, act III, scene iii, lines 322–4. BF had written most of the second line in his draft, but deleted it.
5. BF interlined this word in his draft.
6. Article 4 of the first draft of the preliminary articles (XXXVIII, 193–4), whose subsequent revision had been lamented by Livingston: XXXIX, 394. It called for American ships and merchants to be treated as British while in Britain and vice versa.

different Principles succeeding, a Commercial Proclamation totally different from those Bills has lately appear'd. I send inclosed
a Copy of it.[7] We shall try what can be done in the definitive
Treaty towards setting aside that Proclamation: But if it should
be persisted in, it will then be a Matter worthy the attentive Discussion of Congress, whether it will be most prudent to retort
with a similar Regulation in order to force its Repeal (which
may possibly tend to bring on another Quarrel) or to let it pass
without Notice, and leave it to its own Inconvenience, or rather
Impracticability in the Execution, and to the Complaints of the
West India Planters, who must all pay much dearer for our Produce under those Restrictions. I am not enough Master of the
Course of our Commerce to give an Opinion on this particular
Question; and it does not behove me to do it; yet I have seen so
much Embarrassment and so little Advantage in all the restraining & Compulsive Systems, that I feel myself strongly inclined
to believe that a State which leaves all her Ports open to all the
World upon equal Terms, will by that means have foreign Commodities cheaper, sell its own Productions dearer, and be on the
whole the most prosperous.[8] I have heard some Merchants say,
that there is ten per Ct. difference between *Will you buy?* and
Will you sell? When Foreigners bring us their Goods, they want
to part with them speedily, that they may purchase their Cargoes & dispatch their Ships which are at constant Charges in our
Ports; we have then the Advantage of their *Will you buy?* and
when they demand our Produce we have the Advantage of their
Will you sell? and the concurring Demands of a Number also
contribute to raise our Prices. Thus both these Questions are in
our Favour at home, against us abroad.— The employing however of our own Ships and raising a Breed of Seamen among us,
tho' it should not be a matter of so much private Profit as some
imagine, is nevertheless of political Importance & must have
Weight in considering this Subject.

The Judgment you make of the Conduct of France in the
Peace, and the greater Glory acquired by her Moderation than

7. The July 2 Order in Council; see Falconer to BF, July 8.
8. An elaboration of an opinion expressed in 1781: XXXV, 83.

even by her Arms, appears to me perfectly just.[9] The Character of this Court and Nation seems of late Years to be considerably changed. The Ideas of Aggrandisement by Conquest, are out of Fashion; & those of Commerce are more enlightened, and more generous than heretofore. We shall soon, I believe, feel something of this, in our being admitted to a greater Freedom of Trade with their Islands,[1] The Wise here think France great enough; and its Ambition at present seems to be only that of Justice and Magnanimity towards other Nations, Fidelity & Utility to its Allies.

The Ambassador of Portugal was much pleased with the Proceedings relating to their Vessel which you sent me, and assures me they will have a good Effect at his Court. He appears extreamly desirous of a Treaty with our States; I have accordingly proposed to him the Plan of one, (nearly the same with that sent me for Sweden) and after my agreeing to some Alterations, he has sent it to his Court for Approbation.[2] He told me at Versailles last Tuesday[3] that he expected its Return to him on Saturday next, and anxiously desired that I would not dispatch our Pacquet without it, that Congress might consider it, and if approved, send a Commission to me or some other Minister, to sign it. I venture to go thus far in treating, on the Authority only of a kind of general Power, given formerly by a Resolution

9. XXXIX, 394.
1. On July 15 Vergennes informed the commissioners that two free ports were being secured to the United States as provided by Article 32 of the Treaty of Amity and Commerce (XXV, 624–5). According to JA's account, these were on Saint Lucia and Martinique: JA to Livingston, July 16, *Adams Papers*, XV, 123. In fact, this new French policy was less liberal than what had occurred during the war, when American ships had enjoyed access to all ports in the French West Indies. In early 1783 France had quietly reverted to the regulations of 1767 which permitted access only to Port-du-Cârenage, Saint Lucia, and Môle-Saint-Nicolas, Saint-Domingue. These regulations also limited what cargoes could be carried, although colonial officials were slow to impose these restrictions. A permanent policy, however, was still under debate; see the editorial note in *Morris Papers*, VIII, 681–4.
2. See the Portuguese Counterproposal for a Treaty of Amity and Commerce, [c. June 7].
3. July 15.

of Congress, to Messrs. Franklin, Dean, & Lee:[4] but a special Commission seems more proper to compleat a Treaty, and more agreable to the usual Forms of such Business.

I am in just the same Situation with Denmark: That Court by its Minister here has desired a Treaty with us. I have proposed a Plan formed on that sent me for Sweden;[5] it has been under Consideration some time at Copenhaguen, and is expected here this Week, so that I may possibly send that also by this Conveyance. You will have seen by my Letter to the Danish Prime Minister that I did not forget the Affair of the Prizes. What I then wrote produced a verbal Offer made me here, of £10,000 Sterling proposed to be given by his Majesty to the Captors, if I would accept it as a full discharge of our Demand. I could not do this, I said, because it was not more than a fifth Part of the estimated Value.[6] In answer I was told that the Estimation was probably extravagant, that it would be difficult to come at the Knowledge of their true Value, and that whatever they might be worth in themselves, they should not be estimated as of such Value to us, when at Bergen, since the English probably watch'd them, and might have retaken them in their Way to America; at least they were at the common Risque of the Seas and Enemies, and the Insurance was a considerable Draw-Back: That this Sum might be considered as so much saved for us by the Kings Interference; for that if the English Claimants had been suffer'd to carry the Cause into the common Courts, they must have recover'd the Prizes by the Laws of Denmark: It was added that the Kings Honour was concerned; that he sincerely desired our Friendship, but he would avoid, by giving this Sum in the Form of a Present to the Captors, the Appearance of its

---

4. The resolution of Oct. 16, 1776: XXII, 629–30.

5. As BF wrote to Livingston on April 15: XXXIX, 468. See the annotation of Walterstorff to BF, May 20.

6. BF had sent Livingston a copy of his letter to Rosencrone with his April 15 letter cited above. The verbal offer described here was made on May 29; see the annotation of Rosencrone to BF, July 8. Ever since the prize ships were seized, the Danish ministry had known that BF valued them at £50,000 sterling; he had written this explicitly in his initial protest: XXXI, 264–5.

being exacted from him as the Reparation of an Injury, when it was really intended rather as a Proof of his strong Disposition to cultivate a good Understanding with us. I reply'd that the Value might possibly be exaggerated; but that we did not desire more than should be found just upon Enquiry; and that it was not difficult to learn from London what Sums were insured upon the Ships & Cargos which would be some Guide; and that a reasonable Abatement might be made for the Risque; but that the Congress could not in Justice to their Mariners deprive them of any Part that was truely due to those brave Men, whatever Abatement they might think fit to make (as a Mark of their Regard for the Kings Friendship) of the Part belonging to the Publick: that I had however no Instructions or Authority to make any Abatement of any kind, and could therefore only acquaint the Congress with the Offer & the Reasons that accompanied it, which I promised to state fully and candidly, (as I have now done) and attend their Orders: desiring only that it might be observed, we had presented our Complaint with Decency, that we had charged no Fault on the Danish Government but what might arise from Inattention or Precipitancy, and that we had intimated no Resentment but had waited with Patience & Respect the King's Determination, confiding that he would follow the equitable Disposition of his own Breast, by doing us Justice, as soon as he could do it with Conveniency; that the best and wisest Princes sometimes err'd, that it belong'd to the Condition of Man, and was therefore inevitable; and that the true honour in such Cases consisted not in disowning or hiding the Error, but in making ample Reparation. That tho' I could not accept what was offer'd on the Terms proposed, our Treaty might go on, and its Articles be prepar'd and consider'd; and in the meantime I hop'd his Danish Majesty would reconsider the Offer and make it more adequate to the Loss we had sustained. Thus that Matter rests; but I hourly expect to hear farther, and perhaps may have more to say on it before the Ship's Departure. I shall be glad to have the Proceedings you mention respecting the Brig. Providentia.[7] I hope the Equity and Justice of our

7. Which Livingston had offered to send, if it seemed necessary: XXXIX, 395–6.

Admiralty Courts respecting the Property of Strangers will Always maintain their Reputation; and I wish particularly to cultivate the Disposition of Friendship towards us apparent in the late Proceedings of Denmark, as the Danish Islands may be of use to our West India Commerce, while the English impolitic Restraints continue.

The Elector of Saxony, as I understand from his Minister here, has Thoughts of sending one to Congress, and proposing a Treaty of Commerce & Amity with us.[8] Prussia has likewise an Inclination to share in a Trade with America, and the Minister of that Court tho' he has not directly proposed a Treaty, has given me a Paquet of Lists of the Several sorts of Merchandize they can furnish us with, which he requests me to send to America for the Information of our Merchants.—[9]

8. See Schönfeld to BF, July 20.

9. Actually, BF had requested these lists. On May 26 Frederick II had instructed Goltz, his minister in Paris, to propose to BF that America designate a European port through which Prussia could continue the trade that formerly had been handled through Britain and Holland: fabrics and woolens exchanged for Virginia tobacco, leather, rice, and sugar. As Prussia had no treaty with the Barbary states, the king was unwilling to risk sending ships to America. Goltz had to wait some weeks before he could meet with BF. (His June 13 dispatch explained that the American had been ill.) On June 20 he reported that BF requested "an exact and extensive" list of Prussian merchandise with prices marked in English and German, which he would forward to American merchants and which Congress could consult before formulating their instructions. BF clarified that only tobacco, rice, and indigo were products of the continent; sugar and coffee could be supplied from the islands. He knew the reputation of fine Silesian fabrics but surmised that less expensive woolen cloth from Westphalia would find a larger market; woolen products and hardware were needed. By contrast, BF assured Goltz that Americans did not need beeswax and honey from Poland. As for setting up a depot in a European port, BF predicted that American merchants would not want to incur the extra expense. They would certainly prefer to ship goods directly to Prussia, even if Prussian outfitters were unwilling to risk encounters with Barbary pirates, who were (it seemed to BF) "quite far off the route." Frederick responded on June 30 that he was having lists of Prussian merchandise printed according to BF's wishes, and would send them to Paris. One of them reached Bache & Shee by Sept. 22, when the firm advertised that it had received a price list of Prussian linen, cotton, and woolen goods: Marvin L. Brown, Jr., ed. and trans., *American Independence through Prussian Eyes: . . . Selections from*

I have received no Answer yet from Congress to my Request of being dismissed from their Service.[1] They should methinks reflect, that if they continue me here, the Faults I may henceforth commit thro' the Infirmities of Age, will be rather theirs than mine.

I am glad my Journal afforded you any Pleasure, I will as you desire endeavour to continue it.[2]

I thank you for the Pamphlet.[3] It contains a great deal of Information respecting our Finances. We shall as you advise avoid publishing it. But I see they are publishing it in the English Papers. I was glad I had a Copy authenticated by the Signature of Secrey. Thomson, by which I could assure M. De Vergennes that the Money Contract I had made with him[4] was ratified by Congress, he having just before express'd some Uneasiness to me at its being so long neglected. I find it was ratified soon after it was received; but the Ratification, except in that Pamphlet, has not yet come to hand.—[5]

I have done my best to procure the farther Loan directed by the Resolution of Congress. It was not possible. I write on that Matter to Mr. Morris.[6]

I wish the Rest of the Estimates of Losses and Mischiefs were come to hand; they would still be of use.[7]

Mr Barclay has in his Hands the Affair of the Alliance &

---

the *Prussian Diplomatic Correspondence* (Durham, N.C., 1959), pp. 202–5; *Pa. Gaz.*, Oct. 8, 1783.

1. XXXVIII, 416–17; XXXIX, 397.

2. He never did. For Livingston's praise of BF's journal of the peace negotiations see XXXIX, 397–8.

3. *Address and Recommendations to the States, by the United States in Congress assembled,* which Livingston sent on May 9: XXXIX, 579.

4. That contract (XXXVII, 633–9) was included in the pamphlet.

5. It was ratified on Jan. 22, 1783: *JCC,* XXIV, 50–64. In February, Vergennes and BF signed a new contract, which Congress ratified on Oct. 31: XXXIX, 201–6.

6. The resolution requested an additional 3,000,000 *livres* from France: XXXIX, 580n. BF's letter to Morris is below, July 27.

7. After concluding the preliminary articles, the commissioners requested estimates from all the states of the losses they had suffered at the hands of the British. Only two states had as yet complied: XXXIX, 580.

Bonhomme Richard.[8] I will afford him all the Assistance in my Power. But it is a very perplex'd Business. That Expedition, tho' for particular Reasons under American Commissions & Colours, was carried on at the King's Expence & under his Orders. M. de Chaumont was the Agent appointed by the Minister of the Marine to make the Out-fit. He was also chosen by all the Captains of the Squadron, as appears by an Instrument under their Hands, to be their Agent, receive, sell and divide Prizes &ca.[9] The Crown bought two of them at Public Sale, and the Money I understand is lodg'd in the Hands of a responsible Person at L'Orient. M. De Chaumont says he has given in his Accounts to the Marine, and that he has no more to do with the Affair, except to receive a Ballance due to him.[1] That Account however is I believe unsettled, & the Absence of some of the Captains is said to make another Difficulty which retards the Completion of the Business. I never paid or received any thing relating to that Expedition, nor had any other Concern in it, than barely ordering the Alliance to join the Squadron at M. de Sartines Request.[2] I know not whether the other Captains will not Claim a Share in what we may obtain from Denmark, tho' the Prizes were made by the Alliance when separate from the Squadron. If so, that is another Difficulty in the Way of making any Abatement in our Demand without their Consent.

8. Barclay received his orders to settle the affair of these prizes (for which see Livingston's May 31 letter) in September, 1782, when he applied to WTF to send him the relevant documentation and provide him with a letter to Castries announcing his assignment. He obtained an audience with the naval minister, who promised to look into it. In March, 1783, when drafting a memorial to the French government at Castries' invitation, Barclay asked BF (once again through WTF) whether he could state that the expenses of the expedition were to be paid by France: Barclay to WTF, Sept. 10, 1782 (APS); Roberts and Roberts, *Thomas Barclay*, p. 106; Barclay to Livingston, Oct. 19, 1782 (National Archives); Barclay to WTF, March 22, 1783 (APS).

9. XXX, 223n, 248n, 459.

1. Chaumont had ceased his involvement with the project in late 1781: XXXVII, 732; XXXIX, 305n.

2. For the request and BF's orders see XXIX, 345–6, 372, 382–3, 383, 780–1; XXX, 68–9.

I am sorry to find that you have Thoughts of quitting the Service.[3] I do not think your Place can be easily well supplied. You mention that an entire new Arrangement with respect to foreign-Affairs is under Consideration. I wish to know whether any Notice is likely to be taken in it of my Grandson. He has now gone through an Apprenticeship of near seven Years in the Ministerial Business, and is very capable of serving the States in that Line, as possessing all the Requisites of Knowledge, Zeal, Activity, Language & Address. He is well liked here, and Count de Vergennes has express'd to me in warm Terms his very good Opinion of him. The late Swedish Ambassador Count de Creutz, who is gone home to be Prime Minister, desired I would endeavour to procure his being sent to Sweden with a Public Character, assuring me that he should be glad to receive him there as our Minister, and that he knew it would be pleasing to the King. The present Swedish Ambassador has also proposed the same thing to me, as you will see by a Letter of his which I enclose.[4] One of the Danish Ministers, Mr. Walterstorf, (who will probably be sent in a Public Character to Congress) has also expressed his Wish that my Grandson may be sent to Denmark.[5] But it is not my Custom to sollicit Employments for my self or any of my Family, and I shall not do it in this Case. I only hope that if he is not to be employed in your new Arrangement, I may be informed of it as soon as possible, that while I have Strength left for it, I may accompany him in a Tour to Italy returning thro' Germany, which I think he may make to more Advantage

3. See Livingston to BF, May 31.
4. Staël von Holstein to BF, June 13.
5. Walterstorff was actually not a minister, but hoped to be permitted to sign the treaty and to be named minister to the United States. In early August, when soliciting these favors from Rosencrone, he claimed that BF had offered to write on his behalf. As for WTF's diplomatic career, Walterstorff's dispatches reflect only that when he pressed BF to send a negotiator to Copenhagen (for which see the annotation of his May 20 letter), BF had told him in confidence that he would send WTF. As the weeks progressed, however, it became clear that BF had no intention of doing so. He argued that the matter could be settled more quickly if the treaty were signed in Paris: Walterstorff to Rosencrone, April 10, May 9, July 20, Aug. 3, 1783, Statens Arkiver, Rigsarkivet.

with me than alone, and which I have long promised to afford him, as a Reward for his faithful Service, and his tender filial Attachment to me.

July 25th.
While I was writing the above Mr. Walterstorff came in, & deliver'd me a Pacquet from M. de Rosencrone the Danish Prime Minister; containing the Project of the Treaty with some proposed Alterations, and a Paper of Reasons in support of them.[6] Fearing that we should not have time to copy them, I send herewith the Originals, relying on his Promise to furnish me with Copies, in a few Days.[7] He seems to think that the Interest of the Merchants is concerned in an immediate Conclusion of the Treaty that they may form their Plans of Commerce,

6. See Rosencrone to BF, July 8.
7. He did so on Aug. 7. On Aug. 26 they met to discuss them. BF objected to two of Denmark's changes. To the reciprocal Articles 4 and 5, which in Congress' draft guaranteed mutual protection of ships "upon all occasions," Denmark inserted a clause restricting protection of ships to occasions "where there may be a common enemy." BF also objected to a restriction they placed in Article 13, the revised version of Congress' draft Article 11 (itself essentially identical to the first part of Article 19 of the Franco-American commercial treaty: XXV, 612–13). Whereas America and France had allowed that ships of war or privateers could carry into each other's ports ships and goods taken from their enemies without paying any duties, Denmark specified that they would pay no other duty "than such as the most favored nations." (Wharton, *Diplomatic Correspondence*, VI, 520–1, 522–3.) After debating both issues, Walterstorff reported (however reliably) that BF yielded and was willing to sign the Danish counterproposal. Walterstorff immediately wrote for powers to sign, while informing his court that BF would not sign until he received special powers from Congress, which he expected to arrive in four to five weeks. In the meantime, BF gave Walterstorff two new articles he proposed for inclusion: the humanitarian articles he had long wished to see in the peace treaty with Great Britain, which he wove into his proposed treaty with Portugal (retained as Articles 11 and 12 in the Portuguese counterproposal, [*c.* June 7]), accompanied by a French translation of the essay later entitled "Thoughts on Privateering" (XXXVII, 617–19). Though the king approved these additions in early October, Walterstorff did not inform BF, as he decided against scheduling another meeting until BF received further instructions from Congress. Walterstorff to Rosencrone, Aug. 7 and 28, Oct. 24, 1783, Statens Arkiver, Rigsarkivet.

and wished to know whether I did not think my general Power above mentioned sufficient for that purpose. I told him I thought a particular Commission more agreable to the Forms, but if his Danish Majesty would be content for the present with the general Authority formerly given to me, I believed I might venture to act upon it, reserving by a separate Article, to Congress, a Power of shortning the Term, in Case any Part of the Treaty should not be to their Mind, unless the Alteration of such Part should hereafter be agreed on.

The Prince de Deux-ponts was lately at Paris, and apply'd to me for Information respecting a Commerce which is desired between the Electorate of Bavaria & America.[8] I have it also from a good hand at the Court of Vienna, that the Emperor is desirous of establishing a Commerce with us from Trieste as well as Flanders, & would make a Treaty with us if proposed to him:[9] Now that our Trade is laid open, and no longer a Monopoly to England, all Europe seems desirous of sharing in it, and for that purpose to cultivate our Friendship. That it may be better known every where, what sort of People, & what kind of Government they will have to treat with, I prevailed with our Friend, the Duke de la Rochefoucault to translate our Book of Constitutions into French, and I presented Copies to all the foreign Ministers. I send you One herewith. They are much admired by the Politicians here, and it is thought will induce considerable Emigrations of substantial People from different Parts of Europe to America. It is particularly a Matter of Wonder, that in the Midst of a cruel War raging in the Bowels of our Country, our Sages should have the firmness of Mind to sit down calmly and form such compleat Plans of Government. They add considerably to the Reputation of the United States.

I have mentioned above the Port of Trieste, with which we may possibly have a Commerce; and I am told that many useful Productions and Manufactures of Hungary may be had extreamly cheap there.[1] But it becomes necessary first to consider

8. On June 14, above.
9. See xxxix, 445–6n.
1. For the opening of a direct trade between the United States and Trieste see xxxvi, 354–5; xxxix, 600–2.

how our Mediterranean Trade is to be protected from the Corsaires of Barbary. You will see by the enclosed Copy of a Letter
I received from Algier, the Danger two of our Ships escaped
last Winter.[2] I think it not improbable that those Rovers may be
Privately encouraged by the English to fall upon us; and to prevent our Interference in the carrying Trade; for I have in London heard it as a Maxim among the Merchants, that *if there were
no Algiers it would be worth Englands while to build one.* I wonder
however that the rest of Europe do not combine to destroy those
Nests, and secure Commerce from their future Piracies.— I
made the Grand Master of Malta a Present of one of our Medals in Silver writing to him a Letter of which I enclose a Copy;[3]
and I believe our People will be kindly received in his Ports;
but that is not sufficient; and perhaps now we have Peace, it will
be proper to send Ministers with suitable Presents to establish a
Friendship with the Emperor of Morrocco, and the other Barbary States if possible. Mr. Jay will inform you of some Steps
that have been taken by a Person at Alicant without Authority, towards a Treaty with that Emperor.[4] I send you herewith
a few[5] more of the abovementioned Medals which have given
great Satisfaction to this Court and Nation. I should be glad to
know how they are liked with you.

Our People who were Prisoners in England are now all discharged. During the whole War, those who were in Forton
Prison near Portsmouth, were much befriended by the constant
charitable Care of Mr. Wren, a Presbyterian Minister there,
who spared no Pains to assit them in their Sickness & Distress,
by procuring and distributing among them the Contributions
of good Christians, and prudently dispensing the Allowance I

2. XXXIX, 419–21.
3. XXXIX, 436.
4. The person was Robert Montgomery; see our annotation of Crocco
to BF, July 15.
5. There is an "X" here keyed to the number 25 written in the margin.
BF had previously sent Livingston 50 medals: XXXIX, 470–1n. In early July
he had additional medals struck in silver and copper (XXXIX, 391n). When
those sent with this letter arrived, Boudinot distributed them "among the
States": Smith, *Letters*, XX, 675.

made them, which gave him a great deal of Trouble, but he went thro' it chearfully. I think some Public Notice should be taken of this good Man. I wish the Congress would enable me to make him a Present, and that some of our Universities would confer upon him the Degree of Doctor.[6]

The Duke of Manchester, who has always been our Friend in the House of Lords, is now here as Ambassador from England. I dine with him to Day (26th.) and if any thing of Importance occurs, I will add it in a Postscript.

Be pleased to present my dutiful Respects to the Congress, assure them of my most faithful Services, and believe me to be, with great & sincere Esteem, Sir, Your most obedient & most humble Servant.   B FRANKLIN

Honble: Robt. R. Livingston Esqr:

---

6. A congressional committee recommended a gift "not exceeding £500," but in the end, Congress voted to confer its thanks. The College of New Jersey awarded Wren an honorary degree: Smith, *Letters*, XX, 703; *JCC*, XXV, 632; Sheldon S. Cohen, "Thomas Wren: Ministering Angel of Forton Prison," *PMHB*, CIII (1979), 279−80, 297−9.

Recommendation for Pierre Sonnerat to the Royal Society[7]

DS:[8] American Philosophical Society

[July 22?, 1783]

M. Pierre Sonnerat, Correspondent of the Academy of Sciences at Paris, Member of the Academy of Lyons, well known by his Voyages to New-Guinea and China, where he was employed by the King of France for the promotion of Natural History, being desirous of Admittance into the Royal Society; we whose names are subscribed do recommend him upon our personal

---

7. Sonnerat, who was planning a trip to India, Tibet, and Central Asia, had been trying to obtain an affiliation with the Royal Society since April, when he asked Joseph Banks to help him become a foreign associate. Banks's answer was delivered by Charles Blagden in June: the number of foreign members was fixed at 100, and no places were currently available. Sonnerat was "chagrined" at this, forcing Blagden to explain it again when they next dined together: Madeleine Ly-Tio-Fane, *Pierre Sonnerat, 1748–1814: an Account of His Life and Work* (Cassis, Mauritius, 1976), pp. 10–11, 30–1; Warren R. Dawson, ed., *The Banks Letters: a Calendar of the Manuscript Correspondence of Sir Joseph Banks* . . . (London, 1958), p. 774; Neil Chambers, ed., *Scientific Correspondence of Sir Joseph Banks, 1765–1820* (6 vols., London, 2007), II, 87–8.

On July 23 Sonnerat wrote to Banks that Blagden had given him hope that he might try for election as a regular member. The present document— written by Blagden in the standard language of such petitions—would have been the first step in this process, which required that at least three fellows sign a recommendation. Blagden noted in his journal on July 22 that he visited Sonnerat and "laid before him the list" (presumably of Royal Society fellows), of whom the Frenchman "knew no one but Franklin." It seems likely that Blagden drafted this document that same day, though it must be noted that he did not sign it himself. Ly-Tio-Fane, *Pierre Sonnerat*, pp. 30–1; Charles R. Weld, *A History of the Royal Society* (2 vols., London, 1848), I, 460–1; Charles Blagden's Journal, entry of July 22, 1783 (Yale University Library).

It is not known who presented this sheet to BF, when he signed, or why it remains among his papers. On Nov. 12, in response to a new letter from Banks explaining the impossibility of his candidacy, Sonnerat requested instead letters of introduction to the British governors of the places he intended to visit: Ly-Tio-Fane, *Pierre Sonnerat*, pp. 30–1.

8. In the hand of Charles Blagden.

371

knowledge, as perfectly qualified to become a Fellow of that
learned Body.   B FRANKLIN
                                                            J. OSBORN.[9]

Lafayette to the American Peace Commissioners

ALS: Massachusetts Historical Society

Gentlemen   Chavaniac[1] july the 22 1783
Having Been Honoured With letters from Congress, it Becomes my duty to Consult You Upon a point Which they Have
particularly Recommended— In the late preliminaries no time
is Mentionned for the American Merchants paying their English
debts— A Matter of Great Moment to our Merchants who Require at least three or four Years to Accomplish the Business—
Upon the Receipt of the letter, I Have Adressed Count de Vergennes, and Represented to Him How important a favorable
decision on this point would Be to the french trade—[2] Knowing the Uneasiness of our American Merchants on that affair, I
Cannot Help Partaking of it, and would Consider it as a great
favor to Be Acquainted With the present Situation of things,

9. John Osborn (1743–1814) was a former British diplomat and a fellow
of the Royal Society since 1777. He and Blagden dined together frequently
in July: G. F. Russell Barker and Alan H. Stenning, comps., *The Record of
Old Westminsters* . . . (2 vols., London, 1928), II, 706; Charles Blagden's
Journal, 1783 (Yale University Library).
    1. The family estate: Idzerda, *Lafayette Papers*, I, xxxv.
    2. In a letter of April 12, Boudinot told Lafayette that the only thing
lacking in the preliminary peace agreement was an article allowing American merchants three to four years to pay their debts. He added that it should
"also be an Object with France," as American merchants would be in the
hands of English creditors if such an article were not included in the definitive treaty: Smith, *Letters*, XX, 168–70. Lafayette wrote to Vergennes
on July 21, urging him to intervene in this matter for the good of Franco-
American trade. Vergennes replied on Aug. 5 that Hartley was not authorized to make such compromises concerning the rights of individuals:
Idzerda, *Lafayette Papers*, V, 144–5, 380–1.

and with the further Measures You Might think proper for me to Undertake.

The General Satisfaction Which Arose from the time of peace, is a Matter of justice to You, Gentlemen, that Affords Me a Most Unfeigned Pleasure— Give me leave to present You With the Assurances of an Affectionate Respect I Have the Honour to Be With Your obedient Humble servant

LAFAYETTE

Their Excellencies the Commissioners for treating with G. B. &c

Endorsed by John Adams: M. De La Fayette 22 July 1783.

From Robert Melville[3]

AL: American Philosophical Society

Paris, Hotel d'Espagne Ruë de Guénégaud
22d. July 1783.

Lieut. General Melville presents his best respects to Doctor Franklin,—And, intending to set out, early in next week, from this place, for London, shall be very glad to receive, before Monday next, the letter which the Doctor mentioned his intention of Sending to Mr. Calder, by G. M. And any other letters or Commands which the Doctor may be pleased to honour him with.

The General has farther to beg that the Doctor will be pleased to present his respects to Mr. Adams, and to Mr. & Mrs. Jay, if still at Passy, and to tell them that he shall be glad to carry any letters or Commands of theirs—[4]

Notation: Melvell 22 July 1783.

3. Who carried a letter of introduction from John Calder when he left London in March: XXXIX, 326–7.

4. Melville sent a near duplicate of this letter on July 25, changing his estimated departure date from Monday to Tuesday and adding a final paragraph: "G. M. sent a former Note, *par la petite Poste,* but believing that the Direction was not proper, & that it may therefore not have reached, troubles the Doctor with this." APS.

From Alexander Small ALS: American Philosophical Society

Dear Sir London July 22d 1783

Tho' we can no longer call ourselves Fellow Subjects of the Same Sovereign, yet I hope we shall never forget that we are Fellow Labourers in the Service of Humanity. This gives a right to claim reciprocaly Good-offices. Now that you have in *some* degree settled the various Interests of great Empires, I hope you will find time to exert Yourself in the Service of Humanity; and consider the Service of the Individuals who compose Empires. Do not You think that the greatest Calamity the Garrison of st Philips Suffered arose from their Inattention to preserve a free Current of Air thro' their Subterranean Lodgements?[5] While greater Matters claimed Your attention, you think you should Stand accquitted for the Neglect of lesser Subjects. There is a time for all things.

This Letter will probably be delivered to you by Patrick Wilkie Esqr, who goes Consul to Alicant, and intends to take Paris in his way. I can promise You that if you have at any time business to transact there, he will puctually and honestly execute the Same: and I told him, that when you go to Your *Terrestrial Paradise*, the *promised* Seat of Liberty, Peace and Plenty, you will be equally ready to Serve him. May You enjoy Health and that *expected* Peace prays Dear Sir Your Faithful and most humble Servant ALEXR SMALL

Mr Baldwin flatters me with the hopes of seeing you here glad that the remembrance of a most agreable Fair-One yet dwells with you, and that you wish to touch her Sweet Lips.[6] Would to God! You would give the Kiss of Peace to all the

---

5. Scurvy had decimated the British troops garrisoned at Fort St. Philip on the island of Minorca in early 1782, forcing them to surrender to the Spanish: XXXVI, 604n; Mackesy, *War for America*, p. 438. Small had earlier served as an army surgeon on Minorca, where he probably wrote "Of Ventilation," incorporating some of BF's observations: XXIII, 486–91.

6. BF must have responded to Baldwin's letter of Feb. 18 conveying his wife's greetings: XXXIX, 183–5.

Natives of your Country. This, on tryal, would be found to be the Soundest Policy.

Dr Franklin

Notation: Alexr. Small 22 Juillet 1783.

To Robert R. Livingston[7]

ALS: New-York Historical Society; copy: Sächsisches Hauptstaatsarchiv

Sir,   Passy, July 23. 1783—
This will be delivered to you by M. Thieriot, who goes to Philadelphia by order of his Court as Commissioner of the Commerce of Saxony, in order to establish a Correspondence between the two Countrys, that may, it is thought, be greatly advantageous to both. We have all along had many well-wishers in that Electorate, and I am told by the Minister here, who is much our Friend, that it is probable M. Thieriot may soon be vested with a Public Character among us. I beg leave therefore to recommend him earnestly to your Countenance & Protection, as well as to those Civilities you have always a Pleasure in showing to Strangers of Merit.— With great Esteem, I have the honour to be, Sir, Your most obedient & most humble Servant

B FRANKLIN

Honble. R R Livingston Esqr

Notations: Docr. Franklin 23d. July 1784 / 23d July 1784 Docr Franklin

---

7. According to a series of notations on the archived copy of BF to Schönfeld, July 23 (the following document), BF provided Thieriot with identical letters addressed to Robert Morris and Michael Hillegas.

To Schönfeld[8]

Copy: Sächsisches Hauptstaatsarchiv

Mr.   [July 23, 1783]

Vous trouverés cy-joint les lettres que Vous m'avés fait l'honneur de me demander pour le Sr. Thieriot. Elles lui procureront, je n'en doute pas, cette reception et consideration qui sont dues à son Souverain ainsi qu'à son merite. Recevés, je Vous prie Mr., l'assurance du très parfait attachemt. avec lequel j'ai l'honneur d'etre Votre &a.

Copie, de la lettre de Mr. B. franklin à Mr. de Schönfeld datée de Passy le 23. Juillet 1783

From Miromesnil

ALS: American Philosophical Society

ce 23 Juillet 1783.

Jai Recu avec bien de la Reconnoissance, Les constitutions des Etats unis de lamérique, que Monsieur Franklin a bien voulu MEnvoier.[9] Je le prie de Recevoir mes Remerciements de Cette

---

8. For background on this letter see Schönfeld to BF, July 20. On July 28 Schönfeld wrote his government that BF had received him and Thieriot with much cordiality, but had refused to do more than provide Thieriot with letters of recommendation. Schönfeld believed that BF was unwilling to risk exceeding his powers; JA had told him that "M. Franklin n'a plus auprès du Congrès l'ancienne influence, dont il jouissoit, et que la meilleure partie, qu'il ait à prendre, est de finir ses jours en France, où il est réellement chéri et vénéré": William E. Lingelbach, "Saxon-American Relations, 1778–1828," *American Hist. Rev.*, XVII (1911–12), 523.

9. Vergennes granted permission to publish *Constitutions des treize Etats-Unis de l'Amérique* on July 18 in a letter to Pierres (AAE). BF presented copies to the foreign ministers at Versailles at their weekly assembly the following Tuesday, July 22 (see his letter to Livingston, July 22[–26]), and may have left a copy for Miromesnil that same day.

Constitutions des treize Etat-Unis was advertised for sale to the public in the July 30 issue of the *Jour. de Paris*. Available from either Pierres or Pissot père et fils, the 540-page octavo volume sold for 4 *l.t.* 4 *s.* on regular paper. A limited number in quarto, on *papier vélin*, were available in sheets for 24 *l.t.* An extensive review on Aug. 24 praised the wisdom of the legislation, quoting by way of example the preamble to the Pa. constitution, and called

CONSTITUTIONS

DES

TREIZE ÉTATS-UNIS

DE L'AMÉRIQUE.

A PHILADELPHIE;

Et se trouve A PARIS,

Chez
{
Ph.-D. Pierres, Imprimeur Ordinaire du Roi,
rue Saint-Jacques.
Pissot, pere & fils, Libraires, quai des
Auguftins.

1783.

Constitutions des treize États-Unis de l'Amérique, Title Page

marque de Son attention. Je lirai avec attention ce Code qui fait une partie tres Interessante du Droit Public du monde, Et qui sera toujours un monument Insigne de La vertu de Monsieur Franklin Et de son amour Pour Sa Patrie.

Je Le prie detre persuadé de la sincerité de touts Les Sentiments quil m'a Inspirés.   MIROMENIL

M. Franklin ministre Plenipotentiaire des Etats Unis de L'amerique a Paris.

To Vergennes

L:[1] Archives du Ministère des affaires étrangères; L (draft):[2] Library of Congress

à Passy ce 24. Juillet 1783.

M. Franklin a l'honneur d'envoyer à Monsieur Le Comte de Vergennes un Exemplaire des Constitutions des Etats-Unis de l'Amerique qu'il le prie de vouloir bien accepter.

M. Franklin prend la Liberté d'envoyer en même tems, ceux destinés pour le Roi et la Famille Royale; et il prie Monsieur le Comte de Vergennes, de vouloir bien les faire parvenir à leur Destination, suivant la Forme qui lui paroitra convenable.

Notations: M franklin. Etats Unis / 1783. 24. Juillet. / Rep

---

attention to the seal of the United States on the title page, which it described as "ingénieusement composé."

The book of constitutions had a great influence in Europe and went through four printings in France by 1789. Of particular interest were the pronouncements on religious liberty in various American states: Raymond Birn, "Religious Toleration and Freedom of Expression," in *The French Idea of Freedom: the Old Regime and the Declaration of Rights of 1789*, ed. Dale Van Kley (Stanford, Calif., 1994), p. 267; Elise Marienstras and Naomi Wulf, "French Translations and Reception of the Declaration of Independence," *Jour. of American History*, LXXXV (1999), 1305.

1. In the hand of L'Air de Lamotte.

2. Or perhaps copy. It was written by WTF.

From the Comte d'Argental[3]

AL: American Philosophical Society

Ce Jeudi 24. Juillet 1783

Le Comte D'argental a Reçû avec autant de reconnoissance que de satisfaction, ce que Monsieur franklin a bien voulu lui Envoyer, il va faire partir celui qui est pour L'Infant[4] a sa Destination, il a deja lû le sien dans lequel il à reconnu, la Sagesse, l'intelligence, et les Excellentes vües d'administration de celui qui la dirigé.[5]

Addressed: A Monsieur / Monsieur francklin Ministre / plenipotentiaire des Etats unis de / L'amerique a la cour de france / A Passy

From the Comtesse de Boufflers[6]

AL: American Philosophical Society

Ce 24 julliet 83 a auteuil

Me [Madame] de Boufflers a reçeu avec un sensible plaisir et une reconnoissance infinie le precieux present dont monsieur

3. Charles-Auguste de Ferriol, comte d'Argental (1700–1788), minister plenipotentiary of the duchy of Parma, was a man of letters and former *conseiller au Parlement de Paris*, known for his friendship with Voltaire: *DBF; Repertorium der diplomatischen Vertreter*, II, 268; III, 299. This is his only extant letter to BF.

4. Ferdinando di Borbone, Duke of Parma and Infante of Spain (1751–1802), was the grandson of Philip V of Spain and, on his mother's side, Louis XV of France: Patrick Van Kerrebrouck, *La Maison de Bourbon, 1256–1987* (Villeneuve d'Ascq, France, 1987), pp. 467, 469–70.

5. BF gave two copies of *Constitutions des treize Etats-Unis de l'Amérique* to the foreign ministers, one to be forwarded to their sovereigns. Other Italian diplomats who received copies, but whose acknowledgments do not survive, include the conte di Scarnafiggi (see the annotation of his Aug. 23 letter) and the representative from Genoa, marchese Cristoforo Vincenzo Spinola (*Repertorium der diplomatischen Vertreter*, III, 151–2). Spinola forwarded a copy to his government on July 28, calling attention to the commercial treaties: Antonio Pace, *Benjamin Franklin and Italy* (Philadelphia, 1958), p. 114.

6. Marie-Charlotte-Hippolyte de Campet (Camps) de Saujon, marquise de Rouveret (Rouverel) and comtesse de Boufflers: XXXV, 20n; *DBF; Med-*

Francklin a bien voulu l'honorer.[7] Personne n'en connoit mieux le prix, et na une plus haute idée de celuy de qui elle le reçoit. Si par un des plus grands efforts que puisse produire lamour patriotique elle a resistè a sa propre inclination pour ne pas se laisser entrainer a lempressement general que Monsieur Francklin a si justement excité, le sentiment rassuré par le succes la rend a son penchant naturel et luy permet de jouir avec une admiration sans melange du beau spectacle ou Monsieur Francklin a représenté un des premiers Personnages.

From Luigi Pio

AL: American Philosophical Society

à Paris ce 24. Juillet. 1783./.
Mr. de Pio a l'honneur d'assûrer de son respect Mr. Franklin, Ministre Plenipotentiaire des Etats-unis de l'Amerique, et de lui dire, qu'il a reçu les trois Exemplaires des *Constitutions*, dont un pour le Roy son maitre, un pour Mr. Filangieri, et un pour lui.[8] Mr. de Pio est on ne peut pas plus sensible a l'honneur que mr. Franklin a bien voulu lui faire en particulier, et il Lui en fait bien des remercimens. Pour ce qui regarde Sa Majesté Sicilienne, Mr. de Pio se fera un devoir de le Lui faire parvenir le plus tôt, et il ose assûrer Mr. Franklin que Sa Majesté en sera très flattée, et Mr. de Pio ne manquera pas dans le tems de communiquer à Mr. Franklin la reponse qu'il en recevra de sa Cour; comme il aura aussi l'honneur de lui adresser celle de Mr. Filangieri./.

---

lin, *Morellet*, 1, 35n; Franco Venturi, *The End of the Old Regime in Europe, 1768–1776: the First Crisis*, trans. R. Burr Litchfield (Princeton, 1989), pp. 330–3.

7. Doubtless the *Constitutions des treize Etats-Unis de l'Amérique*.

8. Pio, the chargé d'affaires of Ferdinand, ruler of the Kingdom of the Two Sicilies, often took charge of correspondence between BF and Filangieri: XXXVIII, 37–8; XXXIX, 360–1.

From Jean Le Rond d'Alembert[9]

AL: Dartmouth College Library

a Paris le 25 Juillet [1783]

M. d'Alembert a l'honneur d'assurer son illustre et respectable confrere de son respectueux attachement, et lui fait mille remercimens du beau présent qu'il a reçu de lui.[1]

Addressed: A Monsieur / Monsieur franklin, / de l'Academie Royale des Sciences, / et Ministre plenipotentiaire / des Etats unis de l'Amerique / a Passy

From Mattheus Lestevenon van Berkenrode

AL: American Philosophical Society

paris ce 25 Juillet 1783.

L'Ambassadeur de Hollande a L'honneur d'assurer Monsieur Francklin de Ses tres humbles Civilités, et celui de Le remercier du Cadeau qu'il à bien voulu lui faire, en lui envoiant Les Constitutions des treize Etats Unis de L'Amerique./

From Baron von Grimm

AL: Harvard University Library

Ce Vendredi 25 Juillet. [1783]

Le Bon. de Grimm a l'honeur de présenter Ses hommages à Monsieur Franklin, et de le remercier très humblement du beau présent qu'il a bien voulu lui faire.[2]

---

9. This renowned *philosophe*, who admired BF (XXVI, 670n) and would have seen him at meetings of the Académie royale des sciences and at the home of Mme Helvétius (whose salon he attended), has left few traces in BF's papers. This is his only extant letter. D'Alembert died on Oct. 29, 1783: *DBF.*

1. Doubtless a copy of *Constitutions des treize Etats-Unis de l'Amérique.*

2. Grimm, minister plenipotentiary of Saxe-Gotha to the French court (XXXI, 398), was undoubtedly acknowledging a copy of *Constitutions des treize États-Unis de l'Amérique.*

From Reuben Harvey

ALS: American Philosophical Society

Respected Friend   Cork 25 July 1783

I am obliged to thee for the favour of thy letter,[3] & may inform thee that two Vessels sailed lately from this Port & Youghal for Philadelphia with upwards of 200 Passengers. I thought, 'till a few days ago, that Hen Laurens Esqr. continued one of the American Commissioners for the United States, And as such, & he being in England, I transmitted to him the 1st. Inst. several Papers concerng. an American Vessel laden wth. Tobacco, which has been detain'd in the Harbour of Castletown near 10 Weeks, whereby a loss of £1500— will accrue, by the fall in value of Tobacco & the prevention of the Ship's return to Carolina with a Cargoe of Merchandize from this Port; The pretence for detaining this Vessel is an *intention* (as the Revenue Officers alledge) of the Captain's to smuggle, & it is only last week that those who possess'd themselves of the Ship & Cargoe gave notice to the Captain that he must prepare for Tryal the 30 of this Month. As I sent a very particular account of this most oppressive Act to H. Laurens Esqr. & requested him to acquaint his brother Commissrs. therewith,[4] I won't now take up thy time in reciting it again, but I beg leave to mention that unless the British Court be apply'd to by the American Representatives touching this Affair, there is little prospect of redress or compensation being obtained here by a Suit at Law, where a poor American has the powers of a Board of Revenue Commissioners to combat.[5] Some more Ships from Carolina & Virginia

3. See Harvey's letter of May 17.

4. Harvey's July 1 letter to Laurens is among BF's papers at the APS, as are a numbered set of 11 documents that were probably enclosed. They include Harvey to the Board of Commissioners of Customs, Dublin, May 29; Harvey to John Gahan, May 30 and June 5; Harvey to Robert, Earl of Northington, June 6; William Windham to Harvey, June 9 and 16; Harvey to Windham, June 13, 21, 22, and 25; and John Gladin to the Earl of Northington, June 22. Also at the APS, separate from this packet, are copies of John Gahan to [the Commissioners of Revenue?], May 27, and Capt. Gladin's deposition, July 2.

5. This complicated affair (as Harvey says in his postscript) involved Capt. John Gladin and his ship *Nancy* of Bath, N.C. Gladin was in

which put into this Harbour lately to seek a market for their Tobacco, were search'd, & all the loose Tobacco taken from on board by Revenue Officers who forcibly broke open their Hatches;[6] I have however after a delay of 10 or 12 days procured this Tobacco again, the Commissioners being afraid to proceed too far in seizing American Vessels. The Revenue Laws of Ireland are so very arbitrary, particularly One Act call'd the *Hovering Act*,[7] that it is realy necessary for Congress to appoint a Consul or such like Person for managing their Commercial Affairs, to reside in Cork,[8] this Port being the most convenient & the most frequented by American Vessels of any in Ireland. No Tobacco in less packages than 500 pounds weight can be imported here by Law; Now as it is the constant custom in America to break up hogshds. of Tobacco & pack them loose in parts

---

Martinique when he received news of the general peace, whereupon he headed for Europe, hoping to sell his cargo of tobacco, staves, and shingles. On May 18, off the southwest coast of Ireland, he tried to engage a pilot to bring him into Cork. Instead, the captain of a Revenue cutter brought him into Castlehaven, where the local customs official found fault with his paperwork, impounded some of the tobacco, and had the vessel detained. On July 14 the *Nancy* was seized and a trial was ordered. Harvey learned this news three days later, whereupon he sent the owners, Thomas and Titus Ogden, copies of all the relevant correspondence (presumably the same documents he sent Laurens) and asked them to urge Congress to protest the injustice. Congress considered the matter in May, 1784, and ordered the American commissioners to investigate the case, sending all the documents to Paris. These are undoubtedly the packet of documents that BF marked "Ship Nancy," gathered under the title "Sundry Papers relative to the Detention of the Nancy at Castletownsend." In addition to the 11 documents described above, this packet adds copies of Harvey's July 1 letter to Laurens, and his July 17 letter to Thomas and Titus Ogden. APS.

6. One of these must have been the *Revolution* from Edenton, N.C., which arrived at Cork on June 28 and was refused entry pending determination of what duties should be charged: Harvey to Laurens, July 1, cited above.

7. The "Hovering Acts" of 1718 and 1721 had been adopted to discourage smuggling. Any vessel under 15 tons found within six miles of the coast was liable to seizure unless she was detained by unfavorable sailing conditions: Geoffrey Morley, *The Smuggling War: the Government's Fight Against Smuggling in the 18th and 19th Centuries* (Stroud, Eng., and Dover, N.H., 1994), p. 6.

8. Harvey had first solicited a consulship in February: XXXIX, 153–6.

of the Ship's hold where a Cask can't be stow'd, & then when she arrives at her destined Port to repack this Tobacco into the Hogsheads again, (wch. are mark'd & set aside in Staves for this purpose), if this Law is carried into effect against American Tobacco Ships which call at the Ports in Ireland for information, whereby they may direct their Voyages, just as they find the best Market likely to be, it will be in the power of every petty Revenue Officer to stop any Ship that shall be found to have loose Tobacco on board, tho' such Ship is bound to another Kingdom, which wou'd in fact amount to a prohibition of your Ships, Tobacco laden, from entering the Ports of this Kingdom.

I write again this post to have the Papers forwarded to the Commissrs. at Paris, if Henry Laurens Esqr. has not already done it, & I hope that thou & the other Gentlemen will see the necessity there is for your interference on this Occasion.

I am very respectfully Thy sincere Friend REUBEN HARVEY

The Vessel under seizure at Castletown is call'd the Nancy of Bath Town, in North Carolina, John Gladin Master; had been a letter of Marque

Benjn. Franklin Esqr.

Addressed: Benjamin Franklin Esqr. / Passy, near / Paris / Post paid

From the Comtesse d'Houdetot

LS: American Philosophical Society

sanois Le 25. Juillet 1783.
J'ay Reçu avec joye Et Sensibilité Le present[9] qu'a Bien Voulû me faire Monsieur franklin il me Sera Cher par Son objet Et par La main qui me le donne. C'est un Monument Du Bonheur De Sa Patrie Et Du Succés De Ses traveaux; Si le Ciel ne nous a point faittes pour Conduire Des Etâts il m'a donné au moins une Ame Bien Sensible pour Ceux qui ont Eclairé Les nations

9. A copy of *Constitutions des treize Etats-Unis de l'Amérique.*

Et Les ont Dirigées Vers Leur Veritable Bonheur La paix Et
La Liberté. C'est a Ces titres que j'offre mes hommages Et mes
Remercimens a Monsieur franklin il m'est Bien doux D'y ajouter
a mon Respectable Amy, quand Verraije Renouveller Les mo-
mens heureux qu'il ma donnés a Sanois.[1] J'attend que L'automne
Luy ait Rendû quelque parure Et quelque fraicheur pour faire
Ressouvenir Messieurs franklin qu'ils m'ont promis D'y Reve-
nir Et je Vais moy même m'En Eloigner pour quelques tems

LA CTESSE DHOUDETOT

From Vergennes   L: American Philosophical Society

A Vlles. 25 Juillet 1783.
M. De Vergennes a reçu l'Exemplaire des constitutions des États
unis de l'amérique que Monsieur franklin a bien voulu Lui envoyer. Il le prie d'en agréer ses justes et sincères remerciments.
   Les Exemplaires du même ouvrage destinés au Roi, à la
Reine, et à la famille Royale, viennent d'être remis à leur destination, conformément au desir de Monsieur franklin.[2]
   M. De Vergennes prie Monsieur franklin de recevoir les assurances de la trés parfaite consideration qu'il lui a vouée./.

1. To the best of our knowledge, BF's last visit to Sannois was in the
spring of 1781: XXXIV, 539–45; XXXV, 512–13.
   2. Two of these are now in the Bibliothèque nationale, one bound with
Marie-Antoinette's arms, the other with the royal arms. The former is
reproduced in Marie-Hélène Tesnière and Prosser Gifford, eds., *Creating
French Culture: Treasures from the Bibliothèque nationale de France* (New
Haven and London, 1995), p. 353.

From the Duke of Manchester

AL: American Philosophical Society

[before July 26, 1783]

The Duke of Manchester's Compts to Dr: Franklin and desires the honor of his company at Dinner Saturday the 26th: inst:[3]

Addressed: Doctor Franklin / à Passy

From Henri-François-de-Paule Lefèvre d'Ormesson

LS: American Philosophical Society

Monsieur   A Versailles le 26. Juillet 1783.

Votre Excellence a bien voulu me destiner un Exemplaire des Constitutions des Etats unis de l'Amerique. Je mets un grand prix à cet Ouvrage et a ce témoignage de l'attention de Votre Excellence; je la prie d'en agréer tous mes remercimens.

J'ai l'honneur d'être avec un très sincere attachement, Monsieur, De Votre Excellence, Le très humble et très obéissant serviteur./.   DORMESSON

A. S. E. M. Francklin Ministre Plénipotentiaire des Etats unis de l'Amerique a Passy Par Paris

Notation: Letters of Thanks for the Constitutions

---

3. BF attended, or at least he planned to: BF to Livingston, July 22[–26]. The Duke of Manchester also sent a pair of invitations to BF and WTF, nearly identical in wording, for "Sunday next the 10th" (APS). This had to have been Aug. 10, the only such Sunday during the seven months of Manchester's mission to Paris.

From the Comte de Rochambeau[4]

AL: American Philosophical Society

Paris ce 26. Juillet 1783.
Le Cte. de Rochambeau prie Monsieur Le Docteur francklin de vouloir bien faire passer la lettre ci-jointe à Mr. le chr. de La Luzerne par la premiere occasion

From Walterstorff

ALS: American Philosophical Society

Sir. Paris July 26th. 1783.

According to Your desire I have the honour of sending You an abstract of the last ordonnance concerning the Trade of the Islands of St. Thomas & St. Johns.[5]

As to the Island of St. Croix I must observe to You, Sir, that all american Vessels are also received there, and although the Suggars of sd. Island are to be exported only to His Majesty's Dominions in Europe, yet there is an Exception in favr. of american Vessels, thus, that half the value of the Cargo imported, when consisting of provisions, lumber, or such things that are to the use of the Plantations or their cultivation, may be exported to America in Suggars. Any quantity of Rum may be exported to America from St. Croix as also all Kind of Europeen or eastindie goods.

I have the honour to be Sir Your most obedt. and most humble Servt. WALTERSTORFF

---

4. The only extant letter to BF from the victor at Yorktown.

5. Rosencrone's explanation of the Danish counterproposal had emphasized that Denmark had granted to those two islands trade privileges with America that gave commerce "a freer course, and very different from that of the commere of the colony": Wharton, *Diplomatic Correspondence*, VI, 526. Walterstorff enclosed a summary of the royal ordinance of Nov. 4, 1782, granting free trade between them and the other islands of the Caribbean and the American continent; trade between those islands and Europe, however, was open only to Danish ships. The fifth and final article specified import and export duties.

386

The right honble. Benjamin Franklin

P.S. It may perhaps be of some service to the Gentlemen merchants in America to know the principal merchants in Denmark
as also in the Danish Westindie Islands. I therefore can recommend the following.[6]

at Copenhagen
The Royal westindie Company, which also has an Adminis-
  tration at St. Thomas.
The Baltic and Guinee Company
The Canal Company, of which I am one of the Directors,
  & which also has an Administration at Altona
Messrs. Jost von Hemmert & Sons
Niels Ryberg
———— Cramer
Conrad Fabritius & Wæver
John Brown.

at Altona
The Royal Canal Company
Daniel Lawaetz
Conrad Mathiesen.

at St. Croix

| Nicholas Cruger | Cornelius Stevenson |
| Behagen & Hage | John Rengger |

at St. Thomas
Messrs. Detlefsen & Limpricht
  John DeWint & Co.
The Royal Westindie Company.
Mathias Kragh.

6. The editors thank Erik Gøbel for reviewing the spellings of these
Danish names.

at Christiania in Norway
The Widow Karen Anker & Sons (has the most considerable
Iron Works.)

Notation: Waterstorf July 26 1783.—

The American Peace Commissioners to Robert R. Livingston

LS:[7] National Archives; copies: Library of Congress, Massachusetts Historical Society

Sir,   Passy, July 27. 1783.
The Definitive Treaties between the late beligerent Powers
are none of them yet compleated. Ours has gone on slowly,
owing partly to the Necessity Mr. Hartley (Successor of Mr
Oswald) thinks himself under of sending every Proposition,
either his own or ours, to his Court for their Approbation; and
their Delay in answering, thro' Negligence perhaps since they
have heard our Ports are open, or thro' Indecision occasioned
by Ignorance of the Subject, or thro' want of Union among the
Ministers. We send you herewith Copies of several Papers that
have pass'd between us.[8] He has for sometime assured us that he

---

7. In WTF's hand.
8. These included Hartley to the American Commissioners, June 14,
and the enclosed memorial of June 1; Hartley's [June 19] propositions for
the definitive treaty and the commissioners' answers of June 29; the commissioners' proposals of June 29; and the Commissioners to Hartley, July
17. They also sent an extract of a May 9 letter from Fox to Hartley, asking
him to request of the commissioners that they intercede in obtaining relief
for a group of British merchants who had twice petitioned the ministry
about the Indian land cessions that had been discussed during the peace
negotiations (XXXVIII, 273–4). Fox enclosed their memorials: identifying
themselves as "merchants trading to South Carolina and Georgia," they
wrote to Shelburne on May 3, 1782, and to Fox on April 11, 1783. (The extract and memorials were copied into the commissioners' letterbooks: Mass.
Hist. Soc., Library of Congress. A sheet filed with the enclosures at the
National Archives bears this notation by WTF: "We promised Mr. Hartley
to forward these Papers to Congress.")

388

is in Hourly Expectation of Answers but they do not arrive. The British Proclamation respecting the Commerce appears to vex him a good deal. We enclose a Copy.[9] And we are of Opinion that finally we shall find it best to drop all Commercial Articles in our Definitive Treaty; and leave every thing of that kind to a future special Treaty to be made either in America or in Europe as Congress shall think fit to Order. Perhaps it may be best to give Powers for that Purpose to the Minister that probably will be sent to London. The Opinion here is, that it will be becoming in us to take the first Step towards the mutual Exchange of Ministers; and we have been assured by the English Minister who treats with us here, that ours will be well received.

The Dutch Preliminaries are not yet agreed on, and it seems to be settled, that we are to sign all together, in the Presence of the Ministers of the two Imperial Courts who are to be complimented with the Opportunity of signing as Mediators, tho' they have not yet, and perhaps will not be consulted in the Negociations. Mr. Adams is gone to Holland, for three Weeks, but will return sooner if wanted. The Propositions you mention as made to us from that State,[1] we suppose he has given you an Account of. Nothing was or is likely to be done upon them here, and therefore it was less necessary to say any thing concerning them. A Minister from thence has been gone sometime to Congress,[2] and if he has those Propositions in Charge, they will best be consider'd there.

With great Esteem, we have the Honour to be, Sir, Your most obedient & most humble Serts. B FRANKLIN
JOHN JAY
HENRY LAURENS.

R. R. Livingston Esqr.

---

9. George III's July 2 Order in Council. This was the final enclosure, according to a list that accompanied this letter (National Archives).

1. See Livingston to the Commissioners, May 31.

2. Pieter Johan van Berckel; see Hogendorp to BF, June 13.

To Richard and Sarah Bache

ALS: Yale University Library; press copy of ALS:[3] American Philosophical Society

Dear Son and Daughter,   Passy, July 27, 1783

I have received lately several Letters from you, which gave me a great deal of Pleasure, as they inform'd me of your Welfare and that of the Children.

Being inform'd that Benny had been ill of a Fever, and that he was dejected & pin'd at being so long absent from his Relations, I sent for him to come to me during the Vacation of the Schools.[4] He is accordingly now here, and I have great Satisfaction in finding him so well grown, and so much improv'd in his Learning and Behaviour.[5] I am not determin'd at present whether to send him back, or procure him Masters under whose Direction he may continue his Studies here.

If the Congress do not dismiss me as I have desired,[6] I wish you would send me in the Fall by any Vessel coming to Havre de

3. Made before WTF added his note below BF's signature.

4. BFB's May 30 letter to BF mentioned his fever, but it was certainly Matthew Ridley's personal account that convinced BF that the situation required intervention; see BF to BFB, June 23, and the annotation there. Pigott also urged BF to remove BFB from Geneva, giving an alarming account of the child's poor health and appalling living conditions: above, June 27.

5. BFB arrived at Passy c. July 19; see the annotation of BFB to BF, July 2. On July 26 Dorcas Montgomery wrote SB a reassuring account of her "Charming Son," whom Montgomery had not seen for 13 months. He was in good health and had grown much taller but was otherwise "very little chang'd," retaining "the same likeness, to the little Ben Bache when in Philada. when his dear Grand-mama used to call him her little *King-Bird*." When Montgomery gave him news of the family dogs, which she learned from hearing BF read aloud William Bache's letter (XXXIX, 345), BFB "much lamented" Pompy's death. When she asked BFB about his grandfather and cousin, "his answer was that he found his G- Papa the same & Cousin likewise, who had made him his *Secretary* and he had wrote that morning three pages.— He found his G- Papa very different from other Old Persons, for they were fretful and complaining, and disatisfy'd. And my G- Papa is laughing, & chearful, like a young person." Dorcas Montgomery to SB, July 26, 1783 (APS).

6. After the preliminary articles were signed at the end of November, BF reminded Livingston of Congress' promise to allow him to retire: XXXVIII, 416–17. That section of his letter was ignored.

grace, some Newtown Pippins, some more Grafts of that Fruit: the former enclos'd in the Tin Case were too dry; they should have had a little moist Earth with them. I have not yet heard how those in Wax succeeded, as they went far into the Country.[7] I wish too for some of our Chestnuts & Hickery Nuts. I also desire another Box of Mr Bartram's Seeds; and let me know the Price.[8]

Mr Restife left your Letters yesterday when I happen'd to be out.— Col. Cambray has been here a long time.[9]

I am frequently solicited for Letters of Recommendation by Friends whom I cannot refuse, tho' I believe they do not always well know the Persons they solicit for;[1] and I trouble you with

---

7. SB had sent grafts in a tin case and a wooden box sealed with wax the previous December: XXXVIII, 404.

8. For the last shipment see XXXVI, 186; XXXVII, 11–12, 168. More than six months earlier (around the beginning of January), BF had received a request that was unrelated to this order. Malesherbes had asked whether BF could procure seeds of the bald cypress tree, which his nephew in Philadelphia (La Luzerne) had been unable to obtain but which Malesherbes had seen on a list of seeds BF had procured for another "amateur." (This was probably the comte de Barbançon, who received his box of Bartram's seeds in April, 1782: XXXVII, 230.) Not wanting to disturb BF, who undoubtedly had more important affairs on his mind, Malesherbes addressed this request to Le Veillard, who answered on Jan. 4 that BF had promised to forward the request to Bartram: Chrétien-Guillaume de Lamoignon de Malesherbes to Louis-Guillaume Le Veillard, undated; Le Veillard to Malesherbes, Jan. 4, 1783 (both at the Archives Nationales). If BF ever did forward the request, no trace of that correspondence survives.

9. SB and RB had entrusted letters to Restif de La Serve dated nearly four months apart (Jan. 2 and April 30), as his departure was delayed: XXXVIII, 535; XXXIX, 537. SB's letter also mentioned the chevalier de Cambray-Digny, by whom she hoped to send another letter; she did so on Jan. 24: XXXIX, 23.

1. Among BF's papers at the APS is an undated, unsigned letter in English, in a hand we do not recognize, that may be an example of such a solicitation. The writer, who is "not personally acquainted with Mess Perrin," has been "assured by good Friends that they are very worthy Men." Sons of a prominent Lyon manufacturer, they intend to go to America to form commercial connections and "wish to be distinguished from the Lump of Emigrants who will resort thither." A notation in French at the bottom of the page indicates that the recommendation should be sent to RB in Philadelphia.

those Letters. I would have you observe, that when I recommend a Person simply to your Civilities & Counsels, I mean no more than that you should give him a Dinner or two, & your best Advice if he asks it; but by no means that you should lend him Money: For many I believe go to America with very little; and with such Romantic Schemes and Expectations as must end in Disappointment and Poverty. I dissuade all I can, those who have not some useful Trade or Art by which they may get a living; but there are many who hope for Offices & Public Employments, who value themselves and expect to be valued by us for their Birth or Quality, tho' I tell them those Things bear no Price in our Markets.— But Fools will ruin themselves their own way.— There is one there at present, whose Father obtain'd of me by means of Friends a Letter recommending him to your Notice, and the Son upon the Strength of it now writes me a long Epistle pressing me to prevail with his Father to send him what he is much in want of, 10,000 Livres. I know nothing of either Son or Father.

I am glad Miss Beckwith is likely to succeed with you. I take her to be a Person of real Merit, and am glad you have been able to render her any Service.[2]

I received duly the Bills you sent me.[3] Let me know whether you have got home my Library: and also whether you have been paid for the Printing Letters sold to Lancaster and Virginia.[4]

I enjoy at present as good a State of Health as I have had for many Years; and I still continue to be esteem'd and belov'd by this amiable Nation, and have probably much more Respect shown me than I should have at home; yet I long to be there before I die, and I wish to set out while I have Strength to bear the Voyage; but I have not as yet receiv'd the Permission of Congress; and the Settlement of my Accts. will I apprehend necessarily detain me another Winter.

2. BF had recommended her; see XXXIX, 23–4.
3. See XXXIX, 24, 325.
4. The Baches had packed BF's library and shipped it to Bethlehem before the British occupied Philadelphia in 1777: XXIII, 279–80, 361. For the current status of the library and printing type see RB's reply of Sept. 9.

Ben writes.[5] I am ever, my dear Children, Your affectionate
Father   B FRANKLIN

[*Note by William Temple Franklin:*] I am afraid I shall hardly
have time to write I therefore here send my most affece. Respects
W. T. F.

To Joseph Banks   ALS: British Library; copy: Library of Congress

In this letter, prompted by Banks's overture of May 28, Franklin re-
joices in the peace, muses on the folly of war, and reclaims his place in
the British scientific community, as he had long wished to do.[6] Eras-
ing eight years of estrangement, he notes with pleasure the recent
discoveries made by "our" Society. By way of reciprocation, he adds
a postscript alluding to an experiment that no one in Paris had yet
witnessed but all were discussing: the "vast Globe sent up into the
Air" in the village of Annonay. The age of flight had begun, and
in the months to come Franklin would be its chief chronicler to the
Royal Society.

The idea for the hot-air balloon came from Joseph Montgolfier,
a scion of the great papermaking family of Annonay with whom
Franklin had corresponded and whose paper he greatly admired.[7]
Unsuited to business (he had failed at several ventures) but fascinated by mathematics, chemistry and mechanics, subjects in which
he was entirely self-taught, the 42-year-old was observing particles
rising up the flue in his fireplace on a cold day in November, 1782,
when he realized that he might be able to harness the power of heated
air. His first experiment consisted of levitating a four-foot-high box

5. BFB wrote a brief and dutiful letter to his father that same day. ("Excuse the schortness of my letter," he wrote in a postscript, "the time don't
permit me to write a Long one.") He had received RB's letter of May 31, had
seen the Morris boys often, had been sick but was now "quitte well," had
left Geneva on July 9, and "saw my Dear Grandpapa the 19 of the same
mounth." BFB to RB, July 27, 1783, APS. BFB added more notes to his family
before the present letter was posted, though none has been found; see RB to
BF, Sept. 9.
6. See BF's previous letter of Sept. 9, 1782: XXXVIII, 84–5.
7. XXXVI, 384–5, 486–7.

made from taffeta stretched around a thin wooden frame. Rushing home to the papermill in Vidalon, he engaged his brother Etienne to collaborate on further experiments. Etienne, five years his junior and the youngest of Pierre Montgolfier's sons, had been in charge of the Vidalon mill since 1772, when their father had called him home from his architecture studies in Paris to manage the family business. While in Paris, Etienne had received formal instruction in science, which would now prove invaluable, and had also met several people who would play key roles in the story of the balloons (not to mention papermaking), most notably Nicolas Desmarest and Jean-Baptiste Réveillon.[8]

Joseph and Etienne experimented with ever-larger "machines" in the confines of the Vidalon compound, careful to keep their trials secret. In mid-December, after a huge box filled with hot air burst its retaining cords and sailed into a neighboring field, Etienne wrote a long letter to Desmarest in Paris, begging him to announce their discovery to the Académie des sciences and establish their priority. Details would follow, he promised. The academician declined to take any further action until Etienne sent a good drawing and a detailed description.[9] The brothers, meanwhile, continued their experiments throughout the spring: calculating forces, modifying designs, and constructing larger vehicles capable of lifting heavier loads. Eventually, with the help of their family, they fabricated a balloon 35 feet in diameter, its four segments made from cloth lined with paper (to prevent leakage) and fastened by 1,800 buttons. This was the "machine aérostatique" that they demonstrated before the *Etats particuliers*, the diocesan assembly of the Vivarais region, on a rainy June 4, 1783.[1]

---

8. The best account of the Montgolfiers and the history of the first balloons is Gillispie, *Montgolfier Brothers;* the information in this paragraph is drawn from pp. 10–17. Our understanding of the story, which will occupy this edition for several volumes, is based on Gillispie's work and the contemporary MSS and imprints that informed it, many of which (the Montgolfier papers, in particular) were deposited by the author in the Princeton University Library.

9. Gillispie, *Montgolfier Brothers*, pp. 21–2.

1. See Gillispie, *Montgolfier Brothers*, pp. 3–4. The experiment is often cited as taking place on June 5, a date that appeared in contemporary newspapers beginning with the *Jour. de Paris*, July 27, 1783. The confusion stemmed from an ambiguity in the assembly's hastily written account. The actual date is clarified by the Montgolfier brothers' petition to the *Etats particuliers*, published and discussed in Auguste Le Sourd, *Essai sur*

The globe, to which they had at the last minute attached a brazier holding the source of heat—straw and shredded wool, set aflame—bobbed to a height of 3,000 feet and remained aloft for about 10 minutes, gently landing in a vineyard more than one and a half miles away. The following morning, at the brothers' request, the *Etats* wrote an official account (*procès-verbal*) of the trial they had witnessed, establishing the Montgolfier brothers of Annonay as the globe's inventors. By June 28 that report was in the hands of Lefèvre d'Ormesson, controller general of finances, who forwarded it to Condorcet, secretary of the Académie des sciences, requesting a response. At its next meeting, July 2, the academy appointed a five-man commission to examine the invention. Three members were well known to Franklin: Lavoisier, Desmarest, and Le Roy. They were joined by mathematicians Gaspard Monge and the abbé Charles Bossut.[2] The following day, July 3, the commission reviewed the *procès-verbal* and a set of observations by the Montgolfiers.[3] Two weeks later, Condorcet

---

les Etats du Vivarais depuis leurs origines (Paris, 1926), pp. 150–2; see also Comte de La Vaulx and Paul Tissandier, *Joseph et Etienne de Montgolfier* (Annonay, 1926). The Montgolfiers' draft petition is illustrated in Gillispie, *Montgolfier Brothers*, facing p. 7. Faujas de Saint-Fond also attributed the experiment to June 5 in his widely read *Description des expériences de la machine aérostatique de MM. de Montgolfier*, published in November, 1783, based on an undated letter he claimed to have received from Etienne Montgolfier, quoted on pp. 3–4.

2. The minutes of the July 2 meeting include the text of d'Ormesson's June 28 letter to Condorcet as well as the names of the commissioners: Académie des sciences, *Procès-verbaux*, CII, 149. Monge (1746–1818) and Bossut (1730–1814) are listed in the *Index biographique des membres et correspondants de l'Académie des sciences . . .* (Paris, 1954), pp. 363–4, 63–4. For Monge, see also *Dictionary of Scientific Biography*. Bossut, assistant director of the Académie des sciences, is identified in the *DBF*. Condorcet served on the commission ex officio. During the fall, Monge left the commission and Tillet, Brisson, and Cadet were added: "Rapport Fait à l'Académie des Sciences, sur la Machine aérostatique, de Mrs. de Montgolfier . . . ," *Histoire de l'Académie royale des sciences* for 1783, p. 5.

3. The "Observations" refer explicitly to the *procès-verbal* and correct certain points. The MS version that circulated in July (BF's copy of which is discussed below) was unsigned. The authors were commonly known, however (see Neil Chambers, ed., *Scientific Correspondence of Sir Joseph Banks, 1765–1820* (6 vols., London, 2007), II, 113), and were identified when the "Observations" were published alongside related documents and commentary in *Jour. historique et politique*, no. 33 [mid-August], pp. 359–63.

reported to d'Ormesson that since Etienne Montgolfier had proposed to come to Paris to repeat his experiment before the commission, they would await his arrival.[4]

News of the Annonay experiment spread quickly in the scientific community. Charles Blagden learned of it almost immediately from members of the Académie des sciences.[5] Franklin was given the *procès-verbal* and "Observations" to read, and had his secretary make copies.[6] His opinion, expressed to Blagden some weeks later, was that the balloon should have been constructed of "fine oil'd Silk,"[7] as indeed the next balloon was.

It would be another several weeks before the general public would read an accurate description of the experiment. In the meantime, what purported to be an eyewitness account was published on July 10 in the *Affiches, annonces, et avis divers*. The anonymous letter, written by an Annonay landowner with no love for the Montgolfiers, portrayed the experiment as a harebrained scheme concocted by a pair of reckless brothers who were determined to go up in the sky and would not stop until one of their necks was broken. Their contraption was shaped like a house, measured 16 × 16 × 36 feet, and had burst into flames upon landing, terrifying the peasantry into believing that the moon had detached itself from the sky, signaling the Last Judgment. A variant of this letter was reprinted on July 26 in the *Mercure de France*, a prominent weekly news journal.[8]

4. Condorcet to d'Ormesson, July 19, 1783, described in Gillispie, *Montgolfier Brothers*, p. 25, and reproduced in Comte de La Vaulx and Paul Tissandier, *Joseph et Etienne de Montgolfier* (Annonay, 1926), p. 35. In an undated letter to Desmarest written during this period, Etienne Montgolfier described the capabilities of the invention, explained the brothers' need for financial assistance for further development, asked Desmarest to intercede with the academy to have a commission named, and expressed his desire to demonstrate the machine before that commission "during [his] visit to Paris." The Montgolfier family decided that Etienne would make the trip alone: Gillispie, *Montgolfier Brothers*, pp. 22–4.

5. Blagden reported these general conversations to Joseph Banks on July 4, 1783: Chambers, ed., *Scientific Correspondence of Sir Joseph Banks*, II, 101–2.

6. Those copies, which include a July 3 notation made by the commission, are in the hand of L'Air de Lamotte (University of Pa. Library).

7. Charles Blagden's Journal, entry of July 25, 1783, where Blagden called the balloon a "flying Sack." Yale University Library.

8. The first letter, dated June 21, has so many factual errors that the author's claim to having been present at the launch cannot be believed. It does

Everything changed once Etienne Montgolfier made his presence known to the academy.[9] Le Roy informed Franklin of his arrival on July 27, the date of the present letter.[1] That same day, the *Journal de Paris* printed a factual account, obviously written by an academician, of both the Annonay experiment and how the academy had learned of it. It included calculations of the balloon's weight, volume, and lifting force taken from the "Observations." Acknowledging Montgolfier's reputation for making the finest paper in France (a subject the academy had investigated in 1781),[2] the article also observed that if he had only been able to fill the balloon with "l'air inflammable" extracted from iron (a technique only recently demonstrated by Lavoisier), it might have achieved greater height.

A team of scientists outside the Académie des sciences immediately formed to do just that. Having studied the *procès-verbal* and "Observations," and having heard rumors that Montgolfier planned to launch a balloon 100 feet in diameter,[3] they knew that whatever gas he would use (the secret was closely guarded) would be the same as what he had used in Annonay, which was only slightly lighter than air. "Inflammable air" was 10 times as light, but was extremely expensive to produce and had so far been generated only in small quantities. On July 28, Barthélemy Faujas de Saint-Fond installed him-

---

not mention the presence of the *Etats particuliers*. It does, however, point out that the Montgolfiers' neighbor (and rival) Mathieu Johannot remained productively engaged in manufacturing what might be the most beautiful paper in France: *Affiches, annonces, et avis divers* (also known as *Feuille hebdomadaire*), July 10, 1783, p. 112; described in Gillispie, *Montgolfier Brothers*, p. 25. The second version, also from an anonymous source in Annonay but dated June 26, dropped the final section about Johannot: *Mercure de France (Jour. politique de Bruxelles)* for July 26, 1783, pp. 176–7.

9. Etienne had left Annonay on July 11, but spent his first days in Paris lodging quietly with an uncle. The newly fabricated balloon he intended to demonstrate was shipped separately, on July 12, but was never used: Gillispie, *Montgolfier Brothers*, pp. 24–5.

1. See the postscript of Le Roy's letter of July 27. That letter mentions the previous day's meeting of the Académie des sciences; Le Roy must have learned the news then.

2. XXXVI, 384.

3. Faujas de Saint-Fond to Joseph Banks, July 28, 1783. He enclosed copies of the *procès-verbal* and "Observations" and reported on Montgolfier's plans: Chambers, ed., *Scientific Correspondence of Sir Joseph Banks*, II, 113. The rumor of a 100-foot-wide balloon was still circulating a month later: *Mercure de France (Jour. politique de Bruxelles)* of Aug. 23, pp. 177–8.

self at a table in the Café du Caveau in the Palais-Royal,[4] soliciting contributions to repeat Montgolfier's experiment, this time with inflammable air and under the expert direction of the popular lecturer in physics Jacques-Alexandre-César Charles. Advertising only by word of mouth, as Faujas would boast in the book he published later that year, the subscription was soon filled by wealthy patrons.[5] Long before Etienne Montgolfier would stage his demonstration, Franklin would witness the spectacular ascension of a 12-foot-wide hydrogen balloon.[6]

Dear Sir,   Passy, July 27. 1783.
I received your very kind Letter by Dr Blagden, and esteem myself much honour'd by your Friendly Remembrance. I have been too much and too closely engag'd in public Affairs since his being here, to enjoy all the Benefit of his Conversation you were so good as to intend me.[7] I hope soon to have more Leisure, and to spend a Part of it in those Studies that are much more agreable to me than political Operations.—

I join with you most cordially in rejoicing at the Return of Peace. I hope it will be lasting, & that Mankind will at length, as they call themselves reasonable Creatures, have Reason and Sense enough to settle their Differences without cutting Throats: For in my Opinion *there never was a good War, or a bad Peace.*—[8] What vast Additions to the Conveniences and Comforts of Living might Mankind have acquired, if the Money spent in Wars had been employ'd in Works of public Utility. What an Extention of Agriculture even to the Tops of our Mountains; What Rivers render'd navigable, or join'd by Canals; what Bridges, Acqueducts, new Roads & other public Works, Edifices & Im-

---

4. Planche XXII, La Vaulx and Tissandier, *Joseph et Etienne de Montgolfier,* pp. 35–6.

5. Faujas de Saint-Fond, *Description des expériences de la machine aérostatique de MM. de Montgolfier* . . . (Paris, 1783), pp. 8–9. The list of subscribers has never been located.

6. See BF to Banks, Aug. 30[–Sept. 2].

7. Blagden carried Banks's letter of May 28. During almost two months in Paris, he visited BF only three times; see the annotation of that letter and BF to Blagden, July 29.

8. For BF's earlier uses of this phrase see XXXI, 437; XXXVII, 457.

provements, rendering England a compleat Paradise, might not have been obtain'd by spending those Millions in doing Good which in the last War have been spent in doing Mischief! in bringing Misery into thousands of Families, and destroying the Lives of so many Thousands of working People who might have perform'd the useful Labour.—

I am pleas'd with the late astronomical Discoveries made by our Society. Furnish'd as all Europe now is with Academies of Science, with nice Instruments and the Spirit of Experiment, the Progress of human Knowledge will be rapid, and Discoveries made of which we have at present no Conception. I begin to be almost sorry I was born so soon, since I cannot have the Happiness of knowing what will be known 100 Years hence.—[9]

I wish continu'd Success to the Labours of the Royal Society, and that you may long adorn their Chair, being with the highest Esteem, Dear Sir, Your most obedient & most humble Servant

B Franklin

Dr Blagden will acquaint you with the Experiment of a vast Globe sent up into the Air, much talk'd of here at present, & which if prosecuted may furnish Means of new Knowledge.

Sir Jos. Banks.

To Robert Morris
AL (draft): Library of Congress

Sir,   Passy, July 27. 1783

I have been honoured by your Letters in the Washington, of the 3d. 11th. 13th. 19th of January, and the 26th & 31st of May.[1] Till that Ship arriv'd, we had been totally in the dark respecting

---

9. BF had voiced a similar regret in his letter to Joseph Priestley of Feb. 8, 1780. Among the discoveries that he anticipated within the next thousand years was an invention "to deprive large Masses of their Gravity & give them absolute Levity, for the sake of easy Transport": XXXI, 455–6.

1. Morris wrote on May 30, not May 31, and BF neglected to acknowledge the letter of May 27, to which he also responds here. Otherwise, all the letters mentioned are published above.

American Affairs for near 6 Months. The Correspondence may henceforth be more regular, as 5 Pacquet Boats are now ordered here, to depart from LOrient for N. York the middle of each Month,[2] which with those that I understand will continue to depart from England the Beginning of each Month,[3] will give Opportunities of Writing every Fortnight. The first from hence is to sail the 3d Tuesday in September.— I have received also your Dispatshes per Col. Ogden; and also a Sett that had been in England, and were opened.[4] They contained all your Correspondence with Gen. Washington & the Contractors relating to the Difficulties in supplying the Army;[5] and I am afraid have had an ill Effect on the Negociations, the conciliating Views of the Ministry respecting our Commerce with their Islands seeming by their late Proclamation[6] to be entirely changed.—

I am happy to find that you had agreed to continue the Exercise of your Office for some time longer:[7] Your Reputation as well as your Abilities is necessary to our Affairs.— I am amaz'd at the Quantity of Business you so well go thorough.

The Affair between you & the Intendant of the French Army, respecting the irregular Transactions of de Mars & de Brassine, is not, as I understand from Gen. de Chatellux, at all spoken of here; and he is of Opinion, that as it is settled by the Event of the Suit, there can be no Use in taking any farther Notice of it

2. The packet service was established by a June 28 *arrêt* of the Royal Council of State, printed on July 22 in the *Gaz. de Leyde* and on July 25 in the *Courier de l'Europe*. (An undated copy in L'Air de Lamotte's hand is at the APS.) The *arrêt* provided that the packet boats would carry mail, passengers, and luxury goods, and depart Port Louis (adjoining Lorient) for New York on the Tuesday of the third week of every month. The service would be administered by Le Couteulx & Cie. and begin in September.

3. On the first Wednesday of every month, as Todd wrote to BF on June 25.

4. For the dispatches that arrived with Matthias Ogden on July 12 see the American Commissioners to Livingston, July 18, and BF to Livingston, July 22[-26]. For the letters that were forwarded from England see John Vaughan to BF, June 10; Falconer to BF, June 23; *Morris Papers*, VII, 698n.

5. See XXXVIII, 575n.

6. The Order in Council of July 2.

7. See Morris to BF, May 26, letter (I).

at present. I shall therefore say nothing of it to the Ministers, unless you shall hereafter think proper to direct it.[8] Mr Grand and myself were for a long time in a most anxious Situation here. Our Funds nearly absorbed, fresh Drafts continually appearing, more foreseen, and all our Worrying of the Ministers with Applications for farther Aids from Government proving ineffectual.[9] We at length however after many Difficulties obtain'd what was wanted from the Loan in Holland.—[1] Upon the Receipt of your Letters I made the fresh Application directed, but without Success; as you will see by the Letters inclosed;[2] and I hope in God that no more such Orders will be sent me. If our People who neither pay Rents nor Tythes, would only pay honestly in Taxes half what other Nations pay in those Articles, our whole Debt might be discharg'd in a Twelvemonth.—[3] But I conceive the great Difficulty lies in the Collection of our Taxes, thro' the dispers'd Situation of our Inhabitants; and the excessive Trouble of going from House to House many Miles

8. See Morris to BF, May 27. De Brassine, imprisoned as a result of the lawsuit, was released in 1787 at the request of France: *Morris Papers*, VII, 568n.

9. At this point in the draft, there is a passage which BF crossed out: "We apply'd to Mr Adams, who alledg'd that the Disposition of Money in Holland was taken out of his Hands, at which he seem'd offended, but agreed to write a joint Letter with Mr Jay & me, to advise the Bankers there to furnish Mr Grand wth what they could; their Answer was that they likewise expected Bills from you, but would do it if we would engage to replace what they should furnish, in case they should want it, which we could not do. I apply'd also to Messrs Le Couteulx who we understood had Money of yours in their Hands, but with as little Success. In fine we were on the point of failing, we lost our Sleep, & Mr Grand grew visibly thinner." The letters to and from the Dutch bankers are above, May 22 and May 29, while those to and from Le Couteulx & Cie. are above, July 2.

1. Grand himself wrote to Morris on July 20 that as a result of JA's letter and one of his own, the consortium promised 1,500,000 *l.t.* within a month's time and indeed had already begun remittances: *Morris Papers*, VIII, 315–16; and see Grand to BF, July 5.

2. These were BF and Jay to Vergennes, June 28; BF to Vergennes, July 4; Vergennes to BF and Jay, July 5; and Vergennes to BF, July 18. Morris forwarded copies of these and other documents to Congress on Sept. 15: *Morris Papers*, VIII, 519.

3. BF contemplated substituting "easily in a very short Period" for "in a Twelvemonth", but then reinstated his original phrase.

to collect a few Shillings from each, often oblig'd to repeat the Calls. Might not this be help'd by some Laws, such as one[4] disabling a Man to take out any Writ or commence any Action, for recovering any Debt, Damage, Legacy, &c. or to receive any other Benefit or Protection from the Laws of the Society, who does not prove that he has duly contributed to its support, by producing the Collector's Receipt for his last Taxes.—

The Farmers-General, who have been extreamly kind & favourable to us, in never urging a Compliance with our Contract or a Repayment of the Million they advanc'd to us, nor demanding any Interest, have lately been with me & intimated that they hop'd now we were in Peace, it might not be inconvenient to us to proceed in discharging the Debt. After some Conversation on the Means, they agreed to write me a Letter, of which I send a Copy.[5] You will understand a Part of it, by knowing that I recommended you warmly to them as a proper Correspondent, after this Affair & your Office should be finished.[6] I ought & do as warmly recommend to you the doing them Justice as speedily as may be, and favouring them where it is practicable, for we are really under great Obligations to them. Inclos'd is a Copy of their Acct. It was sent before, but probably miscarried.[7]

I am content with the Method established respecting the Salaries,[8] and am with sincere & great Esteem, Sir,

honble. R. Morris Esqr

---

4. Here BF drafted but deleted "requiring the People to bring in their Taxes to the Collector".

5. Above, July 17.

6. See BF's memorandum to the farmers general, [before July 17].

7. The Nov. 17, 1781, account (XXXVI, 145n) was signed by BF and representatives of the farmers general; a copy in French is at the National Archives along with an English translation. BF may have sent a copy with his Sept. 26, 1782, letter to Morris, of which only an extract survives (XXXVIII, 142–3).

8. Which Morris explained in his letter of Jan. 13 (XXXVIII, 581–2).

From Richard Bache

ALS: American Philosophical Society

Dear & Hond: Sir   Philadelphia July 27th. 1783.

I have to thank you for a number of introductory Letters received from you lately,[9] all of which have been productive of either pleasure, or profit, or both—in consequence of your recommendations B & Shee have received very considerable consignments from Dunkirk and we have further prospects of extending our Connection.

This will be handed you by Mr. Carter, into whose care I have given a large bundle of News papers, he takes his Wife and Family with him, with an intention of staying some time in Europe; Mrs. Carter is the Daughter of General Schuyler, a Lady you know very well; I am certain, it is unnecessary to sollicit your kindness & Civilities towards them—[1] I have received from the Loan Office, certificates for another years Interest of the Money you lent the public, which by an Act of this State are to be paid before July 1784.[2] As soon as I receive the Money it shall be remitted you— I have the happiness to inform you that Sally and the Children are well— I wrote to Ben lately— my love to Temple and accept yourself the dutifull Affection of Dear sir Your ever affectionate son   RICH BACHE

We should be glad to know when we are to expect you on this side the Water—

Dr. Franklin

9. The only such extant letter is a recommendation for Benjamin Vaughan's brother-in-law: XXXIX, 361.

1. For "John Carter" and his family, who sailed that very day, see Philip Schuyler to BF, July 1.

2. The act passed by Pennsylvania on March 21, for which see the annotation of RB to BF, May 31.

From Lafayette[3]

ALS: Sotheby's, New York (1985)

My dear Sir Chavaniac july the 27th 1783
I Beg leave to Return You My thanks for the Notice You
Give me of An opportunity to America— But find it is too late
to improve it, and My only Hope is that some letters I Have
these past days sent to Paris, Have Been put on Board the Washington— Since we Could not Get Monney Here, I am Glad it
Has Been found in Holland— Mr. Hartlay's dissatisfaction, if
Sincere, arises from a disposition in Great Britain I Have long
foreseen— Time, I fear, Will prove those people are not to Be
Confided in—And for ever I take them to Be Natural ennemies
to America— Inclosed You Will find a paper, the postscript of
Which Contains two letters, that I earnestly Beg You to Have
forwarded to American printers—[4] About the 15th August, and
sooner if I may Be of Service, I Hope to tell You Myself How
Respectfully and affectionately I Have the Honor to Be, My
dear Sir, Yours LAFAYETTE

Notation: Lafayette July 27. 1783

3. Because L'Air de Lamotte wrote the notation, we are confident that this letter was addressed to BF.

4. Lafayette must have sent copies of his April 30 letter to Sir Henry Clinton and Clinton's May 12 response, which he had sent to Henry Laurens on July 6, asking that he get them printed in the British press: Idzerda, *Lafayette Papers*, v, 127, 127–8n, 141–2. They appeared in the *Public Advertiser* on July 17; there, as in all other newspaper appearances we have found, the first letter is dated April 29. Whether or not BF forwarded them, they did appear in the American press beginning (as far as we know) with the Sept. 20, 1783, issue of the Philadelphia *Independent Gazetteer.*

BF also extended his friendship to Lafayette's former aide-de-camp Maj. Michel Capitaine du Chesnoy (XXXI, 391n). On Sept. 1 he certified the signatures on an Aug. 20, 1783, power of attorney nominating Richard Peters to receive $1,600 due to Capitaine on account of his service in the American army (Harvard University Library). Capitaine had been promoted to major and granted leave to visit France on Nov. 5, 1778. He returned to the United States in March, 1780, where he served under Lafayette through the Battle of Yorktown. As a French officer, he served with the army intended to sail from Cadiz with d'Estaing (for which see XXXVIII, 330): Lasseray, *Les Français,* I, 141–2; Bodinier, *Dictionnaire; JCC,* XII, 1105.

From Jean-Baptiste Le Roy

ALS: American Philosophical Society

[July 27, 1783][5]

Voici une lettre Mon Illustre Docteur que M. Cassini Le Pere ma chargé de vous remettre.[6] Votre present a été reçu hier à lAcadémie avec beaucoup de reconnoissance et il a été ordonné au Secrétaire de vous ecrire au Nom de la Compagnie pour vous en remercier.[7]

Le Jeune Dr Home dont je vous ai parlé hier et qui va a Veinne se chargera très volontiers de votre lettre pour M. Ingenhouz et sera bien flatté d'arriver chez lui porteur d'une pareille Lettre. C'est un jeune Médecin d'Ecosse de merite. Si vous comptez ou que votre temps vous le permette de lui donner cette lettre ayez la bonté de me l'envoyer parcequ'il doit envoyer chercher ce matin celles que j'ai écrites pour lui et que je lui ai promises.[8] Recevez Mon Illustre Docteur mille nouvelles assurrances de tout mon attachement   LE ROY

5. The date is certain, based on the conjuction of two clues: Le Roy's allusion in the first paragraph to the Academy of Science's receipt of BF's gift on the previous day, and the postscript about the man who had performed an experiment with a balloon 35 feet in diameter. See the annotation below.

6. César-François Cassini de Thury is identified in XXIX, 323–4, where we published his only known letter to BF—an undated note—at the earliest possible time. We now believe that his letter was written on July 26, 1783, and was the one Le Roy is here forwarding. Written from the Académie des sciences, Cassini de Thury asked BF for a copy of the work that Le Roy had just presented to the Academy (a work he viewed as BF's), and promised to reciprocate with a work of his own, currently being printed. For BF's donation see the following note; Cassini de Thury's work was undoubtedly *Description géometrique de la France* (Paris, 1783).

7. On July 26 the Académie des sciences received BF's donation of *Constitutions des treize Etats-Unis de l'Amérique* and resolved to thank him. BF was not present at the meeting; Le Roy undoubtedly conveyed the volume: Académie des sciences, *Procès-verbaux*, CII, 159. Condorcet, secretary of the Academy, wrote the official letter of thanks on Aug. 20, below.

8. The young doctor was most likely James Home (1760–1844), who earned his medical degree at Edinburgh University. In 1798 he succeeded his father, Francis Home, as professor of medicine there: *ODNB*. If Le Roy had asked BF for a letter of introduction to Ingenhousz for Home, as this letter seems to imply, there is no indication that BF ever wrote it.

L'homme a l'experience du ballon de 35 pieds de diamètre est arrivé et je compte vous le mener un de ces jours[9]

Addressed: A Monsieur / Monsieur Franklin

Notation: Le Roy

To Nathaniel Falconer

ALS: American Philosophical Society; transcript: Historical Society of Pennsylvania

Dear Friend,   Passy, July 28. 1783.
I received your Favour of the 18th. Capt. Barney brought us the Dispatches we so long expected. Mr Deane as you observe is lost: Dr Bancroft is I believe steady to the Interest of his Country, and will make an agreable Passenger if you can take him. You desire to know something of the State of Affairs here. Every thing goes well with respect to this Court & the other Friendly Powers. What England is doing, or means to do; or why the Definitive Treaty is so long delay'd, I know perhaps less than you do; as, being in that Country, you may have Opportunities of hearing more than I can. For my self, I am at present as hearty & well as I have been these many Years; and as happy as a Man can be where every body strives to make him so. The French are an amiable People to live with: They love me, & I love them. Yet I do not feel my self at home, & I wish to die in my own Country.— Barney will sail this Week with our Dispatches. A good Voyage to you, my Friend; and may God ever bless you.   B FRANKLIN

Capt. Falconer

Addressed: To / Captain Nathl. Falconer / at the Pensilvania Coffeehouse / Birchin Lane / London

Endorsed: Benja Franklin Passy 28 July 1783

9. A reference to Etienne Montgolfier. The Montgolfiers' demonstration at Annonay on June 4 was the only experiment involving a balloon with a diameter of 35 feet; see our headnote to BF to Banks, July 27.

From Thomas Barclay

LS: Archives du Ministère des affaires étrangères[1]

Sir   Auteuil 28 July 1783

I have the honor to inform your Excellency that I received last post a Letter from Messrs. Schweighauser & Dobreé of Nantes under whose care the Arsnal belonging to the United States is placed,[2] informing me that their Partner at L'Orient Messr. Puchelberg & Co., had some months ago laid an attachment on all the Arms and other Military supplies under the Care of Messrs. Schweighauser & Dobreé.[3]

I need not inform your Excellency of the Nature of the transaction, as it fell immediately under your own inspection, but I beg leave to say that unless Goverment passes some signal Censure on those persons who have brought attachments against the property of the United States the Execution of my Office will be embarrass'd beyond discription.

I beg Sir you will Lay the matter in its proper light before the Minister's, and obtain as soon as possible the dismission of this attachment and of those laid on the Alliances prize money.[4]

These attachments have been held in suspence several months to the great determent of the Public business under my care, and at the immenent risk of a heavy Loss in the final payment.[5]

I have the honor to be with great respect Your Excellency's Most Obedient Most Huml Sert   THOS BARCLAY

His Excellency Benjamin Franklin Esqr.

1. This letter was forwarded to Vergennes with the note BF wrote to accompany it, immediately below.

2. XXXVII, 450.

3. Puchelberg & Cie. had threatened twice before to take action in order to assure payment for supplies it had furnished to the *Alliance* in 1780: XXXVII, 657–8. See also BF's note, below.

4. See Vergennes to BF, June 20, letter (III).

5. Barclay left for Nantes and Lorient in late September to investigate these issues in person: Roberts and Roberts, *Thomas Barclay*, pp. 130–1. He took with him French translations of the congressional resolutions appointing him to audit the public accounts in Europe. BF attested these on Sept. 11 (Library of Congress).

To [Vergennes][6]

ALS: Archives du Ministère des affaires étrangères; ALS (draft): Library of Congress

[on or after July 28, 1783][7]

Note on Mr Barclay's Letter

When the Ship Alliance belonging to the Congress was at l'Orient, under the Command of Capt. Jones, Moylan & Co Merchants there, were appointed to supply the Ship with what was necessary during her Stay.

Capt. Landais taking Possession of the Ship surreptitiously in the Absence of Capt. Jones, apply'd to one Puchelberg, a Commis of Mr Schweighauser, for some Provisions, who not only *without* Orders either from me or Mr Schweighauser, but *contrary* to express Orders from both, furnished the same, pretending that Landais demanded them in the Name and on Account of the Navy-Board of Boston.

Payment was afterwards demanded of me, which I refus'd, referring the Matter to the said Navy-Board. It was also demanded of his Employer Schweighauser, who it seems refus'd also, probably because the Disbursement was made contrary to Orders.[8]

This Man, Puchelberg, has on this Account, arrested the Property of the United States, in whose Hands so ever he could find any.—

The Consul of the States complains of it as an Injury, and an Insult: And it is certain, that great Inconveniencies will follow, if such Proceedings are permitted, and if every Man who

---

6. Drafted by BF for Barclay to forward to Vergennes, along with the letter he had just received from Barclay (immediately above). Vergennes sent translations to Castries on Aug. 15, requesting that Castries consider this case in the same light as the one that had been decided against Forster frères (for which see Vergennes to BF, July 29): AAE.

7. BF could not have prepared this appeal any later than Aug. 1, the day Barclay left Paris for London; see our annotation of Laurens to the Commissioners, Aug. 9.

8. The story of Landais' seizure of the *Alliance* in June, 1780, and Puchelberg's supplying the ship against orders is told in vols. 32 and 33.

pretends a Demand against any Foreign Power, however ill-founded, may arrest the Effects of that Power in France;—for so the Arms, Ammunition, Clothing, &c. purchased in France, & depended on for important Operations of Government, may be stopt by any private Person, perhaps under Direction of an Enemy, & those Operations defeated; and the United States can never hereafter with Safety make any such Purchases in France.
It is therefore submitted to Consideration, whether the said Arrests ought not only to be immediately discharg'd, but the Arrester punish'd for his Insolence.   B F.

Notation: a raport à la lettre de M. Barclay du 28. Juillet 1783.

From Gian Francesco Cigna[9]

ALS: University of Pennsylvania Library

Monsieur   Turin ce 28 julliet 1783
Les heureuses revolutions que Votre genie sublime, Monsieur, a apporté dans la politique et dans la philosophie, qui feront a jamais epoque dans l'histoire des Nations, et dans celle de l'esprit humain ont fait ambitionner a l'Academie des Sciences de cette Capitale d'illustrer son catalogue avec le nom du plus grand Philosophe du siecle, ce qui lui a été aisement accordé par notre Auguste Souverain a l'ocasion qu'il vient de lui donner un etablissement solide,[1] en vous nommant Monsieur pour une des places destinées aux Savants etrangers. Elle espere que vous voudrais bien agreer ce temoignage de l'estime et de la reconais-

---

9. Physician and professor of anatomy at the University of Turin: XIII, 423n, 453; XIV, 49n. BF's copy of his article on electricity, *De novis quibusdam experimentis electricis* (Turin, 1766), is at the Hist. Soc. of Pa.
1. Just three days earlier, the king of Sardinia, Vittorio Amedeo III, extended his special protection to the scientific organization which since 1761 had been a royal society (and as such had exchanged volumes of transactions with the APS: XIX, 147; XXII, 308). On July 25, 1783, its title became Accademia Reale delle Scienze: Michele Maylender, *Storia delle Accademie d'Italia* (5 vols., Bologna, 1926–30), IV, 390–1; Antonio Pace, *Benjamin Franklin and Italy* (Philadelphia, 1958), pp. 65–6, 87–8.

sance qu'elle a pour vos merites eminents, qui lui est commune avec tous ceux qui s'interessent a l'avancement des sçiences, et au bien de l'humanité. Je suis en particulier bien flatté que la charge de secretaire de l'Academie me procure l'honneur d'être son interprete auprés de Vous, et me presente une ocasion de Vous declarer les sentiments d'admiration, dont je suis de long-temps penetré pour vos talents superieurs, et pour vos immor-telles decouvertes.

J'ai l'honneur d'être avec toute la veneration Monsieur Votre très umble et très obeist Serviteur   J. F. CIGNA

Endorsed: Letters to be answd before I leave France[2]

From Giuseppe Doria Pamphili: Letter and Note

(I) L: Library of Congress; copy and transcript: National Archives; press copy of copy: American Philosophical Society; (II) Copy and tran-script:[3] National Archives; press copy of copy: American Philosophical Society; copy: Archives of the Congregatio de Propaganda Fide

The independence of the United States presented the Holy See with the problem of how to minister to the needs of American Catholics. The colonies had been under the authority of the vicar apostolic in London, but once the political ties were officially dissolved, that re-ligious bond would break. On January 15, 1783, Cardinal Leonardo Antonelli, prefect of the Congregation for the Propagation of the Faith, instructed the papal nuncio in Paris, Archbishop Pamphili, to seek the assistance of the French government on two matters. One was persuading the Americans to include in their peace treaty an article guaranteeing the free exercise of the Catholic religion. The other was devising a plan for the establishment of missions in Amer-ica and appointing a vicar apostolic or bishop (preferably an Ameri-can) in one of the major cities. Vergennes assured the nuncio on Feb-ruary 4 that an article was unnecessary, as all religions were tolerated

---

2. BF let this languish until July 5, 1785, when he acknowledged the honor it contained (Hist. Soc. of Pa.).

3. The English translation made for Congress, also at the National Ar-chives, is published in Wharton, *Diplomatic Correspondence*, VI, 614–15n.

in America, and evidently ignored the nuncio's request that he speak to Franklin.[4] Pamphili himself could not broach these topics with Franklin until the American was recognized by the diplomatic corps.

That general recognition came at the weekly gathering of foreign ministers at Versailles on Tuesday, July 8. Pamphili reported to Rome that Franklin, Adams, and Jay were received by the diplomatic corps without having presented the customary card announcing themselves as ministers of the United States of America, but rather, "in the same manner customarily observed with foreign nobility who present themselves in this capital."[5]

With the way now cleared for diplomatic initiatives, Pamphili sent this note to Franklin for forwarding to Congress. Though the American responded that it would be "absolutely useless" to do so,[6] he nonetheless forwarded the note in his September 13 letter to Elias Boudinot.

I.

Ce 28. Juillet 1783.

M. Le Nonce Apostolique a l'honneur d'envoyer à Monsieur Franklin la note ci-jointe. Il le prie de vouloir bien la faire passer au Congrès des Etats Unis de l'Amerique Septentrionale et l'appuyer de son credit./.

II.

[July 28, 1783]

Note.

Avant la Revolution qui vient d'être consommée dans l'Amérique septentrionale, les Catholiques et les Missionaires de ces Provinces dependoient dans le Spirituel du Vicaire Apos-

---

4. See Jules A. Baisnée, *France and the Establishment of the American Catholic Hierarchy: the Myth of French Interference (1783–1784)* (Baltimore, 1934), pp. 21–4, 45–9, where the correspondence is described as well as reproduced in translation. Antonelli's letter in the original Italian is in Carl R. Fish, ed., "Documents relative to the Adjustment of the Roman Catholic Organization in the United States to the Conditions of National Independence, 1783–1789," *American Hist. Rev.*, XV (1909–10), 801–4.

5. Antonio Pace, *Benjamin Franklin and Italy* (Philadelphia, 1958), p. 99. See also the baron de Thun to BF and Jay, July 7.

6. See BF to Pamphili, [before Aug. 27].

tolique résident à Londres. On sent bien que cet Arrangement ne peut plus avoir lieu, mais comme il est essentiel que les Catholiques Sujets des États Unis ayent un Eclesiastique qui les gouverne en ce qui concerne leur Religion. La Congregation *de Propagandâ Fide*, existante a Rome pour l'Etablissement et la Conservation des Missions, est venue dans la Determination de proposer au Congrès d'établir dans quelque Ville des Etats Unis de l'Amerique septentrionale, un de leurs Sujets catholiques, avec les Pouvoirs de Vicaire Apostolique et avec le Caractere d'Eveque ou simplement en qualité de préfet Apostolique, L'Etablissement d'un Eveque Vicaire Apostolique paroit le plus convenable, d'autant plus que les Sujets Catholiques des États Unis se trouveroient à portée de recevoir la Confirmation et les ordres dans leur propre Pays sans être obligés de se rendre à cet Effet dans des Pays d'une Domination étrangere, Et comme il pourroit arriver quelque fois que parmi les Sujets des Etats Unis, il n'y eut Personne en état d'être chargée du Gouvernement spirituel soit comme Eveque, soit comme Préfet Apostolique; il seroit nécessaire dans une telle Circonstance que le Congrès volut bien consentir à ce qu'on la choisit, parmi les Sujets d'une Nation étrangere la plus amie des Etats Unis.

Notation: Note of Pope's Nuncio 28 July 1783.

From Isabella Strange

ALS: American Philosophical Society

Dear Sir London jully 28 1783

I beg once more leave to trouble you with a Letter to my Friend Mr Hunter.[7] I do not yet know any other way of sending a Letter to Him and all I have hitherto are on Business.

Mr Strange joins with me in presenting our respectful compliments. I have the honour to be Dear Sir Your very humble Sert ISABELLA STRANGE

7. Strange had been using BF as a channel for her correspondence with James Hunter, Jr., her cousin's husband in Virginia, for at least two years— most recently in April: XXXIX, 405, 497. The last of these requests, it would appear, is dated Nov. 2, 1783 (APS).

Addressed: His excellency / Benjamin Franklin Esqr / Paris
Notation: Isabella Strange, 28 July 1783.

To Charles Blagden

AL: James M. Osborn, New Haven, Connecticut (1966)

Passy, July 29. 1783—

Dr Franklin presents his Compliments to Dr Blagden, requests his Care of the enclos'd, and wishes him a good Journey with a happy Sight of his Friends & Country.[8]

To William Strahan

ALS: Mrs. Arthur Loeb, Philadelphia, Pennsylvania (1955)

My dear old Friend, Passy, July 29. 1783.
Whom I shall probably never have the Pleasure of seeing again: You some time since recommended Miss Beckwith to me; I in consequence recommended her to my Children in Philadelphia:[9] the enclos'd will give you some Information of her present Situation.[1] I hope you & yours continue well, as does Your affectionate Friend & humble Servant   B FRANKLIN

---

8. Blagden had paid his final visit to BF on July 25. He was received in the "inner cabinet" where a "Great cover [was] laid out," and the two men discussed the Montgolfiers' "flying sack." BF told Blagden that he would send a letter to England by him. That letter, enclosed with the present note, was undoubtedly BF to Banks, July 27; see also the headnote there. Blagden left Paris on Aug. 1: Charles Blagden's Journal, 1783 (Yale University Library).

9. For Strahan's recommendation of Sally Beckwith in May, 1782, her voyage to Philadelphia that fall, and her warm reception by the Baches, see XXXVII, 425–6, 644–5; XXXVIII, 7; XXXIX, 23, 24.

1. According to Strahan's answer of Feb. 1, 1784 (APS), BF enclosed a letter from SB, which Strahan sent back to him. It may have been hers of June 1, above; BF acknowledged receipt of it on July 27.

Wm Strahan Esqr

Addressed: To / William Strahan Esqr / M. P.— / London

From Jean-Charles-Pierre Lenoir

LS: American Philosophical Society

Ce 29 Juillet 1783

Je joins icy, Monsieur, La permission que vous désirez pour faire retirer de La Douanne un paquet de Livres venant de Strasbourg à votre adresse.[2]

J'ai L'honneur d'être avec un respectueux attachement, Monsieur, votre trés humble et trés Obeissant Serviteur   LENOIR

M francklin ministre Plenipotentiaire des Etats unis

Notation: Le Noir 29 Juillet 1783—

From Vergennes

LS and transcript: National Archives; L (draft): Archives du Ministère des affaires étrangères

A Versailles le 29. Juillet 1783.

Vous vous rapellez, Monsieur, que sur votre demande le Roi a ordonné la Main-levée de la saisie faite à la requête des Srs forsters, freres, de tous les deniers qui pouvoient être dus à la frégate américaine l'Alliance.[3] Ces négociants se sont conformés aux intentions de Sa Mte. à cet égard; mais vous verrez, Monsieur, par les copies ci-jointes de la lettre qu'ils m'ont écrite, ainsi

---

2. Perhaps another book shipment from Hohlenfeld & Embser; see XXX-VIII, 68; XXXIX, 225–6.

3. As July 29 was a Tuesday, Vergennes may be reminding BF of information he communicated earlier that day at their weekly meeting. We do not know when the *conseil des finances* ruled in favor of the United States; Barclay had written to Vergennes on July 19, asking whether a decision had been made (AAE). For background on the case see Vergennes to BF, June 20, letter (III).

que de la requête qu'ils ont addressée au Roi, la demande qu'ils font de l'éxécution de l'arrêt du Conseil qui leur a accordé la restitution avec dommage et interêts de leur Navire *les trois-amis,* dont le Capitaine Landais americain s'etoit emparé, quoiqu'il fût muni de passeports qui devoient le mettre à l'abri de cette entreprise.[4] Vous trouverez sûrement que les représentations des Srs forsters sont on ne peut pas plus fondées, et qu'il est de la plus éxacte équité que le Congrès veuille bien prendre les mesures les plus promptes pour leur procurer le payement qu'ils réclament, et dont la privation met leur fortune dans le plus grand danger.[5]

J'ai l'honneur d'être très sincerement, Monsieur, votre très humble et très obéissant Serviteur   DE VERGENNES

Mr. Franklin

Notation: Count de Vergennes to Doct Franklin 29 July 1783 with Memorial of Forsters—

4. Forster frères' letter to Vergennes was dated June 28, during the time their case was pending; their memoir to Louis XVI, justifying their claim, is undated. The firm explained the illegal seizure of their ship *Les Trois Amis* in 1779. An *arrêt* of May 30, 1780, ruled that they were entitled to the return of the ship and its cargo as well as interest and damages. They claimed that when they presented an account to BF, he admitted the justice of their demand but asked them to wait until the return of peace to pursue it. (When BF forwarded these documents to Congress, he wrote "A Misrepresentation" next to this paragraph.) While they know that they cannot sue the United States in a French court, they argue that Congress has an obligation under the law of nations to pay this debt.

BF forwarded the present letter and its enclosures to Congress in a Sept. 13 letter to Boudinot.

5. Vergennes here drafted, and deleted, a final sentence: "Je vous prie de me mettre en etat de leur faire connoitre les moyens que vous vous proposez d'y employer."

From Jonathan Williams, Jr.

ALS: American Philosophical Society

Dear & hond Sir.   Nantes July 29. 1783.
I have received your kind Letter of the 18 Inst. and thank you for your Advice which I shall always follow.[6] I have had a Consultation with my Creditors here which has terminated in the most favourable Manner possible. Instead of meeting men Angry from disappointment I found myself in the midst of compassionate Friends, & they unanimously offered me 2 Years to pay in, by quarterly payments of 6 months, the first payment to be at the end of 8 instead of 6 Months thereby allowing me two months to collect the Sense of my other Creditors. My Reputation here has suffered but a momentary Check, for the Accot of my Stoppage & the arrangement were know at nearly the same Time, & instead of any Reproaches on my Conduct I have had several friendly Visits congratulating me on the general Satisfaction my Affair had given on 'Change, & the Esteem I appeard to enjoy among the Merchants of this Place.

My Creditors have unanimously reccommended me to renew my Letters of Sûrseance for a Year as soon as possible, and as those I have do not extend further than 6 of September[7] they desire me not to wait their Expiration. This they wish for as a common Security to prevent anyone from obtaining an *hypotheque* by a Sentence against me, which would give such a One a prefference in his Payment. I suppose the same motives which induced the Count de Vergennes to favour me on my first Application will be stronger on my Second, as it is by desire of my Creditors that I make it. I shall be greatly obliged to you if you will apply for me. Billy I doubt not will go to Vesailles & negociate the Business for me & a Letter from you expressing that you have such reliance on my Veracity as to be able to assure the Count that my Creditors desire it for their own Sakes. If it is absolutely necessary I will get them all to sign an Application, but I have not time at present, & as it is no new Favour but only

6. The letter has not been found; for the advice see JW to BF, Aug. 9.
7. For JW's three-month *arrêt de surséance* granted on June 6 see BF to Vergennes, June 3.

a prolongation of one already granted, I have no Doubt of your Success.—[8] What has distressed me more than anything else is the Amount I owe Mr Grand. If I had not realy believed I could have gone on I never would have engaged him, & indeed but for the Disappointment in receiving a considerable Sum I expected I should have made him large Remittances before I thought of Stopping. His Son[9] has written to me very harshly, more so than the Father would have done; however difficult it is, I do & Shall bear all with Patience & Resignation, and I hope from my last Letter to him he will not repeat his Reproaches.

Mr Baches Bill on me is in the hands of Messrs Le Couteulx & Co & is for 25000 *l.t.*, You can run no Risque in paying this Bill[1] so far as relates to me, for if I owe money to Messrs Bache & Shee they have between 4 & 5000 pounds Curny [Currency] of my Property in their Hands but instead of my owing them they owe me considerably, and I am Surprised they should draw on me; It is true I gave them Liberty to draw for the amount of a Cargo of Flour *in case they had previously remitted me* what the owed me: I will not pretend to judge 'till I receive their Accounts.

The Bills I deposited in your Hands for Messrs Barclay & Moylan will be due 10 of next month, care must be taken to receive the amount at the Time otherwise in Case any of the

8. JW enclosed a memoir of the same date, addressed to Vergennes: as the ships he had been expecting from America had still not arrived, his creditors had unanimously encouraged him to request an extension on his *arrêt* for a year beyond its current expiration (*i.e.*, to Sept. 6, 1784) on the same terms as the original. He begged Vergennes for this extension on behalf of himself and Williams, Moore & Co. JW then wrote to WTF, asking him to deliver to Vergennes the memoir and whatever letter BF might write. He gave WTF detailed instructions on how to monitor the stages of the application so that it was granted without delay: JW to Vergennes, July 29, 1783 (AAE); JW to WTF, July 29, 1783 (APS). No letter from BF in favor of this second application has been found.

9. Most likely Jean-François-Paul, as Henry left Paris during the summer (seemingly in late July) for an extended tour of the Continent and England. He was still in England in October: Henry Grand to WTF, Oct. 1, [1783], APS.

1. BF eventually did so. The bill, drawn by Bache & Shee, was paid out of his private account on Sept. 18: JW to Bache & Shee, July 30, 1783 (Yale University Library); Account XVII (XXVI, 3).

Bills Should prove bad the Drawers are not answerable if they are over due before demanded. I inclose sufficient Authority for you to acquit the Bills Signing *par procuration de J. Williams*. If Mr Barclay does not get the arrests taken off,[2] I should be sorry to have the money lay dead, please therefore to get Mr Grand to change it into good Solid Bills at 2 or 3 Usances that I may enjoy the Interest. You will please not to dispossess yourself of this money or its value, without previously informing me as Mr Barclay owes me about 10,000 Livres for my advances for Prisonners[3] which I must deduct.

I beg you will pardon the Trouble I give, & continue to honour me with your Affection; You may depend, that in the most trying Circumstances I will never deviate from those Principles of Honour & Probity, by which only I can hope to enjoy your Friendship.

I am as ever most dutifully & Affectionately Yours.

JONA WILLIAMS J

I beg Sir you will use your Influence with Mr Grand to induce him to agree with my other Creditors agreeable to my Letter to him of this date. He can surely have no Objection to my ob-

2. Of the prize proceeds of the *Alliance*, for which see Vergennes' third letter of June 20 and the one immediately above. Williams, Moore & Co. owed Barclay, Moylan & Co. for a purchase made on behalf of Alexander J. Alexander from the sale of the *Alliance*'s prizes. JW had deposited bills of exchange with BF to complete the transaction, giving him power of attorney to sign them over to Barclay, Moylan & Co. once all claims by French subjects were settled: XXXIX, 423; Chardon to Vergennes, June 17, 1783 (AAE); JW to Barclay, Moylan & Co., July 14, 1783 (Yale University Library). The enclosed power of attorney has not been located.

3. By this time, in fact, JW was owed something closer to 9,000 *l.t.* for the clothing, lodging, board, and passage he had furnished since April to Americans released from British and French prisons. They included Lt. St. Clair (XXXVII, 680–2) and several women and children, most of whom left for Philadelphia on July 13 on the *Hannibal*, Capt. Conyngham. JW submitted his account to Barclay for reimbursement on Dec. 3, 1783: Account XXVII (XXXII, 4); JW to Barclay, June 21, July 12, July 15, and Nov. 6, 1783 (Yale University Library); JW to WTF, Aug. 16, 1783 (APS); M. B. Clark, "Narrative of Captain Gustavus Conyngham, U.S.N., While in Command of the 'Surprise' and 'Revenge,'" 1777–1779," *PMHB*, XXII (1898), 488.

taining an Arrêt de Surseance for a longer Time as it is for his Interest that I go on, and he being my largest Creditor may add a Weight in the Scale in case it should be wanted to succeed with Mr de Vergennes.

Doctor Franklin.

From William Alexander ALS: American Philosophical Society

Dear Sir   Paris 30 July 1783

Our friend W——,[4] has taken his measures & has Already agreed wt most of his people at 6, 12, 18 Months & 2 Years by equal payments— He hopes he will meet no difficulty with the others but thinks that the Extension of his protection to a year (it Expires the 6 septr) woud secure his Object by preventing any troublesome Man from laying by to Catch undue Advantage to the prejudice of his more liberal minded neighbours— I beg You will think of this, And If You approve—suggest it to the Minister—Explaing to Him that Nothing less than full payment is proposed to every body—that W—— Expects to pay much sooner than the time he takes—but as this depends on American remittances, he Chuses Not to run the hazard of Another Stop. I have been in town only Since last night, so that I coud not pay You my respects at Passy, being obliged to Return home to day— I beg my best wishes to Your Son & am wt the warmest Attachment Dear Sir Your most obt hble Sr

W ALEXANDER

From Cambray AL: American Philosophical Society

Paris July 30th 1783

Colo. Cambray's most Respectful Compliments to Doctor Franklin. As he is going in the Country he is deprived of the honor of waiting upon him.

4. JW. For the situation Alexander repeats here see JW to BF, July 29.

He takes the liberty to Send him Some letters for America in consequence of the leave he has been So good as to grant him. If any letters Should arrive from America directed to him he begs they may be Sent to his House rue st. Pierre Hotel de Villers Qr. Montmartre

Notation: Cambray 30 Juillet 1783.—

From Staël von Holstein

L: Library of Congress

Ce 30 Juillet 1783.

Le Baron de Stael est passé chez Monsieur Francklin pour avoir l'honneur de lui faire part qu'il a eu le 29 du courant ses audiences comme Ministre plénipotentiaire du Roy de Suede chez leurs Majestés et la famille royale.

Addressed: A Monsieur / Monsieur Francklin / en son hotel / A Passy

From Herman Heyman's Sons

LS: American Philosophical Society

Sir   Bremen the 31th July 1783.

We beg leave to Refer us to our last Letter which we had the honour to write to your Exelency, by addressing you our most humble thanks for the Letters of Introduction with which you favored us, for our new established House in Nord America.[5]

Beeing convinced of the Patriotism which your Exelency bears for your Country, we hope you'll permit us to trouble you again with the Present, and to lay before your Consideration a Plan which we lately received from one of our principal Glass

---

5. For this Bremen mercantile firm see XXXIX, 145–8, 177–80, 378–9. We believe the letter is in the hand of Herman Heyman, Jr., who wrote again (in his own right) on Jan. 19, 1784 (APS).

Manufactorers in upper Germany, who intend to Establish a Glass Manufactory in Nord America, under the Direction of our House,[6] provided it gets certain Previledges, as well to the ground on which it is to be built, as likewise not to admit at first any other Establishment of that Kind in Nord America, as it would be else not practicable to bring a Manufactory of that Kind to its extends and perfections, and beeing assured that every Manufactory will be advantageous to Nord America, in particular such as we propose, which will make that Country Populous without to be troubelsom or Expensif to it, as they can mentain themselfs easy, whenever the Manufactory is only set in order and any way Flourishing; but such is the sooner and more easy to be brought in Perfection, if Your Exelency great Influence by the Congress could bring it so far, that the Regency of Nord America, grant us for some years a Monopoleye for our Manufactory, Your Exelencys Wisdom & great Intelligence of his Country will teach us, if the Idea which we have of the Progress of such an Manofactory, as we intend to Establish in Nord America, is Regular, or if it is to Precipitant, we therefore can only be Ruled by your Exelency Kind advise, & this will determine our future stepts to this purpose, may we therefore humbly Request from your Exelency, to honour us with an answer as soon as ever Convenient to your Exelency, and if such gives any Prospect that our Intention will be supported by your Exelency and the Congress of the united States, we shall if agreeabel to your Exelency, give the necessary Instructions to our House, to make proper Aplication according to the Direction which your Exelency will be so Obliging to give us, we forwarded however

6. The four-page undated memoir, entitled "Plan To a Compleat Glass Manufactori to be established in one of the 13 United Provinces of Nord America," is written in the first person, though it is unsigned. Its author was undoubtedly Johann Friedrich Amelung, whom Heyman identifies by name in his next letter (cited above), and whom BF would eventually help. Amelung had risen to become the technical director of a mirror-glass factory in Grünenplan renowned for its innovation and quality. Struggling financially because of the war, he determined in 1783 to open a manufactory in America, for which he sought backers: Dwight P. Lanmon and Arlene M. Palmer, "John Frederick Amelung and the New Bremen Glassmanufactory," *Jour. of Glass Studies*, XVIII (1976), 20–3, 134.

allready a part of this Plan to our Partner Mr Arnold Delius at Philadelphia;[7] to be abel to Reflect on it, and to take it in to Deliberation, but he is likewise informed that we took the Liberty to write to your Exelency about it, & was in hopes to receive your Answer and advise.

We have a Vessell now in loading for Philadelphia, which will depart in two month, if your Exelency should wish to have any things forwarded by it, please to Command us, and likewise when ever you find us abel to be of Service to you; having the Honour to suscribe ourselfs with the utmost Regard Sir Your Exelency most Obedt & most humble Servts.

HERMAN HEYMANS SONS

We have taken the Liberty to address the same Content of this to His Exelency John Adams Esq at the Hague,[8] to your Exelency Governmt.

Notation: Herman, Heyman sons 31 July 1783.

From Vergennes: Two Letters

(I) L (draft): Archives du Ministère des affaires étrangères; (II) LS and transcript: National Archives; L (draft): Archives du Ministère des affaires étrangères

I.

A Velle. le 31. Juillet 1783.

J'ai communîqué confidentiellement, M, à M. le Ct. de Mercy la notte que vous m'avez fait l'honneur de me remettre;[9] cet ambassadeur pense qu'il seroit convenable que vous la redigeassies d'après la notte que j'y ai mise: je me persuadé que ni vous ni Mrs. vos Collègues n'y trouveront aucune dificulté.

Mr. franklin.

7. Delius reached Philadelphia in June: XXXIX, 147n.
8. That letter, of the same date, is in *Adams Papers*, XV, 190–1.
9. See the American Commissioners to Vergennes, July 10.

II.

A Versailles le 31. Juillet 1783.
J'ai l'honneur, Monsieur, de vous envoyer une lettre et un mémoire accompagné de piéces qui m'ont été adressés par le Sr. Jean Baptiste Pecquet agent de la nation françoise à Lisbonne. Vous avés été informé, Monsieur, du zele désinterressé avec lequel cet agent S'est porté à rendre les Services les plus essentiels aux matelots Américains que les hazards de la guerre avoient conduits dans le Port de Lisbonne. Vous en trouverés le détail et les preuves dans Son mémoire.[1]

Je ne doute pas, Monsieur, que ces considérations ne vous portent à vous intérésser en Sa faveur, et J'espere que vous trouverés qu'il est de la justice du Congrès d'accorder au Sr. Pecquet quelque dédommagement et un témoignage utile de Satisfaction.

J'ai l'honneur d'être très Sincèrement, Monsieur, votre trèshumble et très obeissant Serviteur. DE VERGENNES

Mr Franklin./.

To Silas Deane

Reprinted from *The Deane Papers, 1774–90* (5 vols.; New-York Historical Society *Collections*, XIX–XXIII, New York, 1887–91), V, 192.

Sir, Passy, August 31st [*i.e.*, 1?],[2] 1783.
I received last night the letter you did me the honor of writing to me the 20th. past, and in answer inform you that I never heard anything of the discourses or resentments you mention, either at Versailles or at Paris; that I do not think your personal

1. Vergennes enclosed a memoir addressed to BF from Pecquet, a number of certificates from local officials, and a June 26 cover letter from Pecquet to the French ambassador at the Portuguese court; see Pecquet's memoir to BF, [c. June 26], above.
2. The date as given cannot be correct; Deane discussed this letter when writing to Barclay on Aug. 28 (*Deane Papers*, V, 187–8). Given that BF mentions having just received Deane's letter of July 20, the month "past," we place this answer at the earliest possible date, knowing that mail often took ten days to travel between the two cities.

safety or liberty would be hazarded from any such resentments by your coming to Paris to settle your accompts; and that, so far as may depend on me, you may rely on the protection you wish for. With best wishes that you may hereafter so prudently conduct yourself as to recover the esteem and respect you once possessed among your countrymen,[3] I am, Sir, Your most obedient and most humble servant,   B FRANKLIN.

Silas Deane, Esq.

From Joshua Johnson[4]   ALS: American Philosophical Society

Sir.   London 1 August 1783.
The Inclosed was sent me from the General Post Office, the Postage being 4/7. I have paid and which you will be pleased to return to Mr. Ridley, It is probable that many more Letters may come for you & which must remain in the Post Office, without the Inland Postage is paid, be pleased to signify whether I may take them up or not & forward them to you. I shall be happy of opportunitys to be usefull to you & I am with the most perfect respect & esteem Sir Your most Obedt. Hb. Servt.

JOSHUA JOHNSON

His Excellency Benjamin Franklin Esqr.

3. On Aug. 10 Deane completed his self-vindicating *Address to the United States of North-America* (XXXVIII, 468), which he had been debating whether to publish for months. He added a postscript and appendix on Oct. 12. The manuscript was carried to America by Deane's son Jesse: *Deane Papers*, V, 142–3, 221, 236.

4. Johnson had recently moved from Nantes to London (see XXXIX, 564–5n, 599), where he continued his partnership in Wallace, Johnson & Muir. By 1785 the firm's financial difficulties were blamed on his mismanagement; two years later he sought protection against legal suits. The firm dissolved at the beginning of 1790. Johnson was named consul in the spring of that year and remained in London until 1797, when he returned to the United States: *Jefferson Papers*, XX, 486.

From Ann Hudson de Lavau[5]

ALS (incomplete):[6] American Philosophical Society

[August 1, 1783][7]

months, the anxiety of my mind Joined with their manner of living brought me very near my Grave, I came here about eight days ago for the recovery of my health, pardon me sir for troubling you with this account of my self, but I think it is necessary I Shoud you be made acquinted with my manner of Living since I left paris mr. hoops[8] in form me that my mother ad sent me letter to your offies permitt me to request it of you sir that if there is any letter for me at your offies you will be so obliging as to order them to be forwarded to me here under the care of Mre. fillath pere.

I have the honour to be with the greatest respect your most obedint servant honoured sir HUDSON DE LAVAU

---

5. A Virginian by birth, Mrs. Lavau (Loviel, Loviet) came to France with her French husband, who later abandoned her. BF first intervened on her behalf in 1781: XXXV, 376–7; XXXVIII, 108–9.

6. The second sheet, transcribed here, is intact. The first sheet, both sides of which were filled, was torn vertically, and only a narrow column on the right-hand side remains. From this we can glean the place names Rochefort and Nantes and a series of words suggestive of a prolonged and frustrating journey, including: "unfortunate," "difficulty," "set out," "opportunity," "recommendation," "procure a pasage," "was addressed," "convent," and "court."

7. Dated by BF's reply of Aug. 10, below.

8. Adam Hoops: XXXVI, 99n. At the beginning of June, Hoops, who knew that BF had letters for her, evidently asked the Lorient merchant Zachariah Loreilhe to help obtain them. Loreilhe wrote as much to WTF on June 4, saying that Mrs. Hudson was in a convent in Lorient and that he would deliver the letters if WTF would forward them to the Lorient firm of Barclay, Moylan & Co. (with which he was associated): Loreilhe to WTF, June 4, 1783 (APS); Matthew Ridley's Journal, entry of May 30, 1782 (Mass. Hist. Soc.); *Jefferson Papers*, X, 304.

From Jean-Paul Marat[9]

AL: American Philosophical Society

Paris ce 1. Aoust 1783.
M. Marat prie Monsieur Franklin de vouloir bien lui accorder un quart d'heure d'audience lundy ou mercredy prochains dans la matinée. M. Marat desireroit Savoir l'heure de la comodité de Monsieur Franklin, au quel il à l'honneur de renouveller les assurances de Son respectueux attachement.

Notation: Marat 1er. Aout 1783.

From John Coakley Lettsom

ALS: American Philosophical Society

Respected Friend   London Aug. 2. 1783
Henry Smeathman, the bearer of this is an ingenious person, who was patronized by Dr. Fothergill and under the Doctor's patronage he visited the coast of Africa, and in consequence of the knowledge he acquired, he seems capable of giving ample information respecting the present trade of Africa, and wishes I believe, to suggest, new sources of extending it into that continent:[1] As I thought such a person might be acceptable to

---

9. To the best of our knowledge, this is the last time Marat's name appears in BF's papers. The purpose of his proposed visit is not known, but he was at this time campaigning to be appointed director of a proposed academy of sciences in Madrid. The conde de Aranda was charged with gathering information about him, and it is possible that Marat was seeking BF's recommendation. In the meantime, Marat continued his scientific work; on Aug. 6 his *Mémoire sur l'électricité médicale* won a prize from the Académie des sciences, belles-lettres et arts de Rouen: Charles Vellay, ed., *La Correspondance de Marat . . .* (Paris, 1908), pp. 16–24, 34–5, 37, 74–9; Charles C. Gillispie, *Science and Polity in France at the End of the Old Regime* (Princeton, 1980), pp. 315–16, 318–19.

1. Smeathman (*ODNB*), the entomologist who had spent from 1771 to 1775 in Sierra Leone on a collecting expedition sponsored by Fothergill, Joseph Banks, and others, returned to England in 1779 and produced the study of tropical termites that established his scientific reputation. In July, 1783, he approached antislavery Quakers in London with a colonization plan

Dr. Franklin, I have taken the liberty of putting this letter of introduction into his hands and am very respectfully &c.

J. C. Lettsom

Addressed: To / Benjamin Franklin

---

for Sierra Leone. While Fothergill and Lettsom, among others, had argued earlier that free-labor plantation colonies in West Africa would be both more ethical and more profitable than the Atlantic slave trade, Smeathman was the first to combine antislavery principles and commercial interests in a concrete project. He proposed to settle 200 to 300 men and women—free blacks from England, America, and the Sugar Islands, along with white tradesmen—in a fertile, deserted area he had identified and cultivate a wide variety of produce for export to England and America. The colony would introduce Africans to civil and religious liberty, education, agriculture, and manufacture, as well as establish a sanctuary for former slaves; within 40 years it would "extend its saving influence . . . wider than even *American Independence"*: Smeathman to Dr. Thomas Knowles, [1783] and July 21, 1783, in *New-Jerusalem Magazine* (London, 1790), pp. 279–94; Stephen J. Braidwood, *Black Poor and White Philanthropists: London's Blacks and the Foundation of the Sierra Leone Settlement, 1786–1791* (Liverpool, 1994), pp. 5–6, 8–9; Christopher L. Brown, *Moral Capital: Foundations of British Abolitionism* (Chapel Hill, N. C., 2006), pp. 260–1.

When the London Quakers as a group refused to support the plan (despite a sympathetic reception by Granville Sharp, among others), Smeathman decided to approach BF and try to raise money in France. As a friend of his put it, "Master Termites is gone to Paris to tell Dr. Franklin of his plan for civilising Africa." Though he stayed nearly a year and developed a friendship with BF and WTF, his efforts led nowhere. On the eve of his return to England he confided his discouragement to Lettsom: his hope of finding support among the wealthy blacks in Paris had dissolved, his attempts to interest Sweden had failed, and even though BF said "he has no doubt I should get it adopted at Boston," Smeathman was loath to "carry my poor brat a-begging from continent to continent on uncertainties": Braidwood, *Black Poor and White Philanthropists*, pp. 7, 10–11, 37; Thomas J. Pettigrew, ed., *Memoirs of the Life and Writings of the Late John Coakley Lettsom* . . . (3 vols., London, 1817), II, 270–6.

From Berkenrode AL: American Philosophical Society

paris ce 3 Aout 1783.
L'Ambassadeur des Etats Generaux, prie Monsieur Francklin, de Lui faire L'honneur de venir diner chez Lui, Jeudi prochain 7 du Mois./.

Addressed: A Monsieur / Monsieur Francklin. / Ministre plenipotentiaire / des Etats Unis de / L'Amerique Septentrionale. / A passy.

From the Comte de Monet[2] LS: American Philosophical Society

Monsieur   Le 3 aoust 1783
   Vous avez prevenu le dessein ou j'etois d'aller vous prier, Monsieur, de me mettre à portée de mettre sous les yeux de sa majesté le roy de Pologne un exemplaire des constitutions des treize etats unis de l'amérique en m'envoyant celui dont j'ai l'honneur de vous accuser la réception et en y en joignant un pour moy. Cette attention obligeante, et la part que toute l'Europe sait que vous avez eue à rendre la liberté à votre patrie et à la formation d'une république fédérative dont vos successeurs sentiront encore mieux tous les avantages, doit ajouter mon estime et ma reconnoissance au plaisir que j'ai eu dès longtemps de faire connoissance avec vous. Je ne doute pas que Sa Majesté le roy de Pologne ne soit sensible à cette attention et ne m'ordonne de vous le témoigner. En attendant je saisis avec empressement l'occasion de vous assurer que personne n'est avec plus d'estime

2. Jean-Antoine Monet (1703–1795) was born in the Savoie region, studied law in Turin, joined the Polish army in 1745, and entered the French diplomatic service in 1755. He joined the "Secret du Roi" (Louis XV's secret diplomatic corps) in 1763 and was named French consul general in Warsaw in 1763–64: Didier Ozanam and Michel Antoine, eds., *Correspondance secrète du comte de Broglie avec Louis XV (1756–1774)* (2 vols., Paris, 1956–61), I, lxxxviii, 124–5n, 127n; *Biographie universelle.*

et de consideration que moy Monsieur Votre très humble et très
obéissant serviteur   LE GENERAL COMTE DE MONET

Rue de Bellefonds Barriere Cadet

Notation: le Cte. de Monet. 3 Août 1783.—

From François Steinsky ALS: American Philosophical Society

MONSIEUR,   Prague le 3me. d'Aoust 1783.

Il y a peu des plaisirs réélles égaux à celui, que me faisoit la
recette de Vos lines;[3] cela m'etoit un vrai soulagement dans une
maladie que je souffrois alors.

Je Vous remercie des louanges que Vous avez la bonté de
faire de nos manufacturiers par raport a une petite chose,[4] a la
quelle hors la bonne volonté il n'y a rien qui merite d'etre re-
gardé de Vous.

Le grand degré de la chaleur effectué par l'air déphlogisti-
qué soufflé sur des charbons est tres remarcable, et pourra aussi
bien que la corde sans fin,[5] si elle est applicable en grand, etre
d'une grande utilité aux mines. Chez nous on donne tres peu
aux études de la Physique, comme sur tout aux sciences, et ce
qui s'en fait c'est pour la plupart par des particuliers amateurs.
Mr. Renner professeur de Mechanique a notre école, a essaye
une Harmonique selon VOTRE modele, et il y a tres bien reussi,
méme il a raffiné quelques petites choses. p. exempl. le mouve-
ment qu'il peut retarder ou accelerer tres egalement moyennant
quatre courbes. Aussi traite il cet instrument divin avec beaucoup d'agilite jusque a des tremblements qu'il sait produire.[6] De

3. BF's letter of Nov. 23, 1782, acknowledged here, was an answer to
Steinsky's of Sept. 12, 1781: XXXV, 468–70; XXXVIII, 337–8.
4. The small tablecloth that Steinsky had sent in 1781: XXXV, 470.
5. The two developments in physics that BF had described in the letter
cited above.
6. Anton Renner of Prague (1745–1828) was a maker of scientific instruments and electrical machines and an early proponent of lightning rods. He

l'Italie j'ai des nouvelles, que Mr. Landriani a Milan a inventé des Barometres, Thermometres, Hygrometres, Electrometres &c. qui marquent par l'application d'un creyon d'eux memes avec la plus grande exactitude leurs degrées. Il donne sur ce soujet une petite ouvrage au jour.[7] Quelques lieues d'ici on a trouvé dans un carriere une monnoie polonoise du 15me siecle parfaitement enfermée dans une pierre. Je l'ai vue, la decouverte est si extraordinaire, que je ne scais pas m'empecher d'en faire inserer la description a un des journaux de Physique.—[8] Je me souviens de Vous etre redevable de la vraie raison que l'Auteur de la description d'une revolution au bord de l'Elbe qui a formé une novelle colline, dont j'avois l'honneur de Vous parler;[9] Il dit que l'humidité de la pluie continue de cette anné 1770 a pénétrée dans une profondeur considerable, ou elle causoit l'effervescence

---

gained a reputation for improving the mechanism of the glass armonica and popularizing the instrument in Bohemia: Constant von Wurzbach, ed., *Biographisches Lexikon des Kaiserthums Oesterreich* (60 vols., Vienna, 1856–91).

7. Among the many instruments Steinsky attributes to Marsilio Landriani, he neglects the one for which the Italian physicist is best known, the eudiometer: *Dictionary of Scientific Biography*. The short work alluded to here may be the article Landriani co-wrote with Pietro Moscati, "Ricerche ed osservazioni sociali fatte per perfezionare il barometro," *Memorie di matematica e fisica della Società italiana delle scienze*, 1 (1782), 225–67.

8. Steinsky eventually submitted his paper to Born, mentioned below, who published it in the proceedings of a private scientific society: "Schreiben an den Herrn Hofrath von Born über eine in Stein gefundene Münze, nebst einigen dadurch veranlassten Gedanken über die Entstehung, der gegenwärtigen Oberfläche der Erde," *Abhandlungen einer Privatgesellschaft in Böhmen, zur Aufnahme der Mathematik, der vaterländischen Geschichte, und der Naturgeschichte*, VI (1784), 377–94.

9. On Jan. 5, 1770, a massive landslide on the steep slope rising above the Elbe River at Veselí (in what is now the Czech Republic) buried houses and created a hill more than 100 feet high at the river's edge. Whatever account Steinsky and BF discussed has not been located. We owe our knowledge of the event to an undated illustrated broadside entitled "Abbildung des am 5ten Januar 1770 bey dem Dorfe Wessel, unweit Aussig in Böhmen hereingebrochenen und bis in die Elbe fortgerückten Gebirges," kindly brought to our attention and interpreted by Professors Jan T. Kozák and Kenneth L. Taylor. We also thank Rhoda Rappaport and Martin Rudwick for their assistance.

de l'acide nitreux avec des sels urineux, dont ces terres la sont bien impregnées, et que cela s'est fait accordant a peu pres aux essais de Mr. Maud dans ses Philosophical transactions No. 318. Dictionaire de l'Enciclopedie.[1] Enfin sommes nous aussi assez heureux de posseder Vos belles Ouvrages en notre langue Mr Walther libraire de la cour a Dresde a soigné l'edition, il m'a prié de Vous faire son tres humble compliment en Vous assurant de la grande éstime qu'il a pour Vous, comme aussi Mr. Wenzel le traducteur, un amateur de Physique.[2] Ces ouvrages cependant ne sont pas encore complettes parce qu'il y manque encore ce tome de Miscellanious Worcks, que j'avois l'honneur de presenter de Votre part a Mr. Martinelli a Florence,[3] et peut etre quelque autre qui a pu

1. Steinsky was looking at the article "charbon minéral" in Diderot's *Encyclopédie*, but miscopied the citation. In talking about underground gases, notably "inflammable air," the article described a terrible mine explosion in 1708, citing *Phil. Trans.*, no. 318. In the next paragraph, the article described John Maud, F.R.S., as saturating the earth with inflammable air, which he synthesized, creating effervescence; this was thought to demonstrate the causes of earthquakes, volcanoes, and other subterranean disturbances. The citation Steinsky gives here is to *Phil. Trans.*, no. 442, p. 282, the first page of Maud's "A Chemical Experiment . . . to illustrate the Phœnomenon of the Inflammable Air . . ." (*Phil. Trans.*, XXXIX [1735–36], 282–5). *Encyclopédie, ou Dictionnaire raisonné des sciences, des arts et des métiers* . . . (28 vols., Genève [*i.e.*, Paris and Neuchâtel], 1754–72), III, 193.

2. *Des Herrn D. Benjamin Franklin's . . . sämmtliche Werke* (3 vols., Dresden, 1780), edited by G. T. Wenzel, reprinted translations from Wilcke's 1758 German edition (XIV, 210n) and added material published by Dubourg and Vaughan, including their editorial notes, many without attribution: Francis S. Philbrick, "Notes on Early Editions and Editors of Franklin," APS *Proc.*, XCVII (1953), 531, 534–35. The Walthers were eminent printers and booksellers in Dresden. Conrad Salomon had inherited his father's position as court printer; his younger brothers Georg Paul and Georg Friedrich managed the family bookstore: Paul E. Richter, "Zur Vorgeschichte und Geschichte der vormals Waltherschen, jetzt Burdachschen Hofbuchhandlung . . . ," *Archiv für Geschichte des deutschen Buchhandels*, XX (1898), 146–9.

3. *Political, Miscellaneous, and Philosophical Pieces* (see XXXV, 469), compiled and edited by Benjamin Vaughan. In fact, the German edition did contain everything Vaughan published, with the exception of "A Reformed Mode of Spelling." Vaughan's name, however, appears nowhere in the edition, whereas Dubourg's name is featured on the title page. Transla-

sortir depuis, de VOTRE fertile plume. Nous osons donc VOUS prier de nous en faire part quand Vous donnez quelque chose au Public, car nos libraires ont peu de commerce avec ceux de Paris, sur tout en matière de Physique.

Avant quelques mois, Mr. de Born[4] a Vienne me marquoit qu'on l'avoit assuré de ce que VOUS voudriez faire une voyage par l'Italie, ce que nous procureroit peut etre le plaisir de VOUS voir. J'ai l'honneur de VOUS assurer que par tout VOUS seriez reçu avec une éstime et joie peu commune.

Si les voeux d'un particulier VOUS pourroient etre de quelque consideration le miens ne seroient certainement pas les moindres. Car ce n'est que de peur d'offenser VOTRE modestie que je n'ose pas laisser le cours a ma plume de VOUS marquer la gratitude, et la parfaite veneration dont mon coeur est rempli vers le liberateur d'une grande partie de l'univers qui surement est un des plus grands hommes que le monde a eu, et de qui la posterité la plus eloignée repetera:

Eripuit cœlo fulmen, sceptrumque tirannis.[5]

Je suis vraiment heureux d'avoir connu ce grand génie— Le ciel qui a conduit Vos heureuses demarches jusque a ce but VOUS conserve, et VOUS assiste dans Vos sages dessins afin que VOUS voyez achevé ce grand ouvrage que VOUS avez si avantageusement commencé. Oh le heureux peuple, qui est le seul dans l'histoire du monde qui est susceptible de la plus parfaite felicité d'etat; car quel peuple se pouvoit jamais dire: nous voici dans le moment de choisir un gouvernement qui nous est le meilleur? Quel peuple avoit jamais a sa tete des heros et des Legislateurs,

---

tions of the first four sections of *Political, Miscellaneous, and Philosophical-Pieces* appeared, in order, in vol. 3; the contents of the fifth section ("Papers on Miscellaneous and Philosophical Subjects") were disbursed throughout vols. 2 and 3 according to their subject matter. BF's famous epitaph was the last item in vol. 3.

4. The eminent geologist Ignaz von Born, who would write to BF in November. Six years earlier, BF had been sent an English translation of his observations on the mineralogy of Hungary and Transylvania: XXIV, 435n; XXIX, 430.

5. Turgot's famous epigram: XXXIV, 419.

qui mieux que Cæsar, Licourg et Solon eussent pu profiter des defautes(?) que l'histoire et l'etat present des impires du monde leur livre? Pour moi je Vous prie Monsieur de conserver toujours votre amicable bienveillance, que je souhaite de meriter, et je ne manquerai pas, comme Vous voyez que je fais, de Vous écrire de tems en tems, selon Votre permission. Cependant j'ai l'honneur d'etre avec l'estime la plus parfaite Monsieur Votre tres humble, tres obeissant serviteur   F. Steinsky.

J'ose Vous ajouter comme à un amateur de Musique quelques Melodies de nos meilleurs Maitres que j'ai fait graver pour un livre de cantiques dont on m'a chargé de faire la compilation, a l'usage des écoles, et du Public.[6]

Notation: Steinsky 3 Août 1783

From the Comte de Pignatelli[7]

L: American Philosophical Society

[after August 3, 1783][8]

Le Comte de Pignatelli a l'honneur de faire part à Monsieur francklin, Ministre plenipotentiaire des Etats unis de l'amerique septentrionale, qu'il a eu Dimanche 3 de ce mois ses premieres

---

6. *Lieder zur öffentlichen und häuslichen Andacht, mit Melodien von Kozeluch, Mozart und anderen vaterländischen Meistern; auf Veranlassung der k.k. Normalschuldirection* was published in Prague in 1784. Some of the melodies were by Steinsky himself: Wurzbach, ed., *Biographisches Lexikon.*

7. Michele Pignatelli, the new minister from the Kingdom of the Two Sicilies, had previously served at the courts of Sardinia (1764–70) and St. James's (1771–81). Ill health forced him to leave France on June 13, 1784: *Repertorium der diplomatischen Vertreter,* III, 424, 426; Jules Flammermont, *Rapport à M. le ministre de l'instruction publique sur les correspondances des agents diplomatiques étrangers en France avant la Révolution . . .* (Paris, 1896), p. 439.

8. The day he presented his credentials: *Repertorium der diplomatischen Vertreter,* III, 423.

audiences du Roi, de la Reine, et de la famille royale en qualité d'ambassadeur Extraordinaire de S. M. le Roi de Naples.[9]

Addressed: A Monsieur / Monsieur Francklin / Ministre Plenipotentiaire des Etats / unis de l'amérique septentrionale / A Passy

Notation: Le Comte Pignatelly—

From William Robertson[1]   ALS: American Philosophical Society

Sir   College of Edinburgh Aug. 4th 1783
My eldest Son[2] will have the honour of presenting this letter to Your Excellency. He has been educated to the profession of Law here, & during the vacation of the Courts of justice, purposes to make a rapid excursion to the Continent. As he will be two or three weeks at Paris, he is ambitious of being introduced to you, & of being able to tell his children that he had the honour of seeing a Man whose name they will often hear mentioned.

If you can trust the partial testimony of a Father, I flatter myself you will find him possessed of such information, & such dispositions as not to be altogether unworthy of your notice. Permit me to hope that it will not be unpleasant to you to allow me to take this opportunity of recalling myself to your remembrance, & of assuring you that notwithstanding the various events which have happened since our acquaintance first commenced that I have the honour to be with great respect &

---

9. Ferdinand IV of Naples; he was also Ferdinand III of Sicily. As Antonio Pace has pointed out, this notification signaled diplomatic recognition of the United States: *Benjamin Franklin and Italy* (Philadelphia, 1958), p. 110.

1. This is the last extant letter from the Scottish historian, identified in IX, 220n. His previous one was written in 1770: XVII, 48.

2. William Robertson, Jr. (1753–1835), had been admitted as advocate in 1775. In 1805 he would be named a judge in the College of Justice of Scotland: *DNB*, under his father.

attachment Sir Your Excellencys most obedient & most humble
Servant   WILLIAM ROBERTSON

From Vergennes

LS and transcript: National Archives; L (draft): Archives du Ministère
des affaires étrangères

A Versles le 5. Aoust 1783.
J'ai l'honneur, Monsieur, de vous addresser la copie d'un mémoire qui m'a été présenté par le Sr. Bayard;[3] Comme les de-
mandes de ce particulier me semblent justes, je me fais un devoir
de vous les transmettre en vous priant de les recommander en
Amérique.
J'ai l'Honneur d'être très sincérement, Monsieur, votre très
humble et très obéissant Serviteur./.   DE VERGENNES

Editorial Note on the American Peace Commissioners' Project for a Definitive Treaty of Peace, [August 6, 1783][4]

In late July, the American peace commissioners obtained Vergennes'
reassurance that France would not sign its definitive treaty with Great

3. BF forwarded it to Congress with his letter to Boudinot of Sept. 13.
The nine-page undated memoir is from François-Louis Bayard, the merchant who had asked BF the previous November to certify certain documents in Garson, Bayard & Cie.'s claim against the state of Georgia; see
XXXVIII, 283–4. In the memoir, Bayard noted that BF had examined the
firm's accounts with him and had certified the powers Georgia had given
the firm's agent Emmanuel-Pierre de La Plaigne. National Archives.
4. The document is published in *Adams Papers*, XV, 151–9, under the
date [before July 19]; in Giunta, *Emerging Nation*, I, 906–13, under [*c.*
Aug. 6]; and in Wharton, *Diplomatic Correspondence*, VI, 601–6, under
July 27. Wharton's source, Jared Sparks, did not ascribe any date at all;
indeed, the document was undated, as discussed below. The only extant
MS versions are copies: the version sent to Congress by the American peace

Britain until the American treaty was ready. On July 31 Vergennes told this to the Duke of Manchester, who immediately informed Hartley. The following day, August 1, Hartley received a letter from Fox—the first in nearly a month—answering his mid-June request to return to London for a face-to-face conference. Fox granted permission, as long as Manchester could affirm that Hartley's absence and the "consequent suspension of negotiation for the definitive Treaty with the United States" would have no effect on the completion of the other treaties, which Fox understood to be "near at Hand."[5]

Hartley, who had suspended negotiations for weeks while waiting for this permission, had no choice now but to stay. In his answer to Fox, he expressed his resentment that so much time had been lost, and with it the Americans' goodwill.[6] He nonetheless would recommence negotiations, even though he still had no concrete instructions. Fox had declined to send any.

On August 2 Hartley reported to Fox that he had met with "the American Ministers." This can only mean that he went to Passy and conversed with Franklin and Jay, as Adams was in Holland and Laurens had returned to England. He delivered Fox's messages: that the Order in Council of July 2 should not be considered the final word, that the commissioners' suspicions were "ill-founded," and that "the points in debate might still be granted if we could agree upon the other parts of the proposed Convention." The Americans were distressed to learn that Hartley had received neither instructions nor specific propositions that he was authorized to sign. "As I had no specific proposition to make to the American Ministers," Hartley told Fox, "I left them to draw up their project in form for their definitive treaty which I expect tomorrow."[7]

Franklin and Jay did not deliver their proposal until the morning of August 6. When sending a copy to Fox that evening, Hartley characterized it this way: "I think there is not much substantial difference in this Project, from the separate propositions from the American Ministers, which I have transmitted to you in former letters; only that these Propositions are now reduced into the specific shape of

commissioners (National Archives), the copy made by Hartley and sent to Fox on Aug. 6 (Public Record Office), and the commissioners' letterbook copies (Mass. Hist. Soc. and Library of Congress).

5. Hartley to Fox, July 31 and Aug. 2, 1783, and Fox to Hartley, July 29, 1783, in Giunta, *Emerging Nation*, I, 902; II, 206–7, 216.

6. Hartley to Fox, Aug. 2, 1783, in Giunta, *Emerging Nation*, II, 217.

7. *Ibid.*

Articles; with a great deal of preambulary recital, which was drawn up by Mr. Adams a long while ago."[8]

Hartley was correct. The "Project for the definitive Treaty of Peace and Friendship between his Britannic Majesty and the United States of America" contained eight articles from the preliminary agreement and 11 others, most of which the Americans had already proposed. The lengthy preamble and the closing paragraphs were taken from the draft language for a definitive treaty that John Adams prepared on February 1. He copied it *mutatis mutandis* from the 1763 Treaty of Paris between Great Britain and France. Adams prepared this draft at a time when the commissioners expected the final treaty to be concluded within a matter of weeks. They were so confident of this, in fact, that Adams wrote "February" into the dateline, leaving only the day of the month and the location blank. He indicated that the preliminary articles were to be inserted as numbers 1 through 9, and added two standard articles adapted from the 1763 British-French treaty, which he numbered 10 and 11, specifying that both parties promised to observe the terms of the treaty and would exchange ratifications within a certain number of months (a number he left blank).[9] In the version Franklin and Jay gave Hartley on August 6, Adams' Articles 10 and 11 were stripped of their numbers but retained in an equivalent location, after the numbered articles, as unnumbered paragraphs.

When Adams returned to Paris, he wrote to Livingston that "nothing further had been done Since my departure but to deliver to Mr: Hartley, a fair Copy, of the Project of a definitive Treaty, which I had left with my Collegues."[1] While this has sometimes been interpreted to mean that Adams prepared the entire text before leaving, no manuscript survives to verify that fact. We think it likely that what Adams left with his colleagues was the draft he had prepared in February, which provided the formal language missing from the preliminary agreement.[2] It would have been left to Franklin and Jay to copy

8. Hartley to Fox, Aug. 6, 1783, in Giunta, *Emerging Nation*, 1, 905–6.
9. See xxxix, 124n, and *Adams Papers*, xiv, 227–30, where the text is published.
1. *Adams Papers*, xv, 216.
2. We base this interpretation on what was copied into the three legation letterbooks prepared by BF's secretaries after the definitive treaty was concluded. Two of the letterbooks (preserved among BF's papers at the Library of Congress) retain the word "February" in the dateline, indicating that the secretaries—L'Air de Lamotte in one case, and BFB in the other—were

this language if Hartley should ask for a proposal, and to insert the articles that the commissioners had already agreed upon. Just when those articles were put into their final form and numbered is not clear. If Franklin and Jay were responsible, it would explain the delay of several days in delivering the proposal.

The body of the proposed treaty consists of 19 articles. Not all of the nine articles from the preliminary treaty[3] were transcribed in full. Those that were to be carried over verbatim or with alterations were noted as such ("the same as . . ."), with the alterations explained. Article 5 was nullified and replaced by the Article 5 that Franklin had proposed, unsuccessfully, on November 29, 1782.[4] Free navigation of the St. Lawrence River was added to Article 8. Article 9, no longer relevant, was deleted without comment.

The new articles, most of them copied from previous communications to Hartley, were as follows:

Articles 9, 10, 11, 12, and 13: The second, third, fourth, fifth, and sixth articles proposed by the American commissioners to Hartley on June 29, above.

Article 14: A new article granting America the same rights to cut logwood as Great Britain had just granted Spain, "on condition that they bring or send the said Logwood to Great Britain or Ireland, and to no other Part of Europe." The American commissioners had raised this issue in the form of a query when submitting their proposed articles on June 29.

Articles 15, 16, and 17: The American commissioners' June 29 revisions to four of the articles (2, 3, 4, and 5) that Hartley proposed to them on June 19.

Article 18: Excerpted from the American commissioners' July 17 letter to Hartley. The proposal is in the paragraph beginning "As it is necessary to ascertain an Epocha, for the Restitutions and Evacuations to be made, we propose that it be agreed . . ."

Article 19: Adapted from the armistice of February 20 (XXXIX,

---

unthinkingly copying the Feb. 1 draft. The third letterbook, also written by L'Air de Lamotte (Adams Papers, Mass. Hist. Soc.), left a blank space for the name of the month, as did the copy on loose sheets that he prepared for the commissioners to include in their Sept. 10 letter to Congress. The fair copy given to Hartley (now missing) also left the month blank, as reflected in the copy Hartley sent Fox.

3. Published in XXXVIII, 382–8.
4. XXXVIII, 375–7.

190–2), concerning the restoration of prizes taken during specified time intervals after the ratification of the preliminaries.[5] When sending this proposal to Fox, Hartley added one final comment: the American commissioners considered all the additional articles to be "optional to either Party," and considered themselves "bound to sign the provisional Articles in *statu quo* as a definitive Treaty of Peace, if called upon by Great Britain to do so." That same day, George III ratified the preliminary articles,[6] setting the stage for an outcome that the commissioners must have realized was inevitable.

From Kéralio

ALS: American Philosophical Society

Paris, Le 7e. août, 1783.

Plaignés notre bonne Douairiere, mon respectable ami; elle part demain et n'a pu vous aller demander votre bénédiction; elle me charge de vous peindre tout le regret qu'elle a de vous quitter; mais comment y parvenir? Il est trop profond; il faudroit sentir comme elle pour le rendre: recevés de sa part les embrassements de L'amitié la plus tendre, et assurès mr. votre petit-fils de son attachement le plus Vrai. Elle part demain pour aller à Tugny en champagne où se fait la noce de son fils,[7] et de là à Forbach ou elle à grand besoin d'arriver—après les peines, les soins et les embarras dont elle a été accablée en ce pays-ci.

Pour moi, mon respectable ami, je suis à vos pieds et j'y dépose l'hommage de la vénération que je vous dois: L'héroisme est sans doute la collection de toutes les vertus, et d'après cette définition, qui fut jamais plus héros que Vous? Vous étes et Vous serés toujours le mien. Continués vos Bontés à l'homme

---

5. This article is equivalent to Article XXII of the British-French preliminary peace treaty and Article X of the British-Spanish preliminary treaty, both signed on Jan. 20, 1783. Fitzherbert exchanged ratifications with the French government on Feb. 3: *Courier de l'Europe*, XIII (1783), 68, 69, 91.

6. Giunta, *Emerging Nation*, I, 904–5.

7. On July 29 the duchesse de Deux-Ponts' eldest son, Christian, married Adélaïde-Françoise-Léontine de Béthune (1761–1823): Bodinier, *Dictionnaire*, under Forbach des Deux-Ponts, Christian.

du monde qui se fera toujours gloire de Vous être le plus respectueusement et dévoué   LE CHR. DE KERALIO

Permettés que j'embrasse le plus tendrement m. votre petit-fils.
Je me recommande à son souvenir et à Son amitié.

Savés vous que le vaisseau *l'américa* est arrivé à Brest. Les
gens de l'art le trouvent d'une belle construction et d'un fini ad-
mirable.[8] De jeunes francois ont dit que les ornements n'étoient
pas de bon gout. Vous les reconnoissés.

William Temple Franklin to Caleb Whitefoord

Reprinted from W. A. S. Hewins, ed., *The Whitefoord Papers* . . .
(Oxford, 1898), pp. 190–1.

My dear Sir,   Passy, 7th Augt, 1783.
I have been so much taken up with Business since the rect of
your Letter, inclosing me an Introduction to Mrs Hesse, that I
have hitherto delay'd answering it.[9] I have not however been
deficient in complying with your request relative to that ami-

---

8. This ship of the line was presented by Congress to France to replace
a French ship of the line lost off Boston: XXXVIII, 70–1n. When surveyed
in 1786 and found to be rotten, it was condemned to be broken up: Morison,
Jones, p. 329.

9. Whitefoord, who had left Paris for London on April 27 (see XXXIX,
604n), wrote WTF on May 9 to introduce Elizabeth Gunthorpe Hesse, a
neighbor who was taking an apartment in Paris for a few months while
her house was being renovated. She hoped to improve her French and was
eager for an introduction to Mme Brillon, about whom her friends had said
many favorable things. Whitefoord reminded WTF that he had introduced
BF to her husband, George Hesse, a clerk in the Pay Office, the previous
fall. APS.

Mrs. Hesse was the daughter of West India merchant William Gunthorpe, and in her husband's obituary was described as "a lady of exquisite
beauty, refined manners, and liberal fortune": Vere L. Oliver, *The History
of the Island of Antigua* . . . (3 vols., London, 1894–99), II, 39; *Gent. Mag.*,
XLIV (1774), 446; LVIII (1788), 563–4.

Two letters from Mrs. Hesse to WTF survive from this trip: on May 29
she rescheduled a visit, and on Aug. 5, writing in French, she asked him to
deliver a note to Mme Brillon and give her best wishes to BF and the Jays.
Both letters are at the APS.

able and accomplish'd Lady: She has form'd with Mr¹ Brillon not merely an Acquaintance, but really a Friendship; and it is impossible for any one to be more universally liked, than she has made herself here by her Person and pleasing Manners. We all exceedingly Regret, that her stay among us has been so short and we are perpetually talking of going all together to England to make her Visit. I really should not be surprised if Mr Brillon and Family should carry this Project into execution in the Fall. As to my Grandfather and myself, I hardly know what will become of us; He has no Answer from Congress to his repeated Applications to Retire, and so continues here, tho' with much Reluctance. I wish ardently to be able to visit England before we Return, were it only for eight Days, to see you and my other Friends, and embrace my Father. He cannot regret more than I do our long Separation, and the interruption in our Correspondence;—he knows the Character of some of our Rulers, and cannot but approve of my discretion.²

Our Negotiations do not go on so well as when Mr. O.³ and you were here. We have lost by the change a worthy Friend, and your Country, an able and upright Minister.

Adieu my dear Sir,—I write in haste in hopes of being in time to request Mrs Hesse to take charge of my Letter.— My Grandfather and Mr and Mrs Jay present you their affectionate Compts as likewise to Mr Oswald, to whom please to remember me in the most affectionate Manner,—and believe me, as ever, Sincerely yours   W. T. Franklin.

Congress have alone Authority to appoint Consuls. The Place at Calais has already been asked for by 50 Persons. If a Frenchman is appointed, it is likely to be Le Veux, our old Correspt.⁴

1. Undoubtedly a mistranscription. Here, and in the next sentence, WTF must have written "Mme."

2. Whitefoord's May 9 letter contained news of WF who, the day before, had called on him and asked him to forward to Passy a letter for BF that had been mistakenly delivered to his address. WF was pleased to hear news of WTF, and "regretted the long interruption of Correspondence, & hoped the Time was near at hand, when it might be renew'd without Impropriety."

3. Oswald.

4. Whitefoord had asked about consulships in Calais. Jacques Leveux had been assisting Americans there since 1778 (see XXVI, 515n), and when

From Benjamin Vaughan

ALS: Library of Congress

My dearest sir, London, Augt. 8th:, 1783.

I beg to introduce to your kind regards one of my best respected friends, Mr Dugald Stewart, who though as yet little known out of Scotland, is one of the best known men in it. He stands in the very first class of their mathematicians & literary men. He has twice at a day's warning taken up Dr. Adam Ferguson's lectures in Moral Philosophy, & twice completely excelled him in the opinion of every one, as was proved in particular by the attendance he had while he lectured.—[5] Perhaps you may remember his father who lectured at Edinburgh in Mathematics, & wrote a treatise on the sun's distance from us as deducible from the theory of gravity. It is very poor compliment to Mr Stewart, to say that in science it is the father who is really the child.[6]

My friend travels with Lord Ancram, the son of the Marquis of Lothian,[7] whom he represents to me as a pretty & very amiable young man. I beg you would extend your notice to him also.

I have extreme confidence in begging your attention to Mr Stewart, because I am sure it is in his power to repay you by the information he can give you of the literary characters in his country, & the objects they are pursuing. He is however very

---

he asked outright about a consulship, BF told him what WTF here confided in Whitefoord: Leveux to BF, March 2, 1784; BF to Leveux, March 8, 1784, both at the APS.

5. Vaughan had already mentioned this eminent mathematician and philosopher: XXXV, 621. Stewart had lectured to Adam Ferguson's classes at Edinburgh University during Ferguson's mission to America in 1778–79, and he assumed his chair in moral philosophy when Ferguson resigned in 1785: *ODNB*, under Ferguson and Stewart.

6. Matthew Stewart (1717–1785) had been professor of mathematics at Edinburgh University until 1772, when poor health forced him to stop teaching. His son took over his classes and in 1775 was appointed to the mathematics professorship. The miscalculations in Matthew Stewart's treatise *The Distance of the Sun from the Earth Determined, by the Theory of Gravity* . . . (Edinburgh, 1763) were first exposed in 1769: *ODNB*.

7. William Ker (1763–1824), Earl of Ancram, whose father was William John Ker (1737–1815), fifth Marquess of Lothian: Sir James Balfour Paul, ed., *The Scots Peerage* . . . (9 vols., Edinburgh, 1904–14), V, 481–3.

diffident, & is very fearful of betraying himself upon subjects which he is not master of, in which list for the present *he* reckons mathematics, & is therefore averse to meeting M D'Alembert on the subject, though he wants to see him.— He is not strong in Natural Philosophy, but he understands every thing in it. He burns to see you as its present father; and as at least *half* the time I spent alone with him in Scotland was employed in conversing about you, I believe he would not think he had been out of his country unless he was allowed to see you at Paris.

I have no news which I have the courage to write you. The way things go on will have sufficiently explained some of the reasons of my past silence.— At present however there is no news which you are not at least as well acquainted with as myself, were I inclined to go into it.— I think the *nation* would in time opens its eyes about improvements in commerce & peace, if pains were taken with them, and the ministry as much in earnest as the last on this point.

Please to remember me very affecty. to Mr Franklin.[8] And for yourself, believe me my dearest sir, your ever respectful, (devoted, grateful,) & affectionate humble sert   BENJN. VAUGHAN

Dr. Franklin.

Addressed: A Monsr / Monsr. Franklin. / &c &c &c / a Passy. / Par faveur de M. Stewart & le Comte Ancram.

8. Here Vaughan heavily crossed out a long sentence. On the same day, both he and his brother William wrote to WTF about various bills. Benjamin had received one from JW that "did not prove good" (University of Pa. Library). William was sending a bill to BF as part of their collaboration to finance the travels of Samuel Vaughan, Jr. He was sorry that he would not see BF in England but, possessing BF's portrait, was often reminded of his advice "Seek & ye shall find." APS.

Henry Laurens to the Other American Peace Commissioners

ALS: New-York Historical Society; two copies[9] and transcript: National Archives; copy: South Carolina Historical Society

Gentlemen.   London 9th. August 1783.

Availing my self of your consent & recommendation I embarked at le Havre on board the Washington & Sailed from thence the 1st. Inst. On the 2d. at 9 o'Clo. AM. we were within six Leagues of Poole in Dorsetshire. The Wind being very favorable, I quitted the Ship, went on board a small Hoy bound to Poole & urged Capt. Barney to proceed on his Voyage, leaving my excellent Post Carriage to take its fate on the Ship's Deck in preference to the risque of delaying him a single hour. Had the Wind been Westerly I might have detained him a few days for dispatching to Congress the result of my applications to the Ministers of this Court. I judge from the state of the Winds since I parted with Capt. Barney, he was clear of the Channel on Sunday Night the 3d. & that he is now 150 or 200 Leagues advanced on his Voyage.[1]

I arrived in London late in the Night of the 3d. on the 5th. had a conference with the Rt Honble. C J Fox Esqr. which I commited to writing as soon as it had ended. I shall give it in short dialogue as the best way, not pretending to accuracy in every word but fully preserving the sense & substance.

Mr. Fox—I suppose Mr. L. you wish to forward the Ratification of the Provisional Articles.

L. I could wish that was done Sir, but tis not the particular business which I have in charge.

F. I understood from Mr. Hartley's Letter which you sent me it was, but he does not speak possitively.[2]

---

9. Made by Henry Laurens, Jr., and signed by Laurens, who sent them to Livingston.

1. Barney arrived in Philadelphia on Sept. 9: *Pa. Packet or the Gen. Advertiser*, Sept. 11, 1783.

2. On Aug. 4 Laurens delivered to Fox an official dispatch from Hartley (no. 15) and a private letter from him dated July 29: Giunta, *Emerging Nation*, I, 904; II, 208–10, 219–20.

L. No Sir, the only business I have in Charge is to enquire, whether a Minister from the US of America would be properly received at this Court.[3]

F. Most undoubtedly, I could wish there was one here at present, I think we have lost much time from a want of a Minister from your side.

L. then Sir, will you be so good as to ask his Majesty the Question & inform me.

F. I'll take the King's pleasure tomorrow & you shall hear from me, I suppose there is already a conditional appointment of some person now in Europe.

L. Not that I know of, tho' I don't know the contrary, but I have an excellent opportunity for writing to Congress & I have no doubt an appointment will be immediately made.

F. that's unlucky, there must be two crossings the Ocean then; If a Minister from Congress had been here we might have done our business in half the time we have already spent, but I shall certainly inform you to Morrow, this is the very time a Minister from your people is most necessary.

L. tho' I have nothing particularly in charge except the business already mentioned, I regret the delay of both the Commercial & definitive Treaty. We had flattered our selves with hopes in March & April that both would have been finished in a few days.

F. Why as to a Definitive Treaty, I don't see any necessity for one, or not immediately. The Provisional Articles are to be inserted in & constitute a Treaty—a Ratification of those I apprehend will answer all purposes of a Definitive Treaty they may be made definitive.— The Case with respect to France

3. The point of this question is explained in what we believe to be an unsent response to this letter, drafted by Jay. After the commissioners learned from Hartley that an American minister would be received at the court of St. James's (see their letter to Livingston, July 27), Laurens had evidently observed that "there was a wide Difference between a Ministers being ceremoniously and formally received, and his being received and treated in a cordial friendly manner." He hoped to clarify this point in a conversation with Fox. See Morris, *Jay: Peace*, pp. 574–5, where this undated draft is published as though sent by the American commissioners.

& Spain differs widely, several articles in our Preliminaries with them refer to a definitive Treaty.

L. I agree with you Sir, the Provisional Articles mutually ratified may by the consent of the Parties be made definitive, but there may be additional articles suggested & agreed to for mutual benefit.

F. that's very true but I don't see any at present. I very much regret the want of a Minister from America.

L. Permit me Sir to ask you, Is it intended by the Proclamation of the 2d July to exclude American Ships from the West India Trade between the United States & the British Islands?

F. Yes certainly it was so intended, in order that we might have something to Treat for, & this will [be] a subject for Commercial Treaty—

On the 6th. I waited upon His Grace the Duke of Portland. His Grace was equally clear & possitive as Mr. Fox had declared himself, that a Minister from the United States of America would be well received at this Court. & also regreted that an appointment had not earlier taken place.— I touched upon the Commercial & definitive Treaty refered to conversations & assurances in March & April, intimated my apprehensions of pernicios effects, which might arise from excluding American Ships from a freedom of Trade between the United States & the British West India Islands, adding what I had learned from Doctor Franklin of the Commerce intended by the Court of France to be permited between our America & the French Islands.[4] I can only say, the Duke seemed to wish that every thing had been settled to mutual satisfaction & to hope that every thing would soon be settled. Yesterday by desire of Mr. Fox I called upon him again, he said he had not seen the King, but that he had transmited an Account to His Majesty of my application, that we might be perfectly satisfied however, a Minister from Congress would be well received, that the appointment of one was much wished for here.[5] That he must take blame to himself

---

4. See our annotation of BF to Livingston, July 22[–26].

5. Not by the king, however. When answering Fox's Aug. 6 letter, George III wrote that he would never find the prospect of an accredited American minister "agreeable," suggesting instead that only agents be

in some degree for the long delay of a Commercial regulation, but that business would now be soon finished. He had no objection himself to opening the West India Trade to the Americans, but there were many parties to please "& you know added Mr. Fox, the people of this Country very well." Yes Sir, I know something of them, & I find not only the West India Planters but some of the most judicios Merchants anxios for opening the Trade, I have been told by some of them they should be ruined without it. "I believe all this, said Mr. Fox but there are other people of a different opinion. As to the Definitive Treaty, there may as you observed be new articles necessary for mutual advantage & we may either add such to the Provisional Articles & make the whole definitive or make a New Treaty, but I understand it is expected this should be done under the Eye of, or in concert with the Court of France which for my own part I don't like and can't consent to."

I replied, "in my opinion a New Treaty definitive would be best as well for incorporating additional Articles as for clearing away some of the Rubbish in the Provisional, which contained if not nonsense, more than a little ambiguity. That tho' I did not see the necessity for it now, yet I had been told it was expected our definitive Treaty should be finished in communication with the French Court. But as I had formerly observed I had received no charge on this head & spoke only the sentiments of Mr. Laurens to Mr. Fox not to a Minister of Great Britain."

I have detailed facts as fully & fairly as memory has enabled me, I leave them with you under this one remark that we are Cooler in the Dog Days than we were at the Vernal Equinox. The Philosophy of Versailles & Passy may account for & guard against the effects of extreme changes.

I have found my presence at this juncture of some use in explaining or attempting to explain the late Mutiny at Philadelphia, the Enemies of this Kingdom & the United States had ex-

---

appointed. Moreover, he would "have a very bad opinion of any Englishman that can accept being sent as a Minister for a Revolted State, and which certainly for many Years cannot have any stable Government." Fortescue, *Correspondence of George Third*, VI, 428–9, 429–30.

447

ulted, the friends to both had too much abandoned themselves to dread that the Soldiery had assumed the Reins of Government & that all the States of America were rushing into Anarchy. Capt. Carbary & Lieutt. Sullivan those rash Young Officers who led on the Mutineers to the State House, arrived a few days ago; the former has been with me expressing deep concern for his misconduct, desiros of returning with an assurance of personal safety & wanting Money for supporting daily expences, alledging that the United States "are indebted to him at least £1200. Currency exclusive of Land." I have recommended to him to return immediately, to demean himself to the Laws of his Country & submit to the Magnanimity of Congress. He expresses a dread of undergoing a Trial. Could I afford it & were to advance Money for his living in London, should I not incur censure at home? I beg you will communicate such particulars of that disturbance & the event of it as you may have learned, & your opinion for my conduct respecting these Officers.[6]

Mr. Barclay[7] will tell you of a display of the American Standard under a triumphant British Pendant at a very Capital Inland Fair. Trifling as the Insult may appear it discovers a little Leaven at Center. With every good wish & with very great Respect & Esteem I have the honor to be Gentlemen Your faithful & Obedient servant   HENRY LAURENS.

Their Excellencies The Ministers Plenepotentiary from the United States of America at Paris.

Endorsed by John Jay: Mr Laurens 9 Augt. 1783

6. For the mutiny see Boudinot to BF, July 15. For Laurens' refusal to loan Carbery money see *Laurens Papers,* XVI, 253n.

7. Who sailed with Laurens from Le Havre, en route to London on private business. Laurens entrusted this letter to Barclay, expecting him to leave London no later than Aug. 12 (as he told BF on Aug. 27, below). He did not leave England until Aug. 20, and was back in Paris two days later: Roberts and Roberts, *Thomas Barclay,* pp. 127–8, 319n.

From Benjamin Vaughan

Incomplete AL: American Philosophical Society

My dearest sir,   London, Augt. 9th:, 1783.

Having heard that you have been told at Paris, that Lord Shelburne had used foul play about the instructions for removing the troops from New York, I have only to state as a fact, that Genl. Gray in a letter I have in my possession addressed to Lord Keppel, requests to know on what means he may depend for removing the troops from New York, which he says make the *grand object of his instructions.*[8] He says that this was the grand object of Sr. Guy Carleton before him, and besides his instructions he names *three* separate dates when the order was sent him, (that is, Sr. Guy Carleton.) The chief embarrassments that prevented the evacuation were, at one time the want of transports, and at another the severity of the season, and at another the want of convoy, especially when the French were on the coast. Nay they were even ordered to go to Halifax at one time, rather than stay at New York, which I suppose was during the unhealthy or the hurricane season in the West Indies.—[9] I think this is strong evidence.— Savannah required 10,000 ton shipping for its evacuation; Charles Town &c 30,000, or three times that quantity; & New York three times that quantity again, (that is, some 300 ships probably as transports.)—[1] The

8. At the end of December, 1782, Sir Charles Grey (XXXVI, 666n) was appointed to succeed Sir Guy Carleton as commander-in-chief of British troops in North America. He promptly informed Augustus Keppel, First Lord of the Admiralty, that the number of transport ships available in North America was insufficient. Keppel replied on Jan. 21, 1783, that no more could be procured: Paul D. Nelson, *Sir Charles Grey, First Earl Grey: Royal Soldier, Family Patriarch* (Madison, N.J., Teaneck, N.J., and London, 1996), pp. 118–19.

9. See Shelburne to Carleton, April 4, 1782, and Townshend to Carleton, Aug. 14, 1782, in K. G. Davies, ed., *Documents of the American Revolution, 1770–1783* (21 vols., Dublin, 1972–81), XXI, 52–4, 109.

1. More than 11,000 tons of shipping were used to evacuate Savannah on July 11, 1782, and 35,785 tons to evacuate Charleston on Dec. 18, 1782. In April, 1783, the gradual evacuation of New York began, using about 40,000 tons; it was completed at the end of November: David Syrett, *Shipping and the American War, 1775–83* . . . (London, 1970), pp. 236–41.

449

whole of Genl Gray's letter, written after his appointment and before his *intended* departure,[2] is in the strain of the evacuation being the great & primary object of his mission.— Ld. Keppels answer was a paltry one.

A second charge I hear of is, that Lord Shelburne put the Spaniards in possession of Florida,[3] to put them in the way of quarrelling with you.— I shall here only relate facts. The preliminaries were signed on a Monday. On the preceding Friday or saturday, Mr. Fitzherbert went to *barter* East Florida for Logwood cutting &c in the Bay. It was a prevailing opinion here, that Florida was a sand-bank; that with Spaniards & Americans for neighbors, it was never worth holding by itself; that its negroes would always be running away; that the Indians woud probably be made troublesome; that the troops would die; and that after all, it would turn out at last *Americas*.— Lord Shelburne in a peace where so much was given away, must be strangely framed to be supposed to give away by choice, and upon such an uncertainty as a quarrel TO *arise* about boundaries.— Lord Shelburne was not a minister for FRENCHmen, *well* understanding him, to relish; nor was he a minister for *ambitious* English *placemen* to relish, or their weaker minded adherents. And to say the truth, for I love frankness, his method of speaking begets often more suspicion of his soundness than is well founded. Of this gentleman I have known a great deal, angry & pleased, hoping & disappointed; & I think him still a real, fair-meaning, *bold* statesman.

I have been silent about his adversaries. I am not inclined to attempt persuading every American, that every other man in England, or at least every present

---

2. Grey, who was supposed to sail in February, never left England, and Carleton was obliged to remain in command of British forces. Grey's ill health may have been a factor in the initial delay, but the fall of the Shelburne ministry called his appointment into question. The king accepted his resignation in mid-April: Nelson, *Sir Charles Grey*, pp. 120–3.

3. This was included in the preliminary British-Spanish peace agreement of Jan. 20, 1783. By failing to specify the borders of West Florida, the British did embroil the Spaniards and Americans: XXXIX, 383–4n.

From Jonathan Williams, Jr.

ALS: American Philosophical Society

Dear & hond Sir.   Nantes Augt. 9. 1783.

I have sent to Billy by this Post a Copy of my last Memoire to M de Vergennes, Supported by those of my Creditors who are of this Town & were of the Meeting, with Copies & Extracts of Several Letters I have received. I send also the originals of these Letters to prove the veracity of the Extracts. As they extend to matters foreign to the Subject and are too lengthy to be given to the Minister, please to certify the verity of the Extracts, after examination, so as the Originals may be immediately returned to me.[4]

You observed to me in your last kind Letter[5] that there was no Situation in Life in which a man might not, by conducting well, do himself honour; this is more my Ambition than any View of Fortune, and I declare to you in the Sincerity of my Heart, that I look forward to the Day I shall have Satisfied all my Creditors, with more eagerness, than ever my Imagination excited me to do in any other View. I beg you will read Attentively the Letters I have Sent, & after considering that not one of the writers knew the others Sentiments you will conceive of the Pleasure I enjoy; I wish you to believe that notwithstanding all this Favour nothing on Earth Shall tempt me to do the Smallest Act in favour of any one Creditor to the Prejudice of the

---

4. See JW to BF, July 29, enclosing a petition to Vergennes seeking an extension of his *arrêt de surséance;* the annotation there describes JW's letter asking WTF to deliver it. WTF evidently did so. As JW anticipated, Vergennes required that the petition be supported by letters from his creditors. WTF informed JW of this in a now-missing letter of Aug. 5, to which JW's letter to WTF of Aug. 9 (APS) and the present letter are the response. In addition to the information summarized in this paragraph, JW asked his cousin to show the extracts to BF, Alexander, and Grand. The only creditor who had not written a letter (he was out of town) was a man to whom he owed but a small sum. WTF should therefore assure Vergennes that "the writers of the Letters, with Mr Grand, (who I suppose will not oppose the Measure) form the majority of what I owe in France." WTF forwarded the memoir and its supporting documents to Vergennes on Aug. 15, with a cover letter expressing the hope that no further obstacle would emerge (AAE).

5. That letter of July 18 is missing; see JW to BF, July 29.

whole,[6] and I expect the Indulgence of my Friends only as my Conduct Shall Answer this Principle. I trust I Shall not reckon among my misfortunes any diminution in your Esteem & am as ever most dutifully and affectionately Yours, JONA WILLIAMS J

Addressed: a monsieur / Monsieur Franklin / Ministre plenipotentiaire / des Etats Unis en Son / Hotel a Passy. / pres Paris

Notation: Jonn. Williams Nantes 9th Aug. 83

To Ann Hudson de Lavau

Press copy of ALS: American Philosophical Society

Madam, Passy, Augt. 10. 1783
I received your Letter dated the first Instant,[7] which I should have answered directly, but had mislaid the enclos'd Letter from your Mother which you desired might be sent you. The Bills mentioned by Mr Beall, came duly to my hands and I have received the Money, Seventy-two Dollars. I imagined you were long since gone to America,[8] am sorry to hear of your Disappointments, and now acquaint you that you may draw on me for three hundred and Sixty Livres Tournois, the Amount of

---

6. On July 31 the Parisian cloth merchant C. J. Morice (XXIII, 200n) had asked for just such preferential treatment, which under French law recipients of bankruptcy protection were prohibited from extending: Morice to JW, July 31, 1783 (APS); Claude Dupouy, *Le Droit des faillites en France avant le Code de commerce* (Paris, 1960), p. 142. After JW refused, Morice and another creditor, Bernier, wrote to Chaumont opposing JW's application. WTF informed JW of this in a now-missing letter of Aug. 16, which JW answered three days later. He sent WTF Morice's incriminating letter of July 31, with instructions to show it to Vergennes if Morice continued to make trouble. He also enclosed a new letter to Vergennes, pleading his case: JW to WTF, Aug. 19, 1783 (APS); JW to Vergennes, Aug. 19, 1783 (AAE).

7. Above.

8. Samuel Beall had enclosed a letter from Ann Evans along with the bills of exchange that were to pay for her daughter's passage to America. By the time Beall's letter arrived, Lavau had already received a pass from BF to travel to Rochefort, from which port she must have intended to leave for America: XXXVI, 380; XXXVIII, 108–9.

the above, which shall be paid on Sight;[9] and this Sum, with Mr Beall's Letter which I also send you enclos'd,[1] will I hope procure you a Passage to your own Country, where I wish you may arrive safe & have a happy Sight of your Friends. I am, Your humble Servant   B Franklin

Mrs Ann Hudson de Lavau

From A. C. G. Deudon[2]   ALS: American Philosophical Society

Monsieur   Paris ce 10 août 1783
   Lors de mon départ de Bruxelles, monsieur Bournons,[3] de l'académie roÿale des Sciences de cette ville, m'a prié de vous faire parvenir la prèmiére partie de ses élémens de mathématiques, que voici; il m'a chargé en même-tems, de vous faire Connoître de Sa part, qu'il aura l'honneur de vous prèsenter les deux volumes Suivans, du même ouvrage, à mesure qu'ils paroitront.
   Il vous souviendra peut-être encore Monsieur, que, sous les auspices de monsieur diderot, vous m'avez fait l'honneur, l'étée passé, de me permettre de voir vôtre armonica, que vous avez eu la bonté de m'en expliquer le méchanisme et que j'ai pris la

9. Her draft of Aug. 21 was paid on Aug. 29: Account XVII (XXVI, 3).
1. See XXXVIII, 108–9.
2. Little is known about this former *échevin* (deputy-mayor) of Mechelen, and no other trace survives of the visit he says he made to BF in the summer of 1782 under Diderot's auspices. He certainly knew Diderot, and served as his intermediary with Prince Gallitzin, the Russian minister to The Hague, in 1780: Gallitzin to Diderot, [Oct. 9, 1780], in Denis Diderot, *Œuvres complètes*, ed. Roger Lewinter (15 vols., Paris, 1969–73), XIII, 955, 956n. How well Diderot knew BF is not known. Though they had many friends in common, this letter contains the only specific mention of contact between the two.
3. The mathematician Rombaut Bournons (d. 1788), born at Mechelen, taught at the Collège Thérésien in Brussels and in 1776 became a member of the Académie impériale et royale des sciences et belles-lettres de Bruxelles: Larousse; *Nouvelle biographie*. The enclosed work was *Elémens de mathématiques à l'usage des collèges des Pays-Bas* (Brussels, 1783).

liberté alors, de vous communiquer les projets, que je m'étois formés d'âjouter quelques perfections, à Ce charmant instrument. Après bien des tentatives et des essais, qui avoient plus ou moins, des avantages ou des deffauts, je me Suis déterminé pour ce qui Suit. Une ou plusieurs bandes de drap mouillé et fixées à la partie antérieure de l'instrument, Sont couchées Sur les verres d'un Bout-à-l'autre et C'est par l'interposition de Ce drap, que les doigts les font sonner. La largeur de ces Bandes, ne doit guerre excéder la partie Supérieure des timbres et la quantité de ces bandes doit être déterminée, Sur les différens verres, d'après quelques essais préliminaires.

Au moÿen de ce procédé Bien Simple, j'obtiens en premier lieu, un Son plus pur, plus doux et également intense qu'avec les doigts nuds. Les doigts nuds, à la vérité, procurant des sons plus argentins, plus pènétrans que le drap; mais celui-ci en revange, en donne des plus moëlleux et des plus tendres. En Second lieu, les tons extrémes, tant Supérieurs, qu'inférieurs, parlent difficilement et n'obéissent que lentement au doigt; le drap au Contraire, les fait chanter plus aisement, Sur-tout les aigus. En troisieme lieu, les verres parlent plus vîte à ma manière et l'intonation en paroit moins Brusque. Enfin le drap une fois mouillé, le reste pour long-tems: il faut au contraire, mouiller Souvent les doigts. Voici du moins les resultats que j'ai trouvé Sur mon instrument fait de verres de la fabrique de liege et j'ai tout lieu de croire, qu'il en Seroit de même, avec des Crïstaux Soufflés ailleurs, d'autant plus que Leurs Altesses roÿales, gouverneurs actuels des paÿs-bas,[4] m'aÿant fait demander quelques mois passés, de remettre deux timbres cassés, à leur Armonica, faite à londres; j'ÿ ai ajouté, après l'avoir racommodé, les Bandes de drap, dont je viens d'avoir eu l'honneur de vous parler et l'on en a été tellement Satisfait, tant pour la beauté des Sons, que pour la facilité du jeu, que les musiciens de la cour, ont totalement abandonné le toucher du doigt nud, pour ÿ Substituer ma méthode.

A Cette petite perfection, j'en ai âjoutée une plus importante, quoi-que de la plus grande Simplicité. Vous connoissez Monsieur, combien les transpositions d'un ton à un autre Sont de difficile exécution en musique et qu'il ne faut rien moins que la très

4. The Duke and Duchess of Saxe-Teschen: XXXVI, 446–7n.

longue pratique, d'un musicien Consommé qui peut la lui rendre facile. Or je transpose Sans peine, dans tous les tons, Sans Sortir même de la gamme naturelle et voici Comment. Vous dites dans vôtre lettre au pere beccaria, en lui donnant la déscription de vôtre charmant instrument,[5] que vous peignez les bords de vos verres, des sept Couleurs prismatiques, les diezés en Blanc et ca pour que l'œil du joueur, puisse aisement reconnoître les tons: Cette ingénieuse idée, m'en a fait naitre une autre et C'est en la généralisant, que j'ai imaginé Ce qui Suit. Au lieu de peindre les verres, je pose derriere eux et en face du joueur, une latte de bois, mince, de la largeur de deux ou trois pouces: cette latte, qui Suit l'inclinaison des verres, est peinte en Blanc, portant Sur toute Sa Largeur, des bandes étroites, colorées des 7 Couleurs du Spectre de newton et dont chacune se trouve vis-à-vis du verre correspondant. Les Semi-tons Sont peints de noir et au lieu d'en faire des Bandes entières, elles n'occupent que la moitié de la largeur de la latte, ce qui imite assez bien l'aspect d'un clavier d'orgue. Si je veux transposer un air quelconque, par exemple d'un demi ton plus bas, que celui dans le quel il est noté, je Substitue à la prèmiére latte que j'enléve, une autre latte, dont les Bandes colorées, Se trouvent toutes placées Successivement un demi-ton plus Bas, que Sur celle-là: de manière, que la bande *rouge*, ou *l'ut* de celle-ci, Se trouve en face du verre qui prècédemment étoit indiqué par le *violet* ou le signe du *Si*. Or comme il Se trouve douze Sémi-tons dans une octave complette, il est clair, qu'au moÿen d'autant de lattes différentes, Sur les quelles on peut reculer autant de fois les couleurs prismatiques, on fera repondre chacune d'elles, à tous les verres, par conséquent à tous les tons de l'instrument; de sorte donc, qu'on pourra transposer à volonté; Ce qui est de la plus grande utilité dans bien des cas et d'un avantage sur tout bien marqué, pour l'armonica, à cause de son peu d'étendu. J'espère Monsieur, que vous voudrez bien pardonner la longueur de ma lettre, à l'enthousiasme qui m'égare, pour le plus flatteur et le plus harmonieux des instrumens, que vous avez si ingénieusement imaginé, ainsi qu'au zèle que j'ai d'ÿ âjouter quelque chose en marchant sur vos traces.

Je crains bien, toute-fois, que peu versé dans la langue

5. X, 129—30.

françoise, qui m'est étrangére, je n'aurai pas eu le bonheur de m'expliquer assez clairement: maûis je me flate en même-tems, qu'au cas que vous soÿez Curieux de voir les détails de mes procédés, vous voudrez bien me permettre que j'aille vous les donner: en ce cas, un mot de reponse, qui m'indiquera le jour qui vous Sera le plus Commode, me fera accourir à passi avec le plus vif empressement, trop flatté de Saisir cette occasion, pour vous donner Cette foible marque du profond respect avec le quel je suis Monsieur Vôtre très humble et très obéissant Serviteur

A: C: G: DEUDON

ancien échevin de la ville de malines, à l'hôtel de lusignan, ruë des vielles étuves st. honoré.

P:S: Si vous me faites l'honneur de me demander, j'apporterai avec moi une des lattes ci dessus, pour servir de modéle.

Notations: M. Deudon, Appointed him to come hither, Thursday the 21. Augt 83—at 1 aClock[6] / Deudon, 10 Août 1783

From Pierre-Samuel Du Pont de Nemours[7]

LS: Library of Congress

Monsieur,   Paris 10 Aout 1783
    Mgr. Le Margrave rêgnant de Bâde[8] me charge de vous prier de vouloir bien faire toutes les démarches qui dépendront de

---

6. This notation was written by WTF. Nothing further is known about Deudon or this visit.

7. Though Du Pont's last letter dates from 1777 (XXIV, 382–3), the old friends presumably spoke more than they wrote. Since 1781, Du Pont served as an economic adviser to Vergennes and in this capacity worked on a commercial plan for Bayonne, including its potential selection as a free port for American merchants (for which see XXXIX, 104–5). In December, 1783, the king rewarded him by conferring *lettres de noblesse:* Ambrose Saricks, *Pierre Samuel Du Pont de Nemours* (Lawrence, Kans., 1965), pp. 76–84.

8. Karl Friedrich (XXI, 387n), whom Du Pont had met in Paris in the summer of 1771. Du Pont periodically visited the margrave in Karlsruhe and wrote to him regularly. In 1783 Du Pont became the unofficial chargé

vous, pour avoir l'Extrait-Mortuaire du Sr. Adam Marggrander, né Sujet de ce Prince, et qui doit être mort noïé à Philadelphie. Ce S. Marggrander est parti pour Philadelphie, en 1774, avec un S. Gucker de Schreck,⁹ et il étoit emploïé à Philadelphie chéz un Brasseur nommé heintz, qui demeuroit dans la rüe du Marché.¹

Son Altesse Sérénissime me charge de vous témoigner d'avance toute la reconnoissance qu'elle aura des peines que vous voudréz bien prendre à ce Sujet.

J'ai bien de l'impatience d'aller vous faire ma cour, et causer un peu sur le Commerce de l'Amérique.

Vous connoissez le profond respect avec lequel je Suis Monsieur De votre Excellence Le très-humble et très-obeissant Serviteur   DU PONT

chever. de l'ordre ral. [royal] de Vaza²
hotel de la Rochefoucaut rue des Petits
Augustins

A Son Excellence Monsieur Francklin Ministre plenipotentiaire des Etats-unis de l'Amérique

---

d'affaires for Baden, despite being an official of the French government: *ibid.*, pp. 57–9, 84.

9. Georg Adam Marggrander and Jacob Gucker (as their names were recorded on the Philadelphia arrivals list) sailed on the *Union* from Rotterdam, arriving in September, 1774: Ralph Beaver Strassburger, comp., "Pennsylvania German Pioneers: a Publication of the Original Lists of Arrivals in the Port of Philadelphia from 1727 to 1808," Pa. German Soc. *Proc.*, XLII (1934), 758–60.

1. Charles Thomson, to whom BF forwarded this letter, understood this to be Market Street brewer Reuben Haines, long known to both of them: XI, 223, 315n; Smith, *Letters*, XXI, 279. Haines (1728–1793) was involved in various real estate and business affairs: Robert E. Wright, "Artisans, Banks, Credit, and the Election of 1800," *PMHB*, CXXII (1998), 221–2; Elaine F. Crane *et al.*, eds., *The Diary of Elizabeth Drinker* (3 vols., Boston, 1991), III, 2158.

2. The Order of Vasa was instituted in 1772 by Gustavus III in recognition of contributions to agriculture, mining, trade, and the arts. Du Pont, who had corresponded regularly with the king, was knighted in 1775: H. Arnold Barton, "Gustav III of Sweden and the Enlightenment," *Eighteenth-Century Studies*, VI (1972), 16; Saricks, *Du Pont de Nemours*, pp. 57–8, 66, 71.

Note in Franklin's hand:[3] Mr. Franklin requests earnestly of Mr Thomson, to procure if possible what is desired in this Letter.

From William Nixon

ALS: American Philosophical Society

Off the Downes, 10th. August 1783.

May it please your Excellency

You will please to call to Mind that I presumed to inclose to your Excellency a little Book, which I published, Viz. *Prosody made easy.* The very polite Answer, which you returned, & your unexpected Liberality at so seasonable a Time can never be forgotten by me.[4] The Mode of paying the Debt due by me to you was such a Proof of Politeness, Liberality, & universal Benevolence, as impressed me with the deepest Sense of the Favour. I take the Liberty of troubling you with a short Specimen of a few little Books, which I humbly hope would facilitate the Acquisition of the Roman Language &, by smoothing the Way, give more Time for other Studies. Should the Plan merit your Approbation, I would be proud of the Honour of being permitted to dedicate all the little Books (mentioned in it, including the Prosody), to your Excellency, for I think your Name would be an Advantage to me, & would be glad to make a public Acknowledgment of your Kindness to me & Mankind in general.[5]

---

3. BF sent this letter to Thomson on Sept. 13. Thomson endorsed it, "Letter from M. Du Pont to Doct Franklin respecting the Sr. Maggrander." It remains among his papers.

4. Nixon, an Irish priest and scholar, had sent this book along with the appeal he addressed to BF from a prison in Normandy in 1781. BF's answer, which he burned (as he says below), enclosed a bill of exchange for a substantial sum. Refusing repayment, BF advised Nixon to give an equivalent sum in the future to a stranger in need: XXXV, 412–14, 445.

5. Nixon enclosed a four-page printed prospectus for a collection of four books that would be printed and sold by subscription under the general title *An Easy Introduction to the Latin Language, Adapted to the Comprehension of Beginners:* a Latin grammar, a prosody (already published and available for sale), a vocabulary, and a translation of Aesop's *Fables.* The prospectus included specimens of the grammer, vocabulary, and fables. (BF's copy is at

The Letter, which you did me the Honour of sending me, when I was a Prisoner at Valognes in Normandy about two years ago, would now, if I had it, be of much service to me, because I am now sailing past the Downes on my Way to Portsmouth in Virginea, but about half a year after I burnt it, on hearing, that some people had been lodged in Newgate in London, on a Suspicion of holding a Correspondence with the Enemy & tho' the Letter, which I had the Honour of having from your Excellency contained nothing political, yet I then thought it prudent to annihilate it, tho' I was very sensible, that, being preserved, it might be one Day useful to me & answer the End of a Letter of recommendation to a Professorship in some of the American Colleges, for you there did me the Honour of saying, that there was no Doubt, but I would make a useful Member of Society in America either as a Professor in a College or as a Clergy-man. The Colleges, I suppose, will be re-established soon, and I humbly hope, that I am not altogether unqualified for undertaking a Professorship in Latin, Greek, Logic, Geometry, Astronomy, Natural or Moral Philosophy. I trust that I can produce such Testimonies, as may not be disapproved of.

Tho' I cannot ask, yet I cannot help wishing for a Letter from your Excellency, which could not but be a most Advantageous Introduction of me into the new World to which I am now bound. Should your Excellency think proper to honour me with an Answer, please to direct to me in Portsmouth Virginea.

I have the Honour of remaining with much Gratitude your Excellency's very much obliged & very humble Servant

WILLIAM NIXON

Addressed: For his Excellency B. Franklin Esqr. / Ambassador at the Court of Versailes / from the united States of America. /

---

the APS, bound in a group of pamphlets.) We have found no evidence that the collection was completed. When *Prosody Made Easy* was republished in 1786, Nixon dedicated it to BF; see XXXV, 445n. He revived the idea for a subscription three years later, issuing *Specimen of a Plan, for Facilitating the Acquisition of the Latin Language* . . . (Charleston, 1789). His vocabulary was published in Philadelphia in 1792: XXXV, 412n.

[*In another hand:*] Inland postage / [*Added by Enoch Story(?):*][6]
Paid— / No 2 Hylords Court London 12th. August 1783
Received and forwarded by Your Excellencys [*torn*]CH STORY
[*torn*] Philadelphia

Notation: William Nixon 10 Augt. 1783.—

From Pio   AL: American Philosophical Society

à Paris ce Dimanche 10. aout./. [1783][7]
Mr. de Pio a l'honneur de renouveller les assurances de son respect à monsieur franklin, Ministre Plenipotentiaire des Etats
unis de l'Amerique et de lui envoyer le 3me. volume des Oeuvres de Mr. filangieri avec une lettre du même, que Mr. de Pio a
reçu hier de naples.

Mr. de Pio est très flatté de pouvoir dire a Mr. franklin, qu'il
y a actuellement un homme de Lettres ici fort de ses amis, qui
travaille à la traduction française des Oeuvres de Mr. filangieri,
et qu'il en est deja au second volume, et le premier paroitra sous
peu de jours./.[8]

6. An old acquaintance of BF's who became a Loyalist and settled in
England during the Revolutionary War: III, 153n; XIV, 308n.

7. Dated by the reference to the third volume of Filangieri's *La scienza
della legislazione* and the author's letter of July 14 (above). The only other
Sunday, Aug. 10, during BF's stay in France occurred in 1777.

8. This statement is puzzling, as the first of Filangieri's volumes trans-
lated into French appeared in 1786. The translator was Jean-Antoine
Gauvin, *dit* Gallois (1761–1828), who would become a close friend of
Cabanis and Mme Helvétius: *DBF*, under Gallois; Quérard, *France litté-
raire;* Eugenio Lo Sardo, ed., *Il Mondo nuovo e le virtù civili: l'espistolario di
Gaetano Filangieri, 1772–1788* (Naples, 1999), p. 243n.

From Jonathan Williams, Jr.: Two Letters

(I) and (II) ALS: American Philosophical Society

I.

Dear & Hond Sir   Nantes Augt 11. 1783.

The Bearer Mr Grand Cannon is a youn Gentleman from Connecticut who passes through paris in his Way to London.[9] He will have the Honour to pay his Respects to you, and I beg leave to introduce him to your kind Notice as a discreet, intelligent worthy young man, and deserving the Esteem of all his Friend; I have this knowledge of him from his Residence for some Time past with me, and have therefore a particular Pleasure in reccommending him.—

I am as ever most dutifully and Affectionately Yours.

JONA WILLIAMS J

His Excellency Doctor Franklin.

Notation: Jonath: Williams Nantes Augst. 11. 1783

II.

Dear & hond Sir.   Nantes Augt. 11. 1783.

I believe you have already Seen Mr Russell of Boston the Bearer of this who will pay his Respects to you in his Way to London. He has for some time Past been in my 'Counting House with a View of commercial Improvement, and from my own Observation I have the pleasure to assure you I think him a very discreet Sensible well informed & good Young Man,[1] I beg

---

9. LeGrand Cannon (1762–1788) was a native of Norwalk, Conn., and the son of West India merchant John Cannon: Lorraine C. White, ed., *The Barbour Collection of Connecticut Town Vital Records* (55 vols., Baltimore, 1994–2002), XXXII, 28; Charles M. Selleck, *Norwalk* (Norwalk, Conn., 1896), p. 410.

1. JW had employed a Thomas William Russell since the summer of 1782. He may have been from the Boston mercantile family of that name, as Jonathan Williams, Sr., had written a letter of introduction for him in early 1781: XXXIV, 346; JW to Russell, July 16, 1782, and JW's cash book for 1782–83 (Yale University Library).

Gurdon Saltonstall Mumford recommended both men to WTF in a letter

leave to reccommend him as such to your kind Notice & am as ever most dutifully & affectionately Yours.   JONA WILLIAMS J

His Excellency Doctor Franklin.

Notation: Jonath. Williams Nantes August 11th. 1783.

David Hartley to the American Peace Commissioners[2]

Copies: Public Record Office,[3] Library of Congress, Massachusetts Historical Society

August 12 and 13 were of far greater diplomatic consequence than this exchange of formal letters about the birth of an English princess (the present letter and the commissioners' answer of the following day) would suggest. On Tuesday, August 12, at the weekly meeting of ministers at Versailles, Franklin and Adams learned that the French and Spanish definitive treaties with Great Britain had been prepared and corrected and were ready to be signed. The Americans presented Vergennes with a copy of their proposal for an Anglo-American definitive treaty, given to Hartley the previous Wednesday, which the French minister promised to review.[4] By the time evening fell, however, all prospects for the success of that proposal had evaporated. A courier from England brought Hartley dispatches from Fox, including (in addition to notification of the royal birth) a letter of August 9 enclosing the king's ratification of the preliminary articles and the text of a definitive treaty with the United States which Hartley was authorized to sign without further instructions. Hartley immediately

----

of Aug. 12. Cannon had worked for JW for a considerable period and was traveling with Russell (whom, Mumford believed, WTF already knew) on private business; they would deliver to BF a box of tea that JW had asked Mumford to forward. In the end they did not take it; JW brought it with him at the end of August: Mumford to WTF, Aug. 12, 1782 [*i.e.,* 1783] (University of Pa. Library); JW to WTF, Aug. 16 and 31, 1783 (APS).

2. Hartley delivered this letter to the commissioners at their meeting of Aug. 13, described in the headnote.

3. This copy and the commissioners' response of the following day were sent by Hartley to Fox in a letter of Aug. 13 (Public Record Office).

4. See the Editorial Note on the Project for a Definitive Treaty, [Aug. 6].

informed Adams of this news, and the two made plans to travel together to Passy the next morning.

On August 13 at Passy, Hartley and the American peace commissioners exchanged ratifications and examined the British proposal. Fox had characterized it as "purposely made out exactly & nearly literally conformable to the Provisional Articles," as indeed it was, with the addition of a preamble and conclusion.[5] Fox instructed that further commercial negotiations be postponed until they could be conducted by British and American ambassadors on their native soil. The Americans agreed, and plans were made to prepare texts of the definitive treaty as soon as possible.

During these discussions, the commissioners informed Hartley that they had agreed to allow the ministers of the two Imperial courts to sign the treaty as mediators. Hartley vigorously opposed the idea, whereupon they assured him that they would be guided by the decision of his government and would wait for its answer. Either way, they said, they would sign the treaty as it stood.[6]

Hartley never did consult Fox on the issue of mediation, believing the concept to be "extremely offensive."[7] When or even if he communicated a final answer to the commissioners is not known. They were still waiting for a response on August 23, when Bariatinskii discussed the topic with Franklin.[8] It is possible that the commissioners themselves dropped the issue, taking their cue from Vergennes. According to Adams' account, when they told him "at last" of Hartley's

5. See BF to Vergennes, Aug. 16, and to Laurens, Aug. 21.

6. For the meetings at Versailles and Passy see JA to Livingston, Aug. 13 (*Adams Papers*, XV, 220–2); Hartley to Fox, Aug. 13, cited above.

7. He was compelled to explain it in a letter of Aug. 20, however, after learning that Manchester had already written to Fox about it. According to Hartley's version of events (which differs from JA's version, related above), it was he who raised the issue of mediation at the Aug. 13 meeting, having heard a rumor that the Americans had been considering it. He gave them an ultimatum, refusing to exchange ratifications unless the American commissioners agreed that mediators would not sign the treaty: Hartley to Fox, Aug. 20, 1783, in Giunta, *Emerging Nation*, I, 922.

8. BF assured the Russian minister that they "would always consider it a particular honor that the foundation of our independence had been confirmed," and were "exert[ing] all our efforts toward this goal," but Hartley was "opposing us in this, responding that England has no need of mediation." Bariatinskii to Osterman, Aug. 24, 1783, in Nikolai N. Bolkhovitinov, *The Beginnings of Russian-American Relations, 1775–1815*, trans. Elena Levin (Cambridge, Mass., and London, 1975), pp. 23–4.

objections, Vergennes turned to Franklin and—using a tone that strongly suggested that "he did not wish the Mediation should take place"—pointed out that mediation could not be employed unless Hartley agreed.[9] If that meeting took place on Tuesday, August 26, and Vergennes left it believing that no further obstacles would prevent his scheduling a signing ceremony, this would explain why he, Manchester, and Aranda had settled on a date by the following day.[1]

Gentlemen   Paris Aug 12 1783

I have the honour of transmitting to you a Copy of a Letter which I have received from Mr Fox, containing an Account of the Queen having been happily delivered of a Princess, and that her Majesty & the young Princess are as well as can be expected.[2]

Since the reconciliation which has happily taken place between our two Countries, I am happy in the opportunity of communicating to you such an occasion of our joint congratulations, as the first token of that satisfaction which your Country (and you as the Ministers of it in the present case) will receive from this and from every event, which may contribute to the happiness and honour of the King, the Queen & all the Royal Family of Great Britain.

I am Gentlemen with the greatest respect and consideration Your most obedt Servt   D HARTLEY

To their Excellencies the Ministers Plenipotentiary of the United States of America &c &c &c

9. *Adams Papers*, XV, 255. A month earlier, Vergennes had written to La Luzerne that in his opinion the settlement of the Anglo-American treaty would be easier without mediation: Giunta, *Emerging Nation*, I, 893.

1. See JA to BF and Jay, Aug. 27.

2. Princess Amelia (1783–1810), King George and Queen Charlotte's fifteenth and final child, was born on Aug. 7: E. B. Fryde *et al.*, eds., *Handbook of British Chronology* (3rd ed., London, 1986), pp. 46–7.

From Sir James Nicolson[3]

AL: American Philosophical Society

August 12. 1783. Grande Rue de Passy La maison près celle De Monsr Le Comte Destaing

Sir James Nicolson presents Compliments to Doctor Franklin and is somewhat surprized to find out, only since his visit to the Doctr., that his Grandson had been received, out of respect to the Doctor's great merit, by Lady Nicolson and that he had concealed her Ladyship's portrait in miniature, under pretence of putting a glass to it. Sir James insists on the restoration of it, as his Lady does on all letters, that may have passed on the subject. He hopes that the Doctr. will grant all the merit due to the prudent method he has taken, having no time to lose, being on his departure for England.

N.B. an immediate answer is expected. as the Doctor's grandson, long before this, has refused complying with Lady Nicolson's request—[4]

Addressed: Doctor Franklin / &c / à son Hotel / a Passy

Notation: J. Nicolson Passy 12 Aug. 83

---

3. This indignant husband and his indiscreet wife have eluded scholars' efforts to identify them, largely because of inconsistencies in the evidence. For a discussion of some of the problems see Lincoln Lorenz, *John Paul Jones, Fighter for Freedom and Glory* (Annapolis, Md., 1943), pp. 774–7. WTF may have known her since 1781; in that year, he introduced David Salisbury Franks to a pair of charming women, a Lady Nicolson and a French countess who won the visitor's heart: Franks to WTF, Dec. 23, 1781, and May 22, 1782 (both at the APS). She is not the comtesse de Nicolson with whom John Paul Jones became entangled, and who also entertained WTF (Capt. de Stark to WTF, July 24, 1784, APS).

4. The next day Sir James wrote directly to WTF: propriety demanded the immediate return of his wife's portrait, and upon its receipt, he would offer "something appertaining to you." WTF replied on Aug. 14, insisting that Lady Nicolson first send back *his* portrait, which "would convince me she did not wish me to retain hers." Nicolson to WTF, Aug. 13, 1783; WTF to Nicolson, Aug. 14, 1783 (both at the APS).

The American Peace Commissioners to David Hartley

LS:⁵ Public Record Office; copies: William L. Clements Library, Library of Congress, Massachusetts Historical Society

Sir, Passy, 13th. Augt. 1783.

We have received the Letter which you did us the honour to write on the 12th. Inst. and shall take the first Opportunity of conveying to Congress the agreable Information contained in it.⁶

The Sentiments & Sensations which the Re-establishment of Peace between our two Countries, ought to diffuse thro' both, lead us to participate in the Pleasure which the Birth of a Princess must naturally give to the Royal Family & People of Great Britain; and we sincerely congratulate their Majesties, on that Addition to their Domestic Happiness.

We have the honour to be, with great Regard, Sir Your most obedt & very humble Serts. JOHN ADAMS.

B FRANKLIN

JOHN JAY

His Exy D. Hartley Esq.

5. In WTF's hand.
6. JA included this news in one of the three long letters he wrote to Livingston on Aug. 13: *Adams Papers*, XV, 222. He had returned from Holland with JQA on the evening of Aug. 9, and the two of them went the next morning to Passy, where they found BF and Jay breakfasting with "a great deal of company": Taylor, *J. Q. Adams Diary*, I, 179, 181.

From Alexandre-Théodore Brongniart[7]

AL: American Philosophical Society

paris le 13 aoust 1783.
Brongniart a L'honneur de présenter Son tres humble Respect a
Monsieur franklin, et de le prier de lui faire Sçavoir Si il Se don-
nera la peine de passer chez Lui Ce Matin Mercredi, et a quelle
heure, Comme m. Son fils le lui a fait espérer La Semaine derniere. Il S'agit d'aller ensuitte a L'Ecole militaire et aux invalides
relativement aux paratonnere que m. Le Maréchal de Ségur est
dans L'intention de faire Etablir dans Ces deux maisons,[8] et pour
Les quels L'avis de Monsieur franklin Lui Sera bien precieux. Si
Monsieur franklin etoit Libre a L'heure du diner apres L'examen
de Ces deux maisons, M. Le gouverneur des invalides Seroit infiniment flatté que Monsieur franklin Voulu Lui faire L'honneur
de Rester a diner chez Lui.[9]

Monsieur franklin en Se donnant La peine de passer chez
M. Brongniart Rue St Marc y Verra Le Modele de la Colonne
projettée a la Gloire de Louis XVI. pacificateur.[1]

Notation: Brognart 13 Août 1783

---

7. The architect who had helped BF find artists for his *Libertas Americana* medal: XXXVIII, 128–9, 577–8. Since 1782, he had served as *architecte
et contrôleur général* of the École militaire and architect of the Hôtel royal
des invalides: Jacques Silvestre de Sacy, *Alexandre-Théodore Brongniart,
1739–1813. Sa vie—son œuvre* (Paris, 1940), pp. 48–51, 155.

8. The marquis de Ségur, minister of war, oversaw the general administration of the Invalides and the Ecole militaire: *Almanach royal* for 1783,
pp. 190–1.

9. Charles-Benoît, comte de Guibert (1715–1786), governor of the Invalides from 1782 through 1786, succeeded the baron d'Espagnac (XXXVIII,
325n): *DBF; Almanach royal* for 1784, p. 192.

1. If he means the monument destined for the place de Breteuil, it was
never built: Silvestre de Sacy, *Brongniart*, p. 50.

From Jonathan Williams, Jr.: Two Letters[2]

(I) and (II) ALS: American Philosophical Society

I.

Dear & hond Sir.   Nantes Augt. 13. 1783.

I received your Favour by young Johonnott who unluckily arrived two days too late for the last Vessell to New England, we have now only one Opportunity & that is for Philadelphia and I will get him away with as little Expence as possible unless you direct otherwise; if he were to miss this Occasion it would be a long time before he could probably have another, and as is [his] Father is in Baltimore he may as well be there as any where else, though I believe it would be better for the Lad in a moral View if he was Fatherless.[3]

I am as ever most dutifully & affectionately Yours.

JONA WILLIAMS J

Addressed: A Son Excellence / Monsieur Franklin / en son Hotel / A Passy. / prés Paris

Notation: Jonath: Williams Nantes August 13. 1783.

II.

Dear & hond Sir.   Nantes Augt. 13. 1783.

I have made a second application to obtain a Passage for master Johonnott at a smaller Rate but without Success, though I

---

2. For the background to these letters see Gabriel Johonnot to BF, May 25. Samuel Cooper Johonnot came to Paris with BFB and remained with the Franklins at Passy for about three weeks before continuing his journey to Nantes: Claude-Anne Lopez, *My Life With Benjamin Franklin* (New Haven and London, 2000), pp. 51–2. BF's letter to JW, mentioned at the beginning of (I), has not been located.

3. Gabriel Johonnot was so delinquent in repaying JW a large debt that JW, galled by his silence and enraged by rumors of his extravagance and mendacity, had asked RB to help him press charges: JW to RB, April 13, Dec. 6, 1782, and July 7, 1783 (Yale University Library). JW was still pursuing this debt two years later. On March 7, 1785, BF certified the signature of a Nantes magistrate who authenticated Johonnot's mortgage to JW dated March 13, 1782. Two copies, both signed by BF, are at the Hist. Soc. of Pa.

think the price extravagant, I think it is the only Opportunity we shall have a long Time, it may therefore be in the End cheaper to send him off at once, and Shall prepare accordingly— If You think otherwise please to let me know in Time.

I am as ever most dutifully & affectionately Yours

J WILLIAMS J

Addressed: A Son Excellence / Mr le Docteur Franklin / Ministre Plenipotentiaire des Etats- / Unis de l'Amerique, prés sa Majesté / trés chrétienne. / à Passy / prés Paris

From Samuel Cooper Johonnot[4]

ALS: American Philosophical Society

Respected Sir   Nantz 14 Aug 1783.

I reach'd this Place the 11th, & waited the same Day on Mr Williams. He was kind enough to think of my Passage & sent Me to the Gentleman that fits out the Ship Le Comte D'Estaing,[5] to agree for my Passage to Philadelphia, as there is no Vessel here bound to the Northward.

The Price is 600 Livres.— Mr Williams thinks it exorbitant, & desires to know whether I must go or wait for a more convenient Opportunity.

I board here at Mrs McCarty's—pretty good Accommodations, & am employ'd under Mr Williams's Eye in perfecting my Hand Writing.

Penetrated with the highest Sense of Gratitude I have the Honour of subscribing myself with Submission & Esteem Your most humble Servant   SAM'L COOPER JOHONNOT.

4. For background see JW's letters immediately above.
5. The name of the outfitter was Peltier: Gouhard to WTF, Sept. 2, 1783 (APS).

From Edward Nairne

ALS: American Philosophical Society

Dear Sir   London Augt. 14th. 1783
Mr Sikes of Paris has been so obliging as to undertake the care of delivering a Book to you. It is directions for using my Patent Electrical Machine which I hope before this you have received safe.[6] There are some experiments in the Philosophical part, which I hope will give you pleasure, as they tend to confirm your Theory of Electricity. If it were necessary to add any thing more to your account of the similitude of Lightning & Electricity, I think the experiment which I have published in the Phil. Trans. Vol: 70 for the year 1780 of the Effect of Electricity in shortning of wire,[7] & likewise the same effect, which I have since observed produced by Lightning, which will be published in the next Phil: Trans:[8] is another confirmation.

I have lately met with a circumstance of the effects of Lightning, which I never heard of before. My Authority is part of a letter from the Duke of Marlborough to Professor Hornsby of Oxford[9] who is now at Ramsgate for his Health, where he read it to me. A Gentleman told the Duke that in the Storm of Lightening which happened lately in Oxfordshire he had several of his Sheep killed under a Tree, I think it was thirteen, & that when

---

6. Nairne had recently published *The Description and Use of Nairne's Patent Electrical Machine: with the Addition of Some Philosophical Experiments and Medical Observations* (London, 1783). A MS version of the description accompanied the machine, which was sent by Benjamin Vaughan in June; see the annotation of Dessin to BF, June 15. Nairne had probably engaged Sykes, the English optician and dealer of scientific instruments in Paris (XXVIII, 430–1n), to market the new electrical machine in France.

7. Edward Nairne, "An Account of the Effect of Electricity in Shortening Wires," *Phil. Trans.*, LXX (1780), 334–7.

8. Edward Nairne, "A Letter from Mr. Edward Nairne, F.R.S. to Sir Joseph Banks, Bart. P.R.S. Containing an Account of Wire Being Shortened by Lightning," *Phil. Trans.*, LXXIII (1783), 223–5. It was read to the Royal Society on Feb. 3.

9. The duke, who had long been interested in electricity, had invited BF to witness experiments in 1765: XII, 96. Thomas Hornsby (XVI, 196n), who had held a professorship in astronomy since 1763, was by this time also a professor of natural philosophy and the Radcliffe Librarian. *ODNB*.

they come to examine them, they found that every one of them had the Balls of their eyes forced out.

I know your time is much taken up, otherwise I should esteem it greatly if you would favor with a line Your much obliged Hble Servt. Edwd: Nairne

Addressed: Pour Son Excellence / Monsr. Le Docteur Franklin / a Passy / pres / Paris.

From Pamphili
L: Library of Congress

Ce 14. Aout 1783.

M. Le Nonce a l'honneur de faire bien des complimens à Monsieur Franklin, et Se fera un devoir de faire passer par la premiere occasion à Sa Sainteté[1] Le livre qu'il vient de lui envoyer./.[2]

To François-Louis Teissèdre de Fleury
Reprinted from *Courier de l'Europe*, xiv (November 4, 1783), 290.

This letter has puzzled editors for years. Its subject is the silver medal that Congress ordered Franklin to have struck for Lt. Col. de Fleury. Fleury himself delivered the congressional resolution to Franklin in early 1780 when he was on leave, but he was called back to America before Duvivier, the engraver, completed the work. At the end of May, 1780, when the medal was ready, Franklin had it delivered to Fleury's father, according to the officer's instructions. Just before leaving Paris, however, Fleury had informed Franklin that he wanted a second medal struck in gold at his own expense; he would pay Duvivier in advance and retrieve the medal from the engraver upon his return. Duvivier, for his part, exhibited the medal at the Salon of 1781, where it was singled out for praise.[3]

1. Pope Pius VI.
2. Doubtless the *Constitutions des treize Etats-Unis de l'Amérique.*
3. See xxx, 416–17; xxxi, 422–3, 424–5, 489–91; xxxii, 200–1, 435–6; xxxiii, 164, 174.

In the fall of 1783, four months after Fleury's regiment returned from America, a succession of articles appeared in the French press that described the congressional medal Fleury had "lately" received, emphasizing that he was the only foreigner to have been so honored by Congress. The first of these appeared on October 17 in the *Mémoires secrets*. It was paraphrased the following week in the *Gazette de France*.[4] On November 1 the *Journal Politique de Bruxelles* section of the *Mercure de France* ran a fuller story which quoted a letter of presentation from Franklin, without a date or full salutation.[5] Three days later, another version of the story appeared in the *Courier de l'Europe*. This one offered a slightly different text of Franklin's letter and included a full dateline and salutation. That is the text we publish below. The differences between the two French versions, many of them stemming from the uncertainty about whether the word "Congress" is singular or plural, suggest that they were independent translations of a now-missing English original.

Given the firm dateline on this letter in the *Courier de l'Europe*, we earlier supposed that Franklin must have retrieved the gold medal from Duvivier and sent it to Fleury upon the chevalier's return.[6] The puzzling aspect was that he here refers specifically to a medal struck by order of Congress (which, strictly speaking, the gold medal was not). We now recognize two other possibilities. Fleury may have retrieved his gold medal from Duvivier as planned but solicited the present letter when he discovered that Franklin had neglected to write one to accompany the silver medal in 1780, as he had requested.[7] The second possibility is that Franklin did write this letter in 1780, but three years later, when Fleury or someone else provided a copy to the newspapers, the date was altered (or, in the case of the *Journal Politique de Bruxelles*, omitted altogether) to foster the harmless fiction that the medal had been presented after the war's conclusion. This, in fact, was the thrust of the news stories. Many of them included other documentation in addition to this letter from Franklin: a complete

4. Bachaumont, *Mémoires secrets*, XXIII, 208–9; *Gaz. de France*, issue of Oct. 24.

5. The article also included information about a medal for the chevalier de Cambray that proved to be false; it was retracted on Nov. 22, after the *Courier de l'Europe* exposed the error on Nov. 18. The undated version of BF's letter was published in Smyth, *Writings*, VIII, 71, where it was attributed to [May, 1780] and the erroneous information about Cambray's medal was repeated.

6. XXXI, 490n.

7. XXXII, 200.

list of men whom Congress had honored with medals during the war (only eight in all, and Fleury the only foreigner), and a testimonial to Fleury's bravery written by George Washington.

The article in the *Courier de l'Europe* was soon translated into English. That translation, containing a retranslation into English of Franklin's letter, appeared in the November issue of the *Universal Maga{zine of Knowledge & Pleasure.*[8] From there it spread to the American press, where it circulated widely. Congress may have been surprised to read it, as Franklin had informed them in 1780 that the medal had been delivered.[9]

Monsieur,   A Passy, le 15 Août 1783.

J'ai l'honneur de vous envoyer, conformément aux ordres du Congrès, la Médaille qu'ils m'ont ordonné de faire frapper, en mémoire de votre belle action à l'attaque du fort de Stony-Point, pour vous la présenter en leur nom.

Je remplis ce devoir avec plaisir, ayant moi-même une haute opinion de votre mérite. Je desire que vous puissiez porter pendant une longue vie cette marque honorable de leur considération.

Je suis, avec une grande estime, &c.   (Signé) B. Franklin

From Berkenrode   AL: Library of Congress

paris ce 15 Aout 1783.

L'Ambassadeur de Hollande a L'honneur d'assurer Monsieur Francklin de Ses tres humbles civilités. Il S'acquittera tres exactement de La Commission en question, et fera parvenir a Leur adresse Le paquet qu'il Lui à envoié hier.

Court un bruit ici, depuis 24 heures, de nouvelles reçues d'une rebellion dans Les troupes Americaines au nombre de 5000 hommes, aiant des bas Officiers a Leur tete, qui doivent avoir commis des desordres a philadelphie.[1] L'Ambassadeur desire Sincerement que la Nouvelle Soit fausse, et, S'il n'y à pas

---

8. LXXIII (1783), 280–1.
9. XXXII, 450.
1. See Boudinot to the Commissioners, July 15. Items about the insurrection (giving the number of insurgents as 500) appeared in the *Public Advertiser* on Aug. 8 and the *Ga{. de Leyde* (sup.) on Aug. 12 and 15.

d'indiscretion, il prie Monsieur Francklin de vouloir bien Lui
dire S'il Sait quelque chose de positif a ce Sujet.

From Elias Boudinot

LS: Library of Congress; copy: National Archives

Sir,   Princeton 15. August 1783.
I had the honor of your favor of the 7th. of March last enclosing the treaty between the United States and the King of
Sweden,[2] the ratification whereof has been retarded for want of
nine States present in Congress. This Act has now taken place,
and I am honored with the commands of Congress to transmit
it to you for exchange, which I now have the pleasure of doing,
and hope it will meet with a safe and speedy conveyance.[3]
On revising the Treaty a manifest impropriety struck Congress in the Title of the United States being called of *North*
America, when it should have been only America; and also in
the enumeration of the different States, wherein the Delaware
State is called "The three lower counties on Delaware." As
there is no such State in the union, Congress were at a loss how
they could ratify the Treaty with propriety, unless they should
alter the transcript, which might be liable to many exceptions;
they have therefore, to avoid all difficulties, passed a seperate
Resolve, empowering you to make the necessary amendments.[4]
A certified copy of this Resolution I do myself the pleasure to
enclose.

2. BF's letter to Livingston of March 7 announced only that the treaty
had been concluded; it did not enclose a copy (though BF promised to send
one "by the first good Opportunity"). His next extant letter to Livingston,
dated April 15, enclosed what he called "another Copy" of the treaty. That
was the first (and, as far as we know, the only) copy to arrive. Congress
received it on July 18: XXXIX, 300, 467, 472.
3. Two delegates having arrived from Connecticut, the treaty was ratified on July 29: *JCC*, XXIV, 457–77.
4. *JCC*, XXIV, 477. See also our discussion of this issue in XXXIX, 255.

Congress are entirely at a loss to account for the silence of their Commissioners at Paris since February last, being without any official information relative to the Treaty with Great Britain since that time.

I had the honor of writing you very fully on the 15th. of July last, giving the reasons for our removal to this place at length, which I hope got safe to hand.

Congress having determined not to fix the place of their permanent residence till the first Monday in October next,[5] is the reason of deferring the appointment of a Minister for Foreign Affairs till that is done.—

I have the honor to be, with high respect, & Esteem Sir, Your most obedient & very humb. Servt.— ELIAS BOUDINOT

P.S.[6] I have sent by this Oppertunity, the News Papers to this Date.

The Honorable Benjamin Franklin, Esq.

From Ingenhousz

ALS: American Philosophical Society

Dear Friend   Vienna Aug. 15th. 1783.

I wrote to you a note some weaks ago[7] to accompany the request of mr. Veinbrenner, which you allready had granted. His commissionary is allready gone to Hamburg and will set out with the first vessel for Philadelphia, waiting only for the introductory lettres you promish'd— Your last was dated may 16th, of Which I first recieved the copy. Reciev my thanks for the medal, which was much and justely admired— I recieved this days a lettre from mr. Le Roy dated juin 9th by which I am rejoiced to see you continue in good health— However strongly

---

5. After the disorders in Philadelphia (for which see Boudinot's July 15 letter), Congress reassembled in Princeton on June 30; on Aug. 13 and 14 a motion to return to Philadelphia was defeated: *JCC*, XXIV, 410–11, 506–9.

6. In Boudinot's hand.

7. Above, June 23.

the printer of my book, *Didot le jeun*, promis'd to work close at the printing of it, he does not perform it; so that it may possibly become a posthumus work. This is vexing to the utmost. The german translation of it is allready nearly sold out. Mr. le Begue says he does what he can to press the printer. I thank you for the leave of dedicating it to you, of which I am proud—[8] I doe not think it probable that one of my letters to you could have been lost, as it went thro the hands of mr. Brantzen. I think reather you may have forgot it or misled.— I have red an extract of our common Friend Sir john Pringle's biography by Dr. Kipi, his theological Friend, who contributed the most to fix his anxious mind upon Socinianisme as being in his opinion the most rational and the only good religion. His caracter seems to me drawn in a masterly way. You and I are good judges of it—[9] In collecting what philosophical anecdotes I possess of you, I find it difficult, how to comply with your request of not mentioning your name in the paper you adressed to me on father Barletti's work.[1] I can not, consistent with the rules of equity and veracity, give it for my own, and even less for a performance of an anonimous author; for than your name would be equaly gessed, and it would have some appearence of mystery. As it is written in a Very polite, and at the same time very modest stile it can't hurt any one, and therefore you would oblige me to withraw your request and give me leave to publish it as it is. The notes, which I will add to it, will be what I wrote to you about my perfectely imitating the effect of the lightning at Cremona by a strong electrical explosion.[2] Father Barletti him Self will

8. See BF to Ingenhousz, May 16 (where BF claimed to have lost his friend's original request for a dedication, mentioned in the next sentence), and the references there. For the German translation see XXXIX, 88n.

9. Benjamin Vaughan had already sent BF a copy of this work, a recently published collection of Pringle's discourses together with "The Life of Sir John Pringle, Bart." by Andrew Kippis; see Vaughan to BF, June 16, letter (II). Kippis mentioned Pringle's particular friendship with both BF and Ingenhousz: *Six Discourses Delivered by Sir John Pringle, Bart...* , (London, 1783), pp. xcii, xcv.

1. "An Attempt to explain the Effects of Lightning on the Vane of the Steeple of a Church in Cremona": XXXVII, 504–12.

2. XXXIX, 528–30.

recieve it with pleasur. It will give him a new specimen of putting explications of natural phenomena in a clear and obvious
light. He is very far from being a clear headed philosopher. All
his writing are nearly as dark, diffuse and perplexed as those
of Father Beccaria.[3] They vex and tire the readers mind, without clearing up the difficulty. I have observed, that those who
extol'd the most their works, had in reality not had the courage
to goe thro them— If you should remember some particularities about the circonstances and consequences of the two electrical explosions, by which you was hit by accident, and struk to
the ground, you would oblige me to communicate them to me,
as I doe not find them in your works.[4] As the effect of a Similar
stroke by which I was struk, was followed by some remarcabel
particularities I should like to compare them which those you
have experienced. The jarr, by which I was Struck, contained
about 32 pints, it was nearly fully charged when I recived the
explosion from the Conductor supported by that jarr. The flash
enter'd the corner of my hat. Then, it entred my fore head and
passed thro the left hand, in which I held the chaine communicating with the outward Coating of the jarr. I neither saw,
heared, nor feld the explosion, by which I was Struck down.
I lost all my senses, memory, understanding and even sound
judgment. My first Sensation was a peine on the forehead. The

3. This was not Ingenhousz' first complaint about Beccaria's obscurity;
see XXIII, 256.

4. BF did not answer this until April 29, 1785 (Library of Congress),
when he referred Ingenhousz to the fifth edition of *Exper. and Obser.* (1774),
pp. 161–2, for the first of his electric shocks. That reference is to an undated
"Appendix" in the middle of the volume (appearing, in fact, on pp. 160–1),
a third-person, unattributed summary of a description BF had written
"some time since" in a letter to Collinson. BF excerpted this summary from
a review of his work by William Watson, who had read the Feb. 4, 1751,
letter when Collinson presented it to the Royal Society. BF first used the
extract in the 1754 edition of *Exper. and Obser.* because, as he noted in the
Appendix, he could not locate the original. It remained in all subsequent
editions. For the text of the original and Watson's summary see IV, 112–13,
136, 140–2.

As for the second incident, BF had made only a passing allusion to it in
a letter to John Lining, reprinted in *Exper. and Obser.* (1769): V, 525. BF described it in detail when answering Ingenhousz on April 29, 1785.

first object I saw Was the post of a door. I combined the two ideas togeather and thaught I had hurt my head against the horizontal piece of timber supported by the postes, which was impossible, as the door was wide and high. After having answered unadequately to some questions, which were asked me by the people in the room, I determin'd to go home. But I was some what surprised, that, though the accident happened in a hous in the same street where I lodged, yet I was more than two minutes considering whether, to go home, I must go to the right or to the left hand. Having found my lodgings, and considering that my memory was become very weak, I thaught it prudent to put down in writing the history of the case: I placed the paper before me, dipt the pen in the ink, but when I applyed it to the paper, I found I had entirely forgotten the art of writing and reading and did not know more what to doe with the pen, than a savage, who never knew there was such an art found out. This Struck me with terror, as I feared I should remain for ever an idiot. I thaught it prudent to go to bed. I slept tolerably well and when I awaked next morning I felt still the peine on the forehead and found a red spot on the place: but my mental faculties were at that time not only returned, but I feld the most lively joye in finding, as I thaught at the time, my judgmement infinitely more acute. It did seem to me I saw much clearer the difficulties of every thing, and what did formerly seem to me difficult to comprehend, was now become of an easy solution. I found moreover a liveliness in my whole frame, which I never had observed before. This experiment, made by accident, on my self, and of which I gave you at the time an account, has induced me to advise some of the London mad-Doctors, as Dr. Brook,[5] to try a similar experiment on mad men, thinking that, as I found in my self my mental faculties improoved and as the world well knows, that your mental faculties, if not improoved by the two strooks you recieved, were certainly not hurt by them, it might

---

5. Probably Dr. Thomas Brooke (d. 1781), a fellow of the Royal College of Physicians, who was consulting physician from 1764 to 1781 at St. Luke's Hospital for the Insane: William Munk, *The Roll of the Royal College of Physicians of London* . . . (3 vols., London, 1878), II, 258–9; C. N. French, *The Story of St. Luke's Hospital* (London, 1951), pp. 4–23, 183.

perhaps become a remedie to restore the mental faculties when lost: but I could never persuade any one to try it.[6] I should like to know allso, whether the clok of your invention, showing hours, minutes and seconds by three weels only, has been publish'd as your invention,[7] and whether you think it my [may] be publish'd now. If you give me leave, I will add to it the idea mr. whitehurst gave us at Derby,[8] who to prevent the pendulum becoming shorter by Cold and longer by heat, by suspending the superior flexible part of it from an iron rod standing behind it, which, by extending or contracting in the same ratio as the pendulum, carries it higher or lower in proportion. I get it executed here. If you Could furnish me with some farther reflexions on this head it would be a satisfaction to me and an advantage to the public. What doe you think of publishing allso, the philosophical curiosity of the globe, formed as an earth globe, swimming in a large glass globe filled with water and æther, and having two magnets, within it and one in the pedestal to keep the globe in the center and preventing it from swimming to the sides?[9]

6. BF had this passage translated into French, beginning with the sentence "The jarr, by which I was Struck . . ." A copy by L'Air de Lamotte, a press copy of it, and a press copy of another version by L'Air de Lamotte are among BF's papers at the APS.

7. Unbeknownst to BF, a description of the clock was published in 1773: VIII, 216–19.

8. In 1771: XVIII, 113–16, 190n.

9. BF's answer of April 29, 1785, gave Ingenhousz permission to publish "the Experiment of the Globe floating between two Liquors," even though it was "a Matter of no Utility." He supposed that Ingenhousz had seen it on his chimneypiece, adding that "Something of the same Nature has been done more than 100 Years since by another Person, I forget who." BF was undoubtedly thinking of Athanasius Kircher, whose description (in his *Magnes, siv de arte magnetica* . . . [Rome, 1641]) was quoted in Otto von Guericke, *Experimenta nova (ut vocantur) Magdeburgica de vacuo spatio* (Amsterdam, 1672), a book BF owned and bequeathed to BFB: "List of Books for B. F. Bache" (APS).

Kircher's invention astounded his contemporaries: a small sphere appeared to be suspended in the center of a glass globe filled with water, just as "the earth rests immobile in the center of the universe." In fact, the globe contained equal portions of water and a clear, immiscible liquid of a higher density. The sphere, which was magnetized, was weighted to have an intermediate density, and came to rest between the two liquids. Kircher stopped

I remember I heard you more than once speak of an easy why of finding the different gravity of bodies in the time of the Conjunction of different planetes or of the sun and moon, by means of a spiral elastic wire, at whose end should hang a whight. I doe not recollect enough the manner of Constructing Such Contrivance to be able to describe it in a clear way. Would you be soo good as to furnish me with some hints about it?

You have certainly concieved some more new ideas regarding Nature's laws, which it would be a pity to be lost to philosophy. It is not common in philosophers to possess an inventive genius. Those who have it live seldom to an age, in which the judgment has become to its full vigour. You live to such an age. It would be a pity your ideas should sink with you into the grave. If some of them should return to your mind, pray, make a note of them.

If to the above articles, and Such as you may still furnish me with, I could add those reflexions you begun to work at, about chimneys; and some few, which I may recollect, or I may find in your lettres, I could present the public with a set of usefull notions from a man, whose memory will be everlasting, and I would have some share in the merit of having saved them from being lost— Pray, in some leasure hours, subtracted from the whimsical potilical world, take now and than a trip again into the world of Nature. In the one you served your country, but in the other mankind— I wish for nothing more than to see you once more. I want only, to come over, more courrage than I have, to ask leave from my imp. master.[1] If we goe here to war with the Turks, we will very likely have soon the Plague

---

short of fully explaining the magnetic component, though it was suggested. The maker of BF's globe (or BF himself, if he commissioned it) knew that the sphere would remain in the center only if another magnet were placed at one of the poles—in BF's case, concealed in the pedestal. For a modern translation of the quoted passage see Margaret Glover Foley Ames, *The New (So-Called) Magdeburg Experiments of Otto von Guericke* (Dordrecht, Boston, and London, 1994), p. 202. See also Thomas L. Hankins and Robert J. Silverman, *Instruments and the Imagination* (Princeton, 1995), pp. 14–36, where other applications of this technique by Kircher, Galileo, and Francis Line are described.

1. Joseph II.

here. The foreign ministers and many people are alarm'd at the danger of this dreadfull calamity; the more so, as it is ordred no more to open at the frontiers the letters coming from the easteren countries or to Smoak them;[2] as some folks have inspired our Prince with a belive, that the plague can not be conveyed by a letter; for, say they, if this was possible, all other nations, to which such letters are dayly conveyed without being Smoaked and purifyed, would constantely have the plague among them. Some people would perhaps suspect those men, who are the advisers of so extraordinary a resolution, in the very time of the plague raging all over the turkish dominions, to be gained by the Ottomans, whose policy it has allways be to send the plague to their ennemies.

One may now soon exspect, that the quarantaine, till now so strictly observed, and with so good a succes, will soon be taken away allso, as it would be strenge to belive, that a lettre, written by a man labouring under the plage or of having its infection about him Could not Convey the Contagion, and to apprehend at the same time that a living man Coming thro the open air from Constantinople to Vienna or Belgrade, could still keep the poison about him without being himself affected by it. This believe that a lettre sealed up can convey no contagion, seems to me as extravagant as would be a believe that, among all the wearing appearel of a traveller, his nightcap only must necessarily be excepted of conveying this contagion. Not long ago my brother in law recieved a lettre from the Archipel written by a traveller labouring actualy under the plague but being nearly out of danger. He should have shuddred in reading it, if the lettre had not been opened at the frontiers (as it has been an invariable custom since a long while), and tho roughly perfumed; which is done by burning brimstone, juniper wood, myrrha, succinnan(?) &c. By the want of those salutary precautions, the plague used to break out at least every 10 years here or there

2. The epidemic, which had killed about one-third of Istanbul's population in 1778, had spread in each succeeding year and was now threatening Austrian dominions: Daniel Panzac, *La Peste dans l'empire Ottoman, 1700–1850* (Louvain, 1985), pp. 58–68; the map on p. 591 shows the sanitary cordon established at the Austrian border.

in Europe in the former centuries. Whole Europe is now again in the same danger, as allmost all the Correspondence by letters from Alappe, Egypt and all those Countries, which are so often infected by the pestilential contagion, goes over Belgrade. I find now written upon all letters these dreadfull words, *netto di fori, sporco di dentro*,[3] which strikes every one with terror, who recieves them. Many people who are much about the Souverain, approove of this extrordinary and erroneous opinion, thinking probably that nothing pleases more a great man than to approove of his opinions. If the plague will thus be carried into the French dominions, your American brethren may take by times salutary means to prevent this calamity passing the ocean. If you should hear speaking about this affaire, as you may likely, when the terror will spread thro Europe, I begg that my name be not mentioned. Writers on the plage give incontestable prooves that the plage has been communicated by parcels, boxes, and letters sealed or shut up during several years. The Contagion of the small pox is of the same nature.

Some weaks ago, Lady Dowager Penn wrote a lamentable letter to the Princess dowager of Lichtenstein,[4] (who has allways shown me civilities and frienship) in which she complains of the hardship of finding her husband's possessions confiscated; and I belive she has endeavoured to find here some high protection or recommendation to mitigate her fate. If the Emperour's protection or recommendation has been Sollicited, I should find it not unreasonable; but you will be surprised, that the Princess of Lichtenstein applyed to me, asking me in the most pressing way my endeavours, to obtain from you a recommendation in behalf of Lady Penn. I told her it was unbecoming in me to trouble you about Such thing, and that even you yourself could be of little use in the case, as those confiscations are made by the legislature in the Country it Self. As I Could by no means persuade her of

---

3. Clean outside, dirty within.
4. Lady Juliana Penn, who had requested help of BF directly (XXXVIII, 343–4, 464n), and Maria Leopoldine von Liechtenstein (Lichtenstein) (1733–1809), the widow of Prince Franz Josef von Liechtenstein (d. 1781): Gerald Schöpfer, *Klar und fest: Geschichte des Hauses Liechtenstein* (Graz, 1996), pp. 89–90.

the inutility of fulfilling her request, I was obliged, if I would not break with her, to promish her to write you in her name, and to sollicite your intercession. She has, she says, the highest opinion of your humanity and your moderation which you publikely show'd in recommending to congress the fate of all the Loyalistes. To Content her about me, I begg only to write in a line or two in your lettre some thing, I may Show her, that I may not be Suspected of having not fulfilled what I promis'd. You know the delicacy of people of superior rank. Remember what jule Cæsar say'd when king Ptolomie did send him the head of Pompeus as a compliment, when he arrived in Ægypt, after the battel of Pharsales.

> Aufer ab aspectu nostro funesta, Satelles!,
> Regis donæ tui . . . .
> . . . . unica belli
> Præmia civilis, victis donare salutem,
> perdidimus.   Lucanus[5]

I recieved as yet no answer from Sam. Wharton, nor any satisfactory account from mr. Coffyn of Dunkerque. However, as I understood from former informations of mr. Coffyn, that our goods were disposed of *to a handsome profit*, and as I can not believe that mr. wharton, a Senator of your Congress, a man of great worth and property, could become an infamous Sharper, I doe still expect getting Soon Som returns thro your hands.[6] If they Should arrive, I should like to know your advise, whether I could not employ the money to a good intrest on Some American loans or in purchassing som peace of land in Mary land or near Philadelphia, which could be let out to advantage, on purpose to secure me some things in the new world if Common sense should fly from the old world. I can not believe what newspapers spread through Europe, that the American people

---

5. Marcus Annaeus Lucanus, *Bellum civile*, book 9, lines 1064–8: "Minion, from my sight remove your king's disgusting gift. Your crime deserves worse . . . ; the one reward of civil war—to grant survival to the conquered—we have lost." *Lucan: Civil War*, trans. Susan H. Braund (Oxford and New York, 1991).

6. Ingenhousz had long been waiting for his share; see XXXIX, 89, and the references there.

are unwilling to contribute any thing to support public credit: tho I may very well believe, that your ennemies will not cease artfully fomenting dissensions, distress, and anarchy, to bring you back to your old rulers.

I am very respectfully your most obedient humbl servant and affectionate friend.   J. INGEN HOUSZ

I beg the favour to forward the inclosed by the penny post as soon as possible[7]

To his Excellency Benj. Franklin a Passy

Endorsed: Aug. 15. 83.

From John Jebb[8]

ALS: American Philosophical Society

Sir   15 Aug. 1783

Mr. Baynes[9] the bearer of this Letter has conceived that I am honoured with a share of your confidence & friendship—& has sollicited from me an introduction to you. I am at a distance from him—and if I were to assure him that I had only the pleasure of being twice in company with you when in England, he might imagine that I underrated the nature of my acquaintance in order to avoid performing an act of friendship which his virtuous attachment to the cause of freedom, & long acquaintance with me intitle him to expect. If you will excuse this act of presumption in me, you will receive him as a young man of excellent principles—modest in his deportment—& a sincere admirer of your character & virtues—

I am with great respect your obedt. Servant   JOHN JEBB.

7. The enclosure was addressed to Lebègue de Presle: Ingenhousz to BF, Sept. 1 (below).

8. The English radical and supporter of the American cause: XXXII, 380n; XXXIII, 409–13.

9. Baynes had been one of Jebb's pupils at Cambridge. He delivered this letter on Aug. 27; see Extracts of John Baynes's Journal, Aug. 27–Sept. 15, below.

Addressed: To / His Excellency / Benjamin Franklin / at Paris.
Notation: Jebb Mr. John 15 Août 1783.

From Samuel Potts[1]   ALS: American Philosophical Society

Dr Sir   Paris Aug. 15: 1783
    In consequence of the conversation I had the honour of hav-
ing with your Excellency last Wednesday, I beg leave to submit
my thoughts to your consideration on the arrangements necessary to take place between the Post Offices of England and
America in respect to the mode of establishing a regular correspondence with the two Countries and if they should meet with
your Idea on the subject, it will give me the highest pleasure
to be the means of conveying to England for the information
of His Majestys Postmaster General any regulation which you
may deem essential towards promoting a permanent intercourse
with Great Britain and the United States—in the first place, as
the English Packet Boats are prohibited from carrying of any
sort of merchandize, I presume they will be allowed the same
priviledges in America as they now enjoy under the British
Government. Secondly as I believe its intended an Agent shall
be appointed by the Postmaster General to reside at New York,
the Mail of course on the arrival of the Packet will be carried to
him, he then will deliver it imediately to the proper Officer—
at the Post Office at New York, who will take charge of the
Letters, and he must account with the Agent for the Amount
of the Postage thereof—this Account to be settled at least once
in every three Months and those Letters which have not been

---

1. Potts, controller of the Inland Office of the British Post Office,
is writing here in his official capacity. The purpose of his trip to Paris,
however, was to ask BF whether he could "prevent Mr. Antills Estate in
America from being confiscated" (as he later recalled). He had written to BF
about this matter in May: XXXIX, 580–2; Potts to BF, July 26, 1785 (APS).
BF asked John Jay to intercede on behalf of his old friend, and Jay did so on
Aug. 15 in a letter to Egbert Benson, attorney general of New York, invoking BF's name (Ind. University Library).

delivered either for want of proper direction or that the Parties cannot be found shall be received as Cash in the said Account. Thirdly as the Correspondents in England have an Option of forwarding their letters either with paying the Inland and Packet Postage or not,[2] I am of opinion the same mode should be adopted in America as the fewer restraints there are the more beneficial to commerce, and that the American postage may be accounted for, I propose that the Agent make himself answerable for the Amount and it may be brought forward in discharge of the postage of letters received from England, but there must be the same proviso in regard to the American returned Letters as to those above mentioned sent by the Packets—these are I think the general heads necessary for the arrangement, if you should think proper to establish others I shall be very happy to attend you on the subject.

I have the honour to be with much truth & Respect Your Excellencys Most Faithful and Most Obedt. & Most Hble servt

SAM POTTS

To Vergennes ␣␣␣ ALS: Archives du Ministère des affaires étrangères

Sir, ␣␣␣␣␣␣␣␣␣␣␣␣␣␣␣␣␣␣␣␣␣␣␣␣␣␣␣␣ Passy, Augt. 16. 1783
I have the honour to inform your Excellency, that the English Ministry do not agree to any of the Propositions that have been made either by us, or by their Minister here; and they have sent over a Plan for the definitive Treaty, which consists merely of the Preliminaries formerly signed, with a short Introductory Paragraph, & another at the Conclusion, confirming and establishing the said preliminary Articles.[3] My Colleagues seem

2. As the Post Office did not enjoy a monopoly on the carrying of mail, its services were optional: Kenneth Ellis, *The Post Office in the Eighteenth Century: a Study in Administrative History* (London, New York, and Toronto, 1958), p. 38.

3. Hartley delivered this plan on Aug. 13; see the headnote to Hartley to the American Peace Commissioners, Aug. 12.

enclin'd to sign this with Mr Hartley, and so to finish the Affair. I am, with Respect, Sir, Your Excellency's most obedient & most humble Servant B FRANKLIN

His Excelly. the Count de Vergennes

From Séraphin-Guillaume Hooke, Chevalier de L'Etang[4]

AL: American Philosophical Society

a Paris Ce 17 aoust 1783 rue des Blancsmanteaux au Marais.

Le chier. de hooke Letang Mestre de Camp, attaché au Regiment de Berwick Irlandais Prie son Excellence Monsieur Franklin De Vouloir Bien Lui indiquer l'heure et Le jour ou elle pourroit Lui accorder une audience. Il a deja eu lhonneur De La voir et Desireroit Conferer avec Elle sur Les moyens De former un etablissement soit Dans La Virginie soit Dans La Pensilanie. Il espere que son Excellence Voudra bien L'aider De ses Lumieres et agreer Les asseurances De son respect.[5]

4. Born on Martinique into a branch of the Hooke family that had fled Ireland under Cromwell, Hooke de L'Etang was a colonel in the Berwick regiment in France, a chevalier de Saint-Louis, and from 1773 to 1776 a member of the prestigious Paris lodge *Les Amis Réunis:* Nicolas Viton de Saint-Allais, *Nobiliaire universel de France* . . . (21 vols., Paris, 1872–78), I, 21; Le Bihan, *Francs-maçons parisiens,* under Hooke.

5. Hooke de L'Etang was joined in this project by the chevalier de Saint-Olympe, who had already requested an interview on the same subject. In a note to WTF obviously written on Aug. 16, 1783 (dated "Samedy 16"), Saint-Olympe mentions having seen WTF at Charles's lecture and requests a brief meeting on Wednesday the 20th for "des eclaircissements" on acquisitions in North America that he and Hooke are considering together. He also asks for a minute of BF's time to discuss the project. If the 20th is not convenient, WTF should name another day (APS).

Whether BF discussed the venture with him on Aug. 20 is not known. That day, however, Saint-Olympe thanked BF and WTF for agreeing to sign his wedding contract. The ceremony was to take place early the following morning. See the annotation of the [*c.* Aug. 21] marriage announcement addressed to WTF, below.

Notations: De kooke.— / [*In William Temple Franklin's hand:*]
Appointed him, Thursday next at ½ pst. 10.—[6]

To Samuel Cooper Johonnot

ALS: Yale University Library

My dear young Friend,   Passy, Augt. 19. 1783.
I received your Letter of the 14th. Instant, and am glad to
hear of your safe Arrival at Nantes; it gives me Concern however to learn that you were too late for the Boston Vessel. If you
had gone in the first Diligence after you came here, as I directed
when I sent Lamotte[7] with you to Paris to secure a Place for
you, which you would not suffer him to do, you would have
been at Nantes in time to have gone in that Vessel which sail'd
but two days before you got there for Boston, and might now
have been far on your Voyage, and have sav'd your Father all
the Expence of your waiting for the Philadelphia Ship, and of
the Journey from thence to Boston, which your Wilfulness must
now cost him. You are yet too young to reject safely the Advice
of your Friends. You should continue to comply with it till you
are wiser, which I doubt not you will be in time. In hopes of
which I am still Your affectionate Friend   B FRANKLIN
Mr Cooper Johonnot

Endorsed: Dr Franklin Passy Augt 19th Nantes Aug 26th

---

6. The day of Saint-Olympe's wedding.
7. BF's secretary Jean L'Air de Lamotte.

From Madame ———— Düeil[8]

ALS: American Philosophical Society

Moncegneur   a epernay le 19 aout 1783

Sont escellance cerapelles [se rappellera] sandoutte que le 14
juilliet jeus lhonneur dele voir apasÿ et deluy aufrir duvin de
chanpangne de mont Creux [mon Cru]. Monsieur le Compte de
Mallebois qui citrouva, voulleu bien asurré sont escellance que
je meritté sas [sa] Confiance et vous Mordonnate devous adressé
un pannier de 60 bouttelles jes choisÿ Cellecy que les marchant
devin duroÿ ont tachetté [ont achetées] pour labouche duprince
et jay lhonneur de vous en nadresser un pannier de 62 bouttelles dont 50 de 1775 et 12 de 1778 qui sont ettiquetté vous vous
dret [voudrez] bien choisir Celluy qui vous plerat [plaira] pour
une plus grande Cantitée sis Contre mont atante il ne cetrou-
vet pas avostre gouc [à votre gout] je vous ran veret [renverrai]
dautre bouttelles dessé [d'essai] ayant a Coeur devous bien Cer-
vir demeriteé vostre Confiance inis [ainsi] que celles detous Ce
qui vous interesse aboston je suis en mes mes [à même] devous
livreé tous Ce qui vous Conviendrat pour lamerique est autre
lieux Commes vous latres [l'a très] bien dit Mr le Compte de
Mallebois lafrance ayant fait un tretteé dalliance avec boston je
cerret tres flatté dans [d'en] faire un de Commerce avec vous
Monsieur et demeritté vostre Confiance vous trouveret en moy
la franchize milliterre tenant a cest etta [cet état] de tous Cotteé
Commes vous Ceriez peutetre enbarassé de mefaire par venir
les fons de Ce pannier je chargeret Mr dueil directeur des nouvelles aux [eaux] de passÿ de recevoir lemontans [le montant]
qui me ferat passé.

Je recevré vos hordre [vos ordres] avec lerespect que vous
mave inspiré et je noré rien tans a Coeur que daprandre que ce
vin vous pleze degne [daignez] mefaire lagrasse demes'crire sis

---

8. A wine merchant who, as she says here in phonetically spelled French,
sold BF an order of Champagne wine on July 14 and was now shipping a
pannier of her choicest vintages. She was also hoping to export wine to
America, in consideration of the "tretteé dalliance" that existed between
their two nations. She may have been the wife of Philippe-Henry-Michel
Dueil: Bodinier, *Dictionnaire*, p. 128.

[la grâce de m'écrire si] vous en nette [en êtes] contans et agrez lasurance du profont respect avec lequel jay lhonneur detre Monsieur Vostre tres hunble et tres obeisante servante

DÜEIL

famme delaide major de gravellines
prez antemant aepernay en chanpangne

Le pannier ariverat le 24 aout et part le 20 despernay il est Composé de 62 bouttelles qui a 50 sous laboutteles font 152 lt pour pallettes panier en palliage a clicer [clisser?] part bouttelles 413 sous total 156 lt 13 sous[9]

Notation: Dueil 19 Aout 1783

From Jonathan Williams, Jr.

ALS: American Philosophical Society

Dear & hond Sir.   Nantes Augt. 19. 1783.

The Situation of the american Merchants in France is not the Effect of the ill Conduct of any one but a general Consequence of the Peace, and I believe there is no Exception. Mr Grubb[1] is one of us, and with a full Intention as well as Capacity to pay all, intends to apply for Letters of Surseance to prevent any little Creditor arresting his Property as it may arrive, to the prejudice of the others. In case any Reference should be made to you as to Mr Grubbs Character, I have pleasure in assuring you I think him an honest honourable Man, & I believe his Representations perfectly true.

Mr Harrison[2] who will present you this, has been some time with Mr Grubb with a View to improve himself in Commercial

9. This sum is listed on Finck's account of household expenditures for August; cartage fees came to 9 *l.t.:* Account XXXI (XXXVIII, 3). On the verso of the present letter, WTF figured the cost per bottle, estimating the pannier with delivery charges to be 165 *l.t.*

1. James Grubb, a Nantes merchant whom JW introduced to BF in 1782: XXXVI, 553.

2. Most likely George Harrison of Philadelphia, who came to France in 1781 with enthusiastic recommendations. After several months in Holland,

Knowledge. I reccommend him to you as a very worthy discreet
& Sensible young man.
I am as ever most dutifully & affectionately Yours
JONA WILLIAMS J

His Excellency Dr Franklin.

Notation: Jona. Williams 19 Augt. 1783.

From the Marquis de Condorcet

ALS: American Philosophical Society

Mon cher et illustre Confrere;   Ce 20 Aoust [1783]
L'academie m'a chargé de vous exprimer toute sa reconnaissance pour le beau present que vous lui avez fait.[3] Elle verra avec
plaisir dans sa biblioteque ce premier monument de L'histoire
d'un peuple auquel les sciences auront un jour tant d'obligation,
et cet ouvrage lui rappelera La part distinguée qu'un des membres a eue, à la plus grande revolution politique dont on ait Con-
servé La mémoire, et La seule qui ait eu La conservation des
droits des hommes pour motif, et le bonheur du genre humain
pour objet.
Daignez, agreer, mon cher et illustre confrere L'homage de
mon tendre attachement et de mon respect
LE MIS. DE CONDORCET

M. fauchet ajusteur de La monnoie de Paris[4] a entendu dire, Mon
cher et illustre Confrere, que vous désiriez avoir en Amérique

---

he traveled to Nantes, where in April, 1782, he was welcomed into the American mercantile community: XXXV, 183–4, 417; *Adams Papers*, XII, 400.
    3. Condorcet had waited nearly a month to write this acknowledgment of
Constitutions des treize Etats-Unis de l'Amérique; see Le Roy to BF, July 27.
    4. At this time the French Mint employed 27 *ajusteurs*, who prepared the
blank coins, and 26 *monnayeurs*, who struck them. These positions were
passed down in families, the position of *monnayeur* being reserved for the
eldest son: *Almanach royal* for 1783, pp. 338–9; Fernand Mazerolle, *L'Hôtel
des Monnaies: les bâtiments, le musée, les ateliers* (Paris, 1907), p. 153.
    Turgot had appointed Condorcet *inspecteur général des Monnaies* in 1775,

des ouvriers exercès dans la fabrique des monnoies. Il a plusieurs enfans et désirerait qu'un d'entre eux pût vous Convenir pour cet objet. Permettez-moi de vous le recommander. Si ce bruit est fondé et Que vous désiriez avoir des eclaircissemens sur Le talent et La Conduite des enfans de M. fauchet, Ceux qui sont à la tête de La monnoie de Paris vous en procureraient don je crois que vous auriez Lieu d'être Content. Agréez encore une fois mon cher et illustre Confrere L'homage de mon tendre attachement.

From Caleb Davis[5]   ALS: American Philosophical Society

Sir   Boston August. 20th. 1783
    The Liberty I take in Addressing your Excellencey and incloseing the within to your Care, is in Consequence of Mr. St. Johns request and information that he had obtained your permission for that purpose, and I most Ardently Wish the inclosed May reach him as it Contains information of Much importance for him to Know and Several Letters which have been Wrote him on the Subject have Miscaried—[6]

asking him to establish a unified system of weights and measures. When Necker replaced Turgot as director general of finances, Condorcet resigned his position (though not his official lodgings), but he was reinstated in 1784 under Calonne: Elisabeth Badinter and Robert Badinter, *Condorcet (1743–1794): un intellectuel en politique* (Paris, 1988), pp. 113–16, 143, 184–5.

    5. Davis (1738–1797) was a prominent Boston merchant, shipowner, and member of the legislature: George C. Shattuck, "Caleb Davis and His Funeral Dinner," Mass. Hist. Soc. *Proc.*, LIV (1920–21), 215–18.

    6. In April, 1782, Crèvecœur sent Davis (whom he did not know, but who had been recommended to him) a bill of exchange for 25 guineas, with instructions on cashing it and on giving the sum to a close friend in New York to use for the care of Crèvecœur's two children. The following November, frantic at having heard nothing, Crèvecœur wrote Davis a second time, begging him to make inquiries. See XXXVII, 75; St. John de Crèvecœur to Caleb "Davies," April 7 and Nov. 20, 1782 (Mass. Hist. Soc.).

I have the Honor to be With every Sentiment of Respect your Excellenceys Most obedient and Most Humble Servant—
CALEB DAVIS

His Excelly. Benja. Franklin Esqr.

Addressed: His Excellencey / Benjamin Franklin Esquire / Paris / Pr. Capt Randall / Via London—

Notation: Caleb Davis Augt. 20. 1783.—

From the Vicomte de Rochambeau[7]

AL: American Philosophical Society

le 20 août 1783

Le vcte. de Rochambeau a l'honneur d'Envoyer a Monsieur le Docteur franklin un livre que Monsieur Telles Dacosta a fait sur les bois.[8] Comme il n'a pas l'honneur d'estre connu de Monsieur franklin il a este requis de le lui faire passer.

To Henry Laurens

ALS: New York Public Library; press copy of ALS and copy: Library of Congress

Dear Sir, Passy, Augt. 21. 1783.

I do not doubt but you have written to some one or other of your Colleagues since your Arrival in England; and as we have

---

7. The general's son: XXXIV, 205n.

8. Dominique-Antoine Tellès d'Acosta (b. 1719), *grand maître des eaux et forêts* of Champagne, was the vicomte's uncle. His *Instruction sur les bois de marine et autres* . . . (Paris, 1782), an expanded edition of a work published two years earlier, proposed new forestry practices and management techniques to increase the yield of shipbuilding timber: XXXIV, 233n; Jean-Claude Waquet, *Les Grands Maîtres des eaux et forêts de France de 1689 à la Révolution suivi d'un dictionnaire des grands maîtres* (Geneva and Paris, 1978), pp. 123, 287, 293–8, 408–9, 413. BF's copy is at the Hist. Soc. of Pa.

heard nothing from you, I thought it necessary by a Line to inform you that none of your Letters are come to hand.

After making and sending over many Propositions of ours & of Mr. Hartley's, and long Delays of Answers, it is come finally to this, that the Ministers propose our signing as a Definitive Treaty the Preliminary Articles, with no Alteration or Addition, except a Paragraph of Preamble setting forth that the following Articles had been agreed to, & a concluding Paragraph confirming them. Thus I suppose the Affair will be concluded. Wishing Health & Happiness to you & yours, I am ever, with sincere & great Esteem, Dear Sir, Your most obedt humb Servt.

B. FRANKLIN

Honble. H. Laurens Esqr

Addressed: Honble. Henry Laurens Esqr / at / Bath / Per favour of Mr Hartley

Endorsed: Doctor Franklin. Augt. 21st. 1783. Receivd. 26th. Answd. 27th.

From Jonathan Nesbitt   ALS: American Philosophical Society

Sir,   Paris Augt: 21st: 1783
    I had the honor to furnish your Excellency a small Account, I think it was in the year 1781, of some articles shipped by your orders for Mr. Richd Bache of Philada.—[9] In the Letter which accompany'd the Account I mention'd my intentions of drawing for the amount, which however never was done;— Your Excellency will oblige me greatly by ordering said Account to be look'd for, and if it has been found free of Errors, I beg that you

9. For BF's order and Nesbitt's acknowledgment of it see XXXV, 483, 587–8. The articles were cases of tea shipped on the *Hope* and the *Polly* and probably did not reach their destination: XXXVI, 422; *Pa. Gaz.*, March 20, 1782.

will send me an order on your Banker for the amount.—[1] I mean to depart for L'Orient on Saturday morning, for which place, if you have any orders I shall be happy to execute them.— I have the honor to remain with great Respect—Sir Your most hble Servt: JONATN: NESBITT

Addressed: A Son Excellence / Le Docteur Franklin, Ministre Pleni / potentiaire des Etats Unis de l'Amerique / a son Hotel. / a Passy

Notation: Johath: Nesbitt Paris August 21. 1783

From Félix Vicq d'Azyr

L.S: American Philosophical Society

Monsieur   21 aoust 1783.

La societé Royale de medecine m'a Chargé d'avoir l'honneur de Vous adresser des Billets pour sa séance publique qui aura lieu le 26 de ce mois; elle Vous prie d'en agréer l'hommage et de Vouloir bien en Disposer.

La societé toujours flattée lorsque Vous Voulez bien l'honorer de Votre Présence Vous prie d'assister à Cette séance. J'y Lirai l'Eloge de feu M Pringle Votre illustre ami.[2] Ne sera-ce pas un motif de plus pour que nous aions le bonheur de Vous y posséder.[3]

J'ai L'honneur d'etre avec respect Monsieur, Votre tres humble et très obeissant serviteur   VICQ DAZYR

1. Nesbitt's draft of Sept. 13 for 606 *l.t.* 10 *s.* was paid by BF on Sept. 20: Account XVII (XXVI, 3).

2. See XXXVIII, 291–2. The meeting is described in the *Jour. de Paris* of Aug. 29 and 31, and the eulogy appears among Vicq d'Azyr's "Eloges historiques" in *Œuvres de Vicq-d'Azyr,* ed. Jacques L. Moreau (7 vols., Paris, an XIII–1805), III, 171–216.

3. BF was unable to attend because of a recurrence of the gout and the stone. The society charged Vicq d'Azyr, their perpetual secretary, with sending BF an expression of their concern. He did so on Sept. 8, adding his own personal good wishes: APS.

M franklin.

Notation: Vicq-d'azir 21 Août 1783.

Rose-Aimée Du Buc d'Enneville, the Comtesse de Choiseul-Meuse, and Jean-Baptiste Du Buc[4] to William Temple Franklin

Printed announcement: American Philosophical Society

M   [*c.* August 21, 1783][5]

Madame D'ENNEVILLE, Madame la Comtesse DE CHOISËUL, & M. DU BUC, Intendant Général des Colonies, sont venus pour avoir l'honneur de vous faire part du Mariage de M. DU

---

4. The Du Buc (Dubuc, Dubuq, Dubucq) family was one of the most powerful planter families in Martinique, and Jean-Baptiste Du Buc (b. 1717) was at this time its most prominent member. Known as "le Grand Dubuc" and widely praised for both intellect and character, he had been president of the island's Chamber of Commerce before being sent to Paris as its representative in 1761. Choiseul soon appointed him *premier commis de la Marine.* He was the author of the *exclusif mitigé,* which relaxed the laws prohibiting trade between France's colonies and other nations, and in 1784 and 1785 helped maintain a direct sugar trade with the United States. Mme d'Enneville was his sister-in-law, legally separated since 1754 from his brother Félix-André Du Buc d'Enneville (b. 1726). Their daughter, his niece Marie-Anne, twice widowed, became a countess by virtue of her third marriage in 1769 to the comte de Choiseul-Meuse. Mother and daughter may have met BF in June, 1777: XXIV, 148–9 (where we speculated that the daughter married the vicomte); XXVI, 28. See the *DBF,* under Dubuc (Les); Jean Tarrade, *Le Commerce colonial de la France à la fin de l'Ancien Régime: L'évolution du régime de "l'Exclusif" de 1763 à 1789* (2 vols., Paris, 1972), I, 185, 190–211; Jacques Petitjean Roget, *J'ai assassiné la Sultane Valide* (Sarreguemines, 1990), p. 112.

5. The date of the wedding is established by the bridegroom's Aug. 20 letter thanking BF and WTF for agreeing to sign the marriage contract. As the ceremony was scheduled for 5 A.M. the next morning and he had much to do, he apologized for not bringing the contract in person: Saint-Olympe to WTF, Aug. 20, 1783, APS.

Buc-Saint-Olympe,[6] leur Cousin-Germain, avec Madame DE
Longpré.[7]

Addressed: A Monsieur / Monsieur franklin, Secretaire / de
Légation americaine / a Passy

To Graf von Brühl[8]   ALS: Scottish Record Office

Sir,   Passy, near Paris, Augt. 22. 1783
M. de Kempel, the ingenious Author of the Automaton that
plays Chess, will have the Honour of putting this Line into the
Hands of your Excellency; and I beg leave to recommend him to
your Protection, not merely on Account of that wonderful Machine, but as a Genius capable of being serviceable to Mankind
by more useful Inventions which he has not yet communicated.[9]

---

6. Jean-Baptiste-César (Cézar) Du Buc, chevalier de Saint-Olympe
(1756–1834), was *sénéchal* and lieutenant general of the admiralty of Gre-
nada; in September, 1783, he was appointed *procureur du roi* of the admiralty at Guadeloupe: Tarrade, *Commerce colonial,* I, 222; Elisabeth Escalle
and Mariel Gouyon Guillaume, *Francs-Maçons des loges françaises "aux
Amériques," 1770–1850: Contribution à l'étude de la société créole* . . . (Paris,
1993), p. 425. The chevalier had known WTF since at least the beginning of
the year; on Jan. 14 he wrote to thank WTF for lending him a copy of Paine's
Letter Addressed to the Abbe Raynal . . . (APS). He and his wife remained on
close terms with the Franklins and their circle for the duration of BF's mission.
7. The bride may have been related to the Le Vassor de La Touche
Longpré family, Martinique planters related by marriage to the Du Bucs:
Jacques Petitjean Roget, *Le Gaoulé: la révolte de la Martinique en 1717* (Fort
de France, 1966), pp. 105–6, 529.
8. Hans Moritz Graf von Brühl (1736–1809) served in London as envoy
extraordinary from the elector of Saxony from 1764 to his death. He also
enjoyed an international reputation as a chess player and was a patron of science: *ODNB; Repertorium der diplomatischen Vertreter,* III, 374; R. Marsham-
Townshend, "Count de Bruhl," *Notes and Queries,* 9th ser., XII (1903), 275.
9. For Kempelen's chess-playing "automaton" and his speaking machine
see his letter of May 28. The mechanical chess player created a sensation in
London, as well; see Tom Standage, *The Mechanical Turk: the True Story of
the Chess-Playing Machine That Fooled the World* (London, 2002), pp. 61–2.

With great Respect, I have the honour to be, Sir, Your Excellency's most obedient & most humble Servant   B FRANKLIN

His Excelly. Count Bruhl, Minister of Saxony

To Joseph-Mathias Gérard de Rayneval

LS:[1] Archives du Ministère des affaires étrangères

Dear Sir,   Passy, 22. Augt 1783.
Mr Carnes[2] having informed me that my Application is necessary to his obtaining a Personal Safety or *Sauf Conduite*, in order to afford him the Time necessary to get the Consentment of his distant Creditors, to his obtaining Lettres de Sur-seances for the space of Six Months: I hereby request you would comply with his Request, not doubting but that he is worthy of the Goodness you are pleased to shew him.

I have the honour to be, with great and sincere Esteem Dear Sir, Your most obedient & most humble Sert.   B FRANKLIN

M. De Raynevalle

To Benjamin Vaughan   ALS: Yale University Library

Dear Friend,   Passy, Augt. 22. 1783
This Line will be presented to you by a very ingenious Gentleman, M. Kempel,[3] inventor of the Automaton that plays at Chess. He has other Inventions in Mechanics of a more useful

---

1. In the hand of WTF.
2. Burrill Carnes (b. 1761), a young merchant from Massachusetts, was currently established in Nantes. He would be named American consul in that city in 1790: Carnes to WTF, Aug. 23, 1783 (APS); George H. Lewis, "Edmund Lewis of Lynn and Some of His Descendants," *Hist. Coll. of the Essex Institute*, XLIII (1907), 129; Walter B. Smith II, *America's Diplomats and Consuls of 1766–1865: a Geographic and Biographic Directory* ... (Washington, D.C., 1986), p. 145.
3. See Kempelen to BF, May 28, and BF to Graf von Brühl, Aug. 22.

Nature, which he has Thoughts of communicating in England, if he can meet with Encouragement. I beg leave to recommend him to your Civilities & Counsels, and am ever, with sincere Esteem & Affection, My dear Friend, Yours most truly

B Franklin

Mr. B. Vaughan

To John Whitehurst[4]

ALS: Descendants of the Rawle and Corning Families, Connecticut (2010)

Sir,   Passy Augt. 22. 1783.

The Bearer, Mr Kempel, is the Creator of the Wooden Man who plays so well at Chess; but he is very ingenious in other Matters of more Importance, and has some useful Inventions to communicate to the Publick. I beg leave to recommend him to you Civilities, and to request your Advice to him, as to the Manner of making those Communications so as to produce some Benefit to himself. With great Esteem, I am ever, Dear Sir, Your most obedient & most humble Servant   B Franklin

Mr Whitehurst.

From the Comte de Bruet[5]   AL: American Philosophical Society

a paris le 22 aoust 1783.

M. Le cte de Bruet a reçû avec la plus grande sensibilité lexemplaire[6] que Monsieur franklin a eu lattention et lhonnetteté de luÿ adresser il luÿ en fait mile remerciements et il seroit

---

4. The Derbyshire clockmaker and scientist: XXXIX, 330.

5. Most likely Joseph-Clément-Marie, comte de Bruet, a gentleman in waiting to the comte de Provence: *Dictionnaire de la noblesse; Almanach de Versailles* for 1781, p. 150. This is his only letter to BF, though his wife sent New Year's greetings on Jan. 1, 1784, and eight months later the comte informed WTF of the birth of their son. (Both letters are at the APS.)

6. Probably a copy of *Constitutions des treize Etats-Unis de l'Amérique.*

bien flatté de trouver les occasions de luÿ en marquer toute Sa reconoissance.

Mde de Bruet fait mille et mille Compliments a messieurs franklin et ne pouvent etre plus sensible a leur souvenir

Notation: Le Cte. de Bruet

From César Bucquet[7] L(?): American Philosophical Society

Monsieur,   Paris quai Peltier Ce 22 aoust 1783

Après un travail assidu de plus de trente années Je Suis parvenu a perfectionner la Mouture économique et a la faire Connoitre dans les Provinces ou elle étoit ignorée. Ce fait est Constaté tant par des Procès Verbaux qui ont eu lieu dans Ces Provinces que par le Rapport des administrateurs de l'hopital Général de Paris. Par Mes procèdés Cet hopital épargne annuellement des sommes Considérables. Je Ne Me Suis pas borné, Monsieur, au Seul objet de la Mouture économique, J'ai porté Mes Vuës Sur la Conservation des grains et farines, par des ex-

7. Though the handwriting does not resemble that of his earlier letter and the signature is different, this "Buquet" is without question the César Bucquet to whom BF was introduced in 1777, after Bucquet submitted (through a friend) a memorandum for Congress about the advantages of "la moûture économique." He was elated when BF accepted his invitation for a simple dinner at his home: XXIV, 139–40, 236, 346–7.

Given the formal nature of the present text, it may have been a generic cover letter written by a friend (perhaps Béguillet, his collaborator) to accompany copies of the "Mémoire imprimé" it mentions: César Bucquet, *Traité-pratique de la conservation des grains, des farines, et des étuves domestiques . . . : Avec des notes & observations sur l'agriculture & la boulangerie*, ed. Edme Béguillet (Paris, 1783).

For more on Bucquet, who by this time was bankrupt, and the complicated history of economic milling in the eighteenth century, which pitted Bucquet and Béguillet against Parmentier and Cadet de Vaux in 1782, see Steven L. Kaplan, *Provisioning Paris: Merchants and Millers in the Grain and Flour Trade during the Eighteenth Century* (Ithaca, N.Y., and London, 1984), particularly pp. 72–3, 429–32, 457–65.

périences Reïtérées J'ai enfin Reussi a les préserver de la Cor-
ruption qu'ils Contractent dans les Magasins ou pendant leur
Transport soit par Mer soit par Terre. En Conséquence J'ai
Cru devoir Consigner le Resultat de Mes expériences dans Ce
Mémoire imprimé cy Joint. J'ai l'honneur, Monsieur, de Vous
l'adresser et de vous prier de vouloir bien agréer Mon hommage.

Je suis avec un profond Respect Monsieur Votre très humble
Et très obeïssant serviteur   BUQUET

Notation: Buquet 22. Août 1783.——

From the Marquis de Deux-Ponts[8]

ALS: American Philosophical Society

Sir   Tugny near Reims August the 22d. 1783
I put so much confidence in your Excellencys friendship to
me, that I depend on your forgiveness, for the freedom I take, to
beg of you the conveyance of the inclos'd to Chevr. La Luzerne
which includes some Lines to my american friends. I shall be
very particularly oblig'd to you for it and am with wery respectfull sentiments Your Excellencys Most obedient Servant
                                               DE DEUXPONTS

From Anthony Todd

LS: American Philosophical Society; copy: Royal Mail Archive

Dear Sir,   General Post Office August 22nd 1783
This Morning Mr. Potts delivered to me your kind Letter of
the 17th. Instant.[9] I now inclose according to your desire with-

---

8. The newly married eldest son of the duchesse de Deux-Ponts; see
her letter of May 24 and Kéralio's of Aug. 7. He was named a chevalier de
Saint-Louis on June 13, by which time, it seems, he had already been elevated from a comte to a marquis: Mazas, *Ordre de Saint-Louis*, II, 349–50.

9. See Potts to BF, Aug. 15. BF's letter has not been found.

out loss of Time a Copy of mine to you which you happen to have mislaid of the 25th. of June last, and I should be very much obliged to you for your opinion of the Matters therein as soon as it may be in your power, particularly as the French Packet Boats are to take place between Port Louis and New York in the Course of next Month.

I thank you very much for your valuable and kind offer to assist any Person with your advice whom The Post Master General may send over to Paris with Instructions for settling such Points as respect the American Packet Boats both English and French and the Exchange of Letters conveyed by them.

These and other Negotiations with the Post Office of Paris appear at present very properly to pass through the Hands of Mr. Maddison Secretary of our Embassy at Paris,[1] who with the Approbation of the Secretary of State here, and of our Ambassader at that Court, will be induced to take Charge of them, and being my Nephew also, will engage you from my antient Experience of your Friendship to afford him every consistent Aid in Your Power and if You have an Opportunity to shew him this Letter you will oblige me very much, and I do assure You I remain with true Respect Dear sir Your most obedient and most humble Servant   ANTH TODD Secy

I should imagine Mr. Foxcroft[2] will remain at New York merely as Agent to the Packet Boats.

Dr. Franklin Paris.

1. George Maddison died unexpectedly on Aug. 27. His death was attributed to poisoning, which George III supposed accidental: *Gent. Mag.,* LIII (1783), 805; Manchester to Fox, Aug. 26, 1783, in Lord John Russell, ed., *Memorials and Correspondence of Charles James Fox* (4 vols., London, 1853–57), II, 146; George III to Fox, Sept. 1, 1783 (Fortescue, *Correspondence of George Third,* VI, 439–40).

2. John Foxcroft, the former joint deputy postmaster general of North America (IX, 378n), had been imprisoned as a Loyalist and paroled in New York: Sabine, *Loyalists; Pa. Arch.,* 1st ser., VII (1853), 377.

To Horace-Bénédict de Saussure[3]

ALS: Bibliothèque de Genève

Sir,   Passy, Augt 23. 1783
Reflecting with Pleasure on the agreable and instructive
Conversation you favour'd me with, when I had the Happiness
of seeing you in London,[4] I embrace this Opportunity of recalling myself to your Remembrance, & of requesting your Acceptance of a Copy of the American Constitutions. With great and
sincere Esteem I have the honour to be Sir, Your most obedient
and most humble Servant   B FRANKLIN

M. de Saussure

3. The physicist, geologist, mountaineer, and professor of philosophy
and natural sciences at the Académie de Genève, who discussed atmospheric electricity with BF in London around 1768 and in 1771 introduced
the first lightning rod to Geneva. He and BF exchanged several letters on
scientific matters around that time, but to the best of our knowledge they
had no subsequent communication until the present letter. BF may have
heard news of him from BFB, who attended the Collège in Geneva which
Saussure (as rector from 1774 to 1776) had tried unsuccessfully to reform;
it was that failed attempt that inspired him to found the Société des arts in
1776. Fascinated by the scientific potential of balloons, he went to Lyon in
January, 1784, to witness an experiment by Joseph Montgolfier. Later that
year he wrote a theory of atmospheric electricity as related to earthquakes:
XIX, 324–7; XX, 75–9; Douglas W. Freshfield, *The Life of Horace Benedict
de Saussure* (London, 1920), pp. 75–6, 116–19, 312–21, 352–3; Albert V.
Carozzi, *Horace-Bénédict de Saussure (1740–1799)* (Geneva, 2005), pp. 81,
92–6, 222.

4. Saussure described their time together in a Feb. 6, 1770, letter to
Giambatista Beccaria: "J'ai eu le bonheur de voir souvent à Londres le Célèbre Franklin & même de faire bien des expériences avec lui, nous nous
sommes Souvent entretenus de vous, Monsieur, il m'a paru rempli pour
vous de la plus grande estime. L'Expérience qui a été le germe de vos cu-
rieuses recherches sur le Puits électrique, & à l'occasion de la quelle vous
me faites l'honneur de parler de mes Théses, est bien de son invention, mais
il n'en avoit pas tiré le parti, et ne l'avoit pas poussée aussi loin que vous
l'avès fait." (APS).

From Elias Boudinot   Two ALS:[5] American Philosophical Society

Dear Sir   Princeton August 23d 1783.
Having a Nephew (Mr John M. Pintard)[6] connected with the
House of Mr. John Searle & Co Mercht: in Madeira,[7] who has
earnestly requested an Introduction of this House to your Excellency, I do myself the honor of complying with his desire, as
from my long Knowledge of the Character of Mr. Searle, I am
certain any Services you can with propriety render the Company, will be extremely well placed, and will be conferring an
Obligation on me; as their extreme attention to those American
Prisoners who have been carried into that Island, and their singular attachment to the american Cause, when in the midst of
our Struggles and difficulties,[8] render this Notice of them but a
Payment of Gratitude for their disinterested Services—

5. One of which (doubtless the one Boudinot marked "Duplicate") was
enclosed in John Marsden Pintard's letter of May 16, 1784 (APS).
6. John Marsden Pintard was the son of N.Y. merchant Lewis Pintard,
who imported Madeira wines, and Susanna Stockton Pintard, the sister of
Boudinot's wife, Hannah. The elder Pintard sent his son to Madeira to establish a branch of the business. He was there by at least the fall of 1782,
when Boudinot promised to intercede in getting him appointed consul; on
Boudinot's advice, he had been active in assisting American prisoners put
on shore. In April, 1783, he wrote to John Jay petitioning the American
peace commissioners to appoint him acting consul and mentioning a now-
missing letter he had written to BF (to which he had not received a reply)
about a group of American prisoners: *ANB* and *DAB*, under Lewis Pintard; Morris, *Jay: Peace*, pp. 526–9.
Pintard was elected as American commercial agent in Madeira on Oct.
31, 1783 (*JCC*, XXV, 779–80). He remained there until 1786, then returned
to New York, where he received a new appointment as American consul
in Madeira in June, 1790: W. W. Abbot *et al.*, eds., *The Papers of George
Washington*, Presidential Series (16 vols. to date, Charlottesville and London, 1987–), III, 216–17n.
7. Boudinot and other members of Congress, as well as George Washington, did business with the firm: Smith, *Letters*, XX, 255–6; Fitzpatrick,
Writings of Washington, II, 398–9, 412–13; XXVI, 448, 450–1. John Searle's
younger brother James, who had spent several years with the company, was
the Pa. agent whom BF had met and recommended in 1780: XXXIII, 63, 287,
380, 385, 413. Their mother was a Pintard: *DAB*, under James Searle.
8. The duplicate ALS uses "Distress."

I have the honor to be with every Sentiment of Respect &
Esteem Your Excellency's Most Obedt & very Hble Servt
ELIAS BOUDINOT

His Excellency Dr. Franklin &c

From Gérard de Rayneval: Two Letters

(I) and (II) ALS: American Philosophical Society

I.

A Vsailles le 23. août 1783
J'ai reçu, Monsieur, la lettre que vous mavez fait l'honneur de
mecrire en faveur de Mr. Carnes;[9] je pense que pour procèder
en règle, il conviendroit que vous écrivissiez directement à Mr.
le Cte. de Vergennes; ce ministre m'a parû disposé à accorder les
lettres de Sauf-conduit à votre recommandation. J'ai lhonneur
dêtre avec un sincere attachement Monsieur, votre très-humble
et très-obeissant serviteur   DE RAYNEVAL

Notation: De Rayneval 23 août 1785.—

II.

A Versailles le 23. aout 1783
J'ai l'honneur, Monsieur, de vous renvoyer votre projet de traité
deffinitif: Mr. votre fils vous aura sûrement rendu compte de mes
observations concernant la manière dont l'article de la pêche est
exprimée.
Je joins ici copie de la recette pour la gravelle; je desire qu'elle
vous Soulage; je desirerois bien plus, que vous ne fussiez pas
dans le cas d'en faire usage.[1]

9. Written on Aug. 22. Carnes had carried that letter to Versailles and
brought back the present response, which he left with the porter at the Hôtel
Valentinois. He also left a letter for WTF, asking him to follow up with this
request; he had just received news that required him to return immediately
to Nantes: Carnes to WTF, Aug. 23, 1783 (APS). He was still in Paris a week
later, desperate for news: Carnes to WTF, Aug. 29, 1783 (APS).
1. WTF responded on his grandfather's behalf on Tuesday, Aug. 25, a
day BF would normally have gone to court. BF was grateful for Rayneval's

La demande [*de*] Mr. Williams sera raportée au Conseil des dépêches de Vendredy prochain.[2]

J'ai l'honneur detre avec un sincère attachement Monsieur votre très humble et tres obeissant Serviteur   DE RAYNEVAL

Notation: De Rayneval 23 août 1783—

"kindness and attention." His "gravel" had "now turned into the gout," making travel impossible. BF begged Rayneval to explain to Vergennes the cause of his absence: WTF to Rayneval, Aug. 25, 1783 (AAE; Bigelow, *Works*, X, 154–5).

2. The progress of JW's application, for which see his letters of July 29 and Aug. 9, continued to be complicated. The day Rayneval sent this note, JW learned from WTF that Chaumont himself was opposed. WTF, meanwhile, received from JW his Aug. 19 letter to Vergennes, which WTF forwarded on Aug. 25 with a cover letter stressing how little time remained on the existing *arrêt de surséance*. Vergennes drafted a letter to the Conseil on Aug. 26 requesting an extension of six months instead of the full year JW had sought. Although Rayneval believed that the Conseil would consider the matter at the end of that week (as he writes here and on Aug. 29, below), it did not rule until Saturday, Sept. 6 (the final day of JW's current *arrêt*), granting a new *arrêt* valid for six months. JW had rushed to Paris at the end of August in case his presence was needed, remaining in seclusion with his in-laws at Saint-Germain until he had the *arrêt* in hand. On Sept. 22, before returning to Nantes, he wrote a letter thanking Vergennes: JW to WTF, Aug. 23 and 31, Sept. 1 and 8, 1783 (all at the APS); WTF to Rayneval, Aug. 25, 1783 (cited above); Vergennes to the Conseil, Aug. 26, 1783, draft and fair copy marked "6 7bre 1783 accordé pour Six mois" (AAE); Rayneval to WTF, Aug. 29, 1783 (APS); JW to Vergennes, Sept. 22, 1783 (AAE).

From the Conte di Scarnafiggi[3]

L: American Philosophical Society

Ce 23. Août [1783][4]

L'Ambassadeur de Sardaigne prie Monsieur Franklin de lui faire l'honneur de Venir Diner chez lui Jeudi 28. Août.[5]

R.S.V.P.

Addressed: A Monsieur / Monsieur Franklin / En son hotel

From Jonathan Williams, Jr.

Copy: Yale University Library

D & hond: Sir./.— Nantes 23 Augt: 1783./.— Inclosed is an Acct: of the Expenses of Master Johnnott including his passage to Philadelphia amouting to £752 *l.t.* 2.— for which I have this day drawn a bill on you in favour of Messr:

---

3. This is the first letter in our edition from the Sardinian diplomat who had served in London while BF was there in 1773, and whose connection to BF had hitherto been as an intermediary for correspondence with Beccaria: XX, 355; XXI, 150–1n; XXXIV, 380. Scarnafiggi was accredited at Versailles from 1777 until his death in 1788. In a 1778 report to the king of Sardinia, he related that BF, while negotiating for an alliance with France, had told the ministers that "England was like a duck which had two immense wings, one extending to America and the other to Asia." The Americans had undertaken to break the first wing. If France would break the other, the duck would "tumble into the water with a splash": Antonio Pace, *Benjamin Franklin and Italy* (Philadelphia, 1958), p. 101.

4. The year is certain, as Aug. 28 fell on a Thursday only once during BF's mission.

5. Such an invitation would not have been issued before BF was recognized by the diplomatic corps; see the annotation of Pamphili's letter and note, July 28. On June 21 Scarnafiggi reported to his court that America was negotiating treaties with other countries, and requested instructions on what to do when BF made his first official call as minister of the United States. On July 26 he reported that BF had sent him a copy of *Constitutions des treize États-Unis de l'Amérique*, without a cover letter. Assuming that it was for the king, Scarnafiggi forwarded it along with two unbound copies that he purchased for the minister of foreign affairs: Pace, *Benjamin Franklin and Italy*, p. 115.

Laval & Wilfelsheim.[6] It was not possible to get his passage at a Cheaper Rate, though extravagant & unreasonable all have been obliged to Submit. Another Lad of the Same age of Johnnot has also been made to pay it. I thought best to Send him as there is no prospect of another Opportunity Soon & the Difference would be Soon Swallowed up in daily Expenses./.— I am as ever &c

M Benj franklin

To Samuel Cooper

LS:[7] Reprinted from Earl P. L. Apfelbaum, *Public Auction* (June 3–4, 1976).

⟨Passy, August 24, 1783: Recommends M. Bertaud, a surgeon, to Cooper's⟩ Notice and Civilities, and request you would assist him with your good Counsel & Advice. You will thereby much oblige, Dear Sir, Your most obedient & most humble Servant

B Franklin

To Vergennes: Two Letters

(I) and (II) LS:[8] Archives du Ministère des affaires étrangères

I.

Sir,   Passy, 24. Augt 1783.
Mr: Carnes, an American Merchant settled at Nantes, who has already presented your Excellency with a Petition request-

6. The Parisian banking firm: XXXIX, 300n. BF paid JW's draft on Sept. 5: Account XVII (XXVI, 3). On Sept. 13 he sent a bill drawn on Samuel Cooper to Jonathan Williams, Sr., under cover of a now-missing letter: Jonathan Williams, Sr. to BF, Dec. 20, 1783 (APS).

7. Only the second sheet of this letter was reproduced as an illustration; it is in WTF's hand, with BF supplying the end of the complimentary close. We transcribe that portion below. Our summary of the first sheet is based on the description on p. 5 of the catalog.

8. In WTF's hand.

ing *un Arrêt de Sur-seance*, informs me that it cannot be complied with unless he first obtains the Consentment of a third of his Creditors; that in order to do this, his Presence is necessary at Nantes; but that his Liberty will be in danger if he has not a Personal Security from Government.[9] I therefore take the Liberty of requesting your Excellency to afford him a *Sauf-Conduitte* 'till he can obtain the Consentment of the Majority of his Creditors, to his being favour'd with Lettres de Sur-Seance.

I have the honour to be, with great Respect Sir, Your Excellency's most obedient & most humble Sert.   B FRANKLIN

His Exy. Count de Vergennes

Endorsed: M De R

II.

Sir,   Passy, 24th. Augt 1783.

Mr: Harrison, an American Merchant, who will have the honour of presenting this to your Excellency, is connected in the House of Grubb & Co. at Nantes,—who have sent him to Paris on Business similar to that of Mr. Carnes.[1] He is well recommended to me as a worthy young Man, and I cannot but wish your Excellency to give him a favourable Hearing.

With great Respect I have the honour to be Sir, Your Excellency's most obedt & most humble Sert.   B FRANKLIN

M. le Cte. de Vergennes

Endorsed: M. De R.

From Joseph Banks

ALS: University of Pennsylvania Library

Dear Sir   Soho Square Augst. 25 83

It was with regret & not without sensations of displeasure that I Learnd from Dr. Blagden in Conversation your not having receivd the Volumes of the Philosophical Transactions

9. See BF to Rayneval, Aug. 22, and his answer of Aug. 23.

1. See JW to BF, Aug. 19. Both men were granted safe-conduct passes: Vergennes, Memorandum, Aug. 27, 1783 (AAE).

which as you had not appointed any one to receive them when they were publishd, were applied for in your name some months ago the Counil of the royal Society orderd them with the most perfect unanimity but I am not able to find that any one has since applied to the Clerk for their delivery.

To Obviate all dificulties however I have taken them myself & deliverd them to Mr. Elmsley Bookseller in the Strand who has already dispatchd them for paris & I hope will have an opportunity of delivering them to you about the second or third week in the next month.[2]

For the future sir if you chuse to appoint Any one to receive them as publishd for you they will be deliverd on application I myself will willingly undertake that office if you will tell me by whose means they may be forwarded to you.

We are anzious here to know the event of Mr. Montgolfiers experiment & that of his Competitor Should you be as much inclind to Philosophical Amusements as we wish you to be you may possibly find time to give me a Line concerning them.[3] General Washington has we are told Cincinnatus like returnd to Cultivate his Garden now the emancipated States have no farther occasion for his Sword how much more glorious would it be for you to return to your more interesting more elevated & I will say more usefull pursuit of Philosophy the head of the Philosopher guides the hand of the Farmer to an more abundant Crop than nature & instinct or unguided reason could have producd he leads the sailor to riches & Luxuries which he brings home to his Countrey would I could see you abdicate the Station of Legislator to States whose internal turbulence will not I fear give to the Cool dictates of prudence & experience & return to your Friends here & to those Studies which raisd you formerly to a hight less elevated perhaps but I am sure far more satisfac-

2. Elmsly was on his way to Paris; see his letter of Sept. 12.
3. He did; see BF to Banks, Aug. 30[–Sept. 2]. Banks learned of the goings-on in Paris from Blagden, who on Aug. 23 passed along information he had just received from a French visitor. The entire city was "in an uproar about the flying machines," he reported. Charles's balloon was being made "upon Dr Franklin's plan of silk covered with elastic gum": Neil Chambers, ed., *Scientific Correspondence of Sir Joseph Banks, 1765–1820* (6 vols., London, 2007), II, 124–5.

tory to one who loves peace & good will towards men than the Precipice on which you now stand.

Adieu good Sir be assurd that while Friends of Philosophy exist you will have abundance here Few maybe more warm than Your Faithfull & Obedient   JOS: BANKS

Addressed: Dr. Franklin / &c &c &c. / Passy / near Paris

Endorsed: Sir Joseph Banks Balloons &c

From Charles-Guillaume-Frédéric Dumas

AL (draft): Nationaal Archief

Lahaie 25 Aout 1783

Mr. Adams, après une apparition subite & courte ici, m'ayant déclaré son intention de rompre son ménage ici,[4] & averti de prendre mes mesures pour m'y tirer d'affaire comme je pour-rois avec le peu qui m'est alloué jusqu'ici pour vivre, cet ordre imprévu & la necessité de sauver autant qu'il est possible les ap-parences & garder quelque ombre de [*illegible*] pour le credit des Etats-Unis comme pour le mien & quelques autres embarras, me mettent dans le cas Monsieur de devoir pour cette fois avoir recours à votre &c un mois plutôt que je n'ai coutume pour mon entretien pendant les 6 derniers mois de cette année. Cependant,

4. In February, 1782, at JA's request, Dumas located and negotiated the purchase of a mansion for the American legation, thereafter called the Hô-tel des Etats-Unis. JA (then in Amsterdam) asked Dumas and his family to live there as well, with Mme Dumas serving as household manager. The couple and their daughter moved in when the property was transferred on May 1, 1782, and were joined by JA about two weeks later: *Adams Papers,* XII, 228, 240, 263–4, 272–3, 284, 293; XIII, 1, 21. The Dumas family stayed on after JA went to Paris the following October, and looked after JQA dur-ing the young man's stay there in the spring and summer of 1783: *Adams Papers,* XIV, 287, 438, 465; *Adams Correspondence,* V, 160–1.

JA arrived at The Hague on July 22, 1783, intent on settling financial matters and bringing his son back to Paris, as he did not expect to return to Holland. He and JQA left on Aug. 6; on the morning of Aug. 10 they called on BF and found him breakfasting with John Jay: Butterfield, *John Adams Diary,* III, 141, 142n; *Adams Correspondence,* V, 202; Taylor, *J. Q. Adams Diary,* I, 176–81.

afin que la chose revienne au même, j'ai tiré à deux usances, au lieu d'une, ces £2700 [*l.t.*] à l'ordre de Mrs. Wm. & Jn. Willink, & l'interêt ne peut être un objet quentre ces Messieurs & moi.[5] J'ai reçu successivemt, de Mr. L. R. Morris les Traites suivantes à mon ordre de la part du Departemt. des affaires étrangeres sur Mr. Grand Banq. à Paris, savoir

No. 397. Pre. & 2e. du 11e. Oct. 1782 . . . signée Rob. Morris S.G. of Finance de £.1380 tournois a 30 jours de vue pr. compte des Etats unis

No. 138. 1e. & 2e. du 25 Mars 1783 comme la precedte. de 1380 *l.t.*

No. 229. 1e. du 21e. May . . . comme dessus . . . 517 *l.t.*

Je les aurois toutes jointes ici, si je n'avais réflechi qu'il valoit mieux attendre vos ordres, M, pour savoir si je dois vous les faire tenir telles qu'elles sont, ou si je dois y ajouter mon endossemt. en blanc.

J'ai aussi reçu de Mr. L. R. Morris un compte du montant des remises qui ont été faites à Vre. Exce. pr. moi depuis le 6 Juillet 1782 au 21e. May 1783. Outre que j'y trouve de l'obscurite & une erreur considérable d'addition, il me paroit par son total réel, qui comprend, dit-on, mon salaire du 1er. Janv. 1782 jusqu'au 31e. Mars 1783, il devoit y avoir un deficit de 700 £ & plus. à mon désavantage, pendt. ces 15 mois-là. Si vous desirez, M, copie de ce compte, je vous en enverrai une, qu'une indisposition ne m'a pas laissé la force de faire depuis 3 jours que j'ai reçu ce compte avec des Lettres du Departemt. des mains de Mr. Bingham, qui venant d'Am. [Amérique] ici par Londres, est allé à Amst. [Amsterdam], d'où il repassera sous peu de jours pour se rendre à Paris. Il seroit superflu de m'etendre pour vous faire remarquer M combien le susdit defisient, retranché du peu que je tire jusqu'ici me seroit insupportable, & qu'il me seroit impossible de subsister, si je ne pouvois compter au moins sur les 225 Louis d'or net jusqu'à-ce que le Congrès ait pensé à me faire un sort plus honnête. Une autre chose qui

---

5. On Sept. 1 BF ordered Grand to transfer to the bankers 2,700 *l.t.* on Dumas' behalf; it was paid on Nov. 10. In 1779 BF raised Dumas' salary to 225 *louis d'or* (5,400 *l.t.*) per year which was paid biannually in late April or May and November: XXIX, 101, 257; Account XXVII (XXXII, 4).

m'inquieté, M, c'est votre départ, qu'on m'a fait craindre, pour l'Amérique;[6] & comme M. Adams paroit de même disposé à ne pas revenir ici, je suis en peine de savoir où il faudra m'adresser alors, si c'est à Paris ou à Amsterdam pour continuer de tirer ce petit salaire provisionnel. J'espere, M, que vous voudrez bien me tirer de cet embarras, & conférer là-dessus avec Mr. Adams.

A l'heure où j'écris les Etats d'holl. sont à resoudre leur accession au Traité définitif.[7]

J'ai eu le plaisir d'apprendre de Mr. Ad. le bon état Monsieur de vre. santé. Je prie Dieu de vous la conserver, & suis avec tout l'attachement respecteux que vous connoissez de V.E. &c.

J'ai fait de mon mieux, pour procurer à Mr. Wheelock une petite recolte.[8] Pr. la faire meilleure il auroit dû venir quelque temps après la paix. Il s'estoit trop pressé pour le credit des Etats unis, comme pr. son profit.

Passy à S.E. Mr. Franklin

From Matthias Ogden

ALS: American Philosophical Society

Sir   Paris 25th. August 83

I take the liberty to ask if it will be perfectly agreeable to your Excellency, to present me to the King tomorrow.

The Marquis de la Fayette is at Versailles & will be present at the ceremony.[9] If it should not be the least inconvenient, I

6. This information must have come from JA, who wrote to his wife in July that BF was "determined to go home": *Adams Correspondence*, V, 198, 202.

7. On Aug. 26 the States of Holland and Friesland advised acceptance of the terms offered by Great Britain (which were similar to those imposed on the Netherlands in January): *Gaz. de Leyde*, Aug. 29, sup. The Dutch had tried in vain to obtain the restitution of their Indian post of Negapatam: Andrew Stockley, *Britain and France at the Birth of America: the European Powers and the Peace Negotiations of 1782–1783* (Exeter, 2001), pp. 195–7.

8. BF had recommended John Wheelock to Dumas, who sent 457 f. to Morris on Wheelock's behalf: XXXIX, 176–7, 333; *Morris Papers*, IX, 845.

9. Ogden had brought Lafayette letters from America: XXXIX, 519n; Idzerda, *Lafayette Papers*, V, 140n, 142.

will be much obliged for the honor of a seat in your Excellencys Carriage from Passy.

I have the honor to be with the utmost respect & esteem your Excellencys most obedient humble servant   M. OGDEN

His Excellency Doctor Franklin

Addressed: His Excellency / Doctor Franklin / Passy

Notation: Ogden Paris 25 August 1783

From Pierres

ALS: American Philosophical Society

Monsieur,   Paris 25 aoust 1783.

M. le Duc de la Rochefoucauld m'a fait demander de votre part une Douzaine d'Exemplaires des Constitutions de l'amérique. Comme je pense que c'est votre Intention de les lui donner en papier fin, & que Ceux que j'ai fait tirer par dessus le nombre que j'ai imprimé pour vous sont destinés, Je vous prie de les lui faire passer directement.

J'esperois, monsieur, que vous me feriez l'honneur de me donner votre jour Comme vous me l'aviez promis: sans doute que des raisons importantes vous en ont empêché jusqu'ici,[1] mais je ne perds pas l'esperance, & j'attendrai avec Confiance l'honneur que vous voulez bien me faire.

Je suis avec un profond respect, Monsieur, Votre très humble & très obeissant serviteur   PIERRES

M. franklin

Notation: Pierre 25 Aout 1783

---

1. The postponement may have been due to BF's poor health. He was unable to travel to Versailles on Aug. 25, and had WTF send his apology to Gérard de Rayneval; see the annotation of Rayneval to BF, Aug. 23, letter (II). The following week, after signing the definitive treaty, JA reported to his wife that BF had "fallen down again with the Gout and Gravel. He is better, and has been to Versailles and Paris, but he breaks visibly": *Adams Correspondence,* V, 233–4.

From [Edmund Burke]   ALS (fragment):[2] Library of Congress

Dear Sir,   Beconsfield Augst. 26. 1783.

My friend & Depu[ty? *torn*][3] a few days at Paris, & is extr[*torn*] =ly knowing you whom he has [*torn*] admiration. I approve very mu[*torn*] cannot refuse him the best [*torn*] it. I am not a little anxiou[*torn*] may have had in your regard [*torn*] revive myself in your re[*torn*] by introducing to your acquain[*torn*] worth & abilities. On this occ[*torn*] with some degree of Envy. [*torn*] the highest regard & Esteem Dr. Sr. y[*torn*]

2. Since publishing Burke's letter of August, 1782, which we believed to be his last (XXXVII, 726–7), we identified this fragment in his hand. It is the left side of a single sheet, torn cleanly down the center. The signature is missing.

3. Richard Champion, the former ceramics manufacturer who sent porcelain portraits of BF and Washington to Passy in 1780: XXXIII, 207, 302, 384. In 1782 his longtime friend Edmund Burke appointed him deputy paymaster general of the British army. Champion solicited the post of consul to the United States as soon as the Coalition ministry took office in the spring of 1783, citing his decades as a merchant in the American trade. The Duke of Portland was favorably inclined, and during the summer's negotiations for a commercial agreement, gave him "papers relative to the American trade" and asked for an analysis. Champion's report countered Sheffield's *Observations on the Commerce of the American States*. In early 1784, following the dissolution of the Coalition ministry, he published this report anonymously as *Considerations on the Present Situation of Great Britain and the United States of North America, with a View to Their Future Commercial Connections* . . . (London, 1784). See Hugh Owen, *Two Centuries of Ceramic Art in Bristol* . . . (London, 1873), pp. 155, 259–67; Richard Champion, *Comparative Reflections on the Past and Present Political, Commercial, and Civil State of Great Britain* . . . (London, 1787), pp. 5–8.

Champion had wanted to emigrate to America since at least 1782, but Henry Laurens had been advising him—even as recently as July 5, 1783—to gather as much information as possible before embarking: *Laurens Papers*, XV, 562n; XVI, 226–8. Champion did meet with BF at the end of August and was back in London by Sept. 11: Champion to BF, Sept. 27, 1783 (APS); Thomas W. Copeland *et al.*, eds., *The Correspondence of Edmund Burke* (10 vols., Cambridge and Chicago, 1958–78), V, 113.

To Pamphili: Observations and Note on American Catholics[4]

(I) and (II) Copy:[5] Archives of the Congregatio de Propaganda Fide

[before August 27, 1783][6]

I.

Observations Sur la Notte de M. Le Nonce Apostolique

M. Franklin après avoir lu la notte de M. Le Nonce et y avoir murement réflechi, croit absolument inutile d'envoyer cette notte au Congrés, qui d'après Ses Pouvoirs et Ses constitutions ne peut ni ne doit dans aucun cas Se mêler des Affaires Ecclesiastiques d'aucune Secte ni d'aucune Religion établie en

4. The only known versions of these undated responses to Pamphili's note of July 28 are the copies that Pamphili sent to Cardinal Antonelli on Sept. 1. In his cover letter Pamphili explained that after acknowledging receipt of them, he had communicated their contents to Vergennes and begged him to facilitate the establishment of a college in France that would educate priests destined to serve in America. Vergennes had pledged his assistance and suggested that the nuncio consult the bishop of Autun, who might help establish a college in one of the coastal cities such as Saint-Malo or Nantes. First, however, the church would have to raise the requisite funds and determine how many priests would be needed. Pamphili met with Marbeuf, the bishop of Autun, on Aug. 27. Three days later they met with Vergennes, and all agreed on the importance of the project. Having explained this history, Pamphili asked Antonelli to send whatever information was available on the mission in North America; after receiving his response, the nuncio would ask Vergennes to consult La Luzerne on how many priests were already in America and how many were needed. English translations of the nuncio's Sept. 1 letter and BF's memoranda are in Jules A. Baisnée, *France and the Establishment of the American Catholic Hierarchy: the Myth of French Interference (1783–1784)* (Baltimore, 1934), pp. 50–4; see also pp. 27–31. For the letter in its original Italian see Carl R. Fish, ed., "Documents relative to the Adjustment of the Roman Catholic Organization in the United States to the Conditions of National Independence, 1783–1789," *American Hist. Rev.*, XV (1909–10), 805–8.

5. Enclosed in Pamphili's Sept. 1 letter to Antonelli; see the annotation above. The nuncio prefaced them with a copy of his own July 28 note, marked "A". BF's responses were marked "B" and "C".

6. The day Pamphili met with the bishop of Autun, after having discussed BF's responses with Vergennes; see the annotation above. The date of his initial meeting with Vergennes is not known.

Amèrique. Chaque Etat particulier S'est reservé par Ses propres constitutions le droit de protèger Ses membres, de tolérer leurs opinions Religieuses, et de ne S'en mêler en aucune façon tant qu'Elles ne troubleroient point l'ordre civil.

M. Franklin pense donc que la Cour de Rome peut prendre d'elle même toutes les mèsures utiles aux Catholiques d'Amèrique, Sans blesser les Constitutions, et que le Congrés ne manquera pas d'approuver tacitement le choix qu'Elle voudra faire de concert avec le Ministre des Etats unis, d'un Ecclesiastique françois toujours residant en france, qui conduira par l'entremise d'un Suffragant residant en Amèrique toutes les affaires Spirituelles des Catholiques qui vivent ou qui voudront S'établir dans ces Etats.

Outre beaucoup de raisons politiques qui peuvent faire dèsirer cet arrangement M. Le Nonce Apostolique doit y en voir beaucoup d'autres qui peuvent être favorables aux intentions de la Cour de Rome./.

II.

Notte Sur les Catholiques Américains.

La Revolution d'Amèrique Sèparant les interêts des Colonies de ceux de la Métropole, change ainsi les rapports qui lioient les Catholiques Amèricains avec ceux qui vivent Sous la domination Angloise. L'unité du gouvernement actuel Semble mème èxiger qu'on tende a diminuer et affoiblir ces Liaisons en ôtant toute influence au Ministère Britannique Sur les Sujets des Etats unis.

Il n'existe dans la plupart des Colonies aucune fondation, aucun revenu fixe pour l'entretien d'un Clergé de quelque Religion que ce Soit, la Lègislation envisageant cet objet Sous le point de vüe d'une liberté plus gènérale, n'a point voulu faire une Surcharge publique d'une imposition qui pourroit n'être que volontaire et particuliere.

Il n'existe point non plus de Collége ni d'ètablissement public pour l'instruction nècessaire à un Ecclèsiastique Catholique, voila deux points ègalement essentiels à considerer.

Il existe en France 4. Etablissemens de moines Anglois dont le revenu total peut se monter à 50. ou 60 mille livres. Ces Moines

Sont en petit nombre. La disette de Sujets rend ceux qui restent au moins inutiles.

Il Seroit possible que le Roi de France pour complaire à la Cour de Rome et resserrer les liens d'amitié avec les Etats unis permit que ces ètablissemens Servissent à former, instruire et faire Subsister en partie les Ecclesiastiques qui Seroient employés en Amérique.[7]

Il conviendroit pour mieux remplir l'objet qu'un des Evêques nommè par le Saint Siége fut un Sujet du Roi residant en france, toujours à portée d'agir de concert avec le Nonce de sa Sainteté, et le Ministre Amèricain, et de prendre avec eux les moyens de former les Ecclesiastiques agrèables au Congrés et utiles aux Catholiques Amèricains./.

John Adams to Franklin and John Jay

ALS: Columbia University Library; copy: Massachusetts Historical Society

Gentlemen   Paris August 27. 1783

As I am informed that next Wednesday[8] is appointed for the Signature of the definitive Treaties of Peace, I Suppose it will be thought proper to think of Some Conveyance of the Ratification of the Provisional Treaty, and of the Original of our definitive Treaty as Soon as it Shall be Signed to Congress. By what Vessell it will be proper to Send it, deserves to be considered as soon as possible, as it is of Importance to the Publick that the News of it, Should reach Philadelphia, without Loss of Time.

I presume too, it will be thought proper to send The Treaties and Dispatches which may accompany them by Some carefull Hand, and the Choice will fall naturally among the younger Gentlemen who have been imployed abroad in the service of

---

7. Pamphili warned against this suggestion in his cover letter to Antonelli. The cardinal's reaction was unequivocal: "The proposition of Mr. Franklin, to suppress the four monasteries of English Benedictines that exist in France, should be rejected, without further discussion." Baisnée, *France and the Establishment of the American Catholic Hierarchy*, pp. 52, 54.

8. Sept. 3.

the Publick, in the Way of Negotiation. On this Supposition I beg Leave to propose to your Consideration, Mr John Thaxter, who had been for Some time in the service of Congress at Philadelphia, before he came to Europe, who embarked with me at Boston about four Years ago, and has accompanied me constantly from that Time to this in a dangerous Voyage and many fatiguing Journeys, and has ever been in the highest degree industrious and faithfull in the Publick service.[9]

With the greatest Respect, I have the Honour to be, Gentlemen, your most obedient and most humble servant

JOHN ADAMS.

Their Excellencies Benjamin Franklin and John Jay Esquires, Ministers Plenipotentiary from the United States of America, for making Peace with Great Britain

Endorsed by John Jay: Mr. Adams to Messr. Franklin & Jay 27 Aug. 1783

From Samuel Cooper Johonnot

ALS: American Philosophical Society

Respected Sir   Nantes 27 Aug 1783. 5 o Cl. A. M.

I now acknowledge my Fault with Sorrow. However 'twill be a Lesson for Me & I have already profited of it.— I am going this Minute in a Barge to Paimbœuf thence to St Nazair, where the Vessel lies. We are now retarded by contrary Wind. The first fair Wind We weigh.[1] Forgive the Shortness of my Letter as Time hinders Me from lengthening it. Be persuaded, Worthy Sir, that I am, with the highest Sense of Gratitude & Esteem Your repenting obliged humble Servant.

SAM'L COOPER JOHONNOT

9. JA had thought Thaxter deserving of the position of secretary to the peace commission: XXXVIII, 165n.

1. In fact, the ship's destination was changed to Baltimore, occasioning additional expense to BF. It did not sail until Sept. 16: Gouhard to WTF, Sept. 2, 1783; Johonnot to BF, April 21, 1784 (both at the APS).

P.S. Your kind Favour of 19 Inst. came to hand. My Compliments if You please to your Grandsons

Addressed: A Son Excellence / Benjamin Franklin Esqr. D.D. / Ministre Plenipotentiare des Etats unis / de L'Amerique prés Sa Majesté trés chre / tienne. / à Passy / près Paris.

From the Duc de La Rochefoucauld

L: American Philosophical Society

ce 27. Aoust. 1783.

Le Duc de la Rochefoucauld reçoit en partant pour sa Campagne les Exemplaires des Constitutions americaines que Monsieur franklin à la bonté de lui envoyer[2] et qui sont en nombre bien suffisant.

Il a appris avec chagrin son incommodité et il sera tres Empressé daller sçavoir lui même de ses nouvelles dans son prémier Sejour à Paris.

Addressed: A Monsieur / Monsieur franklin, / Ministre Plénipotentiaire / des Etats unis d'amerique / a Passy.

Notation: La Rochefoucauld

From Henry Laurens

ALS: Library of Congress; copy: University of South Carolina Library

Dear Sir.   Bath 27th August 1783.

My thanks are due for the justice you did me, in beleiving I had written to some one or other of my Colleagus since my last return to London, altho' it appears by the Letter you have honored me with under the 21st Inst. mine of the 9th. addressed to the whole had not reached them, an unlucky circumstance which gives me much concern. I say I wrot to the American

2. See Pierres to BF, Aug. 25.

Ministers on the 9th. made up my Letter with a News Paper or two into a small Packet which I delivered on Sunday Morning the 10th. to Mr. Barclay who assured me he would leave London on Tuesday the 12th. at latest— You say nothing & I have not heard any thing of his arrival at Paris[3] wherefore I now transmit a Copy of my said Letter, tho' with a slender prospect of its being serviceable since 'tis probable, that before this can arrive, your Phœnix Treaty will be finished.

I was actually in Treaty for the Cabin of a Ship intending to have embarked very early in October for Philadelphia or New York, but three days ago I received a Letter from my Sister in Law in the south of France intimating that my Brother had desired her to inform me he was growing weaker & weaker every day & found himself near his End & therefore earnestly wished to see me before I left Europe.[4] I cannot refuse to gratify the wish of a dying freind. I dare not turn my back upon a Widowed Sister, a most valuable worthy Woman—so long a journey will be rather too heavy for me, but I must encounter it, therefore I shall once more have the honor of paying my Respects at Passy, perhaps about the 10th. September.

You may possibly have seen before this time a little Printed Paper, which the Mr. Jenings has been privately circulating under the Title—The Candor of Henry Laurens Esqr—poor Devil he is as weak as wicked, he has now compeled me to display his wickedness in a more public manner than ever I had intended—the most painful part to me is his involving a third person the friend he pretended to be so much attached to on your side.[5]

3. Barclay arrived on Aug. 22 and that same day delivered a personal letter to Jay, which the latter endorsed with the date he received it: Morris, *Jay: Peace*, p. 577. Since Jay also endorsed the Aug. 9 letter from Laurens (above), it is reasonable to suppose that Barclay delivered it at the same time.

4. Laurens here quotes from Mary Laurens' letter. James Laurens, Jr. (XXVII, 468n), died on Jan. 25, 1784: *Laurens Papers*, XVI, 269–70n, 373n.

5. This dispute was of long standing. Laurens had accused Jenings of writing two anonymous letters: XXXVI, 499. Jenings retaliated in a pamphlet published in July, entitled *The Candor of Henry Laurens, Esq. . . .* Laurens' rejoinder, dated Sept. 3, was published as *Mr. Laurens's True State*

My Son & Daughter unite with me in the most Respectful Cordial Salutes to yourself & Mr. Franklin & I have the honor to be with sincere Esteem & affection Dear sir Your obedient humble servt.   HENRY LAURENS.

His Excellency Benjamin Franklin Esquire Passy.

Addressed: His Excellency / Benjamin Franklin. Esqr: / Minister Plenepotentiary from / the United States of America at / the Court of France. / Paris.

Endorsed: H. Laurens Esqr to B.F.— Aug. 27. 83

From [John Mehegan][6]   L: American Philosophical Society

Brest August the 27th 1783—

A Monsieur Franklin Ministre
plénipotentiare des treize états unis de l'Amerique.

Comme vous êtes dans ce pais ci le représantant des Americains vos compatriotes, ils ne peuvent pas faire mieux que de s'addresser à vous, lorsqu'ils ont besoin de protection. C'est d'apres celà, Monsieur que je vais prendre la liberté de mettre

---

of the Case . . . . In the opening paragraph he explained that as soon as he arrived in London, he received from Edward Bridgen one of Jenings' pamphlets, which Bridgen had been instructed by Jenings to deliver. For Laurens' pamphlet see *Laurens Papers*, XVI, 277–333; see also James H. Hutson, ed., *Letters from a Distinguished American: Twelve Essays by John Adams on American Foreign Policy, 1780* (Washington, D.C., 1978), pp. 61–2.

6. A Carmelite from Brest who had served as chaplain to the comte d'Orvilliers: [Frederick] Gouhard to WTF, Sept. 2, 1783 (APS); Morison, *Jones*, p. 183. This plea on behalf of American sailor Richmond Springer came through a circuitous route. Father Mehegan sent it to JW in Nantes for forwarding; JW's clerk forwarded it to WTF on Sept. 2 (the letter cited above) because JW was in Paris. JW had interested himself in Springer's case since mid-1782, when a prize taken by the sailor and his companions was confiscated. JW wrote twice to BF on Springer's behalf: XXXVII, 555–6, 603–4. He followed those letters with two to WTF (Aug. 31 and Sept. 16, 1782, APS).

sous vos yeux l'affaire d'un Americain, dont la situation meritera peut-ètre votre attention. Voici le fait.

Au mois de May 1782 il arriva ici un sloop monté par sept Americains dont un étoit Mousse; ces hommes échappés de prisons de Kinsale etoient venus au Cove de Cork, s'etoient emparé de ce sloop, et avoient fait route pour les côtes de France.[7] Arrivés ici àprés avoir essuyé bien de difficultés, leur petit batiment fut enfin déclaré *bonne prise* par l'amirauté.

Ces Americains trouvant une occasion de renvoyer dans sa patrie ce Mousse qu'ils avoient sauvé avec eux par charité, ils en profiterent et le firent partir en lui fournissant ce qui lui etoit nécessaire.

Deux des six restant remirent leurs interêts entre les mains du sieur Riou qui est ici interprète anglois;[8] les quatre autres s'adresserent à un procureur de cette ville nommé Lelay et lui donnerent leur procuration. Comme il se passa bien du tems avant que les droits de l'amirauté fussent reglés à l'égard de la prise en question, et avant que la vente en fût faite, et que la quotité des pars fut réglée; trois de ces Americains àprés avoir touché quelques avances, prirent le parti de s'embarquer sur des batiments françois. Les autres resterent ici, toucherent leurs parts et partirent.

Les parts à raison de six se trouverent être de 2900 *l.t.* Le sieur Springer pour lequel j'ai honneur de vous écrire étoit parti des premiers, et n'avoit touché qu'un accompte sur sa part, après avoir ètè fait de nouveau prisonnier et detenu en Angleterre pendant deux mois, il vient d'arriver ici pour réclamer le reste de ce qu'il lui révenoit. Mais il rencontre maintenant des difficultés aux quelles il ne devoit pas s'attendre.

Le sieur Springer est un de quatre qui avoient mis leurs interêts entre les mains du Sr. Lelay procureur. Celui-ci àprés avoir remis aux trois autres les 2900 *l.t.* qui révenoient à chacun d'eux, fait maintenant difficulté pour se dessaisir de la part de celui-ci, sous pretexte que le Mousse, dont il a été question

7. Springer and his companions stole the cutter *Bourke:* XXXVII, 555–6n.

8. Pierre Rïou: XXXVII, 556n.

cy dessus ne vienne un jour à demander sa part de la prise. Le sieur Riou qui n'a pas encore reglé ses comptes avec les deux Americains, qui lui avoient remis leurs interêts s'accorde en cela avec le sieur Lelay, et pretend qu'ils ne doivent rien determiner definitivement dans la crainte que ce mousse ne vienne un jour à leur demander sa part.

Mais qui ne voit pas que ce n'est qu'un subterfuge de la part de ces-Messieurs. 1°. pourquoi N'ont ils pas fait cette difficulté dans le tems qu'ils auroient dû la faire? 2°. ils n'ont traité qu'avec les six Americains en question du fond desquels ils ont eté les dépositaires, ainsi quand même ce mousse auroit droit de revendiquer un part de la prise, il ne pourroit pas l'exiger des Srs. Riou et Lelay et n'auroit son récours que sur les six autres. 3° en supposant donc qu'il ait droit á cette prise, pourquoi faut-il, que le sieur Springer en soit le seul responsable? Mais ni le Sr: Lelay ni le sr. Riou n'ont point entendu parler du mousse qui probablement s'est trouvé fort heureux que des hommes forts et hardis l'aient sauvé avec eux, en s'exposant aux dangers qu'ils ont couru. Ainsi ce nouvel incident de leur part n'est qu'un pretexte supposé.

Le sieur Lelay à d'ailleurs fait offre àu sr. Springer de lui remettre 1250 *l.t.* à condition, que celui-ci se desistera de toute autre pretention. Pourquoi une telle proposition? Ou le sieur Lelay a droit de garder pour sa guarantie la part du sieur Springer, ou il ne l'a pas? S'il l'a, il ne se dessaisiroit pas d'une portion aussi considerable? S'il ne l'a pas, pourquoi ne pas remettre au sr. Springer tout ce qui lui révient?

Le sr. Lelay allegue en outre qu'il ne veut rien terminer definitivement avant que le sieur Riou n'ait rendu ses comptes: Mais le sr. Riou n'a de comptes à rendre qu'aux deux Americains qui lui ont laissé leur procuration, et ces comptes ne regardent en aucune maniere le sr. Lelay. Les comptes de la vente du batiment ont été reglés, et les parts en ont èté determinés, que faut-il de plus?

Le sieur springer implore votre sécours et votre protection. Il est ici sans la moindre résource, et presque sans espérance, quoi de plus à plaindre que sa position? Dans un païs ètranger dont il ignore la langue et les rubriques de la chicane, que voulez vous qu'il fasse si vous ne lui pretez une main Sécourable? Il espere, Monsieur, que vous voudriez bien faire employer l'autorité nécessaire pour que le sr. Lelay lui remette le restant de sa part qui se monte à 2246 *l.t.* Ce sera un service dont il vous aura une éternelle reconnoissance.[9]

To his Excellency Doctor Franklin

Extracts of John Baynes's Journal[1]

Reprinted from *The Life of Sir Samuel Romilly, Written by Himself. With a Selection from His Correspondence. Edited by His Sons.* (3rd ed., 2 vols., London, 1842), I, 447–58.

[August 27–September 15, 1783]

Wednesday, August 27. Hired a coach for the day, and went to visit the ambassador (the Duke of Manchester), who received me very politely; asked me to dine on Friday. From thence I went to Passy (a pleasant town, two miles from Paris, and on the Seine)

9. Springer sailed back to America in November without having received payment in full: JW to Betsy Rhoades, Jan. 3, 1784 (Yale University Library).

1. The political reformer John Baynes (1758–1787) formed a close friendship with fellow student Samuel Romilly when they were both reading law at Gray's Inn. In August, 1783, when Romilly set off for Lausanne on family business, Baynes accompanied him as far as Paris, carrying a letter of introduction to BF (mentioned below). Baynes remained in Paris for two months, visiting BF several times and keeping a detailed journal of their conversations. Romilly was with him for the introductory visit and recorded his own impressions (quoted in annotation below). When Baynes died of a fever four years later, in the bloom of a promising legal and literary career, his friend considered it a great loss to the public: *DNB* and *ODNB* for both men; *The Life of Sir Samuel Romilly, Written by Himself*... (3rd ed., 2 vols., London, 1842), I, 48–50.

Baynes never married, and the disposition of his Paris journal is not known. Romilly's sons had access to it from "its present possessor" when, decades after their father's death in 1818, they were preparing the third edition of their father's memoirs. Believing Baynes's entries to be of general interest, they added an appendix containing selections from the journal "which refer principally to conversations with Benjamin Franklin": *Life of Sir Samuel Romilly*, I, 447. Principally but not entirely. In reprinting these selections,

to present Dr. Jebb's letter to Dr. Franklin.[2] Mr. Romilly went with me, having inquired most particularly into the propriety of his going, and finding that there would be nothing improper.[3] His house is delightfully situated, and seems very spacious; and he seemed to have a great number of domestics. We sent up the letter, and were then shown up into his bedchamber, where he sat in his nightgown, his feet wrapped up in flannels and resting on a pillow, he having for three or four days been much afflicted with the gout and the gravel. He first inquired particularly after Dr. Jebb, which led us to the subject of parliamentary reformation. I mentioned that Dr. Jebb was for having every man vote: he said he thought Dr. Jebb was right, as the all of one man was as dear to him as the all of another. Afterwards, however, he seemed to qualify this by expressing his approbation of the American system, which excludes minors, servants, and others, who are liable to undue influence. He said that he much doubted whether a parliamentary reform at present would have the desired effect; that we had been much too tender in our economical reform,—that offices ought never to be accompanied with

---

we omit several paragraphs that do not relate to BF, indicating those omissions with ellipses. The rows of asterisks, on the other hand, are original to the published text and signal the editorial decisions of 1842. The journal continues through Oct. 17; the latter portion will be published in vol. 41.

2. Of Aug. 15, above.

3. Romilly described the visit thus: "Dr. Franklin was indulgent enough to converse a good deal with us, whom he observed to be young men very desirous of improving by his conversation. Of all the celebrated persons whom, in my life, I have chanced to see, Dr. Franklin, both from his appearance and his conversation, seemed to me the most remarkable. His venerable patriarchal appearance, the simplicity of his manner and language, and the novelty of his observations, at least the novelty of them at that time to me, impressed me with an opinion of him as of one of the most extraordinary men that ever existed. The American Constitutions were then very recently published. I remember his reading us some passages out of them, and expressing some surprise that the French government had permitted the publication of them in France. They certainly produced a very great sensation at Paris, the effects of which were probably felt many years afterwards." *Life of Sir Samuel Romilly*, I, 50.

such salaries as will make them the objects of desire. In support of this he read the 36th article of the Pennsylvania Constitution (a most wise and salutary rule).[4] He mentioned the absurd manner in which the *Courrier de l'Europe* had spoken of General Washington's resignation and retirement, as if it were a dissolution of the original compact:[5] he said that the General was an officer appointed by the state, and no integral part of the constitution, and that his retirement could affect the state no more than a constable, or other executive officer, going out of office. I observed how some of our papers had affected to depreciate his motives in retiring,[6] and added that I should always suppose a man to act from good motives till I saw cause to think otherwise. "Yes," said he, "so would every honest man;" and then he took an opportunity of reprobating the maxim that all men were

4. "As every Freeman, to preserve his Independence, (if without a sufficient estate) ought to have some profession, calling, trade or farm, whereby he may honestly subsist, there can be no necessity for, nor use in establishing offices of profit, the usual effects of which are dependence and servility, unbecoming Freemen, in the possessors and expectants; faction, contention, corruption and disorder among the people. But if any man is called into public service, to the prejudice of his private affairs, he has a right to a reasonable compensation: And whenever an office, through increase of fees, or otherwise becomes so profitable as to occasion many to apply for it, the profits ought to be lessened by the legislature." *The Constitution of the Common-wealth of Pennsylvania* ... (Philadelphia, 1776), p. 27.

5. The Aug. 15 issue of the *Courier de l'Europe* printed a translation of Washington's June 18 circular letter to the state governors announcing his resignation (which had been widely reprinted in the British press the previous week). It also reported on the general belief that the United States was now without a legitimate government, and raised the question of whether any definitive peace treaty could be signed: *Courier de l'Europe*, XIV (1783), 106–9, 111–12. For Washington's circular letter see the annotation of Boudinot to the Commissioners, July 15.

6. Some newspapers went so far as to suggest that Washington's retirement was "fictitious," and that like Julius Caesar, Richard III, and Oliver Cromwell, he was plotting to become absolute ruler by popular acclaim. That accusation appeared in identical language in at least two English-language newspapers on Aug. 19: the *Public Advertiser* and *Public Ledger*. The *Courier de l'Europe* printed a translation of the latter, explaining that it was the most concise rendition of what all the papers were saying: *Courier de l'Europe*, XIV (1783), 116.

equally corrupt. "And yet," said Mr. Romilly, "that was the fa-vourite maxim of Lord North's Administration." Dr. Franklin observed that such men might hold such opinions with some de-gree of reason, judging from themselves and the persons they knew: "A man," added he, "who has seen nothing but hospitals, must naturally have a poor opinion of the health of mankind."

Mr. Romilly asked as to the slave-trade in America, whether it was likely to be abolished?[7] He answered that in several states it now did not exist; that in Pennsylvania effective measures were taken for suppressing it;[8] and that, if it had not been for the Board of Trade, he believed that it would have been abolished everywhere.[9] To that board he attributed all our misfortunes, the old members corrupting the young ones.

He seemed equally liberal in religious and in political opin-ions. The excellence of the constitution of Massachusetts in point of religious liberty being mentioned, he observed that they had always shown themselves equally so; that the land was originally granted out to them subject to the payment of a small sum for the support of a presbyterian minister; that, many years ago, on the application of persons of other religions, they agreed that the sum actually paid by any congregation should

7. Romilly was an ardent abolitionist. He had translated Condorcet's *Réflexions sur l'esclavage des negres. Par M. Schwartz*... (Neufchâtel, 1781), which he acquired on a previous trip to Lausanne, but was unable to find a publisher: *Life of Sir Samuel Romilly*, I, 51n.

8. On March 1, 1780, Pennsylvania passed "An Act for the Gradual Abolition of Slavery," which banned the importation of slaves and pro-vided for gradual emancipation of newborn slave children, who remained indentured to their former owners for 28 years: Gary B. Nash and Jean R. Soderlund, *Freedom by Degrees: Emancipation in Pennsylvania and Its After-math* (New York and Oxford, 1991), pp. 105, 110–11, 137–8.

9. In the years before the Revolution, American colonists, including BF, came to believe that the British government had coerced them into main-taining slavery and the slave trade against American efforts to limit or abolish both. (BF had made this argument in his 1770 "Conversation on Slavery": XVII, 38–40.) In fact, the Board of Trade and the Privy Coun-cil had vetoed only some, but not all, duties on imported slaves that the colonies had levied to raise revenue and slave prices or to better control the slave population: James A. Rawley, *The Transatlantic Slave Trade: a History* (New York and London, 1981), pp. 316–18.

go to its own minister, whatever was his persuasion.[1] This was certainly a great act of liberality, because they were not bound to do it in point even of justice, the annual payment being in fact the price or rent of the land. He mentioned his having had a conversation with Lord Bristol (the Bishop of Derry) on a similar subject; that the Bishop said he had long had in hand a work for the purpose of freeing Roman Catholics from their present state, and giving them a similar indulgence.[2] "And pray, my Lord, while your hand is in, do extend your plan to dissenters, who are clearly within all the reasons of the rule." His Lordship was astonished—no—he saw some distinction or other, which he could not easily explain. In fact, the revenue of his Lordship would have suffered considerable diminution by suffering dissenters to pay their tithes to their own pastors. He reprobated the statute of Henry VI. for limiting votes to forty-shilling freeholders, and observed that the very next statute in the book was an act full of oppression upon poor artificers.[3]

He conversed with greater freedom and openness than I had any right to expect, which I impute partly to Dr. Jebb's friendly letter, partly to his own disposition. I never enjoyed so much pleasure in my life as in the present conversation with this great and good character. He looked very well, notwithstanding his illness; and, as usual, wore his spectacles, which made him very like a small print I have seen of him in England.[4] He desired us on tak-

1. In 1727 the Mass. legislature allowed Anglicans to use the mandatory tax levied on behalf of the Congregational Church for their own ministers. A year later, the legislature exempted Baptists and Quakers from the tax: John D. Cushing, "Notes on Disestablishment in Massachusetts, 1780–1833," *W&MQ*, 3rd ser., XXVI (1969), 169–72. However, the 1780 constitution put an end to these exemptions, as BF explained to Baynes on Sept. 15.

2. The only subjects who were excluded from the liberty of conscience granted by the Mass. charter were Roman Catholics: Cushing, "Notes on Disestablishment in Massachusetts, 1780–1833," p. 171.

3. BF attacked these statutes in his marginalia in Allan Ramsey's pamphlet, *Thoughts on the Origin and Nature of Government . . .* ; see XVI, 312–13.

4. The 1777 "fur hat" engraving by Augustin de Saint-Aubin, the frontispiece of vol. 24, inspired many copies: XXIV, xxx; Sellers, *Franklin in Portraiture*, pp. 109–10, 227–30.

ing leave to come and visit him again, which we resolved to do....

*****

Monday, September 15. Called on Lieutenant Hernon, and walked with him as far as the *Barrière de la Conférence*, on the way to Passy. He left me there, and I proceeded to Dr. Franklin's house. On entering, a confounded Swiss servant told me to go up stairs and I should meet with domestics. I went up, but not a domestic was there; I returned and told him there was nobody. He then walked up with me, and pointing to the room before me told me I might enter and I should find his master alone. I desired him to announce me. "Oh! Monsieur, ce n'est pas nécessaire; entrez, entrez;" on which I proceeded, and, rapping at the door, I perceived that I had disturbed the old man from a sleep he had been taking on a sofa. My confusion was inexpressible. However, he soon relieved me from it, saying that he had risen early that morning, and that the heat of the weather had made a little rest not unacceptable; and desiring me to sit down. He inquired if I had heard from Dr. Jebb. I then showed him an excellent letter which I had just received from him, containing some noble sentiments on the American war, with which he seemed much pleased. The letter contained some sentiments on the American religious constitution, particularly noticing the liberality of that of Massachusetts Bay. Dr. Franklin observed that, notwithstanding its excellence, he thought there was one fault in it: that when the government of that colony had, thirty or forty years ago, upon the application of the dissenters, permitted them to apply their portion of the sum raised for religious purposes to the use of their own minister (as he had mentioned in his former conversation), the Quakers likewise applied for a total exemption from this burden upon this ground, that they did, one among another, *gratis*, the same duties as the other sects paid a duty for performing. "The government," said he, "considered their case and exempted them from the burden, the person claiming an exemption being obliged to produce a certificate from the meeting that he was really *bonâ fide* one of that persuasion. The *present* constitution of Massachusetts Bay does not appear to me to make any provision of this sort in favour of Quakers. Now I own I think this a fault;[5] for if their regulations, one among another, be such that they answer the ends of a minister, I see no good reason why they should be obliged to contribute to a useless expense. We find the Quakers to be as orderly and as good subjects as any other religious sect whatever; and indeed," said he, "in one respect I think their mode of instruction has the advantage; for it is always delivered in language adapted to the audience, and consequently is perfectly intelligible. I remember once in England being at a church near Lord Despencer's with his Lordship,[6] who told me that the clergyman was a very sensible young man, to whom he had just given the living. His sermon was a sensible discourse and in elegant language; but notwithstanding this, I could not perceive that the audience seemed at all struck with it. The Quakers in general attend to some plain sensible man of their sect, whose discourse they all understand. I therefore rather incline to doubt of the necessity of having teachers, or ministers, for the express purpose of instructing the people in their religious duties.

"All this is equally applicable to the law: the Quakers have no lawsuits except such as are determined at their own meetings; there is an appeal from the monthly to the annual meeting. All is done without expense, and nobody grumbles at the trouble of deciding. In fact, the honour of being listened to as a preacher, or of presiding to decide lawsuits, is in itself sufficient. A salary only tends to diminish the honour of the office; and this, if considered, will tend to support the doctrine, held in the Penn-

5. Article III of the Declaration of Rights of the 1780 Mass. Constitution, which mandated the raising of taxes for the support of religious establishments, reversed the exemptions secured by Baptists and Quakers (discussed above). The tax was now compulsory for all citizens; if they did not have a minister of their own, their contributions would go to the Congregational Church. Article III was the only article that JA declined to draft: *Adams Papers*, VIII, 231; Samuel Eliot Morison, "The Struggle over the Adoption of the Constitution of Massachusetts, 1780," Mass. Hist. Soc. *Proc.*, L (1916–17), 368–71. In 1780 BF had made a similar criticism of the Mass. constitution's religious tests, arguing in a letter to Richard Price that "When a Religion is good, I conceive that it will support itself": XXXIII, 389–90.

6. The late Sir Francis Dashwood, Baron Le Despencer, with whom BF had collaborated on *Abridgement of the Book of Common Prayer:* XX, 343–5.

sylvania constitutions, which I mentioned to you in our last conversation. Persons will play at chess, by the hour, without being paid for it; this you may see in every coffee-house in Paris. Deciding causes is in fact only a matter of amusement to sensible men."

I mentioned the mode in France of buying seats in the Parliament for the purpose of ennobling themselves. He observed that that very practice would confirm the ideas he had just thrown out. Here a *bourgeois* gives a sum of money for his seat in Parliament as a *conseiller*. The fees of his office do not bring him in 3 per cent., or at least not more. Therefore for the *noblesse* or honour which his seat gives him, he pays two-fifths of the price of the office, and at the same time gives up his labour without any recompense.

In the course of our conversation I asked if they did not still imprison for debt in America? He answered that they did; but he expressed his disapprobation of this usage in very strong terms. He said he could not compare any sum of money with imprisonment—they were not commensurable quantities. Nobody, however, in America who possessed a freehold (and almost everybody had a freehold) could be arrested on mesne process.[7] He inclined to think that all these sorts of methods to compel payment were very impolitic—some people indeed think that credit and consequently commerce would be diminished if such means were not permitted, but he said that he could not think that the diminution of credit was an evil, for that the commerce which arose from credit was in a great measure detrimental to a state.

* * * * *

He mentioned one instance to show how unnecessary such compulsory means were, and he seemed to think that it would

7. Under English law, a creditor could have a debtor arrested and held to bail or imprisoned on mesne process, *i.e.*, before the suit came to trial, which could take several months. In the United States, laws on this matter varied from state to state: Joanna Innes, "The King's Bench Prison in the Later Eighteenth Century: Law, Authority and Order in a London Debtors' Prison," in *An Ungovernable People: the English and Their Law in the Seventeenth and Eighteenth Centuries*, ed. John Brewer and John Styles (New Brunswick, N.J., 1980), pp. 252–3; Peter J. Coleman, *Debtors and Creditors in America: Insolvency, Imprisonment for Debt, and Bankruptcy, 1607–1900* (Washington, D.C., 1999).

be better if there were no legal means of compelling the payment of debts of a certain magnitude. In the interval between the declaration of independence and the formation of the code of laws in America, there was no method of compelling payment of debts, yet, notwithstanding this, the debts were paid as regularly as ever; and if any man had refused to pay a just debt because he was not legally compellable, he durst not have shown his face in the streets. Dr. Jebb having requested me to inquire if there were any good political tracts or pamphlets, I took the liberty to ask if he knew any. He told me that there were a good many upon one particular subject, which had been fully discussed, but which was little known in England as yet. Of these he said one might make a little library. The subject was on the giving information to the public on matters of finance. The books in question had given rise to a set of persons or to a sect called economists, who held that if the people were well informed on matters of finance, it would be unnecessary to use force to compel the raising of money; that the taxes might be too great—so great as in fact to diminish the revenue—for that a farmer should have at the end of the year not only wherewith to pay his rent and to subsist his family, but also enough to defray the expense of the sowing, &c. &c., of next year's crop; otherwise, if the taxes are so high as to prevent this, part of his land must remain unsown, and consequently the crop which is the subject of taxation be diminished, and the taxes of course must suffer the same fate. Some of their principles, he observed, were perhaps not quite tenable. However, the subject was discussed thoroughly. The Marquis de Mirabeau was said to be the author of the system. Dr. Franklin waited on him, but he assured him that he was not the author originally—that the founder was a Dr. Chenelle, or Quenelle. The Marquis introduced Dr. Franklin to him, but he could not make much out of him, having rather an obscure mode of expressing himself.[8]

8. BF met physiocrats Victor de Riquetti, marquis de Mirabeau, and Quesnay during a trip to Paris in the fall of 1767. Du Pont de Nemours sent him Quesnay's *Physiocratie* the following spring, which he read with great interest; he had a copy of Mirabeau's *Les Économiques* on his bookshelf at Passy: XV, 118–20, 181–2; XXXVI, 340.

He said that he was acquainted with an *Abbé* now abroad, but who would return in a fortnight or so, and who would give him a list of the principal pamphlets on both sides.

I then left him, and he desired me to call from time to time during my stay at Paris.

* * * * *

"Une Abonnée"

AL (draft): Library of Congress; copy: American Philosophical Society

Letters to the editor written in the guise of a woman were one of Franklin's earliest and favorite forms of satire. The present example is the only instance we have seen of his crafting this sort of spoof in France. Whether it was truly intended for publication or simply meant to amuse his friends is not known; no mention of it has been found in any of his correspondence, and it never appeared in print. Despite its obvious appeal, the piece lay unidentified among Franklin's papers until the present edition was launched.[9]

Franklin drafted this letter in French. The heavily labored manuscript shows him trying to refine his wording, correct the genders of his nouns, and wrestle his verbs into the proper form. He had his grandson Benny Bache prepare a fair copy, which suffers from Benny's occasional spelling errors, and that copy was shown to a Frenchman—possibly Le Roy—who interlined a few suggestions, which we note in annotation. We publish the text as Franklin wrote it.

The problem so ingeniously solved by this female "subscriber" ("abonnée" is in the feminine) was one that French scientists were considering in the summer of 1783: how to generate the lightest and least expensive gas to fill a balloon. In late July, when Montgolfier announced his plan to demonstrate a *machine aérostatique* in Paris, scientists began speculating on what mysterious substance he could be using. Based on the calculations he had submitted, they realized that whatever it was, it could never achieve the levity of the newly discovered *air inflammable* (hydrogen), which was ten times lighter than air. Generating a sufficient quantity of hydrogen, however, would be painstaking and very expensive. As noted elsewhere in this volume, a team led by

---

9. Claude-Anne Lopez recognized this piece in our archive and published an English translation in Lopez, *Mon Cher Papa*, p. 222.

the physicist Jacques-Alexandre-César Charles raised public money to fabricate a balloon and fill it with *l'air inflammable*. Their highly publicized work culminated in a launch on August 27 witnessed by thousands of delighted spectators who, it seems, could talk of little else for weeks. When describing the experiment to Joseph Banks on August 30, Franklin mentioned a few of the fanciful applications that were being discussed, ranging from manned flight to refrigeration.[1]

Ascribing a date to this manuscript has posed its challenges, but we think it likely that Franklin wrote it in the giddy aftermath of Charles's August 27 experiment. According to this "abonnée," even a fool such as herself knew that there existed a substance ten times lighter still than *l'air inflammable* and available in abundance.

Messieurs, [after August 27, 1783]
On dit que les Chemistes font tous leurs efforts pour trouver un Air plus leger & moins dispendieux que l'air inflammable pour remplir les *Aerostats* (nom donné aux Ballons par notre savante Academie.) Il est vraiment Singulier que les hommes aussi eclairés que ceux de notre Siècle cherchent continuellement dans l'Art ce que la Nature offre partout à tout le monde, & qu'une Sotte telle que moi soye[2] la premiere a en trouver l'Application. Mais je ne ferai pas un Secret de mon Invention, ni ne demanderai aucune Recompence du Gouvernement, ni aucun Privilege exclusive. Si vous desirez remplir vos Ballons d'une *Matiere* dix fois plus leger que l'Air inflammable, vous la pouvez trouver en grande quantité dans les Promesses des Amans & des Courtisans, dans les Soupirs de nos Veufs;[3] dans les bonnes Resolutions faites pendant une Tempete en Mer, ou dans une Maladie à Terre; & surtout dans les louanges contenus dans les Lettres de Recommendation.[4]

Je suis, &c UNE ABONNÉE.

1. See BF to Banks, July 27 and Aug. 30.
2. BF meant "soit." The correction was made on the fair copy.
3. Interlined on the fair copy is the suggestion: "ceux qui deviennent veufs".
4. Within months of arriving in Paris, BF satirized the French convention of writing empty letters of recommendation in his "Model of a Letter

From Jean-François de Cailhava d'Estandoux[5]

Printed invitation, signed: American Philosophical Society

MONSIEUR,

A l'hôtel du Musée de Paris, rue Sainte-Avoye, le 28 Août 1783.

LE Musée de Paris ayant transporté ses Séances au local de M. Pilatre de Rozier, rue Sainte-Avoye, vis-à-vis la rue du Plâtre;[6] vous êtes prié de vouloir bien vous y trouver aux Assemblées ordinaires des Jeudis, & nommément à celle du 11 Septembre prochain, dans laquelle on fera un appel général pour fixer le nombre des Muséens.

Si vous ne pouvez pas vous y trouver, vous êtes prié de me faire réponse d'ici à cette époque,

J'ai l'honneur d'être, Monsieur, Votre très-humble & très obéissant serviteur CAILHAVA Président.

Addressed: A Monsieur / Monsieur franklin / ministre plenipotentiaire / des etats unis de lamerique / a passy

Notation: Musée de paris

---

of Recommendation of a Person You Are Unacquainted with": XXIII, 549–50. See also BF to RB and SB, July 27, above. In this piece, he is playing on the French expression "en l'air" (idle, empty, shallow, silly) as applied to words or ideas, which had its English equivalent in the adjective "airy."

5. Cailhava (1731–1813) was a playwright, literary critic, and founding member of the Neuf Sœurs. He was also the leader of a dissident faction of the Musée de Paris, as explained below. *DBF;* Amiable, *Une Loge maçonnique*, pp. 21, 26, 193–4.

6. At a "tumultuous" meeting of the Musée de Paris in July, Cailhava and his followers staged a coup and elected him president, ousting Court de Gébelin who, since his elected term had expired (XXXIX, 342n), was continuing as *président perpétuel.* Court de Gébelin quickly retaliated, reestablishing his presidency and, as he owned the building, expelling the dissidents. They merged with Pilatre de Rozier's scientific museum, still calling themselves the Musée de Paris. The original Musée, having "regained its tranquility," continued to meet and on Sept. 2 hosted an elaborate fête in honor of the king of Poland. In 1785, after Court de Gébelin's death, the dissidents were welcomed back: Bachaumont, *Mémoires secrets,* XXIII, 77–8, 96–7, 135–6; XXV, 13–14; Anne-Marie Mercier-Faivre, *Une Supplément à l'"Encyclopédie": le "Monde primitif" d'Antoine Court de Gébelin . . .* (Paris, 1999), pp. 66–7.

From John Calder[7]

AL: American Philosophical Society

London Aug. 28 1783

Dr. Calder presents his respectful Compts to Dr. Franklin, & begs leave to remind him, by favour of his particular friend Mr P. Elmsley,[8] that there was a letter sent, or to be sent to the Hotelle D'Espagne for L. G. Melville which has never come to the hands of Dr. C. who takes this favourable opportunity to inform Dr. F. that now after his having been for many years employed in a most delicate situation all his friends are his friends still, & his enemies, such of them as survive, relinquished by their friends, are objects of his pity & generous recommendation. If Dr. F. has any letters which he wishes to be safely transmitted to any of his many friends here, Dr. C. can assure him that he may most entirely confide in the bearer of this.

Addressed: Dr. Franklin / Paris.

Notation: Calder August 28 1783.

From Cambray

ALS: American Philosophical Society

Monsieur   Paris ce 28 Août 1783

J'ay l'honneur de Vous écrire pour le même sujet qui fit une partie de notre entretien il y a deux jours. Je suis très occupé d'obtenir de l'avancement de la Cour; Mr. le Marechal de Segur est on ne peut pas mieux disposé en ma faveur; j'ay réussy particulierement à mettre Mr. le Cte. de Vergennes dans mes interêts, je dois lui être présenté par Mr. le Mis. de la Fayette. Vous seul êtes dans le cas de mettre la derniere main à cet ouvrage. Vous connoissés avec quel Zele j'ay servy les Etats Unis, vous avés lu tous les témoignages flatteurs que j'ay rapportes du Congrès, des Legislatures des deux Carolines, du Général Washington, et du General Lincoln, et particulierement les ré-

7. Calder was waiting for an answer to his March 13 letter: XXXIX, 326–30.
8. Peter Elmsly.

solutions par lesquelles il m'a été décerné une medaille portant des Inscriptions on ne peut pas plus flatteuses, par l'Assemblée de la Caroline du Sud, pour avoir été l'instrument de la sureté de Charlestown dans la premiere invasion des Anglois.[9]

Je reclame à cette heure votre témoignage dans une lettre que je Vous prie de vouloir bien m'envoyer pour Mr. le Comte de Vergennes; mon Memoire lui a été présenté hier; ainsy je ne pourray pas le faire apostiller par Vous comme nous en étions convenus; Votre lettre sera suffisante. Je demande que Vous me rendiés justice, et comme votre lettre va être préponderante, puisque mes services ont eu le bonheur d'être approuvés par les Etats Unis, j'espere que Vous voudrés bien ne pas menager les expressions favorables à mes interêts.

Je remettrois sous vos yeux tout ce que Vous avés déjà lu à mon arrivée, si mes papiers n'étoient point entre les mains de Mr. le Duc de la Rochefoucault, qui ne doit me les rendre que la semaine prochaine.

J'attends de Vous, Monsieur, cette marque de bonté que je reclame dans cette lettre comme une recompense de mes services en Amerique par les effets qu'elle doit produire. J'espere qu'en mème tems vous voudrés bien m'informer de l'état de votre santé, et être persuadé du très profond respect avec lequel je suis Monsieur Votre trés humble et tres obéissant serviteur

LE CHEVR. DE CAMBRAY/.

Hotel de Villers rue St. Pierre quartier Montmartre

P.S. Je vous prie de vouloir bien mentionner que j'ay le brevet de Colonel au service des Etats Unis./.[1]

---

9. Cambray was awarded a gold medal by the state of South Carolina for his service during the defense of Charleston. The documents he describes here, including Washington's certificate of October, 1782, and the testimonial by Benjamin Lincoln, were translated into French and published in the *Mercure de France (Jour. politique de Bruxelles)*, Nov. 22, 1783.

1. Congress promoted Cambray to the rank of colonel on May 2. He was honorably discharged from service on Nov. 15 and remained in France: *JCC*, XXIV, 324; Lasseray, *Les Français*, I, 140.

S. E. Mr. Franklin Ministre Plenipotentiaire des Etats Unis.

Notation: Le Chevr. de Cambray 28 Août 1783.—

Response to a Memorandum of Sabatier fils & Després[2]

D: Archives du Ministère des affaires étrangères

[*c.* August 29, 1783?]³

Apostille proposée par Monsieur Le Docteur Francklin Sur le Mémoire de MM. Sabatier fils et Desprez.

2. This copy of an undated note by BF concerns a debt incurred by Sabatier fils & Després in 1782 when, under orders from the French government, they replaced the military stores for the American army that had been captured in May, 1781, aboard the *Marquis de Lafayette*. The question under discussion was whether France or the United States was liable for the debt. (For background, see XXXV, 172, 244–5, 395.)

Sabatier fils & Després explained the problem in an Aug. 29, 1783, memorandum to Palteau de Veimerange (AAE). They reminded the former *commissaire* (now *intendant des armées du roi: État militaire* for 1783, p. 9) that in September, 1781, he had contracted with them to furnish military supplies for the United States which would be purchased by the royal treasury. They had received the full contract price by the end of 1782, as scheduled, but their actual costs were higher by 134,065 *l.t.* Initially, they were told to apply to BF to collect the difference. BF had referred them to Barclay, who had been delaying. They now demanded payment from the French government, with whom they had the contract.

The circumstances under which BF wrote the present note are still unknown. It is filed with the Aug. 29, 1783, memorandum at the AAE, giving the impression that it was written in response to it. However, because BF mentions the firm's demand on *him*, it seems more likely that this note was written in early 1783 and submitted to the French government by Sabatier fils & Després as evidence that BF had disclaimed responsibility. Calonne had certainly seen this "apostille" when describing the situation to Vergennes on Feb. 1, 1784 (AAE). If BF had initially disclaimed the debt, however, he acknowledged it as an American expense by May, 1783; see XXXIX, 589. In 1784, the French treasury paid Sabatier fils & Després and applied for reimbursement to Congress, which acknowledged the claim: Vergennes to Marbois, Oct. 12, 1784 (AAE); Marbois to John Jay, Feb. 22, 1785 (Wharton, *Diplomatic Correspondence*, I, 161, 197); *JCC*, XXIX, 602–3.

3. A clerk in Vergennes' office wrote "1783. Août 29" in the top left-hand corner of this sheet, undoubtedly when filing the sheet with the memoir.

Je pense que MM. Sabatier fils et Desprez dirigent Irrégulierement Leur demande Sur moy qui n'ayant jamais eté partie dans le marché dont il Sagit, et n'ayant pas dû m'attendre à La répétition de La somme qui en est L'objet, n'ait fait aucune disposition, pour me pourvoir des fonds nécéssaires pour L'acquitter./.

David Hartley to the American Peace Commissioners

ALS: William L. Clements Library; copies: Library of Congress, Massachusetts Historical Society, National Archives; press copy of copy: National Archives

Gentlemen   Paris August 29 1783

As the day is now fixed for the signatures of the Definitive treaties between Great Britain France and Spain[4] I beg leave to inform you that I am ready to sign the Definitive treaty between Great Britain and the united States of America whenever it shall be convenient to you. I beg the favour therefore of you to fix the day.[5] My Instructions confine me to Paris as the place appointed to me for the exercise of my functions[6] and therefore whatever day you may fix upon for the signature I shall hope to receive the honour of your Company at the Hôtel de York.[7]

I am Gentlemen with Great Respect and Consideration Your most obedt Servt.   D HARTLEY

4. The day was set for Wednesday, Sept. 3.

5. BF immediately applied to Vergennes on this point; see Gérard de Rayneval's response, the following document.

6. Hartley's instructions contained no such restriction. His claim that he was obliged to perform all official functions at Paris was a ruse to forestall the Americans' proposing that they sign the treaty at Versailles: Hartley to Fox, Sept. 1, 1783, in Giunta, *Emerging Nation*, 1, 930. BF later observed to the president of Congress that Hartley's refusal to sign at Versailles was evidence of the English ministers' mounting irritation that "all their Treaties for Peace were carried on under the Eye of the French court." The American commissioners complied with Hartley's insistence on signing at Paris with "good Humour": BF to Thomas Mifflin, Dec. 25, 1783 (National Archives).

7. Hartley's residence was at 56, rue Jacob, in the Latin Quarter; see Hillairet, *Rues de Paris*, 1, 667.

To Their Excellencies The Ministers plenipotentiary of the United States of America.

From Gérard de Rayneval[8]

Copies:[9] Massachusetts Historical Society, Library of Congress

Versailles le 29. Aout 1783.

J'ai rendu compte à M. le Cte. de Vergennes, Monsieur, de la difficulté que fait Mr. Hartley de signer à Versailles et ce Ministre m'a chargé de vous mander, Que rien ne devoit vous empêcher de signer à Paris mercredy prochain, Jour designé pour la Signature des autres Traités; mais il vous prie d'indiquer à M. Hartley 9. heures du Matin, et d'envoyer ici un exprès immediatement apres votre Signature faite: M. de Vergennes veut être assuré que votre besogne est consommée en même tems que la Sienne. Vous recevrez pour Mercredy un Billet d'Invitation, ainsi que Mrs. vos Collegues et M. Hartley:[1] Je presume que celui ci n'y trouvera aucune difficulté.

Vous trouverez ci-Joint, Monsieur, les deux Sauf-conduits que vous avez demandés; la Demande de M. Williams sera portée demain au Conseil.[2]

J'ai l'honneur d'etre avec un parfait Attachement, Monsieur, Votre tres humble et tres obeissant Serviteur,

(signé) DE RAYNEVAL

To Mr. Franklin

8. Obviously written in response to a now-missing note from BF to Vergennes regarding Hartley's letter, immediately above.

9. In the peace commissioners' letterbooks. We publish the copy made by L'Air de Lamotte, whose French is more accurate than that of the other copyist, BFB.

1. The only one of these that has been found is Vergennes' invitation to Jay, dated Aug. 28: Morris, *Jay: Peace*, p. 581.

2. For the requests for *sauf conduits* see BF to Rayneval, Aug. 22; Rayneval to BF, Aug. 23, letter (I); BF to Vergennes, Aug. 24.

The American Peace Commissioners to David Hartley

Copies: National Archives,[3] William L. Clements Library, Library of Congress, Massachusetts Historical Society; press copy of copy: National Archives

Passy 30. August 1783.

The American Ministers Plenipotentiary for making Peace with great Britain, present their Compliments to Mr. Hartley. They regret that Mr. Hartley's Instructions will not permit him to sign the Definitive Treaty of Peace with America at the Place appointed for the Signature of the others.[4] They will nevertheless have the Honour of waiting upon Mr. Hartley at his Lodgings at Paris, for the Purpose of signing the Treaty in Question, on wednesday Morning at Eight oClock.

3. Enclosed in the commissioners' letter to Boudinot, Sept. 10. WTF noted at the top of this copy, "Answer to Mr. Hartley's Letter of the 29. Augt 1783—"

4. The American commissioners evidently believed Hartley's claim that his instructions required him to sign the treaty at Paris and refuse mediation. Thirty years later, JA recalled that they had thought these orders unbecoming to "a great nation and a great monarch," but Hartley had "glossed these things over with ingenuity and good humor. We knew they were not his own projects, and received his apologies with equal good humor." See Hartley to the American Commissioners, Aug. 12 (headnote) and Aug. 29; to Fox, Aug. 20, in Giunta, *Emerging Nation*, 1, 922–3; and *Adams Papers*, XV, 250–1n, which quotes JA's recollections from February, 1812, published in the *Boston Patriot*.

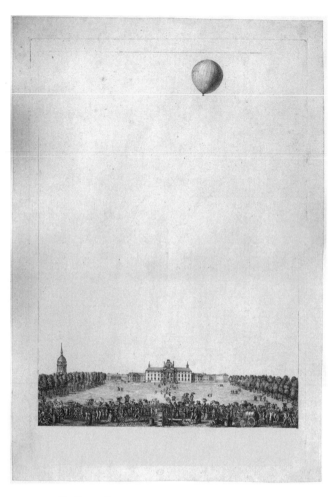

Balloon Rising over the Champ de Mars

To Joseph Banks

LS:[5] Royal Society; press copy of LS: Harvard University Library; AL (draft): University of Pennsylvania Library;[6] copy: Library of Congress

During August, while Etienne Montgolfier was conferring with the Académie des sciences, working on his new balloon, and pursuing his business interests as a papermaker,[7] his competitors were scrambling to figure out how they could safely generate the 900 cubic feet of hydrogen needed to fill the globe they had constructed, financed through private subscription.[8] It is unlikely that Franklin was among

5. In L'Air de Lamotte's hand. BF added the last seven words of the complimentary close and two subsequent notes as indicated. We have silently supplied from BF's draft one word that was dropped ("an"), and have removed occasional punctuation that conforms to French usage and was inadvertently added by L'Air de Lamotte. Otherwise, the minor copying discrepancies are preserved as written.

6. The press copy and AL (draft) lack the second postscript and the enclosure. The complete copy at the Library of Congress contains an additional section describing the engraving that BF sent to Banks two weeks later by way of Richard Price, reproduced on the facing page. It begins with a general description: "The print contains a view of Champ de Mars and the ball in the air." Next, the copyist transcribed the legend engraved on the print (quoted in the List of Illustrations), which credited the Robert brothers with the execution of the balloon and ended with the names "Mr. Faujas de Saint Fond & M. Charles." To this was added a final note explaining that Charles's name was "wrote with pen, not engraved." BF must have inserted that name, and with good reason. Charles was not named in many of the articles published in the *Jour. de Paris* and reprinted elsewhere. The indignant Robert brothers countered with a public letter correcting the articles and "Estampes éparses de tous côtés," insisting that it was Charles alone who had directed their operations, and that Faujas de Saint-Fond's role was limited to raising the subscription and issuing tickets: *Jour. de Paris*, Sept. 14, 1783.

7. For background on the Montgolfiers' hot air balloon see the headnote to BF to Banks, July 27. Etienne's family, concerned that he was too focused on how his name "vole par toute l'europe," pressed him to visit customers and talk to BF about marketing paper in America: Jean-Pierre to Etienne Montgolfier, Aug. 30, 1783, described in Gillispie, *Montgolfier Brothers*, p. 39; see also pp. 34–6.

8. Charles had technical assistance from the brothers Anne-Jean and Marie-Noël Robert, instrument makers, who supplied the materials. See the headnote cited in the previous note, as well as Gillispie, *Montgolfier Brothers*, pp. 27–9; Faujas de Saint-Fond, *Description des expériences de la machine aérostatique de MM. de Montgolfier . . .* (Paris, 1783), pp. 7–9.

the subscribers, as he makes no mention of it in this report. (By contrast, he did tell Banks in October that he had subscribed to Charles's next experiment.)[9] He certainly was acquainted with Faujas de Saint-Fond, however, who managed the subscription, and knew Charles by reputation and in person, having attended at least one of his lectures.[1]

By August 23, when materials for Charles's balloon were finally ready and Paris was "in an uproar about the flying machines," the press had begun alerting readers that a public demonstration of the rival balloon was imminent.[2] On August 25 all of Paris (according to one reporter) made its way to Charles's home on the place des Victoires, where people glimpsed the marvelous *globe aérostatique* suspended. It was transported under escort to the Champ de Mars in the middle of the night of August 26–27. As soon as it was properly situated and anchored, the team of scientists and assistants began the laborious generation of hydrogen. By the time the globe rose "majestically" from its moorings at five o'clock in the evening, the size of the crowd exceeded anything most witnesses had ever seen.[3]

9. BF to Joseph Banks, Oct. 8, 1783 (Royal Society).

1. For BF's attendance at Charles's lecture in December, 1781, see XXXVI, lxii. After Charles died, the story was told of how BF had attended one of his lectures in company with the Italian physicist Alessandro Volta. BF was so impressed with the experiments that he remarked: "La nature ne lui refuse rien, il semble qu'elle lui obéisse": Baron Joseph Fourier, "Eloge historique de M. Charles . . . ," *Mémoires de l'Académie des sciences de l'Institut de France* (2nd ser., 40 vols., Paris, 1816–78), VIII, lxxiv, lxxvi. WTF knew Charles as well, having attended one of his courses: Chevalier de Saint-Olympe to WTF, Aug. 16, 1783 (APS).

2. For the quotation, see the annotation of Banks to BF, Aug. 25. Until this time, the press had reported only on the Montgolfiers' experiment at Annonay and the fact that Etienne Montgolfier would soon be staging a repetition of it. See, for example, Bachaumont, *Mémoires secrets*, XXIII, 85, 88–9, 108, 116–18; *Jour. historique et politique*, no. 33 [mid-August], pp. 359–63; *Jour. de Paris*, Aug. 27, 1783.

3. *Jour. de Paris*, Aug. 28, 1783; Bachaumont, *Mémoires secrets*, XXIII, 117–18; Tourneux, *Correspondance littéraire*, August, 1783, p. 348. The crowd remained transfixed in spite of the rain, which wilted plumes, hats, and dresses: Bachaumont, *Mémoires secrets*, XXIII, 128–9. See also Gillispie, *Montgolfier Brothers*, pp. 30–1.

In light of BF's problems with gout and kidney stones (see the Aug. 27 entry in Baynes's journal, published above under that date), he probably observed the experiment from his own terrace, which afforded an unobstructed view

Even in the midst of the overwhelming "enthousiasme public," however, there were enough detractors that their grumblings were reported along with the machine's success. Where would this lead, they asked. What possible utility could be derived from these experiments? When this question was posed to Franklin on the day of the demonstration, he was said to have replied, "Eh! à quoi bon l'enfant qui vient de naître?" ("Eh! Of what use is a new-born baby?")

This famous *bon mot* was recorded by Baron von Grimm in his *Correspondance littéraire*, a handwritten paper circulated privately to a select group of European aristocrats. Grimm went on to observe that the infant might die in his cradle or perhaps turn out to be an "imbécile," but he might equally turn out to be the glory of his country, the light of his age, the savior of humanity.[4] A few weeks later, after the next balloon ascension inspired a frenzy of new commentary, Franklin would see his witticism quoted in the mainstream press in slightly altered form and become transformed over time, as elements of Grimm's own comments were incorporated and the phrase was embellished and burnished.

The wit of the original version, whose essence lay in its being posed as a rhetorical question, was flattened when the quip appeared publicly for the first time in the *Mémoires secrets* on September 24: in this retelling, Franklin "ingeniously" replied, "C'est l'enfant qui vient de naitre." This phrase was printed the next day in the *Journal de Paris*.[5] In the September 27 issue of the weekly *Mercure de France (Journal politique de Bruxelles)*, the "penseur profond" was quoted as saying, "Peut-être sera-t-il un imbécile ou un homme de beaucoup d'esprit; attendons pour le juger que son éducation soit achevée."[6] It was in this distorted form that the expanded phrase appeared twice more in other journals with widespread distribution, to the indigna-

---

across the river. That view was reproduced in "Premier Voyage Aérien En présence de Mgr. le Dauphin . . . Vüe de la Terasse de Mr. Franklin à Passi," an engraving depicting Montgolfier's experiment of Nov. 21, 1783.

4. Tourneux, *Correspondance littéraire*, August, 1783, p. 349.

5. Bachaumont, *Mémoires secrets*, XXIII, 171; *Jour. de Paris*, Sept. 25, 1783.

6. The following week, in another article about balloons, the journal referred to the baby who was still awaiting its education, before which, "selon un homme célèbre," one could not judge whether it would amount to something or nothing: *Mercure de France (Jour. politique de Bruxelles)*, Sept. 27, 1783, p. 178; Oct. 4, 1783, pp. 36–7.

tion of an earnest inventor from Picardy whose objections filled two long letters.[7]

Franklin's *mot* continued to circulate as the balloon craze grew and the expense of the trials kept alive the question of whether glorified kites could be justified in light of society's pressing needs.[8] Balloons and babies became so closely associated, in fact, that both enthusiasts and skeptics used the metaphor, with or without attribution, either to support their views or to cast ridicule on the entire phenomenon. Thus, *Lettre de M. Joly de Saint-Vallier . . . à Madame La Princesse de ***, à Pétersbourg, sur les ballons appellés globes aëro-statiques*, published in Ostend in November, declared that the balloon was an infant that had already reached maturity and would never be anything but a toy. A reviewer, explaining the allusion, combined previous versions into a smoother formulation. "Le mot célebre de M. Francklin," he explained, was *"Ce n'est encore qu'un enfant: peut-être ne sera t-il qu'un imbécille, peut-être deviendra-t-il un grand homme."*[9]

Even Franklin played off the remark, it seems, after witnessing Charles's manned flight on December 1. Enchanted at the sight (according to the *Mémoires secrets*), he said that the first balloon had been an "enfant," but this one was a "géant." Not wanting to appear partisan, however, he added that "le machine aérostatique étoit un enfant dont M. Montgolfier étoit le pere & M. Charles la mere nourrice."[1]

Franklin also invoked the metaphor when shrugging off a question posed to him by Condorcet at a session of the Académie des inscriptions et belles-lettres in November. When asked if he thought it would ever be possible to steer a balloon, he was quoted as saying: "la chose est encore dans son enfance, ainsi il faut attendre."[2] Why would

7. Ducarne de Blangy, October 3 and 7, 1783 (University of Pa. Library). He cited the *Jour. de Genève*, Sept. 27, 1783, p. 609. The same quotation, with minor variations, appeared in the *Jour. historique et politique*, no. 40 [early October, 1783], p. 23.

8. This question was discussed at length in the *Jour. historique et politique*, no. 40 (cited above), and still nagged at La Sablière de la Condamine on March 8, 1784 (APS), when he sent BF a memoir on the subject.

9. Métra, *Correspondance secrète*, XV, 270.

1. Bachaumont, *Mémoires secrets*, XXIV, 65.

2. Giacomo Casanova, *Ma voisine, la postérité: à Léonard Snetlage . . .* (Paris, 1998), p. 47. The session was described as taking place shortly after d'Alembert died, which was on Oct. 29, 1783. The *Jour. de Paris* of Nov. 14 reported a public session of the Académie on that day.

a chronicler preserve such an unremarkable statement if not for its allusion to the by-then famous expression?

In the present letter reporting on the events of August 27, Franklin gives Joseph Banks a sense of the crowd's speculations and begins to muse on the implications of the balloon experiment. But neither here nor in any other letter does he so much as allude to the witticism for which his name was yet again being celebrated, concurrently with the peace treaty and the image of the United States as an infant emerging from its cradle that was circulating around Europe on his *Libertas Americana* medal.

Did Franklin actually utter this *mot*, and if so, in what form? Sixteen years after the fact, and nine years after Franklin's death, a speech delivered by Le Roy confirmed that he had said something of the kind. On 21 Prairial, An 7 (June 9, 1799), when asked by the minister of the interior to report to the first class of the Institut national des sciences et des arts on the utility of the balloon and Montgolfier's role in its invention, Le Roy reminded his audience of "ce mot de l'illustre Franklin, interrogé par un savant qui lui faisoit la même question sur leur mérite que celle que le Ministre de l'Intérieur a faite à la Classe: *C'est un enfant*, répondit-il, *qui vient de noître, on ne peut pas dire ce qu'il deviendra.*"[3] This formula certainly captures the meaning, but did Le Roy remember his friend's exact words? In our view, the rejoinder noted immediately after the fact by Grimm sounds the most Franklinian—succinct, wise, and ironic.[4]

SIR,   Passy, August 30.[–September 2,] 1783

On Wednesday the 27th. Instant, the new aerostatic Experiment, invented by Messrs. Mongolfier of Annonay, was repeated by Mr. Charles, Professor of experimental Philosophy at Paris.

A hollow Globe 12 feet Diameter was formed of what is called in England Oiled Silk, here *Taffetas gommé*, the Silk being impregnated with a Solution of Gum elastic in Lintseed Oil, as is said. The Parts were sewed together while wet with the Gum,

---

3. *Procès-verbaux des séances de l'académie tenues depuis la fondation de l'Institut jusqu'au mois d'août 1835* (10 vols., Hendaye [Basses-Pyrénées], 1910–22), I, 586.

4. Seymour L. Chapin, who traced the many different iterations of BF's remark, concluded the opposite, citing Le Roy's close friendship with BF: "A Legendary Bon Mot?: Franklin's 'What Is the Good of a Newborn Baby?'" APS *Proc.*, CXXIX (1985), 278–90.

and some of it was afterwards passed over the Seams, to render it as tight as possible.[5]

It was afterwards filled with the inflammable Air that is produced by pouring Oil of Vitriol upon Filings of Iron, when it was found to have a tendency upwards so strong as to be capable of lifting a Weight of 39 Pounds, exclusive of its own Weight which was 25 lb, and the Weight of the Air contain'd.

It was brought early in the Morning to the *Champ de Mars*, a Field in which Reviews are sometimes made, lying between the Military School and the River. There it was held down by a Cord till 5 in the afternoon, when it was to be let loose. Care was taken before the Hour to replace what Portion had been lost, of the inflammable Air, or of its Force, by injecting more.

It is supposed that not less than 50,000 People were assembled to see the Experiment. The Champ de Mars being surrounded by Multitudes, and vast Numbers on the opposite Side of the River.

At 5 a Clock Notice was given to the Spectators by the Firing of two Cannon, that the Cord was about to be cut. And presently the Globe was seen to rise, and that as fast as a Body of 12 feet Diameter with a force only of 39 Pounds, could be suppos'd to move the resisting Air out of its Way. There was some Wind, but not very strong. A little Rain had wet it, so that it shone, and made an agreable Appearance. It diminish'd in Apparent Magnitude as it rose, till it enter'd the Clouds, when it seem'd to me scarce bigger than an Orange, and soon after became invisible, the Clouds concealing it.

The Multitude separated, all well satisfied and delighted with the Success of the Experiment, and amusing one another with discourses of the various Uses it may possibly be apply'd to, among which many were very extravagant. But possibly it may pave the Way to some Discoveries in Natural Philosophy of which at present we have no Conception.

A Note secur'd from the Weather had been affix'd to the Globe, signifying the Time & Place of its Departure, and

5. The fabric had been devised by a M. Bernard: Faujas de Saint-Fond, *Description des expériences de la machine aérostatique*, pp. 7–9.

praying those who might happen to find it, to send an Account of its State to certain Persons at Paris. No News was heard of it till the next Day, when Information was receiv'd, that it fell a little after 6 a Clock at Gonesse, a Place about 4 Leagues Distance, and that it was rent open, and some say had Ice in it. It is suppos'd to have burst by the Elasticity of the contain'd Air when no longer compress'd by so heavy an Atmosphere.

One of 38 feet Diameter is preparing by Mr. Mongolfier himself, at the Expence of the Academy, which is to go up in a few Days. I am told it is constructed of Linen & Paper, and is to be filled with a different Air, not yet made Public, but cheaper than that produc'd by the Oil of Vitriol, of which 200 Paris Pints were consum'd in filling the other.[6]

It is said that for some Days after its being filled, the Ball was found to lose an eighth Part of its Force of Levity in 24 Hours; Whether this was from Imperfection in the Tightness of the Ball, or a Change in the Nature of the Air, Experiments may easily discover.

I thought it my Duty, Sir, to send an early Account of this extraordinary Fact, to the Society which does me the honour to reckon me among its Members; and I will endeavour to make it more perfect, as I receive farther Information.

With great Respect, I am, Sir, Your most obedient and most humble Servant   B FRANKLIN

P.S. Since writing the above, I am favour'd with your kind Letter of the 25th. I am much obliged to you for the Care you have taken to forward the Transactions, as well as to the Council for so readily ordering them on Application. Please to accept and present my Thanks.

I just now learn, that some observers say, the Ball was 150 seconds in rising, from the Cutting of the Cord till hid in the Clouds; that its height was then about 500 Toises, but, being moved out of the Perpendicular by the Wind, it had made a Slant so as to form a Triangle, whose Base on the Earth was

---

6. A French "pinte" was roughly equivalent to 47 cubic inches or 0.93 liters: Ronald E. Zupko, *French Weights and Measures before the Revolution: a Dictionary of Provincial and Local Units* (Bloomington, Ind., 1978).

about 200 Toises. It is said the Country People who saw it fall were frightned, conceiv'd from its bounding a little, when it touch'd the Ground, that there was some living Animal in it, and attack'd it with Stones and Knives, so that it was much mangled; but it is now brought to Town and will be repaired.[7]

The great one of M. Mongolfier, is to go up, as is said, from Versailles, in about 8 or 10 Days; It is not a Globe but of a different Form, more convenient for penetrating the Air. It contains 50,000 cubic Feet, and is supposed to have a Force of Levity equal to 1500 pounds weight. A Philosopher here, M. Pilatre du Rozier, has seriously apply'd to the Academy for leave to go up with it, in order to make some Experiments. He was complimented on his Zeal and Courage for the Promotion of Science, but advis'd to wait till the Management of those Balls was made by Experience more certain & safe.[8] They say the filling of it in M. Mongolfier's Way will not Cost more than half a Crown. One is talk'd of to be 110 feet Diameter. Several Gentlemen have ordered small ones to be made for their Amusement. One has ordered four of 15 feet Diameter each; I know not with what Purpose; But such is the present Enthusiasm for promoting and improving this Discovery, that probably we shall soon make considerable Progress in the art of constructing and using the Machines.[9]

Among the Pleasanteries Conversation produces on this Subject, Some suppose Flying to be now invented, and that since Men may be supported in the Air, nothing is wanted but some

7. To reassure the public, the government issued a statement describing the two experiments that had already been conducted and giving notice that more were being planned with even larger balloons. The "machines" were harmless, being made of fabric and paper, and presumably one day would serve a useful purpose for society: *Mercure de France (Jour. politique de Bruxelles)* for Sept. 6, 1783, pp. 32–5.

8. This exchange took place at the meeting of the Académie des sciences on Aug. 30: *Procès-verbaux*, CII, 194–5.

9. The baron de Beaumanoir lofted a balloon of one and a half feet diameter on Sept. 10, and announced public demonstrations on the next two days: *Jour. de Paris*, Sept. 11 and 12, 1783. Smaller balloons, eight inches across, were soon being sold by M. Blondy for 6 *l.t.* apiece: *Jour. de Paris*, Sept. 14, 1783.

light handy Instruments to give and direct Motion. Some think Progressive Motion on the Earth may be Advanc'd by it, and that a Running Footman or a Horse slung and suspended under such a Globe so as to have no more of Weight pressing the Earth with their Feet, than Perhaps 8 or 10 Pounds, might with a fair Wind run in a straight Line across Countries as fast as that Wind, and over Hedges, Ditches & even Waters. It has been even fancied that in time People will keep such Globes anchored in the Air, to which by Pullies they may draw up Game to be preserved in the Cool, & Water to be frozen when Ice is wanted. And that to get Money, it will be contrived to give People an extensive View of the Country, by running them up in an Elbow Chair a Mile high for a Guinea &c. &c.   B F

[*In Franklin's hand:*] A Pamphlet is printing, in which we are to have a full & perfect Acct of the Experiments hitherto made, &c. I will send it to you. M. Mongolfier's Air to fill the Globe has hitherto been kept secret; some suppose it to be only common Air heated by passing thro' the Flame of burning Straw, and thereby extreamly rarefied. If so, its Levity will soon be diminish'd, by Condensation, when it comes into the cooler Region above.

Sir Joseph Banks, Bart.

[*Enclosure:*]¹

Calculs du Ballon de 12. Pieds de Dametre
enlevé le Mercredy 27. Aout 1783.

Circonférence du	
grand Cercle	37. Pieds
Diamétre	12.

	74
	37.
Surface	444. Pi.

1. In L'Air de Lamotte's hand.

Tiers du Rayon   2.

Solidité   888. Pieds cubes.
Air atm. à 12.
gros le Pi.   12.

1,776.
888

Pesanteur de
l'air atm.   10,656. gros $\begin{cases} 8 \\ \overline{1332.} \text{ onces} \end{cases} \Big/ \begin{matrix} 16 \\ \overline{83.} \end{matrix}$ lb 4. onces
              26
             25,6   52

L'air Atmospherique dont le Ballon occupoit la Place pesant 83. lb 4. ces [onces] et sa force pour s'élever étant de 40. lb il falloit que son Eveloppe et l'air inflammable qu'elle contenoit ne pesassent que 43. lb 4. onces l'Enveloppe en pesoit 25, rèste pour l'air inflamable 18. lb 4. onces.

En supposant le Ballon de 6 Pieds de diametre, son Volume étant le 8eme. du 1er., Le Poids de l'air dont il occupoit la Place seroit le huitieme de 83. lb 4. onces   = 10. lb 6. onces 4. gros
L'air inflammable ⅛ de 18. lb 4. onces = 2. lb 4. onces 4. gros
L'Enveloppe   ¼ de 25. lb   = 6. lb 4. onces
     Les dernieres valeurs reünies sont 8. lb 8. onces 4. gros qui otés de 10. lb 6. onces 4. gros pèsanteur de l'Air atmospherique dont le Ballon occupoit la place, laissent pour sa force d'élevation une Livre quatorze onces.

[*In Franklin's hand:*] Sept. 2. I add this Paper just now given me
B F

From Jean-Pierre Duplan   ALS: American Philosophical Society

Monsieur   Lausanne 30e. Aoust 1783.
     Vous étes trop grand dans toutes vos demarches pour avoir oublié les Esperances flatteuses que vous nous donnates de bouche en *1778.* Qu'étant honorés de vôtre presence, vous Souscrivites Monsieur pour un Exemplaire de nôtre Enciclopedie 8°.

en 36 vol: de discours, & 3 de planches, comme conste la lettre cy inclus que nous avons l'honneur de vous mettre sous les yeux pour vous rapeller Monsieur de la chose.[2]

En même tems vous nous fites Monsieur la grace d'encourager nôtre Edition, en nous laissant esperér vôtre Protection pour l'écoulement de cet excelent Dictionaire dans vos Provinces libres.

Nous osons Monsieur aujourdhui reclámer vos bontés a cet egard, & vous demander de nous ouvrir une Correspondance avec une Maison de Vos Provinces, avec laquelle nous puissions traitter pour un certain nombre d'Exemplaires, de ce livre, que nous avons de surnumeraires de la 2de. Edition, qui ne le cede en rien a la premiere.

Comme ce livre ne peut S'établir par quique Ce Soit au prix que nous l'avons, et que nous pouvons le céder, nous n'hesiterions pas Monsieur de Vous en offrir environ 2 à 300 Exemplres. qu'il nous en reste, si vous pensiés Monsieur a en faire l'acquisition pour l'usage de vos Provinces libres Vû que c'est le moment d'y introduire Cet article qui jusques icy n'y à pas été importé, et qui ÿ sera accueilli tant par sa grande utilité, que par le bas prix auquel nous pouvons Monsieur vous le Céder. Pardonnés Monsieur la liberté que nous avons Osé prendre devous parler de cet article, si nous n'étions convaincus d'avance, que vous Cherchés en tout le bonheur des hommes Americains, que nous Aimons par la gloire, & le bonheur qu'ils ont sçû s'acquerir par leur grande valeur & sagesse que tout vray Republicain doit admirer, & admire dans ce paÿs, nous n'oserions vous en parler mais sachant Monsieur jusqu'où vous mettés d'interêt pour avancer le bonheur de vos Compatriottes, & des hommes en general, ce motif est Suffisant pour nous excuser aupres de vous Monsieur dans l'offre que nous nous permettons, d'un nombre de 300 environ d'Exemplaires complet que nous desirons de voir passer dans les mains de cette Colonie respectable:

En attendant nous avons l'honeur de vous rapeller Monsieur

2. Duplan, who obviously had not received a reply to his letter of Nov. 10, 1782, may have enclosed a copy of it: XXXVIII, 297–8.

de vôtre souscription d'un Exemplaire a compte duquel il à eté livré dans votre maison à Passy les Tome 1 a 10—par M Dassy Darpajan de Fontainebleau, & pour completter il vous sera remis Monsieur Sous peû par Mr Marechal Avocat Biblioteq: mazarine à Paris[3] les T. 11 à 36. de discours avec les 3 vol. de planches qui complettent l'exemplaire, lequel vous servira Monsieur d'Echantillon pour le nombre que nous proposons, car c'est un comme tous; Le prix de cet Exemplaire est de £ 225. de france, que Mr. Marechal encaissera, en livrant les Volumes; daignés Monsieur Nous honorer d'un môt de reponse sur nôtre proposition, que vous aurès la bonté de diriger soùs envelope a l'adresse cy bas Au Directeur en chef de nôtre societé, L'Ecrivain de la presente, qui s'estimera heureux de meriter cette faveur de vôtre part Monsieur, & celle d'etre accueilli dans son offre;

C'est avec la plus respectueuse Consideration que j'ay l'honneur d'etre Votre trés humble & trés Obeissant Serviteur Monsieur

pour La Societé Typographique de Lausanne
DUPLAN Directr. en chef d'icelle

Passy Monsieur Le Docteur Francklin

Notation: Duplan 30 Août 1783

From Pierres

ALS: American Philosophical Society

Monsieur, Paris 30 aoust 1783
J'ai l'honneur de vous envoyer l'Exempl. in 40. pour le Grand Duc de Russie.[4] Je vous renvoye aussi l'Ex. in 80. que vous m'aviez fait passer.

3. The radical poet and essayist Pierre-Sylvain Maréchal (1750–1803). His first collection of poems helped secure him a position as an assistant librarian at the Bibliothèque Mazarine of the Collège des Quatre-Nations in 1770; his religious satire *Livre échappé au déluge* . . . (Paris, 1784) caused him to lose it: Larousse; Alfred Franklin, *Histoire de la Bibliothèque Mazarine et du palais de l'Institut* (2nd ed., Paris, 1901), p. 238.
4. Grand Duke Paul of Russia, whom BF had met in the summer of 1782: XXXVII, 311–12, 316, 445–6.

Je suis avec un respect infini, Monsieur, Votre très humble &
très obeissant serviteur   PIERRES

M. Franklin./.

Notation: Pierres 30 Août 1783.

From Philipp Thieriot   ALS: American Philosophical Society

Monsieur   Bordeaux ce 30e Aoust 1783.
Je crois de mon devoir de vous prevenir que je suis sur mon
depart pour Philadelphie. Je serai tres flatté, Monsieur, si vous
vouliés bien m'honnorer de vos ordres. Tout ce que vous daignerés me confier sera soigné avec la plus grande exactitude.
    S'il n'arrive pas de contretems imprevu, je partirai sans faute
Jeudi prochain en huit; de maniere que l'honneur de votre reponce peut me parvenir la veille de mon depart.
    Le batiment par lequel je dois partir, est Americain, et un des
meilleurs voiliers.[5]
    J'ai l'honneur d'etre avec la Consideration la plus distinguée
Monsieur Votre tres humble & tres obeissant serviteur
                                                PH THIERIOT

Le Navire se nomme la Nancy de Bath, Cape J: L: B: Moignard.

Notation: Thieriot 30 Août 1783

5. The ship proved no match for the autumn storms, however. Even after
he was rescued by an American fishing boat off the West Indies, severe
weather continued to plague Thieriot's journey. He finally arrived in Philadelphia on March 18, 1784, carrying letters of introduction from BF and
Carmichael. Robert Morris and Michael Hillegas received him cordially,
and Morris provided letters of introduction to governors in New York and
New England. Thieriot soon realized that the desultory state of the American economy doomed prospects for trade with Saxony, and he returned to
Europe at the beginning of 1785: William E. Lingelbach, "Saxon-American Relations, 1778–1828," *American Hist. Rev.*, XVII (1911–12), 525–30;
Morris Papers, IX, 193–4, 227, 441–2.

To Elias Boudinot[6]

LS,[7] press copy of LS,[8] and transcript: National Archives; copy: University of South Carolina Library

Sir,   Passy, Augt. 31. 1783.

After a continued Course of Treating for 9 Months, the English Ministry have at length come to a Resolution to lay aside for the present all the new Propositions that have been made & agreed to, their own as well as ours; and they offer to sign again as a Definitive Treaty the Articles of Novr 30th. 1782, the Ratifications of which have already been exchang'd. We have agreed to this, and on Wednesday next, the 3d. Septr. it will be signed with all the other Definitive Treaties, establishing a General Peace, which may God long continue.

I am with great Respect Sir, Your Excellency's, most obedient and most humble Servant   B FRANKLIN

His Exy The Presdt. of Congress.

Notation: Letter Aug 31. 1783 B Franklin definitive treaty agreed on

From Octavie Guichard Durey de Meinières[9]

ALS: American Philosophical Society

aux Pavillons de chaillot Ce 31 aoust 1783

Illustrioux Legislator of your Country, I Would be Very obliged to you, if you Would and Could give me, the book,

---

6. WTF sent a copy of this letter to Henry Laurens at Bath so that "Mr. Lawrens will be made acquainted with what is going on here." WTF to Laurens, Aug. 31, 1783, S.C. Hist. Soc.

7. In WTF's hand.

8. Made before the signature was added.

9. A spirited member of Mme Helvétius' circle and former translator of English works: XXXII, 297–8. For a study of some of her earlier correspondence see Marie-Laure Girou Swiderski, "De la 'gazette' au 'commerce des âmes': les lettres de la présidente de Meinières à la marquise de Lénoncourt," in *Femmes en toutes lettres: les épistolières du XVIIIe siècle,*

of the Constitution, translated by M. de la Rochefoucault. Some body told me, that it is not Sold. I Should be lofty[1] to have it of your hand, and gratefull to you for your Kindness, my dear Neighbour, loved and revered by your most humble Servant   GUICHARD DE MEINIERES

Addressed: A Monsieur / Monsieur franklin / ministre plénipotenciaire des états / unis de l'amérique / a Passy

Notation: De mainieres.

To Madame Durey de Meinières   ALS: Yale University Library

Passy, Augt 31. 1783.—
I send with great Pleasure the Constitutions of America[2] to my dear & much respected Neighbour, being happy to have any thing in my Power to give that she will do me the honour to accept, and that may be agreable to her. I am, ever, with sincere Esteem, my dear Friend, Yours most affectionately

B FRANKLIN

---

ed. Marie-France Silver and Marie-Laure Girou Swiderski, *Studies on Voltaire and the Eighteenth Century* (Oxford, 2000), no. 4, pp. 119–39, 254–6.
    1. By which she means proud (*fière*).
    2. Which she had requested in the letter immediately above. BF's inscription (presumably in that work) read: "A Madame / Madame la Présidente de Manières de la part du B. FRANKLIN." The loose flyleaf is quoted in Charles Hamilton Autographs, Inc., catalog 31 (1959), item 72.

Notes on Establishing a Packet Boat Service to and from New York[3]

AD (draft): American Philosophical Society

[c. August 31, 1783]

American Postmaster at New York to receive and distribute all Letters brought by the Pacquets of England & France
    To give Receipts for the Amount, & keep an Account with each
    Settle & pay every three Packets
    Allow'd for dead, return'd or missent Letters.—

All preceding Postage of Packet Letters to be paid on both sides before they are sent forward by the respective Offices So that when the Letters arrive in America or Europe they may have no Charge on them but the Pacquet Postage, for the more easy & clear keeping of[4] the Accounts—

The American Postmaster at New York shall send all American Letters that come to his Hands by the first Pacquet that sails whether French or English, unless otherwise directed by Words on the Superscription, such as *via England* or *via France*, or *by the English Packet*, or *French Pacquet* &c[5]

3. On Sept. 19, 1783 (APS), Anthony Todd answered a now-missing letter of Aug. 31 in which BF outlined his thoughts on a coordinated French and British packet boat service to the United States. Todd's answer makes it clear that BF's proposal was based on the ideas outlined here.

4. This phrase is interlined above another ("which will save much Trouble in"), which BF underlined and presumably was considering deleting.

5. This entire paragraph was written below one that BF deleted with a single line. He had originally given the American postmaster the job of sorting overseas mail and routing it accordingly: "The American Postmaster at New York to sort all American Letters that come to his hands, and send by the French P. Boats all directed for France or the Continent of Europe, and all by the English P. Boats all directed for England, Scotland or Ireland, unless the writer has signified a different Intention by writing on the Superscription via France or via Engld." When Todd answered on Sept. 19, he objected to the "first Pacquet" idea and proposed what BF himself had originally written.

England & France to add their respective Inland Postages on Letters receiv'd by Packet according to their respective Regulations—

From Thérèse Aerts

ALS: American Philosophical Society

Monsieur, Bruxelles ce Aout 1783.

La confience que vous inspire à toutes les personnes qui ont l'honneur de vous connaitre m'enhardit à recourir une seconde fois à vos bontés. Ma reconnoissance ose vous rappeller Monsieur La lettre que vous m'avez fait la grace de m'écrire en datte du 28 Aout 1782.⁶ Le Sentiment en est profondement gravé dans mon Coeur. Cette lettre a fait Longtêms mon espoir et ma consolation; je croÿois voir approcher le jour qui devait mettre un terme à toutes les engoises de ma scituation; helas! le sort semble L'emporter sur les demarches plaines de bonté et de commiseration que vous avez daignez faire en ma faveur. Il s'agissait de trouver les moÿens de retracer un epoux qui s'est expatrié pour aller se fixer à boston, vous aviez ut la bonté de vous addresser pour cet effet à Mr. Williams à nantes, et de le charger de correspondre avec moi. Apres huit mois d'attente Mr: Williams m'a fait l'honneur de m'écrire qu'il n'avoit jusqu'à lors rien recu touchant l'existence du nommé Smith mon epoux—⁷

6. Neither her earlier letter nor BF's response has been located.

7. With the present letter (as she says below), she enclosed a copy of the three-page memoir she had sent earlier. It states that her husband, François Joseph Aerts of Brussels—who had taken the name Smith—had written from St. Pierre, Martinique, to a merchant in Brussels on April 21, 1778, saying that he was sailing for Boston aboard the privateer *America*, Capt. John Allen Hallet, with a cargo of goods consigned to William and Godfrey Hutchinson of Boston. If after a year there was no word from him, the merchant was to get his will, made out in favor of his wife and children, and arrange for them to claim what was due to him by the Boston firm. All this could be done through BF in Paris. Mme Aerts begged for BF's help, as all attempts to contact her husband had failed.

WTF forwarded Mme Aerts's first letter and memoir to JW, on the day BF answered her appeal. JW in turn forwarded her memoir to a correspondent

Je suis donc sans espoir de ce coté la apres cinq années de souf-
frances et d'incertitudés. La derniere lettre de mon mari en datte
du 24. Avril 1778. me marquait que si après une année révolue je
n'apprenois point de ses nouvelle, ce seroit une preuve certaine
qu'il auroit cessé de vivre. Quatre années se sont écoulées depuis
la revolution de cette fatale année, sans qu'il m'ait été possible
de decouvrir si mon epoux est en vie, ou si ajant cessé de vivre,
les personnes qu'il avoit rendu depositaires de ses fortunes sont
en même au point de remplir ses dernieres volontés. Jugez Monsieur de ma situation; abbandonnée de mon epoux étrangere à
ses parens qui se vangent par le cruel delaissement du chagrin
que leurs à causé un fils denaturée, je languis sans secours, et
sans appuis, je vois s'éloigner chaque jour la faible, et la seule
ressource sur laquelle il m'étoit permis dans ma misere de jetter
les ÿeux, mon mari vivant m'avoit promis des de secours il savoit
combien il m'étoient necessaires, la justice la pitie lui faisoient
un devoir de m'assister depuis cinq ans je n'ai plus aûcune de ses
nouvelles, s'il est mort qu'on me rende son bien il en à disposé en
ma faveur, toutes les loix divines et humaines viennent à l'appuis
de ma juste réclamation, mais pourquoi vous importuneraisje de
mes peines; j'en ai dit asséz pour interesser l'âme du plus grand
des hommes, du plus sensible du plus genereux. Comme la mul-
tiplicité de vos affaires ne peut que vous avoir fait perdre de vue
les details de ma demande, je prends la liberté Monsieur d'en
joindre ici la copie telle que j'ai eu l'honneur de vous l'envoier.
J'ai l'honneur d'être, Monsieur, Vôtre très-humble et tres-
obeissante servante[8]   M: T. AERTS NÉE SPEECKAERT

---

in Boston: JW to WTF, Sept. 16, 1782 (APS); JW to Joshua Eaton, Sept. 16,
1782 (Yale University Library).

8. "Smith" (c. 1750–1802) abandoned his family and settled in Pennsylvania, where he took Elizabeth Brodhead as his common-law wife around
1780 and, as "Dr. Francis Smith," became a well-respected physician.
According to a statement he wrote near the end of his life, he was born
Josephus Jacobus Aerts; he was intelligent, fluent in many languages, and
anti-authoritarian by nature. A six-month stint in a dungeon for an unspecified offense inspired him to change his name; in 1777 he went to America,
where he was commissioned in the Continental Army on July 29, 1778.
One of his sons from his first marriage, Francis Alexander Smith, emi-

P.S. Je vous prie, Monsieur, d'adresser l'honneur de vôtre reponce sous le Couver de Mr Vain Controlleur au Bureau Général
des Postes des Paÿs-bas, à Bruxelles.

Notation: Aerts Mde. Bruxelles Aout 1783.—

From Jean-Jacques Caffiéri

ALS: American Philosophical Society

Monsieur   Paris ce Premier Septembre 1783
Aÿent appris votre indisposition j'ay eté pour avoir lhonneur
de vous assurer de mes Civilité, j'ay appris avec Satisfaction que
votre Santé alloiest beaucoup mieux, je vous en filisite.

Permette de vous Reiterée mes instance et vous prier Monsieur de vouloir bien vous Resouvenir de moy Dans le Cas que
le Congrés Des Etats Unis de L'amerique fit elevér quel que
monument a la Gloire De La Nation ou des Generaux qui y on
Contribuer.[9]

Je Suis avec Respect Monsieur Votre tres humble et tres
obeïssant Serviteur   CAFFIÉRI

Notation: Caffieri 1er. Sept. 1783

---

grated to the United States in the early 1790s and settled near his father:
Alfred Mathews, *History of Wayne, Pike and Monroe Counties, Pennsylvania* (Philadelphia, 1886), pp. 880, 1002–3; *JCC,* XI, 730; Anne Goodwill
and Jean M. Smith, eds., *The Brodhead Family: the Story of Captain Daniel
Brodhead, His Wife Anne Tye and Their Descendants* (8 vols. to date, Port
Ewen, N.Y., 1986–), II, 130–4; Francis Alexander Smith to Stephen Girard, Feb. 27, 1812, Stephen Girard Papers, Girard College.
    9. For his earlier solicitations see XXXIX, 9, 386.

From Ingenhousz   ALS: American Philosophical Society

Dear Friend   Vienna Sept. 1. 1783.
The inclosed note and bill of exchange of 150 florins on
Messrs. Goll & Verbrugge at Amsterdam are delivred to me by
his Excellency Count Chotek chanchellor of Bohemia and Austria,[1] one of our first Noblemen, and, what more is, a true Lover
and encourager of Sciences; deserving therefore very highly
your attention in fulfilling his desires, by sending the inclosed
list of American plantes to a good botanist or nursery man, and
to engage him in a pressing way to forward, as soon as possible,
by the first vessel bound to Amsterdam, all, or as many of such
grains or seeds mentioned in this list, as he will be able procure
immediately, principaly those marked L. You will be so good as
to send by the Same way the inclosed bill of Exchange, after having endossed it, the amount of which must balance the expenses
of the Commission, shipping included. What the Commissioner
may not be able to collect immediately, must not stop in the least
the sending of those he may procure immediately, as the remain-
dre is to be Sent in the autum of 1784. Those which he will send
by the first oportunity will be made use of in the spring of 1784.
    I hope you have recieved my last dated August 5th,[2] with an
inclosed to mr. Le Begue de Prèsle.
    I hope you will now disentangle your Self from the boister-
ous and capricious Political world, and finish in a more elevated
sphere, the last revolutions of years, Providence has reserved to
you for the good of Mankind. You have done enough. (Spec-
tatum satis est et donatum Iam rude)[3] Elevated on the highest
pinnacle of human Grandour, which a private man can attain,
you can, at your age, not be so fond of it as of the immortal

---

1. Johann Rudolph Graf Chotek von Chotkowa und Wognin (1748–
1824) was also the president of the Royal Bohemian Society of Sciences.
He owned several estates on which he experimented with agricultural inno-
vations and landscape design: Constant von Wurzbach, ed., *Biographisches
Lexikon des Kaiserthums Oesterreich* (60 vols., Vienna, 1856–91).
    2. Actually, Aug. 15, above.
    3. One who has proved himself and now received a badge of service:
Horace, *Epistolae*, book 1, epistle 1, line 2.

name of a Philosopher of the first rang— Fulfill now your ardent wishes, and finish your Glorious carriere in philosophical tranquillity. After having now given the finishing stroke to the greatest revolution which the world ever beheld, and after having had a grate share in the foundation of an immense empire on the basis of Liberty and independence, you have acquired the greatest right to enjoy the remnant of life left to you, in a way the most suited to your inclination— My ardent wishes are Still to enjoye once more your company— If, according to your plan, I may Still hope to embrace you here, you will be eye witness of those immense labours, which I have undertaken, and still pursue with unremitting assiduity and attention, to the sole purpose of enlarging human knowledge; and you will be pleased to see, that I have not laboured quite in vain— Contented with what I have acquired by saving the most illustrious Princes of the world from the dangers of a disease so fatal to their family,[4] I enjoye, tho in a philosophical obscurity, more real happiness, than a Conquerour of the World.

That you may enjoye still many years of health, happiness and tranquillity, is the wish of Your old and affectiona friend.

J. INGEN HOUSZ

to his Excellency B. Franklin Ministre Pleny of The United states of America at Passy.

Endorsed: Sept. 1. 83

From Lewis Littlepage[5]   AL: American Philosophical Society

Monday 1st. September 1783—
Mr Littlepage presents his most grateful & respectful thanks to his Excellency doctor Franklin for his polite & friendly

4. Probably a reference to his inoculation of the Austrian royal family against smallpox: XIV, 4n.
5. Littlepage, a Virginian, sailed to Europe in 1780 anticipating the patronage of John Jay, with whom he stayed in Spain: XXXI, 476–7, 489;

acquiescence in Mr Littlepage's request of being sent with the definitive Treaty to Congress, but as Mr Jay has declared himself decidedly in favor of Mr Adams's Clerk,[6] Mr Littlepage request's his Excellency not to take the trouble to propose him—

Mr Littlepage will ever retain the warmest sense of gratitude for this generous instance of friendship from doctor Franklin, & will with the greatest pleasure inform the Marquis de La Fayette of the deference which his Excellency has been pleased to pay to his recommendation—[7]

Addressed: His Excellency / doctor Franklin

XXXII, 52–3. He served under the duc de Crillon at the sieges of Minorca and Gibraltar, joined Lafayette for his proposed expedition to the West Indies, and traveled to Paris with Lafayette in the spring of 1783, where he met BF and attended his Independence Day celebration. The antagonism that developed in Spain between Jay and Littlepage escalated during this stay in Paris and continued long afterward: *DAB;* Morris, *Jay: Peace,* pp. 218–20; Idzerda, *Lafayette Papers,* V, 96; and see the note below.

6. JA proposed John Thaxter, Jr., on Aug. 27, above.

7. If BF ever intimated to Lafayette that he would support Littlepage's candidacy, knowing the impossibility of its success, it might have been at the dinner Lafayette hosted on Aug. 30. (The invitation is cited in the annotation of Lafayette to BF, June 6.) Whatever BF may have said, the impression he created had unforeseen consequences and was a matter of public dispute in an acrimonious exchange of pamphlets years later between Jay and Littlepage.

Littlepage had been angling for the honor of carrying the treaty since mid-July, when Jay told him that it would be decided by vote. According to Jay's account, on Sept. 1 Littlepage told him that he had secured BF's support and asked Jay to cast the deciding vote in his favor. Jay insisted that there had to have been a misunderstanding: BF had told JA (when the latter delivered his letter of Aug. 27, above) that "he had no objections" to Thaxter, whom Jay also preferred. The next day, Littlepage sent Jay a letter accusing him of lying and challenging him to a duel. Shortly thereafter, he appeared at Jay's chambers, where he found Jay and JA together. JA confirmed Jay's account, and Littlepage withdrew the challenge. In Littlepage's version, after his initial conversation with Jay on Sept. 1, he went straight to BF, who denied supporting Thaxter and assured him that he would be pleased to have an occasion to show "deference to [Lafayette's] request." Littlepage then confronted Jay, who "confessed" that he had already declared his support for Thaxter. The rest of Littlepage's account, including his challenge and its retraction, is similar to what Jay had written:

To Ingenhousz   ALS: Mrs. James A. de Rothschild, England (1962)

Dear Friend,   Passy, Sept. 2. 1783.—
Inclos'd I send you a Copy of a Letter to Sir Joseph Banks,
concerning the Ballons that at present occasion much Conversation here.[8] I imagine that if you make one, and fill it with inflammable Air, you will contrive to fire it by Electricity when it is
up, and by that means match in Report the Thunder of Nature.
    To morrow is to be signed our Definitive Treaty, which es-
tablishes for the present the Peace of Europe & America. Long,
long, may it continue!— Adieu. Yours most affectionately,
                                                    B FRANKLIN

Dr Ingenhauss.—

[John Jay], *Letters, being the Whole of the Correspondence between the Honorable John Jay, Esq. and Mr. Lewis Littlepage* . . . (New York, 1786), pp.
40–1; [Lewis Littlepage], *Answer to a Pamphlet, Containing the Correspondence between the Honorable John Jay, Secretary for Foreign Affairs; and Lewis
Littlepage, Esquire, of Virginia* . . . (New York, [1787]), pp. 20–2.
    8. BF to Banks, Aug. 30[–Sept. 2], above. According to Ingenhousz'
reply of Nov. 19, 1783 (APS), BF also enclosed a print of the "allarm" of
the peasants at Gonesse, where the balloon landed. "Allarme générale des
habitants de Gonesse," a print described in the Sept. 13 article on the Montgolfiers' experiment in the *Jour. de Paris,* depicted a terrified populace at-
tacking the semi-deflated balloon with pitchforks, guns, and stones, having
been told by two monks that it was a monstrous animal. It is reproduced in
François-Louis Bruel, *Histoire aeronautique par les monuments peints, sculp-
tés, dessinés et gravés des origines à 1830* (Paris, 1909), plate 30.
    Ingenhousz' Nov. 19 reply also indicated that BF forwarded a letter
for him from Samuel Lewis Wharton, along with a bill of exchange for
8,000 *l.t.*

From David Hartley

ALS: Historical Society of Pennsylvania; copy: William L. Clements Library

My Dear friend   Hotel de Yorck Sept 2 1783

I find that the Answer wch I received in form from the American Ministers to that note wch I transmitted by Mr Adams, runs, that they will come to my Lodgings at Paris, tomorrow morning, for the purpose of signing the Treaty in Question. Mr Adams and Mr Jay understand it so and propose to come.[9] Upon so great a Crisis leading to the Reconciliation of our two Countries I shall be very happy to see you too. I hope the inconvenience will not be very great to you, or in any degree commensurate to the occasion.

I am ever Your most affectionate friend[1]   D Hartley

To Dr Franklin &c &c &c

Definitive Treaty of Peace between the United States and Great Britain

DS: Massachusetts Historical Society,[2] National Archives (two), Public Record Office; copies: Library of Congress, Massachusetts Historical Society, National Archives (two).)

Early on the morning of September 3, Benjamin Franklin, John Jay, and William Temple Franklin rode into Paris carrying four official

---

9. The only extant versions of the commissioners' Aug. 30 response to Hartley's letter of Aug. 29 are copies that do not indicate signatures. If it was delivered without any, that would explain Hartley's clarification here.

1. WTF answered this note on behalf of his grandfather. BF would "do his utmost" to be present at the signing the next morning. In addition, WTF accepted Hartley's invitation (now missing) for "Thursday next": WTF to Hartley, Sept. 2, 1783, Clements Library. For BF's current sufferings with the stone and gout see Pierres to BF, Aug. 25. The Thursday invitation was undoubtedly for Sept. 4, when JA wrote his wife, "To day We dined with Mr. Hartley and drank Tea with the Duchess of Manchester. Thus you see We are very good Friends, quite free, easy and Social": *Adams Correspondence*, v, 233.

2. We have silently corrected a few minor copying errors.

without Difficulty and without requiring any Compensation.

Article 10th.

The solemn Ratifications of the present Treaty expedited in good & due Form shall be exchanged between the contracting Parties in the Space of Six Months or sooner if possible to be computed from the Day of the Signature of the present Treaty. In Witness whereof we the undersigned their Ministers Plenipotentiary have in their Names and in Virtue of our Full Powers signed with our Hands the present Definitive Treaty, and caused the Seals of our Arms to be affixd thereto.

Done at Paris, this third Day of September, In the Year of our Lord one thousand seven hundred & eighty three.—

D Hartley John Adams. B Franklin John Jay—

Definitive Peace Treaty between the United States and
Great Britain, September 3, 1783

copies of the treaty that would end the War for American Independence.[3] Joined by Adams, they convened at Hartley's chambers at the Hôtel de York. There the texts were reviewed, and the two secretaries—William Temple Franklin and George Hammond—attested the copies of the commissions that would be appended to them. At half past ten o'clock, the four principals signed the treaties and affixed their seals "with the most perfect cordiality on both sides," as Hartley wrote. Cordiality may have reigned, but this was not the treaty any of them had hoped for.

Hartley assured the Americans that morning, on Fox's behalf, that all the points that had been under consideration since the previous spring and any others they might wish to raise would be "immediately resumed in negotiation."[4] In the meantime, they were signing essentially the same document they had signed on November 30, 1782.[5] The nine articles of the provisional treaty were retained nearly verbatim, the chief difference being the shift of a portion of text from the end of Article 1 to the beginning of Article 2, where it belonged thematically. The British added a tenth article stipulating standard terms for ratification and dropped the separate article concerning the borders of West Florida. Fox had worried that the Americans would object to the crown's priority in the preamble he supplied, but they did not.[6]

3. The four copies known to have been signed on Sept. 3 were either written by WTF or prepared under his supervision. Two are entirely in WTF's hand: the primary copy kept by the American commissioners (published here) and one of the two copies marked "Duplicate" that they sent to Congress (National Archives). The treaty that Hartley would carry to England (Public Record Office) and the second congressional copy (National Archives) were written by BF's French secretary Jean L'Air de Lamotte, with WTF adding the final dateline. On the version given to Hartley, WTF also penned the opening lines.

4. He told Fox that he intended to put this in writing, as indeed he did: Hartley to Fox, Sept. 3, 1783, in Giunta, *Emerging Nation*, II, 222; Hartley to the Commissioners, Sept. 4, below.

5. XXXVIII, 382–8.

6. "When a treaty is signed between two crowned Heads," Fox explained to Hartley, "in order to prevent disputes about precedency, the name of the one stands first in one instrument, & that of the other in the other, but when the treaty is between a crowned Head & a republick, the Name of the Monarch is mentioned first in each Instrument. I believe if you will inquire upon this subject among the *Corps Diplomatique*, you will find this to have been the constant Practice." Hartley answered that he never had occasion to employ this argument, as the Americans never

Another matter of protocol which caused concern on both sides was the question of gifts. Fox knew that royal portraits were out of the question, but he thought it would not be excessive to present each of the four American peace commissioners with the sum of £1,000 sterling that was customary for a sole ambassador. Manchester and Hartley recommended that each commissioner receive half that sum, for a total of £2,000. Hartley promised to broach the subject with Franklin. As the American commissioners had no means to reciprocate and did not wish to insult the king by refusing, they were in a quandary. "So much was said against it," according to Adams' later account, "that we never saw the presents and heard no more about them."[7]

Once the treaties were signed, the commissioners dispatched a messenger to Versailles, as Vergennes had requested.[8] The British and Spanish ambassadors and their secretaries convened at Vergennes' chambers between noon and one o'clock to sign their own treaties. (The preliminary Anglo-Dutch treaty had been signed the previous day.) That business was concluded at three o'clock in the afternoon, after which Vergennes hosted a dinner for those who had been involved in all four negotiations. There were 31 at table.[9]

None of the American commissioners left descriptions of the evening's celebration, other than Adams' recollection 30 years later that they traveled to Versailles in company with Hartley and "dined amidst

---

raised the issue: Fox to Hartley, Aug. 21, 1783; Hartley to Fox, Sept. 1, 1783 (Giunta, *Emerging Nation*, I, 923, 930). In fact, this was not a change from the preliminary articles.

7. The Americans also worried about their obligation toward the mediators, should they have been employed, as "we had no money to spare for the purchase of gold tobacco boxes, set with pictures and diamonds": *Adams Papers*, XV, 251n. See also Lord John Russell, ed., *Memorials and Correspondence of Charles James Fox* (2 vols., Philadelphia, 1853), II, 129–30, 132–3.

8. See Gérard de Rayneval to BF, Aug. 29.

9. Manchester dispatched a courier to London as soon as the signing was concluded: Giunta, *Emerging Nation*, II, 137. The number of guests, 11 of whom were named, was reported in the *Gaz. de Leyde*, Sept. 12, 1783. It has been claimed that the duc de Croÿ was also present and exchanged witty remarks with Vergennes. In fact, the duc was not in Paris at the time; he had dined with Vergennes the previous February, after the preliminary treaty was printed: Stacy Schiff, *A Great Improvisation: Franklin, France, and the Birth of America* (New York, 2005), pp. 349–50; Emmanuel, duc de Croÿ, *Journal inédit du duc de Croÿ. . .* (4 vols., Paris, 1906–7), IV, 270–1.

mutual congratulations."[1] Franklin anticipated the day's events with a degree of resignation. When informing Henry Laurens, he wrote that after so many frustrating months, "it is come finally to this." When Laurens wrote to Congress, he expressed regret at the outcome. Adams was overtly gloomy when writing to his wife the day after the signing: "We have negotiated here, these Six Months for nothing." Jay said nothing of his disappointment when writing to Robert Morris, but did offer a reflection. "We are now thank God in the full Possession of Peace and Independence," he wrote. "If we are not a happy People now, it will be our own Fault."[2]

[September 3, 1783]

IN THE NAME OF THE MOST HOLY & UNDIVIDED TRINITY.

IT HAVING pleased the divine Providence to dispose the Hearts of the most Serene & most Potent Prince George the third, by the Grace of God, King of Great Britain, France & Ireland Defender of the Faith, Duke of Brunswick & Lunebourg, Arch-Treasurer, and Prince Elector of the holy Roman Empire &ca. and of the UNITED STATES of AMERICA to forget all past Misunderstandings and Differences that have unhappily interrupted the good Correspondence and Friendship which they mutually wish to restore; and to establish such a beneficial and satisfactory Intercourse between the two Countries upon the Ground of reciprocal Advantages and mutual Convenience as may promote and secure to both perpetual Peace & Harmony; and having for this desirable End already laid the Foundation of Peace & Reconciliation by the Provisional Articles signed at Paris on the 30th. of Novr. 1782 by the Commissioners empower'd on each Part, which Articles were agreed to be inserted in and to constitute the Treaty of Peace proposed to be concluded between the Crown of Great Britain and the said United States, but which

1. *Adams Papers*, XV, 250–1n. JA mentioned nothing about the dinner at Versailles when writing to his wife the next day, though he did say that he had just had tea with the Duchess of Manchester: *Adams Correspondence*, V, 233–4. Hartley had written to Fox on Sept. 1 that they would all travel to Versailles together after the signing, and that he would entertain the Americans the following day: Giunta, *Emerging Nation*, I, 930–1.

2. BF to Laurens, Aug. 21; *Laurens Papers*, XVI, 337; *Adams Correspondence*, V, 233; *Morris Papers*, VIII, 506.

Treaty was not to be concluded until Terms of Peace should be agreed upon between Great Britain & France, and his Britannic Majesty should be ready to conclude such Treaty accordingly: and the Treaty between Great Britain and France having since been concluded, His Britannic Majesty & the United States of America, in order to carry into full Effect the Provisional Articles above mentioned, according to the Tenor thereof, have constituted & appointed, that is to say His Britannic Majesty on his Part, David Hartley Esqre: Member of the Parliament of Great Britain; and the said United States on their Part John Adams Esqre: late a Commissioner of the United States of America at the Court of Versailles, late Delegate in Congress from the State of Massachusetts and Chief Justice of the said State, and Minister Plenipotentiary of the said United States to their High Mightinesses the States General of the United Netherlands; Benjamin Franklin Esqre: late Delegate in Congress from the State of Pennsylvania, President of the Convention of the said State & Minister Plenipotentiary from the United States of America at the Court of Versailles; John Jay Esqre: late President of Congress, and Chief Justice of the state of New-York & Minister Plenipotentiary from the said United States at the Court of Madrid; to be the Plenipotentiaries for the concluding and signing the present Definitive Treaty; who after having reciprocally communicated their respective full Powers[3] have agreed upon & confirmed the following Articles.

Article 1st.

His Britannic Majesty acknowledges the said United States, viz. New-Hampshire, Massachusetts Bay, Rhode-Island & Providence Plantations, Connecticut, New-York, New Jersey, Pennsylvania, Delaware, Maryland, Virginia, North Carolina, South Carolina & Georgia, to be free sovereign & Independent States; that he Treats with them as such, and for himself his Heirs & Successors relinquishes all Claims to the Government Propriety and Territorial Rights of the same & every Part thereof.

3. For the Americans' commission of June 15, 1781, see XXXV, 163–5; for Hartley's of May 14, 1783, see XXXIX, 605–7.

ARTICLE 2D.

And that all Disputes which might arise in future on the Subject of the Boundaries of the said United States may be prevented, it is hereby agreed and declared, that the following are and shall be their Boundaries Viz: From the North West Angle of Nova Scotia, viz: that Angle which is formed by a Line drawn due North from the Source of St Croix River to the Highlands along the said Highlands which divide those Rivers that empty themselves into the River St. Lawrence from those which fall into the Atlantic Ocean, to the Northwesternmost Head of Connecticut River; Thence down along the Middle of that River to the forty fifth Degree of North Latitude; From thence by a Line due West on said Latitude until it strikes the River Iroquois or Cataraquy; Thence along the middle of said River into Lake Ontario; through the Middle of said Lake until it strikes the Communication by Water between that Lake & Lake Erie; Thence along the middle of said Communication into Lake Erie; through the middle of said Lake, untill it arrives at the Water Communication between that Lake & Lake Huron; Thence along the middle of said Water Communication into the Lake Huron, thence through the middle of said Lake to the Water-Communication between that Lake and Lake Superior thence through Lake Superior Northward of the Isles Royal & Phelipeaux to the Long Lake; Thence through the Middle of said Long Lake, and the Water Communication between it and the Lake of the Woods, to the said Lake of the Woods, Thence through the said Lake to the most Northwestern Point thereof, & from thence on a due West Course to the River Mississippi, Thence by a Line to be drawn along the middle of the said River Mississippi until it shall intersect the Northernmost Part of the thirty first Degree of North Latitude. SOUTH, by a Line to be drawn due East from the Determination of the Line last mentioned, in the Latitude of thirty one Degrees North of the Equator to the Middle of the River Apalachicola or Catahouche: Thence along the middle thereof to its Junction with the Flint River; Thence strait to the Head of St Mary's River, and thence down along the Middle of St Mary's River to the Atlantic Ocean. EAST by a Line to be drawn along the Middle of the River St Croix, from its Mouth in the Bay of

Funday to its Source, and from its Source directly North to the aforesaid Highlands, which divide the Rivers that fall into the Atlantic Ocean from those which fall into the River St. Lawrence; comprehending all Islands within twenty Leagues of any Part of the Shores of the United States, & lying between Lines to be drawn due East from the Points where the aforesaid Boundaries between Nova Scotia on the one Part and East Florida on the other, shall respectively touch the Bay of Fundy and the Atlantic Ocean, excepting such Islands as now are or heretofore have been within the Limits of the said Province of Nova Scotia.

ARTICLE 3D.

It is agreed that the People of the United States shall continue to enjoy unmolested the Right to take Fish of every kind on the Grand Bank and on all the other Banks of Newfoundland, also in the Gulph of St. Lawrence and at all other Places in the Sea where the Inhabitants of both Countries used at any time heretofore to fish. And also that the Inhabitants of the United States shall have Liberty to take Fish of every kind on such Part of the Coast of Newfoundland as British Fishermen shall use, (but not to dry or cure the same on that Island) and also on the Coasts Bays & Creeks of all other of his Britannic Majestys Dominions in America, and that the American Fishermen shall have Liberty to dry & cure Fish in any of the unsettled Bays Harbours and Creeks of Nova-Scotia, Magdalen Islands, and Labrador, so long as the same shall remain unsettled, but so soon as the same or either of them shall be settled, it shall not be lawful for the sd: Fishermen to dry or cure Fish at such Settlement, without a previous Agreement for that purpose with the Inhabitants, Proprietors or Possessors of the Ground.

ARTICLE 4TH.

It is agreed that Creditors on either Side shall meet with no Lawful Impediment to the Recovery of the full Value in Sterling Money of all bona fide Debts heretofore contracted.

ARTICLE 5TH.

It is agreed that the Congress shall earnestly recommend it to the Legislatures of the respective States to provide for the Restitution of all Estates, Rights and Properties which have been confiscated belonging to real British Subjects; and also of the Estates Rights & Properties of Persons resident in Districts in the Possession of his Majesty's Arms, and who have not borne Arms against the said United States. And that Persons of any other Description shall have free Liberty to go to any Part or Parts of any of the thirteen United States and therein to remain twelve Months unmolested in their Endeavours to obtain the Restitution of such of their Estates, Rights, and Properties as may have been confiscated. And that Congress shall also earnestly recommend to the several States, a Reconsideration and Revision of all Acts or Laws regarding the Premises, so as to render the said Laws or Acts perfectly consistent not only with Justice and Equity but with that Spirit of Conciliation which on the Return of the Blessings of Peace should universally prevail. And that Congress shall also earnestly recommend to the several States, that the Estates Rights & Property's of such last mentioned Persons shall be restored to them, they refunding to any Persons who may be now in Possession the bona fide Price (where any has been given) which such Persons may have Paid on purchasing any of the said Lands, Rights or Properties, since the Confiscation.

And it is agreed that all Persons who have any Interest in confiscated Lands either by Debts, Marriage Settlements or otherwise, shall meet with no lawful Impediment in the Prosecution of their just Rights.

ARTICLE 6TH.

That there shall be no future Confiscations made, nor any Prosecutions commenced against any Person or Persons for or by Reason of the Part which he or they may have taken in the present War and that no Person shall on that Account suffer any future Loss or Damage either in his Person Liberty or Property; and that those who may be in Confinement on such Charges at the Time of the Ratification of the Treaty in America shall be immediately set at Liberty, and the Prosecutions so commenc'd be discontinued.

ARTICLE 7TH.

There shall be a firm & perpetual Peace between his Britannic Majesty and the said States & between the Subjects of the one, and the Citizens of the other, wherefore all Hostilities both by Sea & Land shall from hence forth cease: All Prisoners on both sides shall be set at Liberty, and his Britannic Majesty shall with all convenient Speed, and without causing any Destruction, or carrying away any Negroes or other Property of the American Inhabitants, withdraw all his Armies, Garrisons and Fleets from the said United States, and from every Port, Place and Harbour within the same; leaving in all Fortifications the American Artillery that may be therein. And shall also order & cause all Archives, Records, Deeds & Papers belonging to any of the said States or their Citizens, which in the Course of the War may have fallen into the Hands of his Officers, to be forthwith restored and deliver'd to the proper States & Persons to whom they belong.

ARTICLE 8TH.

The Navigation of the River Mississippi, from its Source to the Ocean shall forever remain free and open to the Subjects of Great Britain and the Citizens of the United States.

ARTICLE 9TH.

In Case it should so happen that any Place or Territory belonging to Great Britain or to the United States should have been conquer'd by the Arms of either from the other before the Arrival of the said Provisional Articles in America it is agreed that the same shall be restored without Difficulty and without requiring any Compensation.

ARTICLE 10TH.

The Solemn Ratifications of the present Treaty expedited in good and due Form shall be exchanged between the contracting Parties in the Space of Six Months or sooner if possible to be computed from the Day of the Signature of the present Treaty. IN WITNESS whereof we the undersigned their Ministers Plenipotentiary have in their Name & in Virtue of our full Powers signed with our Hands the present DEFINITIVE TREATY, and caused the Seals of our Arms to be affixed thereto.

DONE AT PARIS, this third Day of September, In the Year of our Lord, one thousand seven hundred & Eighty three.

[seal] D HARTLEY   [seal] JOHN ADAMS.
                              [seal] B FRANKLIN
                              [seal] JOHN JAY

To Henry Laurens   ALS: South Carolina Historical Society

Dear Sir,   Passy, Sept. 3. 1783

This Line is just to acquaint you that the Definitive Treaty between England and the United States was signed this Morning at Paris, and the others are suppos'd to be sign'd at the same time at Versailles. I shall write to you fully in a Day or two. With great & sincere Esteem, I have the honour to be Dear Sir, Your most Obedt & most humble Servt

B FRANKLIN

Honble Henry Laurens Esqr

Addressed: Honble. Henry Laurens, Esqr / Minister Plenipotentiary from the / United States of America, &c / Paris.

Endorsed: Doctr. Franklin 10th. Septem 1783. Recd. from him & answer 21st.—

From the Committee of the Sufferers in Falmouth, Casco Bay[4]

ALS: American Philosophical Society

Sir Falmouth Casco Bay Sept 3 1783[5]

From a consideration of the great attention and regard you have shewn to the just Rights of Human Nature, as well as the benevolent Character you sustain, among the People of America whom in a very eminent Station you represent, we are induced to transmit to your Care the inclosed Address—[6]

It comes from Men who have suffered exceedingly, not only by the common Calamities of War, but by an extraordinary Event peculiarly awful and distressing— We trust the unhappy circumstances of our Case will justify our Application for Relief

4. Elected on Aug. 23, this committee was charged with soliciting donations from Europe and the West Indies for the relief of the inhabitants whose town had been burned by the British in 1775. Enoch Freeman (1706–1788), chairman, was a merchant; his eldest son, Samuel (1742–1831), was postmaster and a delegate to the Provincial Congress in 1775–76 and 1778. Jedediah Preble was either the major general (1707–1784) or his eldest son and namesake. Timothy Pike was undoubtedly the colonel who commanded the Fourth Cumberland County regiment in 1776. John Waite (1732–1820), a militia colonel and former sea captain, was sheriff of Cumberland County and a delegate to the Provincial Congress in 1776: John Frothingham's certificate, Sept. 13, 1783 (APS); William Willis, *The History of Portland, from 1632 to 1864: with a Notice of Previous Settlements, Colonial Grants, and Changes of Government in Maine* (2nd ed., rev. and enl., Portland, Me., 1865), pp. 746–7n, 805–7, 835–6, 850–2, 903; Nathan Goold, "History of Col. Edmund Phinney's 31st Regiment of Foot," Maine Hist. Soc. *Coll. and Proc.*, 2nd ser., VII (1896), 175.

BF was well aware of the atrocity they described; see XXII, 242, 246–7, 392–3.

5. Though written on Sept. 3, this letter went back and forth to Boston before being sent under cover of James Bowdoin's letter to BF of Sept. 23 (which will appear in vol. 41). Initially, the committee wondered about who in France should receive it. Concerned that JA might have already left, they decided to address it to BF: Willis, *History of Portland*, pp. 902–3.

6. The petition, addressed "To all Friends of Humanity and charitable Persons in the Kingdom of France," described the torching of Falmouth and the "unspeakable Distress" it caused, estimated the property losses at £54,600 (irrespective of the loss of livelihoods), and sought contributions to help the town rebuild.

to the generous and humane part of the Nation to whom it is directed— And we more especially flatter ourselves it will be honored with that patronage from you which will ensure it the success we wish—

You have been pleased to manifest a concern for the United States in general—and we hope our sufferings will excite your attention to this part of them in particular—

We judge it would be expedient to have our Address published throughout the Kingdom, and we doubt not, most of the Printers in France would cheerfully do us this favour without a Fee—

We have left a Blank in it for the name of the Gentlemen who will consent to have it inserted—and we request that he would appoint such Persons in the different Parts of France as he should judge best, to receive any Donations that may be offered, and publish their appointment with the Address— We wish it might be filled with yours, if it be agreeable[7]—If not that you would be so kind as to prevail with some other Gentleman to honor us with his Assistance in this Respect—

If any other measures for our Relief should seem to you more eligible, we beg the favour of you to adopt them in our name—

The Sufferers have authorized us to receive whatever may be presented, and it may be sent by such Opportunities as may offer for this place, or any other within this State, directed "To the Honbl. Enoch Freeman Esqr. and others a Committee of the Sufferers in Falmouth Casco Bay."

That you may be fully satisfied of our being duly authorized for this purpose we forward this through the hands of our worthy Friend The Honorable James Bowdoin Esqr. who will transmit you this with proper Certificates for that end—

We should have been glad to have sent some Person from hence specially upon this Business—but in our present Circumstances it would be extremely difficult to collect a Sum of Money sufficient to defrey his necessary Expences—

---

7. In fact, by the time the packet of papers was sent, one of the committee had already filled in BF's name and title.

Wishing you the best of Heavens Blessings We are with great Respect Your most obedient and very humble Servants

ENOCH FREEMAN
JEDIDIAH PREBLE
SAML FREEMAN
TIMOTHY PIKE
JOHN WAITE

His Excellcy. Benjamin Franklin Esqr

David Hartley to the American Peace Commissioners[8]

Copy[9] and press copy of copy: National Archives; copies: William L. Clements Library, Library of Congress, Massachusetts Historical Society, Public Record Office

Gentlemen, Paris Septr. 4. 1783.

It is with the sincerest Pleasure that I congratulate you on the happy Event which took Place Yesterday, viz., the Signature of the Definitive Treaty between our two Countries. I consider it as the auspicious Presage of returning Confidence, and of the future Intercourse of all good Offices between us; I doubt not that our two Countries will entertain the same Sentiments, and that they will behold with Satisfaction the Period which terminates the Memory of their late unhappy Dissensions, and which leads to the renewal of all the Ancien ties of Amity & Peace. I can assure you that his Britannic Majesty, and his confidential Servants, entertain the strongest Desire of a cordial good understanding with the United States of America. And that nothing may be wanting on our Parts to perfect the great Work of Pacification, I shall propose to you in a very short time, to renew the Discussion of those Points of Amity and Intercourse which have been lately suspended, to make way for the Signature of

8. This letter reiterates what Hartley had told the American peace commissioners in person the previous morning; see the headnote to the Definitive Treaty of Peace, Sept. 3.

9. In L'Air de Lamotte's hand and enclosed in the American commissioners' Sept. 10 letter to Boudinot.

the Treaties, between all the late belligerent Powers which took Place Yesterday. We have now the fairest Prospects before us, and an unembarassed Field for the Exercise of every beneficient Disposition, and for the Accomplishment of every Object of reciprocal Advantage between us. Let us then join our hearts and hands together in one common cause, for the reunion of all our antient affections, and common Interests. I am Gentlemen, With the greatest Respect and consideration Your most obedt. Servt. (signed) D. HARTLEY.—

To their Excellences the Ministers Plenipotentiary of the United States of America.

No. 7.

The American Peace Commissioners to David Hartley

Copies: Public Record Office,[1] William L. Clements Library, Library of Congress, Massachusetts Historical Society, National Archives; press copy of copy: National Archives; copies of draft:[2] Library of Congress, Massachusetts Historical Society

Sir,   Passy Septr 5 1783
We have received the Letter which you did us the Honour to write yesterday.

Your friendly Congratulations on the signature of the definitive Treaty, meet with cordial Returns on our Part; and we sincerely rejoice with you in that event, by which the Ruler of Nations has been graciously pleased to give Peace to our two Countries.

1. Enclosed in Hartley to Fox, Sept. 7 (Public Record Office).

2. Preserved in the legation letterbooks, where they precede the final texts; both are dated Sept. 5. In the letterbook at the Mass. Hist. Soc., this version is labeled "Copy of the Letter to Mr. Hartley, as 1st. sent", while the final version is labeled "Copy of the Letter to Mr. Hartley, with the Alterations." When JA reprinted both versions in 1812, he called the first a draft; see *Adams Papers*, XV, 260n. The difference is in the rewritten central section concerning the Americans' authority to conclude a commercial treaty; see the following note.

We are no less ready to join our endeavours than our wishes with yours, to concert such measures for regulating the future intercourse between Great Britain & the United States, as by being consistent with the Honour and Interest of both may tend to increase & perpetuate mutual Confidence & good-will.[3] We ought nevertheless to apprize you that as no construction of our Commission could at any Period extend it, unless by Implication, to several of the proposed Stipulations; and as our Instructions respecting commercial Provisions however explicit, suppose their being incorporated in the definitive Treaty, a Recurrence to Congress, previous to the signature of them will be necessary, unless obviated by the Dispatches we may sooner receive from them.

We shall immediately write to them on the Subject, and we are persuaded that the same disposition to Confidence and Friendship, which has induced them already to give unrestrained Course to British Commerce, and unconditionally to liberate all Prisoners, at a time when more caution would not have appeared singular, will also urge their attention to the objects in question, and lead them to every proper measure for promoting a liberal & satisfactory intercourse between the two Countries.

We have communicated to Congress the repeated friendly assurances[4] with which you have officially honoured us on those subjects, and we are persuaded that the Period of their being

3. The revised section runs from this point through the end of the following paragraph. The copy of the draft (Library of Congress) reads: "We must nevertheless candidly inform you that we consider our Commission as terminated and therefore without further Authority from Congress will not be able to sign and conclude. All we can at present do is to confer with you and recommend to Congress such Propositions as may appear to us to merit their Assent and we shall propose to them to send a Commission to Europe without Delay for these important Purposes.

"The unrestrained Course already given by the States to the British Commerce with them and the unconditional Liberation of Prisoners, at a Time when more Caution would not have been singular are marks of Liberality and Confidence, which we flatter ourselves will be equalled by the Magnanimity of his Majesty and the People of Great Britain."

4. Changed from "warm & repeated assurances." For those assurances see the commissioners' July 27 letter to Livingston.

realized, will have an auspicious & conciliating influence on all the Parties in the late unhappy dissensions.

We have the honour to be Sir, with great Respect & Esteem Your most obedt & humble Servants   JOHN ADAMS
                                                    B FRANKLIN
                                                    JOHN JAY

Honble D Hartley Esqr His Britannic Majesty's Minister Plenipotentiary

To Charles James Fox

ALS: Public Record Office; copies: Library of Congress (two), Massachusetts Historical Society

Sir   Passy, Sept. 5. 1783—

I received in its time the Letter you did me the honour of writing to me by Mr. Hartley:[5] And I cannot let him depart without expressing my Satisfaction in his Conduct towards us, and applauding the Prudence of that Choice which sent us a Man possess'd of such a Spirit of Conciliation, and of all that Frankness, Sincerity and Candour which naturally produce Confidence, and thereby facilitate the most difficult Negociations. Our Countries are now happily at Peace, on which I congratulate with you most cordially; and I beg you to be assured, that as long as I have any Concern in Publick Affairs, I shall readily & heartily concur with you, in promoting every Measure that may tend to promote the common Felicity.

With great and sincere Esteem & Respect I have the honour to be, Sir, Your most obedient & most humble Servant
                                                    B FRANKLIN

Hon: Cha. J. Fox Esqr

Endorsed: Passy Sept 5 1783. Dr. Franklin. R. 13t: by Mr. Hartley

---

5. The letter of introduction Hartley brought with him in April: XXXIX, 481–2.

To David Hartley[6]

Copies: Massachusetts Historical Society, William L. Clements Library (two), Library of Congress (two)

My dear friend,   Passy Sept. 6. 1783

Inclosed is my Letter to Mr. Fox.[7] I beg you would assure him, that my Expressions of Esteem for him are not mere Professions. I really think him a *Great* Man; & I could[8] not think so, if I did not believe he was at Bottom, and would prove himself, a *good* One. Guard him against Mistaken Notions of the American People. You have deceived yourselves too long with vain Expectations of reaping Advantage from our little Discontents. We are more thoroughly an enlightned People, with respect to our political Interests, than, perhaps, any other under Heaven. Every man among us reads, and is so easy in his Circumstances, as to have Leisure for Conversations of Improvement, & for acquiring Information. Our domestic Misunderstandings, when we have them, are of small Extent; tho' monstrously magnified by your microscopic Newspapers. He, who judges from them that we are on the Point of falling into Anarchy, or returning to the Obedience of Britain, is like one, who, being shown some Spots in the Sun, should fancy that the whole Disk would soon be overspread with them, and that there would be an End of Day Light. The great Body of Intelligence, among our People, surrounds and overpowers our petty Dissensions, as the Sun's great Mass of Fire diminishes and destroys his Spots. Do not, therefore, any longer delay the Evacuation of New York, in the vain hope of a new Revolution in your Favour, if such a hope has indeed had any Effect in occasioning the Delay. It is

6. BF wrote this letter on the morning of a day when Hartley had planned to come to Passy for one final meeting with the American commissioners before leaving for England. Instead, ill health forced Hartley to send word to JA asking whether the commissioners could come to him as early as they could arrange it, after which he would be bled: *Adams Papers*, XV, 264.

BF did not take this letter and its enclosure with him to Paris. He sent it the next day; see his letter (I) to Hartley, Sept. 7.

7. Immediately above.

8. We have corrected this word (miscopied as "would") based on all other copies of the letter.

now nine Months since the Evacuations were promised.[9] You expect, with Reason, that the People of New-York should do your Merchants Justice in the Payment of their old Debts; consider the Injustice you do them, in keeping them so long out of their Habitations, and out of their Business, by which they might have been enabled to make Payment. There is no Truth more clear to me than this, that the great Interest of our two Countries is a thorough Reconciliation. Restraints on the Freedom of Commerce & Intercourse between us can afford no Advantage equivalent to the Mischief they will do by keeping up Ill Humour & promoting a total Alienation. Let you and I, my dear Friend, do our best towards advancing and securing that Reconciliation. We can do nothing that will in a dying Hour, afford us more solid Satisfaction.

I wish you a prosperous Journey & a happy Sight of your Friends.[1] Present my best Respects to your good Brother & Sister,[2] & believe me, ever, with sincere & great Esteem, Yours affectionately　　　　　　　　　　(signed) B. FRANKLIN

To D. Hartley Esqr.—

From the Chevalier Du Ponceau[3]

ALS: American Philosophical Society

Monsieur　　　　　　　　　sarre Louis 6. 7bre. 1783.

Depuis que je suis arrivé D'amerique avec L'armée de Rochambeau, Je n'ai point reçu de nouvelles de mon frere qui

9. By Article 7 of the preliminary peace agreement of Nov. 30, 1782 (XXXVIII, 386).

1. Hartley's intention, as he wrote to Fox on Sept. 1, was to leave for England a few days after the signing, to deliver the treaty and receive further instructions: Giunta, *Emerging Nation*, I, 930–1.

2. His half-brother Winchcombe Henry Hartley (XXXVI, 624n) and his half-sister Mary Hartley (XXVII, 343n).

3. Jean-Michel Du Ponceau, as he says here, fought in America under Rochambeau: XXXVI, 582n. He was captured at sea in January, 1783, and there is no record of when he arrived in France. He returned to America

est employé à philadelphie dans les affaires étrangeres.[4] Tout m'engage à croire que mes lettres ne lui sont pas parvenues Sans doute parceque j'ai employé de mauvais moyens. Jose prendre la liberté Monsieur de lui en addresser une sous votre envelope. L'offre obligeante que vous avés fait à ma Soeur m'est un sur garant que vous voudrés bien lui faire parvenir.

Je suis avec un très profond respect Monsieur Votre Très humble & très obeissant Serviteur

LE CHR. DU PONCEAU
offr. au regt. de saintonge

Notation: Duponceau 6. 7bre. 1783

From the Comtesse d'Houdetot

LS: American Philosophical Society

Le 6. 7bre. 1783

J'implore Mon Cher Docteur Votre protection pour un Malheureux Matelot attaché au Service D'un Batiment americain Et que des Circonstances Malheureuses Et la Difficulté De s'Expliquer font Detenir injustement Dans une prison Cruelle je Gemis pour mon paÿs qu'il Soit possible qu'il y ait Des Malheureux de Ce Genre mais Enfin sauvons Celuy Cy Si nous Le pouvons. C'est L'honêste st. Jean De Crevecœur mon Ameriquain qui me L'a adréssé avec une Lettre tres pathetique Et Les informations que j'ay L'honneur De Vous Envoyer[5] il Sagit de

---

in 1803, joining his distinguished brother Pierre-Etienne, and stayed until 1815. In 1823 he was elected an international member of the APS: Bodinier, *Dictionnaire*, p. 170; APS membership records.

4. Their sister Louise-Geneviève wrote to BF on May 27, above, also asking about Pierre-Etienne; see the annotation there.

5. The enclosure, now separated from the present letter, was Louis Le Févre des Mars to Crèvecœur, Sept. 1, 1783, written from Caen, and bearing notes by Crèvecœur clarifying some of the names (APS). It concerns the Irishman John Hammon, who was serving on the American vessel *McClenachan*, commanded by Capt. Houston and second captain Connoly, when the vessel was captured and the crew incarcerated in England: XXXVIII, 569–70. Hammon escaped to Le Havre. Because he had no money

luy procurer la Liberté Et les moyens De Retourner a L'Orient ou il pourra s'Embarquer; il faut pour Cela que Vous ayéz La Bonté D'Ecrire un Mot a L'intendant De Caen[6] pour Reclamer Cet homme Et quant aux frais pour le mettre En Etât de Retourner a Lorient ou il trouvera Des Ressources s'il n'y a pas De fonds Destinés a Cela par Vos Concitoyens, nôtre Charité y supléera, je n'ay point oublié Ce que les Dames Anglaises ont fait pour les Matelots français Et je Seray De plus fort aise De Rendre a Ma Chere Amerique un homme qui Est dit-on Encore En Etat De la Servir. Dailleurs la Somme n'est pas forte Et ne Monterait qu'a dix Ecus. Il faudrait que Vous Eussiés la Bonté De M'Envoyer Vôtre Lettre pour L'intendant De Caen Lieu De la Detention De Cet homme je me Charge De L'Envoyer Et D'En avoir Reponse. Je Vois avec plaisir s'aprocher Mon Cher Docteur Le tems De La petite Course que Vous M'avés fait Esperer a Sanois ou je Retourne Enfin Le Vingt Deux De Ce Mois sy Vous pouviés y Venir avec Monsieur Vôtre petit fils Dans L'Espace Du Vingt quatre au trante il fait Encore un assés Beau tems pour que la Campagne Vous offre quelques Agréemens Et Vous scavés Mon Cher Docteur Combien Vôtre presence me Rend heureuse. Recevés Les assurances De ma tendre Veneration Et De mon immuable attachement

LA CTESSE D'HOUDETOT

Je Vous prie D'Envoyer Votre Reponse Chez Moy a paris

Notation: La Cesse d'Houdetot 6 7bre. 1783.

---

and no passport, could not name the prison he had been in, and did not understand a word of French, he was thrown in jail, then transferred to Caen for examination by a judge. At first he was considered an imbecile, but the judge decided, without due process, that he had to be a thief, and ordered him imprisoned. Le Févre des Mars, who had exhausted his own attempts to help the *misérable*, assures Crèvecœur that Hammon is well-spoken and seems honest. Moreover, he has friends at Lorient, and if he could be released and his travel expenses provided, he could find a berth home.

6. Charles-François-Hyacinthe Esmangart (1736–1837): *DBF.* A month later, after the comtesse reminded him, BF complied with her request; that now-missing letter will be described in vol. 41.

From David Hartley

ALS: William L. Clements Library

My Dear friend   Hotel de Yorck Sept 7 1783

I beg of you not to forget your letter to Mr Fox:——[7] The purpose of my journey to England will be to do the best in my power for things & persons & particularly for my friends.—— If you have any other private letters, send them to me. I will deliver them. I hope likewise be personally charged with the answers. I am better this morning[8] and shall certainly set off very early tomorrow morning. Pray give my best compts to Mr & Mrs Jay & to Mr Willm Franklin. I wish you all health till I shall have the pleasure of seeing you again.

Your ever most affecte friend   D HARTLEY

To Dr Franklin &c &c &c

To David Hartley: Two Letters

(I) Copies: Library of Congress (two), William L. Clements Library, Massachusetts Historical Society; (II) Copies: Library of Congress (two), William L. Clements Library, Massachusetts Historical Society, Public Record Office

I.

My dear Friend,   Passy Septr. 7th. 1783

The enclosed Letters to you and to Mr. Fox[9] were written before I saw you yesterday. On my return home last night I found despatches from Congress which may remove the Difficulties

---

7. BF to Fox, Sept. 5; see BF's letter to Hartley of Sept. 6 and his letter (I) immediately below.

8. Hartley had started feeling ill on the evening of Sept. 5 and had been bled after meeting with the American commissioners the next day. See the annotation of BF to Hartley, Sept. 6.

9. Written on Sept. 6 and Sept. 5, respectively.

we were entangled with.[1] Mr. Adams will be here this Morning, when you will hear from us.

I am ever Yours sincerely   (signed) B. FRANKLIN

To David Hartley Esqr.

II.

My Dear Friend   Passy Septr. 7. 83.

Enclosed I send you an Extract of a Letter to me from the President of Congress[2] in which you will observe the moderate disposition of that Body towards the Loyalists with the Causes of Aggravation in the People's Resentments against them: I am always invariably Yours most sincerely

(signed) B. FRANKLIN

David Hartley Esqr.

The American Peace Commissioners to David Hartley

Copies: Massachussetts Historical Society, Library of Congress

Sir,   Passy 7th Septr. 1783

We have the honour of transmitting herewith enclosed an Extract of a Resolution of Congress of the 1. May last, which we have Just recd.[3]

1. The commissioners were undoubtedly discussing with Hartley their lack of a commission to conduct further negotiations. Boudinot's letter of June 16, informing them that a commission was forthcoming, had just arrived; see their letter to Hartley immediately below.

2. The penultimate paragraph of Boudinot to BF, June 18, beginning, "You will receive herewith a Number of our late News-Papers."

3. A resolution that ordered Livingston to prepare a commission and instructions for the commissioners to negotiate a commercial treaty with Great Britain. Boudinot enclosed it in his letter of June 16; see the headnote and annotation there.

JA lamented that the resolution had not been sent with Capt. Barney; its earlier arrival would have saved much anxiety. He now believed that he would have to spend another winter in Europe, both for negotiations with the British and for raising another loan in the Netherlands, and asked his wife and daughter to join him: JA to Abigail Adams, Sept. 7, 1783, in *Adams Correspondence*, V, 236–8.

You will perceive from it that we may daily expect a Commission in due Form, for the Purposes mentioned in it, and we assure you of our Readiness to enter upon the Business, whenever you may think proper.

We have the honor to be with great Respect & Esteem, Sir, Your most obt. & humble Servts

(signd) J ADAMS, B. FRANKLIN, J JAY

To D. Hartley Esqr

To Mary Hewson

ALS: Yale University Library

My dear Friend,   Passy, Sept. 7. 1783

I received your kind Letter of the 9th past.[4] I am glad that the little Books are pleasing to you and your Children, and that the Children improve by them. I send you herewith some more of them.[5] My Grandson Bache has been four Years at School at Geneva; and is but lately come home to me here. I find Reason to be satisfied with the Improvement he has made in his Learning. He translates common Latin readily into French: but his English has suffer'd for want of Use; tho' I think he would readily recover it if he were a while at your School at Cheam, and at the same time be going on with his Latin and Greek. You were once so kind as to offer to take him under your Care; would that be still convenient to you?[6] He is docile and of gentle Manners, ready to receive and follow good Advice, and will set no bad Example to your *other* Children. He gains every day upon my Affections.

I long much to see you & yours, and my other Friends in England, but I have not yet determin'd on the Journey. Our de-

4. Missing.
5. Probably more installments of Berquin's *L'ami des enfants;* see XXXIX, 67n, 504n.
6. BF and Hewson had been discussing this possibility for some time; see XXXVII, 471–2, 652–3; XXXVIII, 567.

finitive Treaty of Peace, being now sign'd, I have indeed less to confine me here, & might make a short Excursion without much Inconvenience: but short Days & Winter are coming on, and I think I can hardly undertake such an Expedition before the Spring of next Year.

With regard to the future Establishment of your Children, which you say you want to consult me about, I am still of Opinion that America will afford you more Chances of doing it well than England. All the means of good Education are plenty there, the general Manners more simple & pure, Temptations to Vice and Folly fewer, the Profits of Industry in Business as great and sure as in England; and there is one Advantage more which your Command of Money will give you there, I mean the laying out a Part of your Fortune in new Land, now to be had extreamly cheap, but which must be increas'd immensely in Value before your Children come of Age, by the rapid Population of the Country. If you should arrive there while I live, you know you may depend on every Assistance in my Power to afford you, and I think my Children will have a Pleasure too in serving their Father's Friend. I do not offer it as a Motive that you will be much esteem'd and respected there, for that you are & must be every where; but give me leave to flatter myself that my being made happier in my last Years by your Neighbourhood and Society, may be some Inducement to you.

I forwarded your Letter to Mr. Williams. Temple is always with me, being my Secretary. He presents his Respects to you. I have been lately ill with a Fit of the Gout, if that may indeed be called a Disease; I rather suspect it to be a Remedy; since I always find my Health & Vigour of Mind improv'd after the Fit is over. I am ever, my dear Friend, Yours most affectionately,   B FRANKLIN

PS. You say you are a little afraid that our Country is spoiled. Parts of it have indeed suffered by the War, those situated near the Sea; but the Body of the Country has not been much hurt; and the Fertility of our Soil, with the Industry of our People, now that the Commerce of all the World is open to us, will soon repair the Damages receiv'd, and introduce that Prosperity which we hope Providence intends for us, since it has so remarkably favour'd our Revolution.

Mrs Hewson

Endorsed: B F Sept. 7 — 83 42

From the Comte d'Angiviller[7]

AL: American Philosophical Society

ce 7 7bre. 1783.

M. D'angiviller est bien flatté de pouvoir procurer à Monsieur francklin la facilité de voir plus commodement les beautés du sallon. Il doit prendre interêt au succès des arts, ils sont faits principalement pour consacrer à la posterité les hommes et les actions illustres et celebres,[8] monsieur francklin a bien quel ques droits sur eux. Mr. D'angiviller a bien du plaisir à reconnoitre ceux qu'il a à la profonde vénération de tous les hommes qui attachent un prix à la vertu active et au merite utile. Il a l'honneur de luy en offrir l'hommage./.

Notation: D'Angivilliers 7. 7bre. 1783.

---

7. Director of royal buildings, gardens, and manufactures, the comte d'Angiviller was also the director of the Académie royale de peinture et de sculpture: XXXV, 529n; *DBF.*

8. D'Angiviller actively (or as his critics argued, authoritatively) promoted this aesthetic program as director of the Académie; in particular, he commissioned statues and paintings of great men and significant actions that treated French history with the grandeur usually reserved for classical subjects: Jacques Silvestre de Sacy, *Le Comte d'Angiviller: dernier Directeur Général des Bâtiments du Roi* ([Paris], 1953), pp. 100–14; Francis H. Dowley, "D'Angiviller's *Grand Hommes* and the Significant Moment," *Art Bulletin,* XXXIX (1957), 259–77; Thomas E. Crow, *Painters and Public Life in Eighteenth-Century Paris* (New Haven and London, 1985), pp. 189–92. This kind of history painting dominated the Salon of 1783: *Jour. de Paris,* Sept. 15, 1783.

From the Marquis de Castries

LS: Library of Congress

Versailles Le 7 Septembre 1783.

J'ai l'Honneur, Monsieur, de vous envoyer les pieces qui m'ont été adressées par M.M. De Bellecombe et De Bongars Commandant et Intendant à St. Domingue,[9] relativement à la prise du Bateau le St. Thomas, arrêté sous Pavillon Danois par le Corsaire Américain la Lady Gréen, dans le mois de février de l'année derniere, et conduit au Port de jérémie où il a été vendu.[1]

Les administrateurs de St. Domingue ont ordonné provisoirement que le produit de ce Bateau Seroit déposé entre les mains du Trésorier de la Colonie, et ils pensent qu'il Seroit juste d'en faire la remise au Né. [Négotiant?] Moreau qui avoit obtenu la permission d'acheter ce Bateau à la Jamaïque, et de le faire naviguer sous Pavillon neutre, pour le récompenser du Zêle et de l'intelligence avec laquelle il a rempli les différentes missions secretes dont il a été chargé pendant la guerre.

Je vous prie, Monsieur, de me faire connoitre si la procédure qui a été faite par les officiers de L'amirauté de jérémie vous est parvenue.[2]

J'ai l'honneur d'être avec la considération la plus distinguée, Monsieur, votre très humble et très obéissant serviteur.

LE MAL. DE CASTRIES

M. Franklin.

Prises. Envoi des Pieces relatives à la prise du Bateau le st. Thomas par le Corsaire américain la Ladi Gréen / 4. Pieces.[3]

---

9. Bellecombe and Bongars were listed as *gouverneur général* and *intendant* of the French Windward Islands in the *Almanach royal* for 1783, pp. 170–1. Pierre-Guillaume-Léonard Sarrazin de Bellecombe (1715–1796) remained in Saint-Domingue until 1788: Larousse.

1. As Capt. Smith, commander of the *Lady Greene*, had told BF in 1782: XXXVII, 456–7.

2. Smith had sent BF an English translation of the Admiralty Court's judgment with the letter cited above.

3. The enclosures have not been located.

From Benjamin West ALS: American Philosophical Society

Dear Sir London. Sepr. 7th. 1783—

I could not deprive myself the pleasure of convaying these few lines to you by my friend Mr. Dagge,[4] he means to see you, and has been so Obliging to promis he would give this letter to you; I told him the jurney he was about to take, I almost envyed, as I should be happy to see you once more; Your friends hear have been flattering themselves with the pleasing expectation of seeing you once more among them on the return of pice; And altho they have been disappointed in that pleasure, are still loth to relinquish the pleasing thought and live in expectation of that indulgenc at some future period—. I shall be happy to hear from you, and that you are in health— My Dear Betsey[5] desires to be kindly remembered to you, her health is much as usual, my Eldest son is well, I bring him up to my Profession he has great Abilities. My Youngest son (your Godson) I have at school, what will be his lot in life is not yet determined—he is in health—and upon the whole, they are promising Boys.[6] Mr and Mrs. Aufrere of Chelsea have ever retained you in their good wishes and esteem, and desired when I last saw them, that whenever I wrote to you, their names might be mentioned, they are worthy people, and I have the greatest esteem for them.[7] My Eldest son desires to be remembered to your grandson, his old

4. Henry Dagge, a member with BF of the Walpole Company and its legal representative; see, for example, XVI, 166–7; XXII, 102.

5. His wife, the former Elizabeth Shewell: XII, 43n.

6. Raphael Lamar West was 17; Benjamin West, Jr., BF's godson, was 11: XIX, 274; XXXIII, xxviii; Robert C. Alberts, *Benjamin West: a Biography* (Boston, 1978), p. 72.

7. George Aufrere, a wealthy London merchant and banker (*ODNB*), was for many years the partner of BF's banker and friend John Sargent. In the early 1760s their firm handled financial affairs for Pennsylvania: IX, 359n, and X, *passim*. Aufrere and his wife, Arabella Bate, knew BF well and owned a portrait of him: David Hancock, *Citizens of the World* (Cambridge and New York, 1995), pp. 99, 100, 314; Sellers, *Franklin in Portraiture*, pp. 333–4, 336–8; Namier and Brooke, *House of Commons*, II, 34. For portraits and busts of George and Arabella Aufrere see Hancock, *Citizens of the World*, pp. 72, 78, 365, 366.

Schoolmate,[8] and flatters himself with the pleasure of seeing him in Paris in a year or two more, my compliments likewise to him.— And be Assured I am, with the greatest respect and esteem—Dear Sir Your Obliged and Obedient Humble Servent

BENJN. WEST

Dr. Benjamin Franklin—

From Richard Bache

ALS: American Philosophical Society

Dear & Hond. Sir Philadelphia Septr. 8. 1783.

The inclosed Packet directed for yourself I received a few days ago, from Cape Francois; the other Packet for the Compte de Barbençon, Mr. Bartram requested me to forward to your care—[9] We have had several Arrivals lately from France, without the pleasure of a Line from you, Mr. Williams writes me however that you are well; we would rather have this information under your own hand & Seal, but we content ourselves with supposing that it is business that deprives us the pleasure of hearing from you, as often as we could wish—

Sally and the Children are in perfect good health. The Season has been rather sickly, more frequent & sudden changes from hot to Cold were never known in America, these have produced

---

8. Raphael must have attended James Elphinston's boarding school in Kensington, where WTF was a student until February, 1775: XIII, 443.

9. With BF, WTF, and RB serving as intermediaries, the comte de Barbançon had received boxes of seeds of North American plants and trees from Bartram in 1782: XXXVII, 11–12n, 168n, 230. This packet from Bartram probably contained his printed broadside "Catalogue of American Trees, Shrubs and Herbacious Plants, most of which are now growing, and produce ripe Seed in John Bartram's Garden, near Philadelphia." BF had that broadside reprinted in Paris, with the title line translated into French, the common English names eliminated, and the date "1783" added. One example of the French reprint survives (APS); see Gilbert Chinard, "Recently Acquired Botanical Documents," APS *Proc.*, CI (1957), 520–22. For Bartram's original see Joel T. Fry, "Bartram's Garden Catalogue of North American Plants, 1783," *Jour. of Garden History*, XVI (1996), 1–66.

fevers of various sorts, which have carried off a great number of People—[1]

Mr. Jos: Turner & Mr. Hamilton[2] have slipped off, but they had been invalids for some time preceding their death— Notwithstanding the mortality of the Season, our numbers have increased in a most astonishing degree; such an influx of Foreigners from every Country in Europe, exceeds every expectation;—in short our City is as full as it can hold.

I herewith send you the News papers, and remain Dear sir Your affectionate Son   RICH BACHE

Dr. Franklin

From Charles Jackson[3]   AL: American Philosophical Society

Septemr. 8. 1783

The unfortunate Chas. Jackson whom his kind Friend Dr. Franklin Remembered one of the happiest of Mortals when possessed of the dearest most amiable lovely & best beloved of Women, now full at heart with sorrowful Reflection on his Loss, yet full of regard & esteem likewise for his real Friend, gladly

---

1. On Sept. 16 Benjamin Rush attributed what he called an epidemic of scarlet fever to the "crowds of strangers which our commerce has invited to our city," as well as other unnamed "circumstances." The Baron de Beelen-Bertholff, writing the following summer about how unhealthy Philadelphia was, reported that illnesses in August, 1783 (just before he arrived), claimed the lives of up to 30 people a day: L. H. Butterfield, ed., *Letters of Benjamin Rush* (2 vols., Princeton, 1951), I, 311; Hanns Schlitter, ed., *Die Berichte des ersten Agenten Österreichs in den Vereinigten Staaten von Amerika Baron de Beelen-Bertholff* . . . (Vienna, 1891), p. 330. See also Elaine F. Crane *et al.*, eds., *The Diary of Elizabeth Drinker* (3 vols., Boston, 1991), I, 413–15, where Drinker notes the symptoms of many members of her household who fell ill during September with what doctors were calling "the fall Fever." None of these cases was fatal.

2. Joseph Turner (II, 154n; XVIII, 217n) and James Hamilton (III, 327–8n). Hamilton died on Aug. 14, after battling cancer (*DAB*).

3. Who had sent his regards to BF in June, through Nathaniel Falconer; see Falconer to BF, June 7.

embraces the opportunity this moment afforded him of sending his most sincere & affectionate Respects to dear Dr. Franklin, by the hand of their mutual Friend—

Addressed: Benjamin Franklin Esqr. / Paris.

From Neufville & Cie.   L: American Philosophical Society

Sir   Amsterdam 8th. Sepr. 1783
    His Excellency John Jay Esqr. having given us his address at passy, we beg leave to put a letter under Your Excellencys Cover, requesting in case said Gentleman Should be moved from thence, you Will please to cause it to be forwarded, and as we Have not had the honour of addressing you since the Change of the firm of our House we pray you to observe that it is now De Neufville & Compy. the Signature of Which is given by procuratn. as at foot to Messrs Rolland & Compy.[4] to which we have only to add the respectful Sentiments with Which we have the honour to be your Excellency's Most Obedient Humble servants   By procuratn. of Messrs. De Neufville & Compy.
                ROLLAND & COMPE

His Excellency Dr. B Franklin Minister plenipo: at the Court of Versailles Passy

Notation: Neufville & Compy. Amsterdam 8th. Septr. 1783

4. In May, 1783, Leendert de Neufville (who took charge of the family firm after his father Jean retired in June, 1782: XXXVII, 572–3) was forced to seek protection from creditors. While the son went to America hoping to collect payments due, the father reorganized the firm under his own name, making an agreement with Rolland & Cie. to settle its affairs. Jean Rolland, the leading partner, became a partner of Neufville & Cie. in September, 1784: Pieter J. van Winter, *American Finance and Dutch Investment, 1780–1805* . . . (2 vols., New York, 1977), I, 150, 194.

From Richard Bache

ALS: American Philosophical Society

Dear & Hond: Sir   Philadelphia Sept. 9th. 1783.

I did myself this pleasure yesterday; and late last Evening, the Washington packet brought us your acceptable favor of the 27th. July, with several pleasing inclosures from Benny, whom you had with you at Passy, a circumstance, he seems much to be delighted with—

Mr. Vaughan, (your old Friend) and his family arrived here yesterday,[5] they have taken up lodgings with us 'till they can be better accommodated; they send their respectfull Compliments— As this Vessel is just pushing off, I have only time to say—that the Apples, Nuts &c. shall be sent you this fall via Havre, if such an opportunity should present— I have got your Library home;[6] the Types you sold to the Lancaster Man are paid for, those sold to Virginia are yet unpaid, and indeed I am at a loss what to demand for them, as they were sent away without being weighed on account of the hurry & confusion we were in at that time, you can probably recollect what they cost you, & let me know what you suppose their real value at the time they were spared to the State, a Bill from under your own hand, would I am certain, obtain a speedier payment, than any thing I could exhibit.[7]

Sally is so occupied with her new friends that she has not time to write,[8] nor have I time to add more than with Love to Temple & Ben I remain ever Dear sir Your affectionate Son

RICH: BACHE

I sent the News papers Yesterday Via L'Orient

---

5. They sailed on July 9: William Vaughan to WTF, Aug. 8, 1783, APS. For the family's preparations see Samuel Vaughan to BF, June 14.

6. According to RB's "Day Book," the books were brought back from Bethlehem on June 4: Penrose R. Hoopes, "Cash Dr to Benjamin Franklin," *PMHB*, LXXX (1956), 63.

7. We cannot trace any type BF sold to a Lancaster printer, nor does RB's "Day Book" record any payment for it. For the type sold to Virginia see XXIX, 598–9; XXX, 363–4.

8. On the contrary: her letter of the same date is below.

Addressed: His Excellency / Dr. Benjamin Franklin / Minister Plenipoy. from the United / States of No: America at / Passy—

From Sarah Bache

ALS: American Philosophical Society

Dear & Honoured Sir   Philadelphia Sept 9 1783

Your Friends the Vaughan Family are now under our roof, the pleasure we take in entertaining every body that you love and that loves you, make us happy in their Company, they are come to settle among us, and what little I have seen of them promise a very agreable addition to our Society— My letter to day on their account will rather be short as I have a good deal to attend to, my dear Nephew on this account will excuse me by this Vessel, we shall shortly have an opportunity by which I will write Longly, being as ever Your Afectionate Daughter

S BACHE

Addressed: Dr. Franklin / Passy

From Bariatinskii

L: American Philosophical Society

Mardy 9. 7bre. 1783./.

Le Prince Bariatinskoy a l'honneur de remercier Monsieur franklein de la communication, qu'il a bien voulû Lui faire du Traite de Paix.[9]

Notation: Bariatinskoy 9. 7bre 1783—

9. The next day, Bariatinskii sent Empress Catherine II two gifts from BF: a *Libertas Americana* medal with its explanation (XXXIX, 549–55) and a copy of *Constitutions des treize Etats-Unis de l'Amérique.* Nina N. Bashkina *et al.,* eds., *The United States and Russia: the Beginning of Relations, 1765–1815* ([Washington, D.C., 1980]), p. 209.

From Elias Boudinot

AL (draft):[1] Princeton University Library; copy: National Archives

Sir   Philada. 9. Sept. 1783

Being by Accident at this City and an Opportunity offering, I do myself the Honor of enclosing a duplicate of the Ratification of the Treaty with Sweden, the original of which I transmitted some time since,[2] but not having the Copy of the Letter attending it by me, I am prevented from sending duplicate of it, unless this Opportunity is risqued.

I am happy to enclose you some Resolutions of the Assembly of P. [Pennsylvania] by which you will see that all the difficulties that arose on Acct of the Mutiny have happily subsided, without producing the least ill Consequences.[3]

The Soldiers were very penitent & two of the Serjeants are now under Sentence of Death but I believe will be pardoned by Congress on Acct of the Means used by Capt Carberry & Lieut Sullivan to induce these poor wretches to behave as they did under Expectations of great personal Advantages—[4] I hope these two Officers will meet with proper detestation by all good Men—

The Honble Benjamin Franklin, Minister &c. Paris

1. The dateline and esquire line were added by the secretary who made the letterbook copy (National Archives).

2. On Aug. 15.

3. Three resolutions of Aug. 29 encouraging the Continental Congress to return to Philadelphia: *JCC*, XXV, 530–1. Congress, however, remained in Princeton until early November and then moved to Annapolis: *Morris Papers*, VIII, 662–8.

4. Sergeants John Morrison and Christian Nagle, who had been condemned to death, and four soldiers, who had been sentenced to be flogged, were pardoned by Congress on Sept. 13: *Morris Papers*, VIII, 226, 235n; *JCC*, XXV, 565–6. For Carbery and Sullivan, who fled to England, see Boudinot's July 15 letter and Laurens' Aug. 9 letter.

From Pierres

ALS: American Philosophical Society

Monsieur,   le 9 7bre. 1783.

J'ai l'honneur de vous envoyer la Copie du Traité, la Composition est faite & l'Epreuve est à moitié lüe.[5]

Je vous fais passer par le porteur[6]

	1. arithmetique . . .	2. *l.t.*	15.
Bezout	1. Géométrie . . .	3.	15.
	1. algébre . . .	4.	15.
	1. Mécanique 2 vol.	9.	10.
		20.	15.

Il n'y a pas actuellement de *Navigation* du même auteur, parce qu'il est à la campagne.

Je suis avec un respect infini, Monsieur, Votre très humble & Très obeissant serviteur   PIERRES

Le Porteur a payé.

Notation: Pierre le 9. 7bre. 1783

---

5. Pierres' printing of *The Definitive Treaty between Great Britain, and the United States of America, Signed at Paris, the 3d day of September 1783,* was not issued until *c.* Sept. 27. The title page is reproduced as the frontispiece to this volume, but the publication itself will be discussed in vol. 41. See also Luther S. Livingston, *Franklin and His Press at Passy* (New York, 1914), pp. 188–90.

6. BF had evidently ordered Pierres' recent edition of Etienne Bézout's popular *Cours de mathématiques à l'usage des gardes du pavillon et de la marine,* which consisted of five parts. The first four, listed here, were reprinted by Pierres in 1781–82: "Elémens d'arithmétique," "Elémens de géométrie . . . ," "L'algèbre . . . ," and "Principes généraux de la méchanique . . . ." The fifth part, "Traité de navigation," did not appear until 1784.

Bézout (XXIV, 142; XXXIII, 49n) died on Sept. 27, 1783. BF's set of these volumes has not been located, but his copy of Bézout's *Théorie générale des équations algébriques* (Paris, 1779) is at the APS: Wolf and Hayes, *Library of Benjamin Franklin,* p. 128.

The American Peace Commissioners to Elias Boudinot

LS[7] and press copy of LS: National Archives; copies: Library of Congress, Massachusetts Historical Society

Sir,   Passy, 10th. Septr. 1783.

On the third Instant, Definitive Treaties were concluded, between all the late belligerent Powers, except the Dutch, who the Day before settled and signed Preliminary Articles of Peace with Britain.

We most sincerely & cordially congratulate Congress and our Country in general, on this happy Event, and we hope that the same kind Providence which has led us thro' a vigorous War, to an honorable Peace, will enable us to make a wise & moderate Use of that inestimable Blessing.

We have committed a Duplicate Original of the Treaty to the Care of Mr. Thaxter, who will go immediately to L'Orient, whence he will sail in the French Packet to New-York. That Gentleman left America with Mr. Adams as his Private Secretary, and his Conduct having been perfectly satisfactory to that Minister, we join in recommending him to the Attention of Congress. We have orderd Mr. Grand to pay him one hundred and thirty Louis d'ors, on account of the reasonable Expences to be incurr'd by his Mission to Congress, and his Journey from thence to his Family at Hingham in the Massachusetts Bay.[8] For the Disposition of the Money he is to account.

The Definitive Treaty being in the Terms of the Provisional Articles, and not comprehending any of the Objects of our subsequent Negociations, it is proper that we give a summary Account of them.

When Mr Hartley arrived here he brought with him only a set of Instructions signed by the King. We objected to proceeding with him until he should have a Commission in Form. This occasioned some Delay—a proper Commission was however transmitted to him, a Copy of which was shortley after sent to Mr. Livingston.

---

7. In WTF's hand.

8. The payment is recorded in Account XXVII (XXXII, 4) under the date of Sept. 12.

We having been instructed to obtain if possible an Article for a Direct Trade to the West Indies, made to Mr. Hartley the Proposition No 1.[9]

He approved of it greatly and recommended it to his Court, but they declined assenting to it.

Mr. Hartley then made us the Proposition No 2.[1] but on being asked whether he was authorised to sign it, in Case we agreed to it, he answer'd in the Negative. We therefore thought it improper to proceed to the Consideration of it until after he should have obtained the Consent of his Court to it.— We also desired to be informed whether his Court would or would not comprehend Ireland in their Stipulations with us.

The British Cabinet would not adopt Mr Hartley's Propositions but their Letters to him were calculated to inspire us with Expectations, that as nothing but particular local Circumstances, which would probably not be of long duration, restrained them from preferring the most liberal System of Commerce with us, the Ministry would take the earliest Opportunity of gratifying their own Wishes as well as ours, on that Subject.—

Mr Hartley then made us the Proposition No 3.[2] At this Time we were informed that Letters for us had arrived in France from Philada. We expected to receive Instructions in them, and told Mr. Hartley that this Expectation induced us to postpone giving him an Answer for a few Days.

The Vessel by which we had expected these Letters, it seems had not brought any for us. But at that Time Information arrived from America, that our Ports were all opened to British Vessels. Mr Hartley thereupon did not think himself at Liberty to proceed, until after he should communicate that Intelligence to his Court and receive their further Instructions.

Those further Instructions never came, and thus our Endeavours as to commercial Regulations, proved fruitless. We had many Conferences & recd. long Memorials from Mr Hartley on

9. The first article that the commissioners presented on April 29: XXXIX, 524–5. For Livingston's instructions and the congressional resolution on this issue see XXXVIII, 71–2, 537n.

1. Above, [May 19].

2. Hartley's revised article of June [14–18], above.

the Subject; but his Zeal for Systems friendly to us, constantly exceeded his Authority to concert and agree to them.

During the long Interval of his expecting Instructions, for his Expectations were permitted to exist almost to the last, we proceeded to make & receive Propositions for perfecting the definitive Treaty. Details of all the Amendments, Alterations, Objections, Exceptions &ca. which occurr'd in the Course of these Discussions would be Voluminous. We finally agreed that he should send to his Court, the Project or Draft of a Treaty No 4.[3] He did so, but after much Time, and when pressed by France, who insisted that we should all conclude together, He was instructed to sign a Definitive Treaty in the Terms of the Provisional Articles.

Whether the British Court meant to avoid a Definitive Treaty with us, thro' a vain Hope from the exagerated Accounts of Divisions among our People, and Want of Authority in Congress, that some Revolution might soon happen in their Favour; or whether their dilatory Conduct was caused by the Strife of the two opposite and nearly equal Parties in the Cabinet is hard to decide.—

Your Excellency will observe, that the Treaty was signed at Paris & not at Versailles. Mr Hartley's Letter No. 5, & our Answer No 6. will explain this.[4] His Objections, and indeed our Proceedings in general, were communicated to the French Minister, who was content that we should acquiesce, but desired that we would appoint the signing early in the Morning, and give him an Account of it at Versailles by Express, for that he would not proceed to sign on the Part of France, 'till he was sure that our Business was done.

The Day after the Signature of the Treaty, Mr. Hartley wrote us a Congratulatory Letter No 7. to which we returned the Answer No. 8.[5]

He is gone to England, and expects soon to return—which for our Parts we think uncertain. We have taken Care to speak to him in strong Terms, on the Subject of the Evacuation of New-

3. Summarized above, [Aug. 6].
4. Hartley's of Aug. 29 and the commissioners' reply of Aug. 30.
5. Hartley's of Sept. 4 and their reply of Sept. 5.

York, and the other important Subjects proper to be mentioned to him.— We think we may rely on his doing every thing in his Power to influence his Court, to do what they ought to do, but it does not appear that they have as yet formed any settled System for their Conduct relative to the United States.— We cannot but think that the late & present Aspect of Affairs in America has had, and continues to have, an unfavourable Influence, not only in Britain but throughout Europe.

In whatever Light the Article respecting the Tories may be reciev'd in America, it is consider'd in Europe as very humiliating to Britain, and therefore as being one which we ought in Honour to perform and fulfil with the most scrupulous Regard to good Faith, & in a manner least Offensive to the Feelings of the King and Court of G. Britain, who upon that Point are extremely tender.

The unseasonable and unnecessary Resolves of various Towns on this Subject, the actual Expulsion of Tories from some Places, and the avow'd Implacability of almost all who have published their Sentiments about the Matter, are Circumstances which are construed, not only to the Prejudice of our national Magnanimity and good Faith, but also to the Prejudice of our Government.[6]

Popular Committees are consider'd here as with us, in the Light of Substitutes to constitutional Government, and as being only necessary in the Interval between the Removal of the former and the Establishment of the present.

The Constitutions of the different States have been translated & published, & Pains have been taken to lead Europe to believe, that the American States not only made their own Laws, but obey'd them. But the continuance of popular Assemblies conven'd expressly to deliberate on Matters proper only for the

6. Since March, opposition to Article 5 of the preliminary treaty had found expression in newspaper editorials and local public meetings throughout the United States. Some of these meetings issued resolutions banning Loyalists from their town or state and petitioned elected officials to pass anti-Loyalist legislation: Roberta Tansman Jacobs, "The Treaty and the Tories: the Ideological Reaction to the Return of the Loyalists, 1783–1789" (Ph.D. diss., Cornell University, 1974), pp. 71–9.

Cognizance of the different Legislatures & Officers of Government, and their proceeding not only to ordain, but to enforce their Resolutions, has exceedingly lessen'd the Dignity of the States in the Eyes of these Nations.

To this we may also add, that the Situation of the Army, the Reluctance of the People to pay Taxes, and the Circumstances under which Congress removed from Philadelphia,[7] have diminish'd the Admiration in which the People of America were held among the Nations of Europe, & somewhat abated their Ardor for forming Connections with us, before our Affairs acquire a greater Degree of order & Consistance.

Permit us to observe, that in our Opinion the Recommendation of Congress, promised in the 5th. Article, should immediately be made in the Terms of it and published; and that the States should be requested to take it into Consideration as soon as the Evacuation by the Enemy shall be compleated. It is also much to be wished that the Legislatures may not involve all the Tories in Banishment and Ruin, but that such Discriminations may be made, as to entitle the Decisions to the Approbation of disinterested Men, and dispassionate Posterity.

On the 7th. Inst. we received your Excellency's Letter of the 16th. June last, covering a Resolution of Congress of the 1st May directing a Commission to us for making a Treaty of Commerce &ca with G. Britain. This Intelligence arrived very opportunely to prevent the Anti-American Party from ascribing any Delays on our Part to Motives of Resentment in England to that Country. Great Britain will send a Minister to Congress as soon as Congress shall send a Minister to Britain, & we think much Good might result from that Measure.

The Information of Mr Dumas, that we encouraged the Idea of entering into Engagements with the Dutch to defend the Freedom of Trade, was not well founded.—[8] Our Sentiments on that Subject exactly correspond with those of Congress; nor did we even think or pretend that we had Authority to adopt any such Measures.

7. See Boudinot to the Commissioners, July 15.
8. See Livingston to the Commissioners, May 31, and their reply of July 27.

We have Reason to think that the Emperor and Russia, & other Commercial Nations, are ready to make Treaties of Commerce with the United States. Perhaps it might not be improper for Congress to direct that their Disposition on the Subject, be communicated to those Courts, & thereby prepare the Way for such Treaties.

The Emperor of Morrocco has manifested a very friendly Disposition towards us: He expects and is ready to receive a Minister from us, and as he may either change his Mind, or may be succeeded by a Prince differently disposed, a Treaty with him may be of Importance. Our Trade to the Mediterranean will not be inconsiderable, and the Friendship of Morrocco, Algiers, Tunis & Tripoli, may become very interesting, in case the Russians should succeed in their Endeavours to Navigate freely into it by Constantinople.[9]

Much we think will depend on the Success of our Negociations with England. If she should be prevailed upon to agree to a liberal System of Commerce, France & perhaps some other Nations, will follow her Example; but if she should prefer an exclusive monopolizing Plan, it is probable that her Neighbours will continue to adhere to their favorite Restrictions.

Were it certain that the United States, could be brought to act as a Nation, and would jointly and fairly conduct their Commerce on Principles of exact Reciprocity with all Nations, we think it probable that Britain would make extensive Concessions—but on the Contrary, while the Prospect of Disunion in our Councils, or want of Power and Energy in our Executive Departments exist, they will not be apprehensive of Retaliation, and consequently lose their principal Motive to Liberality. Unless with respect to all foreign Nations and Transactions, we uniformly act as an entire united Nation, faithfully executing and obeying the Constitutional Acts of Congress on those Subjects, we shall soon find ourselves in the Situation in which all Europe wishes to see us, Vizt. as unimportant Consumers of

9. It was widely feared that Russia's annexation of the Crimea on April 8 would lead to a war with the Turks in which the Russians would seize Constantinople and partition the Ottoman Empire: Alan W. Fisher, *The Russian Annexation of the Crimea, 1772–1783* (Cambridge, 1970), pp. 135–7.

her Manufactures & Productions, and as useful Labourers to furnish her with raw Materials.

We beg leave to assure Congress that we shall apply our best Endeavours to execute this new Commission to their Satisfaction, & shall punctually obey such Instructions as they may be pleased to give us relative to it.— Unless Congress should have nominated a Secretary to that Commission, we shall consider ourselves at Liberty to appoint One; and as we are satisfied with the Conduct of Mr Franklin, the Secretary to our late Commission, we purpose to appoint him, leaving it to Congress to make him such Compensation for his Services as they may Judge proper.

Count de Vergennes communicated to us a Proposition[1] (Viz No 9 herewith inclosed) for explaining the 2d & 3d Articles of our Treaty with France, in a manner different from the Sense in which we understand them. This being a Matter in which we had no Right to interfere, we have not express'd any Opinion about it to the Court. With great Respect, We have the honor to be, Sir, Your Excellency's most obedient & most humble Serts.

JOHN ADAMS.
B FRANKLIN
JOHN JAY

To his Excellency Elias Boudinot Esqr: President of Congress.

To John Adams

LS:[2] Massachusetts Historical Society

Sir,   Passy, Sept. 10. 1783.

I have received a Letter from a very respectable Person in America,[3] containing the following Words, Viz

---

1. Above, [May 20].

2. In L'Air de Lamotte's hand.

3. Samuel Cooper. The only portion of that May 5 letter to have survived is the lengthy extract BF sent to Vergennes; see the extract and annotation in XXXIX, 561–3, and for further background see *Adams Papers*, XV, 289–90n. In the passage quoted below, BF condensed Cooper's open-

"It is confidently reported, propagated, and believed by some among us, that the Court of France was at bottom against our obtaining the Fishery and Territory in that great Extent in which both are secured to us by the Treaty; that our Minister at that Court favoured, or did not oppose this Design against us; and that it was entirely owing to the Firmness, Sagacity & Disinterestedness of Mr. Adams, with whom Mr. Jay united, that we have obtained those important Advantages."—

It is not my Purpose to dispute any Share of the Honour of that Treaty which the Friends of my Colleagues may be dispos'd to give them; but having now spent Fifty Years of my Life in public Offices and Trusts, and having still one Ambition left, that of carrying the Character of Fidelity at least, to the Grave with me, I cannot allow that I was behind any of them in Zeal and Faithfulness. I therefore think that I ought not to suffer an Accusation, which falls little short of Treason to my Country, to pass without Notice, when the Means of effectual Vindication are at hand. You, Sir, was a Witness of my Conduct in that affair. To you and my other Colleagues I appeal, by sending to each a similar Letter with this,[4] and I have no doubt of your Readiness to do a Brother Commissioner Justice, by Certificates that will entirely destroy the Effect of that Accusation. I have the honour to be, with much Esteem, Sir, Your most obedient & most humble Servant.   B. FRANKLIN

His Excelly. J. Adams Esqe.

Endorsed: Dr Franklin 10 Sept. 1783 concerning a Letter he recd from America.[5]

---

ing phrases: "It is then confidently whispered among us that Letters have been received from Paris, both in this State and at Philadelphia, which mention, that the Court of France . . . "

4. He sent nearly identical letters to John Jay (Columbia University Library) and Henry Laurens (S.C. Hist. Soc.). He wrote the one to Jay himself; the one to Laurens was copied by L'Air de Lamotte.

5. That same day, JA maligned BF in three more letters to America that warned against allowing the doctor to continue negotiating commercial treaties on his own, a situation "contrived by Vergennes on purpose to throw slights upon Jay and me, & to cheat you out of your Carrying Trade." BF had been "secretly contriving" to gain the exclusive manage-

From Jean Rousseaux[6]   ALS: American Philosophical Society

Monsieur Brest le 10 Septembre 1783—
Je metois fait l'honneur de vous Ecrire de dunkerque au Sujet de mes appointemant et part au prize que nous avons fait Sur vottre fregatte du Congre lexemton Cape. henry Jonson pour que vous ayé la Bonté de massister de quelque Chose Etant Sans aucune resource. Jesperre Monsieur que vous vouderez Bien massister je crois monsieur que je ne vous demande rin de ce que jay nay pas gagnié et que vous ette Trop Juste pour me faire pairdre cella. Jattant cette Bonte de vous.
Je vous prie de me faire lhoneur dune Reponse. Mon adresse est Chez Monsieur Rousseaux La Combe perre a Blaye.
Jay lhonneur dettre avec Respect Monsieur Votre tres heumble et tres obt. Servt. ROUSSEAUX

Je vous prie de ne me pas oublie je vous prié—

Addressed: A Monsieur / Monsieur Bayamain / frankellin Embasadeur / du Congré demeurant a / pasy pres paris / a Passy

Notation: Rousseaux 10. 7bre. 1783.

---

ment of the negotiations with Denmark and Portugal, as he had those with Sweden. He was "cunning, but very malicious to every Man and every Project, calculated for the public Good." Anyone who objected to his acting as sole plenipotentiary in these matters was "persecute[d] . . . with a Malice and Rancour that is astonishing." Indeed, JA professed himself astonished "that Jealousy Envy and Vanity could have gone such Lengths": JA to Elbridge Gerry, William Gordon, and James Warren, all of Sept. 10, in *Adams Papers*, XV, 276–7, 278–9, 280.

6. A sailor who had been twice captured while in the American service, the first time while serving under Capt. Henry Johnson on the *Lexington* in 1777. He and his father, Étienne Rousseaux Lacombe, with whom he was presently living (as he mentions here), had been sending appeals to BF since 1778; see, for example, XXVI, 147–8; XXVIII, 514–15, 636–7; and for his most recent letter, XXXVII, 69.

From Jacques-Etienne Montgolfier

L:[7] American Philosophical Society

By the second week in September, Etienne Montgolfier was ready to offer members of the Académie des sciences a preview of the balloon he had constructed.[8] He had been aided in this effort by Jean-Baptiste Réveillon, the wallpaper manufacturer, who put his expertise, ingenuity, and workforce at Montgolfier's disposal.[9] As the Ministry of Finance had now assumed the expense of the experiment,[1] it was arranged that the official demonstration would take place before the royal family at Versailles on September 19. The preliminary demonstration would be conducted in the courtyard of Réveillon's wallpaper manufactory on the rue de Montreuil.

This *montgolfière* was substantially redesigned and elaborately decorated. Weighing 1,000 pounds and constructed of three geometric segments, it was 70 feet tall, tapered at the nose and base, and swelled to 40 feet in diameter at its midsection. Having experimented with various kinds of coatings, Montgolfier and Réveillon rejected varnishes in favor of the original concept of taffeta lined with heavy paper. This time, however, rather than lining the balloon with two layers of paper, they placed the layers on either side of the cloth. With the outer layer of paper serving as his canvas, Réveillon sent into the sky a resplendent vision of gold ornaments against an azure field. The trial they conducted on the cloudless morning of September 11 went perfectly. Montgolfier immediately issued invitations to the members of the Académie des sciences for the next morning—providing, as the present example says, that the weather continued fair.

---

7. This generic invitation is in a secretarial hand. The address appears to have been written by Montgolfier.

8. The information in this headnote is from Gillispie, *Montgolfier Brothers*, pp. 36–9; Barthélemy Faujas de Saint-Fond, *Description des expériences de la machine aérostatique de MM. de Montgolfier . . .* (Paris, 1783), pp. 29–35.

9. Another important collaborator was the chemist and physicist Ami Argand. While working on the balloon, Argand was also honing his own invention, an improved oil lamp: John J. Wolfe, *Brandy, Balloons, & Lamps: Ami Argand, 1750–1803* (Carbondale and Edwardsville, Ill., 1999), pp. 2–7.

1. They did so when it became clear that the Académie des sciences would be overburdened.

Though Franklin returned an acceptance (the following document), there is no evidence that he attended. He would not have been the only person to stay away, given the unsettled weather.[2] The day dawned overcast, with intermittent light rain. Despite black clouds on the horizon, a crowd of academicians and other distinguished guests gathered in Réveillon's courtyard. The balloon filled magnificently, but strong winds and heavy rain arrived just as it began to ascend, carrying 500 pounds of weight. As Montgolfier and his assistants wrestled it back down, strips of waterlogged paper began detaching from the fabric. The members of the commission who were present wrote an encouraging *procès-verbal* on the spot, emphasizing that the failure of the experiment did not stem from defects in the invention itself.[3]

Monsieur   Ce Jeudy 11. 7bre. [1783]

M. De Montgolfier a l'honneur de vous prévenir que si le tems continue à être favorable, il se propose de faire demain vendredy entre huit et dix heures du matin rue de Montreuil, l'expérience de sa machine aerostatique, vous priant de vous rendre de bonne heure, la matinée etant le moment le plus convenable.

Addressed: A Monsieur / Monsieur Francklin / Ministre Plenipotentiaire / des Etats Unis de Lamerique / A Passy

To Montgolfier[4]   Copy: Musée de l'Air et de l'Espace

Passy 11 septembre 1783

Mr. Franklin remercie monsieur de Montgolfier de son attention et se rendra a l'heure prescripte pour voir l'experience a laquelle il veut bien l'inviter.

---

2. According to press reports, several invited guests and certain commissioners from the Académie des sciences did not attend, persuaded that "le temps étoit trop mauvais pour risquer d'elever en l'air cette grande machine": *Gaz. de Leyde*, Sept. 23, 1783 (sup.); *Mercure de France (Jour. politique de Bruxelles)* for Sept. 27, 1783, pp. 175–6. Le Roy must not have gone, as he did not sign the *procès-verbal*.
    3. The *procès-verbal* was signed by Cadet, Bossut, Brisson, Lavoisier, and Desmarest: Faujas de Saint-Fond, *Description*, pp. 35–6.
    4. See the preceding document.

To Josiah Quincy, Sr.[5]   ALS: American Philosophical Society

My dear Friend,   Passy, Sept. 11. 1783.——

Mr Storer told me not long since that you complain'd of my not writing to you.[6] You had reason; for I find among your Letters to me two unanswered, viz. those of May 25, and Dec. 17. 1781.[7] The Truth is, I have had too much Business to do for the Publick, and too little Help allow'd me; so that it became impossible for me to keep up my private Correspondencies. I promis'd myself more Leisure when the Definitive Treaty of Peace should be concluded: But that it seems is to be followed by a Treaty of Commerce, which will probably take up a good deal of Time & require much Attention. I seize this little Interim to sit down & have a little Chat with my Friends in America.——

I lament with you the many Mischiefs, the Injustices, the Corruption of Manners, &c &c that attended a depreciating Currency. It is some Consolation to me that I wash'd my Hands of that Evil by predicting it in Congress, and proposing Means that would have been effectual to prevent it if they had been adopted.[8] Subsequent Operations that I have executed, demonstrate that my Plan was practicable. But it was unfortunately rejected. Considering all our Mistakes and Mismanagements, it is wonderful we have finish'd our Affair so well, and so soon! Indeed I am wrong in using that Expression, *WE have finish'd our Affairs* so well. Our Blunders have been many, and they serve to manifest the Hand of Providence more clearly in our Favour; so that we may much more properly say, *These are* THY *Doings, O Lord, and they are marvellous in our Eyes!*——[9]

Mr. Storer, whom you recommended to me is now in England. He needed none of the Advice you desired me to give

5. This is BF's final letter to his old friend, who died the following March: *Adams Correspondence*, V, 305n.

6. The last letter of which we have a record is from 1779: XXIX, 358–9. Charles Storer, who had ceased duties as JA's secretary in July, was a correspondent of Quincy's: *Adams Correspondence*, V, ix, 148n.

7. Neither of which has been located.

8. BF detailed these in a 1779 letter to Samuel Cooper: XXIX, 355–6.

9. Psalms 118:23.

him. His Behaviour here was unexceptionable, and he gain'd the Esteem of all that knew him.—

The Epitaph on my dear and much esteemed young Friend, is too well written to be capable of Improvement by any Corrections of mine.— Your Moderation appears in it, since the natural Affection of a Parent has not induc'd you to exaggerate his Virtues. I shall always mourn his Loss with you; a Loss not easily made up to his Country.[1]

How differently constituted was his noble and generous Mind from that of the miserable Calumniators you mention! Having Plenty of Merit in himself, he was not jealous of the Appearance of Merit in others, but did Justice to their Characters with as much Pleasure as these People do Injury. It is now near two Years since your Friendship induc'd you to acquaint me with some of their Accusations. I guess'd easily at the Quarter from whence they came; but conscious of my Innocence, and unwilling to disturb public Operations by private Resentments or Contentions, I pass'd them over in Silence; and have not till within these few days taken the least Step towards my Vindication. Inform'd that the Practice of abusing me continues, and that some heavy Charges are lately made against me respecting my Conduct in the Treaty, written from Paris and propagated among you; I have demanded of all my Colleagues that they do me Justice, and I have no doubt of receiving it, from each of them.— I did not think it necessary to justify my self to you; by answering the Calumnies you mention'd. I knew you did not believe them. It was improbable that I should at this Distance combine with any body to urge the Redemption of the Paper on those unjust Terms, having no Interest in such Redemption. It was impossible that I should have traded with the Public Money, since I had not traded with any Money, either separately or jointly with any other Person, directly or indirectly to the Value of a Shilling, since my being in France. And the Fishery which it was said I had relinquished, had not then come in

1. Josiah Quincy, Jr. (XXI, 283n), an ardent young patriot who went to London in the winter of 1774–75 and got to know BF well, became ill in England and died on the return voyage: XXI, 513.

question, nor had I ever dropt a Syllable to that purpose in Word or Writing: but I was always firm in this Principle, that having had a common Right with the English to the Fisheries while connected with that Nation, and having contributed equally with our Blood and Treasure in conquering what had been gain'd from the French, we had an undoubted Right on breaking up our Partnership, to a fair Division.— As to the two Charges of Age and Weakness, I must confess the first; but I am not quite so clear in the latter; and perhaps my Adversaries may find that they presum'd a little too much upon it when they ventur'd to attack me.

But enough of these petty Personalities. I quit them to rejoice with you in the PEACE God has blest us with, and in the Prosperity it gives us a Prospect of. The Definitive Treaty was signed the third Instant. We are now Friends with England and with all Mankind. May we never see another War! for in my Opinion *there never was a good War, or a bad Peace.* Adieu, & believe me ever, my dear Friend, Yours most affectionately

B FRANKLIN

Honble. Josiah Quincey Esqe—

Notation: Dr. Franklin

From Dumas

AL (draft): Nationaal Archief

M,   La Haie 11e. 7br. 1783.

Me référant à celle que j'ai eu l'honr. de vous écrire le 25e. du passé, celle-ci est pour prendre la liberté de faire passer par vos mains l'incluse pour le Congrès, comme j'ai fait jusqu'ici par les mains de S.E. [Son Excellence] Mr. Adams pour celles que j'ai fait passer par la France, & comme je croirois devoir continuer de faire, si je ne craignois que quelque voyage de son côté, maintenant que la grande oeuvre est accomplie, n'exposât ma Lettre a être égarée ou du moins [*exposée*] à des retards & détours. Voulez-vous donc, Monsieur, avoir la bonté, s'il est encore à

SEPTEMBER 11, 1783

Paris, de la lui communiquer, après quoi, je voudrois qu'elle fût fermée & acheminée, soit par Mr. J. Thaxter, s'il peut encore la recevoir, ou par Mr. Barclai à l'Orient, ou par le Paquebot qui partira du Port-Louis vers la fin de ce mois, selon qu'il paroîtra le plus sûr & le plus expéditif.

J'aurois écrit à Mr. Thaxter en réponse à la Lettre amicale par laquelle il m'annonce son départ de Paris, fixé à 10 jours de la date de sa Lettre, qui est du 31e. Août. Mais comme je ne reçus sa dite Lettre que mardi 9e. peu avant le départ de la poste, j'ai craint d'écrire à pure perte.

J'écris par Amsterdam à Mr. L. R. Morris Secretaire au Département des E.U. pr. les affes. étrangeres, que je continuois de tirer sur V.E. [Votre Excellence] les 225 L. [Louis] d'or qui me sont alloués provisionnellement pr. ma subsistance annuelle,[2] en attendt. qu'il ait plu au Congrès de la rendre plus supportable. Je fais bien des voeux pour la continuation de votre bonne santé, & suis avec tout l'attachement respectueux qui vous est connu, De V.E. &ca

Paris à Son Exce. Mr. Franklin M.P [Ministre Plénipotentiaire]

From John Jay

AL (draft):[3] Columbia University Library

Sir   Passy 11 Septr. 1783

I have been favored with your Letter of Yesterday,[4] & will answer it explicitly—

I have no Reason whatever to believe that you was averse to our obtaining the full Extent of Boundary & Fishery secured to us by the Treaty.— Your Conduct respecting them throughout the Negociation indicated a strong & steady attachment to both those objects, & in my opinion promoted the attainment of them.

I remember that in a Conversation which Mr. de Rayneval,

2. See his letter of Aug. 25.
3. For the changes Jay made while drafting this letter see Morris, *Jay: Peace*, pp. 584–5.
4. Identical to the letter to JA of that date, above.

614

the first Secretary of Count De Vergennes, had with you and me, in the Summer of 1782, you contended for our full Right to the Fishery, and argued it on various Principles.

Your Letters to me when in Spain, considered our Territory as extending to the Missisippi, and expressed your opinion against ceding the Navigation of that River, in very strong and pointed Terms—[5]

In short Sir: I do not recollect the least Difference in Sentiment between us respecting the Boundaries or Fisheries.— On the contrary, we were unanimous and united in adhering to, and insisting on them—nor did I ever percieve the least Disposition in either of us, to recede from our Claims, or be satisfied with less than we obtained—

I have the Honor to be with great Respect & Esteem Sir Your most obedient and very hble Servt

His Exy Dr. Franklin—

To Dr. Franklin 11 Sepr. 1783 in ansr. to 10 Inst

From Madame Durey de Meinières

ALS: American Philosophical Society

aux Pavillons de chaillot Ce Vendredi 12. 7bre 1783
Une famille patriarchale, dont le mérite et la tendre union Vous causérent, Monsieur, il y a quelques jours un attendrissement, qui passa dans tous les Cœurs, Cette famille, disje, Se rassemble et dine aux Pavillons, dimanche prochain. Vous ajouteriés beaucoup, Monsieur, au bonheur de *my husband*,[6] et au mien Si Vous Vouliés nous faire le même honneur que Messieurs, Mesdames, et Mesdemoiselles de Guibert.[7] J'ose l'espérer, quoique Vous

---

5. See XXXIII, 357, and XXXIV, 315.

6. Jean-Baptiste-François Durey de Meinières: XXXII, 297n.

7. Possibly the family of the comte de Guibert, who invited BF to dine with him at the Invalides a month earlier; see Brongniart to BF, Aug. 13. His son Jacques-Antoine-Hippolyte (François-Apolline) (1743–1790),

nous ayés longtems oubliés. Mais on Court après Ses bienfaits, et Comme Vous avés bien Voulu me donner, de la meilleure grace du monde, les Constitutions américaines,[8] Vous Voudrés peutêtre bien encore en Venir recevoir mes remercimens, en attendant qu'un rhumatisme me permette de Vous les porter chez Vous, quand il ne me retiendra plus Courbée en deux. Je Vous écris en françois pour que Vous m'entendiés; Car je Crains d'écorcher maintenant Votre *tongue*, et de Vous être inintelligible, ou au moins désagréable quen m'en Servant or je ne Veux Vous paroitre ni l'une, ni l'autre, lorsque j'essaye de Vous engager à Voisiner cordialement dimanche prochain avec your most humble and most obedient Servant and friend

GUICHARD DE MEINIERES

To [Madame Durey de Meinières]

ALS: American Philosophical Society

Passy, Sept. 12. 83—

My Friend Made [Madame] Helvetius tells me that I do wrong to dine abroad, as it hurts my Health; and I much respect her Counsels: But I cannot resist the double Temptation you offer me of dining with you and with that amiable Family. So that if alive and well I shall certainly render my self on Sunday at the Pavilions of Chaillot, when I hope your Rhumatism will have left you, so as to permit your standing upright, that you may enjoy more Ease, and I more Pleasure in the greater Convenience of Embracing you. I hope also to find your good Husband well; for I respect and esteem you both, as all do who know you. Your English is better than you think it. I wish my French were equal to it.— My Heart however is good, and you have always a Place in it. B FRANKLIN

---

a celebrated officer and author best known for *Essai général de tactique* (London, 1772), was married to Louise-Alexandrine Boutinon de Courcelles (1758–1826), who became a novelist after her husband's death: *DBF*.

8. See their exchange of letters on Aug. 31.

From Peter Elmsly[9]

AL: American Philosophical Society

Paris 12 Septr. 1783.

Mr. Elmsly presents his respects to Dr. Franklin and Sends him the inclosed,[1] if the Dr. has any Parcel for England, that Mr E. Can take with him, He will be So good as send it to Mr Pissots[2] & great care Shall be taken of it. Mr E. has sent to Mr P. four parts of the Phil: Transact: from Sr. Joseph Banks for Dr Franklin,[3] they will be Sent him as Soon as the Bale arrives.

Addressed: Dr Franklin

Notation: Elmsey 12 Sept. 1783

From George Hobart[4]

AL: American Philosophical Society

Septr 12 1783. Hôtel de Chartres

Mr Hobarts Compliments wait upon Mr Franklin, not knowing where to find Mr Adams He takes the Liberty in Governor

---

9. The important London bookseller who specialized in the French trade: XXV, 91; *ODNB*.

1. Probably John Calder's letter of Aug. 28.

2. The Paris bookseller Noël-Jacques Pissot (1724?–1804) worked with his son Laurent-Noël and specialized in trade with England. He was Joseph Banks's preferred source for French books, and after the war handled the subscriptions to French journals for Banks as well as the king and queen of England: XXXV, 367n; Jean-Dominique Mellot and Elisabeth Queval, *Répertoire d'imprimeurs/libraires XVIe–XVIIIe siècle: état en 1995* (Paris, 1997); Neil Chambers, ed., *Scientific Correspondence of Sir Joseph Banks, 1765–1820* (6 vols., London, 2007), II, 143, 262.

3. See Banks to BF, Aug. 25. The four volumes must have been parts I and II of *Phil. Trans.*, LXXI (1781) and LXXII (1782). The last of these was issued in early August, 1783, and was the last volume BF had received when he next inquired about his subscription: *Gazetteer and New Daily Advertiser*, Aug. 6, 1783; BF to Banks, Aug. 21, 1784 (British Library).

4. Who traveled to France periodically and brought BF correspondence and printed matter from Thomas Pownall. He is identified in XXXV, 627, where we tentatively published an undated letter from him preceding his first fully dated letter. We now realize that the items Hobart mentioned there, which he was delivering on behalf of Pownall, are those to which

Pownalls Name to forward to him the Memorial address'd to the Sovereigns of America.[5] Governor Pownall is also very desirous of knowing whether his Letter & Power of Attorney was ever forwarded to Mr Bowdein and Doctor Cooper, for if they should have been lost, He will send Duplicates.[6]

Notation: Hobarts 12 7bre. 1783

From John Shaffer[7]

LS: American Philosophical Society

Monsieur De lhotel de la force ce 12 7bre. 1783

Je pris hier la liberté de vous écrire pour reclamer l'honneur de Votre protection, quoique je Sente bien que je ne l'a mérite

Pownall alerted BF on July 5, 1782 (XXXVII, 582–4), the letter that Hobart undoubtedly enclosed. Hobart's undated letter should therefore be ascribed to [after July 5, 1782].

5. *A Memorial Addressed to the Sovereigns of America* (London, 1783). Pownall told BF about his intention to write it in February, and it was published in June: XXXIX, 228; *Gazetteer and New Daily Advertiser,* June 20, 1783. On Oct. 6, when Pownall had still not heard from BF, he wrote to inquire whether he had received the pamphlet; Pownall mentioned having also sent a copy to "each of Your Colleagues" (APS). By the time Hobart wrote the present letter, he must have already conveyed BF's copy.

6. BF never answered Hobart, who wrote again two weeks later to ask about these letters to Bowdoin and Cooper (which Pownall had sent BF in February with a power of attorney: XXXIX, 228–9): Hobart to BF, Sept. 26, [1783], APS. In the Oct. 6 letter cited above, Pownall repeated the question, reminding BF of his promise to forward them in March.

7. The unscrupulous, dull-witted Philadelphian who had first seen the inside of a French jail two years earlier, when he imposed on BF for assistance. For his failed attempts to make a dishonest living see, in particular, XXXIV, 364n; XXXV, 440–2. As of 1783, he spells his name Schaffer; we continue to use his original spelling for consistency.

BF had no intention of forgiving the loan Shaffer received in 1781: XXXV, 620; XXXVI, 375–6. WTF tried to collect payment in the spring and summer of 1783, but the bills Shaffer gave him were all rejected: Shaffer to WTF, [before March 13] and March 13, 1783; comte Charles de Polignac to [WTF?], July 19, 1783; APS. In March (to judge by the letters just cited),

plus. Je vous ai instruit Sur le Sujet de ma Détention,[8] c'est une circonstance malheureuse qui m'a entrainé dans l'etat triste et déplorable ou je me trouve réduit, circonstance d'autant Malheureuse qu'on m'a depouillé de mon portefeuille dans lequel Se trouve un effet accepté par vous Monsieur, et plusieurs autres Sur les meilleures Maisons de Paris; et cela pour être Soupconné Seulement d'etre de la compagnie du Sr. St. iver: j'ai deja prouvé au ministere que je n'etois réellement pas Son associé, et une Seule parole de vous Monsieur, Suffit pour me rendre ma liberté. Si jeusse Suivi vos conseils, je ne Serois point aujourd'hui dans la triste situation ou je Suis reduit. Je me jette â vos genoux et vous Suplie en grace de vouloir bien vous intéresser à moi qui Suis plus malheureux que coupable, Si je ne mérite pas cette grace de vous Monsieur, aumoins que ma famille que vous con-

---

Shaffer had taken refuge in the Temple, a privileged enclosure providing immunity from the police and sanctuary to insolvent debtors (Hillairet, *Rues de Paris*, II, 547).

8. He did indeed, and at great length. The undated letter was written, as this is, by a Frenchman; in a postscript of his own, Shaffer explains that he is too "indisposed with the feaver" to write himself. The story he tells is as follows: the king exonerated him on July 30 and gave him a *sauf conduit*, whereupon he returned to his lodging at No. 5 rue des fossés Saint-Marcel, staying for about six weeks. During that time a certain "St. Iver"—a complete stranger—sought to rent a neighboring apartment, and Shaffer offered him a room in his own. On Aug. 25 a police inspector came to arrest Saint Iver and, to Shaffer's astonishment, arrested him as well. Saint Iver, it seems, had "borrowed" his name in connection with shady commercial dealings of which he was ignorant. Desperate to prove his innocence, he pleads for BF to intervene with the authorities. In his postscript, Shaffer promises that as soon as he is released from prison, "I will go to my Country you may depend upon it." Shaffer to BF, [Sept. 11, 1783], APS. As the case unfolded over the next several months, it would come to light that since 1782 Shaffer had been listed in the *Almanach royal* as the principal of a fictitious banking firm claiming an official link to the United States of America. (Shaffer denied knowledge of this.) Menier de Saint Yver, who tried to protect Shaffer while declaring his own innocence, told BF that he had known Shaffer since June, thereby contradicting the story Shaffer tells here: Menier de Saint Yver to BF, Nov. 28, 1783 (APS); BF to Vergennes, Jan. 17, 1784 (AAE).

noissez (Surtout Mr. Mulinberg mon frere membre du congrès[9]) vous interesse.

Vous pouvez croire qu'aussitôt mon élargissement je me rendrai dans le Sein de ma famille pour y goutter la douce Satisfaction qu'elle est capable de me procurer.

Que votre cœur compatissant pour l'humanité Se laisse encore une fois flechir à la vue des peines qui m'environnent de toutes parts, une Seule parole de Vous Monsieur Suffit pour me rendre ma liberté Si chere à tous les hommes. J'ose encore esperer tout indigne que je Suis de vos bontés que vous vous intéresserez à moi, ma reconnoissance en Sera éternelle et rien ne pourra jamais effacer de mon cœur le doux Souvenir de tenir ma liberté d'un protecteur aussi bienfaisant.

Je Suis très respectueusement Monsieur Votre très humble Et très obt. Serviteur   J. SCHAFFER

Daignez Monsieur mhonorer d'une reponce

To Elias Boudinot

LS,[1] press copy of LS, and transcript: National Archives; ALS (draft) and transcript: Library of Congress

Sir,   Passy, Septr. 13. 1783.
I received a few Days since the Private Letter your Excellency did me the honour of writing to me of the 18th. June. I regret with you the Resignation of the late Secretary. Your present Cares are encreased by it, and it will be difficult to find a Successor of equal Abilities.

We found no Difficulty in decyphering the Resolution of

---

9. Frederick Augustus Conrad Muhlenberg (1750–1801), an ordained Lutheran minister married to Shaffer's sister Catharine, entered politics partly owing to Shaffer's influence. He was elected in March, 1779, to serve out the term of Edward Biddle in the Continental Congress and was reelected in November of that year: *ANB;* Paul A. W. Wallace, *The Muhlenbergs of Pennsylvania* (Philadelphia, 1950), pp. 176–8.
1. In WTF's hand, with minor corrections by BF.

Congress. The Commissioners have taken Notice of it in our Public Letter.[2]

I am happy that both the Device and Workmanship of the Medal are approv'd with you, as they have the good Fortune to be by the best Judges on this side the Water. It has been esteem'd a well-timed as well as a well-merited Compliment here, and has had good Effects. Since the two first which you mention as received, I have sent by different Opportunities so many as that every Member of Congress might have One. I hope they are come safe to hand by this time.[3]

I wrote a long Letter to Mr. Livingston by Barney,[4] to which I beg leave to refer, inclosing a Copy.

We had before signing the Definitive Treaty received the Ratification of the Preliminary Articles by his Britannic Majesty, exchanged with us by Mr. Hartley for that of the Congress. I send herewith a Copy of the first & last Clauses.[5]

In a former Letter I mentioned the Volunteer Proceedings of a Merchant at Alicant towards obtaining a Treaty between us & the Emperor of Morocco. We have since receiv'd a Letter from a Person who says, as you will see by the Copy inclosed, that he is sent by the Emperor to be the Bearer of his Answer to the United States, & that he is arrived in Spain in his Way to Paris. He has not yet appear'd here, and we hardly know what Ansr. to give him. I hope the sending a Minister to that Court, as recommended in my last, has been taken into Consideration, or at least that some Instructions respecting that Nation have been sent to your Minister in Spain, who is better Situated than we are for such a Negotiation.[6]

The Minister from Denmark, often speaks to me about the

2. Above, Sept. 10.

3. By mid-September Boudinot had received and distributed about 20 *Libertas Americana* medals: Smith, *Letters*, XX, 675n.

4. Above, July 22[–26].

5. BF here drafted but deleted "the rest consisting merely of those Articles [*interlined:* word for word,] is omitted for the present; but may be".

6. See Crocco to BF, July 15, and BF to Livingston, July 22[–26]. The minister in Spain was acting chargé d'affaires William Carmichael.

proposed Treaty, of which a Copy went by Barney.[7] No Commission to sign it, nor any Instructions from Congress relating to it are yet arrived: And tho' press'd I have not ventur'd to do any thing farther in the Affair.

I forward herewith a Letter to the Congress from the City of Hamburgh.[8] I understand that a good Disposition towards us prevails there, which it may be well to encourage.

No Answer has yet been given me from the Court of Portugal, respecting the Plan of a Treaty concerted between its Ambassador here & me. He has been unwell and much in the Country, so that I have not seen him lately. I suspect that the false or exaggerated Reports of the distracted Situation of our Government, industriously propagated thro'out Europe by our Enemies, have made an Impression in that Kingdom to our

7. Neither Jay nor JA had been shown BF's proposal or the Danish counterproposal. The day after Walterstorff delivered the latter to BF, Jay wrote to JA (in Holland) that he believed a draft treaty had been prepared and would be sent to America with Barney: *Adams Papers*, XV, 172. This enraged JA, who confronted Walterstorff at Versailles on Aug. 12, shortly after his return. Upon learning that a proposal for a commercial treaty had been delivered to BF two weeks earlier, JA asked whether it was addressed to BF alone (as it had been) or to all the American commissioners. Within earshot of the entire diplomatic corps, he then berated the Danes for conducting diplomacy in such a deaf ("sourde") and clandestine manner, insisting that BF had no authority to treat (a point he had made months earlier; see Walterstorff to BF, May 18). Walterstorff defended his country's actions but revealed no details, having no orders to discuss anything with JA. He then informed BF of the exchange; BF made excuses for not having shown JA the counterproposal and assured Walterstorff that he would do so, adding that they would discuss the matter on the carriage ride back to Paris: Walterstorff to Rosencrone, Aug. 15, 1783 (Statens Arkiver, Rigsarkivet). JA wrote a strong letter of protest to Livingston the next day, Aug. 13, urging that all the American commissioners be consulted on such treaties. He feared a conspiracy to limit American power and saw the commercial treaties under discussion as a way for European powers to increase their trade at American expense. He made the same point in several private letters he wrote to members of Congress on Sept. 10: *Adams Papers*, XV, 223–5, 276–80.

8. Of March 29; see XXXIX, 417–18.

Disadvantage, and inclined them to hesitate in forming a Connection with us. Questions asked me, and Observations made by several of the foreign Ministers here, convince me that the idle Stories of our Disunion, Contempt of Authority, Refusal to pay Taxes &ca. have been too much credited and been very injurious to our Reputation.

I sent before a Copy of the Letter I wrote to the Grand Master of Malta, with a present of our Medal; with this you will have a Copy of his Answer.[9]

I send also a Copy of a Note I recd from the Pope's Nuncio.[1] He is very civil on all Occasions and has mentioned the possibility of an advantageous Trade America might have with the Ecclesiastical State which he says has two good Ports, Civita Vecchia and [*blank*].[2]

This Court continues favourable to us. Count de Vergennes was resolute in refusing to sign the Definitive Treaty with England, before ours was signed. The English Ministers were offended but comply'd. I am convinced that Court will never cease endeavouring to disunite us. We shall I hope be constantly on our Guard against those Machinations, for our Safety consists in a steady Adherence to our Friends, and our Reputation in[3] a faithful Regard to Treaties, and in a grateful Conduct towards our Benefactors.

I send herewith sundry Memorials recommended to my Care by M. le Comte de Vergennes, Viz.

9. XXXIX, 436, and Rohan-Poulduc to BF, June 21; see also BF to Livingston, July 22[–26].

1. See Pamphili to BF, July 28.

2. The other main port in the Papal States was Ancona. BF here drafted the start of a new paragraph, but then deleted it: "The Congress will probably instruct me what Answer I should give to his Note".

3. We have corrected this word (which WTF copied as "is") from the draft. At the end of the paragraph BF wrote but deleted the following passage: "The Malignity of the Refugees in England, is outrageous. They fill the Papers with Falshoods to exasperate that Nation against us, & depreciate us in the Eyes of all Europe. They may do us some present Mischief, but Time & Prudence will draw their Teeth, pare their Claws, & heal the Scratches they are making upon our National Character".

One respecting a Claim of Messrs. Forsters of Bordeaux.
One   Do—   of M. Pecquet; &
One—   Do—   of M. Bayard.[4]
The Congress will take such Notice of them as they shall think
proper.

With great Esteem & Respect I have the honour to be, Sir,
Your Excellency's most obedt & most humble Servant.

                                                                                                B FRANKLIN

His Excellency Elias Boudinot Esqre: President of Congress.

To Jane Mecom   ALS: Massachusetts Historical Society

Dear Sister,   Passy, Sept. 13. 1783
I received your kind Letter of April 29. and am happy that
the little Supplies I sent you, have contributed to make your Life
more comfortable.[5] I shall by this Opportunity order some more
Money into the Hands of Cousin Williams, to be dispos'd of in
assisting you as you may have Occasion.[6]

Your Project of taking a House for us to spend the Remainder of our Days in, is a pleasing one; but it is a Project of the
Heart rather than of the Head. You forget, as I sometimes do,
that we are grown old, and that before we can have furnish'd
our House, & put things in order, we shall probably be call'd
away from it, to a Home more lasting, and I hope more agreable
than any this World can afford us.

Tell my Cousin Colas, that the Parson she recommended to

---

4. BF enclosed Forster frères' June 28 letter to Vergennes, their undated
memoir to Louis XVI, and Vergennes' July 29 covering letter to BF, above.
For the enclosures regarding Pecquet and Bayard see Vergennes' second
letter of July 31 and his letter of Aug. 5.

5. See XXXIX, 532–5.

6. BF wrote a letter to Jonathan Williams, Sr., on Sept. 13 (now miss-
ing), enclosing a bill of exchange for 2,722 *l.t.* 16 *s.* 8 *d.*, drawn on Samuel
Cooper. This was reimbursement for what BF had spent on Samuel Cooper
Johonnot's education and travel expenses: Jonathan Williams, Sr., to BF,
Dec. 20, 1783 (APS).

me is gone to Rome, and it is reported has chang'd his Presbyterianism for the Catholic Religion.[7] I hope he got something to boot, because that would be a sort of Proof that they allow'd our Religion to be, so much at least, better than theirs.— It would be pleasant, if a Boston Man should come to be Pope! Stranger Things have happened.—

Cousin Williams went back for Boston from London about the Beginning of June, so that probably he is with you before this time. He laid out, by my Desire, the Money he receiv'd for you, in Goods, which you will receive of him.[8] When you have sold them, perhaps it may be adviseable to put the Money at Interest, that it may produce you a little Income.—

My two Grandsons are now both with me, and present their Duty. I am ever, my dear Sister, Your affectionate Brother

B FRANKLIN

To Charles Thomson

ALS: Library of Congress

My dear old Friend, Passy, Sept. 13. 1783.

Mr Livingston having resigned, I am obliged to trouble you with some Notes of Enquiry, and other Papers that have been put into my Hands from time to time.[9] If you can procure any

---

7. Jane Mecom Collas had provided Boston minister John Thayer (xxxv, 127n) with a letter of recommendation to BF in June, 1781. Jane Mecom met him a few months later, just before he sailed for France, and gave him a letter for BF, as well: xxxv, 127–8, 642, 667; xxxviii, 507. Thayer had been in Rome since at least the beginning of 1783 and converted to Catholicism in May: John Thayer, *An Account of the Conversion of the Reverend Mr. John Thayer . . . on the 25th of May, 1783 . . .* (London, 1787; 5th ed., Baltimore, 1788).

8. Jonathan Williams, Sr., explained this to BF on May 14: xxxix, 604.

9. After receiving this packet, Thomson referred in his correspondence to eight letters or petitions BF had sent him, dating from as far back as 1780. Two of them concerned Frenchmen who had fought for America and whose families were desperate for news: Mlle Poliange's memoir about Gabriel Vigeral (see xxxiii, 212–13, 346–7) and the sieur d'Averton's query about his son (see xxxvii, 36). Du Pont de Nemours' Aug. 10 letter, seeking documentation about the death of an immigrant to Philadelphia,

625

of the Informations desired, you will much oblige me and some of my Friends.—
With great Esteem, I am ever, Yours most affectionately

B FRANKLIN

Cha. Thomson, Esqr

Endorsed: Letter from Doct Franklin Sept 13. 1783.—

From John Adams

Copies: South Carolina Historical Society,[1] Massachusetts Historical Society; press copy of copy: Henry E. Huntington Library

Sir,   [September 13, 1783][2]
I have received the Letter which you did me the Honour to write me, on the Tenth of this Month, in which you say, you have received a Letter from a very respectable Person in America, containing the following Words vizt. "It is confidently

---

is above. Stromeyer and Straub had begged BF to force Gen. von Steuben to pay a longstanding debt (their letters are summarized in the headnote to Du Berruyer's letter of May 18, above); BF simply forwarded their complaint. Several supplicants petitioned about land claims: Lotbinière (for whom see XXXIX, 124–6, 150–1, 398–9, 401); Dr. David Barry, born in England, and his wife, Ann Hellier Barry, born in Wilmington, N.C., who wanted to pursue a claim on several tracts her father had owned (an undated petition from them, in French and addressed to Congress, is among BF's papers at the APS); and the heir of Earl Granville, who was claiming vast tracts in North Carolina. Finally, BF forwarded a July 5, 1783, petition to Congress, in Latin, from Gioanni de Bernardi, who had first offered his services to the United States in 1779 (see XXIX, 170). Now that the war had ended, de Bernardi was offering to supply America with artists, artisans, scientists, and scholars from his native Italy, which had plenty of such people to spare. He directed Congress to send its reply, in secret, care of BF; if it was encouraging, de Bernardi would set forth immediately, bringing with him an Italian mathematician (National Archives): Thomson to Michael Hillegas, Dec. 30, 1783; to Reuben Haines, Jan. 1, 1784; to BF, Jan. 14 and 15, 1784; published in Smith, *Letters*, XXI, 245–6, 254–5, 279–80, 283–5.

1. In L'Air de Lamotte's hand. The press copy is of this text.
2. The dateline is present on the Mass. Hist. Soc. copy, written by Thaxter in JA's letterbook; see *Adams Papers*, XV, 291–2.

reported, propagated and believed by some among us, that the Court of France was at Bottom, against our obtaining the Fishery and Territory in that great Extent in which both are secured to us, by the Treaty; that our Minister at that Court favoured, or did not oppose, this Design against us, and that it was entirely owing to the Firmness, Sagacity & Disinterestedness of M. Adams, with whom Mr. Jay united, that we have obtained those important Advantages."—

It is unnecessary for me, to say any Thing upon this Subject more than to quote the Words which I wrote in the Evening of the 30 of November 1782 and which have been received and read in Congress, vizt.[3] "As soon as I arrived in Paris, I waited on M. Jay & learned from him, the Rise and Progress of the Negotiation.— Nothing that happened, since the Beginning of the Controversy in 1761 has ever struck me more forcibly or affected me more intimately, than that entire Coincidence of Principles and Opinions, between him and me. In about three Days I went out to Passy, and spent the Evening with Dr. Franklin, and entered largely into Conversation with him, upon the Course and present State of our Foreign affairs. I told him my Opinion without Reserve, of the Policy of this Court, and of the Principles, Wisdom and Firmness, with which Mr. Jay had conducted the Negotiation, in his Sickness and my Absence; and that I was determined to support Mr. Jay, to the utmost of my Power, in Pursuit of the same System. The Dr. heard me patiently but said Nothing.

"The first Conference we had afterwards, with Mr. Oswald, in considering one Point and another, Dr. Franklin turned to Mr. Jay and said, I am of your Opinion, and will go on with these Gentlemen in the Business, without consulting this Court. He has accordingly met us, in most of our Conferences, and has gone on with us, in entire Harmony & Unanimity, throughout, and has been able and useful both by his Sagacity and Reputation, in the whole Negotiation."

I have the honour to be, very respectfully, Sir, your most obedient & most humble Servant.   (signed) JOHN ADAMS.

3. The following quotation is from JA's journal of the peace negotiations, received by Robert R. Livingston on March 12, 1783: Butterfield, *John Adams Diary*, III, 41–3n, 82.

Copy of a Letter from his Excellency John Adams to B. Franklin Esqr. dated Paris, Sept. 13. 1783.—

Notation by Henry Laurens: Copy of Mr. Adams's Letter of 13th. Septr 1783 to Doctr Franklin given to me by the Doctor 5th. Novr 1783—

From Joseph Banks

ALS: American Philosophical Society

Dear Sir   Soho Square Sept. 13 1783

For having it in my power to Answer with precision the numerous questions which are askd me by all sorts of people Concerning the Aerostatique Experiment which such as they may be are suggested by every newspaper now printed here & considerd as a part of my duty to Answer is an Obligation for which I am indebted to you & an Obligation of no small Extent I consider it. I Lament that the vacation of the Royal Society will not permit me to Lay your paper before them as a Body immediately but it shall be the first thing they see when we meet again as the Conciseness & intelligence with which it is drawn up preclude the hopes of any more Satisfactory being receiv'd.[4]

Most agreeble are the hopes you give me of Continueing to Communicate on this most interesting Subject. I consider the present day which has opend a road into the Air as an epoche from whence a rapid increase of the Stock of real Knowledge with which the human Species is furnishd must take its date & the more immediate Effect it will have upon the Concerns of Mankind greater than any thing since the invention of Shipping which opend our way upon the face of the water from Land to Land.

If the rough Effort which has now been made meets with the improvement that other Sciences have done we shall see it usd as a Counterpoise to Absolute Gravity a broad wheeld waggen traveling with 2 only instead of 8 horses the breed of that Rival

---

4. Banks read BF's letter of Aug. 30 and his next of Oct. 8 at the Royal Society's meeting on Nov. 6, but they were not published in the *Phil. Trans.*, at BF's request: Banks to BF, Nov. 7, 1783 (University of Pa. Library); BF to Banks, Nov. 21 [*i.e.*, 22–25], 1783 (Library of Congress).

Animal in Course diminishd & the human species incread in proportion.

I have thought as soon as I return from my Present banishment[5] of constructing one & sending it up for the purpose of an Electrical Kite a use to which it seem particularly adapted.

Be pleasd to direct your Favors to Soho Square they are sent to me without delay Whereever I am beleive me Your Obligd & Obedient Servant   Jos: Banks

Addressed: Dr. Franklin / Passy / near Paris / France

From Edward Bridgen   ALS: American Philosophical Society

My Dear Sir   London Sepr: 13 1783

As your Excellency & the rest of the Commissioners were so obliging as to second my former proposals I think it my duty to inform you Sir and them of the additional step we have taken towards accomplishing our wishes.[6]

The preceeding[7] I laid before Mr Laurens which meeting

---

5. Banks was recuperating from recurring chest pains and a fall at his country estate, Revesby Abbey, in Lincolnshire: Harold B. Carter, *Sir Joseph Banks, 1743–1820* (London, 1988), p. 185.

6. Bridgen had been proposing to supply America with copper coinage since 1779. In 1782 he sent a proposal in the name of himself and John Waller to various members of the American commission, who discussed it after the preliminaries were signed. JA, acting on his own, sent it to Congress in mid-December. Some days later, the American commissioners as a group forwarded the proposal under all their signatures. BF sent an additional copy to Livingston on Dec. 24 along with his ideas on coin design and samples of the copper: XXXVIII, 74n, 243–4, 481–2, 492–3.

7. Bridgen wrote the present letter below a copy of Bridgen & Waller to Livingston, Sept. 8, 1783. Wondering whether Congress' silence was due to "the want of Cash," the partners offer an alternative: they would strike the coins in England (according to terms they specified) and launch them into circulation, trusting that English merchants would exchange them for American goods. In this way, the "whole Continent" would eventually be supplied, at no risk or expense to America.

BF wrote extensive calculations on the bottom of this letter, evidently struggling to figure out the advantages of this scheme.

with his approbation I immediately dispatched the same under Mr Ls: cover, as a vessell was just then taking away the Bag for Philadelphia and gave me no time to consult with the other Gentlemen whose friendship I had experienced.[8]

Would you do me the favour Sir to make my Apologies to the other Gentlemen and believe that I am with great truth Your Excellency's and their Much Obliged & faithful Hum: Sert.

EDWD: BRIDGEN

His Excellency Benjn: Franklin

Addressed: His Excellency / Benjn: Franklin / at Passy.

Endorsed: E Bridgen to R R Livingston Esqr. Sept. 8. 83. Copper Coinage

From James Hutton   ALS: American Philosophical Society

Dear Old Friend   13. Septr. 1783

I am desired by a 50 years dear friend to recommend to you a Mr Blount & his Lady[9] who intend residing some years in France, they are People of Fortune and Mr Blount is a man of Science & very ambitious for the Honour of your Acquaintance; He is of a very ancient and Respectable Family in Oxfordshire. Now

---

8. Laurens sent Bridgen & Waller's revised proposal with a group of dispatches he forwarded to Congress along with his own letter to Livingston of Sept. 11; that letter (which does not mention coinage) is filed at the National Archives with copies of the original and revised proposals from Bridgen & Waller. Another set of the proposals is filed at the National Archives with a copy of BF's Dec. 24, 1782, letter to Livingston. When Congress finally took up the matter of manufacturing copper coinage in 1787, they considered Bridgen & Waller's bid among the many they had received, referring to it as the one communicated by BF. In the end, another proposal was selected: *JCC*, XXXII, 160–4, 221, 223–4, 225.

9. Probably Joseph (b. 1752) and Mary Canning Blount. Joseph was from a Catholic family of Mapledurham, Oxfordshire, and died somewhere near Lyon during the French Revolution: Tony Hadland, *Thames Valley Papists: from Reformation to Emancipation* ([England], 1992), p. 142; Bernard Burke, *A Genealogical and Heraldic History of the Landed Gentry of Great Britain and Ireland* (2 vols., London, 1875), I, 115.

I know your kind Regard for me, and there fore I beg the Favour of you to give Mr Blount the Happiness of your acquaintance. I can trust the Character given of him to me by my old 50 years Friend, as if I knew him myself. I give you again Joy of Peace.

Peace is my dear Delight—not Fleury's more.[1] It has pleasd God to take away our senses for a time may He restore them to us, when He sees what He has not seen yet that we may know when we are well. Now all is so far over I shall look for next Spring to have the Happiness of seeing you. Once more I am in earnest when I desire you to recieve Mr Blount as one who I am assured will answer the warmest Praises I could give him. You will I hope have opportunity of introducing him if He desires it, to some of your French Friends especially to our dear Du Pont.[2] I am with all that old personal Friendship & Gratitude I have long felt for you Dear Old Friend your most obliged & affectionate Servant   JAMES HUTTON

Dr Franklin.

Addressed: To / Dr Franklin / Passy

To Lewis R. Morris   ALS and transcript: National Archives

Sir,   Passy, Sept. 14. 1783.
I receiv'd by the Washington the Bills and Accounts men-tioned in yours of the 5th of June, and shall soon send you an Account of the Disposition of the Money. My Account as stated by you appears to be right. With much Esteem I have the hon-our to be, Sir Your most obedient & most humble Servant
                                               B FRANKLIN

L R Morris Esqr

1. A line from Alexander Pope, *The First Satire of the Second Book of Horace, Imitated in a Dialogue between Alexander Pope, of Twickenham in Com. Midd. Esq. . . .* (London, 1733), p. 13.

2. Du Pont de Nemours, an old friend of Hutton's. The previous spring, BF had sent Hutton his book on Turgot: XXXIX, 543.

Index

Compiled by Philipp Ziesche.

(Semicolons separate subentries; colons separate divisions within subentries. A volume and page reference in parentheses following a main entry refers to an individual's first identification in this edition.)

689

THE PAPERS OF
BENJAMIN FRANKLIN

SPONSORED BY

The American Philosophical Society
and Yale University